PSYCHOLOGY
The Science of Who We Are

2nd edition

Charlton • Sobel • Sobel

FOUNTAINHEAD PRESS

Cover and Text Design: Susan Moore

Developmental Editor: Amy Salisbury-Werhane

Illustrations: Carol Hill

Some photos provided by Shutterstock and Getty Images.

ISBN: 978-1-68036-635-8

Printed in the United States of America

ABOUT THE AUTHORS

Ken Sobel earned a B.S. in electrical engineering from Carnegie Mellon University in Pittsburgh, PA, then an M.S. in information science from the University of Pittsburgh. While at Pitt, he became interested in cognitive science, which explores the interaction between human brains and minds from several perspectives, including computer science, philosophy of mind, and cognitive psychology. Seeking to extend his training in cognitive science, he next earned an M.A. in philosophy from the University of Wyoming and a Ph.D. in cognitive psychology from Vanderbilt University. Dr. Sobel has been a professor at the University of Central Arkansas since 2005, where he studies human attention and perception, and in his free time enjoys riding his bicycle when the weather isn't too hot.

Susan Sobel earned a B.A. in psychology from Gustavus Adolphus College and a Ph.D. in clinical psychology from the University of Wyoming. In order to open up more professional opportunities, she obtained an Ed.S. in School Psychology from Middle Tennessee State University. Dr. Sobel has worked in community and school-based mental health, private practice, and as a professor of school psychology. She joined the Counseling Center staff at the University of Central Arkansas in 2013, and has been the director since 2014. Her interests outside of psychology include reading, travel, and watching her daughter play softball.

Shawn R. Charlton earned a B.A. in psychology from Utah State University (2001) in Logan, UT, and both an M.S. (2003) and Ph.D. (2006) in experimental psychology from the University of California, San Diego. His interest in psychology was planted through conversations with his father, Robert Charlton, Ph.D., a Clinical and School psychologist. It took two years living in Santiago, Chile, for this interest to blossom into a full passion for understanding the role of the environment in shaping our behavior. This interest has become a research and teaching program focused on the evolutionary and environmental events that shape decisions. Dr. Charlton is an advocate for undergraduate research and for supporting career development among undergraduates. Dr.Charlton spends his free time playing, laughing, and travelling with his wife, Veda, and three children, Ashlin, Jaxon, and Jeron.

PREFACE

We wrote the preface for the 1ˢᵗ edition of this text weeks after the United States finished the 2016 presidential election. This was one of the most contentious presidential races America had ever experienced. The past year has not been much different with the political tensions continuing—and even expanding. While the political process can be frustrating at times, the pure psychology is absolutely wonderful. What influences the parties to nominate the candidates that they do? What motivates the candidates to behave as they do, and what motivates voters to respond as they do? Watching politics during times like national elections provides a prime window to observe how psychology plays out in real life.

Of course, the wealth of human behavior available to observe isn't limited to politics (it is just such a rich place for observing the breadth of human behavior). As you read through this book, we hope you will come to view psychology as more than just a subject you study in the classroom. A major goal for us as we work on this book is to demonstrate that psychology is truly all around you. Whether you are asking questions about your own behavior and personal experiences, or those of friends, colleagues, and national leaders, you are asking questions about psychology. Our hope is that your study of this text will help you appreciate psychology as something that happens in your daily life.

To meet this goal, we focused on the ideas that are most fundamental to the ways that psychology helps you relate to the world around you. Chapter 1 provides a general overview of the history and philosophy of psychology. Chapter 2 describes the scientific tools used by psychologists to understand behavior. The next two chapters (3 and 4) provide an overview of the working of the brain and sensory systems. Chapters 5 and 6 provide an overview of how we develop and the role of sexuality and gender. Chapter 7 describes how we learn and change our behavior as we experience the world. Chapters 8, 9, and 10 discuss memory, cognition, and consciousness, the skills that enable us to remember, process, and adapt to the information around us. Chapters 11 and 12 provide a general overview of what motivates us, our emotions, and our personality— the enduring characteristics that shape our interactions with the world. Chapters 13 and 14 discuss mental health issues and what we can do about them. Finally, chapter 15 talks about how we manage the social world around us.

You can see from this overview of the contents in each chapter, we cover a lot of psychology in this text. Unfortunately, we cannot cover it all. Writing an introductory text about a subject as broad as psychology requires many decisions about what to include and what to leave out of the discussion. We felt like we were walking on a tight rope between broad coverage and sufficient depth of topic. We aimed to strike this balance by focusing on what you, the reader, need to know to be able to use your growing understanding of psychology to change your behavior and how you interact with others and to build a solid foundation for those of you who endeavor into more advanced psychology courses.

Another goal was to integrate the different areas of psychology into a coherent whole, so while you read each section, you will understand how each area influences the others. Psychological scientists typically look at their area of interest in isolation from all other areas, but you experience the world as a single whole person. By pointing out the connections between different *levels of analysis* throughout the text, we hope to encourage you to see behavior as a product of multiple influences (e.g., biology, learning, and culture) acting on you in a number of different ways.

In order to help you understand psychology, we have built the text around several specific learning technologies (pedagogical elements):

Critical Thinking Questions

We weave questions throughout each chapter to help you think critically about the information you learn, as well as to give you practice in communicating your thoughts about psychology. Psychological science has demonstrated that learning is most efficient when students personally engage with the material. We hope that the critical thinking questions encourage you to actively engage the material.

Chapter Openings

Each chapter opens with a set of questions that will be answered as you read through the chapter. These questions were designed in light of what psychological science has revealed about how people learn. The questions "prime" your attention to look for particular information in the chapter, improving your retention of the material by piquing your interest.

Introductory Narratives

At the beginning of each chapter, we introduce the key components of the material through an explanatory story that exemplifies chapter content. As you read the chapter introductions, the material prepares you for more detailed study of its elements while offering a real-life example of what you're about to learn.

"This is Psychology"

Throughout the text, you will find brief sections that provide more depth into how psychological science applies to real world problems and situations. These sections help you to appreciate the role of psychology in your life, the major historical events in psychology, and the unexpected oddities of behavior. We also try to point out ways that psychology is applied in the workplace as well as trying to convey that psychology is influenced by culture, and can help us to understand each other and conduct ourselves in a manner that is respectful and responsible.

Concept Recall

Each chapter contains several sections that each end with a series of open-ended review questions that can be answered by referring to the material in the section. Serious attention to these questions will both help consolidate the information as well as provide a quick assessment of understanding.

From the Desk of Dr. Stith

Dr. Randy Stith of the Aurora Mental Health Center in Aurora, Colorado has been practicing psychology for more than 40 years. The Center has been at the forefront of a number of the nation's most traumatic public tragedies over several decades, including Columbine, and more recently, the Aurora theater shooting. Not only are the tragedies Dr. Stith and his team address impactful to the Denver area community, but also, they have garnered national and international interest as issues surrounding mental health. As a result, the field of Crisis Management emerged, which is an amalgam of mental health support, public safety, emergency management, and security. Dr. Stith contributed his expertise in boxed moments throughout the text that are related to chapter content. We felt this emerging sub-field of psychology would both be of interest to students and offer timely, real-world examples of psychology at work.

Cross-Cultural Cases

Since the audience of this textbook is primarily American students, we wanted to give them the opportunity to explore how other cultures relate and respond to elements of psychology. In each chapter, narratives relating to the chapter material present current events, studies, and cultural aspects that provide points for further study and discussion.

Review/Reflect/Write

The end of each chapter provides readers an opportunity to assess their recall of the information using both open-ended questions and multiple-choice questions, and to engage in deeper processing of the information. The "reflect" questions ask you to engage more deeply with the material as you process your opinions and feelings regarding the material. These questions will help you to apply the concepts into your life in a meaningful way. Finally, the "write" questions encourage you to seek out new information, integrate these findings with course materials, and then write out your thoughts.

Integration with the American Psychological Association Guidelines for the Undergraduate Major—Version 2.0

In August 2013, the American Psychological Association created a new set of guidelines to help undergraduate programs prepare students for professional careers in psychology. We were mindful of these guidelines, and used them as a framework for our decision-making as we shaped this text. The goals outlined by the APA include:

Goal 1: Knowledge Base in Psychology

Goal 2: Scientific Inquiry and Critical Thinking

Goal 3: Ethical and Social Responsibility in a Diverse World

Goal 4: Communication

Goal 5: Professional Development

As you read this text, you will find these themes appearing throughout the narrative. For example, we discuss throughout the text the scientific nature of psychology and the importance of asking questions about how the world works, independent of our perceptions and opinions regarding behavior (*Goal 2*). Another theme that you will find in the text is the importance of culture and diversity (*Goals 3 and 4*). Finally, we have built into the narrative discussions of the career options available in psychology as well as ways to apply psychology to whatever professional path you select (*Goal 5*).

We used what we know about psychology to build a text that facilitates your learning. The success of this book is determined by the degree to which you are able to use the information from these pages to engage with the world around you. We hope to convince you that psychology is not just a vibrant and exciting science, but can also help you achieve your personal goals and improve your relationships.

TABLE OF CONTENTS

1

Understanding Psychology

After reading this chapter, you will be able to answer the following questions:

- How is psychology the study of you?
- What are the three characteristics of psychology?
- How is psychology a science?
- What does it mean to say that psychology is an integrative study of behavior?
- How do the subfields of psychology help us understand behavior?
- What are some of the key events in the early history of psychology?
- How did psychology expand from the laboratory to become an applied science?
- Where do psychologists work and what do they do?

Psychology is the scientific study of you. It is the study of how you learned to walk, how you talk, how you make decisions about what to eat, who to be friends with, and what types of products to buy. And psychology is so much more. Psychology is also the study of how you fall in love, why some situations make you scared, and what it is that makes you intelligent (or not). Psychology helps to understand exceptional moments in your life, such as when you choose to help someone else or when you are able to overcome challenges. It also helps us to understand your greatest challenges—such as dealing with your own mental illness or that of a friend or family member—and your darkest experiences—such as prejudice, discrimination, hatred, bullying, and conforming to peer or other social pressures. Psychology truly provides insight into all of the different experiences, thoughts, beliefs, and behaviors that are part of what it is to be you.

To appreciate how psychology can help you understand who you are, take a moment to think of what you did, thought, and felt over the past 24 hours. As you think about the number of different things you did and the experiences that made up your previous day, you will be making a list of the things psychologists study. For example, think about the last time you watched television. As you watched your favorite show, sporting event, news program, or movie, you were engaged in many activities examined by psychologists. As you read the following paragraphs, consider some—but not all—of the ways a psychologist might study your television-watching behavior.

As you watched the television, the sensory receptors in your eyes and ears received the electromagnetic radiation emitted by the television (light) and the molecular motion produced by movement of the speakers (sound). Once the sensory organs were stimulated by this environmental information, the neural signals passed to your brain to be processed. Psychologists interested in sensation, the conversion of real-world energy into a neural code, and perception, the processing of neural sensory information, study how the sensory organs, nervous system, and brain are able to receive, encode, transfer, and make sense of the information in your environment. One of the major challenges in understanding the viewing of television, computer, and movie screens is comprehending how the brain transforms the two-dimensional screen image into the perception of a three-dimensional world. This transformation is a major perceptual challenge, but one that occurs so automatically we hardly ever stop to think about it.

While psychologists interested in studying sensation and perception are researching how you process the sensory information received as you watch television, a cognitive psychologist would be more interested in studying the neural process that results in you correctly understanding an actor who says, "You can see the sea from seat 3C." Despite all those "sees" in the same sentence, you are able to understand that each identical-sounding

"see" has a distinct meaning. Yet another psychologist, a social psychologist, might analyze your reaction to the aggressive discussion between a male and female character on the show or investigate how the staged aggression between the actors influences your behavior in the real world. Another psychologist might study your emotional reaction to this interaction based on your racial, cultural, or sexual background. Or, maybe, the psychologists studying your behavior are interested in how your reaction changes based on the people with you while you watch the television program.

The possible questions raised by your television watching, as identified above, are only a small sample of the questions psychologists can ask about this behavior. And notice that they are not exclusive of one another. A psychologist investigating your sensory experiences and one investigating your social experiences will come up with different explanations of what is influencing your television watching because they are looking at what you are doing in different ways. Television watching may seem like a simple task to you, but the behaviors involved are complex and of great interest to a variety of psychologists.

With so many questions we can ask about your television watching, imagine what would happen if we looked at a more complex behavior, such as falling in love, dealing with a school bully, or handling the loss of a loved one. Highlighting the types of questions asked by different types of psychologists illustrates just how much about you can be understood through psychological science.

WHAT IS PSYCHOLOGY?

psychology
the scientific study of the behavior of individual organisms and how environmental, physiological, mental, social, and cultural events influence these behaviors

Defining psychology as the scientific study of what you do captures both the breadth and focus of psychology, but it is a little too informal for an academic introduction to the discipline. More formally, we can say that **psychology** is the scientific study of individual organisms' behaviors and how environmental, physiological, mental, social, and cultural events influence these behaviors. Take a moment to look back at the definition of psychology, and you will notice that psychology is a complex discipline with three main characteristics.

1. Psychology is a science.
2. Psychology studies individual behavior.
3. Psychology studies the variables that influence behavior (environment, physiology, mental processes, social interactions, and cultural practices).

Understanding these three characteristics of psychology is critical to appreciating fully how psychology can help you understand yourself, your friends and family, and others in your world.

Psychology Is a Science

A key component of psychology's definition is that it is a scientific discipline. As a science, psychology aims to accomplish its goals through systematic observation and measurement. Psychologists conduct their research using the scientific method as a framework for exploring the world through developing and testing hypotheses. Depending on the research question, a psychologist may use many of the same tools as other scientists, including the same types of technology, methodology, and philosophy. Similar to other scientists, research psychologists aim to describe, predict, explain, and control behavior (we will explore this topic more fully in Chapter 2). However, while psychologists share the same goals as other scientists, their area of study is unique. As already established, their area of focus is you and what you do. Because your behavior is so complex and you live in such a complex world, psychologists frequently use methods and technologies that are distinct from those used by other scientists. For example, psychologists often rely on surveys and self-reported experiences, two tools that are rarely employed in the disciplines of physics and chemistry.

While psychology is a science, the majority of psychologists are not interested in the strictly scientific side of psychology. Instead, a large portion of those who work in psychology-related fields are interested in how to apply the discoveries made by psychological researchers. For example, most therapists and counselors are not directly engaged in research, but they study the work done by research psychologists and apply it to developing ways to work with their individual clients. In this way, psychological practice is informed by basic psychological research. At the same time, the challenges and difficulties experienced by psychological practitioners often generate questions for the basic scientists to explore. Regardless of whether the psychologist is working on the production or the application of psychological science, his or her work is driven by what we know based on our scientific explorations of human behavior (Figure 1.1).

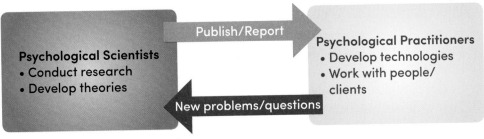

1.1 The generation of future research
The connection between psychological science and application.

While psychology uses the basic ideas, technologies, and procedures of science, there is a challenge in psychology that is unique to the social sciences. Psychology seeks to understand how people behave, but the psychologists doing the research are themselves people. This creates major challenges because we all have theories and ideas about why people do things. In fact, it is very difficult to watch any object in motion without developing an explanation for why it behaves the way it does. When conducting psychological research, the explanations psychologists have for how people behave can interfere with developing a scientific understanding of their behavior. Instead of focusing on science-driven explanations, people have a tendency to take their observations and informal explanations and use these to form theories to rationalize other people's actions. Sometimes these insights are valid, but often, they fail to accurately explain the real reasons for behavior.

Take a moment and consider how odd it is for the researcher and the research focus to be the same type of object. If we were geologists studying rock formations, we would likely not be tempted to project our feelings and experiences onto the rock. However, as the similarity between us, as the observer, and the object of our study grows, the tendency to project our feelings, thoughts, and emotions into the situation gets stronger (the projecting of human experience and abilities onto nonhuman objects is formally called **anthropomorphization**). As psychological scientists, we must separate ourselves carefully and purposefully from the topic of our study. While our experience can give us insights into behavior, it is essential that we compare these insights with the outcomes of well-designed scientific studies.

anthropomorphization
the projecting of human experience and abilities onto nonhuman objects

Another major challenge in conducting psychological science lies in the reactivity of the subject to the study's demands. Participants in psychological studies are influenced by the way the study is designed, what happens before the study, and experiences from their past. Associations between the study and other events, as well as unrelated experiences (such as traffic, conflicts with coworkers or family members, or the length of time since the participant last ate) can impact how a participant behaves during the study. Because of the dynamic nature of human behavior, psychologists must use different sets of tools and procedures to conduct their research than those we often think of when we contemplate how and where a scientist works.

As you read this book and other psychological works, you will find some ideas that confirm your beliefs about human behavior and others that challenge them. When you find your ideas about behavior challenged, we encourage you to ask yourself, "Why is this different from what I thought about behavior?" and "Where did my ideas about how people behave come from?" By developing the habit of asking questions about what you believe and the origin of those beliefs, you will gain confidence in using scientific knowledge guide your decisions and actions. A similar set of questions should be asked about other people's beliefs about behavior: "Why do they believe this?" and "Where did their ideas about behavior come from?"

Psychology Is about the Individual

As highlighted by the formal definition of psychology and the introduction to this chapter, psychology is about the individual: you. Other sciences, such as sociology, economics, and anthropology focus on how groups of people interact with one another. Psychology does look at groups, but the focus of these studies is always how the group influences the individual's behavior. For example, psychological science has shown that people tend to take on the characteristics of groups that are important to them, such as their style of dress, political ideas, and manner of speaking. Psychologists are interested in understanding why this happens at individual level. Is this tendency to conform an attempt by the individual to gain support and protection from the group? Does conformity reflect an attempt by the individual to bolster his or her self-esteem? As we saw in the television-watching example, these two questions regarding the function of our conformity behavior are not exclusive of each other, but they could be the focus of two different lines of study. While much of the psychological literature involves collecting data from a group of participants, the goal of a psychological study is to understand how an individual behaves in a given situation and why.

Psychology Is Interested in Interaction

To understand the various influences on individual behavior, psychologists take an integrative approach. Thanks to the breadth of psychological research, we now understand that behavior is a product of many influences. Psychology separates these influences into five general categories (Figure 1.2):

- **Environment**: The natural world around the individual, which can include illumination, temperature, sounds, weather, air quality, and other features
- **Physiology**: The individual's biological structure, organ functions, and genetic makeup
- **Mental processes**: The information-processing systems and structures that are part of the individual's mental capacities and process sensory information
- **Social interactions**: The groups and individuals we interact with throughout our lives
- **Cultural practices**: The norms and rules that have been adopted by the individual's social group and that have become part of the social structure of his or her environment

1.2 The five interacting behavioral influences An integrated view of psychology states that while we only have one experience of reality, our behavior is simultaneously influenced by our biology, the environment around us, our mental processes, the people who surround us, and our cultural norms.

While we are not aware of all of these different elements' influences at any given moment, our behavior is continuously influenced by each of them. It is tempting—and easier—to think of these influences in isolation, such as occurs in nature/nurture debates when people wonder whether a particular behavior is inherited (nature) or learned (nurture), but the belief that one of these influences can act in isolation from the others is mistaken. All of the aspects of our environment we can detect are part of the context that influences our behavior. Because we need to understand how all of the aspects of the environment work together to produce our behavior, we say that psychology is an integrative study of behavior.

We discussed our tendency to adopt the characteristics of the social group in the previous section. The degree to which we conform to the characteristics of the group is influenced by available sources of shelter/protection, our biological susceptibility to stress, amount of information that needs to be processed, the size of the group, and our cultural attitudes about the individual's value compared to the group's. For scientific purposes, we may isolate one or two of these influences to better understand how they impact behavior, but in understanding real world behavior, it is important to remember that our actions are a product of all of these influences acting together.

Concept Recall

1. What is the formal definition of psychology?
2. Why must psychologists and other social scientists be vigilant regarding their own biases when conducting their research?
3. How does psychology differ from other social sciences, such as sociology and anthropology?
4. What are the five types of interactions psychologists view as shaping our behavior?

Psychology Is the Study of Behavior

While psychology is a complex field representing scientists asking a broad range of questions about you, all psychologists share one thing in common: They focus on the study of what you do—your behavior. What exactly is behavior? Broadly defined, behavior is anything that the organism does. Ogden Lindsley, a behavior analyst (a scientist within a branch of psychology that focuses on the interaction between behavior and the environment, described in more detail in Chapter 7), defined behavior as anything that passes the dead person's test (Lindsley, 1991). According to Lindsley, a behavior is anything that a dead person cannot do. Can a dead person walk? No. Can a dead person talk? No. Sing? Think? No and no. So, walking, talking, singing, and thinking are all behaviors. Table 1.1 gives several examples of both behaviors and nonbehaviors according to Lindsley's dead person's test.

Table 1.1   The dead person's test

Behavior	Nonbehavior
Passes Dead Person's Test (Cannot be done by a dead person)	**Fails Dead Person's Test (Can be done by a dead person)**
Running, walking, playing	Not moving
Raising hand before speaking	Not talking during class
Sleeping	Lying on the ground
Eating fruits and vegetables	Not eating foods high in calories or sugar

Awareness of what is and is not behavior is particularly useful when we aim to change our behavior. People frequently decide that they would like to lose weight, and to meet this objective, they will set a goal that goes something like this: "I will not eat any junk food." Is "not eating junk food" a behavior? Notice that a dead person does not spend much time eating junk food, so this intention isn't actually a behavior. Instead, you will have more success adopting a specific goal, such as eating healthy food or increasing your daily exercise, both of which are behaviors as neither of these are things that a corpse can do. As living beings, behavior is what we do, so when trying to change behavior, we have more success swapping one behavior for another than swapping one behavior for a nonbehavior.

While eating healthy and exercising are directly observable behaviors, psychologists focus on the full breadth of what an organism can do. As we look at the complexity of behavior, we note that behavior ranges from complex, full-body movements—such as those we would see from a professional dancer—to the microscopic changes that occur inside a neuron, the cells that make up our nervous system (described in Chapter 3). To appreciate the range of complexity in our behavior, think again of when you last watched television. One large-scale behavior you were engaged in was to move your arm toward the remote, securing the remote with your hand, lifting it, and pressing the buttons. At the same time, the muscles surrounding the pupil of your eye were adjusting to the brightness of the scene on the television. On the smallest level, neurons in your brain were firing in response to the lights and sounds from the television. While different in size and complexity, all of these behaviors are part of what you do (notice that a dead person does not do any of these things), and all are important parts of the experience we call watching television.

Not only do psychologists study behaviors of different size and complexity, but they also study behaviors that occur outside the organism, such as movement of the limbs, eye blinking, and talking, as well as the behaviors that occur inside the organism, such as hormone secretion, changes in neurotransmitter levels, and changes in heart rate. External, public, easily observable behaviors and internal, private, hard-to-measure behaviors are part of what the organism does—its behavior. Figure 1.3 illustrates the relationship between simple and complex behaviors as well as internal versus external behaviors. All of these behaviors are important parts of understanding how we interact with the world. Returning once again to the television-watching experience, if we changed the way you interacted with the remote control, the way your pupils dilated,

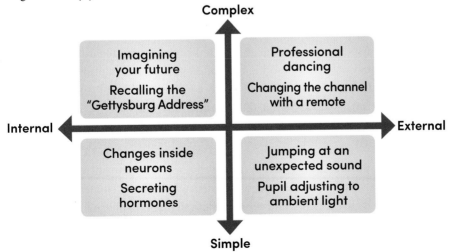

1.3 Two major dimensions of behavior
Behaviors range from simple to complex, internal to external. Behaviors organisms exhibit interact to increase the complexity of those behaviors.

or the neurons that are active as you watch your television show, we would change your experience. As we think about our experience with the world, it is important to note that: there are many behaviors occurring both outside and inside as we interact with the world, and while we are not aware of all of the behaviors we engage in, we use all of our behaviors to create a single, unified experience of the world.

BREADTH OF PSYCHOLOGY

Everything you do, whether big or small, outside the body or inside your skin, is of interest to, and studied by, psychologists. Not only are psychologists interested in everything you do, but they are also interested in all of the places where you engage in behavior. If there is a place where you could behave, there is a psychologist who studies the effect of that context on your behavior. For example, the United States space program employs a large team of psychologists who work on a variety of projects, including understanding the effect of being in space on behavior. We will discuss many of the current areas in which psychologists work at the end of the chapter. In order to understand the breadth of psychology and psychology studies, consider the major perspectives of the discipline.

Major Perspectives of Psychology

perspectives of psychology
philosophical ways of thinking about the goals of psychology and the nature of human behavior

Each subfield of psychology represents a unique focus and set of methodologies brought to bear on the study of the individual. Although psychologists might identify themselves as members of one or more particular subfields, their work parallels the work of psychologists in other disciplines, as psychology strives overall to produce a broader understanding of human behavior.

Over the years since its founding, psychology has seen the rise and fall of a number of different **perspectives of psychology**: philosophical ways of thinking about psychology's goals and the nature of human behavior. While there are a number of different perspectives at any given time, psychology is typically dominated by a particular perspective at any given moment. Understanding the different perspectives of psychology is an important step in appreciating modern psychological thought. These psychological perspectives represent formalized philosophies regarding the primary goals of psychology as well as specific methodologies for accomplishing those goals. The six major historical perspectives of psychology are structuralism, functionalism, gestalt, behaviorism, psychodynamic theory, and humanism.

structuralism
the view that psychology's goal should be to identify and understand the basic elements of human experience

Structuralism

As the oldest perspective of modern psychology, **structuralism** suggests that psychology's goals should be to: reduce experience to its basic elements, discover the laws that govern these elements, and connect these elements to physiological conditions (Schultz & Schultz, 2004). As you can see from these three objectives, structuralism's founder, Edward B. Titchener, believed that there are basic components to our experience, and these components can be organized in a lawful way to produce our behavior, no matter how complex. Frank J. Landy (1999) described structuralism as "an

Edward B. Titchener

attempt to outline the elements of consciousness from the inside out." Titchener was strongly influenced by chemistry's periodic table of the elements and argued that psychology should similarly strive to identify and understand the basic elements that make up our experiences of the world and reduce conscious experience to its most elementary components (Cummins, 1991).

Functionalism

Functionalism asserts that psychology's goal should be to study how consciousness and experience aid in adjusting to the environment (Schultz & Schultz, 2004). Rather than focusing on experience itself, as suggested by Titchener, the functionalists believed psychology's emphasis should be on why we have experiences and what they accomplish. The functionalists emphasized understanding how mental operations work, why they work that way, and how they help the organism to survive in its current environment. Functionalists focused on how mental activities, such as memory, perception, imagination, and judgment, enable us to evaluate, organize, and act on experience. William James, considered by many historians to be the father of American psychology, was the best-known proponent of the functionalist view. Today, the ideas of functionalism are embodied in the field of **evolutionary psychology**: a subfield of psychology that aims to understand the evolutionary pressures that shaped behavior and the adaptive function of behavior. With its heavy emphasis on how our behavior adapts to the world around us and what a given behavior's function is in that world, functionalism became a strong influence on the development of psychological approaches to solving real-world problems (Landy, 1999).

functionalism
the view that psychology's goal should be to study how consciousness and experience aid in adjusting to the environment

evolutionary psychology
a subfield of psychology that aims to understand the evolutionary pressures that shaped behavior and the adaptive function of behavior

William James

Gestalt

The **gestalt** perspective argues that psychology's goal should be to study experience as a whole rather than the sum of its parts. Gestalt psychologists rejected the structuralist claim that consciousness could be broken down into its elemental components, and instead they claimed human experience is more than the sum of its component parts (Schultz & Schultz, 2004). A good way to understand the gestalt movement is to imagine eating all the ingredients of your favorite food separately. If you particularly enjoy apple pie, you would likely be disappointed in the experience you would get from eating apple chunks, then sugar, cinnamon, eggs, and butter. You have all the right ingredients, but there is more to a pie than just the ingredients (and you really should avoid eating raw eggs). Similarly, human experience is not the same if we try to break it down into just the basic sensory components.

gestalt
the view that psychology's goal should be to study experience as a whole rather than the sum of its parts

behaviorism
the view that psychology's goal should be to study directly observable behavior and to understand how the events in the environment outside the organism produce behavior

Behaviorism

Behaviorism suggests that psychology's goal should be to study directly observable behavior and to understand how the events in the external environment produce behavior. American psychologist John Watson, who coined the term "behaviorism," argued that psychology could not become a science if it continued to focus on nonobservable, subjective mental experiences. Thus, while structuralism, functionalism, and gestalt psychology argued about how best to understand the unobservable mental

John Watson

behavior analysis
a scientific approach to the study of learning that focuses on laws and processes of behavior across species and the development of behavior technologies

psychodynamic theory
Freud's argument that our psychological experience is the product of the conflict between our id and our superego

world, Watson and the behaviorists focused on the associations between environmental events and behavior. Watson argued that a scientific study of behavior should first be able to predict what behavior will follow a given environmental stimulus, and second, be able to predict what stimulus produced a given behavior.

Behaviorism became a dominant perspective in psychology in the United States until the 1960s when the American perspective began to change with the invention of the digital computer and the cognitive revolution that followed. Today, behaviorism's ideas have evolved into the field of **behavior analysis**: a subfield of psychology that aims to understand both external (observable movements) and internal behaviors (thoughts and feelings).

Psychodynamic theory

From the perspective of **psychodynamic theory**, psychology's goal should be to attempt to understand patients' mental health issues. Psychodynamic theory was developed by the Austrian physician, Sigmund Freud, who argued that our psychological experience is the product of the conflict between our *id*—the desire to find physical satisfaction and fulfill biological needs—and our *superego*—the need to meet the demands of society. As these two sources of demands are in conflict with each other, our personality becomes a product of the balance struck by our *ego*—the component of our self that seeks compromise between the id and superego, between satisfaction and conformity. According to Freud's theory, the majority of this conflict occurs in the subconscious mind, but the side effects of the conflict become evident in our psychological problems. Much of Freud's theory is no longer considered accurate, but the idea of unconscious influences on our behavior is very much a part of modern psychology and can be seen in such situations as the conflict between our emotional desires and our more rational thought processes (Kahneman, 2011).

Sigmund Freud

Humanism

humanism
the view that psychology's goal should be to understand human strengths, aspirations, conscious experience, free will, and potential

positive psychology
the subfield of psychology that aims to understand the strengths, virtues, and values of human behavior

The perspective of **humanism** argues that psychology's goal should be to understand human strengths, aspirations, conscious experience, free will, and potential (Schultz & Schultz, 2004, pg. 460). Abraham Maslow, one of humanistic psychology's founders, is best known for his work on the Hierarchy of Needs, in which he discussed our journey from our most basic needs to self-actualization, or the full realization of our hopes and dreams. Similarly, Carl Rogers, also a humanistic psychologist, is best known for the idea that we can attain our best self through unconditional positive regard. Today, many of humanism's ideals and beliefs are present in the field of **positive psychology**: a subfield of psychology that aims to understand the strengths, virtues, and values of human behavior.

Recognizing the basic views of these historical perspectives in psychology is important as they continue to shape the way psychologists and people think about what determines our behavior. As you have the opportunity to interact with psychologists, either in person or through reading their work, pay careful attention to how they talk about behavior and what interests them, and you will get a feel for how these historical perspectives influence their thinking.

You are likely wondering what is the current, dominant perspective. This is difficult to answer. In many ways, it is easier to pinpoint the historical perspectives that have shaped psychology than it is to identify what the major influence is today. Thanks to improved communications technology and the greater accessibility of information, our thinking about psychology (and pretty much all other topics) is not as strongly influenced by a single theory as it was in the past. Furthermore, improvements in our research technologies have allowed us to better conceptualize psychology as a complex process with influences from a number of different sources. Because of this greater breadth of thinking, most current psychologists would likely agree that psychology's dominant perspective is the **bio-psycho-social-cultural perspective**. As suggested by this mouthful of a name, this perspective includes the many factors that work together to influence our behavior. Pause for a minute and look at the name of this perspective again, and you will notice how closely it matches the five behavioral influences mentioned in the definition of psychology earlier in this chapter. The "mental processes" in the definition of psychology uses and the "psycho" in the bio-psycho-social-cultural perspective both refer to the same set of internal behaviors, such as thinking, feeling, and motivation, and can be viewed as synonyms of each other in this context. This modern view of behavior conceives of our actions as a product of our biology, our environmental and social interactions, and the cultural context in which we live.

From the Desk of Dr. Stith

My name is Dr. Randy Stith, and I'm glad to introduce you to the psychology subfield of crisis management. I'm the CEO and Executive Director of the Aurora Mental Health Center, where I have worked for 40 years. Here in Aurora, Colorado, our staff has been on the front lines of some of the nation's most pressing tragedies directly or indirectly related to mental health issues and in support of the victims.

Crisis management, at its core, is an element of crisis intervention where trained professionals apply strategies toward the address of a significantly negative event. It combines elements of security, emergency management, mental health support, and public safety, and demand for professionals with the crisis management specialty is growing. Throughout *Psychology: The Science of Who We Are*, I've written commentaries on the role of crisis management within the context of the core concepts of the book to give you a sense of the place of crisis management in the discipline. I hope you find the notes from my desk enlightening and of interest as you stake out your career path.

bio-psycho-social-cultural perspective
this perspective is inclusive of the many factors that work together to influence behavior

Subfields of Psychology

Due to the complexity of human behavior, psychologists cannot focus on all the variables that influence behavior, or all the different behaviors that make up our experience of any given event, in each study. Instead, psychologists typically break the human experience into different behaviors and influences. The separation of complex behavior into smaller parts is a necessary element of managing the scope of a given research project. These different areas of research that focus on a specific set of influences on behavior represent the **subfields of psychology**. The subfields of psychology addressed in this textbook include the following:

- **Biopsychology** (Chapter 3): How the physical systems (the brain, nerves, and hormones) produce behavior

- **Sensation and perception** (Chapter 4): How the senses collect energy from the environment and then process this sensory information to create a mental model of the world

subfield of psychology
areas of research that focus on a specific set of influences on behavior

biopsychology
how the physical systems produce behavior

sensation and perception
the study of how the senses collect energy from the environment and then process this sensory information

developmental psychology
the study of how the individual changes physically, cognitively, and emotionally over the life span

cognitive psychology
the study of memory, thinking, reasoning, and other mental activities

psychology of intelligence
the study of individual differences in mental capacities and abilities

personality psychology
the study of the relatively consistent patterns of thinking, feeling, and behaving within an individual

abnormal psychology
the scientific study of psychological problems, including mental illness, and their treatment

social psychology
the study of how the social environment, including individuals and groups, influences the behavior of the individual, including how they think, act, and feel

multicultural/diversity studies
a subfield of psychology that explores how behavior is influenced by culture, ethnicity, sexual orientation, gender, and disability

- **Developmental psychology** (Chapter 5): How the individual changes physically, cognitively, and emotionally over the life span
- **Behavior analysis** (Chapter 7): How behavior changes over time and across species in response to environmental influences
- **Cognitive psychology** (Chapters 9 and 10): How psychological information is processed, stored, and interpreted
- **Psychology of intelligence** (Chapter 10): How individuals differ in their mental capacities and abilities
- **Personality psychology** (Chapter 12): How consistent patterns of thinking, feeling, and behaving exist within and across individuals
- **Abnormal psychology** (Chapters 13): How psychological problems, including mental illnesses, develop, impact life, and are treated
- **Social psychology** (Chapter 15): How the social environment—including individuals and groups—influence individual behavior, including how a person thinks, acts, and feels

The listed subfields covered in this text are only a sampling of the many different areas of psychological study. Even as we directly address these subfields, you will also read about other fields, such as **multicultural/diversity studies**, a subfield of psychology that explores how culture, ethnicity, sexual orientation, gender, and disability influence behavior and cuts across the traditional subfields, strongly representing the growing integration within psychology as modern research tools allow psychologists to ask more complicated and comprehensive research questions. Just as behavioral influences are too various to study in a single field of psychology, the number of subfields in psychology is too numerous to cover fully in a single introductory text. Rather than trying to cover all of the specialties and interests of psychology, the goal of this text is to cover the major fields needed to build a sufficient foundation to both appreciate the power of the science of psychology and to understand how you can begin to apply psychology in your life to better manage your behavior and your interactions with others.

Concept Recall

1. What is the dead person's test, and how does it help us to identify what are and are not behaviors?
2. How is focusing on behavior beneficial when setting goals?
3. What are the similarities and differences among the six historical perspectives of psychology?
4. What is a subfield of psychology? What nine subfields are discussed in this text?
5. Why is it beneficial to study a limited range of behavior and environmental influences in a given study?

This Is Psychology

One way to appreciate the breadth of psychology is to look at the professional organizations representing psychologists' interests today. To do this, we encourage you to visit the websites of the American Psychological Association (www.apa.org) and the Association for Psychological Science (www.psychologicalscience.org). These are the two largest organizations representing psychology in the United States today. The American Psychological Association has fifty-four divisions that exemplify the broad interests of its membership. Take a minute and visit the website listing of these divisions: www.apa.org/about/division. Did any of these divisions surprise you? Did any catch your interest? Why?

A BRIEF HISTORY OF PSYCHOLOGY

Modern psychological science is often considered to have begun in 1879 when German physiologist, politician, and philosopher (though he will forever be best known as a psychologist), Wilhelm Maximilian Wundt (1832-1920) established a laboratory at the University of Leipzig (Hothersall, 1990). While Wundt gets the credit for the founding of psychology, it is important to note that his work was strongly influenced by the changing nature of thought and science in Europe at the time. The academic climate at the time when Wundt was working saw a major shift in the **zeitgeist** (spirit of the times) of European thought. While we do consider Wundt as the originator of modern psychology, his work was really the emergent product of the research and thinking of many scholars before him.

Wilhelm Wundt

zeitgeist
the major intellectual theories and philosophies that dominate an area during a specific time in history

Intellectual Influences on Psychology

John Stuart Mill, a popular British philosopher interested in mental activity (Hothersall, 1990), was one of a number of European philosophers and scientists whose ideas about how to understand human behavior became the foundation of psychology. Mill helped set the stage for the development of psychology through both his arguments in favor of applying the scientific process to the exploration of human behavior and his application of ideas and concepts from chemistry to psychological exploration (Schultz & Schultz, 2015). Mill believed mental experiences, like chemical compounds, have characteristics greater than the sum of their individual parts. Mill's ideas regarding how human experience builds in complexity were a direct reflection of changes in how chemists understood the synthesis of chemical compounds from basic elements. Mill's father, James Mill, had similarly borrowed from the ideas of physical scientists in his arguments that the mind was a machine, responding in a robotic fashion to environmental inputs. While both father (James) and son (John) were influenced by the work of contemporary physical scientists (physicists and chemists, respectively), they differed significantly in their views of the mind as either a machine responding to the environment (James) or as an active player in synthesizing new information from the basic inputs of the environment (John) (Schultz & Schultz, 2015). Wundt read the philosophies and ideas

John Stuart Mill

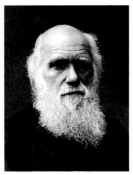

Charles Darwin

discussed by John Stuart Mill (such as his book *A System of Logic*, published in 1843), and those ideas, therefore, had a direct impact on how psychology developed.

While philosophers such as James Mill and John Stuart Mill influenced the developing ideas of a scientific view of human behavior, Charles Darwin's presentation of evolution by natural selection in *On the Origin of Species* (1859) strongly influenced the changing views on the connection between mind and body. Darwin's work on natural selection had broad appeal as an explanation for the origin of mental and physical activities in humans and animals. Prior to the shift in thinking represented by Darwin's work, the dominant view held that behavior was driven by both a physical component and a mental element. This way of thinking was founded on René Descartes's theory of dualism: the idea that humans are a combination of physical and nonphysical components. (You'll read more about dualism in Chapter 8.) Darwin's theory of evolution demonstrated how both the physical and behavioral aspects of an organism change over time in response to the environment. Darwin's work was critical in creating the discipline of psychology as it repaired the separation resulting from Descartes's dualistic view of human nature, thus reconnecting our physical bodies to our behavior.

Wundt's Laboratory

As we consider the intellectual changes in Europe as evidenced by Darwin's work on evolution as well as the work of philosophers such as William James and John Stuart Mill, we can appreciate how the founding of psychology in Wundt's laboratory was the synthesis of a number of different ideas and pressures. Today, we find that Wundt's interests and experiences with physiology and philosophy, coupled with the changing view of human behavior as the product of natural selection, forged psychology into a connecting science between biology, philosophy, and the social sciences. Indeed, psychology has been referred to as a "hub science," perched at the intersection between many other fields of scientific inquiry (Cacioppo, 2007).

Wundt's and his students' early work was based on the premise that most knowledge can be doubted, so the only certainties are the result of direct experience (Blumenthal, 1975). Wundt argued that psychological science should rely on observable, replicable measurements of behavior and mental events. Because of Wundt's focus on using physiological methods to study mental behavior, the research in Wundt's lab made use of the scientific technology of the day, including "tachistoscopes, chronoscopes, electrical stimulators, pendulums, timers, and sensory mapping devices" (Hothersall, 1990, pg. 97). These tools connected the psychological work of Wundt's students to the physiological methodology of Wundt's training. Much of the research in Wundt's lab focused on questions that would be of interest to cognitive psychologists and sensation and perception researchers, including the measurement of memory, the limits of our senses and perceptual systems (including color vision and afterimages), speed at which participants could complete mental tasks, perception of time, and the sense of touch (Blumenthal, 1975; Hothersall, 1990). As this list indicates, Wundt's laboratory had a broad interest in the spectrum of human behavioral abilities. While Wundt did not explore questions about higher mental functions with experiments in his laboratory,

Cross-Cultural Case

The Science of Who We Are

It's no secret that the development of modern psychology as a discipline occurred primarily within Western culture, most notably Europe, in the nineteenth and twentieth centuries. As such, the behavioral data of Western people helped construct many of the "baselines" of behavior that psychologists used and continue to use, a clear limitation of psychology's ability to integrate into non-Western nations' cultures. The American Psychological Association (APA) addresses this limitation in the updates to the fifth edition of the Diagnostic and Statistical Manual of Mental Disorders (DSM-5). You can read more about this in Chapter 13, Abnormal Psychology.

But the origin of psychological study dates back more than a millennium and spans a number of societies and cultures. Ancient studies from Greek, Persian, Chinese, Indian, and other civilizations contributed to the philosophical study of psychology as early as 400 BCE! To put that timeline into perspective, Alexander the Great hadn't even been born yet, war raged between the Spartans and Persians, and the Julian calendar—the precursor to what we currently use, the Gregorian calendar—had yet to be invented. Despite modern psychology's focus on empirical scientific data, much of the development of psychological philosophy occurred in the context of religion, such as Buddhism in China and Hinduism in India. Throughout nearly all of human history, we've reflected on the way we "work" and how we interact with our environments and each other, turning a critical eye on what makes humans *human*.

While we'll see throughout the book that cross-cultural theories of psychology have revealed significant parallels across world cultures, it's important as one who studies psychology to consider context. As you learn about psychology and theories of psychology, remember to recognize the importance of not only the context in which the treatment or theory developed but also the context of use as we continue to understand the science of who we are.

Nong2 / Shutterstock.com

he did write extensively about these topics. Some of Wundt's broader interests included language, concept formation, culture, religion, and art (Hothersall, 1990). Because of the difficulties designing controlled experimental studies of these topics, Wundt used historical analysis, naturalistic observation, and logical inference in his study of complex human behavior (Blumenthal, 1975).

Wundt's work has had a profound influence on how we think about psychology. In addition to Wundt's published works, Wundt influenced psychology by training many of the leaders in the field as graduate students. James Cattell, Wundt's first PhD. student in psychology, returned to the United States after completing his degree to become the first professor of psychology in the United States and a major influence

From the Desk of Dr. Stith

Ever wonder who you really are? After fifty years as a psychologist, the cliche, "With experience comes the knowledge of how much you don't know" seems pretty accurate. What also seems pretty accurate is everyone and everything human I've encountered is somewhere along a continuum. Imagine long strings with everything that makes up your personality as a knot on the string. You are smart, but there are others smarter—and others not as smart. You are funny, and there are others funnier and those not as funny. You are where you are on the intelligence continuum and on the humor continuum. I am basically an optimistic person; one of my cousins is seriously cynical. We are at different places on the continuum string called optimism—pessimism.

What do I know if I say you are funny? Do I know how smart you are? How optimistic you are? Or how happy, sad, depressed you are right now? Every one of us is somewhere on multiple continua. Some aspects of personality stay relatively stationary on the string. Other parts of our identity, feelings, skills, and needs can move rapidly up and down a particular continuum.

Likewise, every event that involves humans also falls along a continuum. In crisis management, the personal differences of every victim, survivor, responder, and crisis helper make their experience of a disaster unique to them. There is no "generic" victim. Joe's disaster event and trauma and recovery are different from Heather's or Jason's. It may have been the same hurricane or tragic shooting incident, but the event and feelings are uniquely their own.

It's so very important for all of us to remember not to over-generalize; it is important not to treat people as a diagnosis or just a victim. Everyone is an individual with varied uniqueness moving along multiple continua—their own "Gordian Knots" of complexity.

So, who are you right now?

Randy C. Stith, PhD

in the development of intelligence testing (Boakes, 1984). Edward Titchener, an English psychologist, immigrated to the United States, where he founded the psychology department at Cornell University and mentored Margaret Floy Washburn, the first woman to receive a PhD in psychology. She received her degree in 1894 and went on to publish more than 130 articles and several books, was elected president of the American Psychological Association, and became a member of the National Academy of Sciences (Pillsbury, 1940).

In the end, Wundt's contributions to psychology have proven to be paradoxically vast and negligible (Hunt, 1993). Vast because he provided the emerging field with a champion who emerging psychologists could either rally behind or challenge, and negligible because Wundt's psychology has been widely replaced by newer ideas and approaches (Benjamin, 1988). Wundt was also able to attract and train high-quality graduate students who developed the theories and perspectives that became the backbone of modern psychology (Richards, 2009).

The Expansion of Psychology

While Wundt receives credit as the founder of psychology, other scientists and philosophers across both Europe and the United States were also working on the development of a scientific study of psychology at the same time. Gustav Fechner, a physicist in the early stages of his academic career, conducted pioneering research on sensation and perception throughout the 1860s. Fellow German Franz Brentano, a philosopher by training, published *Psychology from an Empirical Standpoint* in 1874, the same year Wundt published his first psychology textbook. However, though the two early psychologists published their first books in the same year and were of the same nationality, their perspectives on psychology were very different (Hothersall, 1990).

As it turns out, 1874—the year that Brentano published his text—was a big year for the development of psychology both in Europe and in the United States. In the United States, William James, who is now considered the father of American psychology, presented a series of lectures on psychology at Harvard University. These lectures represent the formal introduction of psychology to the United States and led to James being asked to write the first American textbook on psychology. James originally trained as a medical doctor, though he never actively practiced medicine (Hothersall, 1990). Despite his tremendous impact on psychology, James was not a fan of experimental work, as he found the details of research tedious (Landy, 1992). In 1890, James formalized his ideas regarding psychology with his publication of *Principles of Psychology*. The table of contents alone provides a glimpse of the breadth of James's thinking regarding psychology, as it includes topics as diverse as habit, attention, the conscious self, memory, imagination, reasoning, instinct, emotions, will, and hypnotism, to name just a few. As the variety of topics in his text demonstrates, psychology has asked broad questions about human behavior since its earliest days.

Psychology was an established science by the start of the 1900s in both Europe and the United States. By the start of the new century, a number of professional publications and a formal association, the American Psychological Association, founded in 1892, represented psychological science (Landy, 1992). With its formal founding by Wundt in 1874, psychology is now more than 140 years old. While this may seem like a long time in the life span of an individual, psychology's short history as a discipline makes it a relatively young science. As we will see throughout this text, both our understanding of psychology and our technologies for conducting psychological research are changing rapidly. In many ways, psychology no longer resembles what was originally envisioned by Wundt and his students, despite their original ideas continuing to serve as the foundation of the science.

Psychology Leaves the Laboratory

Wundt's work helped to establish psychology as a laboratory science; however, with its early growth came questions about its value in addressing real-world problems. In 1904, Charles Spearman, a British psychologist who made major contributions to our understanding and measurement of intelligence, directly addressed the disconnect between the lab and real-world applications of psychology in a published paper that was highly critical of laboratory work that made no effort to contribute to real-world questions. Similarly, William James, with his functionalist views of psychology, was especially vocal in this criticism as his views on the importance of the function of behavior often pointed to application. With the growing interest in the application of psychology, the early 1900s saw a huge growth in applied psychology.

One of the first demonstrations of experimental psychology's power to solve real-world problems came in the early 1900s through Carl Stumpf and Oskar Pfungst's work in solving the problem of Clever Hans. Clever Hans was a horse trained by his owner, Wilhelm von Osten, to answer questions by tapping with his hoof. Hans was able to answer almost any

Clever Hans the horse was able to respond to almost any question that could be answered through a series of hoof taps.

question that could be answered by hoof tapping, including math problems, spelling, geography, and recall tasks (Schultz & Schultz, 2015). Thanks to his great "intelligence," Hans became all the rage in Europe. However, even as he astounded audiences across the continent, people questioned the validity of his performance. Certainly, there must have been some trick. Several studies were conducted, including one commissioned by the German government, and the result appeared to confirm that Hans was, indeed, answering the questions.

Stumpf and Pfungst were not content with the results of these tests and set out to use the tools of science to understand what Hans was doing. Through their research, they discovered Hans was cleverer than anticipated. While Hans was not actually able to do the mental work required to calculate a reply to the question, he did reliably produce the correct response. So how did he do it? Pfungst's research found that when the audience knew the answer to the question, Hans was able to respond to 98 percent of the questions correctly. However, when the audience, including the questioner, was unaware of the answer, Hans's accuracy dropped to just 8 percent. These outcomes provided clear evidence that the questioner, not Hans, was doing the calculations, and Hans was somehow extracting the right answer from members of the audience. The final insight came when Hans was blindfolded. When blindfolded, Hans was unable to produce the correct response regardless of whether the audience knew the answer or not. Apparently, Hans had learned that while people were looking at his foot, he should continue tapping. When people moved their eyes away from his foot to look at his face, as the audience unintentionally reacted as soon as he reached the correct number of taps, he should stop tapping. Hans turned out to have a very simple strategy for solving very complex problems.

Experimental psychology's success in solving the problem of Clever Hans was an important step forward in psychology's development. Not only were Stumpf and Pfungst able to explain clearly what was going on with Hans, but they also did so in a public way that clearly demonstrated the advantages of applying scientific methodologies to mental problems.

**industrial/
organizational
psychology**
the subfield of psychology that examines the application of psychological principles to work and business

The importance of psychology as an applied field grew as our world became more technologically complicated. Early work in the area of **industrial/organizational psychology**—the subfield of psychology that examines the application of psychological principles to work and business—attempted to improve the efficiency of workers in factories and other settings created by modern technology. Examples of this early work include W. L. Bryan's report in 1897 on how telegraph operators learn Morse code, one of the first applied psychology papers ever published, and the work of Walter Scott, who focused on the application of psychological concepts in advertising (Muchinsky, 2003). Perhaps most influential at the time was the work of Hugo Münsterberg, considered by many to be the father of industrial/organizational psychology.

Münsterberg was a German-trained medical doctor who earned his PhD with Wundt and then left Europe to work with William James at Harvard University. He was a very prolific writer who extended the application of psychology to business, education, and

Hugo Münsterberg

the beginnings of the field of legal psychology with his work on eyewitness testimony, lie detection (a topic Oskar Pfungst also studied after his initial work with Clever Hans), and jury persuasion (Landy, 1992). In many ways, Münsterberg's life reflected the general growth trend of what was to become psychology in North America. His initial ideas and influence came from Wundt's lab and theories of structuralism, but then he moved across the Atlantic to the United States, where the concepts and ideas of functionalism came to dominate his approach to psychology. Similarly, having established psychological laboratories in both Germany and Massachusetts, Münsterberg began his career as a strict experimentalist and later shifted to a greater focus on applying psychology to real-world problems.

Concept Recall

1. What influence did the general intellectual changes in Europe have on Wundt's ideas regarding psychology?

2. How did Darwin's views of human nature differ from Descartes's dualism?

3. What types of research did Wundt conduct in his initial studies of psychology?

4. How did the case of Clever Hans impact the development of psychology?

5. What role did developing technology have on the history of psychology?

This Is Psychology

The history of psychology has had a direct impact on your life, even though you are likely unaware of this influence. For example, you probably completed the SAT, ACT, or another type of college entrance exam. The college entrance exam movement is based on work conducted by psychologists during World War I. Commissioned by the US government, Robert Yerkes led a group of psychologists in developing the Army Alpha and Army Beta tests, which were aptitude tests for determining how best to use new recruits (Schultz & Schultz, 2015). These tests were so successful that, after the war, the concepts, procedures, and technologies used in the army tests were applied to college acceptance exams. Thus, the SAT, ACT, and other entrance exams find their origins in the history of psychology (Popham, 2002).

PSYCHOLOGY TODAY

Psychology has changed a great deal since its inception in the late 1800s. Thanks to technological advances, we can explore questions about behavior that are more complex than could be imagined when the science began. The types of questions psychologists ask both in the lab and in the world outside the lab relate to all aspects of life. Psychologists now work in settings ranging from airports to zoos. However, while psychology may be much bigger and broader than when it began, its foundation remains the same—as an empirical, science-based approach to understanding human behavior.

As the largest association in the world representing psychologists' interests, the American Psychological Association (APA) is particularly interested in the growth of the field. In 2016, the APA published research on where psychologists work, based on level of education. Three of the top fields for individuals with a bachelor's degree in psychology are: sales (20 percent), professional services (mental health counselor, addictions counselor, etc.; 17 percent), and management/supervision (16 percent). In contrast to this distribution, psychology majors with a master's or doctorate in psychology work largely in professional services (45 to 54 percent) with only a handful working in sales positions (1 to 8 percent). The major reason for this shift in job distribution lies in the additional training and possibility of gaining a professional license that comes with completing a graduate program. Most professional services positions require the participant to complete at least a master's degree in their chosen field before they can work in that area. A doctoral degree is required before someone can say he or she is a "psychologist." Individuals with a master's degree are typically called a counselor, mental health professional, or one of a number of other professional titles.

As you read through this text, you will learn about the many different questions psychologists try to answer and the different work settings where they are employed. Some of the main jobs you will see psychologists performing are teaching, conducting research, counseling, consulting, conducting psychological assessments, working in schools, designing user interface systems, and many, many more (APA, 2011). Figure 1.4 shows the breakdown of work tasks by psychologists in eight categories. Most psychologists complete several of these tasks as part of their daily work responsibilities. Ken and Shawn split their days between research and teaching activities. Susan spends her work days providing mental health services and engaging in management and administrative activities. One value of training in psychology is that the knowledge and skills acquired can be used in a very broad range of work responsibilities.

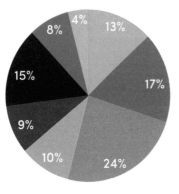

- Research
- Educational Services
- Other Employment Activities
- Education (Teaching)
- Other Applied Psychology
- Not Specified
- Health/Mental Health Services
- Management/Administration

1.4 Work tasks reported by psychologists
Adapted from Table 4 of the 2015 American Psychological Association Member Profiles Report.

Before finishing this chapter, we encourage you to take a few minutes and visit the news feeds hosted by the American Psychological Association (www.apa.org/news/psycport) and the Association for Psychological Science (www.psychologicalscience.org/index.php/news). These newsfeeds provide a great overview of the current work being done by psychologists.

PSYCHOLOGY IN CONTEXT

Psychology is a systematic study of what it means to be you. Researchers in the field use the scientific method and best practices of scientific research to develop and test hypotheses about our behavior. The information gained from these studies can be used to understand why we act the way that we do and how to build technologies based on this information. You will see throughout this text that psychological science is used to improve education, health, and personal relationships. Psychology is also used to sell you products, convince you to vote for certain candidates, and encourage you to spend more time in a store, online, or playing certain games. Psychology explores all of the influences that surround you. Because of the breadth of this science, understanding psychological research is an important step in better understanding yourself.

As you begin your study of psychology, we challenge you to ask yourself the following question: "How does this information help me better understand my behavior and experiences?" Psychology is an extremely personal science. Approaching your study of psychology with an emphasis on better understanding you is an ideal way to get the most out of this text. Not only will developing the habit of seeking the personal connection between what you are reading and your experiences help with appreciating psychology, it is also an excellent learning tool.

Review/Reflect/Write

REVIEW

- What is the formal definition of psychology?
- How do personal experiences and the reactivity of the participant create unique challenges that psychologists must overcome?
- Identify the five types of behavior influences that psychologists use to study behavior. How do these factors combine to make up our experience?
- What is the major difference between psychology and the other social sciences?
- What is the dead person's test? How does it help us to understand what psychologists study?
- Which of the five influences on behavior included in the definition of psychology would be of the most interest to a social psychologist? What about to a behavior analyst?
- What is the bio-psycho-social-cultural perspective of psychology?
- Why were the events of Clever Hans important in the development of applied psychology?
- What impact have changes in technology had on the development of psychology?
- What are: the major job functions of psychologists and the major work settings for psychologists today?

1. The study of how the senses collect energy from the environment and then process the sensory information in order to create a mental model of the world is represented by which subfield of psychology?

   a. biopsychology
   b. cognitive psychology
   c. developmental psychology
   d. sensation and perception

2. Mental processes are:

   a. The natural world around the organism, which can include lighting, temperature, sound levels, and other features

b. The groups and individuals who we interact with throughout our life

c. The biological structure of the organism, functioning of the organs, and genetic makeup

d. The information-processing systems and structures that are part of the mental capacities of the individual and serve to process sensory information

3. What is a potential source of challenge that is unique to psychologists studying behavior compared to other scientists?

   a. The types of tools that the psychologist uses to study behavior

   b. The psychologist's own personal experiences and behavior

   c. The particular culture that the psychologist lives in while conducting his or her research

   d. The subfield of psychology that the psychologist studies

4. If a psychologist was studying a group of individuals, which of the following would be a potential research question?

   a. How is the culture of the group affecting the choices that are made as a group?

   b. How are the dynamics of the group affecting the choices of the individuals?

   c. How could group efficiencies be increased in a way that would lead to stronger decision-making?

   d. How would this group interact if divided into two groups?

5. According to what we know about behavior, which of the following goals would be most likely to elicit a behavioral change?

   a. "I want to do better in school, so I won't watch TV."

   b. "I want to do better in school, so I will not go out on the weekend."

   c. "I want to do better in school, so I will study for two hours a day."

   d. "I want to do better in school, so I will stop drinking."

6. In terms of the effect of culture on behavior, how do psychologists conceptualize culture?

   a. The geographic region that the organism comes from that affects processing of the world

   b. The norms and rules that have been adopted by the social group and have become part of the environment

   c. The ways various groups can change the interaction patterns within a larger region

   d. The biological predisposition to behave in a certain way

7. Which of the following statements would Edward B. Titchener most agree with?

   a. The human experience loses its essence when it is broken down, and it should be looked at as a whole.

   b. The elementary components of experience will best help us understand consciousness.

   c. Psychology should focus on higher mental processes, because these tell us more about conscious experience than physiology.

   d. Rather than focusing on the "what" of experience, we should focus on the "why."

8. The idea that the goals of psychology should be the study of how consciousness and experience aid in adjusting to the environment is known as:

   a. functionalism   b. structuralism   c. gestalt   d. behaviorism

9. Dr. Cross focuses on the strengths of her clients, including their potential. Her therapy highlights the goals, aspirations, and free will of her clients. Dr. Cross is most likely a:

    a. behaviorist   b. humanist   c. gestaltist   d. structuralist

10. Oskar Pfungst found that Clever Hans's correct answers were produced by:

    a. what he had learned in his training

    b. secret prompts that he had been taught

    c. unconscious cues from the audience

    d. auditory signals given by a plant in the audience

REFLECT

1. Psychologists have to be very careful not to allow their personal experiences to bias their interpretations. Why do you think this is a problem? What are two ways that you could apply the scientific perspective of psychology in your life to help keep your personal experiences from biasing your interpretations of other people's behavior?

2. The various perspectives of psychology represent different ways of thinking about the origins of behavior. So, are you a structuralist, functionalist, behaviorist, humanist, psychoanalyst, or gestaltist? Why? What experiences from your life make you identify with that particular perspective?

3. The early history of psychology was strongly influenced by cultural changes in Europe. What current cultural and social events and changes do you think might influence the future development of psychology?

WRITE

1. Psychology views behavior as a product of the influence of five factors: biology, mental processes, the environment, the social world, and our cultural experiences. Pick three everyday behaviors that you engage in, and write an analysis of how each of these five influences affects that behavior.

2. The brief history of psychology presented in this chapter focuses on the development of psychology in the United States. Europe and the United States are not the only places where psychology is studied. Choose two non-North-American and non-European countries, and investigate what psychology looks like there. Do those countries have similar themes to those that we see in the United States? Are there differences in their approaches compared to what is discussed in this text? Why do you think psychology might differ across cultures?

Key Terms

abnormal psychology   20
anthropomorphization   12
behavior analysis   18
behaviorism   17
bio-psycho-social-cultural perspective   19
biopsychology   19
cognitive psychology   20
developmental psychology   20
evolutionary psychology   17
functionalism   17
gestalt   17
humanism   18
industrial/organizational psychology   26

multicultural/diversity studies   20
personality psychology   20
perspectives of psychology   16
positive psychology   18
psychodynamic theory   18
psychology   10
psychology of intelligence   20
sensation and perception   19
social psychology   20
structuralism   16
subfields of psychology   19
zeitgeist   21

Chapter

2 Science of Behavior

After reading this chapter, you will be able to answer the following questions:
- What are the steps of the scientific method?
- What are the four goals of science?
- What is the difference between internal and external validity?
- Why are external and internal validities important in evaluating studies?
- What are the different types of research methods that psychologists use?
- What are the major characteristics of experimental research?
- What does studying animals have to do with human behavioral research?
- Why are research ethics important in the study of psychology?

On January 15, 2016, Anna Stubblefield was sentenced to twelve years in prison for sexually assaulting a man with cerebral palsy (Engber, 2016). The actions that led to Stubblefield's conviction were founded on her claim that D.J.—the man she was convicted of assaulting—had communicated to her his consent and desires, despite his being considered by most people to be completely non-communicative. At the beginning of her trial, Stubblefield's attorneys argued that they should be allowed to present typed communications that they asserted were authored by D.J. giving consent for both the relationship and the sexual activities. The judge for the case, however, ruled that none of these communications would be allowed as evidence because they were produced by facilitated communication (FC), an assisted communications technology that the state of New Jersey does not recognize as a scientifically verified form of communication.

FC arrived in the United States from Australia in the early 1990s. During facilitated communication, a facilitator supports the arm of a nonverbal individual while he or she, the communicator, types out messages on a keyboard. The facilitator's role is to provide support for the communicator, enabling him or her to use the device despite physical disabilities. Unfortunately, because the facilitator is in contact with the communicator, there are concerns regarding who produces the communication, the communicator or the facilitator. These questions of authorship are exactly why the New Jersey court disallowed the communications that Stubblefield argued were produced by D.J.

Stubblefield's case is the most recent example in a long history of facilitated communication in courts of law. Shortly after FC became popular in the United States, facilitators started reporting instances in which the communicators typed allegations of physical and sexual abuse by educators, treatment providers, and family members. These reports were investigated and, at times, resulted in arrests and family separations, using the messages typed through facilitated communication as key evidence. The seriousness of the allegations required immediate action by legal authorities. However, they also raised concerns about the validity of the communications. If the FC reports were true, FC was saving children from abuse and maltreatment. If the FC reports were fabricated, individuals and families were being harmed. But how could scientists and courts determine the true source of the messages? Were communicators actually conveying their own thoughts, or instead were facilitators concocting the messages from scratch?

As you read the story of Anna Stubblefield, D.J., and facilitated communication, you may have noticed some similarity between the stories of facilitated communication and Clever Hans from Chapter 1. Just as Oskar Pfungst was charged with determining the truth of Hans's communications, psychologists, special educators, and other behavioral scientists took the charge of determining the authorship of communications produced by FC. In the case of Hans, Pfungst discovered that Hans could only answer questions when his audience knew the right answer. A similar test was devised for FC.

An illustrative example of how scientists approached the study of facilitated communication occurred in 1994. Howard C. Shane and Kevin Kearns (1994) worked with a facilitator and a thirty-four-year-old client to test the origins of the messages typed during an FC session. Shane was an advocate for the use of FC when it first became popular but later developed major reservations regarding the technique and wanted to investigate whether the tool was valid. Using both visual and auditory cues, Shane and Kearns presented the communicator and facilitator with two experiences: both facilitator and communicator were given the same questions; and, facilitator and communicator were given different questions.

The facilitator and the communicator were "blind" to the other's questions. In other words, the facilitator did not know what question the communicator was asked, or even that the communicator might receive a different question than the facilitator, and likewise for the communicator. In a visual task, the facilitator and communicator individually viewed a picture. For half the trials, both were shown the same picture. For the other half of the trials, each saw a different picture (Figure 2.1). Remember, though, that neither the communicator nor the facilitator knew that different pictures were being shown.

Take a minute and think about why the researchers designed the study this way. What are the possible outcomes when you give a prompt to an FC team? If the facilitator is asked one question and the communicator is asked another question, which question should the communicator answer? That is, if an FC team tapped out an answer to the question asked of the facilitator but not the communicator, do you think that indicates that the communicator was conveying his own thoughts, or instead that the facilitator was concocting the answer from scratch based on what she believed the communicator was thinking?

	Facilitator	Communicator
Control Trials		
Experimental Trials		

2.1 Examples of possible stimuli shown to facilitator and communicator in an experimental test of facilitated communication (FC)
If FC works as believed, the communicator types "key" in the control trial and "cat" in the experimental trial. If the communicator is influencing the typing, the communicator types "boat" in the experimental trial. The picture shown to the facilitator is the answer given on almost every experimental trial.

The trials in which the facilitator and communicator received the same question are a control condition. If FC is working, then it is expected that the level of accuracy would be extremely high in this condition. That is exactly what Shane and Kearns found: When both members of the team received the same question, the response was correct on almost every trial. In the example shown in Figure 2.1, both the facilitator and the communicator were shown a picture of keys. In the subsequent test, the facilitated response was "keys." These results show that under laboratory conditions, FC was operating as expected. This result was extremely important in demonstrating the validity of the FC method. However, these experiences do not provide evidence to the research regarding the source of the message: facilitator or communicator.

In other trials, the facilitator and communicator received different questions. This is the the experimental condition. There are three possible outcomes in this trial: the wrong answer could be given, the correct answer to the question given to the communicator could be given, or the correct answer to the question given to the facilitator could be given. The researchers found that in almost all experimental trials, the typed answer matched the question given to the facilitator. For example, imagine that you showed a picture of a boat to the facilitator and a picture of a cat to the communicator. If the communicator is doing the typing—as argued by the proponents of FC—the answer typed should be "cat." On the other hand, if the facilitator is providing the answer, the typed answer would be "boat." In Shane and Kearns's research, the typical answer given was what the facilitator, not the communicator, was shown. In the example shown in Figure 2.1, the majority response would have been "boat" rather than "cat." This pattern of outcomes is very strong evidence that the typed messages in FC come from the facilitator, not the communicator.

Shane and Kearns's results were surprising. One study, though, was not enough to conclude that the facilitator, not the communicator, was providing the answer. Fortunately, Shane and Kearns's work has been repeated in dozens of studies using a variety of different tests. The evidence that the content of FC messages is strongly influenced by the facilitator in most cases (some cases of communication using FC seem to be legitimate) is extremely strong. Like the New Jersey court system, the majority opinion regarding FC is that it is not a valid communication tool. The use of the scientific approach allowed us to understand how to evaluate the message produced during FC sessions. This realization improved understanding of how FC works, thereby improving the outcomes for individuals with disabilities, their families, and society as a whole. This is the power of a scientific approach to understanding human behavior.

THE SCIENCE OF PSYCHOLOGY

In Chapter 1, we explored psychology's historical roots and the general definition of the field. As you remember, we highlighted that psychology is a science focused on the factors influencing a person's behavior. Also, we noted that psychology's history has often been determined by the struggle to define the scientific focus and direction of psychology. Now that we understand the historical roots of psychology, it is time to consider the scientific foundations of the field.

science
the systematic, organized approach to understanding the physical and natural world through direct observation and measurement

Science is a systematic, organized approach to understanding the physical world through direct observation and measurement. Science can be practiced with electron microscopes, orbiting telescopes, chemical assays, clipboards, or by watching the events in the world around you. Science can be practiced in a vacuum chamber, under the ocean, in a classroom, or at home. Despite the fact that science can be practiced anywhere and with any number of tools, we find that most people have a very particular stereotype of what science looks like. (See Chapter 15 for more on stereotypes.) For most people, science looks like a sterile lab with people in white lab coats surrounded by weird-looking microscopes and other machines. This is one context in which science occurs; however, science is not limited to that stereotypical context. Indeed, in psychological science, very little of the actual work takes place in a laboratory. Instead, it is more common to see psychologists conducting their research in classrooms, clinics, hospitals, businesses, factories, and anywhere else that people behave.

The Scientific Method

scientific method
an organized way that helps scientists (or anyone) answer a question or begin to solve a problem

The critical elements of science are not the tools or the location, but the discipline and approach of those conducting the study. A scientist, regardless of specialty, tools, or location, seeks knowledge through direct experience with the matter of interest. Scientists organize their work using the general guidelines of the **scientific method** (Figure 2.2):

1. **Observe** the world around you.

2. **Ask** a question about the physical world.

3. **Look** for relevant information in the existing scientific literature.

4. **Develop** a testable hypothesis.

5. **Conduct** an empirical test of the hypothesis.

6. **Objectively evaluate** the results of the test.

7. **Compare** your results with what is already known.

8. **Decide** on future action: publish your findings to the scientific community or revise your question, and repeat Steps three through seven.

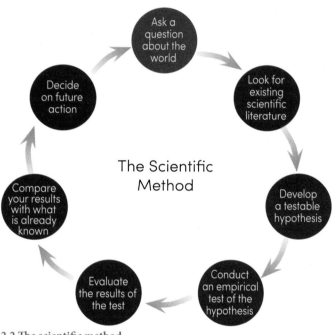

2.2 The scientific method
The scientific method is a general approach to systematically observing, testing, and evaluating the physical world.

These eight steps are a broad outline of the process scientists follow as they work to understand the physical world. Most scientists do not follow a checklist that includes each of these items; rather, the scientific method tries to capture the way scientists think about their work and the general development of a research project as it proceeds from informal observation to scientific investigation.

In order to fully appreciate the power of the scientific method, consider how we might use these steps to help us understand how people behave. For example, imagine that Mary, an undergraduate psychology student, recently made her first visit to Las Vegas, Nevada. During Mary's visit to a casino on the Las Vegas Strip, she was surprised that the electronic slot machines mimic the sound of coins falling into a metal dispenser, even though no actual coins fell into a tray. Instead of physical, noise-producing coins, Mary's winnings were recorded on a plastic card. Why does the casino play the recorded sound of coins dropping into the metal dish? (Step 1— observe the world around you.)

As Mary observed this, she wondered whether the sounds were intended to encourage players to insert more money into the machines. (Step 2—ask a question about the physical world.) Once she returned to her hotel room, Mary logged into her university's PsycINFO database (an electronic database for psychology-related publications) and looked for existing research relevant to her question. (Step 3—look for relevant information in the existing scientific literature.) Mary's search led her to a paper (Dixon et al., 2013) reporting that the sounds of the casino can produce an increase in heart rate and other physiological responses in experienced gamblers. Consistent with Mary's observation, this paper provided evidence that the casino sounds could, indeed, influence how gamblers react to the casino environment.

While the research Mary found gave some information related to her question, Mary did not find a complete answer in her search of the scientific literature. Mary reflected on her own behavior in the casino and anecdotally (based on personal experiences rather than scientific investigation) observed that the casino really did not have an impact on her heart rate or gambling behavior. If the sounds of the casino influence behavior, why didn't they influence her? Or did they have an influence on her that she might not have noticed? As Mary thought about the difference between what she read in the literature and her experiences in the casino, she developed a hypothesis: the sounds of the casino will produce a physiological change and influence gambling behavior, but only in people who are established gamblers. (Step 4—develop a testable hypothesis.) Mary's hypothesis contains a hallmark of good scientific thinking: it is directly falsifiable. **Falsifiability**—the ability to test a hypothesis with an objective, empirical observation that could demonstrate the hypothesis to be incorrect—is a defining characteristic of scientific inquiry.

Upon returning home, Mary decided to collect some information to help test her hypothesis. (Step 5—conduct an empirical test of the hypothesis.) With the approval of her university's **Institutional Review Board**—a committee composed of scientists and administrators that oversees all human research at an institution in order to protect the rights of research participants—Mary made a trip to the casino nearest her home, where she randomly approached twenty-five casino patrons and asked each of them two questions. (1) How serious a gambler are you? (This was scored on a scale from zero, indicating that they hardly ever gamble, to ten, indicating that they gamble every day.) (2) On a scale of zero to ten, how exciting do you find the sounds of the casino? The results from Mary's study are presented in Figure 2.3 as a **scatterplot**—a graph that shows the relationship between two continuous variables.

Mary evaluated the results of her test by both looking at the scatterplot of her results and by using **statistics**, a type of mathematics used to describe and evaluate data. (Step 6—

falsifiability
the ability to test a hypothesis with an objective, empirical observation that could demonstrate the hypothesis to be incorrect

Institutional Review Board
a committee composed of scientists and administrators that oversees all human research at an institution in order to protect the rights of research participants

scatterplot
a graph that shows the relationship between two variables

statistics
a type of mathematics used to describe and evaluate data

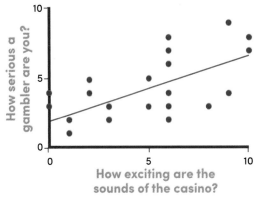

Mary's question: are casino sounds more exciting for serious gamblers?

2.3 Scatterplot of the results of Mary's gambling study
This graph shows a moderate positive relationship, with excitement tending to increase as experience with gambling increases.

objectively evaluate the results of the test.) Based on her results, Mary determined there is a correlation between how serious a gambler is and how excited he or she feels by the sounds of the casino. This result was consistent with Mary's hypothesis and helped her understand how her personal reaction to the casino's sounds (unexcited) could relate to the conclusions found in her research, suggesting that habitual gamblers do find the sounds of the casino to be exciting. (Step 7—compare your results with what is already known.)

Mary's scientific exploration of the observation she made while in Las Vegas provides a good example of applying the scientific method to reason through a problem. Mary's test was a respectable first step in examining the relationship between the sights and sounds of the casino and gambling behavior. However, it was just preliminary exploration into her project. Mary later met with her research advisor and began to design a more detailed, and controlled, test of her hypothesis. (Step 8—decide on future action.) As Mary and her advisor discussed her future research plans, they cycled back to the beginning of the scientific method, using the results of Mary's small survey as Step 1 (observe the world around you) in their next cycle of scientific reasoning. By using the scientific method as a framework for building her investigation of the world around her, Mary is able to ensure that her work has not been done before, is related to what we already know about how the world works, and is protected from her personal biases and beliefs about the world.

Concept Recall

1. What is science?
2. What are the eight steps of the scientific method?
3. What is the role of previous scientific knowledge in the scientific method?
4. What is falsifiability, and why is it important in science?
5. What information is shown on Mary's scatterplot, and what does this graph suggest about Mary's hypothesis?
6. How does the scientific method help improve the quality of questions that scientists ask?

This Is Psychology

Advertisements play a major role in our exposure to media. A popular technique used by advertisers is to suggest that their products have been "scientifically" tested. As potential consumers, we should carefully evaluate these claims. Pseudoscience is a term used to describe arguments that have the feel of science but without the rigor of real science. Commercials, advertisements, and many arguments are often filled with pseudoscientific claims. One of the best ways to identify these false scientific claims is to look for the hallmarks of the scientific method: direct observation, testable (falsifiable) hypotheses, and built on a foundation of existing, published scientific research. Without evidence of these elements, you're likely viewing or reading the result of pseudoscience.

THE FOUR GOALS OF SCIENCE

Thanks to the exceptionally large variety of behaviors we engage in, psychologists have a virtually unlimited range of questions they can ask and answer. As they do so, psychologists typically focus on finding answers consistent with the four general goals of science.

1. **Description:** *Psychologists aim to provide a clear understanding of when and where the observed behavior occurs.* Mary's study of gambling behavior was aimed at description. Based on her work, she was able to clearly describe some of the conditions associated with greater excitement about gambling (i.e., the sounds of the casino).

2. **Prediction:** *Psychologists work to anticipate the occurrence of the behavior and the magnitude of the behavior that might be observed.* Mary's next study could possibly focus on predicting under what conditions a novice gambler would transition into a problem gambler. For example, it might be that people who show elevated levels of excitement to the casino early on are more likely to become problem gamblers later in life.

3. **Explanation:** *Psychologists produce theories and models providing causal reasons for why the behavior happens the way it does.* The goal of explanation is met as the psychologist becomes able to understand the mechanisms responsible for the behavior. For example, Mary might focus on the role of changes in novice gamblers' physiological systems (e.g., nervous system, muscular system, cardiovascular system) as they develop problematic gambling behaviors. Studies aiming to explain behavior typically focus on either more fundamental levels of the behavior (physiological systems, genetics, biochemistry) or higher levels of explanation (culture, family systems, friends).

4. **Control:** *Psychologists apply the knowledge gained in scientific research to our daily lives through the development of psychological technologies.* These technologies can range from apps on your phone that influence how much you engage in a certain behavior (e.g., a therapeutic intervention app used by a professional counselor to work with a person with a mental illness). In this sense, technology refers to any system or tool built by a person. These technologies can take the form of anything from computers to building blocks. All engineered systems are technologies, no matter how simple.

In order to understand the four goals of science, consider the role of psychologists in political elections. A *New York Times* article published on November 12, 2012, discussed the role of psychologists in President Barack Obama's election to a second term as president of the United States. Just what would a psychologist do in working with a political campaign? The psychologists employed by President Obama's campaign team focused on the fourth goal of science: control. They were actively engaged in using behavioral science to develop technologies—flyers, advertisements, face-to-face dialogues—designed to influence a particular type of human behavior (voting). To succeed in this task, the psychologists had to understand behavior at each of the analytical levels scientists use. First, they had to develop a clear picture of what voting entails. Political psychologists describe voting behavior as more than just clicking a box on the voting machine. Rather, successful voting is a process that extends to learning about the candidates, understanding the voting system, and making a plan to vote. After describing what is involved in voting, the research team focused on predicting who would successfully accomplish these behaviors, who would not, and what conditions would influence these groups (weather, polling location, type of election).

Once the team of political psychologists consulting with President Obama's campaign was able to successfully describe and predict voting behaviors, the team was well-positioned to develop hypotheses about why voting is influenced by the particular events they identified through their research. The theoretical explanations of voting behavior provided the political psychologists a framework on which to develop technologies to influence behavior. President Obama's team of psychologists used their understanding of voting behavior to motivate a group of voters who are typically pro-Democratic but have poor turnout rates for elections. President Obama's team succeeded in motivating this group of voters by understanding that there is often a breakdown between intended and executed actions. (You have likely experienced this when you make plans to complete your homework, a workout, or an entrepreneurial project, but then fail to actually complete your homework, workout, or entrepreneurial project.) This disconnect is often caused by a failure to create detailed action plans. President Obama's campaign staff created a behavioral technology that included a planning session in their door-to-door visits, in which they helped potential voters develop a concrete plan for getting to the polling station and casting their vote. The success of this new approach in motivating the target population to vote is considered by many political historians as one of the keys to President Obama's successful re-election in 2012. Table 2.1 gives several examples of questions that psychologists can ask about voting behavior for each of the goals of psychology.

Table 2.1 Examples of questions psychologists might ask about voting behavior

Description	Prediction	Explanation	Control
What is voting?	When do people vote?	Why do people vote?	How do we encourage people to vote?
• What is involved in casting a vote? • What does the voter have to do to get to the voting location?	• What types of people vote? • Does the type of election matter?	• Why do some people choose to vote? • Why do more people vote in some types of elections than others?	• What strategies can be developed to increase turnout by underrepresented groups? • How do we increase access to information about candidates to encourage greater participation in elections?

HOW PSYCHOLOGISTS STUDY BEHAVIOR

As psychologists strive to understand behavior, they use scientific tools to observe and record what their participants do. Direct observation of behavior provides verifiable evidence that can be analyzed and discussed in order to address the four goals of science (description, prediction, explanation, and control). When we observe the world, there are several important considerations that we must keep in mind.

First, in order to measure behavior, we must clearly define exactly what it is that we intend to measure. The process of creating an **operational definition**—a statement that clearly explains what is being measured and how to measure it—is a critical first step in conducting any observation. A useful operational definition includes a clear statement of the target behavior that clearly describes what the behavior is and a statement about how the behavior will be measured. In the opening of this chapter, we discussed Dr. Shane's research on FC. In that study, he operationally defined a "correct answer" as any time the typed response on the keyboard matched the question provided to the communicator. If the communicator was shown a key and then typed "key," this was a correct answer. But, what if the communicator typed "kei"? Should this be counted as correct? Or what about "*llave*," the Spanish word for key? A good operational definition will specify how to deal with these types of cases.

operational definition
a statement that clearly explains what is being measured and how to measure it

A great example of the problem with poor operational definitions is the conflict that can arise when parents tell their teenage children to clean their rooms. What exactly is a clean room? For a teenager, "cleaning" typically means moving items out of eye sight (e.g., into the closet or under the bed). For a parent, cleaning a room typically includes putting items away (in the correct spot), dusting, and vacuuming. Much conflict occurs between parents and teenagers when a sufficient operational definition is not given before the task begins. The conflict over whether the room is sufficiently clean can be minimized by clearly specifying the outcome and the expected behaviors.

Second, any time we observe the world, we need to be careful that what is being observed is a true representation of behavior. The act of observing someone creates a risk of **reactivity**—changes in behavior that occur because of being observed and recorded. You have experienced reactivity in your life. Think about the last time someone started to take a picture or a video of what you were doing. The creation of this permanent record of your behavior likely caused a change in how you acted. You may become more outgoing and energetic while being filmed, or you might find yourself shyly trying to avoid the camera.

reactivity
changes in behavior that occur because of being observed/recorded

experimental control
the ability of the researcher to control the environment and minimize outside influences on the behavior of interest

Third, when psychologists observe behavior, they want as realistic a representation of the natural environment where the behavior occurs as possible, and they want to control as many of the variables that could influence the behavior as possible. Unfortunately, these desires are in opposition to each other. In order to have control of the variables influencing behavior, scientists have to create artificial environments in which to test the behavior. While this creates a controlled testing environment, it also creates a setting that is not similar to the natural environment. On the other hand, observing behavior in the real world maximizes realism, but it also limits the amount of control the scientist has over the environment and the behavior. In designing their research, psychologists must decide how to balance the demands of **experimental control**—the ability of the researcher to control the environment and minimize outside influences on

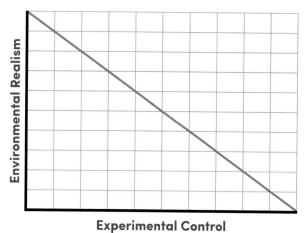

2.4 The relationship between environmental realism and experimental control
Environmental realism and experimental control are in opposition to each other. Highly controlled studies are not representative of the real world. Highly realistic studies make it very difficult to establish experimental control.

environmental realism
the degree to which the testing environment is similar to the real-world context where the behavior typically occurs

functional Magnetic Resonance Imaging (fMRI)
a technology that uses MRI techniques to measure changes in blood flow in the brain during mental activity

internal validity
the ability to minimize the influence of variables other than those involved in the research question

the behavior of interest—and **environmental realism**—the degree to which the testing environment is similar to the real-world context where the behavior typically occurs—in order to develop an answer to their research questions (Figure 2.4).

In order to understand the tradeoffs between control and realism, consider fMRI research. **Functional magnetic resonance imaging (fMRI),** a technology that measures changes in blood flow in the brain during mental activity, is one of several brain observation techniques that have revolutionized modern psychological science. However, fMRI research scores are extremely unrealistic since, during the fMRI session, participants are inserted into an extremely long, narrow, and loud metal tube that is often frightening even for participants who don't suffer from fear of closed-in spaces. During the imaging session, participants are required to lie as still as possible. This technology allows for very accurate, objective measures of brain activity; however, the results do not accurately reflect behavior in the real world. While fMRI allows for a great deal of experimental control and scientific precision, it does so in an artificial context, so without further research, we would not know how strongly the results from our controlled research apply to the complex context of the real world.

Choices made regarding the realism and control of the research study have a strong impact on the internal and external validity of the research study. A major goal of any research project is to design the study in a way that eliminates possible confounding variables. **Internal validity** refers to the ability to minimize the influence of variables other than those involved in the research question. If a researcher is interested in the effects of sleep on exam performance, the internal validity of the study will depend on the researcher's ability to control other variables that might influence exam performance, including recent food consumption, temperature of the testing environment, and stress level.

As a researcher, one way to optimize internal validity is to increase the experimental control. If all participants were forced to live in the laboratory during the study, where they would experience identical diet, exercise, time demands, temperature, and so on, then the researchers would be able to demonstrate strong internal validity. Unfortunately, it would be very difficult to recruit participants for this study or to sufficiently compensate them for their participation.

A second approach to increasing internal validity is to randomly assign participants to study conditions. Random assignment does not eliminate possible differences across participants, but instead spreads the differences across the study conditions.

For example, the diet of participants randomly assigned to the sufficient-sleep and insufficient-sleep conditions are likely to be comparable, so the main variable that systematically differs between groups is that one group had enough sleep and the other did not.

External validity refers to the degree to which findings from the study can be applied to situations and participants outside the original group of participants. A study that has high external validity will have results that can be used to understand the behavior of groups and situations that differ from those in the original study. External validity is critical to understanding the application of research to the real world.

external validity
the degree to which findings from the study can be applied to situations and participants outside the original group of participants

A classic example of an experiment with limited external validity is the Pepsi Challenge (Kirchner, 1995). In the late 1970s, Pepsi representatives set up tables in grocery stores across the United States and asked shoppers to compare the taste of Pepsi to Coke in a blind taste test. A blind taste test is one in which the participant is not told beforehand which cup contains Pepsi and which contains Coke. The results showed that most participants preferred the taste of Pepsi. As you might imagine, executives at Coca-Cola responded to these results with disbelief and vowed to carry out their own blind taste tests. To their horror, when Coke ran its own taste tests, the results matched those from Pepsi's taste tests: most participants preferred the taste of Pepsi. These results caused a crisis at Coca-Cola, leading the company to change its formula for the first time in nearly 100 years. The classic formula of Coke remained in stores only until April 1985, when new Coke was scheduled to appear. The switch to new Coke aroused widespread panic among Coke's faithful customers, who pressured the company for the next two months to restore the classic formula. In July, Coca-Cola gave in to the pressure and released Classic Coke to be sold alongside new Coke. Following the entire episode, Coke and Pepsi resumed their relative market shares, with Coke predominating and Pepsi in second place. Even though Pepsi is consistently preferred to Coke in blind taste tests under experimental conditions, these results fail to generalize to the everyday situations in which people drink cola. Under experimental conditions, people sip one cola then the other, but in real life people often guzzle one can after another. Because Pepsi tastes sweeter than Coke, a sip of Pepsi is typically judged to taste better than Coke, but when people drink large quantities of cola over long periods of time, the sweetness can become cloying. The Pepsi Challenge was not externally valid because the experimental results, in which Pepsi is preferred to Coke, failed to generalize to the world outside in which Coke is preferred to Pepsi. While the Pepsi Challenge shows the pitfalls associated with an experiment that is not externally valid, experimental psychologists always strive for their experiments to be externally valid so that their results can be used to describe how people act in their everyday lives.

Concept Recall

1. What are the four goals of science, and how do they build on one another?
2. Why is an operational definition important when observing behavior?

3. How does reactivity impact our observations of behavior?

4. What is the relation between experimental control and environmental realism?

5. What are internal and external validity, and how are they important in psychological science?

This Is Psychology

It is especially important that we consider the external validity of a study when reading about science in popular media. Most experimental research is constrained to very specific conditions in order to control for confounding variables. Real life is not similarly constrained. When generalizing the findings from a scientific report to the real world, reporters and science writers have to make a generalization. For example, Brad Tuttle did just this in his article "The Simple Mind Trick That Will Boost Your Savings in No Time" published on time.com (2015). Based on a published science report, Tuttle's article advises that we should think of important financial decisions—such as saving for retirement—in terms of days, not years. This suggestion is based on research by Neil A. Lewis Jr. and Daphna Oyserman (2015). Tuttle's story claims that this report showed that thinking in days will help you save money. And it might. But that is not what the original report showed. Lewis and Oyserman reported that people who were asked about *hypothetical* savings situations would start saving earlier if they thought in days as opposed to years. To what degree is what you report in a hypothetical situation the same as what you would do in a real scenario? Tuttle's interpretation of the research report assumes that they are very similar. Tuttle is making a large assumption regarding the external validity of the original work. Unfortunately, to scientists, the external validity was an unknown at the time Tuttle wrote his article. Lewis and Oyserman's findings had only been published a few weeks before the article, not giving enough time to replicate the study with different participants and in different settings.

Behavioral Research Methods

naturalistic observation
a research method in which behavior is observed and recorded in the context where it typically occurs with as little interference from the researchers as possible

case study
a detailed observation of a single individual or group of individuals

One way that psychologists balance the demands of control, realism, and validity is in how they decide to study the behavior of interest. For example, researchers must decide whether to study behavior in the laboratory or in real-world situations. By studying the behavior in the real world, the research team can see the behavior as it really happens, but they lose the ability to control variables that might be important to understanding the behavior. If they choose instead to study the behavior in the laboratory, they can control the variables that might influence the behavior, but they create an artificial environment. Researchers must think carefully about these choices because where and how they study the behavior impacts the research process, the types of questions that can be addressed, and the answers that can be gained from the study.

Behavioral observation

Research studies that aim for high realism often use the naturalistic or case study approach. Both of these approaches provide a great deal of realism that allows for thorough descriptions of the behavior. However, both research designs lack sufficient control to address the scientific goals of explanation, prediction, or control. For example, during a **naturalistic observation**—a research method in which behavior is observed and recorded in the context where it typically occurs with as little interference from the researchers as possible—of shopping behavior, the research team might monitor where people walk through the store and what products they evaluate and purchase. (Paco Underhill and his employees at Envirosell have mastered the use of these techniques; see *Why We Buy* [2008] by Underhill for examples of their work.) During these observations, the research team would be as unobtrusive as possible while recording the behaviors of interest. The research team would then use their observations to build a description of shopping behavior. Imagine that our naturalistic observation of shopping behavior found that shoppers tended to enter the store, turn immediately to the displays on their right, and then continue moving through the store in a counterclockwise direction. This is an interesting description of shopping, but why do the shoppers behave this way? Is the counterclockwise shopping pattern a general trait of shopping behavior? Or maybe this is something unique to this particular store? Our naturalistic study can give us a great description of behavior, but without more work, it does not provide sufficient control to explain what causes the behavior.

Similar to a naturalistic observation, a case study is another technique for describing behavior through systematic observation. A **case study** is a detailed observation of a single individual or group of individuals. Case studies tend to be extremely useful for studying behavioral differences found only in a small group of people. While the study is of a small

From the Desk of Dr. Stith

Why do we tend to slow down and look at an accident scene as we drive by? Are we afraid we'll recognize one of the cars? Glad it wasn't us? Vicariously excited by the mayhem? All of the above?

These same elements of curiosity influence our desire for information and constant news coverage during disasters. Those directly involved in natural disasters (hurricanes, tornadoes, or fires) and those victims and survivors of perpetrated mass tragedies, defined by three or more unrelated persons intentionally harmed, experience significant and immediate trauma. Some portion (approximately 20 percent) may develop persistent PTSD. But why do so many of us not directly involved also get caught up in the trauma and emotions of those who are? We all experience disasters and crises as an interaction of four personal factors: our geographic distance from the event, our emotional distance from the event, our history of trauma, and our unique blend of nature/nurture aspects of personality.

Geographic distance is measured not just in miles but also feet and inches. The impact of stress immediately and in the long term is different if you are in the hurricane, or are an evacuee, or are watching it unfold on TV. It's different if you are present during a tragic event or experience it on the news. It is easy to understand that the trauma is immediate, both emotional and physical, for the people injured in the car accident you drove by. But even though you passed close by, unless you recognized the car or were recently an accident victim yourself, any reaction you have is minimized and fleeting. Likewise, emotional distance is experienced differently if you are there or your loved one has been harmed or is at serious risk of being harmed—even if you are 1,000 miles away. The fear of harm to you or the ones you love can feel overwhelming and immobilizing. The sense of helplessness makes everything seem "out of control," and the stress can result in extremes from volatile emotionality to numbness. Safety and doing something to get some control back should be our first concerns.

Research shows that early childhood traumas and/or multiple exposures to trauma can wear down a person's physical and emotional immune systems. Likewise, previous experience of similar traumas can either accelerate the impact of negative reaction or provide resilience skills to help cope more quickly and help others begin to regain some control.

Each of us is a complex combination of these elements, the genetic makeup our parents gave us, and the support we received during and after a disaster. We may have been born with a higher tolerance to physical pain. We may be physically stronger in a situation that requires strength. We may naturally be optimistic and assume others will help and make support easier for us and for that support to occur.

Randy C. Stith, PhD

group of people, or maybe just a single individual, what is learned from these studies can have a huge impact on our understanding of our behavior. For example, one of the most famous case studies in the history of psychology involved a detailed study of the memory of H.M. (Squire, 2009). An experimental participant for most of his adult life, H.M.'s identity was hidden from the public by referring to him by his initials until his death in 2008, when it was revealed that his real name was Henry Molaison. H.M. lost his ability to create new memories following an attempt to treat his epileptic seizures through the surgical removal of his hippocampus. Careful observations of the specific types of memory deficits H.M. experienced following his surgery provided important insights into the role of the hippocampus in memory formation. Many of these observations became the inspiration for more controlled research that led to much of our modern understanding of how memory works. Note that the study of H.M.'s case led to the development of hypotheses about the function of memory that were later tested with larger samples and more controlled situations in order to develop a better scientific understanding of behavior.

Naturalistic observations and case studies can be powerful research tools. Both techniques can provide detailed descriptions of behavior. These descriptions can then be used to develop testable hypotheses that can be used in predicting, explaining, and controlling the behavior. However, there are also important limitations to these methods. First, observations from naturalistic studies and case studies often lack generalizability. **Generalizability** refers to the degree to which findings from one context can be applied to a different context. The findings from our hypothetical shopping study, indicating shoppers tend to go to the right after entering the store, would be generalizable if this were true not only for shoppers in the store that was studied, but also for other types of stores in other locations. Similarly, findings from H.M. would be generalizable if the same memory deficits were observed in other individuals showing similar types of brain damage. Generalizability is typically identified by conducting the study again, but in a different context or with different participants. If the findings continue to be true across different observations in different settings, the findings are said to be generalizable. What was learned from H.M. is a good example of generalizable findings. Over the years, the original findings from H.M.'s case have been replicated with other cases of individuals with damage to the hippocampus.

generalizability
the degree to which scientific findings from one context can be applied to a different context, group of people, or situation

Understanding generalizability is one of the most difficult parts of learning to read and understand scientific literature. Each well-designed study that is conducted is only applicable and accurate within the boundaries of that particular study. A study of the effect of exercise on depression that uses a sample of sixty individuals with mild to moderate symptoms of depression who are enrolled in a small university in the rural midwestern United States will likely be of use in helping individuals who share those same characteristics. However, we would need to be very cautious when applying the findings from this study to work with individuals with severe symptoms of depression in a major metropolitan area. Due to the many differences between the examined group and the new group, we would need to evaluate additional evidence before feeling confident that the results from the study would generalize to our new group of people. Popular media reports of science, especially cutting-edge science, often suffer from overgeneralizing results from research. This is most often the case when we see headlines reporting sensational breakthroughs in scientific understanding or highly unexpected results.

Another form of passive research (research that does not directly manipulate the participant's environment or behavior) is correlational research. In a **correlational study**, the researchers measure two or more variables and then use statistical procedures to evaluate the degree of relationship between the variables. Correlational studies are highly popular research methods, as they help us to understand the degree of relationship between variables. However, because correlational studies only involve measurement of the variables, they cannot tell us anything about what is causing the relationship between the variables. *Researchers must use extreme caution when interpreting the results of correlational studies* because an observed correlation between two measurements could indicate several results:

correlational study
a research study that involves the measurement and comparison of two or more variables

- **There really is a direct relationship between the variables.** Studying and scores on exams are strongly correlated, as time spent studying really does increase exam scores (as long as the time is spent studying the material that is on the exam).

- **The two variables might be related by a third variable that influences both variables.** Time watching television is highly correlated with BMI. However, television watching does not cause weight gain. Rather, both television watching and weight gain are related to level of exercise. People with highly sedentary lifestyles tend to watch television and gain weight.

- **The two variables might represent a spurious correlation** (Pearson, 1897), a situation in which two variables are not directly related but are statistically correlated. Robert Matthews (2000) demonstrated that, consistent with the myth that storks bring babies, there is, indeed, a correlation between the population of storks in seventeen European countries and the birth rate for those countries. Spurious correlations are prevalent enough that there has even been a (humorous) book written about them: *Spurious Correlations* by Tyler Vigen (2015).

spurious correlation
a situation in which two variables are not really related but are statistically correlated

As these different possible outcomes demonstrate, correlational studies can provide information about the relationship between measured behaviors. However, cautious interpretation of the correlations includes remembering that correlations cannot tell us about causation, and all correlations must be interpreted within a theoretical framework.

One of the main statistical tools used to compare data from a correlational study is the **correlation coefficient**. The correlation coefficient summarizes the degree of relatedness between two continuous variables. Figure 2.5 provides a graphical demonstration of a correlation. The graphs on the left and on the right show two instances of correlated variables. The graph in the middle shows two variables that are unrelated. The correlation coefficient is a number that ranges from −1 to +1 and tells us two things about the relationship between variables. First, the sign of the correlation,

correlation coefficient
summarizes the degree of relatedness between two continuous variables

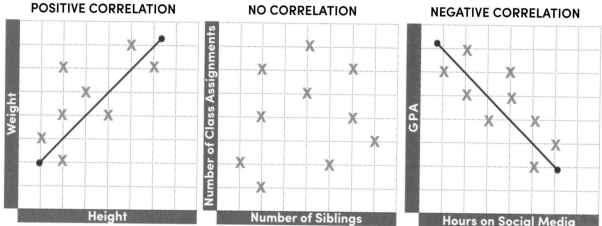

2.5 Examples of correlations between two variables
The left graph shows a positive correlation, where values of both variables increase at the same time. The center graph shows no correlation, where the values do not change in the same way. The right graph shows a negative correlation, where an increase in the value of one variable is associated with lower values of the second variable.

(+) or (–), tells the researchers how the two items change in relation to each other. A positive (+) correlation indicates that the two variables increase and decrease together. If one of the variables goes up, the other variable tends to go up as well. For example, height is positively correlated with weight because taller people typically weigh more than their shorter counterparts, and years of education is positively correlated with wages because highly educated people typically make more money than their less educated peers. A negative (–) correlation tells us that as one of the variables increases, the other variable tends to decrease. For example, the tendency to worry is negatively correlated with happiness because people that worry too much are typically less happy than their unconcerned counterparts, and time spent playing video games is negatively correlated with academic performance because video game enthusiasts have little time left over to study.

The second piece of information we get from a correlation coefficient indicates how strongly the two variables are related. The strength of the relation is indicated by the size of the number after the (+) or (–) sign. This number ranges from zero—suggesting no relation between the two variables—to one—suggesting the variables are perfectly related. For example, two perfectly positively related variables (correlational coefficient = +1.0) are number of birthdays and years of age; someone who has had twenty birthdays is twenty years old, and someone who has had forty birthdays is forty years old. In contrast, the variables mentioned above, such as height and weight, are not as strongly related as number of birthdays and years of age. A person may be very tall and extremely skinny or very short and significantly overweight. These examples indicate that the positive correlation between height and weight is not perfect, but it is a fairly accurate description of the relation between these two variables.

Experimental research

Naturalistic studies, case studies, and correlational studies have relatively high environmental realism but have limited experimental control of other variables.

Experiments are the opposite, insofar as they maximize experimental control, but the experimental setting is very different from the real world. (Remember the loud and tight fMRI tube?) In experiments, researchers manipulate one variable, which means that they expose some participants to a treatment and withhold the treatment from other participants. For example, to test the effectiveness of a new drug therapy intended to treat depression, some participants are given the drug and others are not given the drug. The group of participants exposed to the drug is called the **experimental condition**, and the group of participants not given the drug is called the **control condition**. To measure the effectiveness of the drug, the mood of the experimental condition is compared to the mood of the control condition.

One peculiar aspect of human nature that complicates this experimental design is that we often feel better when exposed to a treatment, even if the treatment doesn't work.

experimental condition
a situation in which the level of one or more independent variables has been changed, while holding as many other variables constant as possible

control condition
a situation in which variables are not changed in order to observe what the behavior looks like in normal circumstances

Cross-Cultural Case

The Mechanism of the Placebo Effect

The placebo effect is a very real phenomenon that psychiatrists and psychologists have studied for decades. We understand how it works, but recent studies have begun asking whether cultural factors influence the placebo effect. In recent studies, researchers have concluded that they can, but not always in the ways we expect. A 2015 study led by Bhugra and Ventriglio of King's College London found that, in addition to such variables as color, name, appearance, and method of administration, a person's cultural expectations for treatment could also affect how he or she responded when given a placebo in double-blind studies. Perhaps even more interesting is a team of psychologists' discovery published in the Proceedings of the National Academy of Sciences of the United States of America in 2012 that a patient's unconscious mind plays just as large a role in the placebo effect as his or her conscious mind. In other words, a person need not know she or he is being given a medical treatment for the placebo effect to work. According to this study, the placebo effect operates via three mechanisms: culture, meaning, and belief. Each culture recognizes certain experts that people from that culture believe are able to treat ailments through a variety of means. Complementing this is the understanding that these experts have access to products, be they

potions, herbs, or chemicals, that can make us better. When we receive something from one of these experts, our unconscious mind signals to us that it should heal us; we believe that it will heal us. Depending on the culture in which you were raised, you will expect different treatments from your expert or healer; however, the simple recognition of the healer can trigger the placebo effect, allowing it to transcend cross-cultural boundaries, leading people to believe they've been healed even when they've received no treatment at all.

placebo effect
a phenomenon in which people often feel better when exposed to a treatment, even if the treatment does not work

In the case of a drug therapy, if a group of depressed participants is given capsules filled with sugar, they will often feel some relief from their depression compared to a group of participants that are not given any sugar-filled capsules. This is called the **placebo effect**, and it raises an important question about the experimental study of drug therapy: Did the participants in the experimental condition feel better because the drug relieved their depression or merely because they were given a pill to swallow? To address this question, experiments intended to establish a drug therapy's effectiveness typically have not just two, but three conditions: one group is given the drug, one group is not given the drug, and a third group is given an ineffective placebo. For the drug to be considered effective, the relief from the drug must exceed the relief due to the placebo.

independent variables
the environmental conditions the researcher manipulates during the experiment

dependent variable
the behavior that is being directly measured and observed

confounding variables
uncontrolled variables that can influence the phenomenon being studied

An experimental study focuses on three main variables: independent variables, dependent variables, and confounding variables. The **independent variables** are the environmental conditions the researcher manipulates during the experiment. In the described experiment, the independent variable is the drug exposure, with three levels: drug, placebo, and none. The **dependent variable** is the behavior that is being directly measured and observed. The research team manipulates the independent variable because they believe it will directly impact the dependent variable. Whenever possible, the dependent variable will be the behavior of interest. If drug exposure is the independent variable, the dependent variable presumed to be affected by the drug is the participants' mood. Do they continue to feel depressed after being exposed to the drug or placebo, or do they feel some relief? **Confounding variables** are environmental factors other than the independent variables that influence the dependent variable. Table 2.2 provides a summary of these three variables and gives examples of each type. A confound is a variable the researcher inadvertently manipulated at the same time he or she was manipulating the variable of interest. That is, the researcher intended to manipulate drug exposure while holding everything else fixed, but perhaps the drug and placebo look different. A drug in a pill looks different than a placebo in a capsule, so while it is true that the researchers manipulated drug exposure, they also manipulated the appearance of the treatment. The confound undermines the experimental results. If the drug group feels better than the placebo group, is that because the drug is effective or because the pill has a stronger placebo effect than the capsule? Because both the drug and its appearance were manipulated between the experimental and control conditions, there is no way to tell. A good experimental study will have clearly defined independent variables, an objectively measured dependent variable, and minimal confounding variables (high internal validity). Due to the strong control of a well-designed experiment, it typically takes a series of experiments with variations in the independent variables, participants, and settings in order to establish the generalizability and external validity of the research.

Table 2.2 Summary of the three major research variables

Independent Variable	Dependent Variable	Confounding Variable
Environmental conditions that are changed during the experiment	Behavior that is being measured during the study	Uncontrolled variable that might influence behavior
Hypothesized cause	Hypothesized effect	Uncontrolled cause
Number of hours of sleep participants are allowed	Scores on a memorization task	Time spent watching television while awake
Presence or absence of a "greeter" as students walk into class	Time spent on task during the class period	Temperature of the classroom

Concept Recall

1. What are the differences and similarities between naturalistic observations and a case study?

2. What can we learn from a correlational study, and what caution should we take when interpreting a correlation between items?

3. How does an experimental study differ from a correlational study, and what impact do these differences have on how we interpret the outcomes of a study?

4. How do the following elements of an experiment work to create experimental control: control condition, experimental condition, independent variable, and dependent variable?

5. How can a placebo effect make it difficult to understand the outcome of an experiment?

This Is Psychology

John Tesh is a musician, television personality, and radio show host. One of his most popular programs is the radio show *Intelligence for Your Life*, on which Tesh presents brief advice statements frequently based on psychological science. This program's popularity lies in its brief, easy-to-digest advice for life. However, what is the validity of his advice? As we consume popular media, it is important to develop habits of asking "How do you know?" and "Is this really what was studied?" Much of the advice we get in the world has strong face validity—it sounds good. Interpreting the information we receive in the media and from others must be an active process. Just as scientists design research studies to test their hypotheses, we need to develop habits of approaching interpretations of science with the same skeptical lens. This will help us to separate the good advice from "good-sounding" advice.

Indirect measurements

While it is always the goal of researchers to directly measure the target behavior represented by the dependent variable, this is not always possible. When direct measurement is not possible, psychologists will often use **indirect measurements** of the target behavior. Intelligence is a good example of a psychological construct that requires indirect measurements. We do not have any way to directly measure a person's level of intelligence, but we do know of various behaviors an intelligent person could be expected to accomplish, such as quickly solving complex problems, coming up with multiple solutions to challenges, and defining lots of words. When using an indirect measure, it is the researcher's responsibility to demonstrate that the method being used is a valid measure of the behavior of interest.

One of the more popular forms of indirect measure used by psychologists and other social researchers is the **survey**. Surveys are found everywhere these days. Many businesses include surveys on their receipts with an offer to receive discounts in exchange for providing feedback on your experience. Many websites have survey pop-up offers to collect information regarding your experience. Surveys are useful because they allow an indirect measurement of important behaviors. As a self-report instrument, surveys also do not require access to the context in which the behavior would normally occur for direct observation. Finally, surveys are beneficial because you can ask about behaviors that would not be possible to directly observe due to time constraints, privacy concerns, or frequency of the action. In short, surveys are powerful instruments because they allow for non-invasive measurement of a wide range of behaviors.

Unfortunately, the strength of the survey method is also its major weakness. Without direct observation of the behavior, it is difficult to assess the accuracy of the responses to the survey items. Sometimes, lack of honesty on surveys is due to the personal nature of the items or fear that complete honesty would result in negative consequences. These concerns tend to be crucial for self-reports of criminal behavior, drug use, and sexual experiences.

Despite the occasional occurrence of active misreporting, this is not the most common form of inaccurate measurement in surveys. In most cases, participants do not purposefully withhold the truth; rather, they may not be completely aware of the accurate answer. Imagine that you are completing a survey that asks you to report how many glasses of water you consumed each day over the past three months. This is not very personal information, and it is unlikely that you would feel a great need to misrepresent the true amount of water you consumed. However, this is a very difficult question, as we tend not to pay much attention to the water we drink. There would likely be a great deal of error in the reports given by participants using this type of survey instrument. Researchers who design survey tools will often build into their instruments a number of items that help them to assess the accuracy of the survey responses.

Comparative research

It is important to note that psychologists study behavior across organisms as well as human behavior. The study of behavior in nonhuman species can be a powerful way to better understand human behavior; thus, researchers often utilize **comparative psychology** as a research method to further their investigation of aspects of behavior. Observations of animal behavior are considered an indirect form of measurement because researchers are not studying what they are actually interested in but something analogous to the behavior of interest.

comparative psychology
an indirect form of measurement with the goal of learning about humans by studying nonhumans

There are several advantages to studying behavior in nonhuman species. One major advantage to this type of research is that the research team can better control the environment. Nonhuman participants can be tested in highly controlled environments, raised in specific ways, and even be genetically modified to allow for testing of the role of specific genes on behavior. For example, behavior analysts often conduct learning studies with pigeons and rats in which the organism is taught to behave a certain way in response to specific stimuli. To ensure experimental control, the animals are tested in special cages that are soundproof, light-controlled, and temperature-regulated. (These chambers are often called "Skinner Boxes" in reference to the scientist who popularized their use.) In this way, the research team can be confident that the only changes in the animal's environment during the study are those that were a part of the study.

Concept Recall

1. How does an indirect measurement differ from direct measurement?
2. Under what conditions is a survey a useful measure of behavior?
3. What are some major considerations when using surveys for research?
4. Why do psychologists study animal behavior?
5. What are some of the advantages of conducting comparative psychological research?

RESEARCH ETHICS

The previous sections discussed the role of scientific research in psychology and the various tools that psychologists use to study behavior. In conducting research with human participants, psychological scientists must take an active role in considering the health and well-being of participants in their research. It is the researcher's responsibility to ensure participants' rights, feelings, and bodies are protected from harm throughout the study.

To help protect research participants, all research conducted for academic purposes in the United States must pass through either an Institutional Review Board (IRB) for research involving human participants, or an Institutional Animal Care and Use

Committee (IACUC) for research involving nonhuman species. These groups have been developed to protect the participants involved in research.

Participants are protected from unethical practices by three main principles.

1. **Pre-participation informed consent:** Prior to beginning a research project the participant, or a legal guardian or caretaker, is told of the requirements of the study, any costs associated with the study, any potential benefits of the study, and any potential for physical, mental, or emotional harm. The participant, parent, or guardian is also provided information regarding how to contact the research staff and assured that their data will be protected. The goal of the informed consent letter is to allow the participant to make an informed decision about consenting to participate in the study.

2. **Post-participation debriefing:** Following completion of the study, participants are provided with a review of what they did in the study, details of how the data will be used, information regarding any deception that was used during the study, information that might have been withheld from the informed consent (such as the research hypothesis), and contact information for the research team.

3. **Minimization of harm:** All research is evaluated using the potential knowledge that can be gained from the study and the potential harm that can be caused to the participants. Researchers aim to maximize the gains from each study while minimizing the potential for harm. All research procedures must be designed in a way that offers maximum protection for the participant, and when options are available, the least risky procedure must be adopted.

While the informed consent cover letter requires the researcher to explain what will be required of the participant and any associated costs, it does not require the researcher to reveal all details of the project. For example, psychological research often requires some form of deception—false information that helps to reduce reactivity during a research study—in order to hopefully create more realistic behavior. For example, imagine you participated in a study measuring how many times you said "um" while talking. If you were told before participating in the experiment what the researcher was studying, do you think that knowledge would influence your behavior? Likely, your speech would be less fluid as you actively worked to avoid saying "um." This reactivity—the tendency to change behavior as a result of being observed—is a direct threat to the research question, as it fails to accurately reflect how the participant would actually respond when not under observation. In this situation, the informed consent would probably rely on slight deception by stating that the researcher is interested in the participant's opinion regarding different issues on campus or the surrounding community. Notice that this statement accurately reflects what the participant is going to do—talk—but it fails to specify fully what is being measured or why.

The debriefing that follows the completion of a research study is designed to ensure that participants are fully aware of what happened during the study. In the "um" study, during the debriefing the researchers would explain to the participant that one objective of the study was to measure how many times the participant said "um" during the conversations. In addition to providing any information that might have been withheld during the informed consent, the debriefing is also a time to gauge how the participant responded to the study. If the study contained any emotionally upsetting material or physical distress, the debriefing is a time when the researcher will minimize any possible harm.

The same principle of minimization of harm is followed when animal models are used to better understand behavior. Due to ethical and methodological considerations, there are questions that cannot be addressed using human participants. However, these questions are critical to understanding behavior and to developing technologies that allow us to improve behavior and the quality of life for both us and other animals. Under these circumstances, researchers and ethics boards must weigh the potential gains to society against the risk of harm to the animal participants. These boards give consideration to alternative models (such as computer simulations) in making their decisions regarding the ethics of proposed research projects. All animal participants must be given sanitary, comfortable living conditions. Psychological scientists are very aware of their responsibility to their animal participants and the needs of society.

Concept Recall

1. What is the psychologist's responsibility regarding the protection of participants in their studies?
2. What is the role of the Institutional Review Board and the Institutional Animal Care and Use Committee in conducting behavioral research?
3. What information needs to be included in the informed consent letter?
4. How does the debriefing letter help participants understand the full extent of their participation?
5. What is the principle of "minimization of harm?"

This Is Psychology

Recent efforts have begun to increase the overall responsibility of psychological scientists in all aspects of their research. An excellent example of these efforts is the creation of the Center for Open Science (http://cos.io). The Center began its work in 2013 and aims to make science more transparent and reproducible by encouraging scientists to make all of their work openly available, including details from the initial planning to final results. Openness in science is important to maintain research ethics and greatly benefits society as a whole by making science more accessible and collaborative.

SCIENCE IS THE FOUNDATION OF PSYCHOLOGY

As you progress in your study of psychology, you will see many of the themes from this chapter appear in the context of other components of psychology. The methods of science discussed in this chapter are the foundation for our understanding of modern psychology. You will notice that as you move from chapter to chapter, the procedures and technologies used by psychologists to understand the behavior of interest will also change. The next two chapters of the text explore the biological foundations of our experience with the world. Chapter 5 discusses the way we change across our life span. These two areas of research use extremely different techniques. However, despite the differences in the scientific tools used by various subfields of psychology, the objective remains the same: to understand the factors that influence how you behave.

As you read the remaining chapters in this book, we encourage you to use the ideas from this chapter to evaluate the information that is presented. Ask yourself what type of scientific technique would be used to come to the conclusions presented in different sections. Ask yourself what types of confounds may have existed in the work of the researchers. And ask yourself what questions the researchers could explore next. This type of active processing will help you to better understand the nature of psychology and to better recall the concepts and ideas presented in this text.

Review/Reflect/Write

REVIEW

- How is psychology a science?
- What are the steps of the scientific method?
- How do the goals of science help researchers move from simple questions to technologies that address important problems?
- What is an operational definition, and why is it an important first step in conducting research?
- Why is it important to balance between experimental control and environmental realism when designing a study?
- How are external and internal validity different? How are they similar?
- When would you use a naturalistic study? A case study?
- What is the difference between a correlational study and an experimental study? What are the strengths and weaknesses of each methodology?
- What are some of the strengths and weaknesses of surveys as a measurement tool?
- What are the three major elements of an IRB application for conducting human research?

1. John discovered a strong correlation between two traits in the participants of his study. If this correlation applied to populations outside of the lab setting, his study is said to have high:
   a. external validity
   b. internal validity
   c. external reliability
   d. internal reliability

2. Jane is performing a study in which half of her participants are randomly assigned to take a newly developed antidepressant while the other half of the participants takes nothing. The group taking nothing is considered to be the:

    a. experimental group

    b. nonexperimental group

    c. neutral group

    d. control group

3. The behavior being measured in a study is the:

    a. independent variable

    b. dependent variable

    c. experimental variable

    d. all of the above

4. Naturalistic observation is performed when:

    a. the observer does not interfere with those being observed.

    b. observers avoid influencing behavior.

    c. behavior is observed in its typical, more natural environment.

    d. all of the above

5. When a researcher uses an indirect measure of a phenomenon, what must they show?

    a. That the direct measure would be unreliable.

    b. That the measure used records an alternative behavior of interest.

    c. That the measure is a valid measure of the behavior of interest.

    d. Measures must be direct in nature.

6. The purpose of the Institutional Review Board is to:

    a. protect the legitimacy of the research conducted on university campuses.

    b. provide legal help for researchers.

    c. protect the rights of participants in psychological science.

    d. provide directions for the future that will be meaningful in the study of psychology.

7. The ability to test a hypothesis empirically and find the hypothesis to be incorrect makes that hypothesis

    a. valid.

    b. reliable.

    c. objective.

    d. falsifiable.

8. In the scientific method, what step comes after you conduct an empirical test of the hypothesis?

    a. Decide on future action.

    b. Look for relevant literature.

    c. Evaluate the results of the test.

    d. Compare results with what is already known.

9. A participant in a research study is placed in a lab and told to perform a task and act normal. He instead is very stiff and is politer than usual. This effect is known as

    a. external validity.

    b. participant bias.

    c. reactivity.

    d. internal validity.

10. The degree to which the testing environment is similar to the real-world context where the behavior typically occurs is known as

    a. environmental realism.

    b. experimental control.

    c. external validity.

    d. internal validity.

REFLECT

1. The original studies providing evidence that the communications produced by facilitated communication were strongly influenced by the facilitators were conducted in the early 1990s. However, FC is still used today. Why do you think the method is still used when most scientists believe it is not a true form of communication?

2. We often develop superstitious behaviors through spurious correlations that occur when something really good (or bad) happens right after another noticeable event. What superstitious behaviors do you have? What events do you think produced these behaviors?

3. How do you feel about the use of animals in research? Under what conditions do you think it is appropriate to use animals in research? Under what conditions do you think it is inappropriate?

WRITE

1. Go to the website for a national news source, such as *The New York Times*, *Los Angeles Times*, or *Time* magazine. Identify three news stories that discuss psychological research. From the news stories, identify the operational definition of the target behaviors, the type of research method used in each study, and the dependent variables and any independent variables (depending on the research type) used in each study. Does the way the articles report the studies seem to be justified by the type of research design used by the researchers?

2. Write a report about how you would use the scientific method to design an experiment to test a behavior of interest to you. Begin with the first step of forming a question, and outline what you would do all the way through the last step of disseminating your findings. While you do not actually need to conduct your experiment, clearly explain your operational definition, independent and dependent variables, and how you would minimize any potential confounding variables.

Key Terms

3 Biopsychology

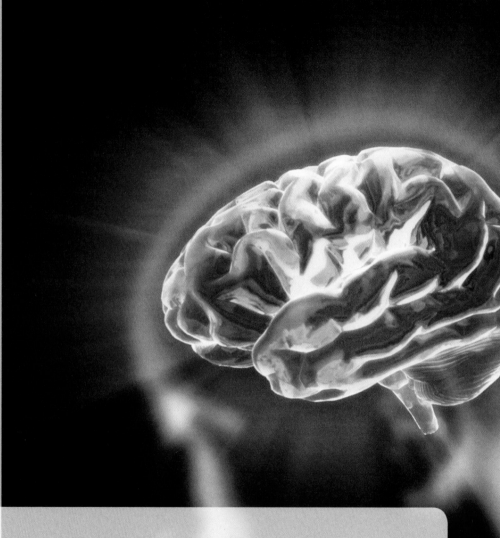

After reading this chapter, you will be able to answer the following questions:
- What are the major components of the nervous system?
- How do the endocrine and nervous systems work together?
- How do action potentials work?
- What are the parts of a neuron?
- How do neurons communicate with each other?
- What are the major parts of the brain?
- What effect do drugs have on brain function?
- How do the left and right hemispheres of the brain differ?

Has your life or the life of anyone you know been improved by receiving transplanted body parts? Transplanted corneas restore lost vision, transplanted kidneys eliminate the constant need for dialysis treatments, and transplanted hands restore lost functionality.

Despite all of the advances in medical transplantation, brain transplants remain the subject of fiction. For example, in the hit sitcom *Friends*, the character Joey Tribiani deals with the consequences of brain transplantation when his *Days of Our Lives* character, Dr. Drake Ramoray, is brought out of a coma by receiving a brain from a person killed in a horse riding accident. While these types of transplants are not possible today, imagine for a moment what you would do if the procedure were available. If medically necessary, would you consent to receive a transplanted brain from a willing donor?

Somehow a brain transplant seems different from other kinds of transplants, primarily because it reverses the relationship between donor and recipient. That is, the person offering a cornea, kidney, or hand is the donor, and the recipient is undoubtedly the beneficiary, but is this the case with a donated brain? If a donated brain were inserted into your skull and connected to your body so that it could perceive and move, would you actually be the beneficiary? Wouldn't it be more accurate to say that you donated your body to prolong the life of someone else's brain? After all, the postoperative fusion of your body with someone else's brain may look like you, but without all the stuff in your own brain (such as your memories, preferences, and personality), it isn't really you. Imagining the possible consequences of a brain transplant highlights just how much of who you are is embodied in your brain. Therefore, the scientific study of psychology depends on understanding how brains work, beginning with an examination of the cellular components of the brain.

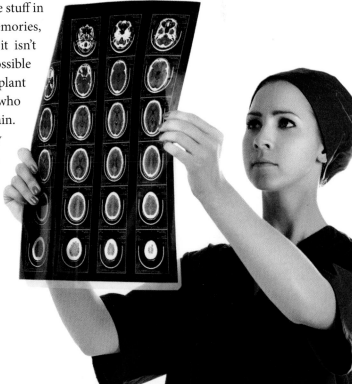

NEURAL STRUCTURE AND FUNCTION

neuron
a brain cell that stores and processes information using an electrical code

glial cell
a brain cell that supports the activities of neurons

soma
part of the neuron that contains machinery to keep the neuron alive and functioning

Like most people, you probably believe that there is just one "you" who woke up this morning and went about your daily routine, but in fact your brain contains about one trillion individual cells that all work together because they are all reading from the same playbook or genome. Your experience of the world, your thoughts and fears, and your dreams for tomorrow are all the product of activity in these cells.

About half of your brain cells are **neurons**, each of which is a tiny electrical device that stores and processes information using an electrical code. The pattern of activity in these neurons determines your experience of the world. Each of the billions of neurons in the brain works like an electrical switch. Even if medical science never achieves brain transplants, perhaps medical science can figure out how to replace an ailing neuron with an artificial electrical switch or transistor. Would you still be the same person if one of your billions of neurons were replaced by a transistor? If a thousand of your neurons were replaced by transistors? What about if all of them had been replaced? As you read about neurons, remember that everything you have ever felt or experienced can be attributed to billions of tiny switches responding to charged particles moving around.

The other half of brain cells (called **glial cells** from the Greek for "glue") do not directly participate in mental processing, but they do support and maintain neurons. Although recent research has shown that the number of neurons and glial cells in the human brain are about equal, for the previous several decades most neuroscientists believed that about 90 percent of brain cells in the human brain are glial cells (Herculano-Houzel, 2014). The outdated belief that only 10 percent of brain cells are neurons that contribute to mental processing may be the basis for the common myth that people use just 10 percent of their brains. The "10 percent myth" seems to capture the popular imagination, perhaps because it implies that anyone learning to harness just a bit more brainpower could accomplish great things. If everyone uses just 10 percent of their brainpower, boosting your brainpower by just a few percent would enable you to accomplish wonderful things. Actually, people regularly use 100 percent of their neurons, and glial cells can't be repurposed to carry out mental processing, so like everyone else, you too are stuck using the half of your brain cells that are neurons.

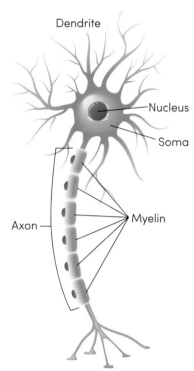

3.1 Parts of a neuron that contribute to an action potential
Dendrites receive electrical signals from other neurons, and the signals from all dendrites converge on the soma. If the signal at the soma is strong enough, an action potential is sent along the axon to the axon terminals, where it makes synapses with the dendrites of other neurons. Myelin surrounds the axon to electrically insulate it from the fluid outside the neuron.

Neurons are further divided into subcomponents, which have their own roles in cellular and electrical neural functioning. Neurons form connections with other neurons, and these neural networks transmit information throughout the brain. Neural communication is both an electrical and a chemical process. Information is transmitted within a neuron using an electrical signal and between neurons using chemical signals.

When seen through a microscope, neurons appear to have three distinct parts, as depicted in Figure 3.1. The **soma**, or cell body, contains the tiny cellular machinery needed for the cell to accomplish its housekeeping chores (protein synthesis, energy regulation, etc.) and the nucleus, which contains the cell's DNA. The branching limbs at one end of the soma are called **dendrites**, from the Greek word for tree. On the opposite side of the soma is a single, microscopically thin filament that extends for great distances. When you stub your toe on the coffee table in the middle of the night, an **axon** conveys the pain signal from your toe all the way up your leg, terminating at the base of the spine, where it connects with other neurons. The dendrites, soma, and axon each have a distinct outward appearance, but they work together to generate the neuron's electrical and chemical behavior.

dendrites
branching neural fibers that collect inputs from other neurons

axon
a single long wire that sends electrical signals from the soma to other neurons

Neural Communication: Electrical Signals

As with other cells in the body, neurons consist of cellular fluid and machinery enveloped by a membrane. Neurons function like tiny versions of the batteries used to power electronic devices. Human-made batteries are manufactured by concentrating positively charged particles on one end of the battery and negatively charged particles on the other end, with a barrier between them. As with batteries, neurons segregate positive charges from negative charges. The cell membrane is the barrier between positive and negative charges, and the neuron continuously pumps charged particles (ions) across the membrane. As a result of the ion pumps, the insides of neurons maintain a negative charge of about seventy millivolts relative to the outside. While seventy thousandths (0.07) of a volt may sound like a tiny amount of charge, a standard flashlight battery delivers one and a half (1.5) volts: only about twenty times the voltage maintained by microscopic neurons. Indeed, by arranging cellular "batteries" in a serial circuit to additively combine their voltages, electric eels can deliver shocks that stun and kill their prey. A neuron maintaining a constant voltage is not actually restful because the neuron must constantly work to pump ions across the membrane, just as a sailor in a leaky boat must constantly bail water out of the boat with a bucket to keep it afloat. Even though a neural battery is not resting, its voltage is called a **resting potential** to distinguish it from a neuron in which an electrical impulse is actively traveling along the axon.

resting potential
voltage maintained by a neuron when it is not sending any electrical messages

Whereas a neuron that is maintaining a constant voltage can be likened to a battery, a neuron that decides to communicate with another neuron acts like an electrical switch, resulting in an **action potential**. Dendrites—the branching limbs on one end of the soma—are the electrical inputs to the neuron. The membrane surrounding dendrites contains **ion channels**, which permit ions to enter the neuron when the channels are open. Dendritic ion channels permitting the inflow of positively charged ions raise the voltage of the neuron above its resting potential, and other channels permitting the inflow of negatively charged ions lower the neuron's voltage. The accumulated dendritic signals converge on the soma, which adds up the positive charges and subtracts the negative charges to calculate a single value for the overall dendritic input voltage. The part of the axon nearest to the soma contains electrically activated ion channels. If the sum of the dendritic inputs exceeds the activation threshold of the axon's ion channels, it triggers the ion channels to open, which lets positively charged ions flood into the neuron.

action potential
electrical impulse that moves from the soma through the axon

ion channels
passageways that enable charged particles (ions) to travel through the neural membrane when opened

Positively charged ions on the outside of the neuron are attracted to the inside of the neuron because of its negative charge, and as with people, opposites attract. With an

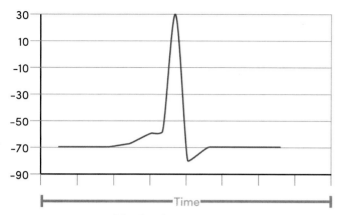

3.2 An action potential displayed on a screen, such as a cardiac neuron displayed on the screen of a heart monitor
Voltages in the soma rise slowly, then when the voltage reaches a threshold value, it opens ion channels. Positively charged ions rush into the neuron, causing a rapid rise in voltage. At the peak voltage, some ion channels close but others remain open, and the outrushing of positively charged ions makes the voltage fall until it reaches the resting potential and all ion channels close.

incoming flood of positively charged ions the neuron's voltage rises steeply until reaching a peak, which activates other ion channels to open, causing an outflow of positively charged ions. The outrushing ions cause the neuron's voltage to fall until it returns to the resting potential, at which point the ion channels slam shut. The shape of an action potential as depicted in Figure 3.2 may look familiar if you've seen heart monitors in hospital room scenes from movies or in real life. Heart monitors display a cardiac neuron's action potentials on a small video screen. Each action potential sent to the heart by a cardiac neuron commands the heart muscle to contract.

After electrically activated ion channels permit a flood of positively charged ions into the part of the axon next to the soma, the ions travel along the axon, bringing their positive charges from one end of the axon to the other. Whereas dendrites are the neuron's electrical input, the resulting output signal is sent through the axon. The movement of charge along the axon means that the axon acts like an electrical wire, and as such, it needs to be electrically insulated from its surroundings to prevent leakage of charge. An axon's electrical insulation is provided by specialized glial cells called **myelin**. Just as with any signal sent by wire, the action potential loses signal strength as it moves along the axon.

myelin
glial cell that provides electrical insulation for the axon

When the action potential reaches the unmyelinated, or uninsulated, part of the axon, it's lost much of its strength but retains enough charge to trigger the opening of electrically activated ion channels. The influx of ions acts like an amplifier, boosting the action potential to full strength and enabling it to continue its way along the axon. When an action potential reaches the axon's terminus (the end of the neuron), the neuron dumps bags filled with chemicals into a gap between it and other neurons as a means of encouraging the postsynaptic neurons to send their own action potentials. With that in mind, we can see that neurons communicate within the cell (intracellular) using electrical signals and between cells (intercellular) using chemical signals.

Neural Communication: Chemical Signals

In the late nineteenth century, the Italian anatomist Camillo Golgi accidentally bumped a beaker filled with a solution of silver, spilling it onto some nearby samples of brain tissue. Disappointed that he'd ruined the samples, Golgi nevertheless examined the slides under a microscope. To his delight, some of the brain cells had absorbed the silver solution and could be seen in great detail. In the years following his fortunate accident, Golgi often noticed the ends of axons entangled with dendrites. He could see no space between axons and dendrites, so he concluded that brain tissue consisted of a single complex, interconnected network. The Spanish anatomist Santiago Ramón y Cajal adopted Golgi's staining techniques but disagreed with Golgi's metaphor of a network. Ramón y Cajal argued that axons are separated from dendrites by a tiny gap, and what appears to be a single network is actually made up of many individual neurons. Later scientific work supported Ramón y Cajal's **neuron doctrine**, and the tiny gap between one neuron's axon and another neuron's dendrite is now called a synapse. Golgi and Ramón y Cajal were jointly awarded the Nobel prize in 1906 for the development of the neuron doctrine but never stopped bickering, each blaming the other in their acceptance speeches for deliberate and malicious errors and omissions.

neuron doctrine
the claim that the network that appears when examining brain tissue under a microscope consists of separate cells

synapse
tiny gap between two neurons where chemical transmission of neural messages occurs

Among the many functions carried out in the neuron's soma is the manufacture of chemicals called **neurotransmitters**, which convey chemical signals between neurons. The soma crams neurotransmitters into bags called **vesicles** and ships the vesicles to the axon terminal where they await the arrival of an action potential. When an action potential arrives, a vesicle binds to the neural membrane and releases its contents into the synaptic gap between the axon and a dendrite on the other side of the synaptic gap. Once released, neurotransmitters diffuse across the gap, then insert themselves into **receptor sites** on the dendrite's membrane like a key in a lock. The lock-and-key metaphor is apt not only because neurotransmitters fit into receptor sites, but also because a neurotransmitter binding to a receptor opens a door, which is called an ion channel. The synaptic transmission of chemical messages is depicted in Figure 3.3. Because neurons use chemicals to communicate, brain activity can be altered by exposure to psychoactive drugs. Examining the effects of drugs on the brain can illuminate how synaptic processes work.

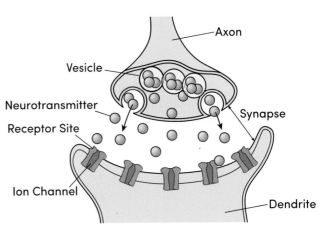

3.3 Chemical transmission of signals across the synapse
When the action potential reaches the end of the axon, vesicles filled with neurotransmitters pour their contents into the synaptic gap between the axon and a dendrite on the other side of the gap. Neurotransmitters fit into binding sites like a key in a lock, opening ion channels that alter the voltage in the postsynaptic dendrite.

neurotransmitters
chemical messengers manufactured by one neuron that communicate with other neurons via synapses

vesicles
tiny bags used to contain and transport neurotransmitters from the soma to the end of the axon

receptor sites
locations where neurotransmitters fit like a key in a lock to activate postsynaptic neurons

Drug Effects on the Brain

Our culture encourages the use of some psychoactive drugs, such as antidepressants, tolerates others, such as alcohol and nicotine, and discourages still others, such as methamphetamine. Given the range of chemicals that alter consciousness, there is nothing inherently evil about drugs; caffeine is just as much a drug as heroin. All psychoactive drugs work by influencing one of several synaptic processes, including neurotransmitter release, binding on the receptor site, deactivation after binding, and reuptake into the presynaptic neuron after release. Here we will see three drugs that affect these synaptic processes and one drug that has such a similar shape to a neurotransmitter that the drug mimics the neurotransmitter. You will read more about the effects of psychoactive drugs on consciousness in Chapter 8.

Of the more than 100 neurotransmitters that have been discovered, dopamine is one of those better known to the general public, largely because of its role in the addictiveness of drugs. Pleasurable activities, such as socializing with friends, eating good food, and sex, stimulate a release of dopamine into the same part of the brain that is targeted by addictive drugs: the nucleus accumbens. Dopamine binding to receptor sites opens ion channels, permitting the entry of positively charged ions to the neuron, raising its voltage. As a result, releasing dopamine into the synapse tends to encourage the postsynaptic neuron to send action potentials. Methamphetamine (also known as meth, crystal, and speed) causes presynaptic neurons to release more dopamine into synapses than normal, thereby increasing the overall number of action potentials across the entire brain. Psychoactive drugs are typically classified by their effect on a specific neurotransmitter. Drugs that increase the overall effectiveness of a neurotransmitter are agonists, and drugs that decrease the effectiveness of a neurotransmitter are antagonists. By raising the level of dopamine in the synapse, methamphetamine is a dopamine agonist. In contrast, a drug that prevents neurotransmitter binding would be considered an antagonist, which is how the drug curare affects the neurotransmitter acetylcholine.

When you make any kind of movement, a motor neuron releases acetylcholine into the neuromuscular junction—a synapse between a neuron and muscle fiber—causing the muscle fiber to contract. Curare, a drug extracted from a plant native to Central and South America, has traditionally been used in hunting practices by indigenous people to paralyze and kill prey animals. It does so by binding to acetylcholine receptors but not activating them, almost as if you stuck a key in a lock then broke off the key handle, leaving the stub behind. Just as the stub would prevent the insertion of any other key in the lock, curare blocks acetylcholine from the receptor, thereby paralyzing the muscle fiber. Because curare paralyzes the diaphragm, an animal pricked by a curare-tipped blowgun dart would die from suffocation. Used with appropriate caution and preparation, curare can be useful in surgery. Surgical incisions cause the patient's muscles to contract, even for an unconscious patient. Administering curare along with anesthetic allows the surgeon to make incisions without having to worry about patients involuntarily clenching in response.

When two neurons communicate, the reception of neurotransmitters from the sending neuron briefly changes the voltage of the receiving neuron, making an action potential either more likely (excitation) or less likely (inhibition). Once the signal has been received, the neurotransmitter releases from the receptor site. The sending neuron vacuums up the used neurotransmitters and repackages them for reuse. This process of reuptake is particularly important to the treatment of depression. Serotonin is implicated in mood, sleep, and appetite and is presumed to be deficient in the brains of people who are depressed. When Prozac (fluoxetine) was released to the market in 1988, it was the first drug classified as a selective serotonin reuptake inhibitor (SSRI). As the name implies, SSRI drugs discourage the removal of serotonin from the synapse, leading to serotonin accumulation in the synapse and a consequent lightening of mood. As a result, SSRI drugs are considered to be serotonin agonists.

Finally, some drugs have such a similar chemical structure to a neurotransmitter that they actually bind to and activate the same receptor sites that the neurotransmitter

nucleus accumbens
part of the brain that underlies feelings of pleasure

agonist
a drug that boosts the effectiveness of a neurotransmitter

antagonist
a drug that reduces the effectiveness of a neurotransmitter

acetylcholine
a neurotransmitter that causes a muscle fiber to contract

neuromuscular junction
tiny gap between a muscle fiber and the motor neuron controlling the fiber

reuptake
the process of the sending neuron reclaiming used neurotransmitters from the synapse

serotonin
a neurotransmitter that affects mood, sleep, and appetite

does. One of the best-known examples of a drug that mimics a neurotransmitter is **morphine**. For hundreds of years, it has been known that scratching the seed case of the opium poppy plant causes it to exude a sticky sap as a defense against further injuries. Although intended to poison the creature attacking its seeds, the sap proved to be an effective pain reliever when ingested in small quantities. In the 1970s, neuroscientists knew that morphine activates certain receptor sites in the brain associated with pain relief, and yet it seemed peculiar that our brains sat around waiting for the sap from a particular flower. It made more sense that these receptor sites are activated by chemicals manufactured by our own brains and that morphine made from poppies just happens to have the same chemical structure. If the brain manufactures its own **analgesic**, or pain-relieving chemicals, what should they be called? They were called endogenous (internally generated) morphine—or endorphins.

When endorphins were discovered in the early 1970s, pharmacologists thought they could be used as analgesics without being addictive like morphine, but unfortunately endorphins are addictive, as is well known to runners and other athletes who skip one of their regular exercise sessions. Our brains manufacture endorphins to be used in stressful situations, such as when being pursued by a predator. Running on an injured leg may aggravate the injury, but with a predator in hot pursuit it is much more important to evade the predator than to rest the injured leg. In the modern world, we run for exercise and recreation, but our brains don't realize this and respond to a run for exercise just as they would for a run to evade a predator: they release endorphins. An athlete who maintains a regular workout schedule gets a shot of endorphins at predictable intervals, so skipping a workout can induce feelings of withdrawal just like ones felt by a morphine addict who needs to get a fix.

In summary, neurons communicate using both electrical and chemical signals. Electrical neural communication occurs primarily within a neuron, with the dendrite as the input to the soma and the axon as the output from the soma. Chemical neural communication occurs primarily between neurons, with the axon as the input to the synapse and the dendrite as the output from the synapse. Drug effects on the brain are attributable to their influence on the synaptic processes of neurotransmitter release (methamphetamine promotes the release of dopamine), binding (curare prevents the binding of acetylcholine), or deactivation (SSRI prevents the reuptake of serotonin), or by mimicking the neurotransmitter (morphine mimics endorphins). Having considered the cellular components of the brain, we turn now to the nervous system at large.

morphine
a drug that relieves pain by mimicking the neurotransmitter endorphins

analgesic
a substance that relieves pain

Concept Recall

1. What are the primary jobs of neurons and glial cells?
2. How are signals communicated within neurons and between neurons?
3. What role do the dendrites, myelin, and axon play in the action potential?
4. What is a neurotransmitter, and how does it communicate information?

central nervous system
the part of the nervous system made up of the brain and the spinal cord

interneuron
a neuron in the spine that is involved in reflexive movements

peripheral nervous system
the portion of the nervous system containing all nerves outside the central nervous system

somatic nervous system
the portion of the peripheral nervous system that controls voluntary behaviors (i.e., walking)

5. What is the difference between an agonist and an antagonist?

6. How do each of the following drugs impact neural communication: methamphetamine, curare, SSRIs, and morphine?

THE NERVOUS SYSTEM

For most vertebrates, the brain and spine are essential to life but delicate enough to be vulnerable to damage, so they are surrounded by the armor plating of the skull, which protects the brain, and vertebrae, which protect the spinal cord. Together, the brain and spinal cord form the **central nervous system**. At first it may seem puzzling to group the spinal cord with the brain because the brain processes information whereas the spinal cord merely seems to convey information to the brain. In fact, the spinal cord does some basic stimulus processing. Did you ever touch something hot—such as a stove you didn't know had recently been used—then jerk your hand back and think, "Oh boy, that's gonna hurt," and sure enough, a moment later the finger begins to throb? How could you jerk your hand back *before* feeling the pain? The reason is that the pain signal was sent through a sensory nerve's axon to the spinal cord, where it synapses with an **interneuron**, which in turn synapses with a motor neuron descending to the arm muscles. When the pain signal reaches the spine, it generates a reflex to jerk your hand back as shown in Figure 3.4, but to *feel* the pain requires the pain signal to ascend all the way to the brain, which requires an extra moment of travel.

The nervous system is divided into the central nervous system (brain and spine) and peripheral nervous system, which is further divided, as shown in Figure 3.5. The **peripheral nervous system** contains all the nerves outside the central nervous system, divided into the **somatic nervous system**, which controls voluntary behaviors such as walking, and the **autonomic nervous system**, which controls involuntary behaviors such as heartbeat, blood pressure, and digestion. The autonomic nervous system can be further divided into the sympathetic nervous system, which controls the body's response to threats, and the parasympathetic nervous system, which controls organ activities when no threat is present. A threatening stimulus could

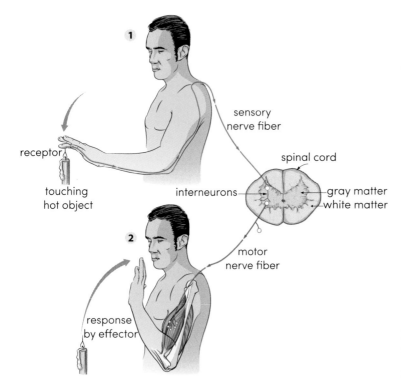

3.4 Reflex arc
Exposure to a sharp pain sends a signal through a sensory neuron to an interneuron in the spinal cord that initiates a motor response. To feel the pain requires that the pain signal ascend all the way to the brain, so the reflexive withdrawal of the hand occurs before you even become aware of the pain.

be a social threat, such as someone calling you names in public, or a dangerous predator, such as a bear chasing you, both of which call for a vigorous response. When responding to a threat by fighting or fleeing, the arms and legs need to work together or in sympathy with each other, which may help you remember that the **sympathetic nervous system** controls organ activities associated with fight and flight. Conversely, after the threat is removed or eliminated, the body needs to calm down. The **parasympathetic nervous system** is associated with rest and digestion.

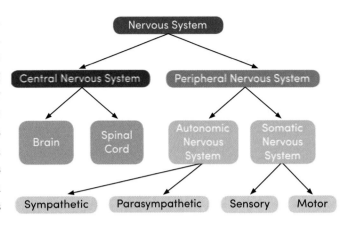

3.5 Divisions of the nervous system

The nervous system is a collection of pairs. The central nervous system consists of the brain and spinal cord. The peripheral nervous system contains the nerves that control organ activities (autonomic) and voluntary activities (somatic). In the autonomic nervous system are organ activities that contribute to fight or flight (sympathetic) or rest and digest (parasympathetic).

The way the sympathetic and parasympathetic systems interact can be illustrated by sorting through some of the puzzling aspects of the drug methamphetamine. You may have noticed that purchasing over-the-counter medicine for relief from cold symptoms has become increasingly complicated in recent years. In most states, when customers want to purchase pseudoephedrine, sold under the brand name Sudafed, they can only purchase a limited amount per day, must provide photo identification, and often must use the same pharmacy where they purchase their prescription medicine so the pharmacist knows them by name. Of course, the heightened security is a response to the fact that methamphetamine can be manufactured by concentrating the pseudoephedrine in the cold medicine. Nevertheless, isn't it odd that lots of people consider concentrated cold medicine to be a recreational drug? Conversely, isn't it odd that diluted methamphetamine provides relief from cold symptoms?

The oddities of this drug become clearer when we consider that methamphetamine stimulates the sympathetic nervous system, which is mutually antagonistic with the parasympathetic nervous system. In other words, stimulating the sympathetic nervous system suppresses the parasympathetic nervous system, and stimulating the parasympathetic nervous system suppresses the sympathetic nervous system. Methamphetamine stimulates the sympathetic organ activities associated with fight or flight, such as the heart and breathing rate, and suppresses organ activities not essential to fight or flight, such as mucus processing and digestion. By suppressing mucous processing, diluted methamphetamine can provide relief from cold symptoms.

Another puzzling aspect of methamphetamine is that heavy users often suffer from widespread and advanced tooth decay, often called "meth mouth." This process also causes the tooth decay commonly observed in meth addicts. Suppressed digestion from the use of meth means suppressed salivation, and to relieve the resulting dry mouth, meth users typically seek to maintain or strengthen the effect of the drug by drinking beverages that have lots of caffeine. To someone with suppressed digestion, coffee and tea seem strong and heavy, and therefore vaguely disgusting, so the drink of choice for meth users suffering from dry mouth is often sugary caffeinated soda.

autonomic nervous system
the portion of the nervous system that controls involuntary behaviors (i.e., digestion)

sympathetic nervous system
the portion of the autonomic nervous system that controls the body's organ activity in response to threats

parasympathetic nervous system
the portion of the autonomic nervous system that controls normal organ activity

As recently as twenty years ago, most dentists thought that dentures were a thing of the past. Unfortunately, recent increases in methamphetamine abuse have led to the combination of dry mouth coupled with drinking gallons of sugary beverages, both of which encourage bacterial growth, making dentures depressingly common for people in their 20s and 30s who abuse methamphetamine.

Concept Recall

1. How can you reflexively withdraw your hand or foot from a painful stimulus before you even become aware of the pain?
2. How do the central and peripheral nervous systems differ?
3. How would the two systems of the autonomic nervous system (sympathetic and parasympathetic) respond to a near accident when driving a car?
4. Stimulation of which part of the nervous system would suppress appetite?

This Is Psychology

In the early twentieth century, neuroscientists were sharply divided over the question of how neurons send signals across the synapse, with some claiming synaptic signals are chemical and others claiming they are electrical. One night in 1920, the Austrian scientist Otto Loewi dreamed of an experiment that would settle the dispute between the "soups" and "sparks," so he briefly woke and jotted down some notes. Unfortunately, in the morning he couldn't read his notes, and he had forgotten all the details from his dream. The next evening, he awoke from the same dream, but having learned his lesson, he rushed to his laboratory. His experiment used two hearts from frogs that continued to beat when extracted and placed in salt water. Loewi stimulated a nerve connected to one heart, and as expected, its beating slowed. The critical part of the experiment came next, when he sucked up some fluid surrounding the slowed heart and squirted it into the beaker holding the second heart. The beating of the second heart slowed, proving that the signal between a cardiac neuron and the heart muscle is chemical.

STRUCTURE AND FUNCTION OF THE BRAIN

Our brains are built from the ground up, with parts that promote basic survival inherited from our most primitive ancestors at the bottom and more sophisticated, evolutionarily recent structures built on top. The spinal cord pokes through a hole in the base of the skull and extends upward like a stick. This extension of the spinal cord is called the brain stem. One of the main structures in the brain stem is the **medulla**, seen in Figure 3.6, which controls basic reflexes such as breathing, heartbeat, digestion, and coughing. The medulla has many receptor sites for opiates, which are depressant drugs derived from the opium poppy plant that include codeine, morphine, and heroin. As

medulla
a brain stem structure that controls basic reflexes, such as breathing and heartbeat

a brain stem depressant, codeine is often prescribed as a cough suppressant. Opiates also suppress digestion, so one surprising side effect of heroin abuse is constipation. This side effect has been harnessed for clinical use in tropical climates, where diarrhea from amoebic dysentery and other maladies can be life-threatening, and a small dose of opiates can prevent death from dehydration. Because breathing is also controlled by the medulla, the most dangerous effect and most common cause of death from opiate abuse is suppression of breathing.

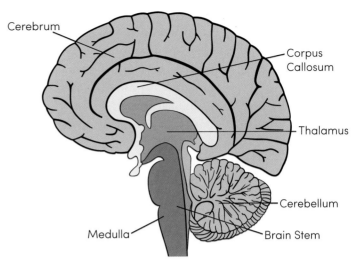

3.6 Half of the human brain
This figure illustrates one half of a human brain, obtained by slicing down through the longitudinal fissure, a deep valley that separates the right and left hemispheres from each other. Slicing the brain reveals deep brain structures, such as the thalamus, corpus callosum, and medulla, which are impossible to see in an intact brain, as in Figure 3.9.

Straddling the brain stem are two prominent orbs that hang down from the rest of the brain called the **cerebellum**, meaning "small brain" in Latin. The cerebellum contributes to movements requiring balance, coordination, and precise timing. Although small, the cerebellum contains more neurons than are contained in the rest of the brain; motion control apparently requires lots of processing power. To appreciate the role of the cerebellum in movement, consider what happens when the cerebellum is suppressed, as when someone is under the influence of alcohol. Ideally, the driver of a car should be in command of movements requiring fine motor control and precise timing, but alcohol eliminates both by suppressing the cerebellum. The field sobriety tests used by police are designed to assess cerebellar suppression. For example, a driver suspected of driving under the influence of alcohol might be asked to hold both arms straight out to the side, then rapidly touch the nose with both index fingers. While seemingly simple, this motion actually consists of two movements: a gross movement of the hands from their starting point to a position near the face, followed by fine motor adjustments to lightly touch the nose. Alcohol suppresses cerebellar function while leaving gross movements relatively intact, so impaired drivers asked to carry out this task will often hit themselves in the face.

cerebellum
a brain structure that contributes to movements requiring balance, coordination, and precise timing

Middle Brain Structures

Medieval Christian authors described limbo as a place at the edge of hell that was not quite in heaven either. The main structure in the middle brain, the **limbic system**, was named to convey a similar idea, that the functions of the middle brain lie between the primitive lower brain and the higher-level processing in the cerebrum. The limbic system contains several structures that contribute to our emotional experience, including the nucleus accumbens mentioned earlier in this chapter as the part of the brain stimulated by pleasurable experiences and addictive drugs. Emotion is a notoriously slippery word to define, so an example may clarify what it means. If you were lying comfortably in

limbic system
a group of midbrain structures that contributes to our emotional experience

a hammock holding a cold drink on a warm summer's day and saw a baby crawling toward the swimming pool, your fear for the baby's safety would motivate you to leap out of the hammock and grab the baby before she tumbles into the pool. In this example, it's clear that one of the primary functions of emotions is to instigate immediate motor responses, so the **thalamus**, located in the midbrain, carries out quick but rough preliminary analyses of perceptual information. Vision and hearing project directly from the eyes and ears to the thalamus, which then forwards the sensory information to several targets in the limbic system and to the cerebral cortex for more sophisticated processing. The limbic system also includes the amygdala, where fear-conditioned associations are stored (LeDoux, 1996). To provoke action, the amygdala turns to the **hypothalamus** (Greek for "under the thalamus," and that is just where it dangles). As shown with the example of the baby and swimming pool, emotions move us to act.

By provoking decisive actions that promote survival under stressful conditions, the hypothalamus is essential to motivated behaviors (what are commonly called the four F's: fighting, fleeing, feeding, and mating). Experienced soldiers in combat often throw themselves to the ground without thinking when they hear incoming artillery. This snap judgment serves the soldiers well during combat because if they had to think about how to respond to the sound of artillery, their responses would be too slow to save them from the storm of fragments that follows an explosion. Unfortunately, the snap judgments afforded by the thalamus-to-amygdala connection are fast but not flexible. When a soldier returns to civilian life with his battle-hardened intuition, he might hit the deck when hearing a clap of thunder. The soldier consciously understands that in the civilian world, hitting the deck is no longer appropriate, but his amygdala has already triggered its command by the time his cortex has had the opportunity to realize this.

The hypothalamus prepares the body for action by activating the sympathetic nervous system, which in turn activates the adrenal gland, which is actually part of the endocrine system. The endocrine system contains all the glands that secrete hormones into the blood; for example, the adrenal gland secretes adrenaline. Hormones are comparable to neurotransmitters in that both act as chemical messengers. The primary difference is that neurotransmitters send their messages from one neuron to another across the tiny synaptic gap, whereas hormones broadcast their messages across the entire body through the bloodstream. For example, a person who is about to engage in physical exertion ought to lower his body temperature in preparation for the forthcoming rise in body temperature associated with the exertion. Sweat glands across the entire surface of the skin respond to adrenaline in the blood by releasing sweat to cool the body, which is why people sometimes complain of a "cold sweat" when terrified.

Do you remember your first kiss? What about your first bowl of rice? If you're like most people, you remember the kiss but not the rice. One noticeable difference between the two is that you were probably emotionally aroused during the kiss but not while eating the rice. As we saw with the amygdala-hypothalamus connection, activity in one component of the limbic system tends to excite other limbic structures. The hippocampus (Greek for "seahorse") stores conscious experiences in memory to be made available for

thalamus
a midbrain structure that receives incoming sensory information and passes the information on to the limbic system and the cortex

hypothalamus
a midbrain structure that is essential to motivated behaviors, such as feeding or fighting

later retrieval. The fact that emotional arousal promotes storage in long-term memory has intuitive appeal; after all, the events associated with strong emotions are almost certainly more important than those associated with humdrum emotions.

It is widely known that memories are closely associated with our sense of smell. This principle is beautifully illustrated in the movie *Ratatouille*. When the restaurant waiter places a dish of ratatouille on the table in front of a food critic, the critic's mind flashes back to a scene from his childhood when his mother gave him a dish of freshly cooked ratatouille. The axons from sensory nerves in the nose project directly to the olfactory bulb that underlies our sense of smell, and its proximity to the hippocampus explains why smells can induce the retrieval of long-buried memories. Less well-known than the connection between smell and memory is the fact that loss of the sense of smell (anosmia) can be emotionally devastating. Indeed, anosmia evokes almost no sympathy; students completing a questionnaire ranked it as equivalent to the loss of a big toe (Wrzesniewski, McCauley, & Rozin, 1999). Permanent anosmia commonly results from a forceful blow to the forehead, just above the nose, which shears off olfactory axons between the nose and olfactory bulb. For people with a normal sense of smell, activity in the olfactory bulb stimulates the amygdala throughout a normal

Cross-Cultural Case

Cultural Neuroscience

Cultural influence on psychology and psychological development is undeniable, and the growing field of cultural neuroscience will use brain-imaging technology to study it. Specifically, cultural neuroscientists hope to increase our understanding of how much influence environmental factors truly have on our behavior and mental functions. Though the field is barely a decade old, researchers have already discovered differences in brain activity between people of different cultures when asked to consider answers to the same question, providing documentable evidence that behavioral theorists can use to support their theories. In short, as Beth Azar of Science Watch notes, "neuroscience can measure cultural differences" and "may even change the way we think about

brain development." However, pioneering cultural neuroscientists, such as Stanford University's Dr. Hazel Rose Markus, caution that "to make progress in our understanding of how cultures shape brains and brains shape culture, we need to know what psychological and behavioral tendencies are associated with these social categories and how these tendencies are linked to brain function." So while cultural neuroscience is an exciting new field of psychology, it is closely entwined with cultural and behavioral psychology as well.

day, but people with anosmia have no such constantly shifting olfactory experience and therefore suffer from blunted emotions. They just can't get excited like they did before losing their sense of smell, to the extent that they can become depressed, even to the point of feeling suicidal. In summary, the fact that components of the limbic system are mutually excitatory can explain why emotionally laden memories are easier to recall than unemotional memories (amygdala-hippocampus), why smell is closely associated with memory (hippocampus-olfactory bulb), and why a blunted emotional life commonly results from loss of the sense of smell (olfactory-bulb–amygdala). Having considered some of the brain areas that are implicated in emotion, we will now look at emotion in more detail.

Emotional Processes in the Brain

As mentioned previously in connection with the example of the baby crawling toward the swimming pool, two aspects of emotion are the tendency for emotions to make you shuffle your priorities and their tendency to provoke responsive actions. The cold drink and hammock had been your primary concerns, but then a moment later the baby became your primary concern, prompting you to abandon the hammock and leap to the baby's rescue. Already, it seems that the single term "emotion" actually refers to more than one experience, and there are still other aspects of emotion: physiological arousal and affect. Autonomic arousal includes such responses as a pounding heart, heavy breathing, and dilated pupils, among others, and somatic arousal includes such responses as facial expressions and running away from the threat. Emotional affect (pronounced with the stress on the first syllable) refers to the internal experience of how the emotion feels: anger feels different from fear, which feels different from disgust, and so on. Common sense suggests that when confronted by a stimulus such as a bear, the visual perception of the bear triggers the feeling of fear, which in turn triggers physiological arousal in order to respond to the threat posed by the bear. William James, who you met in Chapter 1 as the best-known advocate of Functionalism, proposed an alternative account of emotion in which the causal order of emotional affect and physiological arousal are switched, so arousal precedes the feeling rather than the other way around, as shown in Figure 3.7. Around the same time that William James developed his proposal, the physician Carl Georg Lange made a similar suggestion,

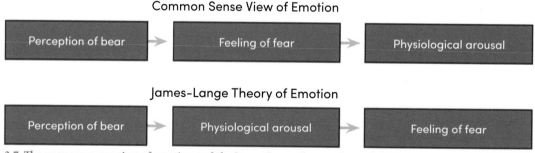

3.7 The common sense view of emotion and the James-Lange theory of emotion
Common sense suggests that a threatening stimulus, such as a bear, induces a feeling of fear, which then leads to symptoms of physiological arousal, such as a pounding heart. James and Lange suggested that instead physiological arousal occurs first, which is then followed by the feeling.

so their ideas were fused into what has become known as the James-Lange theory of emotion. It may seem strange that only after becoming aroused do you realize how you feel, but several different kinds of experimental results support the James-Lange alternative to the common sense account of emotion.

Autonomic arousal

The results from an experiment by Stanley Schachter and Jerome E. Singer (1962) provided the first piece of evidence. In their experiment, participants were injected with epinephrine, a hormone that induces the racing heartbeat, heavy breathing, and sweaty palms associated with autonomic arousal. However, only some participants were accurately informed about what they could expect from the injection, and other participants were not given any information about how the injection would affect them. After being injected, participants were asked to fill out a questionnaire in the same room as another person who was also filling out the questionnaire. The experimenters deceived participants by telling them the other person in the room was also a participant; in fact, the other person in the room was a confederate of the researchers, who pretended to be another participant but who was actually behaving as the researchers wanted. In one condition the confederate acted euphoric, as if filling out a questionnaire was the most fun and exciting activity imaginable, and in the other condition the confederate acted angry, as if the questionnaire were a major inconvenience. Secretly watching the participants through a one-way mirror, the researchers noticed that the epinephrine-ignorant participants behaved similarly to the confederate, euphoric when the confederate was euphoric and angry when the confederate was angry, but the epinephrine-informed group did not.

How would you react if your heart were pounding, you were breathing hard, and your palms were sweating while filling out a questionnaire next to another person who was either acting as if it was either great fun or a major hassle? If you had been accurately informed about what to expect from the injection, you would know why you felt funny and would just consider the confederate's behavior to be a bizarre spectacle. On the other hand, participants who were ignorant of the injection's effect would have no idea why they felt so jittery, so they would look around them to find the reason for feeling so keyed up. When the confederate was acting euphoric, the epinephrine-ignorant participant might think, "So that's why I'm so wound up, because I'm getting such a kick out of filling out this questionnaire!", and when the confederate was acting angrily, the participant might think, "Who do they think they are, asking me to kill myself with this outrageous workload?"

Donald Dutton and Arthur Aron (1974) wondered if the results in Schachter and Singer would extend to a situation in which arousal resulted directly from the circumstances rather than from an injected hormone. In their experiment, male participants walked across one of two bridges to meet the experimenter, who was an attractive woman. Some participants walked across a bridge that was rickety, swayed in the wind, and was located above a deep ravine, whereas other participants walked across a much more stable and secure bridge. Dutton and Aron expected the rickety bridge but not the stable bridge to induce physiological arousal in participants. In the experimenter's debriefing, she gave participants a sheet of paper with her phone number and instructions to call if they had any additional questions. More participants who had walked across the rickety bridge called the experimenter afterward than participants who had walked across the secure bridge. Dutton and Aron argued that the rickety bridge induced autonomic arousal in the participants who had to walk across it, and when participants saw the attractive experimenter, they misattributed their arousal to feelings of sexual attraction for the experimenter.

The results from the Schachter and Singer epinephrine experiment and the Dutton and Aron rickety-bridge experiment support the James-Lange theory by showing that when people experience autonomic arousal, they look to their surroundings to figure out the reason, and only then do they experience the feelings that match the situation. Further support for the James-Lange theory of emotion comes from evidence that somatic arousal in the form of facial expressions can cause people to feel emotions that are consistent with the facial expression.

Somatic arousal

Do you think facial expressions are universal across all human cultures, or instead are they culturally driven? In the early 1960s, Dr. Paul Ekman was a young psychologist just out of graduate school who wanted to study facial expressions. At the time, the consensus among psychologists was that facial expressions were driven by the culture in which a person had grown up. And yet, in his travels outside the United States, Ekman would carry photographs of people displaying various facial expressions, and when he asked anyone he met to describe the emotional experience of the people in the photos, they always agreed on what the facial expressions meant. Although people across the world could determine the way Americans felt based on how they looked, perhaps this merely shows that American culture had spread across the globe so people from far-flung locations had learned how to interpret American facial expressions from American movies and shows. On the other hand, could Americans interpret the facial expressions of people from very different cultures?

To answer this question, Ekman got his hands on some film depicting people from the interior of Papua New Guinea, the enormous island just north of Australia. As recently as the early twentieth century, there were Stone-Age tribes living among the jungles in Papua New Guinea that nobody outside the island even knew existed. In fact, Papuans living on the island's outskirts considered the mountains ringing the island to be impenetrable, and within living memory none of them had ever ventured over the mountains to investigate the interior. When explorers in the 1920s began to fly airplanes over the mountains expecting to find nothing but uninhabited jungle, they were astonished by clear signs of well-established and widespread human settlements. The mountains remained formidable barriers to encroachment from the outside world, keeping Papuans about as remote from Western culture as possible. Nevertheless, when Ekman showed the movies of Papuans to Dr. Silvan Soloman Tomkins, an expert on human facial expressions, Tomkins could accurately describe the cultural experiences of the people in the movies without any previous knowledge. Paul Ekman and his academic collaborator Dr. Wallace V. Friesen immediately decided to develop a catalog of human facial expressions.

Ekman and Friesen began by determining all the facial muscles, then set about learning to flex each muscle one at a time. To make sure each person was flexing the intended muscle, they practiced while seated at a table facing each other. After going home one day, Friesen noticed that he felt terrible, and wondering why, he realized that he and Ekman had spent the day making faces associated with dread. Sure enough, when the two met at work the next morning, Ekman admitted to having had similar feelings as Friesen the night before. Making facial expressions associated with dread seemed to induce a feeling of dread. Although the face is widely considered to be a window into the soul, Ekman and Friesen began to believe that the face doesn't just reveal how a person feels, but actually *is* how a person feels.

To test Ekman and Friesen's hypothesis that making faces can induce feelings consistent with the facial expressions, Dr. Fritz Strack, Leonard L. Martin, and Sabine Stepper (1988) wondered whether people who are smiling would laugh more when reading something intended to be funny than other people who aren't smiling. If you were a participant in a psychology experiment in which you were asked to smile while reading the comics, you would probably figure out what the researchers were trying to accomplish, and as a result you probably wouldn't act naturally. For that reason, the experimenters figured out a clever way to get half of their participants to smile without them even realizing they were. All participants were asked to hold a pen in their mouths while reading cartoons and to rate how funny they thought the cartoons were. Half of the participants were instructed to hold a pen in their mouth by the lips without touching their teeth to the pen, and the other half were instructed to hold a pen by the teeth without touching their lips to the pen. As you can see in Figure 3.8, participants who held the pen in their teeth without it touching their lips needed to maintain a smile, and they didn't realize they were smiling because they focused on keeping their lips from touching the pen. Participants who held the pen in their teeth rated the cartoons as funnier and laughed more than the participants who held the pen in their lips. It seems there is some wisdom in the old song lyric that urges the listener to "Smile though your heart is breaking . . ." because just smiling will make you feel better.

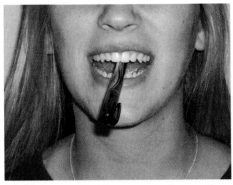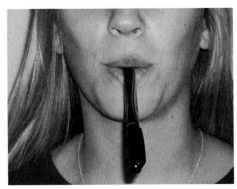

3.8 Two ways of holding a pen in the mouth
Holding a pen by the teeth without touching the lips requires the participant to smile, but holding a pen by the lips without touching the teeth does not.

While it seems that making faces will induce the feelings that match the facial expression, if you were (temporarily) unable to make some facial expression, would that prevent you from feeling the associated emotion? To set the stage for answering that question, consider whether you would eat food from cans that are dented or have bulges. You may realize that eating food from dented cans is probably fine, but if you have any food in cans that bulge, you ought to toss those cans in the trash without opening them, and definitely without eating any of the food if you do open the can. Bulges in canned food are a sign that the food has been infected by botulism, which would kill you if you ate even the tiniest sample. The reason is that botulism, like curare, described earlier in this chapter, paralyzes muscles including your diaphragm, so exposure to botulism would cause death by suffocation. And yet some people are willing to pay cosmetic surgeons hefty fees to inject botulism toxin (commonly abbreviated as BOTOX®) into their faces. BOTOX® which paralyzes facial muscles at the injection site, thereby reducing the wrinkles that are a sign of aging. One well-known side effect of BOTOX® injections is the frustrating inability to frown. A recent study (Havas et al., 2010) showed that people who recently had BOTOX® injections were slower to read sentences describing angry situations than controls whose facial muscles were not paralyzed by BOTOX®. The researchers argued that comprehending a sentence describing an angry situation requires the reader to frown, so the inability to frown interferes with reading comprehension.

Can you imagine feeling any emotion, whether it be anger, disgust, fear, or any other, without also feeling physiologically aroused? Does it even make sense to simultaneously feel emotional and cool as a cucumber? The intuition that emotional experience is necessarily associated with physiological arousal led James and Lange to propose their account of emotion, in which arousal occurs before the emotional feeling arises. Various experimental results support the James-Lange theory of emotion: People who experience autonomic arousal look to their surroundings for an explanation of the arousal, then feel the emotion that is consistent with the explanation. Facial expressions are universal across all human cultures not just because they are all associated with particular emotions, but because in a certain sense, the facial expression is the emotion. Having considered emotional experience, we turn now to brain areas with higher-level mental processing: the four lobes in the cerebral cortex.

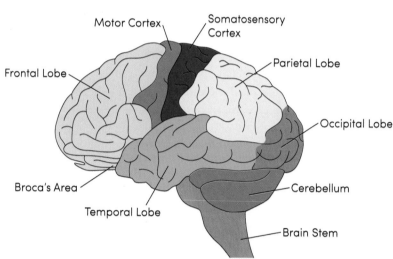

3.9 Intact human brain
An intact human brain, on which can be seen four lobes of the cerebral cortex, the brain stem, and cerebellum. The motor cortex defines the posterior (farthest back) edge of the frontal lobe, and the somatosensory cortex defines the anterior (farthest forward) edge of the parietal lobe. For most people, Broca's area is in the left hemisphere (the hemisphere seen here), at the base of the frontal lobe.

Cerebral Cortex

The most prominent feature of a human brain is its wrinkly surface, or **cortex**, named for the Latin word for "bark" (as in bark like a tree, not bark like a dog). Each person's cortex has a unique set of valleys and ridges that are as distinct from any other cortical landscape as fingerprints. Nevertheless, some features are stable across most brains and serve as landmarks for staking out the boundaries of the four lobes, as seen in Figure 3.9.

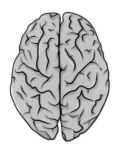

3.10 Human brain as seen from above
The cerebral cortex consists of two hemispheres, one on each side, with a massive valley called the longitudinal fissure separating them.

At the extreme rear or posterior corner of the brain is the **occipital lobe**. The anterior, or forward, edge of the occipital lobe borders on the **parietal lobe** and **temporal lobe**, with the massive **sylvian fissure** separating the two. At the anterior edge of the parietal lobe are two vertical ridges: the **primary somatosensory cortex** and **primary motor cortex**. The somatosensory cortex processes sensations associated with touch, and the primary motor cortex programs voluntary movements. The valley between the two ridges designates the boundary between the parietal lobe (which includes the somatosensory cortex) and the **frontal lobe** (which includes the motor cortex). As seen from above, the cortex is divided by the longitudinal fissure into left and right **hemispheres**, as can be seen in Figure 3.10.

cortex
the wrinkly surface of the brain

occipital lobe
the lobe at the posterior corner of the brain, concerned primarily with basic visual processing

parietal lobe
the part of the cortex that processes visual locations and contains the primary somatosensory cortex

temporal lobe
the part of the cortex that allows us to recognize visual objects, such as faces

sylvian fissure
a structure of the cortex that separates the parietal and temporal lobes

primary somatosensory cortex
lies on the parietal lobe and processes touch sensations

primary motor cortex
lies on the frontal lobe and programs voluntary movements

frontal lobe
the area of the brain that is implicated in impulse control and personality

hemisphere
the division of the cortex into left and right sides

Occipital lobe

The occipital lobe at the back of the brain is concerned primarily with basic visual processing. (Doesn't it seem a little funny that vision is processed at the back of the brain?) As mentioned earlier in this chapter, the thalamus receives neural projections from the eyes. The thalamus then projects to the primary visual cortex (V1) in the occipital lobe. The first systematic studies of V1 were carried out by wartime physicians: Dr. Tatsuji Inouye, a Japanese physician during the Russo-Japanese War of 1904-1905, and Sir Gordon Morgan Holmes, a British physician during World War I (Fishman, 1997). The bullets used in early twentieth-century warfare caused localized wounds that left the victims with small blind spots, almost as if paint had been splattered on their eyeballs. To study the vision of patients with these kinds of bullet wounds, the Japanese and British physicians moved a visual target around and asked patients to indicate when the target was visible and when it was not. By correlating the locations of blind spots with bullet-entry wounds on the back of the head, the physicians inferred that the visual world is laid across the primary visual cortex just like a map, with the center of gaze represented at the back of the brain and peripheral vision farther forward. Also, the right half of the visual field is represented in the left hemisphere, and the left half of the visual field is represented in the right hemisphere.

Temporal lobe

After V1 carries out basic visual processing, the visual signal splits into two streams, one of which flows toward the temporal lobe and the other toward the parietal lobe, as

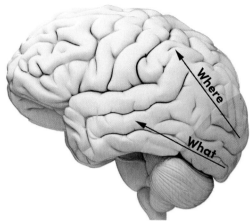

3.11 The "what" and "where" visual processing streams
Initial processing of visual information takes place in the occipital lobe, then proceeds in two visual processing streams. The "what" stream, which projects to the temporal lobe, identifies objects. The "where" stream, which processes object locations and facilitates action, projects to the parietal lobe.

3.12 Does one paddle look more like a face?
Newborn babies will look at a paddle with three circles arranged like facial features more than at one with the same three circles that are not arranged like a face.

in Figure 3.11. The temporal stream recognizes objects, so it is called the "what" stream; the parietal stream enables us to visually navigate our surroundings, so it is called the "where" stream. To recognize an object, the "what" stream connects an image with objects stored in memory. Of all the objects that we can recognize, faces seem to have a high priority. First of all, newborn babies prefer to look at two circles next to each other with a third circle below rather than when the third circle is above the other two, as in Figure 3.12. The first arrangement looks more like a face, implying that newborn babies love to gaze at faces. This is fortunate because parents love to gaze into babies' faces, so parents and babies have lots of fun staring at each other. The importance of faces is also illustrated by the fact that we see faces in places where there are no faces, the most famous example probably being the man in the moon. The special status of face perception was confirmed by brain-scanning experiments that revealed which parts of the brain are active for the task. While viewing images of faces, one part of the brain "lights up," indicating increased activity, so it was called the **fusiform face area** (FFA) to highlight its role in face perception. To get a sense of how your own FFA works, look at the upside-down image of a face on the left side of Figure 3.13. Although the upside-down face looks fine, when right-side up the face looks grotesque, with pieces that don't fit together. Apparently, when viewing upside-down faces we perceive the nose, mouth, eyes, and other features, but when viewing faces in their usual upright orientation we perceive not just the features but also the way the features fit together. Damage to the FFA leads to a condition called **prosopagnosia**, in which victims fail to recognize the faces of close friends, loved ones, and even pictures of themselves.

fusiform face area (FFA)
an area of the temporal lobe that has increased activity when we view faces

prosopagnosia
a condition that causes people to lose the ability to recognize faces

neglect
a visual deficit in which people tend to ignore everything seen in one half of the visual field

Parietal lobe

Damage to the parietal "where" stream leads to a different kind of visual deficit called **neglect**, for which the main symptom is the tendency to neglect everything located in one half of the visual field. In an intact brain the right parietal lobe pays attention to

3.13 Visual processing of faces
Both images are the same, but the upside-down image looks much better than the right-side up image, in which the president's mouth and eyes clearly do not fit the overall organization of his face. When viewing upside-down faces we see eyes, nose, mouth, and other facial features but not how well the facial features fit together; the fit between facial features (or lack of fit, as here) only becomes apparent for faces viewed right-side up.

the left half of the visual field, so damage to the right parietal lobe eliminates visual attention for the left visual field, leaving intact visual attention for the right visual field. If you presented a dinner plate filled with food to someone with right parietal damage, he would neglect all the food on the left side of the plate and eat just the food on the right side. After eating half of the food on the plate, your dinner companion might complain of lingering hunger. In response, you could rotate the plate a half-turn so the uneaten food was now in the right (intact) visual field, and he would be surprised and pleased by the sudden appearance of a "full" plate of food.

The parietal lobe processes not just visual locations but also the locations of touch sensations on the body in the primary somatosensory cortex (S1), which defines the parietal lobe's anterior edge. The organizational layout of S1 was mapped primarily by the neurosurgeon Dr. Wilder Penfield in a series of surgical procedures intended to provide relief from seizure disorders. Seizures often begin when a small population of wayward neurons collectively join in a recurring pattern of activity; these neurons recruit some nearby neurons, which then recruit still other neurons, and the seizure steadily spreads across the brain. For many sufferers of seizure disorders, the point of origin, or **focus**, of seizures is located in S1, so they feel a tingling in a particular part of the body just before each seizure. In the 1920s, Penfield believed that locating and then removing the offending cells at the seizure's focus would eliminate seizures. With that in mind, Penfield designed a surgical procedure that entailed removing a portion of the skull to expose S1. It might seem that such an invasive procedure would require a general anesthetic, but Penfield needed his patients to remain awake and alert during

focus
the point of origin of a seizure

the entire procedure, so he administered just a local anesthetic to deaden sensation in the scalp. No pain relief is needed for the brain itself because it has no pain receptors. With S1 exposed, Penfield lightly touched the surface of the brain with a tiny electrode, which induced a small electrical current at the point of contact, and asked the patient to say what he felt. Electrode stimulation of some locations in S1 induced feelings at body locations that were roughly similar from one patient to another: When stimulating S1 locations near the top of the brain, patients said that they felt a tingling in the toes, then stimulation farther down the surface of S1 induced tingling in the leg, torso, arm, and hand. Below the hand was a discontinuity where the S1 representation jumped from hand to face. After poking around S1 to get his bearings, Penfield zeroed in on the spot that induced the same feeling that preceded the onset of seizures. When he found the right brain location, he knew what tissue he needed to remove. At this point, you may realize that surgical removal of a section of S1 means that the patient will be numb in the associated body part for the rest of his life. Apparently, Penfield's patients considered a small region of lifelong numbness a fair price to pay for relief from their seizures. Just anterior to S1 is the primary motor cortex, (M1), which is mapped in a layout similar to S1: if electrode stimulation of one location in S1 induces a tingling in some body part, stimulating the adjacent location in M1 instigates a movement of that same body part. The valley between S1 and M1 marks the boundary between the parietal lobe and the frontal lobe.

Frontal lobe

The most conspicuous difference between human brains and the brains of our closest evolutionary cousins, chimpanzees, is the comparatively massive frontal lobe in human brains. It seems that the frontal lobe contains what makes us human, and for that reason the functioning of most of the frontal lobe is subtle and mysterious. The person who ushered in the modern study of the frontal lobe was not a scientist but a nineteenth-century railroad foreman.

Phineas Gage, pictured with the tamping rod that caused his unique injury.

In September 1848, Phineas Gage was supervising his gang of workers as they blasted through some rock outcrops near Cavendish, Vermont, to clear a corridor for the railway. Gage set and detonated explosive charges, then his men carted away the rubble. His primary tool was a three-and-a-half-foot-long steel tamping rod commissioned from a local blacksmith. Weighing about fifteen pounds, it was flat on one end and tapered to a point at the other end. Gage followed a routine when setting charges: Sprinkle black powder into a hole, use the pointy end of the rod to snake a fuse into the hole, fill the hole with sand, flip the rod over so the flat end is on the bottom, and use the flat to tamp down the sand. After setting the charge, Gage would light the fuse and run like mad. Late one day, Gage had an accident that would make his name the best known in all of neuroscience. Accounts vary about what happened to cause the mishap, but it seems likely Gage's attention was distracted by his workers' mischief, and he accidentally hit the rock next to the fuse with the tamping rod, creating a spark that prematurely ignited the explosive charge. The explosion transformed the tamping rod into a missile with Gage's head situated directly in its path.

The pointy end of the tamping rod blew upward into Gage's head through his left cheek and exited through his upper left forehead then continued flying through the air, landing about 30 yards behind him. The collision between rod and head knocked Gage to the ground, and his workers were certain that it had killed him. In a certain sense they were right, because the man who inhabited Gage's body for the next 11 years was profoundly different than the man Gage had been prior to his impromptu brain surgery. Victims of recent brain trauma are typically disoriented and shaken up, but Gage walked under his own power to an oxcart, sat upright in the cart during the ride to town, walked up a flight of stairs to his room, and waited patiently for the arrival of the town physician. When Gage met the physician, he even told a joke: "Well, here's enough work for you, Doctor." The doctor could do little for Gage besides delicately reposition some skull fragments, wrap his head with bandages, and hope that he didn't die from infection. After a couple weeks, Gage looked and acted as if he'd recovered from his accident: he could walk, talk, see, hear, remember, and reason pretty much like before the accident. Although Gage seemed to recover, his family and closest friends knew something was deeply wrong with him but found it difficult to express their intuitions in words; the best that anyone could do was to say, "Gage is no longer Gage."

Before his accident, Gage was efficient and organized, mild-mannered, a great leader of men, and was held in high esteem by both his workers and superiors. After his accident, Gage swore like a sailor, could not maintain several ongoing mental tasks at once, and behaved erratically, guided primarily by his emotional state at each particular moment. You might be able to imagine how Gage must have struggled to control his impulses if you, like most people, have been occasionally tempted to tell your boss what you really thought of him or her. While it would have felt wonderful in the short term to plainly state how you felt, you probably realized that doing so would have long term consequences, such as being unable to pay the rent or purchase groceries. Most everyone feels impulses generated by their emotional brains, but those of us with intact frontal lobes are also able to control those impulses by considering how they impact our long-term goals.

With a damaged frontal lobe, Gage was a slave to his impulses and utterly incapable of resuming his career as railroad foreman. For a couple of years, Gage went wherever the wind blew him, ending up in P. T. Barnum's freak show as the "Only Living Man with a Hole in His Head" (Fleischman, 2002). Beginning in 1852, Gage spent seven years as a horse wrangler and stagecoach driver in South America; then in 1859 he appeared on his sister's doorstep in San Francisco. For the last months of his life Gage confected wild tales of adventure to entertain his nieces and nephews, the flow of the stories guided primarily by whatever random ideas popped into his head. After suffering from seizures that were probably a consequence of his previous injury, the frequency and severity of the seizures worsened until one killed him in May 1860. Gage had never intended to become famous, but he provided insight into the question that drove mid-nineteenth-century ideas about the human brain: are mental faculties smeared across the entire brain, with every part of the brain contributing equally, or are they instead localized into independent and segregated modules? By retaining most of his mental faculties but losing the ability to control his impulses and thereby to fit into the social world of adults, Gage showed that these abilities are localized in the frontal lobe. Gage was not well known to the scientific establishment of his time, however, and other case studies were used to settle the argument about whether brain functions are distributed or localized.

Concept Recall

1. Why is respiratory arrest the most common cause of death from opiate overdose?

2. Why does alcohol interfere with the ability to drive a car?

3. Why might a soldier who spent time in combat hit the deck when hearing thunder?

4. What parts of the brain are contained in the limbic system?

5. Why are emotional memories retained better than memories of humdrum experiences?

6. What are the four lobes of the cerebral cortex, and where is each located?

7. What are the major functions in each cortical lobe?

This Is Psychology

Phineas Gage isn't the only person who tended to make bad decisions after suffering damage to the frontal cortex. Dr. Antonio Damasio, a neuroscientist who studies decision-making, described one of his patients (Damasio, 1994) who had been married with a family, a steady job, and a home, when a brain tumor near his frontal cortex caused a radical change in his behavior. After Damasio's patient lost his job, got divorced, and moved out of his house, he married a prostitute. As you might imagine, his second marriage ended badly. Oddly enough, when Damasio asked his patient, "Do you think it would be a good idea to marry a prostitute?" his patient acknowledged that it would be a mistake and he should have known better. Knowing that some behavior is risky and yet doing it anyway is a hallmark of frontal lobe disorder and may be an essential component of drug addiction. Many habitual drug users realize that their drug use is ruining their lives, and yet they continue using the substance. This understanding may explain why warnings on cigarette packaging have less effect than hoped for: smokers already know that cigarettes are harmful.

BRAIN LOCALIZATION

For most of human history, the brain was considered to be an organ, so it was presumed to work just like any other organ. For example, each part of the liver does liver stuff, and each part of the kidney does kidney stuff, so by extension each part of the brain must do brain stuff. The generally held belief that the mind is distributed across the

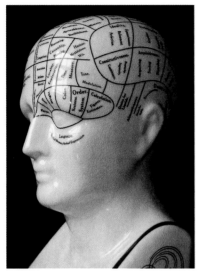

3.14 Phrenological map
Skull bumps in different locations are presumed by phrenology to indicate a bulging brain underneath, which in turn indicates what characteristic abilities that person has.

brain began to change in the early nineteenth century when the ideas of the Austrian physician Dr. Franz Josef Gall captured the popular imagination. Early in his career, Gall was a first-rate neuroanatomist making discoveries that still appear in neuroscience textbooks. Unfortunately for Gall's legacy, he is best known today for his crackpot system of **phrenology**. As a student in medical school, Gall noticed that some students, whom he considered less intelligent than himself, received better grades because they were better at memorization. He also noticed that these students all had protruding eyeballs (Hunt, 1993). Gall concluded that the ability to memorize is isolated to the part of the brain above the eyes and that brain tissue is like a muscle that bulges with repeated and heavy use. Gall manually examined the skulls of hundreds of people to map the mind onto the brain as shown in Figure 3.14, correlating the bumps he found with each person's predominant personality characteristics. Using skull bumps to describe an individual's personality enjoyed widespread enthusiasm among the general population for much of the nineteenth century.

phrenology
an idea created by Franz Josef Gall that postulates bumps on a person's skull are correlated to his or her personality

However, the scientific establishment rejected phrenology on the basis of Gall's shoddy data collection techniques. For example, Gall collected data from cases that supported his theories and discounted cases that did not. (As you read in Chapter 2, one of the hallmarks of good science is data collection from a random sampling of cases.) Repelled by phrenology's slipshod methods and lack of supporting evidence, the scientific community initially refused to believe in brain localization but was slowly persuaded to accept it beginning in 1861 with the case of the patient nicknamed Tan.

His real name was Louis Victor Leborgne, a Frenchman whose ability to speak eroded until at the age of 31 he could only say one word, "Tan," which became his nickname. Losing any means to support himself along with his ability to speak, Tan was committed to the Bicêtre, a combination hospital and nursing home outside Paris, in 1840. Tan's situation only worsened when his right arm and leg became paralyzed, confining him to his bed where he developed bedsores that became gangrenous. The surgeon Dr. Pierre Paul Broca amputated his leg to halt the spread of gangrene, but Tan died soon afterward. In the postmortem examination, Broca found a massive lesion on the left side of Tan's brain at the intersection of the frontal and temporal lobes, implying that Tan's lesion destroyed the language area of his brain. Broca spread the word among his colleagues that he wanted to find other people with the same **aphasia**, or language deficit, as Tan. It was then that he became aware of Lazare "Lelo" Lelong, an elderly ditchdigger who died from complications arising from a broken leg. Like Tan, Lelo was nicknamed for one

aphasia
a language deficit

of the five words he retained the ability to say. The postmortem exam revealed damage in the same location as in Tan's brain: the intersection of frontal and temporal lobes in the left hemisphere. Broca's colleagues began referring their patients with aphasia to Broca, and he eventually performed about two dozen postmortem examinations of aphasics' brains, all but one having damage to what has since been called **Broca's area** in the left hemisphere. This was the first evidence to show that language is localized, and moreover that the brain is *lateralized*, meaning that the functions of the right and left hemisphere are not symmetrical.

Brain Laterality

Are you left-brained or right-brained? Actually, you're both, because your cerebral hemispheres are connected by a bundle of about 200 million nerve fibers at the base of the brain called the **corpus callosum**. Although the corpus callosum facilitates communication between hemispheres, neural communication is more efficient within a hemisphere than between hemispheres. You can demonstrate this for yourself by doing the following: Lift your right foot, and rotate it clockwise around an imaginary circle. While rotating your foot, lift your right arm up high and draw a gigantic number six in the air. You will probably find that the arm motion interferes with the foot's rotation, but now try rotating the *left* foot clockwise while drawing a six shape with the right arm, and it should be much easier. By now you probably realize that asking you to draw a six is really just a sneaky way of getting you to rotate your hand counterclockwise, which interferes with clockwise rotation of the foot—but only when both hand and foot are on the same side of the body. As mentioned earlier in this chapter, the right cerebral hemisphere moves and senses the left side of the body, and the left hemisphere moves and senses the right side of the body. Broca showed that language is generally localized to the left hemisphere. As for the laterality of other mental faculties, our current knowledge is based on experiments with people who have had the corpus callosum surgically severed.

The American paratrooper W.J. jumped out of a plane over Holland in 1944, but unfortunately his parachute malfunctioned so he landed hard, breaking his leg. Soon after W.J. was captured by the Nazis, an enraged guard whacked him on the head with the butt of a rifle, and the resulting head injury received no medical attention during the remaining year of the war. After the war, W.J. suffered from seizures that became increasingly frequent until he was having as many as twenty per day in the late 1950s. As with Penfield's patients, W.J. was desperate for relief and agreed to undergo a risky experimental surgery in 1962. At the time, about the only thing physicians knew about the corpus callosum was that seizures gained strength when they jumped through it from one hemisphere to the other. With this in mind, it was reasonable to conclude that surgically severing the corpus callosum, an operation called a **corpus callosotomy**, might reduce the intensity of seizures. W.J.'s surgeons had only expected the callosotomy to restrict his seizures to one hemisphere, but the operation seemed to eliminate his seizures entirely. Not only was the outcome of the surgery better than expected, W.J. seemed to have recovered all of his mental and physical functioning, encouraging

Broca's area
an area of the cortex typically located in the left hemisphere associated with language, damage to which causes aphasia

corpus callosum
a broad band of fibers that connects the left hemisphere of the brain to the right hemisphere

corpus callosotomy
a surgical procedure in which the corpus callosum is severed

surgeons to perform more callosotomies. The neuroscientist Dr. Roger Sperry and his graduate student Michael Gazzaniga found it hard to believe that hacking through a couple hundred million neural fibers in the central nervous system had left behind no ill effects, so they took it as a challenge to find any abnormalities in the behavior of W.J. and other split-brain patients.

The techniques developed by Sperry and Gazzaniga enabled researchers to discover each hemisphere's particular talents, forming the basis for what is now called right-brained versus left-brained thinking. The left hemisphere is usually better at speech and language, and the right hemisphere is usually better at spatial reasoning and facial recognition (Wolman, 2012). Check out the two faces in Figure 3.15, each of which is a fusion of two half faces. Which fused face looks happier? If you're like many, you might think that the fused face on the right looks happier than the one on the left. Your right hemisphere, which is better at extracting emotional expression from faces than the left hemisphere, processes the left half of each image, so the image in which the left half is smiling is judged by your right hemisphere to be happier.

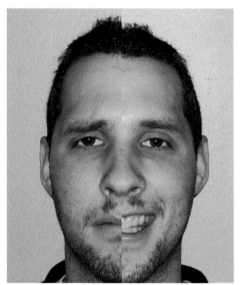 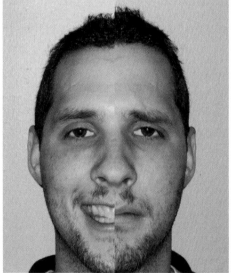

3.15 Which face looks happier?
Although both images are the same (they're mirror images of each other), does the image on the right look happier than the one on the left? If so, this occurs because of the way your right hemisphere views the left side of the world (due to neural crossover). Now look at the left half of each image. The left side of the image on the left is frowning, but the left side of the image on the right is smiling.

Trying to counter the way hemispheric differences are represented in popular culture, Gazzaniga has always emphasized that the two hemispheres are more like two hands working together than two rivals. To see what he means, consider Vicki's postoperative experience (Wolman, 2012.) (She doesn't mind having her first name known.) For about a year following her callosotomy, Vicki had great difficulty selecting an outfit each morning. Each hemisphere would pick a different outfit, and without a corpus callosum, Vicki's hemispheres couldn't talk to each other *inside* her skull, so they took their fight outside. That is, one hand would often grab the other hand to convince it to drop the outfit it was holding. When confronted by a difficult situation, have you ever felt as if you were "of two minds," pulled in two different directions? Perhaps, like Vicki, you really *did* have two minds, but with an intact corpus callosum you were able to blend each hemisphere's contributions to reach an equitable solution.

Concept Recall

1. What is phrenology, and what role did it play in the development of ideas about brain localization?

2. What is aphasia, and how did aphasia guide Broca's work on brain localization?

3. What is the corpus callosum, and what happens to a person after having surgery to sever it?

4. What does each cortical hemisphere do better than the other hemisphere?

BIOPSYCHOLOGY CONNECTIONS

You may have heard that "you are what you eat," but more important than this, you are what your brain does. Neurons in your brain are constantly firing. Activation from one system spreads to the next, and the differing patterns of activation produce new experiences and feelings. As complicated as your feelings and thoughts are, they are all built on the foundation of active and resting neurons.

In this chapter, we reviewed brain systems one at a time. This focus is necessary to help us appreciate the structure and function of each system. Unfortunately, it often gives a false idea of how the brain works. Brain networks run in parallel, meaning that multiple systems are active at any one time. Think about when you walk into a noisy restaurant. Your cerebellum is keeping your feet moving and managing your balance. Your occipital lobe is processing all of the visual information. Your temporal lobe is processing the other diners' faces. Your parietal lobe is processing input from the feel of your clothes as you walk. Your frontal lobe is deciding how best to greet your friends—and so much more. Fortunately for us, we don't experience each of these individual streams, but rather we experience the world as the sum of the interactions between all of these systems.

What we know about the brain and how it creates who we are is growing at an exponential rate. Biopsychologists rely on a dizzying array of tools, techniques, and people with unique medical histories to ply their trade. Soldiers with bullet wounds in their visual cortex, a man who inadvertently drove a spike through his brain, and people who sought relief from their seizures have all provided a precious window into how our brains create who we are.

REVIEW

- What are the parts of a neuron, and what role does each play in neural communication?
- How do signals within and between neurons differ?
- What is the difference between an agonist and antagonist?
- What are examples of drugs that affect neurotransmitter release, reuptake, and binding, and what is an example of a drug that mimics a neurotransmitter?
- What are the major divisions of the nervous system?
- What parts of the brain support basic functions, such as breathing, heartbeat, and coordinated movements?
- What parts of the brain are included in the limbic system, and how does each part contribute to experience?
- What are the cortical lobes, where is each located, and what are the major functions of each?
- Is mental function localized or distributed in the brain?
- How is brain function lateralized, and what is the main experimental technique used to study laterality?

1. The common misconception that people can only use 10 percent of their brain at any given time likely originated from the discovery that
    a. about 10 percent of the human brain is comprised of neurons.
    b. the brain can only activate approximately 10 percent of any given lobe regardless of task difficulty.
    c. 90 percent of neurons remain inactive throughout the life span.
    d. the brain's glial cells serve no purpose.

2. Naomi is looking at brain tissue under a microscope. In the area she is examining, she sees a small space. Naomi is probably looking at
    a. a synapse.   c. vesicles.
    b. damaged tissue.   d. myelin.

3. When Greg is safely watching television in the comfort of his own home, where no threat is present, his _____ is controlling organ activities.
    a. somatic nervous system   c. sympathetic nervous system
    b. parasympathetic nervous system   d. central nervous system

4. A severe injury to the frontal lobe could lead to
    a. paralysis of the legs.   c. a change in personality.
    b. loss of vision.   d. decreased dexterity.

5. American paratrooper W.J. agreed to an experimental surgery to have his corpus callosum removed to decrease the severity of his _____.
    a. PTSD   c. left-hemisphere hemorrhaging
    b. personality change   d. seizures

6. Both hormones and neurotransmitters act as chemical messengers. In what way are they different?

    a. Hormones are distributed throughout the entire body through the bloodstream.

    b. Neurotransmitters are transmitted throughout the entire body through the bloodstream.

    c. Hormones only affect mental processes.

    d. Neurotransmitters only affect mental processes.

7. After a serious car accident in which her head was smashed through a window, Barbara is different than before. While she used to be very polite and even taught etiquette classes, now she has become one of the most impolite people, often swearing and yelling as she sees fit. What could explain Barbara's change in behavior?

    a. Damage to the left hemisphere   c. Damage to the corpus callosum

    b. Damage to the frontal lobe   d. Damage to the parietal lobe

8. Greg was in a horrible car accident. As a result of this accident, he has been declared brain-dead. Although he is still living, he is not consciously aware of the world as he was before the accident. Which part of his brain is driving his functioning?

    a. medulla   c. amygdala

    b. hippocampus   d. somatosensory cortex

9. A cell detects that you have stepped on a hot stone, so it sends a message from the bottom of your foot up to the terminal in your spine. In this cell, which of the following is longer?

    a. dendrites   c. spine

    b. axon   d. They are all the same length.

10. If someone received damage to their occipital lobe, what would it be most likely to affect?

    a. auditory processing   c. motor functioning

    b. visual processing   d. olfactory processing

REFLECT

1. Are you surprised by the fact that everything you have ever sensed, thought, or experienced, such as the taste of pineapple or the way it feels to fall in love, is the result of ions moving one way or another across billions of neural membranes? Why?

2. When your arm itches or your feet hurt, the feeling isn't in the arm or feet but is literally all in your head, specifically in your somatosensory cortex. Does the fact that the pain is all in your head make the pain any less acute?

3. Discuss the evolution of biopsychology and the effects certain scientific developments have had on society and culture. For example, the ancient Greeks believed that epilepsy was the result of the goddess of the moon, Selene, cursing those who offended her (Atsma, 2016). Certainly, we know now that epileptic seizures are the result of disrupted electrical activity in both hemispheres of the brain. What other examples of biopsychological elements can you think of whose societal implications have evolved with the furthering of science? How have they changed? Why do you think those changes took place?

Answer Key

1.a 2.a 3.b 4.c 5.d 6.a 7.b 8.a 9.b 10.b

WRITE

Choose five legal or illegal drugs, and research their effects on biopsychological components of the human brain. Specifically, using what you learned in the chapter, deduce the effects your chosen chemicals would have on the following pathways:

1. Reuptake and/or serotonin activity (p. 66)
2. Somatic nervous system functionality (p. 68)
3. Autonomic nervous system functionality (p. 68)
4. Endocrine activity (p. 72)
5. Frontal lobe development and/or function (p. 79)

Prepare a report that includes your research, being sure to provide reasoning and examples to support your inferences.

Key Terms

acetylcholine   66
action potential   63
agonist   66
analgesic   67
antagonist   66
aphasia   85
autonomic nervous system   68
axon   63
Broca's area   86
callosotomy   86
central nervous system   68
cerebellum   71
corpus callosum   86
cortex   79
dendrite   63
focus   81
frontal lobe   79
fusiform face area   80
glial cells   62
hemisphere   79
hypothalamus   72
interneuron   68
ion channels   63
limbic system   71
medulla   70
morphine   67
myelin   64

neglect   80
neuromuscular junction   66
neuron doctrine   65
neuron   62
neurotransmitter   89
nucleus accumbens   66
occipital lobe   79
parasympathetic nervous system   69
parietal lobe   79
peripheral nervous system   68
phrenology   85
primary motor cortex   79
primary somatosensory cortex   79
prosopagnosia   80
receptor site   65
resting potential   63
reuptake   66
serotonin   66
soma   62
somatic nervous system   68
sylvian fissure   79
sympathetic nervous system   69
synapse   65
temporal lobe   79
thalamus   72
vesicle   65

Sensation and Perception

After reading this chapter, you will be able to answer the following questions:

- How do sensation and perception differ?
- How is the eye similar to and dissimilar from a camera?
- Why does the eye have a blind spot, and why don't we notice it?
- How does the brain make sense of information processed through sensing?
- How do we see colors?
- How does the ear create sounds in the brain?
- How do touch and pain differ from the other senses?
- What are the chemical senses?

Sensation and perception connect us to our world. To appreciate the importance of sensation and perception in your life, try to imagine how different your life would be without them. For example, which do you think would be worse, to be blind or deaf? When confronted with such a dubious choice, most people will say that blindness would be worse than deafness; even with a total loss of hearing, they imagine that they could still navigate their world. Anecdotal support for choosing deafness over blindness can be found by looking at professional football. In 2014, Derrick Coleman, who plays as a fullback for the Seattle Seahawks, became the first professional football player with profound deafness to play in a Super Bowl. Coleman is one of three professional football players with profound deafness in the history of the NFL. In comparison, there has never been a professional football player with severe visual impairments. Similarly, individuals with profound deafness are allowed to operate motor vehicles in some states, but individuals who are blind are not. With these differences in mind, it seems like choosing deafness over blindness can be reasonably justified.

What would someone with more direct experience with deafness and blindness choose? Helen Keller, born in Alabama in June of 1880, lost both her sight and hearing due to illness before the age of two. With the assistance of Anne Sullivan, Keller eventually learned to communicate through touch. Keller continued her education, earning a Bachelor of Arts on her way to becoming an author, public speaker, and political activist. Regarding the question of deafness versus blindness, Keller argued that deafness is a greater affliction than blindness, because blindness separates people from things, but deafness separates people from people (Christie, 1987). Vision enables us to navigate our world, but hearing allows ready access to social connection.

Though each sense plays its particular role, not all senses are created equal. The Greek philosopher, Aristotle, noted that the five senses each harvest a kind of energy from the world: vision (electromagnetic radiation), hearing (vibrations in the air), touch (pressure and heat), taste (chemicals dissolved in water), and smell (chemicals floating in the air). Each species faces its own unique challenges in making a living, which entails unique sensory adaptations to help it meet those challenges. If we were bats or dolphins, our brains would be equipped with sonar-processing hardware capable of analyzing echoes from nearby objects and creating a coherent mental snapshot of our surroundings from these sounds. If we were dogs, we would have about ten times as many olfactory receptors in our noses, and considerably more of our brains would be dedicated to olfactory analysis. In contrast

Helen Keller in 1904

to animals, for whom hearing and smell are so important, humans are endowed with highly sophisticated visual processing hardware in our cerebral cortex. Sensory specialization for bats, dolphins, dogs, humans, and other animals is the consequence of evolutionary adaptation, or the way they make a living. Humans and our ancestors are omnivores, relying on both hunting game and gathering produce. As a result, our brain's visual processing supports skillful exploration of complex visual environments, and our color vision enables us to efficiently find and select fruits based on their ripeness.

sensation
the process of collecting sensory information from the outside world through the five senses

perception
the mental experience of sensory information

Making sense of the world around us involves two overlapping processes: sensation and perception. **Sensation**—the process of collecting sensory information from the outside world through the five senses—is actively engaged in the harvesting of energy from the world around us. **Perception**—the mental experience of sensory information—is concerned with sorting, organizing, and processing all of this sensory data. In many ways, perception is the more complicated task, as it involves making sense of what is coming in from one sense as well as integrating the information from each of the different senses into a single, coherent experience. The fact that human brains expend so much effort on perceptual processing demonstrates that sensation is very different than perception; sensation occurs primarily in the sensory organs (eyes, ears, skin, nose, and tongue), and perception occurs primarily in the brain. When we examine our surroundings we don't consciously perceive the spots of light and color presented to our eyes, but instead we perceive people, objects, and scenes. What your eyes see is visual sensation, and what your conscious mind sees is visual perception. The same can be said of the other senses (e.g., what your ears hear is auditory sensation and what your conscious mind hears is auditory perception).

One way to conceptualize the difference between these two processes is to think of sensation and perception as similar to the televised legal drama *Law & Order*. In this show, viewers are presented with legal cases from the perspective of the detectives who collect information about the case (sensation) and the perspective of the prosecution, who assembles the evidence into a coherent argument about the crime (perception). Just as the final arguments in the televised court scenes are a product of the work of both the police and the prosecutors, our experience of the world is produced by both sensation and perception.

LIGHT AND THE OPTICS OF THE HUMAN EYE

Because humans are highly visual creatures, we begin our exploration of the five senses with vision. Vision begins with the eye reacting to electromagnetic radiation—light—in our environment. The range of light that our eyes can detect occupies only a tiny sliver of the entire electromagnetic spectrum, which also includes microwaves, radio waves, and X-rays, as illustrated in Figure 4.1. Electromagnetic radiation within the small range of the visible spectrum has three qualities that make it an ideal source of sensory information. First, the sun produces a great deal of energy within this spectrum. Second, energy in the visible spectrum passes easily through the Earth's atmosphere with little distortion. Finally, energy at these wavelengths tends to reflect off of objects rather than passing through them, whereas radiation at shorter and longer wavelengths penetrates solid objects rather than reflecting. Thanks to these characteristics of visible light, sensory organs that react to this type of energy are extremely adaptive and useful.

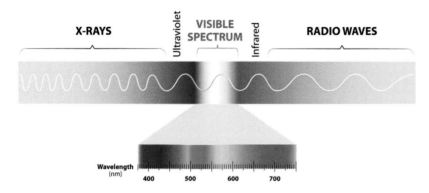

4.1 Electromagnetic spectrum
The electromagnetic spectrum includes many different kinds of energy that could all be considered to be light, but only a tiny sliver (wavelengths between about 400 nm and 700 nm) is visible to human eyes.

Light can act as both a wave and a particle. As a wave, light is defined by its wavelength, which is the distance from one wave crest to the next. When visible light with a relatively long wavelength strikes our eyes it appears reddish, while light with a relatively short wavelength appears bluish. The acronym "Roy G. Biv" is a commonly used memory aid to organize the visible hues from longest to shortest wavelengths: red, orange, yellow, green, blue, indigo, and violet.

Particles of light are called photons. The number of photons emitted by a light source or reflected by an object determines the light's intensity, so intense light appears relatively bright, and less intense light appears relatively dark. With this in mind, the way we use light to create an image of the world works something like this: A source of light (anything from the sun to a light bulb) emits lots of little packages of light energy, called photons, that radiate from the light source in every direction. When the photons reach a solid object some are absorbed by the object, and others bounce off. Some of the photons that bounce off the object travel in just the right direction to reach and enter our eyes. By analyzing these photons, our brains create an account of any objects in the world that reflect light.

In the tenth century CE, the Arab mathematician and scientist known as Al Hazen compared the human eye to a device called a **camera obscura**, which means "dark room" in Latin. One way to build a camera obscura is to construct a small room with walls that do not let any light through (that is, the walls are light-tight, in the same way that airtight walls would prevent any air from entering the room), and then poke a tiny hole in one of the walls. If you were standing in a room built like this, you would see on the wall opposite the pinhole, which acts as a "projection screen," an upside-down

camera obscura
a device created by Alhazen, consisting of a dark room with a tiny hole for light that simulates the human eye

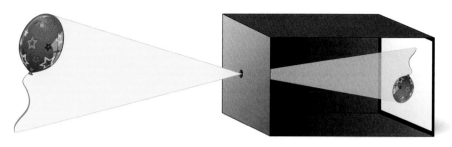

4.2 Camera obscura
A camera obscura, or dark room in Latin. Light-tight walls keep almost all light from entering, but the pinhole in the front wall lets in just enough light to generate an upside-down and backward image of the world on the opposite wall. The optical parts of the camera obscura are analogous to parts in the human eye: the light-tight walls and sclera, the pinhole and pupil, and the projection screen and retina.

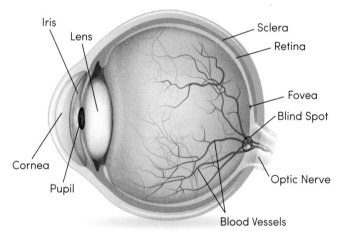

4.3 Cross section of the human eye
The labeled structures constitute the major optical components that project an image onto the retina. The optic nerve toward the back of the eye conveys the retinal image to the brain.

and backward movie version of the world, as in Figure 4.2. The tiny pinhole acts like a gatekeeper, ensuring that just one ray of light is projected on each spot of the "projection screen." Each spot on the projected image has the same color as the location in the world from which the light ray was reflected. When Al Hazen constructed his camera obscura, the projected image was clear but dim, so he tried enlarging the pinhole to let in more light. This made the image brighter, as intended, but it was now blurry because the enlarged pinhole allowed light from a larger area in the world to project onto each spot on the wall. The insertion of a lens both clarified and brightened the image. A camera obscura is a good model for the human eye because each of the camera obscura's optical components (light-tight walls, pinhole, projection screen, lens) has an analogous component in the human eye, depicted in Figure 4.3.

Although the eyeball is spherical, when you look at someone else's eye or your own eye in a mirror, only a small sliver of the eye is visible because it is lodged in a bony socket and covered by the eyelid.

sclera
the outer white portion of the eye

cornea
the transparent bulge at the front of the eye

iris
the colored ring of muscle in the eye that controls the size of the pupil

pupil
the tiny transparent hole in the center of the iris that allows light to enter the eye

The outer layer of the eye, sometimes called the white of the eye, is the **sclera**, and like the walls of the camera obscura, it is impenetrable to light. When light bounces off an object some of it passes through the transparent bulge at the front of the eye called the **cornea**. Behind the cornea is a colored ring of muscle called the **iris** that surrounds a transparent pinhole called the **pupil**. In addition to giving you your own unique eye color, the iris also controls the size of the pupil and, therefore, the amount of light entering the eye. As with the camera obscura, a constricted (small) pupil generates a clear image, which may be dim, while a dilated (large) pupil generates a brighter image, which may be blurry. If you wear corrective lenses, you can try a little experiment to see how a tiny pinhole can sharpen the appearance of the world. Begin by poking a tiny hole in a piece of paper with a pin or nail. Remove your glasses or contact lenses, then hold the paper close to your eye and peer through the hole. The resulting image will be clear even without corrective lenses. Sometimes people take advantage of this fact by squinting, which clarifies the appearance of the world by reducing the area through which light enters the eyes.

After passing through the cornea and pupil, light next reaches the lens, which focuses light onto the retina at the back of the eye. The lens can change its shape in response to either nearby or distant objects to generate a clear image on the retina. Although the process by which the lens changes its shape, called **accommodation**, happens unconsciously, its effect can be observed with the following activity. Look at any relatively distant object, such as a wall or tree, then hold your thumb up at arm's length and in your line of sight, but maintain your focus on the more distant object. You will notice two thumbs, both of which are blurry, but if you then focus on the thumb, the two blurry thumbs will suddenly fuse into a single clear thumb. Accommodation enables your lens to focus on both nearby and distant objects, but only on one distance at a time. Unfortunately, the lens's flexibility only lasts about forty years or so, after which it becomes stiff and inflexible. Most people over the age of forty may retain the ability to focus on distant objects but will eventually lose the ability to focus on nearby objects. After the lens loses its flexibility, a person needs to hold printed words farther and farther from the eyes to generate a clear image. If the lens *inside* the eye can't change its shape, a common therapy is a prescription for two different lenses outside the eye. For this reason, bifocals are commonly associated with aging eyes.

accommodation
a process in which the lens of the eye changes shape to adapt to different viewing distances

The optical components of the eye (sclera, cornea, pupil, and lens) project an image on the **retina**, but the retina is much more complex than a simple projection screen. Remember that in the camera obscura the image projected onto the wall is an upside-down and backward version of the world, and this is true of the image projected onto the retina as well. The retina then transforms the light energy projected onto it into an electrical code that is sent to the brain through the optic nerve for further processing, which includes flipping the image so the world we perceive appears to be upright rather than inverted. The transformation of one kind of energy (in the case of the eye, light energy) into another kind of energy (electrical impulses) is called **transduction**. The eye is an optical device that projects an image onto the retina, which changes the projected image into a collection of electrical signals, much like a digital camera does.

retina
the "projection screen" of the eye, which transforms the light energy received from the outside world into an electrical signal that is passed to the brain

transduction
the transformation of one kind of energy into another kind of energy

photoreceptors
light-sensitive cells in the retina

The Retina and Visual Transduction

Modern digital cameras can generate images containing more than ten million pixels, each pixel representing the output from a single light-sensitive device in the camera. The human eye remains well ahead of current photographic technology, with each eye's retina containing more than 100 million light-sensitive cells, called **photoreceptors**. Photoreceptors come in two varieties, pictured in Figure 4.4, each

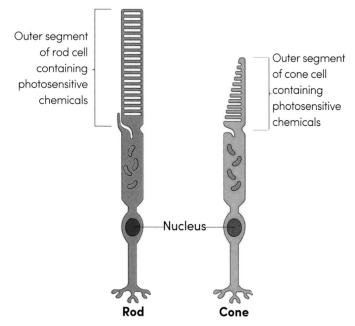

4.4 Photoreceptors in the retina come in two varieties: rods and cones Rods and cones are named after the way they look under a microscope, with rods shaped like a cylinder and cones coming to a point.

cones
a type of photoreceptor found mostly in the foveal region of the retina that is responsible for color vision

rods
a more sensitive type of photoreceptor found mostly on the periphery of the retina

fovea
an area of high-acuity vision in the center of the retina that is tightly packed with photoreceptors

named after the way they look under a microscope: **cones** come to a point, whereas **rods** are shaped like cylinders. Cones and rods differ not only in the way they look but also in their location on the retina and how they work.

At the center of the retina is a small region called the **fovea** that is packed tightly with photoreceptors, most of which are cones; the peripheral region of the retina, away from the center, contains mostly rods. There are three types of cones: one responds best to reddish light, a second responds best to greenish light, and a third responds best to bluish light. These three colors (red, green, and blue, or RGB) may sound familiar because they form the basis for the way colors are represented on television and computer screens, and in fact the RGB system was developed with human color vision in mind. In contrast to cones, rods all respond best to greenish light and are more sensitive than cones, meaning that they can detect light that would be too dim to be detected by cones. Because of the differences between cones and rods, cone-mediated foveal vision emphasizes detail and color while rod-mediated peripheral vision is sensitive under low-light conditions but color blind. As a result, experienced hunters know that instead of looking directly at an animal when hunting at night, they should look just to its side because the more sensitive peripheral vision is better suited than the fovea to seeing objects that are just barely visible. Also, the night-vision goggles used by the military

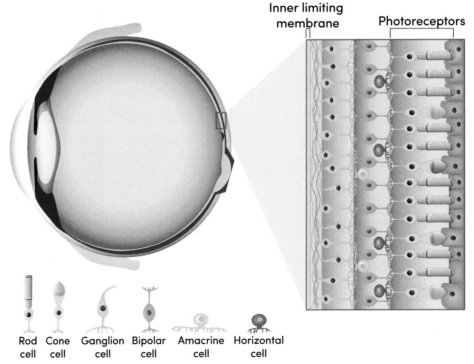

4.5 Retinal cross section
The human retina is built backward, because light must penetrate several layers of cells (ganglion, horizontal, bipolar, and amacrine cells) before finally reaching the photosensitive layer (rod and cone photoreceptors). Photoreceptors then send their information forward to the ganglion cells, which snake their axons through a hole punched in the back of the eye before reaching the brain. Because there are no photoreceptors in the part of the retina through which the bundle of axons, or optic nerve, travels, each eye has a blind spot.

create greenish images because we mostly rely on our rods to see under low-light conditions, and rods are most sensitive to greenish light.

When photons finally reach the retina they may then collide with one of the many **photopigment** molecules in a photoreceptor. The collision with the photon changes the shape of the photopigment, which, in turn, slightly alters the electrical current that constantly flows through its photoreceptor. Photoreceptors are therefore the place where light energy is transduced into chemical energy and then an electrical signal. The electrical signals from more than 100 million photoreceptors converge on about one million retinal ganglion cells. The axons from the retinal ganglion cells are woven together like the fibers in a rope, and the resulting cable is the optic nerve that conveys the visual signal from the retina to the brain.

photopigment
a molecule in a photoreceptor that changes shape when light collides with it

blind spot
an area in the eye without any photoreceptors because of the optic nerve

Curiously, the human retina seems to have been built backward; photoreceptors line the back of the eye, then send their electrical signals *forward* to retinal ganglion cells (Figure 4.5). The ganglion cell axons form the optic nerve that travels backward through a hole punched in the back of the eye on its way to the brain. The hole where the optic nerve exits the eye has no room left for photoreceptors, and with no photoreceptors to collect light, you are blind at that spot in each eye. People are commonly surprised that each of their eyes has a **blind spot** because under normal circumstances most of us never notice any areas of blindness, but you can use Figure 4.6 to locate each of your eyes' blind spots. While holding the book at arm's length, close one eye, and with your open eye gaze at the X. Slowly pull the book toward your face, and at some point one of the discs should disappear. While holding the book at this distance switch the eye that is open and the disc on the other side of the figure should disappear. Although the disc disappears, you don't see any kind of gap in your vision because the place where the disc should be has been "filled in" with the same color as the page. What do you think you would have seen if this figure were printed a different color?

4.6 Blind spots
Find your blind spot. With the book at arm's length, close one eye and look at the x with your open eye. Move the book toward your face while continuing to keep one eye closed and viewing the x with the open eye, and one of the discs will disappear.

Perceptual filling in is one major reason that most people never notice their blind spots. When the brain detects any holes in the visual image it fills them in by "painting" them with the same color that surrounds the holes, which is why the part of the image that projects to the blind spot appeared to have the same color as the surrounding page.

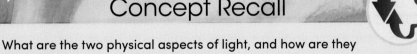

Concept Recall

1. What are the two physical aspects of light, and how are they measured?
2. How is the eye like a camera obscura?

3. What are the optical components of the eye, and how do they contribute to the formation of an image?

4. How is the retina like a digital camera?

5. Why does the eye have a blind spot?

6. What kind of photoreceptor predominates in the fovea? What kind of photoreceptor predominates in the periphery?

This Is Psychology

Given the five senses that are familiar to most people (vision, hearing, touch, taste, and smell), the term "sixth sense" often refers to something beyond these, such as the ability to see dead people (as in the classic movie from the 1990s). However, we all have a sixth sense that doesn't involve dead people but is rarely included among the other five, probably because it is so automatic and familiar that we almost never realize it's even there. To appreciate your sixth sense, called proprioception, clap your hands behind your head. How did you do it, even though you couldn't see your hands? Proprioception enables you to know where your body parts are located so you can do things like clap your hands behind your head or walk without having to look at your legs and feet. Can you imagine life without proprioception? The neurologist and author, Oliver Sacks, described a woman, Christina, who had lost her proprioception in his book about some of his patients with unusual neurological disorders, *The Man Who Mistook His Wife for a Hat* (1985). Christina took antibiotics as a routine preparation for surgery without any expectation of complications, but she soon lost the ability to stand or even sit upright and could hold nothing in her hands. In the years following her unfortunate drug reaction, Christina developed various methods to adjust to her loss. For example, while most people are standing they are actually continually swaying slightly back and forth but maintain their equilibrium by sensing each sway and leaning in the opposite direction. With no way to sense where she is swaying, to merely stand upright Christina flexes all her core muscles as if standing rigidly at attention. Any movements require visual attention, so to walk she watches her feet, and to type on a computer she looks at her fingers on the keyboard. When you think of Christina's plight, perhaps you can give thanks that you have intact proprioception, a sense that you may have never even realized you had.

VISUAL PROCESSING IN THE BRAIN

Perceptual filling in of blind spots is just one of many examples in which our conscious visual experience of the world differs from the retinal image. Most people naively presume that vision works something like this: The camera-like eye projects an image onto the retina, which the retina encodes and ships up to the brain through the optic nerve, almost like a fax machine transmitting an image over a phone line. However, our brains don't just passively receive the retinal "fax" sent via the optic nerve. Instead, our brains are equipped with lots of sophisticated neural hardware that filters and processes the retinal image. Figure 4.7 illustrates how our beliefs and expectations can influence what we see. This picture appears, at first glance, to depict a human skull. The subject of the image is actually an aerial view of two women in white dresses playing cards, but the women can only be seen by someone who knows to look for them. The skull image provides another opportunity to distinguish between sensation and perception. Sensation is the process by which sensory receptors and the nervous system, collect and represent the stimulus energies surrounding us, whereas perception is the process of organizing and interpreting the information provided by sensation. Perception is what enables us to use our expectations to reinterpret the photograph, so what initially appeared to be a skull becomes two women.

The shifting perception of the skull/women is an example of **top-down processing**. Top-down processing occurs as the brain uses previous experiences and expectations to organize sensory information. Like artists, magicians also know how to take advantage of top-down processing by creating illusions that rely on our learned expectations about situations. Creating a seemingly impossible event, such as a coin being conjured from thin air, requires that the magician's audience have a mature understanding of the laws of physics and causation. We know from experience that coins do not magically appear, and that we do not have coins inside our ears. For magic to deceive, the audience must have expectations that the magician can violate. For this reason, children are notoriously difficult for magicians to deceive due to their undeveloped knowledge of the world (Macknik & Martinez-Conde, 2010). Optical illusions can delight the viewer in the same way as a skillful magician because they violate our expectations, specifically the expectation that the mental image should look the same as the retinal image. For example, in the version of White's (1991) illusion in Figure 4.8, although the blue bars on the left that seem to be "painted" on the black fenceposts appear to be much brighter than the bars on the right that seem to be "behind" the black fenceposts, both sets of blue bars are actually the same color.

4.7 The role of expectation in perception
At first glance, this image probably appears to depict a human skull, but the "skull" is actually two women in white dresses playing cards. Can you see the women?

top-down processing
the use of previous experience and expectations about situations to organize sensory information during perception

4.8 White's (1981) illusion
Are both sets of blue bars the same? Actually, they are, even though the bars on the left appear much brighter than the bars on the right.

As with most optical illusions, White's illusion shows us that the image of the world presented to the retina is different from the appearance of the world in our conscious visual experience, and yet we continue to expect that what the mind sees is the same as what the eye sees.

The reason that the mind's view doesn't match the eyes' view is because the retinal image is subjected to lots of processing before being presented to visual awareness. The optic nerve conveys the signals from the retina to a part of the brain called the thalamus, which is dedicated to receiving visual input; other regions of the thalamus receive auditory (hearing) and tactile (touch) information. The visual signal then projects from the thalamus to the **primary visual cortex** (the occipital lobe), the first stage of cortical visual processing. Here, the visual image is broken into its constituent features, so colors are processed in one place in the cortex, shape in another, and motion and distance in yet others. This is surprising because when we look at the objects around us, each object's color, shape, motion, and distance all seem to hang together in a coherent whole. Modern visual neuroscientists have yet to determine satisfactorily how the simple features represented in early visual processing come together to form the objects, people, and coherent scenes that inhabit our visual experience of the world. Nevertheless, we do have some ideas about how each of the simple visual features (color, shape, depth, and motion) is represented and processed by the visual brain.

Perception of Color

Did you ever wonder how colors appear to other people? When you and a friend look at a stop sign, you both probably agree that its color should be called "red." However, if you could somehow see inside your friend's mind, would his or her color experience of the stop sign be the same as what you would call red, or would it be more like what you would call something else, such as yellow or blue? Although colors are part of our everyday experience, there is something distinctly odd about them. In his *Essay Concerning Human Understanding*, the philosopher John Locke distinguished between what he called primary qualities, such as shape, size, and number, and secondary qualities, such as colors, tastes, and pains. The difference between Locke's primary and secondary qualities seems to depend on whether or not we can verify our own perceptual experiences by comparing them with other people's experiences. As with the subjectivity of color, the fact that one person could dislike the taste of chocolate while so many others love it, or that a frying pan just removed from the oven feels painfully hot to one person and only moderately warm to another, shows that secondary qualities seem to vary almost arbitrarily from one person to another.

The fact that almost 10 percent of men have some degree of color blindness indicates that colors must appear quite differently to different people. One of your authors, Ken, can tell you that the term color blind isn't quite right. He and most other people that are called color blind can actually see colors, but just can't distinguish as many colors as someone with normal color vision. Specifically, Ken has some difficulty distinguishing between red and green, so traffic lights indicating "stop" appear to him to be similar

primary visual cortex
the first stage of cortical visual processing in which the visual image is separated into its component parts, such as color, shape, and motion

John Locke

Thomas Young

Hermann von Helmholtz

to the ones indicating "go." Figure 4.9 provides a sense of how traffic lights might appear to someone with color blindness. In constructing this image, Ken put the image on the left through an image processing filter designed to show how the image appears to someone with color blindness, which yielded the image on the right. Though the left image appears different from the right image for someone with normal color vision, Ken and others with color blindness experience both images to be the same colors. To understand why some people are color blind requires an understanding of how color perception works for someone with normal color vision.

4.9 Traffic lights and common color blindness
An image of a traffic light appears on the left, and a filtered image representing the way the original image appears to someone that has a common form of color blindness is shown on the right.

Trichromacy: Three primary colors

At the beginning of the nineteenth century, the English scientist Thomas Young suggested that any visible color could be created by combining various amounts of three primary colors. Later that century, the German physicist Hermann von Helmholtz gathered evidence from a variety of sources that supported Young's idea, including the results from color-matching experiments. In such an experiment, a reference color is projected onto a viewing screen, as depicted in Figure 4.10, and next to the reference color is projected the combined outputs from a reddish, a greenish, and a bluish light. By varying the relative brightness of each of these lights, participants with normal color vision are able to make the combination appear to be identical to any reference color, even though the red-green-blue combination color and the reference color are *physically* different. Helmholtz argued that our eyes are equipped with three kinds of nerves, each of which responds best to one of the primary colors, an idea that is generally called the Young-Helmholtz **trichromatic** (Latin for "three colors") **theory**. We now know that normal color vision relies on three different kinds of cells in the retina, called cones, each of which responds best to a particular wavelength of light. Red cones respond best to long visible wavelengths; green cones respond best to middle visible wavelengths, and blue cones respond best to short visible wavelengths. With three different cone types there are many ways that color vision can go wrong (e.g., one or more of the three cones might be missing from the retina), but the most common form of color blindness is called anomalous trichromacy. For anomalous trichromats like Ken, the red and green cones respond to wavelengths that are closer together than for the red and green cones in eyes with normal color vision. Although trichromatic theory explains many kinds of color perception and how color blindness works, there remain several phenomena that it can't explain.

trichromatic theory the idea that our eyes have three different kinds of nerves that respond to three colors: red, blue, and green

Spotlights

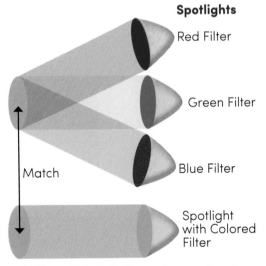

Red Filter

Green Filter

Blue Filter

Spotlight with Colored Filter

Match

4.10 Young-Helmholtz three-color experiment
An observer views a color projected by a single spotlight shone through any color of filter and another color produced by the combined projections of three spotlights, one with a red filter, a second with a green filter, and a third with a blue filter. By adjusting the intensity of each of the red, green, and blue spotlights, the combination of the three spotlights can be made to appear the same color as any other single filter.

Cross-Cultural Case

The Languages Of Color

Colors maintain significance across our lives in a number of ways. Do you don royal blue to go to a Kansas City Royals baseball game? Perhaps you've sent romantic red roses to a young woman you've been dating, owing to the language of flowers originated in Victorian England. But have you ever considered how the language of color itself develops? In 1999, anthropological linguists Paul Kay and Luisa Maffi conducted a study that revealed most languages distribute color naming relatively evenly; most languages have between two and 11 specific color names. As a speaker of English—a language with 11 color names—you might be wondering, do speakers of other languages define and identify colors differently? That was the guiding question cognitive scientists and linguists have asked as they determined the development of color languages. Kay, along with linguist Brent Berlin, determined that a number of languages use just two color words: black and white. When languages define a third color, it's usually closest to what we'd call "red" in English. If a language has four color terms, the fourth will usually be yellow or green. As languages added color terms, Berlin and Kay recognized that languages wouldn't remove a color and replace but would rather build on the existing color terminology. Claire Bowern, Associate Professor of Linguistics at Yale University, extended this research by testing it on aboriginal languages in Australia. Her research generally supported Berlin and Kay's findings about the sequential adding of language terms in the order they proposed. Australian languages showed the same patterns of color naming identified in other parts of the world, with red being the first color to follow black and white. But, Bowern's research showed the likelihood of Australian languages actually losing color terms, contradicting Berlin

and Kay's findings that color terminology is consistent over time. Consider reading about color terminology research, especially that having to do with the environment of the language and culture. How do languages and color references change depending on interactions with geographic factors?

Color opponency

Can you mix blue and green in your imagination, then use your mind's eye to "look" at the result? What about yellow and red? You probably don't have much difficulty carrying out this mental exercise, in which the first combination looks like the color of seawater and the second like an orange. Now, try mixing red and green. You probably found that mentally mixing red with green is much more difficult than mixing blue with green, but why? Why are some color mixtures (e.g., blue and green) easy to imagine and others (e.g., red and green) nearly impossible to imagine?

Karl Ewald Konstantin Hering was a contemporary of Helmholtz who argued that the results from this sort of mind experiment are not readily explained by trichromacy.

Karl Ewald Konstantin Hering

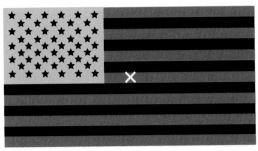 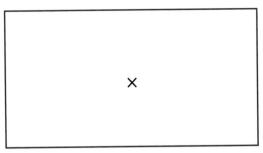

4.11 Color afterimage

Hold your gaze on the ✕ in the middle of the oddly colored flag for about 60 seconds, then shift your gaze to the ✕ in the middle of the rectangle, and you should briefly see a normally colored American flag.

Instead of the three primaries entailed by trichromacy, Hering suggested that color vision is based on two pairs of opponents: red versus green and blue versus yellow, such that the mixtures of opponents are impossible to imagine. You may be surprised that blue and yellow are opponents because you might have mixed blue and yellow crayons or paints with the result being dark green. While mixing yellow and blue pigments yields green, Hering was basing his theory on how colors mix in the mind rather than in a paint can. The effects of **color opponency** can be seen (rather than just imagined) with a color **afterimage**. Look at the X in the middle of the odd-looking flag in Figure 4.11 while counting slowly to sixty. After sixty seconds shift your gaze to the X on the right side of the figure, and you should briefly see an American flag with blue field, white stars, and red and white stripes. The green and yellow that had been visible during the sixty-second extended viewing period have been replaced by their opponents, red and blue. This afterimage effect was known by Hering and Helmholtz, but the answer to why this happens would only be obtained by appealing to neuroscientific knowledge that became available more than 100 years later.

As bitter rivals, Helmholtz and Hering continuously bickered over whether trichromacy or color opponency was a better description of human color vision, and no other scientist could figure out how to reconcile the two accounts of color perception until a better understanding of the retina became available in the middle of the twentieth century (Hurvich & Jameson, 1957). As sometimes happens in science, both descriptions were correct. The presence of three different kinds of cones in the retina explains why three primaries are sufficient for color-mixing experiments. After cones transduce light into electrical impulses, they send their signals to retinal ganglion cells, of which there are two kinds that respond to color. One kind of ganglion cell measures the balance between blue and yellow photons, and another measures the balance between red and green photons. The blue-yellow and red-green channels act somewhat like scales, as in Figure 4.12. So, for example, blue-yellow ganglion cells put all the bluish photons on one side of the scale and the yellowish photons on the other side. If there are more yellow than blue photons, the scale will tip toward the yellow side, and vice versa when there are more blue than yellow photons. If the number of blue photons on one side of the scale equals the number of yellow photons on the other side, the scale will be balanced, and the color will appear to be neither blue nor yellow. The same is true for red-green ganglion cells, so any color that contains blue and yellow and red and green

color opponency
the idea that color vision is based on two pairs of opponents; red vs. green and blue vs. yellow

afterimage
after viewing one color for an extended period its opponent color appears when looking at a colorless surface

4.12 Scales as a metaphor for blue-yellow channel ganglion cells
When more yellowish photons than blue photons strike a ganglion cell, the light appears yellowish, but when equal numbers of bluish and yellowish photos strike a ganglion cell, the scale balances and the ganglion cell registers neither blue nor yellow.

photons will make the blue-yellow scale balance and the red-green scale balance. That is, anything that appears white or gray is actually a combination of colors that balance both the blue-yellow scale and the red-green scale.

The scale analogy for ganglion cells explains both Hering's thought experiments and color afterimages. The red-green scale can only represent red or green, but not both because equal amounts of red and green make the balance rest in the middle, indicating neither red nor green. So, as Hering noticed, we are unable to imagine a color that is a combination of red and green. Furthermore, the red-green and blue-yellow scales are separate from each other, so we are able to imagine combinations such as purple because the reddish photons tip the red-green scale toward red and the bluish photons tip the blue-yellow scale toward blue. As for afterimages, during the extended viewing of the oddly colored flag, your retinal cells are continuously adapting to the yellow and green in the flag, so the ganglion cells get tired and can't respond as vigorously as usual. The part of the retina that gets tired from green retains a normal response to red, and the part that gets tired from yellow retains a normal response to blue, so the afterimage appears to have red stripes and a blue field. This process is called sensory **adaptation** and is, perhaps, most easily understood in reference to smells. When confronted with a strong smell, you might wonder how you could possibly tolerate it for very long, but then, after several minutes of continuous exposure, the smell seems to fade. The odorant molecules that initially caused the sensation of smell remain in your surroundings, but olfactory cells in your brain no longer respond to the presence of the odor. This adaptation to odor mimics the retina's adaptation to color.

adaptation
the process in which the brain becomes less sensitive to a particular sensory feature after being exposed to it for an extended period of time

In summary, trichromacy describes how color is perceived by cones, why some people are color blind, and why three primary colors are enough to generate any other color. Color opponency describes how colors are perceived by retinal ganglion cells, why it is impossible to imagine some color combinations, and how color afterimages work. While Helmholtz and Hering argued over who was correct, the real answer is that trichromacy works together with color opponency to generate our perception of color.

Concept Recall

1. What is top-down perception, and how do magicians rely on it?

2. How do the experienced image of the world and the visual signal in the visual cortex differ?

3. What is the difference between trichromacy and color opponency?

4. Which (trichromacy or color opponency) is the correct version of how we see color? (Hint: trick question!)

5. What is color adaptation, and what color would you see after adapting to red, or green, or blue, or yellow?

This Is Psychology

Why did pirates wear eyepatches? A reasonable guess is that being a sailor in the 1700s was dangerous for the eyes, but if this is the reason, why didn't sailors in the navy wear them? Instead, consider the fact that pirate ships typically had smaller crews than naval vessels, so a pirate might need to man the sails on deck, then step below deck to fire cannons with just a moment's notice. Did you ever come from a bright day outside into a dimly lit room? If so, you may have noticed that you could hardly see anything and had to wait a few minutes for your eyes to adjust to the dark. Pirates who needed to fire their cannons didn't have the luxury of waiting for their eyes to adjust to the dark after coming from the bright sunshine above deck. With one eye covered by a patch, a pirate would always have one eye adapted to the dark, so when stepping into the darkness under the deck they could uncover the patched eye and immediately see their surroundings with the dark-adapted eye.

VISION: PERCEPTION OF MOTION AND FORM

As mentioned in Chapter 1, one of the first major perspectives of psychology was structuralism, which was founded on the belief that the mind could best be understood by breaking sensations into their component pieces. Once all the pieces are discovered and understood, the mind is essentially the sum of the parts. Wilhelm Wundt developed techniques of introspection as a way of closely examining mental experiences by breaking them down into their smallest parts. A modern practitioner of analytic introspection might be a beer enthusiast who describes a favorite beer as hoppy, fruity, and buttery, with just a hint of banana. In response to the structuralist claim that the mind is the sum of its parts, the German psychologist Max Wertheimer argued that when the pieces of experience fit together to form a good gestalt (a German word that roughly translates into English as "whole"), the mind is more than the sum of the parts. Wertheimer based his ideas on his own informal experiments with a toy stroboscope that presented two images, one after another (Hunt, 1993). Even though the stroboscope presented two different images (sensation), they appeared to be a single object moving back and forth between two locations (perception). The eyes only see two alternating images, but the mind generates a sense of motion that is not present in the images themselves. Wertheimer called visual motion produced by alternating static images the **phi phenomenon**. In modern life the phi phenomenon can be seen on strings of Christmas lights when one light flashes, then the next light on the string flashes, and so on from light to light, but the flickering appears to be a single light moving along the string. An even more compelling example of the phi phenomenon can be seen every time you watch a movie in the theater. Although the images on the movie screen generate a robust sense of motion, you are actually seeing a series of still images presented rapidly one after another.

The next time you go to the movies, not only will you get to see the phi phenomenon, but if you stick around to watch the credits you might also catch a motion aftereffect. As with the color aftereffect mentioned previously in this chapter, the motion aftereffect begins with extended exposure to some visual feature, such as the motion of words from the bottom of the screen to the top. At the end of the credits the movie's copyright information will drift upward until it stops in the middle of the screen. Although stationary, the copyright information will appear to drift downward for the same reason prolonged exposure to red will make us see green when we look away. Following the extended viewing of upward motion, the neurons that respond to upward motion will be too tired to respond normally, but the neurons that respond to downward motion will be fresh, so the unmoving copyright information will appear to drift slowly downward.

phi phenomenon
when the brain perceives motion in stationary alternating images, such as lights flashing along a string of Christmas lights

Gestalt and Perception of Form

Although gestalt got its start with motion perception, today it's best known for describing how we perceptually group primitive visual features to form coherent objects and scenes. As mentioned earlier in this chapter, the retina breaks an image down into about 100 million pixels, then ships the individual pixels' signals to the visual cortex, where they are converted into visual features by different areas of the cortex (i.e., colors in one part of cortex, edges in another, and so on). And yet your conscious visual experience of the world is inhabited by people and objects, not colors and edges. How does the brain assemble the primitive features to form people and objects?

4.13 Figure-ground segregation
In the image on the left, do you see white squares on a black background or four black arrows on a white background? The image is ambiguous, so you might go back and forth, seeing squares for several moments, then arrows, and so forth. In the image on the right, the arrows have been separated so that they appear to be arrows in front of a white background.

The first problem that your visual processing must figure out is which colors and shapes are connected to nearby objects and which are in the background. You might think that this is a trivial problem because as you examine this book you can easily distinguish it from the room you're sitting in, but the reason it seems so easy is that your unconscious visual processing does all the hard work before you become consciously aware of the result. Gestalt psychologists have created lots of images intended to demonstrate how hard this problem, called **figure-ground segregation**, is to solve. In the left image in Figure 4.13, based on art by Gaetano Kanizsa (1979), sometimes you might see five white diamonds in front of a black square, and at other times you see four black arrows pointing in four different directions. The image is ambiguous, so you probably see the five white squares in the foreground for a few moments, then the four arrows in the foreground for a few moments, and so on. When the arrows have been separated from one another, as in the right side of the figure, they are no longer ambiguous, so the arrows remain constantly visible.

Sometimes the projection of an object onto the retina is fragmented, so the brain must "glue" the pieces back together to form a coherent mental version of the real-world object. To figure out which pieces belong together, the brain relies on several assumptions, called **gestalt grouping principles**. When you look at the left side of Figure 4.14, what does your retina see? What does your conscious mind see? In this image, also based on Kanizsa (1979), your retina sees nothing more than three sectored circles, or "Pac-Men," but your conscious mind also sees the triangle implied by the way the Pac-Men are arranged. As with the phi phenomenon, when the pieces form a good gestalt the conscious mental image contains more than the sum of its parts.

The three Pac-Men appear to enclose a triangle and your mind does the rest, using the gestalt principle of **closure** to fill in any gaps that appear in the retinal image, thereby generating a mental triangle that is not present in the retinal image. In contrast, the three Pac-Men on the right side of the figure don't form a good gestalt, and your conscious mind does not add anything to the retinal image.

4.14 The gestalt principle of closure
The three sectored circles, or "Pac-Men," on the left fit together so you see a triangle, but the three on the right do not fit together, and all you see are the Pac-Men.

The second gestalt principle, **good continuation**, is based on the assumption that edges are more likely to be smooth than to have abrupt bends or kinks. Sometimes edges do have kinks in them, as in the two shapes that look like apple cores on the left side of Figure 4.15. But when the apple cores are brought together,

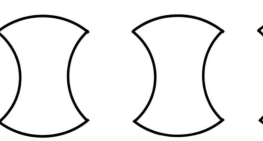

4.15 The gestalt principle of good continuation
Sometimes lines have abrupt corners or kinks in them, as in the two shapes on the left. Your mind prefers to see lines that change smoothly rather than abruptly, so when the two shapes are brought together as in the right side of the figure, the shapes change from two apple cores to two crescent moons.

figure-ground segregation
the ability to distinguish nearby objects from the surrounding background

gestalt grouping principles
methods of grouping disconnected sensory fragments to form a coherent whole

closure
a gestalt principle wherein the brain "fills in" gaps in the retinal image

good continuation
a gestalt principle in which our brain assumes that edges are more likely to be smooth than to have abrupt bends or kinks

the intersections between the two coincide. Your mind prefers to see the lines continue on smoothly rather than bend abruptly, so the apple cores now appear to be two crescents.

Our minds also assume that the same kinds of objects cluster together and have similar appearances. On the top of Figure 4.16 are a group of squares for which the vertical and horizontal distances between squares are the same. When the vertical distance is reduced, the gestalt principle of proximity makes the squares appear to be grouped into columns. In turn, when some of the squares are given the same color, the gestalt principle of similarity groups the same-colored squares into the shape of an arrow. The principle of similarity can be seen when watching a football game in which the members of each team have similarly colored jerseys that are easily distinguished from the other team's jerseys.

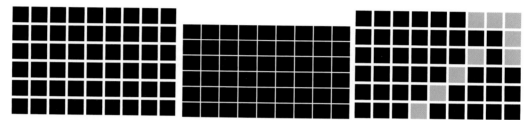

4.16 Gestalt principles of proximity and similarity
When all the squares are the same color and equal distances from each other, they appear to be a cluster of squares. When the vertical distance between squares is reduced, as in the middle of the figure (proximity), the squares appear to be organized in vertical columns, and when some squares have a similar color (similarity) they appear to form their own group.

Depth Perception

stereopsis
the brain's ability to generate a three-dimensional view of the world from two flat retinal images by comparing the two images

Did you ever wonder why you have two eyes? One eye's view of the world is pretty much the same as the other's, so you might reasonably conclude that nature gave us two eyes so anyone who got an eye poked out could still see with the other eye. Actually, the adaptive benefit of two eyes is **stereopsis**, or the ability to generate a three-dimensional view of the world from two flat retinal images. The two eyes' images are very similar to each other, but stereopsis exploits the slight disparities, or differences, between the images viewed by each eye to determine the distances from the viewer to the objects. To see retinal disparities for yourself, close your right eye, hold your right thumb at arm's length and your left thumb about half the distance to your right thumb, and line up the two thumbs so the right is hidden by the left as in Figure 4.17. Now open your right eye and close your left and you'll see two thumbs rather than just one. Every visible object induces retinal disparities, and yet we are generally unaware of any disparities because stereopsis fuses the two retinal images into a single three-dimensional image.

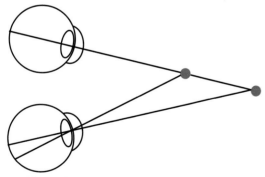

4.17 The world looks differently to the two eyes
With right eye closed, hold one thumb at arm's length and the other thumb about half the distance so the nearer thumb hides the distant thumb. Now open the right eye, and both thumbs are visible.

Stereopsis is the primary binocular (i.e., two-eyed) cue to depth, but you may have noticed that when you close one eye you can still navigate your surroundings based on the information conveyed to your brain by just one eye's (monocular) image. Indeed, Wesley Walker (not to be confused with Wes Welker) was and is legally blind in one eye, yet he had sufficient command of monocular depth perception to be a wide receiver in the NFL (i.e., he was able reliably to catch footballs thrown from various distances) from the late 1970s through most of the 1980s. Though there are many monocular cues to depth, three of the most familiar cues are **atmospheric perspective**, **occlusion**, and **linear perspective**. In Figure 4.18 is a photograph of the Arkansas River valley as seen from the top of Pinnacle Mountain just outside of Little Rock. Atmospheric perspective refers to the detail visible in the landscape corresponding to its distance from the camera. There is much detail

4.18 Atmospheric perspective as a cue to depth
In this image of the Arkansas River valley, nearby rocks and trees have lots of detail, but distant hills appear hazy and indistinct.

visible in nearby rocks, but distant hillsides fade into the haze. Occlusion occurs when one object is closer to you than another so the nearby object occludes, or hides, the more distant object from your vision. Figure 4.19 offers another example of occlusion in an "impossible" triangle based on the one created by the Swedish artist, Oscar Reutersvärd. The blocks hiding, or occluding, the others are perceived by your visual system to be nearer to you than the blocks hidden by them. The triangle is impossible because there is no way in reality to arrange blocks with the same relations of depth as the blocks in the image. Finally, linear perspective refers to the fact that parallel lines that recede into the distance, such as the rails of a train track as in Figure 4.20, appear to converge. Monocular depth cues are all based on assumptions, including the assumptions that nearby objects have more detail than distant objects (atmospheric perspective), hide part or all of distant objects (occlusion), and are further from the convergence of parallel lines than distant objects (linear perspective).

atmospheric perspective
a monocular depth cue wherein objects that are closer have more visible detail than objects in the distance

occlusion
a monocular depth cue wherein objects that are closer may hide or cover objects that are more distant

linear perspective
a monocular depth cue wherein parallel lines appear as if they converge in the distance

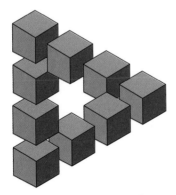

4.19 Occlusion as a cue to depth
When one object is partially hidden behind another object, your brain assumes that the hidden object is farther away than the object in front of it. In this "impossible" triangle, the squares cannot actually be arranged as shown in the image.

4.20 Linear perspective as a cue to depth
Parallel train tracks appear to converge as they recede into the distance.

Concept Recall

1. What is a motion aftereffect, and how is it similar to a color afterimage?

2. What kind of stimulus generates the phi phenomenon, and what does it look like?

3. What are some gestalt grouping principles, and how do they influence the visual experience of the world?

4. What is the primary binocular cue to depth?

5. What is the difference between binocular and monocular cues to depth?

Perceptual Constancy

perceptual constancy
the visual perception that objects remain constant even when their retinal image changes

While visiting a high-end leather goods store, you might have been astonished by a prominently displayed shoulder bag on sale for $7,000 and wondered, "Who on earth would buy a bag for that price?" The store manager cheerfully accepts that almost nobody ever purchases the $7,000 bag because it is really intended to make nearby bags selling for $2,000 seem like bargains, when in fact they are also extravagantly priced (Poundstone, 2011). By using a hyperexpensive bag as a decoy to sell less expensive bags, the retailer is taking advantage of the way human perception works. Although you probably believe that we can perceive features, such as color, brightness, and size, in isolation, in fact, we can only perceive the contrast between one feature and another nearby feature. Under almost all circumstances a $2,000 price tag is exorbitant, but in contrast to a nearby $7,000 price tag, it is comparatively cheap.

Although retailers can exploit human perception to manipulate their customers into purchasing overpriced merchandise, nature endowed us with contrast-based perception because it enabled our ancestors to perceive objects as constant even as the retinal image changes. To understand how our visual systems use contrast to achieve **perceptual constancy**, it is important to recall the difference between sensation and perception described earlier in this chapter. Visual sensation is the harvesting of light energy by the retina, and visual perception is the conscious experience that emerges after the brain has thoroughly processed the raw sensory information. The images of people walking toward and away from you steadily grow and shrink on your retina, but you don't perceive the people to be actually growing and shrinking.

4.21 Perceptual constancy
The retinal image of Allen in the foreground and Jim in the background have different sizes, yet they seem to have the same height. The difference between their retinal images becomes clear when Jim's image is moved so he appears to be the same distance as Allen and appears to be a tiny person.

How is it that your sensations of people change but your perceptions of them as "people-sized" remain constant?

To make Figure 4.21, two men of roughly equal height stood in a hallway at different distances from the camera, Allen nearby and Jim farther away. Notice that the hallway provides the depth cue of linear perspective. The image sizes of Allen and Jim relative to the height of the hallway is about equal, even though the image of Allen is huge relative to the image of Jim. You don't perceive Allen to be a giant and Jim to be an imp because your visual system compares each of their images to their immediate surroundings rather than to each other. When you compare Allen to the *pasted* image of Jim, Allen does appear to be a giant and Jim an imp. When our eyes see large images of people nearby and tiny images of people farther away, both are perceived as people-sized. Under normal circumstances, as people approach and recede from us, the size of their image on the retina (i.e., the sensation) changes, but perceived size remains constant.

HEARING: ANATOMY AND SOUND

As mentioned earlier in the chapter, people with intact vision often believe that loss of vision means losing their ability to navigate the world unassisted. This seemed to be the case for Brian Bushway when he completely lost his vision as a teenager due to optic nerve atrophy (Nestor, 2014).

Prior to losing his vision, Brian had been a typically active, athletic teen. After losing his sight, he had to rely on a guide to help him get around, making him feel depressed and isolated. Then, one day he sensed a pillar just in front of him without having to touch it—and, of course, without being able to see it. Brian's intuition about the pillar was based on the sounds echoing off the pillar. Brian soon began learning how to make a sharp popping noise with his tongue and analyze the sounds he heard when the pop bounced off surrounding objects. Brian is now the subject of online videos in which he can be seen mountain biking around trees and boulders and even riding down a flight of stairs. Brian's use of echolocation and a sighted person's use of vision to navigate their surroundings may seem to be radically different, but they are actually more similar than different: the nearby world is exposed to some kind of radiant energy (light or sound), and a sensory device (eyes or ears) collects the energy that bounces off the objects occupying the scene.

The Nature of Sound

After vision, hearing is probably the sense you rely upon most. While vision relies on the electromagnetic radiation in our environment, hearing collects and interprets energy transmitted as vibrations in the air. We can understand how a sound wave works by examining the simple sound wave made by a tuning fork. As one of the tuning fork's tines moves through the air, it squeezes together the air molecules in front of it, creating a small region of high pressure. The air molecules quickly recoil, expanding outward in all directions. As this is happening, the tine of the tuning fork will have moved away

Lower pitch

Higher pitch

Quieter

Louder

4.22 Sound wave chart
Sound is a wave, and like an ocean wave, it has peaks and valleys. One cycle is the distance from one peak to the next. A wave with fewer cycles packed into each second has a lower frequency—and thus sounds like it has a lower pitch—than a wave with more cycles per second, which has a higher pitch. The amplitude of a wave is the distance between the peak and the valley, so a wave with small peak-to-valley distance has a low amplitude—and thus is not as loud—as a wave with a bigger peak-to-valley distance, which sounds louder.

from the high-pressure region, sucking the air out and creating a partial vacuum or region of low pressure. The wave of low pressure radiates just behind the wave of high pressure. As a result, the pressure near the tuning fork rises steadily until reaching a peak, then falls steadily until reaching a valley, then the cycle begins again. Figure 4.22 illustrates how different pitches and volumes of sounds will produce varied wave patterns. Vibrations like those created by a tuning fork transmit energy from the source of the vibration throughout the environment. These vibrations are sounds if there is a sensory system available to capture and interpret them. Understanding the difference between vibration and sound allows you to correctly answer the question "If a tree falls in the forest and no one is around to hear, does it make a sound?" with, "No. It creates vibrations in the air but not sound." (While this is the correct answer, mentioning it probably won't make you the most popular person at the party.)

frequency
the number of cycles per second of a wave

amplitude
the height of a wave, which corresponds to the loudness of a sound

The physical characteristics of the sound wave are responsible for how we experience the sound. The length of a pressure wave is typically described in terms of **frequency**, which is the number of cycles per second and corresponds to pitch: high frequencies generate high-pitched sounds, and low frequencies generate low-pitched sounds. One cycle per second is called one hertz (Hz) after Heinrich Hertz, the nineteenth-century physicist. The difference between the peak and valley in a wave is called **amplitude** and corresponds to the loudness of a sound. As with light, the physical aspects of sound (frequency and amplitude) are represented by analogous aspects of sound (pitch and loudness) once it enters the mind.

Just as we saw with the limited range of visible light, our hearing is similarly sensitive to only a range of the available vibrations. For persons with normal hearing, the range of sensitivity to audio frequencies extends from 20 Hz to about 20,000 Hz (20 kilohertz, kHz). Human speech sounds range from 250–6,000 Hz (vowels: 250–1,000 Hz; consonants: 1,500–6,000 Hz). Due to differences in size and structural differences caused by higher levels of testosterone during puberty, men typically have deeper voices than women. Aging brings with it a loss of sensitivity to frequencies, with a faster change for higher-frequency sounds. Exposure to high-pitched noises and very loud environments speeds up the course of natural hearing loss.

The loudness of a sound can be measured by how much pressure the sound exerts on your ear. A **decibel (dB)** is a unit of measurement that compares the pressure caused by a sound wave to the normal pressure inside the ear (about twenty micropascals). Decibels are reported as the logarithm of the ratio of pressure caused by the target sound in reference to the pressure in the ear. A sound reading of zero dB means that the pressure in the atmosphere is equal to the normal pressure in the ear. Zero decibels does not imply the absence of sound. If the pressure outside the ear is less than the standard pressure inside the ear, the decibels will be a negative number. As we will see later in the chapter, the inner ear uses a mechanical process to transduce sound waves into neural signals. If the decibel level of sound is too high for too long it can result in permanent damage to the sensory organ. This type of damage is becoming a major health concern as the noise levels in our environment continue to increase with the greater adoption and availability of technology. A particular area of concern is the damage created by extended use and high volume of headphones. Many headphones have a maximum volume level of 115 dB, which is loud enough to damage hearing after just minutes of exposure. Even listening to headphones at a moderate level can create irreparable damage if the time of exposure and the pitch of the music is high enough.

Just as we saw with visible light, sound waves have physical characteristics that make them extremely good sources of environmental information. One major advantage of detecting airborne vibrations is that they both reflect off objects and pass through objects. We have all taken advantage of this characteristic of sound by listening through a door or wall to hear what is being talked about in another room. Unfortunately, this also means that if you are trying to sleep when the neighbors are having a party, the sounds of their revelry will pass through the wall into your room, keeping you awake. The ability of sound to travel through objects provides us details about objects that can be hidden from sight. Similarly, another major benefit of sound is its availability any time there is air through which to travel, such as on the surface of the Earth, at the bottom of an ocean of air. Sound has no need for a giant light source such as the sun, just a moving object and molecules to push around. The fact that sound needs a medium to travel through explains the tagline from the classic movie *Alien*: "In space no one can hear you scream." A final benefit of sound is that it radiates in all directions. As sound waves spread from the point of origin and reflect off objects in the environment, they fill the area around them. This radiation allows organisms with auditory systems to pick up the sound even if they are not pointed in the direction of the sound.

Before we continue with our discussion of hearing, reflect back on what we have learned about the nature of light and sound and why it has been to humans' advantage to develop both vision and hearing. The characteristics of light make vision a great system for detecting motion, color, and fine detail in objects that are directly in front of us during the day (artificial light is a very recent invention, and for most of our evolutionary history, natural light was the only kind of available light). Sound has a huge advantage in that it is available both day and night. Also, we do not have to be facing the source of the sound to detect it. In normal conditions, the two systems provide unique yet highly complementary information. You can easily understand the way these systems work

decibel (dB)
a unit of measurement that compares the pressure caused by a sound wave to the normal pressure inside the ear

together to give us a full picture of your environment by thinking about the last time someone called your name to get your attention. You were likely sitting in a classroom, actively engaged with your smartphone as you waited for lecture to begin. Upon hearing someone say your name, you disengaged from your phone, turned to look behind you, and then smiled as you identified your friend on her way to sit beside you. Despite being visually engaged with your phone, your auditory system was still able to monitor the world around you. Once your attention was captured by the new stimulus, you used your visual system to locate and identify the source. Maintaining multiple sensory systems requires a great deal of neural and metabolic resources and would not be an advantage to the organism unless doing so provided significant advantages.

The Outer and Middle Ear

With a better understanding of how sound works, we are ready to talk about our sound processing systems: the ear and auditory cortex. We begin with a discussion of the outer ear and middle ear.

pinna
the cartilaginous portion of the outer ear, which collect sound

ear canal
conveys sounds from the outer ear to the eardrum

The outer ear consists of the visible outer part that collects sound, called the **pinna** (from Latin for "fin"), and the **ear canal**. The pinna works like a funnel, with its unique shape serving to collect the sound waves into the ear. You may have heard that the famous Dutch painter Vincent van Gogh was reputed to have cut off his ear and handed it to a woman he wanted to impress; we are willing to bet she didn't respond as he had hoped. He didn't actually cut off his whole ear. Rather, he just cut off the pinna, completely neglecting the middle and inner ear. This cosmetic change would not have impaired his ability to hear, but it would have changed his experience of how the world sounds. You experience what van Gogh's world would have sounded like any time you listen to music or a phone conversation using an inexpensive pair of in-ear headphones. The sound coming into your ear from the headphones does not filter through the pinna, so it sounds different than if you heard the music live.

The pinna funnels sound into the ear canal, which allows the delicate eardrum to be buried about an inch below the surface. If you feel your head just behind your pinna you'll notice the bulge that is the hardest part of your skull, which protects the middle and inner ear from damage. When sound waves enter the ear canal the high pressure part of the wave pushes on the eardrum, whereas the low pressure pulls on it; therefore, the position of the eardrum is a moment-by-moment representation of the air pressure reaching it. Obstructions in the ear canal, such as water that remains there after you go for a swim, block the progress of the wave through the ear and thus interfere with the amount of energy available for transduction. This both lowers the perceived volume of the sound and creates the tunnel effect that is so frustrating after you go swimming or when you have a cold.

cochlea
the fluid-filled portion of the middle ear, which transforms sound into an electrical signal to be sent to the brain

Figure 4.23 illustrates the structures of the ear. At the inner end of the ear canal, sound waves impact the eardrum, causing it to vibrate. The sound waves reaching the eardrum are airborne, but the ear's transducers are contained in the fluid-filled **cochlea**, which is named for the Latin word for "snail" because it resembles a snail's shell. Recall from earlier in the chapter that transduction refers to the transformation of one kind of energy to another kind of energy, and the cochlea transduces mechanical vibrations into electrical neural signals. Airborne vibrations are too feeble to induce vibrations in fluid, so you may have noticed while swimming that the ambient noise in the surrounding air is much quieter when your head is underwater than when above the water because most of the sound energy bounces off the surface of the water. For that reason, the middle ear must amplify the airborne vibrations that reach the eardrum before delivering these vibrations to the fluid in the cochlea.

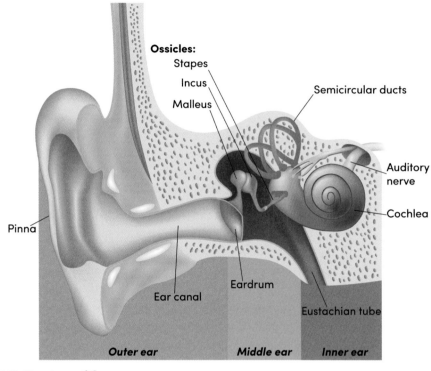

4.23 Structures of the ear
The pinna is the outer part of the ear that is visible. The ear canal conveys sounds to the eardrum, which vibrates in response. The three small bones in the middle ear amplify the eardrum's vibrations and push on the cochlea, where the vibrations are transduced into neural signals. Notice the Eustachian tube, which leads to the throat and balances the pressure on the inside of the eardrum with the pressure on the outside.

The middle ear consists of the eardrum and three **ossicles**, which is Latin for "tiny bones," and in fact the three middle ear ossicles are the three smallest bones in your body. The first of the three ossicles is connected to the eardrum, so it vibrates along with any movement of the eardrum, repeatedly striking the second ossicle like a blacksmith striking steel. This is why the two are called the hammer (malleus) and anvil (incus), respectively. The third ossicle is called the stirrup (stapes) because it looks like a stirrup (yes, the names of the first two bones are based on their function and the third is based on its shape). Working together, the three ossicles provide leverage to amplify airborne vibrations presented to the eardrum so that they have sufficient energy to instigate waterborne vibrations in the cochlear fluid.

ossicles
three tiny bones in the middle ear that amplify airborne vibrations

For the eardrum to vibrate as efficiently as possible, the air pressure in the middle ear needs to balance the average pressure on the outer surface of the eardrum. When you ascend quickly in a fast elevator to the upper floor in a tall building, the air pressure on the outer surface of the eardrum drops slightly, so it is then lower than the air pressure in the middle ear. You may have noticed that as the elevator ascends, sounds become quieter than they had been when you were on the ground floor. That's because the pressure imbalance interferes with the eardrum's ability to vibrate. To balance the pressure on the inner and outer surfaces of the eardrum, you need to vent some of the air out of the middle ear through the Eustachian tube (named after the Italian anatomist who first described it), which connects the middle ear to the throat. If you swallow upon reaching your floor, some air from the middle ear escapes into your throat, and the loudness of sounds returns to normal. A swimmer or scuba diver who descends in the water has the opposite problem: the pressure on the outside of the eardrum is much higher than the pressure on the inside. Scuba divers are taught to continually "clear their ears" as they descend, by blowing air from their lungs but keeping their mouths closed and pinching their noses. The air forced from the lungs can't escape, so it flows up the Eustachian tube into the middle ear, balancing the force of water pushing on the eardrum.

Auditory transduction in the inner ear

One end of the stirrup is connected to the cochlea's oval window, through which the stirrup's vibrations are transferred to the fluid inside the cochlea. As the auditory transducer, the cochlea extracts the frequencies from sounds then encodes them into electrical signals, which are conveyed to the brain via the auditory nerve. The pure tones produced by tuning forks consist of just one frequency, whereas natural sounds are collections of several frequencies blended together. To extract the pitches contained in complex sounds, the cochlea exploits **resonance**. Resonance refers to the tendency for one vibrating object to cause a nearby object to vibrate in response. Every object has its own resonant frequency, which is the frequency at which it will respond most vigorously to nearby vibrations. You may have noticed that sometimes when you hear loud music, deep bass notes can cause your entire chest cavity to vibrate—because the music contains the resonant frequency of your chest cavity. Perhaps the easiest way to understand how the cochlea uses resonance is by first imagining that the cochlea's spiral is "unwound" into a long straight tube (Figure 4.24). In the unwound cochlea, a flat sheet of tissue called the **basilar membrane** runs along the entire length of the tube, varying in width from narrow at the oval window to wide at the other end. Because of the variation in the basilar membrane's width, its resonant frequency varies accordingly, such that high frequencies make the narrow end of the basilar membrane flex and low frequencies make its wide end flex. Resting on the basilar membrane is the organ of Corti, which contains thousands of hair cells; when one part of the basilar membrane bends, it pushes on the corresponding hair cells on the organ of Corti. Each hair cell is such an exquisitely sensitive electrical switch that if it were expanded to the same height as the Eiffel Tower, the hair cell would detect deflections of just a thumb's width. The hair cells' extreme sensitivity entails that they are also extremely fragile. A vigorous flexing of the basilar membrane will snap off its associated hair cell. For that reason, acquired deafness—deafness that occurs as the result of experience—is most often clustered around certain pitches rather than being spread across all pitches.

resonance
a frequency at which something vibrates most energetically

basilar membrane
a flat sheet of tissue in the cochlea that resonates at different frequencies at different ends

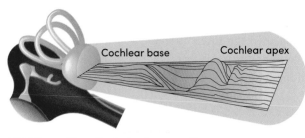

4.24 The cochlea after being "unwound"
It's easier to understand how the cochlea transduces sounds if we first imagine that the coiled cochlear chamber could be "unwound." The stirrup delivers vibrations to the fluid in the cochlea through the oval window, which in turn pushes and pulls the basilar membrane. The resonant frequency of the basilar membrane varies along its length, so one end of the membrane is receptive to low frequencies and the other end to high frequencies, with the part between the two ends receptive to intermediate frequencies.

In summary, the process of hearing works like this: Sound waves reach the eardrum, causing it to vibrate. The vibrations are amplified by the ossicles and delivered to the cochlea through its oval window, and parts of the basilar membrane resonate to the frequencies present in the sound. This pushes hair cells, which act like electrical switches and send electrical signals to the brain through the auditory nerve.

From the ear to the brain

Just as we learned with vision, the processing of the auditory signal begins even before the neural signal arrives in the cortex. In the same way that the first major region of visual processing in the cortex is called the primary visual cortex, the first major region of auditory processing in the cortex is called the **primary auditory cortex**. Tracing the main path of the auditory signal as it goes from transduction to perception is a great way to appreciate the complex processing involved in hearing. The transduced auditory signal begins its journey to the brain along the auditory nerve. The first major structures that the auditory signal encounters are the cochlear nucleus and the superior olive, both located in the brain stem. Both of these structures are engaged in the processing of the neural signal. As the signal passes through these two structures in the brain stem, sound elements are unpacked, analyzed, and then repackaged, often in new bundles and with different components of the sound, and then passed upward in the brain. The neural signal next passes through the inferior colliculus—a structure in the midbrain that is a relay center for auditory and other sensory information—where the neural signal begins to both merge with information from other areas in the brain and to be shipped off to other sensory systems. Further processing occurs as the auditory signal passes through the medial geniculate nucleus—an auditory relay station in the thalamus—before arriving at the primary auditory cortex.

primary auditory cortex the first major region of the auditory processing in the cortex

As we consider the journey from cochlea to the primary auditory cortex, there are a couple of key elements to remember. First, each hemisphere receives auditory information from both ears. As depicted in Figure 4.25, the information from both ears is merged at the brain stem. Because the ears are on different sides of the head, the sound detected in each ear will be slightly different. The merging and subsequent comparing of information from each ear provides important information with regard to locating sounds. Second, not all auditory information is processed in the auditory cortex. Much of the information is directed to other areas of the brain as the information passes through the brain stem, midbrain, and thalamus before arriving at the cortex. Finally, nonauditory information is picked

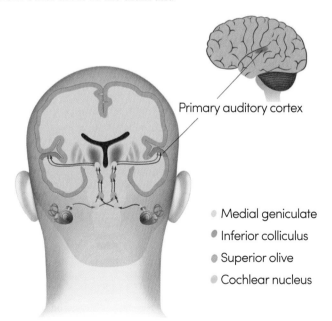

Primary auditory cortex

- Medial geniculate
- Inferior colliculus
- Superior olive
- Cochlear nucleus

4.25 The auditory pathways
Sound information is conveyed from the ear through the auditory nerve to the cochlear nucleus and superior olive in the brain stem. From there, the signal is projected to the inferior colliculus in the midbrain, then the medial geniculate nucleus in the thalamus, and finally to the primary auditory cortex.

up as the signal passes through the various sensory relay stations. The loss and gain of information as the signal travels from the ears to the cortex tells us that what we "hear" is not always what was actually sensed. Instead, top-down processing and inputs from other sensory systems modify the original signal.

Concept Recall

1. What are the parts of the ear, and how do they contribute to the experience of sound?

2. What are the physical aspects of pressure waves, and how do they correspond to the experience of sound?

3. What is echolocation, and how might a blind person use it to get around?

THE CHEMICAL SENSES

Taste and smell are often collectively called the chemical senses. In Chapter 3, you learned that signals between neurons are conveyed via chemicals called neurotransmitters that travel from an axon across the synapse to dendritic receptor sites on the other side. When a chemical with the right shape makes contact with the receptor, it fits into the receptor like a key in a lock, causing ion channels to open and changing the electrical charge of the postsynaptic neuron. This is not only how neurons inside our brains act but also how our taste and smell receptors work. The major difference is that the receptor sites for taste and touch are exposed to the outside world, whereas neurotransmitter receptor sites are buried inside the skull. The chemicals that connect with taste and smell receptors are not neurotransmitters but are rather tiny pieces of objects in the environment. In this way, the chemical senses are much more intimate than vision or sound. In vision, we see the light reflected off of objects. In hearing, we detect the displacement of molecules caused by movement in air. In both cases, we detect the effect of the object on the environment. In taste and smell, we are directly detecting the object itself. For taste, the object itself—or at least a part of the object—is placed in our mouth, where moisture from our saliva and the mechanical process of chewing breaks the object apart, freeing chemicals to make contact with our taste receptors. For smell, something in the environment has separated chemicals from the object, such as a knife slicing into an onion, which then releases chemicals to become airborne and float into our noses for detection.

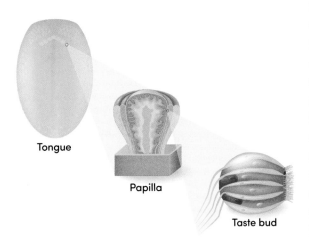

4.26 Taste receptors
If you look at your tongue in a mirror, you will see numerous bumps, each of which is called a papilla and is covered with receptors called taste buds. Chemicals with the right shape bind to the taste bud like a key in a lock, which creates a taste signal.

Taste is a particularly intimate sense, as our interaction with the object to be sensed is direct. We see this direct interaction in the way that babies interact with their world, by placing objects directly into their mouths. Inside the mouth, water-soluble chemicals dissolved on the tongue elicit tastes through the taste buds (Figure 4.26), and chemicals floating in the air elicit smells. Each of five basic tastes indicates the presence of a particular chemical in food. Sweetness indicates glucose, sourness indicates acids, saltiness indicates sodium, and bitterness indicates alkaloids, which are often present in poisons. The fifth basic taste, umami, is the least familiar and the most recently discovered, having been described by the Japanese scientist Kikunae Ikeda in 1908. Umami indicates the presence of the amino acid glutamate, which is a building block of many proteins. To get a sense of how umami tastes, imagine that you dropped a roast into the slow cooker when you left for school or work, then upon your return in the evening the aroma of roast beef had permeated your entire home. Then you grab a big spoon and slurp a mouthful of broth, which is the essence of umami. Although the tongue map (as shown in Figure 4.27) is probably the most recognizable image in the study of taste (Munger), the map doesn't work the way most people think it does. Because the various tastes are segregated into their own little regions (i.e., sweet on the tip, bitter at the back, etc.), most people have mistakenly concluded that each region can sense only one taste. Actually, the tongue map was intended to show that different parts of the tongue are slightly more sensitive to certain tastes than others, but in fact every part of the tongue can sense every taste.

4.27 Don't be misled by the classic tongue map
Although every part of the tongue can sense every taste, some areas of the tongue are slightly more sensitive to some tastes than others.

Our behavioral responses to each of the tastes highlight the role of the corresponding chemicals in our lives. Throughout much of our evolutionary history, food was scarce and unpredictable, so our brains respond to energy-dense macronutrients (sugar, proteins, and fat) very positively by telling us they taste great. While sugar tastes sweet and proteins taste umami, or savory, fat doesn't elicit its own taste sensation, but it does enhance the tastes of other foods by spreading them around on the tongue; a plain piece of bread has the same taste as one on which you've spread butter, but the butter greatly improves the overall experience. The mere mention of a sour food, such as pickles, may make your mouth water because strong vinegars from pickling have the potential to pack an acidic wallop in the digestive tract. Saliva dilutes the acid before it is swallowed. Because we need sodium for electrical transmission of neural signals as described in Chapter 3, salty tastes are generally very pleasant, as evidenced by the fact that restaurant food is designed to make customers happy and is notoriously high in sodium. However, imagine sitting down to a bowl filled with salt and eating it with a spoon. Eating salt by the spoonful probably seems disgusting because high concentrations of sodium in the extracellular fluid can be harmful, causing water to diffuse out of cells. In other words, salt is pleasant up to a point, after which it becomes disgusting. Finally, because alkaloids are typically present in plant toxins, our initial response to bitter tastes is marked by an urge to spit them out. Through the course of evolution, plants that instilled bitter-tasting alkaloids in their leaves enjoyed an adaptive benefit because hungry animals tended to avoid eating them. However, alkaloids often accompany essential nutrients, such as folic acid in leafy green vegetables. With experience, we can override the impulse to spit them out and even acquire a taste for them.

Although there are just five basic tastes, there are an unimaginably large number of flavors because flavor represents the interaction between the five tastes and millions of discernible smells. To see how different taste is from flavor, get a morsel of food

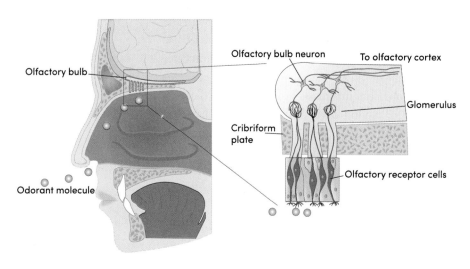

4.28 Olfactory (smell) pathway
Airborne molecules inhaled into the nose become embedded in the olfactory epithelium, thereby stimulating neurons that project through the cribriform plate to the olfactory bulb in the brain.

that has a distinct taste and smell; a jelly bean is a good candidate. First pinch your nose, then pop the morsel into your mouth and start to chew. Without any aroma, the morsel will only elicit a basic taste, such as sweetness. As you continue chewing, release your nose, and you'll be hit with a full-bodied flavor, such as blueberry or bubblegum. Smells enhance the flavors of foods not just before we place them in your mouth but while they're in your mouth because odorant molecules from the food travel through the back of the mouth and enter the nasal cavity over the palate.

Smell is unique from all of the other senses in that it has the most direct access to the brain. Airborne molecules are inhaled through the nose, warmed in the nasal cavity, and then rise to make contact with the olfactory epithelium, a receptor-lined tissue running along the top of your nasal cavity (Figure 4.28). Neurons from the olfactory epithelium project through the cribriform plate to the olfactory bulb in the brain. Pause and take a moment to think about how this relatively straightforward path compares to the complicated series of reorganizations that occur for both vision and hearing.

Smells and taste are very closely tied to our emotional responses. In the 2001 romantic comedy *Someone Like You*, Ashley Judd's character, Jane Goodale, approaches a surgeon with the request to have her sense of smell removed in order to eliminate problems caused by her "erotic brain." After a series of bad encounters with an ex-boyfriend, Jane has reasoned that she will minimize the chances of falling into further problems if she can eliminate the connection between the great smell of her ex and the associated memories. This is not a recommended treatment for relationship problems, but it does highlight how strong the connection is between smells and memory. You have likely had the experience of encountering a smell that reminded you of a good (or bad) childhood memory and were subsequently overwhelmed by the emotions and nostalgia associated with the past event.

4.29 Look of disgust
Facial expressions, particularly those of the six basic emotions proposed by Ekman, are the same across cultures.

Our sense of smell is especially tied to the emotion of disgust. Disgust is one of the six basic emotions proposed by Paul Ekman and his associates. Those emotions are anger, disgust, fear, happiness, surprise, and sadness (1983). Two of the characteristics that led Ekman and his group to consider each of these emotions as basic is that they have a unique facial expression that is recognizable across cultures. In Figure 4.29 is a man with a distinct facial expression that your visual system immediately and automatically processed as one of disgust. If we had captured your face in the moment that you perceived this image, we would have seen a brief mirror of this same expression on your face. These matching microemotions occur almost any time we detect emotion in someone else, and they happen independent of cultural, racial, or educational background. These reactions to the picture provide evidence of the universality of the emotion.

Disgust is strongly tied to certain environmental smells. The following list is not very pleasant. Some odors that trigger disgust include feces, vomit, blood, and rotting food. The association between these smells and a feeling of disgust is unlearned—and for a good reason. Items in this category are strongly associated with infectious agents and toxins. Avoiding items that are associated with these smells is good for our survival and increases our overall fitness. When exposed to these smells, we feel a strong urge to leave the area, turn our heads, and cover our mouths.

While disgust is strongly tied to specific stimuli, regardless of the environmental context of the organism, the emotional triggers for disgust are also highly malleable through experience. In Chapter 7, you will learn about how respondent conditioning can be used to associate novel environmental events with existing physiological responses, such as emotions. Depending on our environmental and cultural context, we experience different tastes and smells. Early exposure to these stimuli can shape the way we respond to them. For example, imagine eating a tarantula or sheep's head. In cultures such as America's, in which these are not a normal part of the diet, thinking about eating them typically elicits a strong feeling of disgust. However, there is nothing inherently "disgusting" about these foods. Prepared correctly, they contain proteins and nutrients that the body can use.

Concept Recall

1. What kinds of chemicals elicit tastes and what kinds elicit smells?
2. Is "flavor" just another word for "taste"? Why not?
3. What are the five basic tastes, and what chemical do each represent as present on the tongue?

TOUCH AND PAIN

Touch is unique among the senses because the other four have specialized sensory organs: eyes for vision, ears for hearing, the tongue for taste, and the nose for smell. In contrast, touch is served by several different kinds of sensory receptors scattered across the entire surface of the body. Commonly considered a single sense, touch is actually the ability to sense heat, cold, pressure, and pain. Because pain is often associated with intense heat, cold, and pressure, it seems reasonable to conclude that we feel pain when those other touch receptors are strongly stimulated, but this is not always the case because pain receptors are distinct from other touch receptors.

Because pain is so unpleasant, it is temping to believe that life would be better without it. This is especially true as the body ages and lingering pains from damaged joints and tissue become constant companions. A life without pain may seem appealing at first, but it comes at a very high cost. The absence of pain receptors can be seen in a rare genetic disorder called congenital insensitivity to pain (CIP). People with CIP typically die young and suffer from many self-inflicted injuries during their brief lives. For example, if you reached for a hot pan handle the painful heat would cause you to immediately withdraw your hand; without any feelings of pain, you would heedlessly continue to hold the pan handle as it burned the flesh on your hand. The information that pain provides about how the environment interacts with the body is extremely important and useful. Ironically, the unpleasantness of pain is the very reason that it is so valuable. The unpleasantness of pain motivates us to remove it, minimize it, and avoid it altogether. Within normal ranges, this motivation is extremely beneficial to our overall health and safety.

Touch receptors are spread across the skin. However, they are not evenly distributed. Some areas contain many more receptors than other areas. For example, the bottom of your foot contains more touch receptors per area than your elbow. Recall Wilder Penfield's pioneering method for easing seizure disorders described in Chapter 3. Penfield removed a piece of the patient's skull to expose the underlying somatosensory cortex, then induced small electrical impulses in different brain regions and

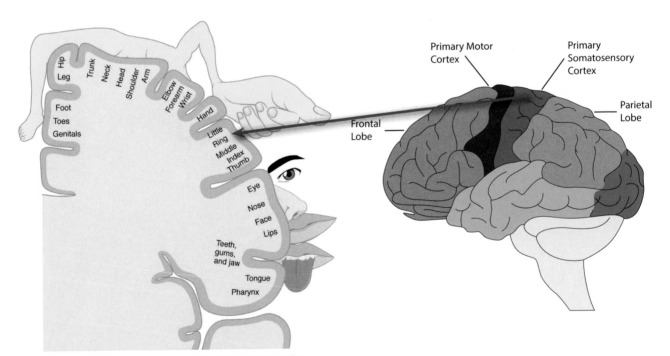

4.30 The map of the body on primary somatosensory cortex
The primary somatosensory cortex forms a stripe of tissue that defines the anterior (forward) edge of the parietal lobe. The primary motor cortex defines the posterior (back) edge of the frontal lobe. Stimulating one part of your body activates the corresponding region in the somatosensory stripe. The primary somatosensory and motor stripes have similar layouts, so for example, the region in the somatosensory stripe that would respond to a feeling in the upper arm lies just posterior to a region in the motor stripe, which, if activated, would cause you to move your upper arm.

asked patients to tell him where on their body they felt the corresponding tingle. Understanding the layout of the somatosensory cortex, illustrated in Figure 4.30, provides insight into the problem of phantom pain (Ramachandran & Hirstein, 1998). People who have lost limbs, such as arms or legs, typically continue to feel the limbs as if they were still attached and often feel pain as well. Unfortunately, phantom pain is not easy to relieve with the usual techniques that you would use for one of your existing limbs. For example, when you feel a pain in your hand, you automatically begin flexing the fingers to reduce muscle tension and rubbing at the hand to help stimulate blood flow. How would you do this if you felt pain in a hand that no longer existed? Phantom pain seems to be due to neural plasticity in the somatosensory cortex. Here the word "plastic" means changeable in form, so in the same way that plastic surgeons change the shape of their patients' faces and bodies, neural plasticity refers to neural connections that change with experience. If a person has lost a hand, the part of the somatosensory cortex that had previously received stimulation from the hand becomes idle from lack of stimulation. Neurons that project to adjacent areas in the somatosensory stripe will take the opportunity to invade the idle region. The hand area in the somatosensory cortex lies next to the arm area, so neural projections from the arm invade the hand area. The face area lies on the other side of the hand area, so neural projections from the face invade the hand area from the opposite direction. Victor S. Ramachandran and William Hirstein describe a patient who lost much of his left arm after a motorcycle accident. Afterwards, Ramachandran would touch his patient's upper arm and cheek, which felt as if the doctor were touching not just the upper arm and cheek, but also the patient's hand that was no longer connected to his arm.

If phantom limbs are a byproduct of neural plasticity of the sensory experience, it may be possible to treat them by creating a new sensory illusion (Ramachandran & Altshculer, 2009). In order to test this possibility, Ramachandran and colleagues created a mirror box, where patients with phantom hands would place both arms into separate receptacles on two sides of a closed box. Inside the box was a mirror that reflected an image of the existing hand. As the patient looked into the box, the visual experience was of two healthy hands: the existing hand and its mirror image. Patients would flex and work their healthy hand and the brain would "see" both hands moving. The results of this study and follow-up work indicate that this treatment reduces phantom limb pain. How does it work? The current hypothesis is that as the visual signal moves forward in the neural pathways, it generates the experience of the missing hand in the conscious mind.

Concept Recall

1. What is the primary sensory organ for the sense of touch?
2. Although you might imagine a life without pain to be attractive, why would the cessation of pain be harmful?
3. Why do people who have lost a limb continue to feel the limb as if it remained attached?

SENSATION, PERCEPTION, AND PSYCHOLOGY

Perception seems so easy: just keep your eyes and ears open, and the world presents itself to your mind. In fact, your brain must expend a great deal of energy and effort to generate your mental model of the world. And it's lucky for us the brain does all that hard work—because without perception, we would become disconnected from our surroundings, lost forever in an internal world.

Sensation and perception maintain a significant role in psychology because they provide a window onto the world and provide a firm foundation on which other psychological processes are built. As we further explore psychology, try to remain conscious of the way the sensation and perception make these other processes possible.

Review/Reflect/Write

REVIEW

- How does the wavelength of light map onto perceived color?
- What is a camera obscura, and how is it similar to the human eye?
- What are the parts of the human eye, and how does each contribute to vision?
- Why does each retina have a blind spot?
- What are the two ways the eyes process color, and where in the retina does each kind of color processing occur?
- How do the gestalt grouping principles contribute to perception of form?
- What is the difference between binocular and monocular cues to depth?
- What are the three main parts of the ear, and how do they contribute to hearing?
- What are the chemical senses, and why are they called that?
- What are the five basic tastes?
- What is meant by "phantom pain," and why do some people experience it?

1. Sensation occurs primarily in
   a. the brain.
   b. the sensory organs.
   c. the sensory organs and brain.
   d. neural networks.

2. When someone says you have beautiful eyes, they are probably referring to your
   a. cornea.   c. sclera.
   b. pupil.   d. iris.

Answer Key
1.b 2.d 3.b 4.d 5.d 6.b 7.d 8.b 9.c 10.d

3. In order to best detect whether an intruder is in a dark house, the homeowner should

    a. look directly at the area where the noise was heard.

    b. look slightly to the side of where the noise was heard.

    c. blink quickly to stimulate the rods and cones.

    d. hide in the closet.

4. After a visit from the police, a band decides to stop practicing so loudly. To get quieter, they should

    a. adjust the frequency.   c. raise their pitch.

    b. lower their pitch.   d. change the amplitude.

5. The process by which energy the brain cannot use becomes a different type of energy that can be perceived by the brain is called

    a. transformation.   c. translation.

    b. transcription.   d. transduction.

6. Which part of the eyes is responsible for turning an image into a collection of signals the brain can interpret?

    a. cornea   c. iris

    b. retina   d. pupil

7. Which of the following is a proper explanation for why we can be fooled by optical illusions?

    a. Our conscious visual experience is identical to our retinal images.

    b. We have the expectation that our mental image will be different than our retinal images.

    c. When an image travels from the optic nerve to the thalamus, it can become warped.

    d. The image we consciously experience is different from the image presented to the retinas.

8. The trichromatic color theory describes all of these *except*

    a. why some people are color blind.

    b. how colors are perceived by retinal ganglion cells.

    c. how color is perceived by cones.

    d. why three colors are enough to generate any other color.

9. Why do we know that a person does not shrink and disappear when they walk farther away from us into the distance?

    a. atmospheric perspective   c. perceptual constancy

    b. occlusion   d. linear perspective

10. In order to taste the full flavor of a food you must

    a. experience the sound of the food being chewed as well as the taste.

    b. experience the sight as well as the taste.

    c. experience the touch as well as the taste.

    d. experience the taste as well as the smell.

REFLECT

1. Top-down processing organizes raw perceptual information to make sense out of it. What do you think would happen to an inmate in solitary confinement who has no visual or auditory input for top-down perception to make sense of? Do you think his top-down processing would shut off, or instead would it create a hallucinatory world?

2. Before reading this chapter, did you believe that the optic nerve was a kind of "fax" line for transmitting the retinal image to the brain? If there were a tiny little person sitting in your brain to read the image transmitted to the brain, how would you explain the way vision works inside his tiny little brain?

WRITE

1. Different cultures have different favorite foods. For example, the durian fruit is prized in Southeast Asia for its custard-like texture and highly flavored pungency. Given to an American, however, the durian is regarded as revolting and rotten-tasting. While the senses of people from different cultures do not function any differently, their perception varies widely, and dramatically, in this case. Research the divergence of sensation and perception. Describe that divergence, and try to identify what factors tend to influence it.

2. Organize a group of your peers, some who use vision correction (contacts or glasses) and some who do not. Locate a collection of brain teaser images (ex: http://brainden.com/eye-illusions.htm), and use the scientific method to determine whether people with vision correction perceive brain teasers differently than people without vision correction. Write a report that details the group of people, the images you used, the steps and reasoning for your methods, and your results and conclusion.

3. Research the sensory/perceptive elements of synesthesia. Using what you've learned, develop a series of tests to see if any of your classmates identify with the phenomenon.

Key Terms

5 Development Through the Life Span

After reading this chapter, you will be able to answer the following questions:

- How do we change over our life spans?
- What is the difference between nature and nurture in development?
- What are the stages of cognitive development?
- What is separation anxiety?
- Why is the attachment process important to socioemotional development?
- What social, physical, and emotional developments occur during adolescence?
- What physical changes take place during middle and late adulthood?

On August 20, 2016, *USA Today* reported the arrest of a 55-year-old woman on a misdemeanor charge. The woman was charged and then released on $500 bail. What was her offense? She was charged with two counts of endangering the welfare of her children, an 8-year-old and 9-year-old, by leaving them alone in their vacation rental while she left to pick up food. The police reported that the children were home alone for at least 45 minutes. The charges against this mother were eventually dropped—but not before the story was reported across the Internet.

This mother is not the only parent whose decision regarding leaving children home alone has been questioned. According to a news report published in the *Telegraph* on March 2015, more than 100 charges were filed in the last three months of 2015 against parents for leaving their children home alone. This is the equivalent of one report per day during that time frame. According to the news story, Great Britain does not have a set legal age for when a child can be left home alone. Instead, this decision is left to the parents' discretion.

So what do you think? Was the mother wrong to leave her two children home alone? At what age do you believe it is safe to leave a child home alone? What factors do you think parents and society should consider in determining when a child can be left home alone? As you think about your answer to these questions, consider at what age you first stayed home alone. Were you ready for the experience?

Questions about when people should be allowed access to certain experiences are driven both by the caregivers and by social and cultural practices. The average age of marriage differs greatly across the world. The age at which people begin to work similarly varies (indeed, child labor laws and advocacy groups exist to try and protect children from being pushed into the workforce). Most of these questions concern the transition from child to adult, a distinction that itself is being examined. At what age does a person cross into adulthood?

At the heart of these questions is the development of the person. The answer to when a person should be allowed access to certain activities is, at its simplest, "When they are ready." But how do we determine this? Does readiness have to do with a certain level of physiological development? A certain level of cognitive maturity? And is it all about the individual, or do we need to take in account the social and cultural context of the individual?

Throughout this chapter, we will explore the changes that occur as we progress in life from conception to death. These developmental events are directly tied to many of the decisions that are made by caregivers, educators, and policy makers. Understanding how you develop and change over time helps you appreciate where you have come from, what caused some of the challenges of your younger years, what you are experiencing now, and what to expect in your future.

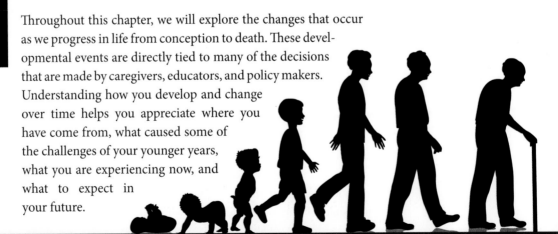

THREE ORGANIZING QUESTIONS OF DEVELOPMENT

It may be one of the great ironies that we leave life, if we live long enough, much as we entered it—bald, wrinkled, and needing others to help with our most basic functions. While there may be some similarities between how we begin and end, what happens physically, cognitively, and emotionally to each of us across our respective life spans involves many different changes.

Developmental psychologists study these and other topics within human development, from changes in the brain to moral development. However, there are three overarching issues that seem to drive theory and research in human development:

1. Nature vs. nurture

2. Stages vs. continuity

3. Stability vs. change

These three comparative questions characterize much of how we think about changes across our life span.

Nature vs. Nurture

The first, nature vs. nurture, is probably the developmental question that gets the most attention. Those who study this issue attempt to determine how much of the change we experience throughout life is due to genetics and how much is due to the people, places, and events we experience. As discussed in Chapter 1, the bio-psycho-social-cultural (integrative) approach to psychology views experience as a product of biology, the current environment, mental processes, social influence, and culture. These influences on our behavior mix together like the different ingredients in a recipe. With all the ingredients mixing and working together, it is difficult to quantify how much each different ingredient contributes to our experience of the recipe. Yes, we may notice some ingredients more than others, but would they taste the same and would we enjoy them as much without the other ingredients? The nature vs. nurture question attempts to determine the degree to which biology influences a particular behavior. For most of us, it is generally accepted that one's biological sex at birth (nature) influences whether he or she will act, dress, and speak in a more masculine or feminine style. However, what is considered masculine or feminine, and how strictly one must adhere to these distinctions, is greatly influenced by the culture in which one is raised (nurture) (Eagly, 2009).

Stages vs. Continuity

The question of nature vs. nurture also influences the second overarching issue in developmental psychology: does development occur in clearly defined, observable stages, or in a gradual, sometimes invisible fashion, differently influenced by experience (continuity)? The stage-versus-continuity argument can be seen in the change from infant to toddler. When does this change occur? Most definitions consider a child who cannot walk to be an infant and a child who has recently learned to walk to be a toddler (hence, one who toddles—moves with short unsteady steps). Most parents feel like the transition from infant to toddler is an instantaneous change: one day an infant, the next a toddler. This categorization would be thinking about development as a series of stages. The transition is not really this abrupt, however. Lots of practice goes into the first steps. Lots of practice comes after the first steps. And, to be honest, the first steps are really more "falling with style" (as Buzz Lightyear from Disney's *Toy Story* would call it). Looking at the transition from infant to toddler this way makes it look more like development is a continuous flow from one skill to the next. Developmental psychologists have found that the answer to this question really depends on the area of development. Let's continue with the example of sex and gender. All of us experience puberty, a biological phenomenon with observable physical stages. Whether our behavior changes significantly in terms of gender roles, however, will vary by culture (Van Leeuwen, 1978).

Stability vs. Change

The final overarching issue in developmental psychology is whether development of our personality (general traits and approaches to situations and events; see Chapter 12) is characterized more by stability or by change. Will a young girl who is a shy "tomboy," who lives for softball and doesn't like dresses, hit puberty and suddenly become an outgoing teenage fashionista who plans to run for homecoming queen? Research has shown that temperament is quite stable (Nave et al., 2010), so it is unlikely that the shy girl will become a bubbly, social teenager. Social attitudes, however, are much less stable (Moss & Susman, 1980), so the interest and dress part of the question is harder to answer. As with many of the questions asked in the field of psychology, the answer is often "It depends" or "Both." Human beings are complex, and as such, there are no simple answers.

Pause and take a moment to think about where you stand on each of these questions. Do you believe that our behavior is influenced more by biology or by our experiences? Do you think that our abilities change in large jumps or that we learn in a gradual buildup of ability? Do you believe that our temperament and approach to situations remains constant, or does it change over time? As these questions are framed here, they are dichotomous choices. It's either one or the other. Most people, though, don't agree with this approach and would prefer to put their answers somewhere in between the two extremes. As you progress through this chapter, keep the three organizing questions of development in mind. Thinking about development along these three dimensions is a great way to organize the information discussed in this chapter.

NEONATAL AND EARLY CHILDHOOD DEVELOPMENT

The first developmental psychologists did not concern themselves with prenatal development, only studying the physical, cognitive, and emotional progress of babies after they were born (Fodor, 1949; Rank, 1952). The absence of research on prenatal development made sense before the invention of modern diagnostic technology.

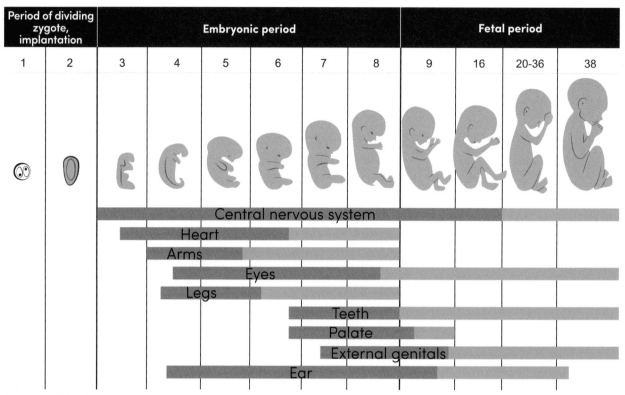

Period of dividing zygote, implantation		Embryonic period						Fetal period			
1	2	3	4	5	6	7	8	9	16	20-36	38

Central nervous system

Heart

Arms

Eyes

Legs

Teeth

Palate

External genitals

Ear

5.1 Prenatal development
This bar graph highlights the milestones of prenatal development. The orange portion of each bar represents the very sensitive periods when teratogens can cause serious abnormalities in development, and the yellow portion indicates that development is still occurring and can be influenced, but less dramatically.

Without the ability to image inside the body, it is extremely difficult to observe the changes that take place during a healthy pregnancy. In the last fifty years, however, developmental psychologists have taken advantage of changes in imaging technology to study the vast amount of growth and change that takes place during the nine months in the womb as well as the importance of environmental factors during prenatal development (Ferreira, 1960; Ward, 1991).

Life Before Birth

In the nine months of neonatal development, a human grows from an embryo the size and shape of a peanut to a seven-pound (on average) newborn, who now has the physical features of a human being rather than a peanut. During this time, the brain develops nerve cells at the astonishing rate of a quarter million per minute (Rabinowicz, et al., 1996, 1999). Even with all of the physical construction taking place during these first nine months, there is still time available for the first bits of learning to occur. Figure 5.1 illustrates the major stages and changes associated with the nine months of neonatal development.

Sounds, stress, calm—all can enhance or detract from prenatal development. By the sixth month of development, the fetus is responsive to sound, and though muffled, it can hear its mother's voice (Hepper, 2005). Further, fetuses appear to become familiar with their mothers' languages, as newborn cries contain intonations that match their mothers' (Mampe, et al., 2009). There is evidence that fetuses adapt to sounds they hear repeatedly; the fetus of a mother living in New York City becomes accustomed to sounds of traffic and people and can sleep through them, just like its mother (Dirix, et al., 2009).

Much of the input from the environment helps the baby prepare for life outside the womb, but even from the earliest stages of pregnancy, environmental factors, such as maternal stress, viruses, or drugs, can adversely affect fetal development. Alcohol and other drugs ingested by a pregnant woman enter the fetus's bloodstream and have similar effects on the fetus's developing central nervous system as they do on the mother's. However, given that the fetus is so small compared to its mother, the impact on it is much greater. Brain development is rapid while the fetus is in utero, and **teratogens**, such as stress and chemicals, can have an epigenetic effect: They can leave chemical marks on the fetus's DNA that cause genes to switch on or off abnormally. For example, caffeine, smoking, and drug use can all lead to low birth weight (Ondeck & Focareta, 2009).

teratogens
environmental factors, such as maternal stress, viruses, or drugs, that can negatively impact fetal development

The Newborn

Babies are born with a variety of automatic reflexes that help them survive (Berk, 2009). They turn toward something touching their cheeks in an effort to get food, and they pull limbs away from something that causes pain, cry when uncomfortable, and turn their heads if something blocks their breathing or vision. All of these skills help the newborn to get the care they need, and babies need a lot of assistance to get through the first few months of life. While babies' reflexes are automatic, their caregivers' responses are not. In fact, many modern adults know very little about newborns until they have one of their own.

Newborns strongly prefer sights, sounds, and touches that facilitate social responsiveness. They turn their heads in the direction of human voices. They gaze longer at objects if they resemble faces (as mentioned in Chapter 3). They prefer to look at objects that are eight to twelve inches away and listen to rhythms that are sixty to eighty beats per minute (Mauer & Mauer, 1988). The latter two correspond to the distance between a nursing baby's eyes and its mother's eyes and its eyes and the mother's heartbeat, respectively; both are inherently and specifically comforting to newborns.

One of the most important things that helps a newborn is the responsiveness of the caregivers (Dunst & Kassow, 2007). Are caregivers able to observe their baby's actions and noises and consistently respond appropriately? Caregiver responsiveness is more than just attending to the safety and distress of the newborn. Indeed, responsiveness includes matching the caregiving responses to the temperament of the infant. Caregiver social attention is most effective when it comes in the doses that fit the newborn's temperament.

maturation
the orderly sequence of
biological growth

We all travel a developmental path from infancy, to childhood, to adolescence, and then to adulthood. We experience the same biological milestones, through a process known as **maturation**—the orderly sequence of biological growth. Maturation is a genetically controlled process. Carefully timed changes are used to move the body through its development from infant to adult. While maturation is controlled by a genetic program that sets the basic course of development, environmental experience can adjust the timing of maturation events (Renner & Renner, 1993; Field, et al., 2007). One way to understand the interplay between genes and environment that produce maturation is to look at how the brain develops. We are born with nearly all of the brain cells we will ever have, and they are mostly where they belong. From birth through early adulthood, the brain is busy making the neural connections that enable us to walk, talk, speak, think, remember, and learn. These connections are new, but they continue to follow the structure that was laid out during neonatal development. As the brain is a use-dependent organ, neural pathways that are used are strengthened; if they are not used, they are shut down. This has far-reaching consequences for overall development, which will be addressed in detail later.

Cognitive Development and Motor Control

The developing brain enables physical coordination, which is why we are able to go from merely waving our limbs around to being able to walk in about a year. With few exceptions, the sequence of physical and motor development is universal, though the exact timing varies. Babies roll over before they sit, and they usually crawl before they walk. These behaviors are reflective of a maturing nervous system—as an increasing number of neural connections are made, our strength and coordination develop and improve. However, parents' actions can also affect the speed at which infants' motor skills develop.

Since 1992, parents have been encouraged to put their babies on their backs to sleep. This recommendation has significantly reduced the number of infant deaths due to Sudden Infant Death Syndrome (SIDS), but it has also impacted motor development (Pin, Eldridge, & Galea, 2007). Parents may have overgeneralized this recommendation and are now failing to provide their babies opportunities to play on their stomachs during the day. Research indicates that this lack of experience can slow motor development. Why is this? Try lying down on your stomach and looking around. In order to see much of the world, you must lift your head and swivel it. This requires back, neck, and abdominal muscles that are similar to those used in walking and supporting yourself upright. Now, flip over to your back and look around at the world. Thanks to the floor supporting your head, all you need to look around from your back are the neck muscles. While the genetic information has provided a blueprint for maturation, the infant needs interactions with the world that strengthen muscles and neural connections. This is why child development experts recommend that caregivers provide "tummy time" for babies from very early on. The American Academy of Pediatrics website recommends "Back to sleep, tummy to play." (healthychildren.org).

Development of Thinking and Memory

Parents often find that when they retell a favorite story from when their child was a toddler, the child responds, "I don't remember that!" Some people do report remembering events from when they were just a year or two old. This is likely not their own memory, but their recall of what they have been told. Our earliest memories seldom predate our third birthdays. Our brains process and store information during our earliest years. (How else would we learn?) However, the hippocampus, the area of the brain responsible for getting memories from short-term to long-term storage, does not fully mature until we are three or four years old.

As noted with motor skills and memory, there are cognitive tasks we can perform as adults that are completely beyond us as babies. **Cognition** is the term used for all the mental activities associated with thinking, knowing, remembering, and communicating. The accepted idea used to be that children were simply miniature adults (Cunningham & Morpurgo, 2006). Once scientists began studying children's abilities, such thinking changed. The most influential scholar in the field of cognitive development is almost certainly Jean Piaget, a Swiss developmental psychologist and philosopher who began his work in 1920.

cognition
all mental activities associated with thinking, knowing, remembering, and communicating

A half century of observing children led Piaget to formulate the theory that children do not think like miniature adults. In fact, they reason quite differently and in ways that make adults wonder, "Why in the world would you think that?" Piaget theorized that children's cognitive abilities develop in a series of stages (remember the stages vs. continuity question from the beginning of the chapter?), as they seek to make sense of their world (Piaget, 1930). As children progress across stages, Piaget believed that they create **schemas**, or mental maps, in which to store experiences. By adulthood, we have countless schemas to help us understand everything from dogs to politics. Our schemas form the foundation of how we view and think about the world around us throughout our entire life, as they are continuously changing and adapting with our experiences.

schemas
the mental maps in which we store our experiences

Piaget suggested that there are two ways in which we change or adjust our schemas: **assimilation** and **accommodation**. To illustrate how each of these processes work, consider your first experience with animals. At about a year old, when first learning language and its usefulness in identifying things, you were likely told that the furry creature with four legs, a tail, and big ears is a "dog." Adults reinforced this when you called pictures as well as actual examples of that animal "doggie." Then you encountered a rabbit. Rabbits have fur, four legs, ears, and a tail. This fit with your rule for a schema, so you proudly pointed and exclaimed, "Doggie!" You then proceeded to do this with each new animal, whether it was a rabbit, cat, or buffalo, with those same features. This is assimilation. You took in the new information in terms of what you already knew and added new examples to the category. The first 50 times you did this, it was cute. Then it wasn't any more, and the adults in your world starting giving you feedback: "No, that isn't a doggie, it's a cat." As you interacted with this differential feedback

assimilation
the process of interpreting new information in terms of what we already know

accommodation
the process of adjusting a preexisting schema to it with new information

and other adults who were not calling every four-legged, furry creature a doggie, you adjusted, or accommodated, your schema to fit the new information. You learned that the original doggie schema was too broad and refined it by creating new schemas for nondoggies and adding details to your existing doggie schema. Today, you are really good at correctly classifying doggies as well as other animals, people, objects, and ideas (we will return to this topic when we discuss stereotypes in Chapter 15).

sensorimotor stage
Piaget's first stage of cognitive development, occurring from birth to approximately age two, in which babies learn about the world through their senses and actions

According to Piaget (1930), children develop their schemas through their interactions with the world and move through up to four stages, each with distinct features that allow for specific kinds of thinking (these stages are summarized in Figure 5.2). The first of these stages is the **sensorimotor stage**. In this stage, which runs from birth to approximately age two, babies learn about the world through their senses and actions. They use a combination of hearing, looking, and touching to learn about the world and their ability to manipulate it.

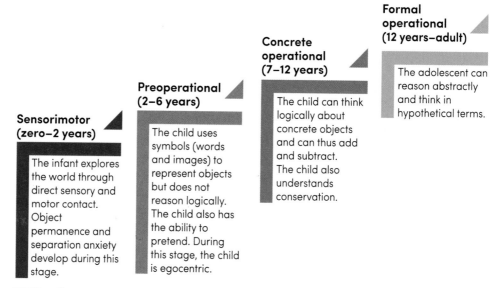

5.2 Piaget's stages
The four major stages of Piaget's theory of development are illustrated above. Also included is the major accomplishment of each stage and general age range.

object permanence
the awareness that objects continue to exist when not seen

Piaget showed that babies do not have a concept of **object permanence**—the awareness that objects continue to exist when not seen—until about eight months of age. We live our first several months of life completely in the present. Out of sight is literally out of mind—if a young baby can't detect something through one of his or her five senses, it doesn't exist as far as the child is concerned (Shawn once had a mother of a three-month-old begin to leave class to return home and be with her child when he first presented this concept). Once object permanence takes root, a baby will look for a toy that has disappeared, and in the case of the "object" being a primary caregiver, get upset, especially when left with someone unfamiliar. More modern developmental researchers still subscribe to the notion of object permanence, but research has shown that the development of this skill is more of a continuous, gradual process than Piaget thought (Wang, et al., 2004). Babies as young as five months old demonstrate brief sparks of understanding that an object exists even when they can't see it. Piaget based his ideas about the timing of object permanence on his observations that babies don't reach for or try to connect with the object that disappears until eight months of age. Attention and expression of surprise, however, are also indicators of understanding object permanence, and these do occur before eight months (Baillargeon, 1987).

The second cognitive stage Piaget believed children go through is the **preoperational stage**. This stage is typically associated with ages two through six or seven. In this stage, children can mentally represent objects (hold a mental picture in their minds), but they cannot mentally operate them. As a result, they lack the concept of **conservation**—the concept that quantity remains the same despite changes in shape. In Piaget's classic example, if you pour liquid from a short, wide container into a tall, narrow container, the average preschooler will tell you there is now more liquid. If you are ever with a child in the preoperational stage who is upset that there are not enough food items, just break them into smaller pieces and spread them across the plate. Voila! From famine to feast in no time.

Once children have mastered the concept of conservation, they move into the **concrete operational stage**. Piaget believed that by age six or seven children develop the ability to perform mental operations, as long as they have tangible (concrete) materials to work with. This is one of the reasons kindergarten, first, and second grade teachers use those colorful blocks or other objects in teaching math. Going back to the liquid task, children in the concrete operational stage now know that changing the shape of the container does not change the volume of the liquid, no matter how it looks. However, if you ask children in this stage to perform mental operations in their heads, with no objects to work with, they won't be able to do it.

Piaget's final stage of cognitive development is the **formal operational stage**. By about age twelve, children should begin to demonstrate the ability to perform mental operations abstractly, without the aid of actual experience. At this last stage, children are able to reach the correct conclusion regarding the liquid task without having to see it in front of them. Piaget also noted that as children move into adolescence, they develop the ability to think like scientists—if this, then that. However, as with earlier stages, modern research supports the idea that children demonstrate abilities from later stages at earlier ages than Piaget theorized.

Egocentrism and Theory of Mind

If young children cannot think abstractly about objects, it follows that they also cannot think abstractly about people. Piaget contended that very young children are **egocentric**: They have difficulty perceiving things from another's point of view, and assume that everyone else sees, hears, and feels exactly as they do. For example, a three-year-old might try to "show" her grandparents her favorite toys when talking to them on the phone (without video), thinking that because she can see the toys her grandparents can see them too.

preoperational stage
Piaget's second stage of cognitive development, occurring between ages two and six, in which children can mentally represent, but not mentally operate, objects

conservation
the principle that quantity remains the same despite changes in shape

concrete operational stage
Piaget's third stage of cognitive development, occurring between ages six and twelve, in which children can perform mental operations as long as they have tangible (concrete) materials to work with

formal operational stage
Piaget's fourth and final stage of cognitive development, occurring at approximately age twelve, in which children should begin to demonstrate the ability to perform mental operations abstractly, without the aid of actual experience

egocentrism
a young child's difficulty perceiving things from another individual's point of view, resulting in the assumption that everyone else sees, hears, and feels exactly as he or she does

Though preschoolers may not be great at understanding how others perceive things, they are somewhat better at inferring what others are thinking and feeling, at least when the others are in front of them. Through understanding of facial expressions and body language, preschoolers are fairly good judges of when someone will share a toy they like, what made a peer upset, and who needs a hug. That said, they don't catch every nuance and won't differentiate between what you said and what you may have meant. When told he or she can't have more juice before emptying what's in his or her cup, a twenty-month-old might solve this problem by pouring the juice in the cup on the floor and then holding it out to get more juice. As a caregiver, you must now make the choice between rewarding creativity and problem-solving or becoming angry at the child for making a mess.

While Piaget felt that children's cognition develops in part through being around others, Russian psychologist Lev Vygotsky focused his studies on children's social environment over their physical world. Vygotsky theorized that much of cognition develops through experience with language and its use in social mentoring. Parents who say, "No, it's hot!" when pulling a child's hand away from the stove are giving the child words as a tool for self-control. Berk (1994) found that second graders who muttered to themselves when doing math problems grasped the next year's math concepts better. When parents and other adults interact with young children and provide them with the language to voice what they are learning, it builds a scaffold the children can use to step to higher levels of thinking (Renninger & Granott, 2005).

Almost 100 years after he began to study children's cognitive development, Piaget was named one of the most important people of the twentieth century by *Time* magazine. We still adhere to Piaget's sequence of stages, even if modern scientists see development as more continuous, and occurring earlier, than Piaget did. In fact, some researchers have proposed that we may be more cognitively advanced overall than Piaget believed from a very young age; we simply do not yet have the motor or language skills to express that knowledge (Carey & Spelke, 1996). Modern scientists also see formal logic as a smaller part of cognition than in Piaget's theory. Both Vygotsky and Piaget's works inform how we teach people today, particularly in formal educational settings. If a teacher had you talk through the steps of a problem out loud in math or build a barometer and observe it over several days in science, they were applying these scientists' theories. From both Piaget's and Vygotsky's work we have learned that children, especially young ones, are incapable of adult logic. This is illustrated in children standing between you and the TV and thinking you can still see it or jumping off a seesaw and being surprised when the person on the other end crashes to the ground. If our goal is to have the best possible interactions we can with children, then we will interact differently with them than we do with adults.

Social and Emotional Development

Human beings are social creatures. The bond they form with their caregivers is essential to the infants' survival (Bowlby, 1969, 1988). Infants know their mother's scent and sound before birth and can distinguish her face from others soon after (Ecklund-Flores, 1992; Hepper, 2005). They cry when hungry, wet, or cold, and they quickly learn to respond to caregiver efforts to fix these things with smiles, coos, and gurgles. Infants incorporate their sense of familiarity with caregivers into their developing schemas and, at about eight months of age, begin to exhibit distress when faced with people they can't assimilate into this caregiver schema (Kagan, 1984). This is known as **stranger anxiety,** and it usually sticks around until at least the preschool years.

The ability to form such a strong **attachment** to caregivers was once thought to be a survival skill linked only to getting nourishment and thus enhancing physical growth, but we now know that the attachment process is critical for cognitive and social development as well (Waters, Corcoran, & Anafarta, 2005). This was discovered, as many phenomena are, accidentally, while trying to learn something else. In the 1950s psychologists Harry and Margaret Harlow were conducting learning experiments with monkeys (if you remember from the research ethics section, researchers often have to use animals to conduct research that would not be possible with human participants). As part of their studies, the Harlows separated the infant monkeys from their mothers shortly after birth and raised them in individual sanitary cages. The Harlow lab provided the monkeys with blankets for warmth and softness and found that the infant monkeys became distressed when the blankets were removed for cleaning (Figure 5.3).

The Harlows, recognizing that this contradicted the idea that attachment occurs because of the association to nourishment, set up a study in which the monkeys were provided with two artificial mothers: one made of wire and wood that provided a feeding bottle and one made of the blanket. Even when feeding, the infant monkeys clearly preferred the blanket mother (Harlow, Harlow, & Suomi, 1971). Human babies also clearly prefer a similar arrangement; most like being wrapped in warmth, cuddled, and spoken to when feeding. Touch is a primary means by which infants and their caregivers communicate emotionally, and thus it is an important part of the attachment process. This understanding helps to explain why babies raised in some orphanages, where little contact is provided, are often delayed in their development.

stranger anxiety
anxiety born of an infant's inability to assimilate people (strangers) into the caregiver schema, beginning at approximately eight months of age

attachment
the association infants make between their caregiver, nourishment, and comfort; this process is integral to cognitive and social development

This critical bond between a baby and caregiver develops in part through responsiveness to the baby's sounds and expressions.

5.3 Attachment and touch
Touch is also very important in the attachment process. This is why a variety of animal babies get comfort from soft objects, such as blankets, particularly if they carry the caregiver's scent.

critical period
an optimal time period within which certain events need to take place to foster healthy development

imprint
a bonding process that occurs between certain birds and their perceived caretakers

Another important aspect of attachment is familiarity. For many animals, attachments based on familiarity form during a **critical period**—an optimal time period when certain events need to take place for healthy development. Konrad Lorenz (1937) explored this process with ducklings and found that birds **imprint** during this critical period, recognizing an individual as a parental caregiver. Lorenz showed that ducklings imprint best with their own kind (ducks), but will imprint on any moving individual seen shortly after hatching. By being present at the hatching of a clutch of chicks, Lorenz got the chicks to imprint on him as their parent. For a time after the imprinting, everywhere Lorenz walked he was followed by a parade of ducklings. While human babies do not imprint, they do attach to what they are familiar with. Repeated exposure correlates with fondness—this affinity is why very young children like to look at the same books, sing the same songs, and play the same games over and over.

Both nurturing contact and familiarity lead to an essential ingredient for healthy social development: a sense of safety. The attachment pattern babies experience with their caregivers is a blueprint for how they will perceive all human relationships. If babies experience consistent, nurturing contact with their caregivers, they will view human interaction as essentially positive and safe. (Consistency breeds familiarity.) As a result, even when they are alone, people with healthy attachment experiences generally do not feel lonely.

strange situation
an experiment conducted by Mary Ainsworth to systematically study attachment patterns in infants

secure attachment
when infants play happily and readily explore new environments in the presence of their mother

insecure attachment
when infants demonstrate behavior marked by anxiety, avoidance, or a combination of both in regard to relationships

temperament
personality characteristics that are made evident shortly after birth relating to emotional reactivity and intensity

Attachment patterns vary from one person to another (Ainsworth, 1973, 1989; De Wolff & van IJzendoorn, 1997). These variations are due to a variety of factors, including the child's temperament, culture, and caregiver characteristics. Mary Ainsworth was one of the first to study attachment patterns systematically, using the **strange situation** experiment. Ainsworth observed mother-infant pairs in their homes for the first six months of the infant's life. When the infant turned one, she observed the pairs in a laboratory playroom (the strange situation). Her research and subsequent studies demonstrate that about 60 percent of infants in American culture demonstrate **secure attachment**. In the presence of the mother, such infants play happily and readily explore the new environment. When the mother leaves, the child becomes distressed and seeks her out for comfort once she has returned. The other 40 percent or so of infants demonstrate some form of **insecure attachment**, marked by anxiety, avoidance, or a combination of both in regard to relationships. In the strange situation, such infants were less likely to explore their surroundings and responded to the mother's departure and return with either continued upset or indifference (Ainsworth, 1973, 1989; Kagan, 1995). Ainsworth and others have found that certain characteristics of the mothers contribute to the attachment pattern. Securely attached infants tend to have mothers who are sensitive and immediately responsive to their infant's expressed needs, while insecurely attached infants tend to have mothers who are responsive on the mother's schedule, not the infant's.

A mother's willingness to be responsive to her baby's needs can depend on the infant's temperament. Babies have evident personality characteristics, or **temperament**, even shortly after birth. Temperament, or emotional reactivity and intensity, is genetically influenced and, in turn, influences caregiver ability to be sensitive and responsive.

Some babies are easygoing, happy, relaxed and easy to settle, whereas others are difficult, irritable, intense in their emotional reactions, and hard to settle. A third category is known as slow-to-warm-up. These babies are calmer than those with difficult temperaments but more cautious than those with easygoing ones (Thomas & Chess, 1977). As you might guess, the easygoing babies are easier for caregivers to be sensitive and responsive to because they reciprocate more readily. The temperament or personality of the caregiver also plays a role, as temperament is something that, while modifiable, influences us throughout our lives. When mothers received personal training in sensitively responding to their temperamentally difficult infants, the rate of secure attachment increased (Stams, Juffer & van IJzendoorn, 2002)

In a small but significant number of cases, the attachment pattern, or lack thereof, is so unhealthy that it severely and negatively impacts a child's socioemotional development (Nelson, Furtado, Fox & Zeanah, 2009). Children can suffer significant abuse and neglect from parents due to anger issues, mental illness, and/or substance abuse. Sometimes children are removed from parents for these reasons, or abandoned by the parents due to their inability to care for them, and placed in a government system, such as foster care or an orphanage (this can be especially problematic in countries with population regulations, such as China or Romania under Nicolae Ceausescu). Such harsh environments can, but do not have to, result in lower intelligence scores and higher rates of emotional and behavioral problems (Nelson, et al., 2009). Many, but not all, abusive parents as well as convicted violent criminals report being abused and/or neglected as children. As previously stated, the brain is a use-dependent organ, and the parts of the brain that help us survive harsh environments are those that make us suspicious and reactive. Abused children exhibit heightened startle responses and decreased ability to calm aggressive impulses. However, if a harsh environment is not the only one a child knows, they can often overcome its negative effects. Even one supportive person in a child's life can build **resiliency**, the ability to overcome stress and trauma (Clancy, 2010; Masten, 2001).

resiliency
the ability to overcome stress and trauma

Self-Concept

The major social achievement of childhood is **self-concept**, preferably a positive one. Self-concept is the image we have of ourselves, consisting of the abilities we believe we have and how we perceive them (Baumeister, 1999). By about age twelve, which most developmental psychologists consider to be the end of childhood, most people have an understanding and assessment of who they are. Children can tell you, with words or actions, whether they see themselves as distinct, a boy or girl, smart or stupid, lovable or unlovable. Children's self-concept is important because it influences their behavior. Children who have a positive self-concept are more confident, independent, optimistic, assertive, and sociable (Myers-Walss, Hinkley, & Reid, 2015). So how do you raise a child who is securely attached and has a positive self-concept? It has already been noted that sensitivity and responsiveness on the part of primary caregivers leads to secure attachment. This is one of the building blocks of a positive self-concept because a securely attached child is one who feels safe exploring his or her environment. This,

self-concept
the image individuals have of themselves, consisting of the abilities we believe we have and how we perceive them

in turn, leads to a sense that he or she can successfully communicate with others and master the skills needed to get along in the world. Primary caregivers, whether biological parents or not, also influence a child's self-concept through how they parent.

Effects of Parenting Styles

parenting style
how caregivers impart beliefs and standards of behavior to their children

responsiveness
warmth, or to what extent parents respond to their children's needs and wants

demandingness
the extent to which parents expect obedience and responsible behavior, regardless of how their children may feel about it

Temperament and attachment are not the only factors that influence a child's personality development. How caregivers impart beliefs and behaviors, or their **parenting style**, plays a role as well. How and to what extent caregivers seek to control their children's values and behavior has been extensively researched. Parenting styles are delineated based on two aspects of parenting: responsiveness and demandingness. **Responsiveness** refers to warmth, or to what extent parents respond to their children's needs and wants. **Demandingness** refers to the extent to which parents expect obedience and responsible behavior, regardless of how their children may feel about it. There are three basic parenting styles according to Diana Baumrind (1971), represented in Table 5.1:

1. **Authoritarian** parents impose strict rules and expect absolute obedience.

2. **Permissive** parents often have few rules or are lax in imposing them and do not expect obedience.

3. **Authoritative** parents have rules and expect them to be followed. However, they explain why they have the rules, accept discussion, and are open to exceptions to those rules.

Table 5.1 Summary of Parenting Styles

	High expectations for self-control	Low expectations for self-control
High sensitivity	**Authoritative:** Respectful of child's opinions but maintains clear boundaries	**Permissive:** Indulgent, without discipline
Low sensitivity	**Authoritarian:** Strict disciplinarian	**Neglectful:** Emotionally uninvolved and does not set rules

A fourth style, uninvolved, was suggested after further research but is not discussed as much (Maccoby & Martin, 1983; Maccoby, 1992). Uninvolved parents impose few rules, show low responsiveness, and rarely communicate with their children. Basic needs, such as food, clothing, and shelter, are met most of the time, but these parents are generally detached from their children's lives. In a very "Goldilocks" sense, the first three styles have been referred to as too hard (authoritarian), too soft (permissive), and just right (authoritative).

Research indicates that authoritative parenting is indeed "just right"—parents using this style tend to produce children with the highest self-esteem, self-reliance, and social competence compared to children with parents in the other two categories (Baumrind, 1996; Buri, Louiselle, Misukanis, & Mueller, 1988; Coopersmith, 1967). Children raised by authoritarian parents tend to have less ability to function independently (particularly in ambiguous situations), fewer social skills, and lower self-esteem. Children of permissive parents tend to be more aggressive and less mature, the proverbial "spoiled brats." Some critics note that the majority of participants in parenting style studies are white middle-class families, and that effective parenting can vary by culture. However, studies have been done in more than 200 cultures around the world, and the results support the social and academic correlates of the authoritative parenting style (Rohner & Veneziano, 2001; Sorkhabi, 2005; Steinberg & Morris, 2001). The effects are even stronger when the authoritative families are embedded in authoritative communities, those that are connected and have adults who model caring and productivity (Commission on Children at Risk, 2003). However, if you remember from Chapter 1, correlation is not causation, so it cannot be said that a certain parenting style directly results in certain behaviors. As with attachment, children's traits can influence parenting. The amount of warmth and control parents exert has been shown to vary with the temperament of the child (Kendler, 1996). Further, some research indicates that parents and children can share genes that predispose social competence (South, et al., 2008). Finally, preferred parenting styles can vary depending on the values of those recommending them. Societies vary in how much they prize obedience or independence as characteristics for all members.

Concept Recall

1. What three main issues are of interest to developmental psychologists?
2. How does exposure to positive and negative external stimuli impact neonatal development?
3. What skills are babies born with, and how do these skills help them?
4. What physical and cognitive changes take place in infancy and childhood?

This Is Psychology

When attachment research began, stay-at-home mothers cared for most babies in our society, perpetuating the idea that secure attachment was best achieved when infants and young children were raised in this fashion. As times changed, more and more women entered the workforce due to both necessity and ambition. An increasing number of children, then, were cared for in daycare settings. Thus, researchers began exploring whether daycare disrupted attachment experiences. This is a very ethnocentric question to ask, as it is only in Western cultures that babies tend to be cared for by one or two caregivers. In other cultures, babies are cared for by multiple people, usually women, and they form multiple attachments (Whaley, et al., 2002). As long as the child's experience is characterized by warm, consistent, supportive interactions with adults and a healthy, safe, and stimulating environment, development will proceed as it should (Whetten, et al., 2009).

ADOLESCENCE AND EMERGING ADULTHOOD

Early in human history, children were often seen as merely small adults. It was thought that our personalities were set in the first few years of life. Further, in most early societies, children took on adult roles and responsibilities as soon as they were physically able. However, as developmental psychology evolved and took on a life-span approach, those views changed. Researchers began to look at a period of development referred to as **adolescence**—the years spent moving from childhood to adulthood. As this suggests, the teen years as you know them did not always exist. The "tween" years are even newer.

adolescence
the years spent moving from childhood to adulthood

Some consider adolescence to be an artificial construct. It starts with the onset of sexual maturity and ends with the achievement of independent adult status. Many cultures in the undeveloped world are like our early civilizations in terms of people taking on adult responsibilities in their early teens. Thus, for some, adolescence is fleeting if it exists at all. For others, particularly those in

While the path to physical and sexual maturity is the same for all adolescents, the end results in terms of height and width can be quite varied.

industrialized societies with postsecondary education available to many, it extends well into their twenties and tends to delay career, marriage, and parenthood as well. They are no longer teenagers but also are not fully independent adults. As many societies moved from being primarily agrarian to primarily urban, the skills needed to survive changed and required more formal education. Adolescents began putting off adult responsibilities until after high school, and now they put them off until after college or even graduate school. Because so many people from eighteen to their mid-twenties are in a more unsettled phase of life, a new term has been coined to describe these years: **emerging adulthood** (Arnett, 2004).

emerging adulthood
an unsettled phase of life occurring between ages eighteen to the mid-twenties

The American psychologist G. Stanley Hall, considered to be the father of adolescent psychology, believed that tension between the physical and cognitive changes and the social dependence (most teens in modern societies are still in the care of parents or other families) made for a period of "storm and stress" (Arnett, 1999). Social interaction with peers also contributes to this tension, as it becomes more complicated and often not that pleasant. Many adults view their adolescent years as a time they are glad to have behind them, having experienced the strain of trying to fit in with peers, being uncertain about the direction of their lives, and feeling alienated from their parents and/or other adults (Arnett, 1999; MacFarlane, 1964). Others look back on it more fondly, recalling a time of rewarding friendships, increased idealism, and excitement regarding the possibilities of life and future.

Physical Development

While the social construct of adolescence may be artificial, there is no denying that significant physical changes occur during this stage of life. The onset of adolescence is marked by **puberty**, the time when we mature sexually, or become capable of reproducing. Puberty follows a surge in hormones, which triggers a two-year period of rapid physical growth and change. This begins at about age eleven for most girls and about age thirteen for most boys, though the exact timing is influenced by physical, social, and environmental factors. One of the first changes seen is a rapid gain in height, more so in some than others, and this is when boys will, on average, become taller than girls. While the growth spurt is occurring in terms of height, the primary sex characteristics—external genitalia and reproductive organs—also develop dramatically. These changes are mostly internal, but the development of secondary sex characteristics—breasts and hips in girls, facial hair and deeper voices in boys, hair under arms and in the genital area for both—are visible. That surge of hormones that precedes puberty also leads many "tweens" to experience their first romantic and sexual feelings toward others (McClintock & Herdt, 1996). In the next chapter, we'll discuss further primary and secondary sex characteristics as well as the development of sexuality in humans.

puberty
the period of sexual maturation within which we become capable of sexual reproduction

The landmark event for girls entering puberty is **menarche**, or the first menstrual period, which occurs, on average, around age twelve. There is evidence that it can occur earlier for girls who have experienced stresses related to absence of a father or father figure, sexual abuse or insecure attachments (Belsky, Houts, & Fearon, 2010; Vigil, Geary, & Byrd-Craven, 2005; Zabin, Emerson, & Rowland, 2005). Historically, the onset age of menarche has dropped due to increased nutrition and better overall health, resulting in increased weight and body fat at earlier ages. Some researchers also attribute this phenomenon to increased hormone-mimicking chemicals in food and increased stress related to family disruption (Biro, et al., 2010). For boys, the landmark is **spermarche**, or the first time sperm is part of ejaculation, which usually occurs in the night. The feelings associated with both events tend to be a mixture of pride, excitement, embarrassment, and apprehension (Grief & Ulman, 1982; Woods, Dery, & Most, 1983). Educating tweens about these upcoming changes can alleviate the latter feelings to some extent and make this time a more positive experience (Fuller & Downs, 1990).

menarche
the first menstrual period, occurring, on average, around age twelve

spermarche
the first time sperm is part of ejaculation

These physical changes in adolescence, like earlier changes, do not vary in sequence but do vary in timing. Some girls start puberty as early as nine, and some boys as late as sixteen. Though these variations have only a small impact on ultimate physical development, they can have a large impact on psychological adjustment to adolescence. For boys, maturing early is a mixed bag. Boys who are stronger and more athletic in the early teen years tend to be more popular, confident, and independent. However, they are also more at risk for alcohol use, delinquency, and premature sexual activity (Conley & Rudolph, 2009; Copeland, et al., 2010; Lynne, et al., 2007). Unfortunately for girls, early puberty seems to be associated only with negative aspects, such as teasing, sexual harassment, and premature sexual activity (Mendle, et al., 2007).

So far, our discussion of physical changes associated with adolescence has discussed the changes that occur below the neck. However, the adolescent brain undergoes significant change as well. Before puberty, brain cells increase their connections; during adolescence, there is a pruning process in which neural connections are selectively eliminated. The connections in parts of the brain that are used flourish, while those that are not are lost (Blakemore, 2008). Remember the kind of nurturing discussed to promote secure attachment in infancy? A similar combination of structure, consistency, and affection is recommended in adolescence. While certain brain changes, such as growth of myelin speeding neurotransmission, result in improved judgment, impulse control, and long-term planning (Kuhn, 2006; Silveri, et al., 2006), others interrupt this progress. Especially in early adolescence, frontal lobe development lags behind limbic system development. The latter houses our emotions, and combined with the hormone surges, makes teenagers emotional and impulsive for a few rocky years. Adolescents can engage in behaviors that make adults exclaim, "What were you thinking?!" It's not that teens don't understand the risks of things such as substance use, fast driving, and unprotected sex; rather, in judging from their feelings, they see the short-term rewards as outweighing the long-term consequences (Reyna & Farley, 2006; Steinberg, 2007).

Cognitive Development

Given what's happening with their brains, it follows that adolescent cognitive functioning, especially in early adolescence, is self-centered and not particularly logical. Declarations such as "You just don't get how I feel!" and "I can't be seen in that—everyone will tease me!" demonstrate **adolescent egocentrism**. For adolescents, this concept involves two things: believing that their private experiences are unique and that others, especially their peers, are always directing their attention toward them. As they move through adolescence, however, most teens begin to think more logically and abstractly.

adolescent egocentrism
the belief that an adolescent's private experiences are unique and that others, especially their peers, are always directing their attention toward them

If and when adolescents reach Piaget's formal operational stage, they begin to apply their cognitive skills to the world around them. This takes them in both idealistic and cynical directions. Adolescents may think about the way things could be in many areas, including society, religion, and philosophy. They may be passionate about possibilities or frustrated by comparison of these possibilities to realities, as well as what they perceive to be the lack of sense in adult rules.

Moral Development

Children and adolescents apply their cognitive skills to moral situations as well. Among the central tasks of growing up are developing character and distinguishing right from wrong—**moral development**. Being a moral person involves both thinking and behavior, and like much in human development, this is thought to occur in stages. Lawrence Kohlberg, an American psychologist, proposed three levels of moral development: preconventional, conventional, and postconventional (Kohlberg, 1981, 1984). These stages make sense in light of Piaget's stages, beginning with a focus on the immediate environment and consequences and moving to a focus on abstract

moral development
the development of the capacity to distinguish between right and wrong

possibilities and justice. However, cognition is not the only player; emotions also influence our moral judgments. **Moral intuitions** are gut feelings that can drive decisions, such as a desire for vengeance when witnessing a deliberately harmful act or an urge to pay it forward after an act of kindness. We see evidence of moral intuition from research on moral paradoxes. Joshua D. Greene (2001) and others used brain imaging to observe people's emotional responses under two conditions. In both conditions, subjects had to decide whether to kill one person in order to save five. In the first condition, they could do this by flipping a switch that diverted a trolley from its current track headed toward five people onto another track where it would be headed toward one person. In the second condition, they could only save the five people by pushing a large stranger on the track to stop the trolley. Most people elected to kill one person to save five, but only in the second condition did the emotional area of their brains light up. In other words, while the subjects' moral decision was the same, they had a stronger emotional response when their choice directly caused a person's death (in the first condition, the person on the track could step off, but in the second condition the stranger was pushed directly in front of the trolley).

moral intuitions
gut feelings that can drive decisions

While cognition and emotion are important in moral development, the proof is in people's actions. Social influence is important here, too. The importance of all three areas is evident in the character education programs seen in schools today. Children, with guidance, will become more mature in their thinking, which leads to behavior that is less selfish and more caring (Krebs & Van Hesteren, 1994; Miller, et al., 1996). Such programs also encourage empathy for others' feelings and the discipline to manage impulses, or delay smaller, immediate gratifications now in order to get bigger rewards later. Children who learn delayed gratification tend to become more academically successful, socially responsible, and productive (Funder & Block, 1989; Mischel, et al., 1988). Results from evaluations of service-learning programs, in which adolescents tutor, assist the elderly, and clean up their neighborhoods, show that the teens who take part in service-learning have an increased sense of competence and desire to serve, as well as improved school attendance and completion (Piliavin, 2003).

Social Development

The physical and cognitive changes that take place in adolescence are bound to impact teens' relationships with others. One of the primary social tasks of adolescence is identity development. Children have some sense of who they are in relation to their families, but it is not until adolescence, if then, that they begin to think about their personal values and life path. In sticking with the stage perspective of development, Erik Erikson (1963) hypothesized that everyone goes through a series of psychosocial crises, or tasks, beginning with trust versus mistrust in infancy and progressing to integrity versus despair in old age. The task for adolescence, according to Erikson, is identity versus role confusion. Many teens explore a variety of roles, having different "selves" for different situations—the self at home with family, the self with friends, the self on social media. If more than one situation occurs at the same time, there can be discomfort, and the teen has to decide which self he or she wants to be. The resolution

identity
an individual's consistent sense of who they are

once a person unifies his or her various selves into a consistent sense of who he or she is, and with which he or she is comfortable, is an **identity**. This exploration is more prevalent in individualistic cultures, where independence and being your own person are valued.

We form both an individual and a group, or social, identity, the latter of which is often based on how we differ from others around us. When living in New Zealand, an American's accent and vocabulary are likely to make him or her much more aware of his or her American-ness (American and Kiwi English can be *very* different). Many adolescents spend a lot of time exploring how they are similar and different from those around them before settling on who they want to be. This can be seen in the different looks they adopt, music they listen to, and peers they hang out with, among other things. But not all teens do this. Erikson concluded that some adolescents settle on who they want to be early on, through adoption of their parents' values and expectations. This is more common in cultures that are collectivistic and traditional, as they tend to teach adolescents who they are rather than encouraging individual exploration. Regardless of a minimal or more extended identity exploration, most American teens (81 percent) develop a sense of contentment (Lyons, 2004).

Education is one factor that tends to extend identity exploration. In fact, some argue that this phenomenon occurs later, in emerging adulthood (Arnett, 2004) for many people, which will be discussed in more detail later. People who pursue a college education are more likely to be exposed to different ideas and ways of life. By their senior years, many college students have a clearer sense of self and more positive self-concept than in their freshman years (Waterman, 1988). College students who have a solid sense of identity are less prone to problems, such as alcohol abuse (Bishop, et al., 2005).

More than one nationwide study has indicated that young Americans' self-esteem falls during the early to middle teen years, and, for girls especially, depression scores often increase. This is not surprising, given the pressure from peers, new body consciousness, and a limbic system that works better than the frontal cortex. Luckily for many, self-image rebounds during the late teens and early twenties (Twenge & Campbell, 2001). Again, this makes sense, as adolescents have had time to adjust to the pressures of adolescence, helped along by increased agreeableness and emotional stability (Klimstra, et al., 2009).

intimacy
the ability to form emotionally close relationships, particularly of a romantic nature

According to Erikson, formation of an identity is followed by a developing capacity for **intimacy**, or the ability to form emotionally close relationships, particularly of a romantic nature. Two out of three seventeen-year-olds in North America report being, or having been, in a romantic relationship. This percentage is lower in more collectivistic countries, such as China (Li, et al., 2010). The importance of early attachment experiences shows up here; those teens who enjoyed (and continue to enjoy) close, supportive relationships with their family are more likely to also have similarly high-quality romantic relationships, or the ability to form emotionally close relationships, particularly of a romantic nature.

Parent and Peer Relationships

So how else do parents impact their adolescent children? For some teens, you wouldn't guess that they have a close, supportive relationship with their parents. In Western cultures, as adolescents seek to form their own identities, they begin to pull away from their parents (Shanahan, et al., 2007). The preschooler who wouldn't let mommy out of her sight, even to play with other children, becomes a fifteen-year-old who doesn't even want Mom to know where she is for hours at a time. The sweet, obedient child becomes an argumentative, rebellious teenager. Parent-child conflict tends to be greater with firstborn children and greater with mothers than fathers (Burke, et al., 2009; Shanahan, et al., 2007). For most families, the conflict, while unpleasant, eventually abates and does not lead to a serious breakdown in relationships (Steinberg & Morris, 2001). In a recent poll, most adolescents from around the world (6,000 of them) said they like their parents (Offer, et al., 1988).

As with romantic relationships, positive parent-teen relationships and positive peer relationships tend to coincide. High school girls who have affectionate relationships with their mothers tend to have more intimate friendships with their girlfriends (Gold & Yanof, 1985), and teens who feel close to their parents tend to be happy, healthy, and successful in school (Resnick, et al., 1997). Having a good parent-adolescent relationship does not necessarily mean that teens actually listen to their parents, especially over their peers. Much of the differences seen in temperament and personality can be attributed to heredity at any age. In adolescence, peers become a dominant source of influence. Most teens like to follow the crowd; they talk, dress, and act like their peers. This tendency has occurred for much of the last 100 years, but the advent of social media has added a new dimension. Instead of hours on the phone, teens now send, on average, more than 1,700 text messages per month (Steinhauer & Holson, 2008). Many teens become absorbed, even obsessed, with social networking. Online communication can stimulate disclosure about very personal details, which can be both positive (in the case of online support groups) and negative (in the case of online predators) (Valkenburg & Peter, 2009).

From the Desk of Dr. Stith

During and after natural disasters, parents need to help each child cope with their fears and anxieties in age-appropriate ways. Toddlers and preschoolers need comfort and constant reassurance that Mom and Dad will keep them safe. It is important at this age to provide lots of physical holding, such as hugs. Try to maintain as much of their routine as possible, especially at bedtime, when being scared can lead to nightmares and night terrors.

Young elementary-age children are sensitive and quickly sense anxiety and fears from not just their parents' words and behaviors, but also from TV and radio reports and the tension often reflected by reporters. At this age, parents have to be especially careful not to voice their own fears in front of the children. Parents should limit children's exposure to media reports of a disaster. Reassure them that you will protect them and that many other grown-ups are working to keep your family safe. It is additionally important to give simple and repeated explanations of what the disaster is. This age can exacerbate children's propensity toward fantasy when, in reality, the threat may not be near their family and they may not be in any imminent danger.

Older elementary and middle-school children are more vocal. They have more specific questions about the disaster and how safe their family is. Parents need to validate their feelings. Yes, they are afraid and anxious: Say, "It's OK to feel that way when scary things are happening." Talk about those fears, and plan for what needs to happen to help children feel less fearful. This age child needs to believe that parents have a plan for how the family will deal with both disaster and recovery.

Teens ping-pong from withdrawn detachment to panic attacks to helplessness to immediate impulses to do something dramatic to help. Parents need to include the teen in "family talk" with questions such as, "How are we going to plan?" "Who is going to do what?" "How to help younger siblings?" Teens, like adults, need to feel they have some control, no matter how slight, that they can hold onto. Listen to their anxiety and frustration. Explain that in a crisis everyone has lots of feelings and irritability. Apologize for your own irritability. Thank them for any patience or calmness they've shown. Enlisting the teen in the family plans for recovery or helping others recover reinforces a sense of control.

Randy C. Stith, PhD

Because a sense of belonging to a peer group is so important, those who feel excluded can suffer significant emotional pain and frustration. Most excluded students simply endure their teen years in silence, at risk for low self-esteem and depression (Steinberg & Morris, 2001). For others, the exclusion and bullying have led to suicide or violent actions toward their peers—the majority of school shooters list feelings of isolation and condemnation as the primary reasons behind their deadly choices. While adolescents may not heed their parents much when it comes to their friends, they do tend to listen in other areas, such as religion, politics, college, and career choices (*Emerging Trends,* 1997; Lyons, 2005).

So, for those societies in which it occurs, what makes emerging adulthood distinct from adolescence? In some respects, the difference is in the age at which some of the previously described changes take place. Late teen/early twentysomethings who live in developed societies and pursue postsecondary education are more likely to go through identity exploration (or continue it) at this stage than in adolescence (Arnett, 2004, Cote, 2006). They may also continue to focus on their needs and wants since they are not yet responsible for someone else. Arnett (2004) refers to this as the self-focused feature. One possibly distinct hallmark of this stage is what Arnett calls the instability feature. Education, career opportunities, desire for independence, and romantic relationships are all unstable aspects of emerging adults' lives as well as reasons they may move multiple times, starting with the move out of their family home (Goldscheider & Goldscheider, 1999). This is less likely to occur for people under eighteen because it is harder to move and live independently when you are not legally an adult. Breaks from university, job loss, and a fluctuating economy mean that many people in their twenties still live with their parents or have moved back in with them. Many readers are likely still on your parents' health insurance due to a change the US government made to accommodate this new developmental phase (Cohen, 2010).

Concept Recall

1. What are the different attachment types, and how do they impact later relationships?

2. What are the parenting styles, and how do children's traits relate to them?

3. How is adolescence defined, and what physical and cognitive changes mark this period?

4. How do parents and peers influence adolescents?

5. What is emerging adulthood?

ADULTHOOD

Psychologists used to view the years between adolescence and old age as one long plateau, where little really changed. They now view our development in areas: early adulthood (roughly twenties and thirties), middle adulthood (thirties to sixty-five), and late adulthood (after sixty-five) (Levinson, 1986). Late adulthood was not widely investigated until recently because most people didn't live that long. While adults may not vary as widely in physical, cognitive, and social development as between infancy and adolescence, we do vary.

The late teen and early adult years are our best in terms of physical development. Most of us have hit our full growth, and we are as strong and flexible as we will ever be. There is a reason that athletes have their greatest success in these years—it's rare to see a forty-year-old medal winner in the Olympics or a World Championship when their competition tends to be about twenty years old. There are exceptions, such as Dara Torres (swimming) and Bernard Lagat (track and field), proving that physical fitness is not exclusively tied to age. As we move into our forties, most of us find that we are not quite as fast or flexible as we used to be. However, nature is smart, and most people have enough physical strength and ability to do what they need to in middle adulthood.

Physical Changes in Middle Adulthood

That said, how able you are physically at any point in adulthood has a lot to do with exercise, health habits, and attitude. Very physically fit fifty-year-olds can complete triathlons, while very unfit twenty-five-year-olds can struggle to walk around the block.

Another physical change we see in middle adulthood is decreased reproductive ability. Fertility declines gradually, especially for women. A woman in her mid to late thirties is only half as likely to get pregnant after a single act of intercourse as a woman in her late teens to mid-twenties. This biological fact can lead to some difficult decisions for women wanting to finish their education and establish a career before starting a family. Women reach **menopause** as their menstrual cycles end, around age fifty, and thus are no longer able to bear children. It is rather ironic that people who are the least likely to be prepared for parenthood (teenagers) are the most likely to become pregnant. While the age range of men's fertility is generally greater, they too experience a decline in fertility through decreased sperm count, testosterone levels, and speed of erection as they age. As hormone levels decrease with age, so does sexual desire. That said, it doesn't end as soon as younger people often think it does. Several studies indicate that around 70 percent of adults forty and older are still sexually active and satisfied, some even in their eighties (Kontula & Haavio-Manila, 2009; Shick, et al., 2010; Wright, 2006).

menopause
the end of the menstrual cycle, resulting in the loss of the ability to bear children

Physical Changes in Later Adulthood

As life expectancy worldwide has increased (from forty-nine years of age in 1950 to sixty-nine years of age in 2010), we have begun to look at what it is like to grow old (PRB, 2010). This is an even more important question in developed countries, where more and more people live into their seventies and eighties. The current life expectancy in America is seventy-eight ("World Factbook,"). Some people consider this increased life expectancy to be humanity's greatest achievement—a real testament to improved ability to provide food, shelter, and good health care. With a decrease in the birthrate, this has significantly increased the aging population; today, one in ten people is sixty or older, and that number is expected to double by 2050 (United Nations, 2001).

Increased longevity does not necessarily equate with increased quality of life, though more people do get to enjoy retirement. No matter how many medical advancements we have made and how hard some people fight aging (vitamin water, anti-aging makeup, BOTOX®, surgery), we still age. Women fare better than men in this area, something that is true throughout the life span (Yin, 2007). Few of us live much past our eighties. The body ages, and its cells stop reproducing. We become more vulnerable to extremes in temperature as well as disease. What would be an inconveniencing injury or infection earlier in life becomes life-threatening in old age. As a developmental colleague of ours once said, "When we live longer, we live sicker." Physical effects of aging are exacerbated by smoking, obesity, negative emotions, and stress. Aging is enhanced by low stress, good health, and a positive outlook.

Although physical decline begins early in adulthood (that peak period is unfortunately short-lived), most people are not aware of it until later—middle age and beyond. Our sensory abilities lose acuity, so hills and stairs get steeper, words on the page or screen get smaller and blurrier, and people talk softer and mumble more. Visual sharpness diminishes, and our ability to perceive distance and adapt to light-level changes is less acute. Our muscle strength, reaction time, and stamina also diminish, as do our sense of hearing and smell. So, it makes sense that our basketball game and driving suffer from the ages of thirty to fifty, and our grandparents often ask us to turn on more lights or put on a sweater when it's eighty degrees.

Physical and Mental Health in Adulthood

Aging brings both good and bad news about health. As previously noted, older people are more susceptible to disease, infection, and injury because the immune system weakens. That's the bad news. The good news is that this same immune system has had a long time to accumulate antibodies, so people older than sixty-five are less susceptible to short-term ailments, such as colds and flu (National Center for Health Statistics, 1990).

While we may have a greater store of knowledge in older adulthood, cognitive processing ability changes. Through adolescence, our brains process information with greater and greater speed (Fry & Hale, 1996; Kail, 1991). Beginning in early adulthood and moving through old age, however, our neural processing slows, resulting in slower reaction time, decreased ability to solve perceptual puzzles, and poorer recall for names and other facts that used to come automatically (Bashore, et al., 1997; Verhaeghen & Salthouse, 1997). Processing speed isn't the only brain function we lose with age; we actually start to lose parts of our brains to atrophy, or wasting away (Schacter, 1996). We begin to lose brain cells gradually, beginning in early adulthood. By age eighty, this results in a brain-weight reduction of about 5 percent, or one and one-half ounces. This loss of mass leads to a decrease in abilities such as impulse control, as much of the loss is concentrated in the frontal lobes, the part of the brain that controls impulses when intact. As a result, the blunt and inappropriate things middle schoolers sometimes blurt out due to a still-developing brain can return in late adulthood due to a degenerating brain (von Hippel, 2007). Then again, perhaps older people are blunt simply because they have less patience and care less about the opinions of others.

There is some good news: physical exercise helps the brain stay limber just like it helps with muscle and bone strength, energy, and good health (Erickson, et al., 2010; Pereira, et al., 2007). Studies have found that older adults who participate in aerobic exercise programs demonstrate enhanced memory, sharpened judgment, and reduced risk of dementia (Nazimek, 2009). Mental exercise, in the form of reading, doing word and number puzzles, stimulating discussions, and even balancing your budget, is good as well. As we have discussed at various times in this chapter, the brain is a use-dependent organ: what we use, we keep; what we don't use, we lose.

Dementia and Alzheimer's disease

While most of us do not live into our nineties, most who do, do so with clear minds. Unfortunately, others suffer a substantial loss of brain cells that goes beyond the small, gradual losses described earlier. There are several negative factors, such as small strokes, brain tumors, disease, alcohol dependence, and heavy smoking, that can progressively damage the brain, causing **dementia** (Rusanen, et al., 2011), which is an umbrella term for symptoms of a degenerating brain, such as impaired thinking and memory (www.alzheimers.net). While many people think this is the same thing as **Alzheimer's disease**, it is not, though Alzheimer's does cause up to 70 percent of all dementia cases. Alzheimer's is a specific form of dementia that is irreversible and includes impaired thought, impaired speech, flat affect, and confusion. We know that in addition to a loss of brain cells, Alzheimer's involves deterioration of the neurons that produce the neurotransmitter acetylcholine, which is critical to memory (including memory of how to do things and events from our past) as well as thinking. While Alzheimer's can't be reversed, researchers are currently looking for drugs and procedures to delay its onset (Kolata, 2010; Stix, 2010). In the meantime, those mental and physical exercises for good health mentioned earlier are useful, as is including fat in your diet, as it helps preserve the myelin sheath that protects and speeds neural transmission. Working longer (into the sixties, not forever) has also been associated with better memory (Rohwedder & Willis, 2010).

dementia
an umbrella term for symptoms of a degenerating brain, such as impaired thinking and memory

Alzheimer's disease
a specific form of dementia that is irreversible and includes impaired thought, impaired speech, flat affect, and confusion

Cognitive Development in Adulthood

We have discussed a little bit about memory as it relates to other brain functions and degenerative conditions, particularly in older adulthood. However, developmental psychologists are interested in what happens to memory, along with other cognitive abilities, throughout adulthood.

Early adulthood is a peak time for some types of learning and remembering. Our frontal lobes are working well, so we have good impulse control and processing speed. It is a good time to learn facts, and we retain important events in memory quite well

(Pillemer, 1998). It makes sense, then, that we tend to remember events from this time in our lives best as we age (Conway, et al., 2005) and look back. We have a harder time encoding newer information as we get older. Nearly two thirds of people older than 40 say their memory is worse than it was ten years ago (KRC, 2001). In actuality, how well memory works in older people depends on the task; one experiment found that subjects showed less memory loss with a recognition task than with a recall task (Schonfield & Robertson, 1966). We have a harder time with prospective memory (remembering to do something), time-based tasks (dentist appointment at 2:00 p.m.), and habitual tasks (take medication at 9:00 a.m. and 3:00 p.m.) than with recognition (Einstein, et al., 1990, 1995, 1998). If older adults are smart, they utilize time management and reminder cues to help with this. Automating memory tasks may be the main reason many older adults learn to use a smartphone.

Regardless of our speed, memory quality also depends on the type of information we are trying to retrieve. We are more likely to remember things if they are meaningful to us, as we have more connections for this information in our memory networks. As you will see in Chapter 9, our memory stores recollections of facts and events in one system and things like skills on a different system. Memory for facts and events degrades faster than skill memory (Graf, 1990). Intelligence is also something that we do not necessarily lose due to age; it appears to be most affected by how close we are to death (Wilson, et al., 2007).

Social Development in Adulthood

There are many social and emotional changes that take place throughout adulthood, and many of these are due to the life events people experience. People are influenced by experiences, such as the first job they get, moving from their hometown, forming a long-term romantic relationship, having children, and losing loved ones. We have already discussed some of what happens in terms of social development in early adulthood when we looked at emerging adulthood. As people in much of the developed world enter their forties, they undergo a transition from early to middle adulthood. For some, this means a continuation of the life events they experienced in early adulthood (marriage, growing family, profession). For others, it can mean changes in these things. Some psychologists have argued that, due to realizing life is mostly behind them, many people experience a "midlife crisis." This is characterized by struggle, regret, and revisiting or trying things missed in youth. The stereotypical image is that of the forty-five-year-old male who gives up his wife, house, and minivan for a younger girlfriend and a red sports car. In fact, unhappiness, job or marital dissatisfaction, divorce, anxiety, and suicide are really no more common in middle adulthood than in other stages of adulthood (Mroczek & Kolarz, 1998). Divorce, for example, is most likely to occur among people in their twenties and suicide among those in their seventies and eighties.

For the one in four adults who do experience a midlife crisis, the trigger appears to be a major event, such as illness, divorce, or involuntary job loss, rather than age (Lachman, 2004). And, because we are living longer, many people in middle adulthood fit the "sandwich generation" mold: they are taking care of their aging parents as well as their growing children and sometimes grandchildren (Riley & Bowen, 2005). Life events will trigger transitions to new stages at a variety of ages. The **social clock**, or appropriate time to leave home, get a job, marry, have children, and retire, depends on the time and culture a person lives in (Neugarten, 1979). That clock will look very different for a young woman from a traditional Middle Eastern background than it will for a young man from a modern American background. In our culture in general, many people still follow the clock, but those who don't feel freer about being "late" or off schedule altogether.

social clock
the appropriate time, depending upon one's culture, to leave home, get a job, marry, have children, and retire

Adulthood's Commitments

Remember Erikson's tasks and psychosocial development from the adolescent section? Well, our task in adulthood is intimacy versus isolation. The other major task we deal with in adulthood, according to Erikson, is generativity, or being productive and supporting future generations. For most people, the task of intimacy involves finding a lifelong romantic partner. For others, it involves the development and nurturing of platonic relationships. For many people today, the stages of intimacy versus isolation and generativity versus stagnation overlap. In some societies, marriage precedes work and having children. In others, these tasks are accomplished simultaneously. Further, not everyone has their own children, but they can still contribute to the success of future generations.

Love and marriage

Love has been the subject of stories for thousands of years. However, it has not been the driving force behind marriage for that long (Illouz, 1997). It has only been in the last couple of hundred years that couples can marry for love, and not in all societies. Many marriages around the world are arranged, for political or property gain or to keep people in a certain economic or social class. That said, it is part of human nature to flirt, fall in love, and commit. This makes sense evolutionarily: parents who cooperate to nurture their children to maturity are more likely to pass on their genes.

Despite the historic and scientific aspects of love and marriage, today's media tends to give us the message that being in love means you meet, feel a strong attraction, and "live happily ever after." Think of any Disney princess movie, or Romeo and Juliet (although their "happily ever after" was quite short-lived). However, romantic bonds of love between adults are most likely to endure and be satisfying when the couple has similar interests and values, shares emotional and material support, and engages in intimate self-disclosure. In other words, the initial infatuation that the media often labels "love" is not enough. Couples who make some sort of legal commitment, whether marriage or civil union, are more likely to stay together longer (Balsam, et al., 2008). Age and education also play a role: couples who are well-educated and marry after age twenty are more likely to stay in a marriage. Over time, however, divorce rates have risen, partly due to lessened economic dependence for women and reduced social stigma for being divorced. Higher expectations also have an influence. Both men and women now expect a lot out of the romantic partner they choose: economic support, caregiving, friendship, and great sex—a lot to live up to.

Given the prevalence of divorce, many may wonder whether cohabitation is a good alternative to marriage. Apparently not, according to Jose, et al. (2010). In Europe, Canada, and America, those who cohabitate before marriage have higher rates of divorce. American children born to cohabiting parents are about five times more likely to see their parents separating than children born to married parents (Osborne, et al., 2007).

In spite of the current divorce rate (about half of all marriages in the United States and Canada), marriage remains a goal for most people (Bureau of the Census, 2007). Nine out of ten heterosexual adults marry worldwide, according to the United Nations. In addition, marriage is a predictor of happiness, sexual satisfaction, income, and physical and mental health (Scott, et al, 2010). Both heterosexual and lesbian couples report greater well-being than those who are single (Peplau & Fingerhut, 2007). Further, neighborhoods with high marriage rates tend to be associated with low rates of social pathologies, such as delinquency, emotional disorders among children, and crime (Myers & Scanzoni, 2005).

That said, being married is not the same thing as being happily married. And marriages that endure are not necessarily lacking in conflict. Some couples fight as enthusiastically

Cross-Cultural Case

Cultural Approaches to Child-Rearing and Development

The culturally accepted norms for raising children are as varied as the countries in which they are born. To Westerners, and Americans in particular, some practices can often seem outlandish and even neglectful. According to research compiled in NPR's "Parallels," "Argentine mothers let their kids stay up until all hours; Japanese parents let seven-year-olds ride the subway by themselves; and Danish parents leave their kids sleeping in a stroller on the curb while they go inside to shop or eat." While these practices tend to deal more with physical boundaries, some mothers in Kenya avoid looking their babies in the eye for more psychological reasons. Researchers report, for the Kisii people of Kenya, eye contact conveys power, and Kisii mothers do not want their babies feeling as though they are the ones in charge. As a result of this practice, researchers have found that Kisii children tend to seek attention less than children in many other cultures. Perhaps even more interesting, however, is a practice subscribed to by many Japanese and some Chinese mothers who train their babies to urinate at the sound of a whistle, thus removing the need for diapers sometimes before a child is even ten months old.

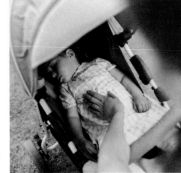

as they show affection, and some seldom fight or show affection. However, passion is not the key to a long-lasting marriage—positive communication is; successful couples demonstrate five times more instances of smiling, complimenting, touching, and laughing than of criticism, insults, and sarcasm (Gottman, 1994).

Parenting

Marriage, or at least love, often leads to children. For most people, most of the time, this is a happy life event. The statement, "I feel an overwhelming love for my children unlike anything I feel for anyone else," was endorsed by 93 percent of mothers in one survey (Erickson & Aird, 2005). Fathers often feel the same. That said, children cause sleep deprivation and worry, and they take lots of time and energy, which often puts a strain on marriages (Doss, et al., 2009). This observation may be especially true for mothers who work outside the home, as they often find that they still carry the bulk of the home and child responsibilities (Hochschild & Machung, 1989). Happy, healthy long-term relationships take work.

Employment

Historically, for most people, work was something done and chosen out of necessity. It is only recently that people have more of a range of choices in terms of career. For example, until the mid-twentieth century, women often had to choose between work and marriage, and their "acceptable" career choices were limited to nursing, teaching, and secretarial work. For a woman to run a business, be a doctor, or become a scientist was rare. Career has become a large part of one's identity for many. Think about the first questions asked when adults meet someone. After learning a person's name, the next question is almost invariably, "So what do you do?" Some of you reading this book may have a clear idea of how you will answer that question in five to ten years. Others may not, and that is normal, as is changing your mind about your major as well as your career later on. It can be difficult to choose a career path, particularly when the economy is bad, as the number and types of jobs are more limited. It can be difficult even in good economic times, due to being in a competitive field, not wanting to relocate, and/or trying to balance work and family.

If you talk to your parents or grandparents, they may describe getting a job straight out of high school or college and staying at it for their entire career. Presently, it is fairly common for people to have ten to twelve different jobs over the life of their careers, or to go back to school to change careers completely. So what sort of work is likely to be satisfying? Contrary to what some people believe, it does not have to be something you are passionate about every day. A job or career you enjoy is one that fits your interests, provides you with a sense of competence and accomplishment, and that you like more days than not (Gable, et al., 2006). People who enjoy their jobs also tend to have a balance with life outside of work—family and/or friends who appreciate them and their accomplishments.

Concept Recall

1. What changes occur in physical development and abilities throughout adulthood?

2. What Eriksonian stage of identity development is thought to occur during adulthood?

3. How do marriage and employment impact our development in adulthood?

This Is Psychology

We live in a world where many are immersed in technology for much of their lives. Televisions, computers, tablets, and cell phones surround us, all with access to the Internet. It has opened up a way to get a lot of information quickly and from many different sources. Online games and activities can also enhance teamwork and creativity (Patrick, 2015). Used wisely, technology is associated with better academic performance, and it certainly makes communication (and shopping) faster and easier. However, the habit many of us have of attending to multiple platforms on one device, or several devices at once, can negatively impact our cognitive development. While you might think this is multitasking, which is focused, productive, and efficient, it is not. Rather, the data gathering is superficial and fleeting, and it actually has a name—continuous partial attention (CPA). Some research has found that too much time engaged in CPA actually makes it more difficult to focus effectively and learn in a way that allows for generalization of new skills (Conley, 2011).

DEATH AND DYING

Death and dying in the twenty-first century look quite different than they did 100 years ago, particularly in industrialized nations. While death is something that people can face at any stage of life, it is a more frequent companion for most of us in older adulthood. We are older and more frail, and many of those we are closest to are also this way. As mentioned earlier, we live longer due to improvements in nutrition and living conditions. In addition, advances in medical care mean that people are more likely to survive illnesses and injuries. During the early 1900s, most deaths in America occurred at home, and many more children died due to infectious diseases ("Achievements in Public Health, 1900–1999: Control of Infectious Diseases"). Now, most deaths impact people over age seventy-five, and more than 70 percent of Americans die in either hospitals or nursing homes ("Not Acceptable!"). However, regardless of where a person dies, grief is soon to follow.

Grief and Coping With Loss

The severity of grief at a death depends on the person's age, whether the death was expected, and how the griever copes with loss in general. Reaction to death is tempered by understanding of it, and understanding is impacted by level of cognitive development. For a child who has not reached Piaget's concrete operational stage, death is not seen as permanent (Grollman, 1967). That said, young children do pick up on the emotions of others around them, and thus, most have an understanding that death is a sad event. Older children and adolescents understand the permanence of death but can have mixed emotions about it. The death of someone they love results in sadness and anger, but the thought of their own death is often met with fearlessness, disbelief, or even anticipation, in the case of suicide (Quadrel, Fischoff & Davis, 1993). By middle and late adulthood, most of us view death as something that will inevitably happen to us (Reker, Peacock & Wong, 1987). While the death of anyone you care about is hard, the death of one's child, particularly when that child is younger than eighteen, is one of the most difficult losses to bear (Li, et al., 2005). The emotional and role changes subsequent to the death of someone we love are known as **bereavement**. For some, bereavement involves several months of mourning and moderate to mild depression (Lehman, 1987). For others, coping with the loss can be difficult enough to warrant inpatient psychiatric care for a short time (Li, et al., 2005). Response to death also varies by culture: intense public displays of grief vs. stoicism, or a year of marked mourning versus a few weeks (Ott. et al., 2007).

bereavement
the emotional and role changes that occur following the death of a loved one

Even so, those who research grief hold that most of us go through a fairly predictable series of stages when we grieve (Kalish, 1985; Kubler-Ross, 1969, 1975). First, people tend to experience shock and denial, lasting two to three months. This stage is followed by a strong focus on keeping the memory of the deceased person alive, a phase that can last up to a year. The third stage, despair and depression, commonly involves confusion and anger. People in this stage may also exhibit seemingly irrational behaviors, such as making a distant move or traveling the world. In the case of terminal illness, bargaining for extra time is another phase that occurs. The final stage, recovery, occurs when people resolve their grief and demonstrate renewed interest in normal daily activities. In the case of terminal illness, the last stage is acceptance, rather than recovery, since by definition, recovery is not going to happen. As with other stage theories, the phases of grief have turned out to be more varied in fact than theory (Friedman & James, 2008).

Social support is a key element in successfully coping with loss (Baddeley & Singer, 2009), so letting others in and allowing them to help, even if only with their presence, is beneficial. For many, the support consists of family and friends, but others benefit from self-help groups and therapy (Neimeyer & Currier, 2009). **Palliative care** is a multidisciplinary support approach that has gained popularity as more people live longer and with more serious conditions (Lynn, 2004). It is similar to the more well-known hospice care, but hospice is provided for patients in cases when the condition is terminal. The palliative care movement is actually an application of humanistic psychology, as it emphasizes the dignity of the individual and the importance of a positive quality of life for the individual and family. Sometimes the person grieving will benefit the most by helping others rather than being the recipient of support (Brown, et al., 2008). And sometimes the most helpful thing is simply the passage of time and acceptance that life and love involve pain and loss as well as comfort and joy. If we can

palliative care
a multidisciplinary support approach to caring for people with serious illnesses, with the goal of improving quality of life for patient and family

achieve this sense of integrity, as Erikson (1963) called it, we will complete our cycle from the cradle to the grave with a sense of contentment.

Concept Recall

1. What physical changes take place during middle and late adulthood?
2. How do cognition and memory change with age?
3. How do social relationships change with age?

WELL-BEING ACROSS THE LIFE SPAN

You are somewhere along the developmental pathway outlined in this chapter. At whatever point you are in your life's journey, there are decisions to be made. Satisfaction with life changes as we age. Life situation and decisions can influence how much and in what direction these changes go. Much of how your life progresses depends on your personality, experience, and outlook as you age. That said, age does have a predictable impact on life satisfaction. A common question once people reach older adulthood is: "Would you live your life over if you could, and what would you change?" Musician Lyle Lovett's response to this was: "I wouldn't—that would be too much work!" Much more frequently, however, people respond that they would have made changes such as "taken my education more seriously and worked harder at it," or "I should have told my father I loved him," or "I regret that I never went to . . ." (Kinnier & Metha, 1989; Roese & Summerville, 2005). Recalling the balance between work and personal life, rarely do people say, "I wish I had worked more."

From adolescence to middle adulthood, most people experience a growing sense of identity, confidence, and self-esteem (Huang, 2010). As people move into older adulthood, more challenges arise: income shrinks due to voluntary or forced retirement, physical ability and energy decline, family and friends move away or die, and we move ever closer to death. Seems like a recipe for decreased life satisfaction, right? It does not have to be. For the majority of people, positive outlook increases as they move into older adulthood (Stone, et al., 2010). This rise may be due to increased emotional control and wisdom. Moods fluctuate with less frequency and intensity as we age (Urry & Gross, 2010). This manifests in less intense anger, stress, and worry as well as fewer problems in social relationships (Fingerman & Charles, 2010).

So it turns out that aging is not all bad. Brain scans of older adults show that the amygdala, the neuroprocessing center for emotions, responds less actively to negative events (but not positive ones), and interacts less with the hippocampus, the neuroprocessing center for memories (Mather, et al., 2004; St. Jacques, et al., 2010; Williams, et al., 2006). Further, at all ages, the bad feelings associated with negative events (unless the event was traumatic) fade faster than the good feelings associated with positive ones (Walker, et al., 2003). This contributes to the majority of older people's sense that life, on average, has been more good than bad.

We started this chapter asking you to think about the age at which people should be allowed to do certain things, like staying home alone. Now that you have studied the developmental life span, we ask you to consider these questions again. Are there specific ages that should be attached to different activities? To what degree should these restrictions be physiologically determined, and to what degree should social and cultural consideration be taken into account? With a better understanding of the complexities of development, you are better prepared to evaluate the complexities of making determinations about age-based abilities and restrictions, as well as how to develop educational and social programs that meet the needs of people at different points of their developmental journeys.

Review/Reflect/Write

REVIEW

- What are the three main issues explored by developmental psychologists?
- What factors can positively or negatively influence prenatal development?
- Describe each of the Piagetian stages of cognitive development in terms of age of occurrence and emerging abilities.
- How do attachment experiences with primary caregivers influence later relationships?
- How do each of the parenting styles influence ability to function as we enter adulthood?
- How do adolescent egocentrism and moral development change our thinking in adolescence?
- What influence do peer relationships have in adolescence?
- What unique challenges do we face in early adulthood?
- How does the aging brain impact cognition in middle and older adulthood?
- What impact does facing death have on older adults?

1. A mother is playing "peek-a-boo" with her baby. Every time she covers her face, the child becomes distraught. This is because the child has yet to develop

   a. a prefrontal cortex.
   b. fine motor skills.
   c. secure bonding with the mother.
   d. object permanence.

2. When Sara, who is four, calls every adult woman "Mama," this is _____. When she finally learns that not all adult women are her mother and do not go by that name, she will _____.

   a. assimilation; accommodate
   b. accommodation; assimilate
   c. accommodation; differentiate
   d. assimilation; differentiate

3. Erika's mom is very open, with rules she strongly enforces, but is flexible enough to talk to her daughter about why the rules are the way they are and is receptive to her daughter's thoughts and input. She is likely a(n) _____ parent.

   a. permissive
   b. authoritarian
   c. uninvolved
   d. authoritative

4. What is true of aging?

    a. Men tend to be healthier than women.

    b. Cells produce more rapidly.

    c. Low stress, good health, and positive thinking can help the aging process.

    d. Negative emotions and stress have no effect on aging.

5. What forms the blueprint for how infants will perceive human relationships in the future?

    a. attachment patterns

    b. sleep patterns

    c. who they imprint on

    d. their ability to problem-solve

6. How do we know it is unlikely that we have memories before the age of three?

    a. The average person reports that they cannot remember anything before the age of three.

    b. The brain has no need for memories that early.

    c. The brain does not develop the area that forms memories until after three years old.

    d. We don't know this. It is our best guess.

7. According to Erikson, which psychological crisis or 'task' is faced by adolescents?

    a. identity vs. role confusion

    b. trust vs. mistrust

    c. morality vs. guilt

    d. integrity vs. despair

8. Which is the correct order of Piaget's stages of development?

    a. sensorimotor, preoperational, formal operational, concrete operational

    b. sensorimotor, preoperational, concrete operational, formal operational

    c. preoperational, sensorimotor, formal operational, concrete operational

    d. preoperational, sensorimotor, concrete operational, formal operational

9. Which of these is NOT true regarding fetal development?

    a. Teratogens can have an epigenetic effect on an unborn child.

    b. The fetus's central nervous system is affected because of the bloodstream it shares with its mother.

    c. Stress is considered a teratogen.

    d. A fetus can recognize sounds, but the nature of the sound (loud, angry, soft, etc.) has no effect on prenatal development.

10. Which of the following is NOT one of the three overarching issues in human development and its research?

    a. Is our development more influenced by our genetic material or our environments after we're born?

    b. Does our development's critical period end after a certain age in childhood, or does it continue through adulthood?

    c. Does development occur in clearly defined stages, or is it a gradual and subjective process?

    d. Do the traits we exhibit early in life stay constant, or can they be changed throughout our lifetime?

Answer Key

1. d 2. a 3. d 4. c 5. a 6. c 7. a 8. b 9. d 10. b

REFLECT

1. Our brains are not capable of making long-term memories before the age of three. Why, then, do you think there is such a market for toys, games, and activities that promote brain development in infancy? Research "the first 1,000 days" and the similarity and divergence between sensory and emotional development. Discuss the value, in your opinion, of sensory experiences in infants.

2. Try to identify the parenting style your parents or other caregivers used when raising you. Did it have the predicted impact described in this chapter? Do you plan to use a similar parenting style, and why or why not?

WRITE

1. Attachment patterns presented here are largely a reflection of white Western values and practices. Choose a different culture, and investigate the types of attachment and its influence on later relationships. Are they similar to or different from what is typically presented in developmental psychology?

2. American culture places a high value on youth and often portrays aging as a decline in development. Investigate why culture—and often media—takes this perspective and why is it not always accurate. Interview adults of different ages; ask them about milestones throughout their lives. Reflect on their milestones and how development progresses and changes through the stages of adulthood.

Key Terms

accommodation   137
adolescence   146
adolescent egocentrism   148
Alzheimer's disease   155
assimilation   137
attachment   141
bereavement   161
cognition   137
concrete operational stage   139
conservation   139
critical period   142
demandingness   144
dementia   155
egocentrism   139
emerging adulthood   146
formal operational stage   139
identity   150
imprint   142
insecure attachment   142
intimacy   150
maturation   136

menarche   147
menopause   153
moral development   148
moral intuitions   149
object permanence   138
palliative care   161
parenting style   144
preoperational stage   139
puberty   147
resiliency   143
responsiveness   144
schemas   137
secure attachment   142
self-concept   143
sensorimotor stage   138
social clock   157
spermarche   147
strange situation   142
stranger anxiety   141
temperament   142
teratogens   135

6 Sexuality and Gender

After reading this chapter, you will be able to answer the following questions:
- How do biological sex and gender differ?
- How do biology and environment influence the development of gender roles and gender identity?
- How do individualism and collectivism influence gender roles?
- How do gender roles and gender typing influence our development in the following areas?
    - Biological Sex
    - Gender Roles and Gender Identity
    - Gender Role Development
    - Sexuality
    - Sexual Orientation

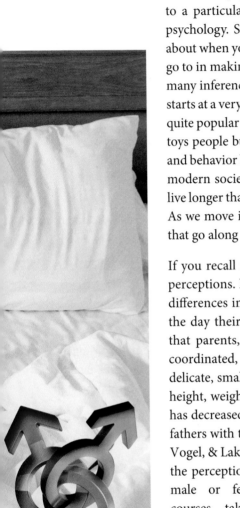

Thus far, this book has discussed the similarities among people, such as the ways in which we take in and manage information and how we develop physically, cognitively, and emotionally. However, we have yet to discuss the psychological aspects of what it means to identify yourself according to a particular gender. Gender is the most researched aspect of diversity in psychology. So why are sex and gender so important to our behavior? Think about when you first meet or hear about a person—one of the first categories you go to in making sense of them is whether they are male or female, and you make many inferences about them as a person based on this category. This distinction starts at a very early age. Gender-reveal announcements and parties have become quite popular in the last decade. From the decor of the nursery to the clothes and toys people buy for the baby, we have different expectations regarding interests and behavior based on whether that baby is identified as male or female. In many modern societies, including the United States, women outnumber and tend to live longer than men. However, the male gender has historically had more power. As we move into the twenty-first century, however, gender roles and the rights that go along with them are changing.

If you recall from Chapters 3 and 5, our expectations strongly influence our perceptions. Learning that a baby is a boy or girl almost automatically triggers differences in how we view that baby. In a classic study that surveyed parents the day their children were born, Jeffrey Rubin and colleagues (1974) found that parents, especially fathers, rated their newborn sons as stronger, better coordinated, and more alert, while newborn daughters were rated as more delicate, smaller, and softer. There were no actual discernible differences in the height, weight, or other physical characteristics of the babies. While this effect has decreased with time, less restrictive gender roles, and more involvement of fathers with their newborns, the stereotypical perceptions do persist (Karraker, Vogel, & Lake, 1995). In relation to gender, these stereotypes not only influence the perception of newborns, as above, but many expectations based on being male or female, such as courses taken in school, careers considered suitable, and activities participated in.

Female Primary Sex Characteristics

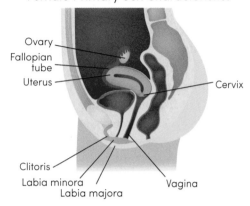

Mammary Gland

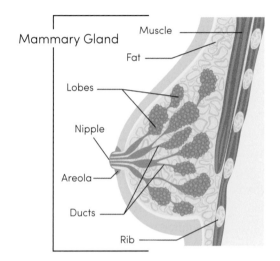

Male Primary Sex Characteristics

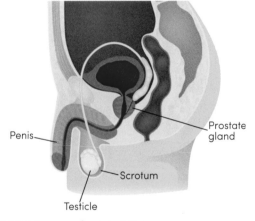

6.1 Primary sex characteristics
Females' primary sex characteristics are the vagina, uterus, ovaries (top image), and mammary glands (middle image). Males' primary sex characteristics are the penis, testicles, scrotum, and prostate gland (bottom image). These primary sex characteristics are directly involved in human reproduction.

BIOLOGICAL SEX

On a physical level, most of us are biologically male or female. Those who have the XX chromosome combination are biologically female, while those with the XY combination are biologically male. This is a person's **sex,** or the biological classification of a person based on genetic composition, anatomy, and hormones. Children themselves become aware of their biological sex around age two or three (Martin and Ruble, 2010). They are able to label themselves and others as either "boys" or "girls" and begin to demonstrate knowledge of culturally prescribed gender roles, which influence the clothes they wear, the toys they play with, the subjects they will study, and the careers they may choose.

Sex Characteristics

Anatomically, a person's biological sex is identifiable via their primary and secondary sex characteristics. **Primary sex characteristics** are present from birth, though many grow or change during puberty, while secondary characteristics develop during puberty. Primary sex characteristics are also directly involved in the reproductive process, while **secondary sex characteristics,** as their name suggests, play only a secondary role since they are not directly involved in human reproduction. Females' primary sex characteristics are the vagina, uterus, ovaries, and mammary glands, while males' are the penis, testicles, scrotum, and prostate glands, as referred to in Figure 6.1.

Though primary sex characteristics are fairly comparable from person to person, how we experience secondary sex characteristics can differ greatly. In most females, the development of secondary sex characteristics starts with a growth spurt that usually begins between the ages of ten and twelve and ends about one year after they complete their first menstrual cycle, known as menarche, usually around the age of twelve or thirteen. Following the growth spurt, increased estrogen levels cause females' breasts to enlarge and their mammary glands to develop the capacity to produce milk, while their hips widen to allow room for a fetus to pass between through the pelvic bones. Other changes include the growth of pubic hair and development of fat deposits on the buttocks and thighs.

For males, increased testosterone production leads to an increase in muscle, bone, and even vocal cord mass, as well as coarser skin. The growth spurt associated with puberty in both males and females begins about two years later for males, but it lasts much longer than that of females, usually resulting in a much greater accumulation of height. Chest, pubic, and facial hair begin to grow; the prostate begins to secrete, and testicles produce sperm.

sex
the biological classification of a person based on genetic composition, anatomy, and hormones

This Is Psychology

While most people who are intersex are born that way, for a very few, it happens shortly after birth. David Reimer (birth name Bruce) was a Canadian born in 1965. His penis was severely burned during a circumcision in infancy, leaving his parents with a significant dilemma—how to raise him when a key physical part of his being male was gone. They consulted John Money, a psychologist at Johns Hopkins University and a pioneer in the field of sexual development and gender identity, based on his work with intersex patients. Money believed that gender identity was essentially a blank slate at birth, developed primarily due to social learning, and thus could be changed with behavioral interventions. Because surgical techniques at the time could construct female genitalia but not male, Money recommended that Bruce's parents raise him as a girl, with accompanying physical changes made through hormonal and surgical intervention at appropriate ages. David's story was chronicled by John Colapinto in *As Nature Made Him: The Boy Who Was Raised as a Girl*. The experiment did not support Money's theory—biology had a much stronger pull than Money anticipated, and David ultimately assumed a male gender identity at age fourteen, after his father finally told him the truth. David later married and adopted his new wife's children. Sadly, he committed suicide at age thirty-eight.

primary sex characteristics
females' primary sex characteristics are the vagina, uterus, ovaries, and mammary glands, while males' are the penis, testicles, scrotum, and prostate gland

secondary sex characteristics
sexual organs and traits that develop at puberty and are not directly involved in human reproduction

Usually, we are born with either identifiably male or female sexual organs, but occasionally, infants' sexes can be ambiguous. Historically, such individuals were referred to as *hermaphrodites* after the Greek gods Hermes and Aphrodite's simultaneously male and female offspring. Recognizing that it is not possible for a human to be both fully male and female, physicians and scientists now refer to people born with ambiguous sexual organs as **intersexed** or intersexual, both of which mean, "between the sexes." People who are considered to be born intersex make up .05 to 1.7 percent of the population, depending on how the condition is defined. Historically, intersexed individuals had a gender and, in more extreme cases, sex characteristics assigned for them when very young. More recently, there is a push to require that intersex people be old enough to give informed consent to any medical interventions designed to alter their sex (www.unfe.org, 2015). Part of the impulse behind this movement is the growing recognition of the differences between physical sex and psychological gender, both within and outside the field of psychology. Indeed, a more common exception regarding sex and gender than intersexuality occurs when an individual identifies as the gender opposite of his or her body's biological sex. This is recognized as a psychological disorder, currently known as **gender dysphoria**. Since people with gender dysphoria will often will often perform and dress according to the gender with which they identify as opposed to their biological sex, people often mistakenly confuse the disorder with **gender nonconformity**, which refers to behaviors that don't match the gender norms

intersexed
people who are born with any of several variations in sex characteristics, including chromosomes, gonads, sex hormones, or genitals, that do not fit the typical definitions for male or female bodies

gender dysphoria
the condition of feeling one's emotional and psychological identity as male or female is different than one's biological sex

gender nonconformity
a phenomenon in which prepubescent children do not conform to expected gender-related sociological or psychological patterns or identify with the opposite sex/gender

or stereotypes of the gender assigned at birth. Though such behaviors were less socially acceptable in the recent past, an increasing number of people accept and understand gender nonconformity (also referred to as gender expansiveness or gender creativity) as merely one option along a nonbinary gender continuum (Ault & Brzuzy, 2009; Langer & Martin, 2004).

Concept Recall

1. What are the primary sex characteristics?
2. How do primary and secondary sex characteristics differ?
3. What does it mean for a person to be intersexed?
4. What's the difference between gender nonconformity and gender dysphoria?

gender
the psychological aspects associated with being male or female

gender role
consist of the attitudes, behaviors, rights, and responsibilities that societies typically associate with each sex

gender identity
the sense of being female or male

gender typing
the process of developing an identity through learned gender roles

GENDER

Though often used interchangeably, sex and gender are not the same. Generally speaking, most cultures hold the popular belief that men and women are very different beings, in terms not only of biology but also of thoughts, feelings, and behavior. If many of men's and women's psychological differences are based more on societal and cultural constructs than biology, what *does* give us our sense of gender? While the physical side of our sexuality, our sex, is made up of the physical characteristics that make us male or female, **gender** refers to the psychological aspects associated with being male or female. Gender affects both our cultural expectations and the development of our individual personalities and identities.

Gender Roles and Gender Identity

Two concepts associated with gender are **gender roles** and **gender identity**. Gender roles consist of the attitudes, behaviors, rights, and responsibilities that societies typically associate with each sex. These roles are not inherent, but are learned through a process referred to as **gender typing**. Gender identity, which is often influenced by gender roles, refers to the gender a person most closely relates to, or feels themselves to be, and is influenced by both biological sex and environmental expectations such as gender roles. Traditionally, gender roles and identity have been considered binary, or separately defined for men and women. One was either a masculine male or a feminine female. However, no matter how strict or lenient a given culture is with its gender roles, there have always been those whose identities and behaviors do not conform with their biological sexes. While many societies have met gender nonconformity with

The development of gender identity through gender typing begins as soon as birth, with hospitals placing pink hats on baby girls and blue hats on baby boys. Further, girls' parents tend to buy them "girl" toys, such as dolls and home-oriented items, whereas parents of boys tend to buy trucks and action figures.

homophobic attitudes and aggressive behavior, there have been exceptions throughout history. Many Native American tribes, for example, not only embraced those who experience gender differently than most, but they also developed roles and held places of honor within their societies specifically for those they described as the "Two-Spirit," or having the soul of both a man and a woman.

Cross-Cultural Case

Gender Across Cultures

The concept known as "gender binary" may seem like the obvious way to categorize sexes from a Western point of view, but a number of cultures worldwide recognize and specifically identify a third or more genders. For example, the indigenous Hawaiian society Kanaka Maoli maintained a multiple-gender tradition sacred to the dissemination of traditional education and rituals. Called māhū, these individuals were responsible for passing on tribal knowledge, were biologically female or male, and inhabited a societal gender role between or encompassing both masculine and feminine traits. In Indonesia, the Buginese people of the Sulawesi island identify four genders and a fifth "metagender" known as bissu. Unique to Buginese culture, bissu are neither male nor female and occupy an androgynous, all-encompassing space reflective of their societal role as wholly human holy people: mediums, sorcerers, or priests. In India, hijras are biological males who undertake "feminized" roles, which have significant social and historical influences. The process of becoming a hijra is physically and financially taxing, with aspiring hijras undergoing castration and other feminizing surgeries and paying hijra gurus for guidance into their new roles. Hijras are purposely present for a number of life events—such as weddings and births—as a means to provide good fortune and were once the guards of holy locations. Despite their importance to Indian culture, they faced discrimination from both Indians and incoming settlers. Hijras' livelihoods were threatened after British colonists passed a law classifying all eunuchs as criminals in 1897, forcing many into extreme financial insecurity, with the effects lasting until the beginning of the twenty-first century as high rates of prostitution and HIV existed among hijra populations. In 2014, the Supreme Court of India ruled that transgender people—including hijras—would be officially recognized under a "third gender" category.

Theories of Gender Role Development

As stated previously, the differences between the physical and psychological aspects of human sexuality become clearer as study of the subject continues; however, it is not possible to completely separate gender from biology. Rather, we need to recognize it as an influencing rather than a deciding factor in gender identity. In addition to the most obvious external differences between men's and women's genitals, there are also hormonal variations that can account for some of our differences in behaviors and desires. Furthermore, studies seem to indicate that exposure to diverse levels of certain hormones during fetal development can affect not only the development of sexual organs but also a person's behavior later in life (Berenbaum & Snyder, 1995; Money & Matthews, 1982; Money & Norman, 1987).

Though the extent to which biology operates on our formation of gender identity is debatable, there is no doubt that environment plays a key role in how humans eventually identify and experience their gender. Most cultures prescribe specific roles for each gender, and the pressure individuals feel to adhere to those roles can be immense. In Western societies, for example, men and boys are expected to be "masculine," subjugating emotion to physicality and preferring activities such as sports to the arts, while women and girls should be "feminine," engaging in such nurturing pastimes as playing house and pursuing motherhood. While children's parents tend to be the key influences on their gender typing, society and culture also play a large role. According to several studies, generally speaking, Western societies that value individuality over collectivism are becoming more nontraditional in their considerations of gender roles, especially where women are concerned. On the other hand, societies that view family and other social ties as more important than individuality and individual achievement tend to be more traditional in their adherence to, and expectation of adherence to, gender roles for both men and women (Forbes et al., 2009; Gibbon et al., 1991; Shafiro et al., 2003). These studies find that the United States, rather than being the progressive, nontraditional country many think it is, falls firmly in the middle of the spectrum between traditional and nontraditional in its peoples' beliefs regarding appropriate behavior for men and women.

Psychodynamic theory

psychodynamic theory of sexuality
suggests children learn gender identity through reconciliation of their own sexual attraction to the opposite-sex parent

It is clear that both biology and environment play a role in the development of gender roles and identity, but there are varying theories regarding how gender roles develop. Early psychologists, such as Sigmund Freud, posited that since children cannot really compete for sexual attention from the opposite-sex parent, they settle for the attention that comes from identifying with the same-sex parent, which is a much more appropriate route from a societal point of view. This **psychodynamic theory of sexuality** essentially suggests children learn gender identity through reconciliation of their own sexual attraction to the opposite-sex parent. More modern theorists, however, shift their focus from the drives and forces within a person, which is the basis for psychodynamic psychology, to cognitive development and learning to identify possible explanations and processes for developing gender roles, behavior, and identity.

Social learning theory

social learning theory
Albert Bandura's theory that suggests that gender roles are learned from the adults who care for us

Contrasting Freud and earlier theories of psychological development, Albert Bandura's **social learning theory**, suggests that gender roles are learned from the adults who care for us. Generally speaking, Bandura's social learning theory argues that behavior is attained from the environment through observational learning and response to stimuli. In other words, children watch people such as their parents and family (models) and "encode" or learn their behavior, which they later imitate or copy. Repetition of this copied behavior will depend on whether it is reinforced or punished. If the child copies the model and is rewarded for its behavior, the behavior will be reinforced and eventually learned; if the child is punished or ignored, Bandura's theory suggests the child will eventually stop copying the model's behavior. So, according to social learning theory, if children are raised by caregivers who demonstrate and reinforce clear divisions between acceptable male and female behaviors, and the children are rewarded when they copy these behaviors, they tend to adopt clearer, and often more traditional, gender roles. If we subscribe to this theory, it follows, then, that if children are raised by caregivers who exhibit nontraditional or nonconforming gender roles, and they are rewarded when they copy those behaviors (or at least not punished or ignored), they will also likely follow suit. It is not just caregivers who influence children's ideas of gender, though. Children are exposed to male and female gender role models on television, in movies, and in other media from a very young age. As a result, in many societies, how characters in such entertainments are allowed to act and what types of entertainment children are allowed to experience are closely monitored and censored. Societies and cultures vary in terms of how clear boundaries are between what is acceptably masculine and feminine, as well as how easily boys and girls can cross that line without disapproval from others.

Cognitive development theory

Lawrence Kohlberg (1966) added a more reflective element to social learning theory, thus **cognitive developmental theory** suggests that children make a conscious decision about their gender identity before they select models from whom to learn their "gendered" behaviors. In other words, once children decide they identify with a particular gender ("I am a boy"), they actively figure out what that means in terms of their behavior, rather than merely reacting to cues from their environment. Kohlberg postulates a three-stage process in which children first identify their basic biological sex around age three, then realize their sex will remain stable over time (boys become men and girls become women), and finally realize that their sex remains constant regardless of changes in activity or appearance (a boy will be a boy even if he's wearing a dress). At this final stage of "gender consistency," children become highly motivated to make their behavior consistent with that of others whom they identify as of their own gender.

cognitive development theory suggests that children make a conscious decision about their gender identity before they select models from whom to learn their "gendered" behaviors

Gender schema theory

A fourth approach to explaining the development of gender roles is **gender schema theory**. This approach, put forth by Dr. Sandra Bem (1981), combines elements of social learning and cognitive developmental theories. If you recall from Chapter 5, a schema is a learned map, or structure, that guides perceptions, memory, and inferences. Bem suggests that children develop schemas or mental patterns of masculine and feminine characteristics, roles, and activities from their experiences in society, and the schemas in turn influence how they interpret and act on new information regarding gender.

gender schema theory suggests that children develop schemas, or mental patterns, of masculine and feminine characteristics, roles, and activities from their experiences in society, and the schemas in turn influence how they interpret and act on new information regarding gender

Once the schemas for "boy" and "girl" are developed, children identify themselves as one or the other and will identify others who also fit that schema and imitate their behavior.

Concept Recall

1. Describe how gender typing relates to gender identity and gender roles.
2. What are some factors that influence gender identity?
3. What theory of sexual identity development suggests that gender roles are learned from adult caretakers?
4. What is gender schema theory?

SEXUALITY

The idea that gender roles are based on actual differences between men and women has lost some ground in recent years. According to Dr. Janet Hyde's (2005) gender similarities hypothesis, whether a person is male or female makes little to no difference on most psychological variables. Only a few differences were evident: compared with women, men could throw farther, were more physically aggressive, masturbated more, and held more positive attitudes regarding sex in uncommitted relationships. This last observation leads into a related area where being male or female has a great deal of influence—sexuality.

sexuality
sexual feelings and attractions to other people

While the difference of one sex chromosome makes most human beings either biologically male or female, all humans experience sexual feelings and attractions to other people, or **sexuality**, to some degree. That said, men and women as a whole differ in their sexual behaviors. Evolutionary psychologists hypothesize that this disparity is due to the different adaptive challenges men and women face in terms of keeping their genes in the pool (Schmitt, 2005). Men aim to have sex with many women because it increases the likelihood of more offspring. Women aim to have sex with a man who will be a good provider because it increases the chances of the offspring they have with that man surviving.

However, the biological drive to continue our family line is not the only driving force behind being sexual—or the differences in how men and women behave sexually. All animals engage in some sort of sexual behavior to procreate, but humans are unique in wanting to engage in sexual behavior purely for pleasure. While Freud has been criticized for placing so much emphasis on the role of sexual drives in our personality development and abnormal behavior, it is hard to argue that sexuality does not influence many areas of our lives. Think about the advertisements we see for clothes, perfumes, and vacations. Many, if not most, use sex or the potential to be viewed as sexually attractive as a motive for purchasing a product. And the most popular issue of *Sports Illustrated* each year has very little to do with sports. Instead, it's the swimsuit issue.

However, how we express our sexuality and our interest in having sex has a great deal to do with gender roles. As with so many other activities stereotypically associated with gender, society enforces a "right" way of behaving sexually for both men and women. As with all stereotypes, in addition to limiting both men and women, these stereotypes ignore that there are a variety of avenues when it comes to sexual attraction, not just being attracted to the opposite sex.

Human Sexual Behavior

As with so much having to do with sex and sexuality in humans, while there are similarities across populations and between people, there are also a number of differences. Prior to Dr. William H. Masters and Virginia Johnson's (1966) foundational study of human sexual arousal, our understandings of the human body's reactions to sexual stimuli and the process of arousal and intercourse itself were fairly vague. Their study outlines **four stages of sexual arousal**, which appear to be very similar between men and women: excitement, plateau, orgasm, resolution.

four stages of arousal
excitement, plateau, orgasm, resolution

During the excitement phase, both males and females experience an increase in heart rate, breathing rate, and blood pressure as well as vasocongestion, or flush of the skin, and hardened nipples. For males, the penis becomes erect, the skin of the scrotum tightens, and the testicles pull up; for females the lips of the vagina open, the walls of the vagina secrete lubricating liquid in preparation for intercourse, and the clitoris swells. The causes of excitement and arousal and the length of time the excitement phase lasts differ from person to person, but the effects are the same.

As we transition from excitement to plateau, many of the effects that began in the first phase continue. Both sexes experience an increase in circulation, heart rate, and respiration. In females, the clitoris becomes extremely sensitive and withdraws slightly into the clitoral hood, while the tissues of the outer third of the vagina swell. In males, the urethral sphincter contracts, preventing urine from escaping during ejaculation, and they may secrete pre-ejaculatory fluid.

Orgasm concludes the plateau phase, and it is the shortest of the four phases. For both males and females orgasm consists of cycles of rhythmic muscle contractions in the lower pelvic muscles, while women also experience contractions of the uterus and vagina. In males, the orgasmic muscle contractions trigger ejaculation. Females tend to take longer reaching orgasm than males; however, orgasm can occur multiple times for females, while men typically experience only one.

Following orgasm, both females and males transition into resolution, the final phase of the sexual arousal cycle, in which the body returns to normal activity. The heart rate, circulation, respiration, and blood pressure return to normal levels. In females, the clitoris retracts and vaginal lips close, while men lose their erections as their testicles descend. While females retain the ability to repeat the arousal cycle immediately, males experience a refractory period, during which they cannot achieve another erection and therefore cannot repeat the arousal cycle for anywhere from several minutes to hours.

As this brief description makes clear, men and women experience many of the same sensations during the arousal cycle, though they experience them very differently. Furthermore, recent research seems to suggest more differences between male and female arousal than previously recognized (Nuwer, 2016; Levin, 2008; and Chivers & Bailey, 2005). However, Masters and Johnson's study remains a cornerstone physiological study and categorization of humans' response to sexual arousal. Even before Masters and Johnson began their research, others had begun studying sexual behavior in and of itself in an effort to better understand the myriad ways humans engage in and define sexual intercourse and attraction. As a result, we came to understand human sexuality not as binary but as a spectrum.

Sexual Behavior and Orientation

In 1947, Alfred Kinsey founded the Institute for Sex Research (ISR), now known as the Kinsey Institute for Research in Sex, Gender, and Reproduction. Though he published multiple works in sexology, Kinsey is best known for *Sexual Behavior in the Human Male* (Kinsey, et al., 1948) and the later *Sexual Behavior in the Human Female* (Kinsey, et al., 1953). Together, these volumes are known as the Kinsey Reports. Kinsey's research laid the foundations for further exploration into both male and female sexuality and dispelled a number of myths previously associated with female sexuality, arousal, and specifically orgasms. As part of their conclusions, Kinsey and his colleagues postulate what would become known as the **Kinsey Scale** (Kinsey, et al., 1948), a spectrum upon which one can measure human sexuality. The scale, which ranges from 0 to 6, where 0 is heterosexual and 6 is homosexual provided the first nonbinary measurement of sexual orientation (a rating of X was later added indicating "no socio-sexual contacts or reactions). See Figure 6.2.

Alfred Kinsey

Kinsey Scale
a spectrum upon which one can measure human sexuality

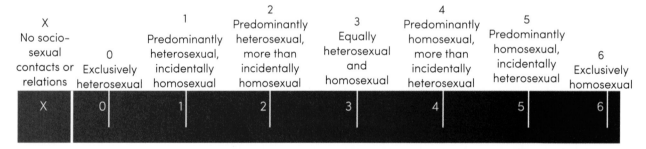

X No socio-sexual contacts or relations	0 Exclusively heterosexual	1 Predominantly heterosexual, incidentally homosexual	2 Predominantly heterosexual, more than incidentally homosexual	3 Equally heterosexual and homosexual	4 Predominantly homosexual, more than incidentally heterosexual	5 Predominantly homosexual, incidentally heterosexual	6 Exclusively homosexual
X	0	1	2	3	4	5	6

6.2 Kinsey Scale
Alfred Kinsey created what is known as the Kinsey Scale, which is a spectrum on which to measure human sexuality. 0 represents exclusively heterosexual, and 6 represents exclusively homosexual. Often, before 0, X will be included to represent asexuality.

sexual orientation
pattern of emotional, romantic, and sexual attraction to others; is part of our sexuality

heterosexuality
sexual attraction to the opposite sex

Sexual orientation, or a pattern of emotional, romantic, and sexual attraction to others, is part of our sexuality. The factors that attract us to someone sexually tend to be a varying combination of physiological arousal and emotional connection. While **heterosexuality**—sexual attraction to the opposite sex—is the most common orientation, it is not the only one. Other sexual orientations include, but are not limited to, **homosexuality** (attraction to the same sex), **bisexuality** (attraction to both men and women), and **pansexuality** (attraction to people regardless of sex, gender, or gender identity). Though terms and definitions change frequently, individuals who place their sexual orientation on the Kinsey Scale anywhere other than zero often identify with the LGBTQIA+ community. Though it is certainly not exhaustive, Figure 6.3 on page 178 contains additional descriptions of various sexual orientations. Estimates vary on the prevalence of the different orientations. This is due to many factors, including differences in how the data was gathered, as well as variations in the perception of homosexuality. One recent study noted that people predominantly attracted to members of the same sex comprise less than 5 percent of respondents in most Western surveys (Bailey, et al., 2016). US rates hover around 1–3 percent who identify as gay, lesbian, bisexual, or "something else." Statistically speaking, then, heterosexuality would seem to be the most common sexual identification, but due to the prejudice, discrimination, and mistreatment so often faced by those who identify as anything other than heterosexual, it is impossible to know how reliable such statistics actually are.

Male and female nonheterosexual orientations differ in some respects. Men are more likely to report an exclusively same-sex orientation, whereas women show the opposite pattern. Men's sexual orientations tend to be closely linked to their pattern of sexual arousal to differing erotic stimuli. Women are more likely to experience same-sex attraction in the context of close affectionate, or emotional, relationships. This pattern holds for heterosexual men and women as well, though remember, there are always exceptions.

Development of sexual orientation

So how does someone's sexual orientation come about? This question is asked much more often for people who are not heterosexual, in part because in spite of advances in acceptance, many still consider any orientation but heterosexual to be abnormal. While nonheterosexuality is certainly less prevalent than heterosexuality, prevailing scientific evidence suggests it is merely a less common part of the continuum of sexuality. There is no causal theory of how sexual orientation develops that has gained widespread support, but there do seem to be some fairly clear correlations. Before detailing these, one important thing to keep in mind is that sexual orientation is different from sexual behavior. As we will discuss in Chapter 9, people's behavior is not always consistent with their personality; people may engage in sexual acts with individuals that do not fit their typical orientations.

According to Bailey, et al. (2016) sexual orientation tends to be influenced by how conforming a person is to expected gender roles. Male and female nonheterosexuality tends to be preceded by gender nonconformity in childhood. In other words, a pattern of behavior that resembles that of the opposite sex. This pattern often emerges at an early age, in spite of conventional gender socialization, and is seen across cultures. Moderate genetic influences are suggested by a higher frequency of a particular orientation in twin studies, and the finding, discussed in This Is Psychology, that when infant boys are surgically and socially altered to be girls, their eventual sexual orientation is unchanged.

homosexuality
attraction to the same sex

bisexuality
attraction to both men and women

pansexuality
attraction to people regardless of sex, gender, or gender identity

Ally
(noun) – A person who supports and stands up for the rights of LGBTQIA+ people.

Asexual
(adj.) – Describes a person who experiences little or no sexual attraction to others.

Bisexual
(adj.) – A sexual orientation that describes a person who is emotionally and sexually attracted to people of their own gender and people of other genders.

Cisgender
(adj.) – a person whose gender identity and assigned sex at birth correspond (i.e., a person who is not transgender).

Gay
(adj.) – A sexual orientation that describes a person who is emotionally and sexually attracted to people of their own gender. It can be used regardless of gender identity but is more commonly used to describe men.

Gender fluid
(adj.) – Describes a person whose gender identity is not fixed. A person who is gender fluid may always feel like a mix of the two traditional genders but may feel more one gender some days and another gender other days.

Heteronormativity
(noun) – The assumption that everyone is heterosexual and that heterosexuality is superior to all other sexualities.

Intersex
(noun) – A term referring to someone whose anatomy or genetics at birth do not correspond to the typical expectations for either biological sex.

Lesbian
(adj., noun) – A sexual orientation that describes a woman who is emotionally and sexually attracted to other women.

Transgender
(adj.) – Describes a person whose gender identity and assigned sex at birth do not correspond. Also used as an umbrella term to include gender identities outside of male and female. Sometimes abbreviated as "trans."

Queer
(adj.) – An umbrella term used by some to describe people who think of their sexual orientation or gender identity as outside of societal norms. Some people view the term "queer" as more fluid and inclusive than traditional categories for sexual orientation and gender identity. Due to its history as a derogatory term, the word "queer," is not embraced by all members of the LGBTQIA+ community.

Questioning
(adj.) – Describes an individual who is unsure about or is exploring their own sexual orientation and/or gender identity.

Intersectionality
(noun) – the idea that identities are influenced and shaped by race, class, ethnicity, sexuality/sexual orientation, gender/gender identity, physical disability, national origin, etc., as well as by the interconnection of all of those characteristics.

6.1 The National LGBT Health Education Center Glossary
The National LGBT Health Education Center (2016) provides a useful glossary of terms to help us understand the spectrum of sexual orientation and many of the key issues being dealt with in LGBTQIA+ communities around the world. Generally speaking, the acronym is agreed to stand for lesbian, gay, bisexual, transgender, queer/questioning, intersex, and either asexual or allies. This figure features definitions for these and some of the other more common terms you may encounter or may have heard.

This Is Psychology

The *TIME* Magazine person of the year for 2017 was not just one person; it was a large group of women and men dubbed "The Silence Breakers." In October of 2017, *The New York Times* reported that more than a dozen women had come forward accusing American movie producer Harvey Weinstein of sexual harassment, assault, or rape. As a result, Weinstein was fired from his own production company, removed from the Academy of Motion Picture Arts and Sciences, and resigned from the Directors Guild of America. The women who came forward against Weinstein catalyzed the #MeToo campaign, which encouraged people to speak out about their own experiences with sexual harassment, spurring a national movement to call out abusers in many circles, particularly in Hollywood. In the months that followed Weinstein's initial allegations, countless women and men shared their stories using the #MeToo hashtag on social media.

While sexual harassment is most often perpetrated by a male toward a female, it can occur between any two people. There are three dimensions of sexual harassment: gender harassment, unwanted sexual attention, and sexual coercion (Gelfand, Fitzgerald, & Drasgow, 1995). Gender harassment consists of verbal and nonverbal behaviors that are usually not aimed at gaining sexual cooperation. Rather, they communicate hostile, insulting, and degrading attitudes about the object of the harassment. Slurs, taunts, gestures, displays of sexually explicit material, and threatening or intimidating acts are types of gender harassment. Unwanted sexual attention ranges from repeated, unreciprocated requests for dates and intrusive letters, texts or calls, to unwanted touching and even physical assault. The third dimension, sexual coercion, is *quid pro quo* harassment: the perpetrator makes some job or academic-related benefit dependent upon sexual cooperation. The Weinstein accusers described sexual coercion as the main type of abuse they suffered in the hopes of securing roles or advancing their careers.

Sexual harassment has long been widespread in occurrence but was quite limited in terms of public recognition until #MeToo emerged. More recently, universities and military communities have implemented Green Dot training—bystander intervention strategies founded by Dr. Dorothy Edwards—to curtail the frequent sexual harassment incidents that can occur in those environments. Despite increased education efforts, rates of having experienced sexual harassment range from 29 to over 50 percent for American adults and adolescents, depending on study and particular behaviors surveyed.

According to the Centers for Disease Control and Prevention (CDC), lesbian, gay and bisexual people experience sexual violence at similar or higher rates than heterosexuals, and approximately half of transgender people and bisexual women will experience sexual violence at some point in their lifetimes. The National Intimate Partner and Sexual Violence Survey—conducted by the CDC—reported the following statistics:

- 44 percent of lesbians and 61 percent of bisexual women experience rape, physical violence, or stalking by an intimate partner, compared to 35 percent of heterosexual women

- 26 percent of gay men and 37 percent of bisexual men experience rape, physical violence, or stalking by an intimate partner, compared to 29 percent of heterosexual men

- 46 percent of bisexual women have been raped, compared to 17 percent of heterosexual women and 13 percent of lesbians

- 22 percent of bisexual women have been raped by an intimate partner, compared to 9 percent of heterosexual women

- 40 percent of gay men and 47 percent of bisexual men have experienced sexual violence other than rape, compared to 21 percent of heterosexual men

sexual dysfunction
difficulty experienced by an individual or a couple during any stage of normal sexual activity, including physical pleasure, desire, preference, arousal or orgasm

paraphilias
a person who can only experience arousal and fulfillment via behaviors generally considered to be socially unacceptable

sexually transmitted infections (STI)
can be a consequence of unprotected sexual contact

pelvic inflammatory disease (PID)
an infection of the female reproductive organs; usually occurs when sexually transmitted bacteria spread from the vagina to the uterus, fallopian tubes, or ovaries

There is much less support for the idea that sexual orientation is primarily determined by environmental factors, such as "recruitment" by homosexual adults, patterns of disordered parenting, or the influence of nonheterosexual parents.

Though we may never know precisely how sexual orientation develops, we do know that young people especially tend to face psychological difficulties coming to terms with identifying as anything other than heterosexual. Though various cultures have become more accepting of a wider range of sexual orientations (Loftus, 2001; Tucker & Potocky-Tripodi, 2006), there are still many in which those who identify as homosexual, bisexual, transgender, and other orientations face harassment, discrimination, and even violence. In this way, sociocultural influences can often create psychological stresses that lead to **sexual dysfunction**.

Sexual Dysfunctions and Problems

The Diagnostic and Statistical Manual of Mental Disorders, 5th ed. (DSM-5) includes a number of physical sexual dysfunctions caused by individual sociocultural influences, organic factors (such as illness), psychological factors (such as traumatic events or relationship problems) and/or, more commonly, a combination of these factors. Some of the more common sexual dysfunctions and problems deal with the functional aspect of sex and include delayed or premature ejaculation, erectile disorder, female orgasmic disorder, and substance- or medication-induced sexual dysfunction. Sexual dysfunctions are typically characterized by an interruption in a person's ability to respond sexually or experience sexual pleasure, and unlike some other psychological disorders, a person can experience several sexual dysfunctions simultaneously. Other sexual dysfunctions deal with sexual behavior and are called **paraphilias**. A person suffering from a paraphilia can only experience arousal and fulfillment via behaviors generally considered to be socially unacceptable. It is important to note that paraphilias are diagnosed when a person's sexual behavior causes distress or risks harm to the self or others, not when their behavior is simply viewed as atypical. Sexual dysfunctions can have a profound effect on a person's enjoyment of sexual activity. Treatment for sexual dysfunctions can include medication, hormone, sex, psychotherapy, stress reduction, and/or behavioral training.

Sexually Transmitted Infections

Certainly not categorized as sexual dysfunctions or problems, **sexually transmitted infections (STI)** can be a consequence of unprotected sexual contact, see Table 6.1. Different STIs affect the body in different ways, with some affecting the sex organs themselves and others affecting larger bodily systems. Furthermore, some STIs, if left untreated, can lead to other diseases with more harmful and long-lasting effects. Many bacterial infections, such as chlamydia, are easily treated with antibiotics, but if left undiagnosed and untreated, they can lead to **pelvic inflammatory disease (PID)**, which can damage the lining of the uterus, the fallopian tubes, and the ovaries, as well as other organs and tissues of the lower abdomen.

This Is Psychology

One of the most infamous of the original gangsters, Al Capone, otherwise known as Scarface, led a lawless, violent, and destructive life. Having begun his career as a bouncer in a Chicago brothel, Capone quickly strayed from his marriage to Mae "Josephine" Coughlin and contracted the STI syphilis before he turned twenty-one. Not only did he neglect to seek treatment for his infection, but before the penicillin era around 1920 (historians are split on the exact timeline of Capone's early career), treatments were rudimentary with no guarantee of a cure. So, the infection festered.

His public infamy emerged during the Prohibition era, where he plunged into the media spotlight as a bootlegger—one who illegally smuggled and sold liquor—and an unforgiving "boss" of an Italian organized crime gang. Over the course of nearly a decade, Capone built his illicit empire on law enforcement bribery, intimidation, and a vast amount of illegally acquired money. He split most of his time between Cicero, Illinois, and a lavish Floridian mansion, becoming increasingly paranoid and concerned for security.

Capone's legacy culminated on February 14, 1929: the day of the infamous St. Valentine's Day Massacre. It's believed that Capone was responsible for the deaths of seven rival gang members led by George "Bugs" Moran. Moran avoided the massacre, but Capone was quickly taken into custody by police on violations of the federal Prohibition laws. Capone was officially diagnosed with syphilis at the age of thirty-three at the Atlanta US Penitentiary. Prison doctors observed signs of neurosyphilis—the end stage of untreated syphilis that usually occurs ten to twenty years after the initial infection. Symptoms include confusion, sudden changes in personality and mood, psychosis, dementia, and indeed, paranoia. The corkscrew-shaped bacterium *Treponema pallidum* is recorded to have infected humans as early as the fifteenth century, but researchers believe it was present in the Americas before Europeans arrived. Syphilis and eventual neurosyphilis were once so prevalent in the US that blood tests were required before couples could obtain marriage licenses in some states. Treated early, syphilis can be completely cured, but in nations where antibiotics are scarce, the infection remains one of the most widespread and deadly STIs.

Al Capone is one of the most famous sufferers of *Treponema pallidum*: syphilis. Because he sought no treatment, the infection spread to his brain, turning into neurosyphilis, causing a host of neurological problems and eventual death.

acquired immune deficiency syndrome (AIDS)
a chronic, potentially life-threatening condition caused by the human immunodeficiency virus (HIV)

human immunodeficiency virus (HIV)
a sexually transmitted infection (STI) that interferes with your body's ability to fight the organisms that cause disease

Though certainly not the most common STI, **acquired immune deficiency syndrome (AIDS)**, the disease caused by the **human immunodeficiency virus (HIV)**, is the most well known. Contracting HIV does not mean that a person will develop AIDS. It simply means s/he is at risk for doing so because HIV wears down the body's immune system, making it easier for infections that can lead to AIDS to take hold. HIV is contagious from the moment it is contracted, regardless of whether a person displays symptoms or not. HIV can be transmitted not only through unprotected sexual activity but also through any other activity that results in contact with bodily fluids other than tears and saliva. While treatments for HIV and AIDS have improved over the years, there is still no cure (Centers for Disease Control, 2013). As with all STIs, the best way to avoid contracting HIV is to avoid unprotected sexual contact.

Table 6.1 Sexually Transmitted Infections

STI	Cause	Symptoms	Treatment
Chlamydia	*Chlamydia trachomatis:* bacterial infection. Can be spread during vaginal, anal, or oral sex and from an infected mother to her infant during childbirth	Most people have no symptoms. When symptoms do occur, they do not present until a few weeks after infection and differ for men and women. **Women:** Vaginal discharge or burning during urination **Men:** Discharge from the penis, burning during urination, and/or pain and swelling of one or both testicles. If left untreated, women can develop pelvic inflammatory disease (PID), which can lead to infertility or ectopic pregnancy.	Antibiotics
Syphilis	*Treponema pallidum:* bacterial infection. Can be spread through vaginal, anal, or oral sex and from a mother to her fetus during pregnancy or to her infant during birth.	Symptoms vary during each of the infection's four stages and often mimic symptoms presented with other diseases. **Primary:** chancre (skin ulceration); **Secondary:** rash, often involving the palms of the hands and soles of the feet. Sores may also develop in the mouth or vagina; **Latent:** The latent stage, in which a person may be symptom-free or show very few symptoms, can last for years. **Tertiary:** gummas (soft non-cancerous growths), neurological, and/or heart symptoms. If left untreated, syphilis can cause lasting brain and/or heart damage and even death.	Antibiotics
Gonorrhea	*Neisseria gonorrhoeae:* bacterial infection. Spread through vaginal, anal, and oral sex, and/or from mother to child during birth.	Many have no symptoms, but when symptoms do present, they are different between men and women. **Men:** burning with urination, discharge from the penis, and/or testicular pain. **Women:** burning with urination, vaginal discharge, vaginal bleeding, and/or pelvic pain. If left untreated, gonorrhea can cause PID in women and inflammation of the epididymis in men. It can also spread to the joints and heart. If left untreated, gonorrhea can be fatal.	Antibiotics
Genital herpes	*Herpes simplex virus* (HSV). Spread through genital or oral contact or through contact with skin or secretions of an infected person.	Symptoms are usually nonexistent or mild, so most do not even know they have the virus. When they do occur, symptoms include small blisters that break open and become painful ulcers. Some also experience flu-like symptoms.	There is no cure for genital herpes, but antiviral medications can prevent or shorten outbreaks.
Trichomoniasis	A parasitic infection caused by *trichomonas vaginalis*. Spread through vaginal, anal, or oral sex and/or genital touching.	Only about 30 percent of those infected present symptoms, which include genital itching, foul-smelling vaginal discharge, burning with urination, and pain during sex. Trichomoniasis infection increases the risk of contracting HIV/AIDS and can cause complications during pregnancy.	Antibiotics

HPV	Human papillomavirus (HPV) infection. The virus has hundreds of strains. A person can be infected by multiple strains at once, and most people are infected with at least one at some point in their lives. It is most commonly spread through vaginal or anal sex but can also be spread through other sustained skin-to-skin contact. It can also sometimes spread from a mother to her fetus during pregnancy.	Most cases cause no symptoms and resolve spontaneously. However, for some, HPV infection can result in warts or precancerous lesions that increase risk for cancer of the cervix, vulva, vagina, penis, anus, mouth, or throat. Indeed, about 70 percent of cervical cancer cases are linked to HPV infection. Though the virus itself is not fatal, the cancers it can cause are.	HPV vaccines prevent the most common strains of the disease and are most effective when administered prior to any contact with the virus.

Concept Recall

1. What are the four stages of sexual arousal?
2. How did the development of the Kinsey Scale affect our understanding of sexual orientation?
3. Do people of all sexual orientations and identities experience sexual harassment in the same way?
4. What bacterial STI can eventually affect the brain?

HUMAN SEXUALITY AND PSYCHOLOGY

Regardless of biological sex, one of the most influential elements of human development is our identification and experience of gender and sexuality. It influences and informs many other aspects of our development and behavior. We've learned in this chapter that, as with most aspects of human behavior and development, gender and sexuality are varied and the result of a combination of biological and environmental factors, and while the biological aspects of sex and sexuality are not that changeable, the roles and expectations set by society are. In the next chapter, we will expand upon how biological, psychological, and sociocultural influences, like those discussed here, also influence our learning and behavior.

Review/Reflect/Write

REVIEW

- How is one's biological sex determined?
- How does biological sex differ from gender?
- What are gender roles, and how are they developed?
- What is gender identity, and how is it developed?
- To what extent does biological sex influence a person's gender?
- What roles do environment and culture play in a person's identification and experience of gender?
- How do each of the four theories presented explain gender development?
- To what extent do men and women differ in their sexual behaviors?
- What is the difference between gender identity and sexual orientation?
- What is sexual orientation, and what factors may contribute to its development?

1. Parents in Westernized cultures are more likely than parents in Eastern cultures to encourage their children to value
   a. nonconformity.
   b. gender roles.
   c. cultural traditions.
   d. enduring friendships.

2. In considering gender differences, you should remember that
   a. no gender difference is common to all human cultures.
   b. gender is NOT the same thing as biological sex.
   c. genetic differences between the sexes do not contribute to differences in behavior.
   d. males are more likely to value relationships than females.

3. When teased by his older sister, Walden does not cry because he has learned that boys are not supposed to cry. Walden's behavior best illustrates the importance of
   a. temperament.   b. testosterone.   c. gender roles.   d. collectivism.

4. People whose gender identity feels mismatched with their biological sex are
   a. transgender.   b. bisexual.   c. heterosexual.   d. lesbian.

5. Through what process are gender roles learned?
   a. heteronormativity
   b. social learning theory
   c. gender typing
   d. collectivism

6. Which of the following is a secondary sex characteristic?
   a. uterus
   b. penis
   c. enlarging breasts
   d. ovaries

7. What is the Kinsey Scale?
   a. A spectrum by which to measure human sexuality
   b. The first nonbinary measurement of sexual orientation
   c. A result of Kinsey's research on sexual behavior in males and females
   d. All of the above

8. According to gender schema theory, upon what do children base their gender schema?
   a. Experiences in society
   b. Their same-sex parent's behavior

c. Their opposite-sex parent's behavior

d. The behavior of those with whose gender they identify

9. According to Rubin and colleagues' 1974 study, what physical differences exist between male and female babies?

a. Male babies tend to be taller.

b. Female babies tend to weigh more.

c. Male babies tend to weigh more.

d. There were no discernible differences.

10. According to psychodynamic theory, how do children learn gender roles?

a. By viewing their same-sex parent's behavior

b. By reconciling sexual attraction to their opposite-sex parent

c. By reconciling sexual attraction to their same-sex parent

d. By viewing their opposite-sex parent's behavior

REFLECT

1. Throughout Western history, those who identify as other than heterosexual have been met with abuse, prejudice, and discrimination. Considering that Western societies tend to be more individualistic rather than collectivist, why do you think many continue to find it difficult to accept those whose gender identity differs from their biological sex?

2. This chapter discussed four learning theories used to suggest how children learn gender roles. Thinking back to your childhood and young adulthood, from whom or what would you say you learned gender roles? Did you embrace the gender roles put forth for you, or did you resist them, and why?

WRITE

1. Many indigenous cultures throughout the Americas and around the world have embraced individuals whose gender identities differ from their biological sex. Briefly research the history of such individuals, referred to today as "Two Spirit," and discuss their treatment as well as the roles and positions held for them within their given societies.

2. While this chapter discusses four learning theories used to suggest how children learn gender roles, there are several others in circulation. Find and research one other learning theory not discussed in this text, and discuss how it explains children's acceptance or rejection of gender roles. How does this theory compare with any of the others that are discussed in this text?

Key Terms

acquired immune deficiency syndrome (AIDS) 172
bisexuality 177
cognitive developmental theory 173
four stages of sexual arousal 175
gender 170
gender dysphoria 169
gender identity 170
gender nonconformity 169
gender roles 170
gender schema theory 173
gender typing 170
heterosexuality 176
homosexuality 177
human immunodeficiency virus (HIV) 181

intersexed 169
Kinsey scale 176
pansexuality 177
paraphilias 180
pelvic inflammatory disease (PID) 180
primary sex characteristics 168
psychodynamic theory of sexuality 168
secondary sex characteristics 168
sex 168
sexual dysfunction 180
sexual orientation 176
sexuality 174
sexually transmitted infections 180
social learning theory 172

7 Learning and Behavior

After reading this chapter, you will be able to answer the following questions:
- What is the formal definition of learning?
- What is classical conditioning?
- What factors influence learning in classical conditioning?
- How is classical conditioning related to emotional responses to situations?
- What is operant conditioning?
- What is the difference between reinforcement and punishment?
- How is the use of punishment potentially problematic?
- How does the timing and availability of reinforcement affect behavior?

Our behavior is strongly influenced by what happens as we interact with our world. At the gas pump, we push a button, hear a beep, and see a change on the screen. As we walk into a dark room, we flip a light switch, and light fills the room. We pull our phones from our pockets, purses, or bags, and the display changes as we tap buttons or swipe the screens. All of these interactions with the world produce small changes in our environment, and as we experience these changes our actions and their outcomes influence what we do in the future.

In order to appreciate the power of feedback in our environment, think about somebody shooting a basketball. The player carefully lines up the shot, extends his or her arm, and watches as the ball moves toward the goal. Upon reaching the goal, the ball swishes through the net, bounces around the rim, hits the backboard, or completely misses the goal altogether. How do these different outcomes affect the player's next shot? If the ball goes through the hoop, the player tries to repeat the same actions the next time she or he shoots. If the ball barely misses, the player makes small adjustments to the shot. If the ball completely misses, the player may decide that basketball is not his or her sport and choose to look for a new activity. For professional basketball players, their entire job depends on how sensitive they are to making the necessary adjustments to keep the ball going through the hoop. And they are extremely good at making these adjustments.

Now, imagine what would happen to a basketball player's game if he or she lost the ability to see the outcome of each shot. She or he can see everything up until the ball is two feet from the hoop, but then the ball just disappears. Yes, this would be a very boring game to play. But more importantly, the player could never fine tune his or her game. Without seeing the outcome of his or her behavior, there is not enough information to make the needed adjustments to become a better player. In basketball—and almost every other situation in which we engage in behavior—the outcome of the behavior provides information about what adjustments are needed for future performances.

Famous American psychologist B. F. Skinner began his influential book *Verbal Behavior* with the following words: "[People] act upon the world, and change it, and are changed in turn by the consequences of their actions" (Skinner, 1957, pg. 1). This process of changing how we interact with the world based on our experience is called learning. Formally, learning is most often defined as a change in how the organism behaves due to changes in the environment produced by their behavior (Chance, 2014, pg. 21). In the section above, we saw how the power of experience in shaping our behavior can be appreciated by thinking about the critical role of environmental feedback in sports performance. Feedback is just as important in improving our academic work. If your instructor never provides feedback on assignments, then you have no way to gauge the outcome of your studying. Experiencing the outcomes of our behavior is critical for changing our behavior and has been a major area of study for psychologists.

BEHAVIOR ANALYSIS AND BEHAVIORISM

behavior analysis
the scientific approach to exploring the laws and principles that govern behavior across species and the development of behavior technologies based on these laws

behavior analysts
the scientists who approach behavior from the perspective of behavior analysis

behaviorism
a subfield of psychology that focused exclusively on the relationship between behavior and environmental events

Today, those scientists interested in studying the impact of learning and environmental changes on behavior are most closely associated with the field of behavior analysis. **Behavior analysis** is the scientific approach to exploring the laws and principles that govern behavior across species and the development of behavior technologies based on these laws (Pierce & Cheney, 2013, pg. 3). **Behavior analysts**—the scientists who approach behavior from the perspective of behavior analysis—work in many different contexts, including animal research laboratories, schools, businesses, and hospitals. In all of these contexts, behavior analysts focus on how they can best understand the ways environmental feedback produces observed behaviors and how the observed behaviors influence the environment. Due to the strong emphasis on understanding the relationship between the environment and directly observable behavior, behavior analysts differ from most psychologists, who put their emphasis on the role of events that occur inside the organism, such as thinking, feeling, and motivation. For behavior analysts, the most important area of study for understanding and controlling behavior is the environment outside the organism both before (antecedents) and after (consequences) the behavior of interest. (This is not to say that the internal environment is not important, just that we can understand and control behavior without focusing on what is going on inside the organism.) Behavior analysts refer to this model as the ABCs of behavior in reference to the Antecedents, Behaviors, and Consequences that are the primary focus of their research (see Figure 7.1).

7.1 The behavior analysts' ABCs of behavior
The ABC framework provides the basic model for behavior analysts. The antecedents and consequences are the environmental events that influence behavior.

Modern behavior analysis developed from the field of **behaviorism**: a subfield of psychology that focused exclusively on the relationship between behavior and environmental events. The emphasis on studying events that occur around the organism before and after it enacts a certain behavior is a common characteristic between modern behavior analysis and behaviorism. However, the two fields differ significantly in the role of private events (thoughts and feelings). Early behaviorists argued that if the event cannot be perceived by an outside observer, it is not scientific and, therefore, should not be explored by a science of behavior. Modern behavior analysts accept that not all behavior occurs outside the organism and behaviors that occur inside the organism are important to a scientific study of behavior and, thus, should not be viewed as different from the publicly observable external behaviors.

The perspective of behavior analysts—and the behaviorists who preceded them—is distinct from the focus of most psychologists. As described in Chapter 1, early psychology was strongly influenced by biology and philosophy. As much of our psychological experience involves thinking and feeling—behaviors that are largely private to us and not directly observable by other people—psychologists often find themselves studying and trying to observe hidden processes. An unfortunate consequence of this internal focus is that psychology struggles with how to make the study of private behaviors a scientific process (we saw in previous chapters some of the ways that modern imaging and physiological techniques are helping solve these problems). Early psychologists attempted to use a variety of external observations, such as **introspection**, a systematic method of providing research participants with an external stimulus and asking them to provide detailed reports of their internal experiences, to provide access to the internal mental processes and experiences of their participants. Unfortunately, for many scientists (both within and outside of psychology) the focus on private mental events led psychologists to rely on techniques that did not provide replicable, verifiable data for use in building explanations of human behavior.

introspection
a systematic method of providing research participants with an external stimulus and asking them to provide detailed reports of their internal experiences to provide access to the internal mental processes and experiences of their participants

One of the opponents to the internal focus of psychology in the early 1900s was John Watson, who argued that rather than focusing on private mental events, psychology needed to change its focus to the external behaviors that could be studied through direct observation (Watson, 1913). Watson argued that introspective psychology should be replaced with a version of psychology based on the following elements:

1. The behavior of organisms adjusts to the environment through both inherited behavioral tendencies and learned behaviors.

2. Psychologists should focus on the relation between environmental events (stimuli) and the behavioral changes (responses) that they cause. Watson argued that psychology should strive to understand these relationships to the point that we could predict behavior based on the events in the environment and predict what the stimuli in the environment were based on the observed behavior.

3. Psychology should make the study of behavior its final objective rather than using behavior only as an indirect measure of unobservable mental processes.

Watson's argument for a new psychology placed greater emphasis on the role of learning in behavior. For example, when you bring a cat home from the animal shelter, the sound of the electric can opener has no meaning for her, but when food appears in a bowl for her to eat after she hears the can opener, her experience has caused her to associate its sound with the appearance of food. The next time you

Watson's emphasis on the role of the environment in behavior is evident in the cat's association between the sound of can openers and dinner.

fire up the can opener, she'll come running in search of the expected food. Likewise, a teacher would argue that students have learned the material when they are able to provide the correct answer to a question related to the target material. The students' ability to provide this response is due to their experience interacting with the material in lecture, reading, or another instructional activity. In this way, the educational experience produced a change in the students' behavior.

Cross-Cultural Case

Cultural Differences to Learning

Have you ever considered how differently you would experience school if it were in a different country? Maybe you've gone abroad yourself and studied in another country for a term in an exchange program, or perhaps some of your peers are from other countries at your school, visiting for a single term or a year. A number of cultural factors not only influence what and how we learn, but also what classroom experience we have. In the United States, university classes tend to fall into two groups: lectures and discussions. Lectures tend to be large groups of students listening to a single instructor with little interaction between them, whereas discussions generally have smaller groups of students matched to an instructor and allow for individuals to respond to instructor questions and break out into interactive groups for activities. Naturally, these two types of classes provide very different experiences to the students taking part. But what if—as an American student—you found yourself in a Singapore classroom, with one instructor and only 18 students? Would you expect to treat this classroom that's, in your assessment, going to be discussion-based?

In a fascinating Canadian study, researcher Luciano Mariani compiled interviews with different cultural student groups, asking them to describe their personal cultural assessments as well as their assessments of the opposite group. A group of Southeast Asians described Americans as believing in freedom of speech, valuing technological advancement, and liking to act and not remain passive. Then, they described themselves as contemplative, peaceful, and enjoying room for silence. Now, flip the previously described scenario around: place a Malaysian student in a small class in a US university. Considering her cultural background, how do you think she would initially treat the learning environment? While instructors maintain awareness of cultural differences across learning styles, as a peer in any environment, remember to take cultural differences into account and understand that adaptation is a necessary part of entering a new classroom.

Remember, whenever we generalize assessments of culture, there is always the risk of oversimplification leading to stereotyping. As researchers, critically assess the data you receive, and qualify that data using objective evaluation techniques.

Behavior analysts distinguish between two main types of learning: classical conditioning and operant conditioning. Both types of learning occur as the organism adapts to its environment. With classical conditioning the stimulus is presented before the animal makes a behavioral response, whereas with operant conditioning the behavior comes first, causing a change in the environment.

classical conditioning
also known as respondent conditioning, Pavlovian conditioning, and associative learning

respondent behavior
an inherited behavior that is directly caused by the occurrence of a specific stimulus in the environment.

reflex
an automatic behavioral response to a stimulus

Concept Recall

1. How do behavior analysts define learning?
2. What is the role of the environment in shaping behavior?
3. What did the behaviorists believe were the problems with introspection?
4. What did Watson believe should be the three goals of psychology?

CLASSICAL CONDITIONING

Classical conditioning—also known as respondent conditioning, Pavlovian conditioning, and associative learning—involves the training of a biologically inherited behavior that is triggered (elicited) by a specific evolutionarily important environmental event to occur in the presence of a new stimulus. Behavior that is influenced in classical conditioning is known as **respondent behavior**: an inherited behavior that is directly caused by the occurrence of a specific stimulus in the environment. Key examples of respondent behavior are constricting pupils in response to a bright light, acting startled in response to unexpected noise or touch, and salivating in response to an appetizing smell. Notice how each of the behaviors (dilating pupils, startling, and salivating) is directly tied to a specific environmental event. This triggering event is typically consistent across members of a species (though the magnitude of the response to the event will vary between individual organisms). If you take a moment to reflect on the last time you engaged in any of these automatic behaviors, you will likely notice that the response occurred as soon as the stimulus was presented, even without your being fully aware of it (such as jerking your hand back from a hot stove even before you experience the pain of the burn).

Respondent behavior is typically described as a **reflex**: an automatic behavioral response to a stimulus. According to this definition, each reflex consists of two parts: the unconditioned stimulus (US) and the unconditioned response (UR), where "unconditioned" indicates that the relation between the stimulus and the response is unlearned. For example, when your pet dog smells fresh meat, the dog will start to drool even without ever having been taught to do so. A very short list of human reflexes is shown in Figure 7.2.

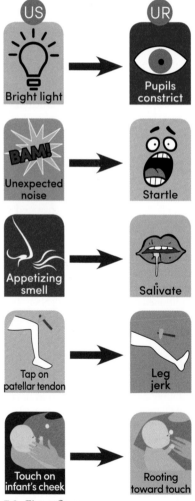

7.2 Five reflexes
Five reflexes are shown above with a US and the UR. For each reflex, an environmental event elicits (triggers) a physiological response.

Ivan Pavlov

There are three items of interest in each of the reflexes shown. First, notice that each behavior was preceded by an environmental event: a stimulus that has roughly the same effect on all members of the species. Second, each environmental event was followed by a specific behavior, which—just like we observed for the US—is largely the same across all members of the species. Finally, the environmental event can be said to have caused the behavior in the sense that the behavior reliably and consistently occurs when the stimulus occurs. When speaking of respondent behavior, the unconditioned stimulus is said to elicit the unconditioned response. This causal relation between the two components of the reflex is shown in the reflex diagram with an arrow like this: →.

While reflexes and their relation to respondent behavior have been recognized for hundreds of years, it was not until the early 1900s that scientists began to really understand how reflexes could be changed by interactions with the environment. The flexibility of respondent behavior was first demonstrated scientifically by the Russian physiologist Ivan Pavlov, who received the Nobel Prize in physiology in 1904 for his work on digestion. Pavlov's work on classical conditioning began in 1897 when some of his students began studying how the type of food presented to dogs influences the observed salivary response (Boakes, 1984). As Pavlov's students presented the food to the dogs, they noted that the dogs began to salivate not when the dogs took the meat into their mouths but before: as soon as they saw or smelled the food. Pavlov and his students referred to these anticipatory salivary responses as psychic secretions.

After studying these psychic secretions for some time, one of Pavlov's students became curious whether any stimulus that preceded the presentation of food could be used to elicit the salivary response. In order to test this, Anton Snarsky presented dogs with acid that had been dyed black. Acid in your food tastes sour, and you might have noticed that sour foods elicit salivation; in fact, if you just think of a sour food you might notice that you salivate. People and dogs salivate in response to sour food because undiluted acid could punch a hole in your digestive system, so saliva in the mouth dilutes the acid before it reaches the stomach. Although sour taste elicits a salivary response, the color black doesn't have any adaptive meaning, so it is a **neutral stimulus (NS)**: an environmental event that does not elicit an unconditioned response. When the dogs were first shown the black-colored liquid, they did not salivate. However, after several presentations of the black liquid onto the tongues of the dogs, the dogs began to salivate as soon as they saw the black acid (Boakes, 1984). The dogs had learned that the color black reliably preceded the sour taste, or, in other words, the color black had become a **conditioned stimulus (CS)**: a previously neutral stimulus that begins to elicit the unconditioned response after being paired with an unconditioned stimulus. The dogs had learned to associate black (neutral stimulus) with sour (unconditioned stimulus), so just seeing black elicited salivation. Salivating in response to a sour taste is unconditioned because the dogs didn't have to learn to respond that way, but salivating in response to the color black is a **conditioned response (CR)**: an unconditioned response that was elicited by the presentation of a conditioned stimulus. It is important to notice that the unconditioned response (UR) and the conditioned response (CR)

neutral stimulus (NS)
an environmental event that does not elicit an unconditioned response

conditioned stimulus (CS)
a previously neutral stimulus that begins to elicit the unconditioned response after being paired with an unconditioned stimulus

conditioned response (CR)
an unconditioned response that was elicited by the presentation of a conditioned stimulus

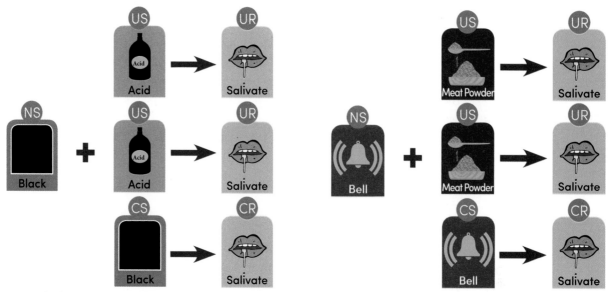

7.3 Pavlov's original two-term contingencies for studying classical conditioning
The two-term contingency framework illustrates how the pairing of the NS + US results in a learned association between the NS and the UR.

are identical behaviors (salivating). The major difference between the two is that a UR is elicited by a US (salivating in response to sour taste) while a CR is elicited by a UR (salivating in response to the color black).

Pavlov's original study used black food coloring and an acid as the NS and US. These stimuli worked, but they limited Pavlov's ability to observe how slight changes to the NS and US might influence learning. To adjust for this, Pavlov replaced the color black and the acid with a bell (NS) and meat powder sprayed into the dog's mouth (US). The behavior of interest (UR/CR) continued to be salivation. Just as we did with the previous learning experience, we can create a two-term contingency demonstrating this learning situation in Figure 7.3.

Take a moment to think about why the bell might serve as a better NS than the black coloring in the water. What do you think? One reason that Pavlov preferred these two stimuli is that the sound of the bell was separate from the taste of the meat powder. In the previous work, the black color and the acid were mixed together, making it difficult to manage the timing of the delivery of the two stimuli. Also, as a visual stimulus, if the dog was not looking at the acid, it would not be able to detect the black coloring. A sound, however, can be detected without the organism being oriented in the direction of the source. By creating greater spatial separation between the US and NS, psychologists have been able to determine several important characteristics of classical conditioning.

Pavlov's studies on classical conditioning proved that a desirable stimulus could be associated with a previously neutral stimulus, such as the ringing of a bell, to elicit certain behavior.

The Importance of Pairing

The most important element of classical conditioning lies in the pairing of the NS with the US. Classical conditioning relies on the relation between the NS/CS and the US. The CS became associated with the US by being repeatedly presented together with the US. The strength of the association between the two stimuli depends on how many times the two stimuli are presented together and the relative timing of when the two stimuli are paired together. Specifically, we can talk about five different dimensions of the pairing process.

The magnitude of the UR

As discussed previously, classical conditioning moves existing behavior into new contexts, but it does not create new behavior. Due to this, the magnitude of the UR determines the upper limit of how much can be learned. For example, the presentation of an unexpected noise might result in a startle response that includes an increase in heart rate from sixty beats per minute to eighty beats per minute. When we later condition a red light to elicit the startle response by pairing it with the unexpected noise, the strongest response we could expect to get from this conditioning is an increase to eighty beats per minute. But what determines the strength of the UR? The strength of the UR is tied to the nature and strength of the US. The more intense the US, the bigger the reaction (UR). Think about how you would react if somebody unexpectedly whispered, "Hey," in your ear while you were focused on reading this text. What if instead of whispering, the person yelled, "Hey"? The unexpected noise is a US, and the size of your startle response would be much larger to the stronger US (yelling) than to the weaker US (whispering). Because yelling produces more of a response, we could use this US to condition a larger CR than what would be possible with the whispered US.

The salience of the NS

salience
refers to how noticeable the neutral stimulus is to the organism

Salience refers to how noticeable the neutral stimulus is to the organism. The more salient the NS, the more quickly the stimulus will become associated with the US. The salience of the NS is determined both by its characteristics and by other stimuli in the environment. For example, consider what would happen if you were studying in the library where it is completely quiet and, moments before your friend yells, "Hey!" in your ear, you hear a quiet scrape on the ground. In the library with very little background noise This scrape would be very salient. However, the same scrape would go largely unnoticed if you were at a party with loud music and people talking.

How many times the NS and US have been paired together

Each time the NS and US are presented together, a greater association is formed between the two events. For example, Pavlov's students had to pair the black coloring with the acid several times before the dogs began to respond to the color black by itself. The amount of learning that occurs with each pairing decreases each time the stimuli are paired together. With each pairing, the organism learns more about the association between the two stimuli; however, the amount learned on each pairing is less than what was learned on the previous pairing. Why is this? An easy way to think about this is to imagine memorizing a list of 100 words. The first time you work on memorizing the list you will learn some of the words: let's say 20 percent—so you now know twenty of the 100 words. The next time you sit down to study the list, you only have eighty words left to learn. As with the previous study session, you learn 20 percent of the words: sixteen words. After the end of two study sessions, you have learned a total of thirty-six words. On each study session, your knowledge of the list grew. However, you learned twenty words the first session and only sixteen words the second session. This is a good analogy of what happens during classical conditioning. Since the US sets an upper limit on how much the organism can learn, the learning that occurs in each session reduces the amount that is left to learn in the next session.

The time between the presentation of the NS and the US

Not only is it important that the NS and the US be presented together, but it is also important that there is a high degree of **contiguity**: the state of being close together in time or space. In general, the closer together the NS and the US occur—the greater the contiguity—the faster learning will occur.

contiguity
the state of being close together in time or space

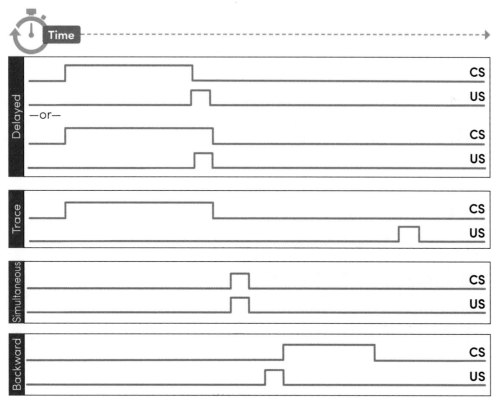

7.4   Four methods for pairing the US and CS in classical conditioning
The timing of the presentation of the CS relative to the US influences learning during classical conditioning. In the figure above, the line moving up indicates that the stimulus (CS or US) turns on.

Classical conditioning researchers typically talk of four ways that the NS and US can be presented together: trace, delayed, simultaneous, and backward. As you read the definitions of these pairing methods, pause and study Figure 7.4. This figure provides a graphical representation of these stimulus presentation methods. Seeing how

trace conditioning
the NS is presented and removed before the US is presented so that there is no overlap between the two stimuli

delayed conditioning
the NS is presented first and then the US is presented while the NS is still present; there are two key elements to delayed conditioning

simultaneous conditioning
the NS and US are both presented at the same time

backward conditioning
the US is presented before the NS occurs

contingency
refers to the degree to which one event predicts the occurrence of another event

these work makes it much easier to understand how these different methods work. In **trace conditioning**, the NS is presented and removed before the US is presented, so there is no overlap between the two stimuli. Trace conditioning may involve the NS ending mere milliseconds before the US begins, or it can be minutes or hours between the two. In general, the greater the time between the NS and the US, the slower conditioning will occur. In **delayed conditioning**, the NS is presented first and then the US is presented while the NS is still present. There are two key elements to delayed conditioning. First, the NS occurs before the US. Second, the NS and US overlap: both are present for a period of time. In **simultaneous conditioning** the NS and US are both presented at the same time. As suggested by the name, simultaneous conditioning involves the greatest degree of contiguity, as both stimuli are presented together. Finally, in **backward conditioning** the US is presented before the NS occurs. Backward conditioning is extremely important because it generally does not work. As a general rule, the NS must occur either simultaneously with or before the presentation of the US in order for conditioning to occur. Ideally, the NS will precede the US by half a second to two seconds and will slightly overlap with the presentation of the US. In this way, researchers generally find that delay conditioning is the most effective way to conduct classical conditioning.

The degree of contingency between the NS and US

In this context, **contingency** refers to the degree to which one event predicts the occurrence of another event. Rescorla (1968) demonstrated that in order for classical conditioning to occur, the NS must provide useful information about the occurrence of the US. This is one reason why delayed conditioning is more effective than simultaneous conditioning and why backward conditioning rarely works. In backward conditioning, the NS is a poor predictor of the US because the US is already occurring. Would Pavlov's bell help the dogs prepare for food if the food is already present? In order to help you review these effects, we provide a brief summary of each in Table 7.1.

Table 7.1 Summary of five factors that influence the strength of the conditioned response (CR).

Factor	Effect
Magnitude of the UR	The magnitude of the unconditioned response (UR) determines the maximum magnitude of the conditioned response (CR).
Salience of the NS	The more noticeable (salient) the neutral stimulus (NS), the faster learning will occur.
Number of NS + US pairings	The more times the NS and US are paired together, the stronger the conditioned response (CR).
Contiguity between NS + US	The closer together in time and space (contiguity) the presentation of the US and the NS, the stronger the conditioned response (CR).
Contingency between NS + US	The better the NS (CS) predicts the occurrence of the US, the stronger the conditioned response (CR).

The degree of learning in classical conditioning is influenced by the nature of the NS and the US and the relation between the two stimuli. It is important to note that the behavior of the organism is not a major determinant of learning. As the US that is selected determines the UR, and thus the CR, it is important to select a US that elicits the behavior that you want to condition at the level that you want it to condition. The preceding sections discussed five factors that influence the degree of learning in classical conditioning.

Extinction of Classical Conditioning

After associating the sound of a bell with the presentation of meat, Pavlov's dogs salivated in response to just the bell. What would have happened if Pavlov repeatedly rang the bell without presenting any meat? After several trials, the dogs would stop salivating to the sound of the bell as it no longer predicted the presentation of meat. This process is known as **respondent extinction** (later we will see another type of extinction), and it occurs any time the conditioned stimulus (CS) is presented without presenting the US. If the CS (bell) is presented enough times without also presenting the US (meat) that it no longer elicits the CR (salivating), the association between CS and US has become extinct.

respondent extinction occurs any time the conditioned stimulus (CS) is presented without presenting the unconditioned stimulus (US)

While the CS will cease eliciting the CR after sufficient extinction trials, that doesn't mean that the animal has completely lost the association between the CS and US. Following extinction (that is, the CS no longer elicits the CR), sometimes the presentation of the CS will elicit the CR, as if the animal has spontaneously recovered the association between CS and US. **Spontaneous recovery** is the reoccurrence of the conditioned response after some time has passed since the last extinction trial. Consider another study of dog salivation conducted by Pavlov (1960, as described by Pierce & Cheney, 2013). Pavlov's canine participants were trained to associate the sight of meat powder with the taste of meat powder, so they would salivate whenever they were shown the powder. Pavlov then gave the dogs five trials in which the meat powder was shown but not delivered. This was a sufficient number of extinction trials to reduce the level of salivation to pretraining levels. He then let the dogs rest for twenty minutes, followed by another visual presentation of the meat powder. Pavlov observed that the dogs once again salivated at the sight of the meat powder, though not as much as they did before the start of the extinction trials. Pierce and Cheney (2013) suggest that there are two possible explanations for this spontaneous recovery of the CS/US relation. First, it is possible that, as Pavlov argued, the response recovery is evidence of persisting neurological connections that are suppressed during extinction. The association remains, but due to experience with the absence of the US, the relation has been paused rather than destroyed. A secondary explanation for spontaneous recovery is that there are other environmental stimuli that were associated with the unconditioned stimulus that do not extinguish as rapidly as the CS.

spontaneous recovery the reoccurrence of the conditioned response after some time has passed since the last extinction trial

Classical Conditioning and Conditioned Emotion

The inability of classical conditioning to produce novel behaviors may seem like a limitation, but classical conditioning can still be a powerful influence on our behavior. Consider the work of John Watson and Rosalie Rayner with "Little Albert," perhaps one of the most famous examples of classical conditioning of human behavior. Watson and Rayner hypothesized that phobia—intense fear of a specific stimulus—could be learned through classical conditioning. In order to demonstrate the learning of an emotional reaction, Watson and Rayner used an unexpected noise as the US to elicit a startle response (UR) from Albert, an eleven-month-old infant they recruited for the project. The two-term contingency demonstrates their training in Figure 7.5.

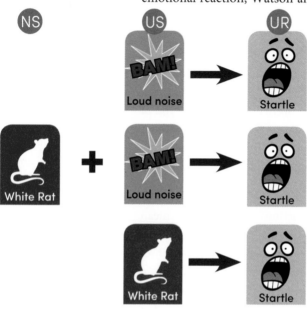

Prior to beginning the conditioning trials, Albert was exposed several times to a white rat. Albert showed no signs of discomfort while the rat was present. During conditioning trials, Albert was allowed to play freely on a carpeted area. After he played for some time, the white rat was placed on the play mat. As Albert reached for the rat, a research assistant standing behind the play area would bang loudly on metal pans. After seven pairing trials between the rat and the loud noise, Albert became agitated as soon as the rat was presented. As predicted by Watson and Rayner, Albert learned to fear the rat through consistent exposure with stimuli that associated a fear response.

7.5 Classical conditioning of a fear response in Little Albert
This figure represents the two-term contingency used to train Little Albert's fear of the white rat.

In addition to testing for the effect of the white rat (CS), Watson and Rayner also tested for two phenomena that are today called discrimination and generalization. **Discrimination** occurs when the behavior is observed in the presence of stimuli used during training, but not in their absence. In the case of Albert, discrimination would occur if he responded to the white rat but did not show the conditioned fear response to other stimuli. Watson and Rayner demonstrated this by presenting Albert with a series of trials in which he was presented with either the rat or a set of building blocks. Discrimination was observed in the occurrence of the fear response when the rat was presented but not when the blocks were presented. The occurrence of the fear response to some stimuli, but not others, demonstrates discrimination. In this case, the discrimination between building blocks and the white rat was fairly easy, as the two do not share many characteristics in common (different color, shape, size, etc.). What would happen if the stimulus were more similar to the CS?

discrimination
occurs when a behavior is observed in the presence of stimuli used during training but not in its absence

generalization
occurs when a CR is observed in the presence of stimuli that were not present during training

In a second set of trials, generalization was observed in Albert's response to the white rat. **Generalization** occurs when the CR is observed in the presence of stimuli that were not present during training. Watson and Rayner presented Albert with a dog, a rabbit, and cotton wool. A fear response was observed with each of these stimuli.

In other words, the association between the US and the CS generalized to stimuli that were similar to the CS used during training. As described in their original paper, Albert showed the greatest distress at the presentation of the rabbit. While the dog elicited a startle response, it was not as significant as that of the rat or the rabbit. This demonstration with little Albert showed that the association between US and CS will generalize to stimuli that share characteristics in common with the CS. The more similar the new stimuli are to the CS in shape, size, color, form, and other dimensions, the greater the degree of generalization.

How strongly the association is generalized or discriminated can be controlled with conditioning. Had Watson and Rayner continued to present the white rat along with the loud noises and occasionally presented the rabbit, dog, and cotton wool without ever following these with the loud noise, the response to the non-CS stimuli would extinguish, while the response to the white rat would be maintained. With sufficient training, the CS would become the only stimulus that would elicit the fear response, indicating strong discrimination. On the other hand, if on occasion the dog, rabbit, or cotton wool were paired with the loud noise, we would eventually see even greater generalization with the fear response occurring to stimuli that were similar to the rat, the rabbit, the dog, and the cotton wool.

Concept Recall

1. What is the relationship between the conditioned stimulus and the unconditioned stimulus? Between the conditioned response and the unconditioned response?

2. How does the timing of the presentation of the neutral stimulus and of the unconditioned stimulus affect learning?

3. Besides timing of the stimulus presentations, what other factors influence learning in classical conditioning?

4. What happens to the learned association when the unconditioned stimulus is no longer presented along with the conditioned stimulus?

5. What is generalization?

This Is Psychology

Joseph Roscoe and colleagues (2011) report that up to 25 percent of cancer patients show anticipatory nausea and vomiting by the fourth chemotherapy treatment cycle. For these patients, the stomach ailments that frequently occur after treatment are triggered as soon as the patient enters the office or clinic. Extensive research indicates that these anticipatory responses are a product of classical conditioning. While the clinic originally serves as a neutral stimulus, it becomes associated with the experienced effects of the chemotherapy (nausea, vomiting) and begins to elicit these feelings as soon as the patient enters. In this context, the patient's body has "learned" to feel sick.

Operant Conditioning

While classical conditioning has a huge, and typically unnoticed, influence on our behavior, it has a major limitation. As we discussed previously, classical conditioning can only move existing behaviors to new contexts; it cannot be used to create new behavior. Fortunately, there is a second type of learning that does allow for the changing of behavior: operant conditioning. **Operant conditioning** focuses on the relation between the behavior and the environmental changes that the behavior produces. The changes in the environment that are caused by the behavior are referred to as the consequences of the behavior. As we will see in this section, operant consequences play an integral role in the shaping of our behavior.

operant conditioning focuses on the relation between the behavior and the environmental changes that the behavior produces

Waving is both a behavior prompted by seeing other people and a signal that cues other people to respond to the waver.

Consider the last time you walked into a social event. As you entered the social event, you likely recognized at least a few people. Imagine that you waved at them. How will their response to the wave influence what you do next? If they wave back, you will likely go over to speak with them. You will also be more likely to wave at them the next time you see them. However, if they fail to wave back, or turn away laughing, this will also impact your behavior. In this case, you likely will find someone else with whom to interact, and you will be less likely to wave at these people the next time you see them. The other people waving were largely influenced by your waving, but your waving was influenced by your past experience with waving at other people. This is operant conditioning.

B.F. Skinner introduced the idea of operant behavior in his work, *The Behavior of Organisms* (1939), in which he made the first formal distinction between classical and operant conditioning. However, the idea that behavior is controlled by its consequences was first presented in 1898 in Edward L. Thorndike's Law of Effect. Thorndike was an American psychologist interested in understanding trial-and-error learning. In order to study this type of behavior, he developed a series of puzzle boxes in which he placed cats. Each box contained a series of objects that the cat had to operate in a set order before it could escape the box. Anyone who has ever tried to take a cat to the veterinarian's office knows how motivated a cat is to escape from a confined space. These boxes ranged from relatively simple (push a lever) to very complex (involving multiple behaviors in a set order). Thorndike placed cats in the same boxes over multiple trials and watched what happened as they learned to escape from the boxes. Most discussions of Thorndike's work focus on the change in the time the cats required to escape from the box. In general, the time needed to escape the box decreased with experience in the puzzle box (see the left side of Figure 7.6). Thorndike graphed the time needed to escape from the box and found that, over time, he could see a learning curve: the time needed to escape from the cage decreased fastest on the first few trials and then slowly leveled off to the final performance. This is an accurate description of Thorndike's findings, but it misses the most important details. Instead of talking about the decrease

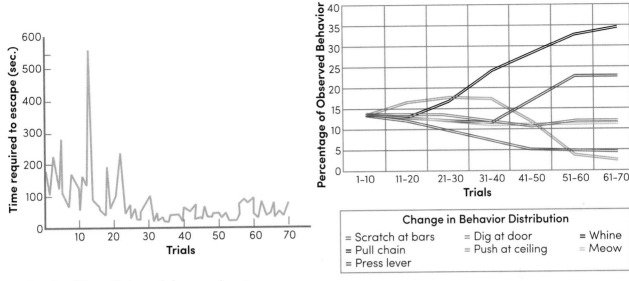

7.6 Results of Thorndike's puzzle box experiments
Thorndike's puzzle box studies with cats showed that cats learned to escape the box faster over trials (left side) and that those responses that produced escape became more frequent, while those that did not became less frequent (right side).

in time to escape, Thorndike focused on what happened to the shape (topography) of the cat's behavior. He noted two important findings (see the right side of Figure 7.6 for a graphical presentation of these two findings):

1. The responses that were "useful" in escaping from the puzzle box began to occur more frequently.

2. The responses that did not facilitate the cat's escape from the box (e.g., howling, crying, hissing, spinning) became less and less frequent.

After several trials in the puzzle boxes, Thorndike's cats were highly efficient at escaping from boxes—even novel boxes. The increased ability to escape was due to the fact that the cats spent the majority of their time engaged in behaviors that had facilitated escape in the past, with only the occasional occurrence of noneffective behaviors. By attending to the topographical changes in the cat's behavior, we can see that the decreased escape time is a product of the increased efficiency of the cat's behavioral responses. Another way to say this is that the cat's behavior adapted to the demands of the puzzle box environment. Thorndike summarized his finding as the Law of Effect:

> Of several responses made to the same situation, those which are accompanied or closely followed by satisfaction to the animal will, other things being equal, be more firmly connected with the situation, so that, when it recurs, they will be more likely to recur; those which are accompanied or closely followed by discomfort to the animal will, other things being equal, have their connections with that situation weakened, so that, when it recurs, they will be less likely to occur. The greater the satisfaction or discomfort, the greater the strengthening or weakening of the bond. (Thorndike, 1911, p. 244)

Over the past more than 100 years since Thorndike wrote this statement, the heart of his eighty-word sentence has been summarized in just seven words: behavior is a function of its consequences.

Operant consequence

As Thorndike demonstrated, and Skinner later elaborated upon, some types of behavior are controlled by how the environment changes after their occurrence. While classical conditioning relies on what happens in the environment before the behavior (the pairing of the NS and the US), operant conditioning is focused on changes in the environment after the behavior occurs. This focus on the environment after the behavior does not imply that what happens before the behavior is unimportant. Rather, the state of the environment before the behavior provides information on what consequences might follow the behavior. For example, consider a stop sign while driving.

The presence of the stop sign tells the driver how to behave as he or she passes through the intersection. Unlike a US or a CS, the stop sign does not make the driver push the brake. Instead, the presence of the stop sign tells the driver that certain consequences may happen, or not happen, if she or he presses the brake. Depending on traffic, pressing the brake may result in the driver avoiding an accident or becoming the source of a major disruption to the flow of traffic. If a police officer is present, pressing the brake may help the driver avoid a traffic ticket and the associated loss of money and gain in driving points on the driver's record. In this way, the information provided by the stop sign is extremely important. The stimuli that precede a behavior and provide information about the available consequences are called discriminative stimuli. These stimuli include stop signs, traffic lights, handicap signs, a person waving at us, open signs on a store, a telephone ringing, time of day, and many, many hundreds of additional environmental events.

discriminative stimuli
the stimuli that precede a behavior and provide information about the available consequences

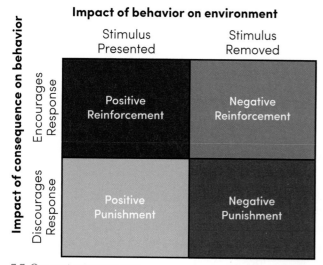

Impact of behavior on environment

	Stimulus Presented	Stimulus Removed
Encourages Response	Positive Reinforcement	Negative Reinforcement
Discourages Response	Positive Punishment	Negative Punishment

Impact of consequence on behavior

7.7 Operant consequences
The four operant consequences are determined by their effect on the response and how they change the environment.

While the **discriminative stimuli** help us to know what consequences may follow, they are not the determining element of the learning experience. That is reserved for the consequences of the behavior. Operant consequences are defined in two ways: by the change that they trigger in the environment and by the impact that they have on the future likelihood of the behavior, as shown in Figure 7.7. The impact of the behavior on the environment is to either add or remove environmental events. When the behavior triggers an increase in the amount of environmental stimulation, the consequence is termed a positive consequence. If the behavior reduces the level of environmental stimulation, then it is a negative consequence. Similarly, if the behavior is more likely to occur in the future due to the change produced in the environment, we call the environmental change a reinforcer. If the environmental change makes the behavior less likely to occur in the future, we call the change a punisher. These two dimensions of the environmental change create four types of operant consequences. Table 7.2 lists each of these consequences and shows how they relate to the future likelihood of the behavior and the consequent change in environmental stimulation.

Table 7.2 Four types of operant consequences

	Future likelihood of behavior	Behavior produces a new stimulus	Behavior removes a stimulus	Example
Positive reinforcer	Increases	Yes	No	Student **given** a sticker for completing homework
Negative reinforcer	Increases	No	Yes	Alarm **turns off** when snooze button is pressed
Positive punisher	Decreases	Yes	No	Name **written on** the board when student speaks out during class
Negative punisher	Decreases	No	Yes	Car keys **taken away** when teenager misses curfew

Positive reinforcer

A **positive reinforcer** is a stimulus or event that, when presented, will increase the likelihood that the behavior that produced it will occur again in the future. In our previous party example, the people waving back at you (adding environmental stimulation) would increase the likelihood that you would wave at them in the future, making the wave a positive reinforcer. Similarly, a student receiving a smiley face on his or her homework for getting all answers correct would likely be a positive reinforcer, as something is being added to the environment (a smiley face), and the student is likely to answer the questions the same in the future. It is important to note that positive reinforcers typically produce an increase in something that the organism likes. Money, food, candy, and drinks all typically serve as positive reinforcers.

positive reinforcer
a stimulus or event that, when presented, will increase the likelihood that the behavior that produced it will occur again in the future

Psychologists often make a distinction between primary and secondary reinforcers. A primary reinforcer is any event that increases the likelihood of the behavior without the organism having to learn the value of the reinforcer. Items that are consumed, like food or drink, are good primary reinforcers. Also, sensory experiences, such as physical or sexual contact with another person, listening to music, changing light displays, and specific odors are all primary reinforcers. Secondary reinforcers are environmental events that influence our behavior only after we have learned that these events are valuable. Money, stickers, certificates of appreciation, and verbal praise are all secondary reinforcers. Until we experience these events paired (classical conditioning) with positive outcomes, we will not find them valuable. Think about it this way. If we were to go to a primitive culture and offer someone a $100 bill, that person would likely see no value in the money. While you would jump up and down for $100 (game shows and reality television have shown us how far people would go for money!), this is only because we have had a great deal of experience with money being related to the future presentation of food, sensory experiences, and other primary reinforcers.

Negative reinforcer

negative reinforcer (NR)
a stimulus or event that, when removed, will increase the likelihood that the behavior that produced its removal will occur in the future

A **negative reinforcer (NR)** is a stimulus or event that, when removed, will increase the likelihood that the behavior that produced its removal will occur in the future. Like a positive reinforcer, a negative reinforcer increases the future likelihood of the behavior. Unlike positive reinforcers, a negative reinforcer is typically the removal of something unpleasant from the environment. Turning off an alarm is a good example of a negative reinforcer. Remember the last time you were awakened by an alarm clock. Prior to the alarm sounding, you were likely sleeping soundly. Then came the rude, disruptive sound of the alarm. Trying not to open your eyes any more than absolutely necessary, you reached out and hit at the alarm until you finally succeeded in turning it off. The likelihood that you will perform this same behavior in the future increases due to the removal of the alarm sound. While the behavior is slightly different, a similar negative reinforcer occurs when you put on your seatbelts to stop the warning sound in your vehicle or clean our room in order to get our roommate or significant other to stop pestering you to clean. Negative reinforcers are considered a type of aversive behavior control as they rely on the use of an aversive situation that the organism will work to escape or avoid.

Understanding how behavior changes as a result of consequences is important to gaining control over the behavior. For example, a professor may think he or she is negatively punishing a student if his or her cell phone rings in class by assigning that student a ten-minute oral presentation, for course points, in the next class meeting. In fact, according to an instructor who employed this policy, it reduced cell phone disruptions to near zero. Let's take a moment and think through this policy. The instructor's goal is to have fewer cell phone disruptions. To accomplish this, the instructor had to increase the frequency with which students turned off their cell phones. However, the instructor was wrong about the type of operant consequence that was responsible for this change. By creating a clear connection between turning off their cell phones and avoiding having to give an oral presentation, the instructor created not a punishment but a negative reinforcer—removal of the possibility of being embarrassed—that increased the rate at which students turned off their cell phones.

Positive and Negative Consequences

The instructor's cell phone policy above highlights what are perhaps two of the most confused concepts in psychology: positive and negative consequences of operant behavior. For many, the confusion comes from the association between "positive" and "good" and "negative" and "bad." With this in mind, it is difficult to imagine how one would get a "bad" reinforcer or a "good" punisher. That is because thinking of these two words as emotional labels is incorrect. It is more accurate—and useful—to think of positive and negative in mathematical terms. In the mathematical sense, a positive number is added to something while a negative number is removed. This is exactly what is meant by the use of positive and negative when discussing operant consequences. When it is presented to an organism following a given behavior, a positive reinforcer causes an increase in that behavior. Conversely, a negative reinforcer is any stimulus or event that, when removed from the environment following the occurrence of a behavior, will make the behavior that produced it more likely to occur. For both positive and negative reinforcers, a change in the stimulus is associated with an increase in probability of the behavior. However, positive reinforcers are associated with the behavior producing a new stimulus in the environment while negative reinforcers are associated with a stimulus being removed from the environment.

One of the best ways to understand positive and negative reinforcement is through the concept of the **behavior trap**: a situation in which two people's unwanted behavior is maintained by both negative and positive reinforcement. One of the most common contexts in which to see behavior traps is relationships. In a column for *The New York Times*, Amy Sutherland (2006) discusses how the power of operant consequences can be used for building a happy, successful relationship. In this article, she mentions that her original attempts to refine her husband's actions were largely to nag at him about what he needed to do differently. This is a behavior that most people have used to get others to change their ways. Whether we nag a significant other, as in Amy's case, a roommate, or a friend, this is a go-to approach to influencing other people since when someone pesters us to do something, this typically creates an aversive situation that

behavior trap
a situation in which two people's unwanted behavior is maintained by both negative and positive reinforcement

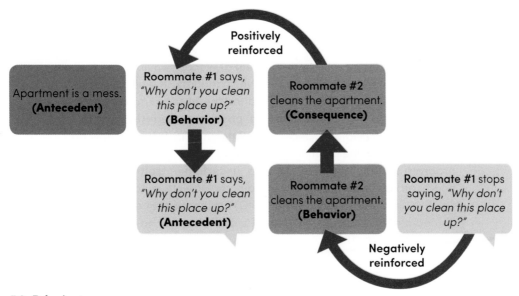

7.8 Behavior trap
This flow chart shows how a behavior trap maintains an aversive interaction between roommates. Neither roommate is happy with the situation, but both are being reinforced by changes in the other's behavior, so the situation continues.

we would like to escape from. The removal of the nagging comments is a negative reinforcer. At the same time, when we get up to do what the person asked, thus removing the nagging, we create a positive reinforcer for the person who is nagging. A visual representation of a behavior trap supporting nagging behavior is shown in Figure 7.8. Think about it this way: the mother who is nagging her child to do his homework receives a positive reinforcer when the child starts to do the homework, while the child receives a negative reinforcer when the mother stops nagging him to do his homework. Neither the mother nor the child are happy with the amount of nagging, but they have a difficult time changing this situation because they are caught in a behavior trap: doing homework is maintained by escape from nagging, which only occurs when homework is not being completed, while nagging is being maintained by doing the homework, which only occurs after being nagged.

Concept Recall

1. How does operant conditioning differ from classical conditioning with regard to creating new behavior?

2. What general behavioral change was responsible for Thorndike's cats becoming more efficient in escaping from the puzzle boxes?

3. What is the difference in how reinforcement and punishment influence behavior?

4. How do positive and negative consequences differ?

5. How are behavior traps responsible for maintaining behaviors, such as nagging and complaining?

This Is Psychology

Aubrey Daniels has worked for the past thirty years applying behavior analysis to the improvement of work behavior. Daniels created the idea of a PIC/NIC® analysis, in which we identify why we do things by evaluating the possible outcomes of each behavior on three dimensions: positive vs. negative, immediate vs. delayed, and certain vs. uncertain. Watching our favorite show on TV is associated with the positive, immediate, certain outcome of enjoying the program and the negative, delayed, uncertain outcome of performing poorly on next week's exam. According to Daniels, outcomes that are positive, immediate, and certain (PIC) and those that are negative, immediate, and certain (NIC) are the ones that will have the most influence on our behavior. Think a moment about the choices you have made today. What were the PICs and the NICs for these choices, and how much of an influence do you think they had on the choices that you made?

Punishment

Punishment occurs when the environmental change produced by a behavior results in the behavior becoming less likely to occur in the future. Just as we have both positive and negative reinforcers, punishers also come in these two types. A positive punisher occurs when something is added to the environment following the behavior, such as a loud noise, an electric shock, a student's name written on the board, or a scarlet letter sewn on the front of someone's dress. A **negative punisher**—a stimulus or event, the removal of which will decrease the likelihood that the behavior that produced its removal will occur again in the future—occurs when something is removed from the environment following the occurrence of the behavior. Time out, such as a child being removed from playing with his or her friends or a favorite toy being removed from the play setting, is the most common example of a negative punisher.

negative punisher
a stimulus or event, the removal of which will decrease the likelihood that the behavior that produced its removal will occur again in the future

In research settings with rats, a common **positive punisher**—a stimulus or event that is produced by the behavior and causes a decrease in the probability of the behavior occurring in the future—is an electric shock received after pressing a lever. We can illustrate this contingency as follows:

positive punisher
a stimulus or event that is produced by the behavior and causes a decrease in the probability of the behavior occurring in the future

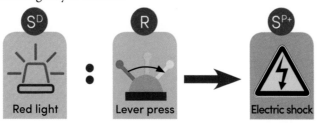

This diagram tells us that when the red light is on, if the rat presses the lever it will receive an electric shock, and, as a result, the rat will be less likely to press the lever in the future. We only label the electric shock as a punisher when it has been shown that this consequence actually reduces the rate of the operant behavior.

Over the years, there has been much debate over the effectiveness of punishment. As stated above, a consequence is only a punisher once its impact on behavior has been demonstrated. In this sense, punishment is an effective process, as it does result in a decrease in the rate of the target behavior. The debate is really over what happens once punishment stops. With reinforcement, failure to deliver the reinforcer results in a weakening of the operant response. If the reinforcer is withheld long enough, the behavior will disappear (this concept, known as "extinction," is outlined in more detail in the section on schedules of reinforcement below). What happens when the punisher is withheld? Over time, the behavior will reappear and will often return to the same level as prior to the onset of the punishment procedure. Why do you think this happens? Earlier in this chapter, we discussed that all operant behaviors that continue to occur are maintained by reinforcement. This is also true of problem behaviors that we are attempting to reduce using punishment. Each delivery of the punisher must compete with the reinforcer elicited by the behavior. For example, consider a child taking a toy from a younger sibling. This behavior is reinforced by acquisition of the toy in the following way:

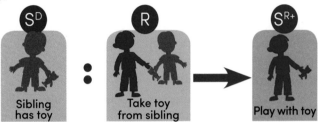

As this contingency shows, the child's toy-taking behavior is reinforced by receiving the toy. A parent may decide to eliminate this problem behavior by adding a positive punisher—yelling at the child—each time the child takes a toy from the sibling. This new contingency is:

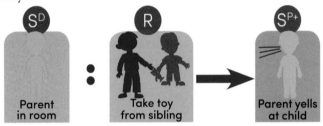

Through the consistent use of this contingency, the child learns not to take the toy from his or her sibling when the parent is in the room. Notice, though, that there are two consequences to taking the toy from the sibling. First, the child gets the toy (but he or she may only have it for a short amount of time until the parent takes it and gives it back to the sibling). Second, the child gets yelled at by his or her parent. If the parent's yelling is more aversive than getting the toy is pleasant, the rate of taking the toy will decrease (be punished). But what will happen if the parent is not in the room? In this case, taking the toy will result in the reinforcer (getting the toy) without the occurrence of the aversive event (being yelled at by the parent). Taking the toy will now be reinforced. For most behaviors that we would punish, the absence of the punisher means that the behavior will be reinforced. For this reason, most punishment contingencies only produce short-term changes in behavior (think about the effect that your last speeding ticket had on your behavior of driving over the posted speed limit!).

Effective punishment typically has four characteristics. These characteristics are immediate, certain, powerful, and surprising. In an operant chamber, it is easy to provide punishers with these characteristics. In the example of the rat discussed on the previous page, as soon as the rat presses a lever, we can present it with a moderate electric shock. This shock is:

Immediate: As soon as the lever press occurs

Certain: We can schedule the mechanism to shock following every lever press

Powerful: We can set the voltage to a high enough level that it does not cause physical damage, but it does induce significant discomfort

Surprising: Without presenting any warning signals or prior experience, the rat would not be prepared for this shock

Under these conditions, we would expect the rat's lever-pressing behavior to immediately stop and to stay depressed for some time. We would not expect the behavior to completely disappear. After some time away from the lever, the rat will try another press. Thanks to the ability to automate the contingencies in an operant chamber, we can arrange it so that the rat is shocked every time it presses the lever. After several shocks, the rat will eventually leave the lever alone entirely, unless this is the only available option for the rat to receive food, in which case we can shock the rat hundreds of times, and it will keep pressing the lever. Due to the biological necessity of food, the reinforcing value of getting food will be greater than the aversiveness of the shock under high enough levels of deprivation.

While it is easy to arrange for immediate, certain, powerful, and surprising punishers in the operant chamber, it is extremely difficult to do so in the real world. Behavior happens in all kinds of contexts, and it is difficult for a behavior manager to create the certainty that would provide the punisher every time the behavior occurs. Also, it is difficult to be able to punish the behavior immediately. Using our example of the child taking a toy from his or her sibling, the child might take the toy from the sibling, begin playing with it, and then minutes later be punished by the parent. In a school setting, a behavior might happen on the playground (fighting, taunting, bullying), and the report to the teacher is not made until after recess or the next day, resulting in a lack of immediacy. Due to the practical constraints in delivering punishment, it is extremely difficult to provide effective punishment in the real world.

In addition to the difficulties of producing lasting change and maintaining effective punishment procedures, the use of punishment is also associated with several unwanted side effects. These problems with punishment are some of the reasons why behavior analysts argue that punishment should be used to change behavior only as a last resort. Here are some of punishment's more common side effects:

1. **Decreased sensitivity to the punisher**: An aversive stimulus that is repeatedly presented will lose its effectiveness if the organism begins to anticipate the occurrence of the aversive event. As the organism acclimates to the aversive stimulus, the trainer needs to use more powerful punishers to get the same effect on the behavior. This escalation cycle is unwanted as it can result in punishment that is physically damaging to the organism.

2. **Counteraggression**: When an aversive stimulus is presented to an organism, we will often observe a retaliatory response. When a rat is shocked, it will often begin gnawing at the response lever. When a person is yelled at, she or he might respond by yelling back or otherwise retaliating against the punisher.

3. **Escape from the punisher**: Through classical conditioning, we develop a negative association between the context in which an aversive event occurs and the aversive event. Over time, the organism may actively engage in responses to avoid the situation in which the punisher is delivered. For example, a child may begin staying away from home in order to avoid the punishment associated with a parent.

4.   **Modeling**: In human behavior, the use of punishment as a disciplinary strategy is associated with greater use of aggressive behavior in peer interactions.

Since punishment is associated with negative side effects and poor long-term outcomes, behavior analysts strongly recommend the use of positive punishment and other nonaversive training techniques as alternatives.

Schedules of Reinforcement

schedules of reinforcement
the rules that specify when reinforcement is delivered and what must be done to earn the consequence

Operant consequences do not happen every time the behavior occurs. For example, we often have to call or text people several times before receiving a response. Similarly, an athlete may need to take several shots before scoring a point, and a video game player may have to push the button multiple times before the enemy is vanquished, the puzzle is solved, or building is finished. **Schedules of reinforcement** refer to the rules that specify when reinforcement is delivered and what must be done to earn the consequence. Overall, the schedules of reinforcement determine how often the reinforcement occurs. In a rich schedule of reinforcement, the probability of a response being reinforced is high, resulting in lots of reinforcement being earned. In a lean schedule of reinforcement, the probability of a response being reinforced is low, resulting in very few reinforcers being earned.

There are dozens of different types of schedules of reinforcement, but we are going to focus specifically on six of the most frequent schedules used in behavioral research. While knowing what the schedule involves is important, it is more important to understand how these schedules influence behavior. Because each schedule is associated with a different pattern of reinforcement, the typical pattern of behavior they generate is also distinct. The six basic schedules of reinforcement are:

1.   Continuous Reinforcement

2.   Extinction

3.   Fixed Ratio

4.   Fixed Interval

5.   Variable Ratio

6.   Variable Interval

The first two schedules, continuous reinforcement and extinction, are the easiest to understand, as they are opposites of each other. Continuous reinforcement (CRF) refers to a schedule in which every occurrence of the target behavior produces reinforcement. In CRF, the probability of the response producing a reinforcer is 1.0, meaning every response will produce a reinforcer. This schedule is particularly useful when teaching new behaviors. CRF is in use when a student is given a point as soon as he or she correctly answers a question. Since reinforcement is received for each correct response, the organism learns quickly which behaviors effectively produce the reinforcers. You most often come into contact with CRF schedules when swiping your credit or debit card leads to an approved transaction that allows you to leave the store with your purchase. CRF is also used when first teaching math concepts to a child. Each time the child correctly answers a question, he or she is rewarded with a smile, sticker, or other recognition of the achievement.

While CRF is a schedule with the probability of reinforcement at 1.0 (happens on 100 percent of trials), extinction (EXT) is a schedule in which the probability of the reinforcer is 0.0 (happens on zero percent of the trials). In EXT, no reinforcers are delivered following an occurrence of the target behavior. EXT is a schedule of reinforcement that is ideal for eliminating the occurrence of the target behavior. According to behavior analytic theory, all operant behavior is maintained by the occurrence of reinforcement. (Remember, not all behavior is operant behavior. Respondent behavior, as previously discussed, is not controlled by the consequences that follow it.) In the absence of reinforcement, the response will eventually disappear. In our discussion, we mentioned swiping your debit/credit card as an example of CRF. Imagine what would happen if the card reader did not respond to your card. This should not be too hard to imagine, as most of us have experienced exactly this situation. This change from a schedule of continuous reinforcement (CRF) to an extinction schedule (EXT) is quite dramatic and results in several major shifts in our behavior. Here are some that you likely experienced:

1. **The Extinction Burst:** Withholding anticipated reinforcers typically results in a sudden increase in the frequency of the operant behavior. While the long-term result of extinction is a reduction in the rate of the behavior, the first change that we see is an increase in the rate of the behavior. What do you typically do after the card reader does not accept your debit/credit card? You slide it several more times. This behavior is an increase extinction burst. While you would normally only slide the card once, you are now sliding it five, six, seven, or more times.

2. **Operant Variability:** After the extinction burst comes a change in the shape or form of the behavior. Typically, this will be other behavior that has produced the desired reinforcer in the past. For example, you might try sliding the card from the bottom up, or maybe sliding your debit/credit card faster, or you might ask the cashier to try running your card for you.

3. **Emotional Responses:** When neither more of the behavior nor different types of behavior serve to produce the reinforcer, the organism will typically begin to show a negative emotional reaction. We most often see behavior that we would label as frustration or anger during this stage of extinction. Some of these emotional responses will be directed toward the response device. For example, we often hear people swear at the card reader or maybe even give it a little shake.

These three characteristics of the extinction cycle are often erroneously perceived as signs that the process is not working, but that is not the case. When you withhold a consequence and see an increase in the frequency of the behavior, operant variability, and emotional responses, it is clear evidence that you have withheld the correct reinforcer and that extinction is working. Rather than giving up, you should continue to withhold the reinforcer until the behavior no longer occurs. When used properly, extinction is a rapid, powerful, and effective method for reducing the frequency of a problem behavior.

While extinction is a powerful tool for reducing the rate of behavior you wish to discourage, there are some cautions that need to be discussed. First, extinction only works when you have the ability to control the reinforcer. If the reinforcer occurs when you are absent or is under the control of something else, then extinction will not work. For example, parents who learn of extinction often try to use this technique to reduce the rate of arguing among their children. They (erroneously) believe that they will impact the behavior by not paying attention to their children when they fight. This will work for the very infrequent cases in which children are fighting in order to get their parents' attention. Most often, children are fighting because of reinforcers that are under the control of their siblings. This might be access to a toy, electronic device, or other activity. You can choose to ignore the fighting, but your inattention will not produce a change in the rate of fighting so long as the behavior continues to produce the desired reinforcers. Remember, ignoring the behavior is only extinction when your attention is the reinforcer.

Second, extinction is not forgetting. When we discussed respondent extinction earlier in this chapter, we pointed out that spontaneous recovery is often observed, in which a relation between a previous CS and CR is seen again after some time has passed since the last pairing of the two stimuli. Something very similar happens in operant extinction. After fully extinguishing a behavior, the response will typically reappear after some time has passed in the situation. This is especially true during extinction for future behaviors in a similar context. When an old behavior reappears during extinction of a new behavior, this is termed **resurgence**. We also know that a behavior put on extinction is not forgotten because subsequent relearning is much faster than when the original association was trained. How much faster learning occurs in subsequent reteaching sessions is often used as a measure of memory (the savings method of memory recall).

Finally, extinction is best used together with positive reinforcement for appropriate behavior. The technique of putting a problem behavior on extinction while adding positive reinforcement is known as differential reinforcement. **Differential reinforcement** works in two ways. First, by adding reinforcement for other behaviors, the organism still has access to desired outcomes. Imagine a rat that has learned to press a lever as its only way of gaining access to food. If we suddenly placed lever pressing on extinction, resulting in the rat no longer getting food for this response, the rat would no longer have access to food. Under these conditions, it would take a long time before the rat would stop pressing the lever for food. Now, consider the same situation, but after putting lever pressing on extinction, we begin providing food whenever the rat approaches the opposite side of the cage. What do you think will happen to the rate of the rat's lever pressing in this new condition? By providing access to the food for a different response, the rate of lever pressing will decrease much faster. The technique described here is termed **differential reinforcement of incompatible (DRI) behavior** because the response that is being reinforced is one that makes it impossible for the rat to engage in lever pressing (the rat cannot be both in the far corner of the operant chamber and pressing the lever on the near wall at the same time).

resurgence
when an old behavior reappears during extinction of a new behavior

differential reinforcement
the technique of putting a problem behavior on extinction while adding positive reinforcement

differential reinforcement of incompatible (DRI) behavior
the technique in which a behavior is identified that cannot occur at the same time as the problem behavior

A second advantage of differential reinforcement is that it provides the organism with a response to engage in instead of the problem behavior. As we saw in the DRI example with the rat's lever pressing, we can often reinforce a behavior that will directly compete with the problem behavior. Another form of differential reinforcement, **differential reinforcement of other (DRO) behavior**, is not concerned with what the other behavior is, but rather provides reinforcement for the organism when it is doing any behavior that is not the problem behavior. In this type of differential reinforcement, the goal is not to increase a specific behavior but simply to get the organism engaged in higher levels of nonproblem behaviors. An ideal situation occurs in **differential reinforcement of alternative (DRA)** scenarios where reinforcement is delivered for behaviors that produce the same reinforcement as the problem behavior targeted. For example, if a child is consistently yelling to get mom's attention, DRA occurs when the child is reinforced—with mom's attention—when she raises her hand or asks politely to speak with mom. As DRI, DRO, and DRA techniques demonstrate, pairing extinction with positive reinforcement is a very powerful, effective, and rapid technique for reducing the rate of problem behaviors.

differential reinforcement of other (DRO) behavior
behavior change technique that provides reinforcement for the organism when it is doing any behavior that is not the problem behavior

differential reinforcement of alternative (DRA)
behavior change technique that provides reinforcement for behaviors that produce the same reinforcement as the problem behavior

Intermittent schedules: Ratio and interval

Continuous reinforcement (CRF) and extinction (EXT) are characterized by their absolute values: either reinforcement is always delivered or reinforcement is never delivered. More common than these schedules are the intermittent schedules of reinforcement in which the probability of a reinforcer is somewhere between zero and 1.00. While there are many types of intermittent schedules, ratio and interval schedules are the simplest and most frequently discussed. Ratio schedules of reinforcement deliver reinforcers based on the number of responses that have occurred. In this way, ratio schedules are based on the frequency of the response. Interval schedules of reinforcement deliver reinforcers based on the time that has passed since the last reinforcer was delivered. In this way, interval schedules are based on the timing of the response. A good example of a fixed ratio schedule of reinforcement is a homework quiz. The quiz has a set number of items—let's imagine it has ten items—that must be completed before you receive the reinforcer (escape from taking the quiz or the score on the quiz, depending on your learning history). No feedback is provided for the first nine items, but once the tenth item is complete, you get the reinforcer. Baking a cake is a good example of an interval schedule. Once you place the batter in the oven, you have to wait for the cake to finish baking before you receive your reinforcer: warm chocolate cake.

The examples of completing a quiz and baking a cake highlight the most important distinction between ratio and interval schedules of reinforcement. While we define these two schedules as being based on the number of responses and time between reinforcers, there is something more important that distinguishes these schedules. Imagine that it is Friday night, and you need to both finish a quiz for your psychology class and bake a cake for your friend's birthday party. How would you get these two tasks done in the most efficient manner? Could you complete one of these tasks faster if needed? Certainly, you could get the quiz done faster by answering the questions faster. If you were not interested in the quality of your answer, you could possibly complete your ten-item quiz in less than a minute. Can you make the cake bake any faster (assuming that turning up the temperature on the oven is not an option)? Not really; the cake needs to bake as long as needed, and no amount of checking, begging, or pleading is going to make the fully cooked cake become available any faster. Because ratio schedules can be completed faster by increasing the speed at which the organism responds, the rate of reinforcement in ratio schedules depends on the rate of the organism's response. This is not true in interval schedules. Instead, the rate of reinforcement in interval schedules is largely independent of the rate of response, so long as the organism is engaging in the minimum response rate required to collect the reinforcer. Given these two characteristics, we could correctly guess that under the pressure of getting ready for the weekend, we would likely take the quiz as fast as possible, but we would not change our rate of cake-baking behavior much.

The effect of response rate on the rate of reinforcement is one distinguishing characteristic between interval and ratio schedules, but there is one more important characteristic. Our guess is that, as you thought about your Friday night preparations, you likely planned to start the cake baking and then work on your quiz. If this is the case, you intuitively took advantage of the second difference between ratio and interval schedules. On an interval schedule, the likelihood of the reinforcer occurring increases with the passage of time. The longer we go between reinforcers, the more likely the next one will occur. This is not true for ratio schedules. If we open the quiz and then go work on the cake, we will not get closer to the quiz being finished. However, if we place the cake in the oven, then go and work on our quiz, we will be making progress toward the completed cake and toward the completed quiz. Interval schedules of reinforcement progress independently of the organism's continued response. Ratio schedules only progress toward reinforcement when the organism is actively engaged in responding to them. Any time we spend away from the quiz will lengthen the time needed to complete the quiz. Time spent doing something else while the cake is baking will not have any effect on the time needed for the cake to finish baking (unless we start an electrical wiring project that results in the oven being accidentally turned off).

Ratio and interval schedules can be set up to provide reinforcers after the same requirement each time or with different requirements. When the requirement for a schedule is set to be constant, we call this a fixed schedule. For example, if you work at a job where you are paid a bonus for every ten items you sell, this would be a fixed ratio of reinforcement. If your instructor schedules an exam every two weeks, this would be a fixed-interval schedule of reinforcement. Schedules in which the requirement changes after each reinforcement are called variable schedules. Slot machines are often given as examples of variable ratios of reinforcement, as you might win two pulls in a row, or you might go for a long stretch before your next pull is a winner. Receiving updates on Facebook is also a good example of a variable interval of reinforcement. Sometimes when you check Facebook your friends have status updates, and sometimes they do not. Since the updates are not predictable, this is a variable schedule.

Schedule specific response patterns

One of the most interesting characteristics of the four main schedules of intermittent reinforcement is that they produce very characteristic patterns of response. These stable patterns are important, as they can help us to identify the reinforcer that maintains the behavior. In the previous paragraph, we identified quizzes scheduled every two weeks as an example of a fixed-interval schedule of reinforcement for your studying behavior. What does your distribution of studying typically look like during the two weeks between quizzes? If you are like most students, you do very little studying immediately after the quiz and for about the next week. Several days before the upcoming quiz, you start doing a little studying, but not much. Several hours before the quiz, you really start studying hard. Look at Figure 7.9 illustrating the response patterns for the four basic schedules. The bottom box on the left is the pattern associated with a

Occurrence of Reinforcer

7.9 Occurrence of reinforcer
The scheduling of reinforcers produces predictable response patterns that can help us identify the reinforcers that can be seen in much of your life. Which pattern looks the most like your typical studying behavior?

fixed-interval schedule. Notice how we see little responding after the reinforcer is earned (the little downward pointing line), as indicated by the flat horizontal line? This is a graph of the number of responses over time. Any time you see a flat horizontal line, this tells you that no responses are occurring. As time passes, the organism starts responding faster, as illustrated by the line bending up toward vertical. The line is at its steepest just before the reinforcer, then it drops back down toward little to no responding for a short time. Look closely at the graph in the fixed interval box below, and imagine that the time between the reinforcers (downward lines) is two weeks. Can you see how closely this looks like the change in rate of your studying behavior between exams?

The figure shows the patterns of responding associated with all four major schedules. As you study this figure, notice that the fixed schedules produce changing patterns of behavior, while the variable schedules produce more constant rates of behavior. Why might this be? Consider a fixed ratio 100 (FR 100) schedule and a variable ratio 100 (VR 100) schedule. Both of these schedules will provide a reinforcer once for every 100 responses. In the FR 100 schedule, however, the first ninety-nine responses are never reinforced. Each response does move the organism closer to the reinforcer, but only the one-hundredth response is ever directly followed by the reinforcer. Due to this, we tend to see long post-reinforcer pauses (the period of no responding shown on the fixed ratio graph, at top-left in Figure 7.9, as a flat horizontal line right after the reinforcer) the higher the response requirement in a fixed ratio schedule. After the pause, the organism jumps right in with a steady, high rate of responding until the reinforcer is earned. In a VR 100 schedule, sometimes the organism is reinforced after just one response, or after four, or after eight, or after sixteen, and so on. In variable schedules, the changing nature of the response requirement makes it so that any response may produce the reinforcement. Since even the first out of the 100 (on average) responses might produce reinforcement, we tend not to see long post-reinforcement pauses and instead see a high, steady rate of responding.

Understanding the patterns of behavior associated with the different schedules of reinforcement is useful for two reasons. First, we can use our understanding of the patterns to better identify the consequences that influence our behavior. Identifying which consequences are responsible for our actions is an important part of being able to predict and control behavior. Second, understanding how schedules influence our behavior can tell as a great deal about how to present the consequences in order to have our intended impact. For example, Zynga, a company that creates popular social media games, such as Farmville and Mafia Wars, makes its money by keeping people interacting with its games on a steady, slow pattern. In order to do so, Zynga fills its games with fixed- and variable-interval schedules. On Farmville, the crops you plant have a set amount of time after which they are ready to harvest (fixed interval), but there are occasional "bonus" items that appear at unpredictable times (variable interval). Because of the arrangement of these two types of schedules, people consistently check their farms and will even rearrange their daily schedules to be able to make their occasional check of their crops' status and to look for unscheduled bonuses.

Concept Recall

1. What are the four characteristics of effective punishment? How do these make it difficult to deliver effective punishment in the real world?

2. What are some of the side effects associated with the use of punishment to manage behavior?

3. How do ratio and interval schedules of reinforcement impact behavior? What about fixed and ratio schedules?

4. What impact does extinction have on behavior, and what are some of the behavioral changes that show us that extinction is working?

5. What are the schedule specific response patterns associated with fixed interval, fixed ratio, variable interval, and variable ratio schedules?

BEHAVIOR, LEARNING, AND PSYCHOLOGY

As we have seen throughout this chapter, behavior is strongly influenced by the environment around us. Conditioned responses are produced by stimuli that have been associated with physiologically important events or uncontrolled stimuli. The power of classical conditioning is often difficult to appreciate as the relation between CS and CR is often something that occurs at a physiological or emotional level. Advertisers and political strategists are well aware of the power of classical conditioning and make use of it in influencing our spending and voting behavior. Much of our nonrespondent behavior is a product of operant conditioning. The consequences that follow our behaviors have a powerful impact on how we behave and how we respond to future situations.

Behavior analysis and learning research demonstrates that we can have a powerful impact on the behavior of an organism by changing the environment surrounding the organism. Behavior analysts argue that powerful technologies for behavior change can be developed by forgoing attempts to change the internal world of the consumer (i.e., how they think, how they feel) and instead focusing on changing the environment before the behavior (antecedent events: discriminative stimuli or conditioned stimuli) or the consequences that follow the behavior (reinforcers, punishers). By changing the context of the behavior, the type of observed behavior will change.

In recent years, the increased focus on the role of the brain in organizing behavior has led to a decreased role for learning research in mainstream psychology. Despite this change in focus, behavior analysts continue to make contributions to designing improved work environments, developing technologies to encourage behavior change, and working with children with developmental disabilities, such as autism.

Despite Skinner's and Watson's arguments that we should look outside the organism for the variables that influence behavior, for the majority of psychologists and even the way we generally think about behavior in our daily lives, we continue to look inside the organism to understand behavior. You likely find yourself reflecting inward to figure out why you do the things that you do or questioning what is going on inside a friend, significant other, or coworker when they behave the way they do. For a change in perspective, try and balance this tendency to look inside with an increased focus on the external factors that influence how we behave. Looking outside the organism for factors that influence the organism's behavior will provide an unexpected—and very useful—perspective of what is going on.

Review/Reflect/Write

REVIEW

- What is learning?
- How does modern behavior analysis differ from the early ideas of behaviorism?
- What are the three elements that Watson argued should characterize scientific psychology?
- How does respondent conditioning create new triggers (CS) for our behavior?
- What are the differences between an unconditioned stimulus, neutral stimulus, and conditioned stimulus? Between unconditioned responses and conditioned responses?
- How do the following aspects influence learning in classical conditioning: (a) the magnitude of the UR, (b) the salience of the NS, (c) how many times the NS and US are presented together, and (d) the time between the NS and the US?
- How does classical conditioning impact our emotions?
- What is the difference between classical and operant conditioning?
- What is the difference between a reinforcer and a punisher? Between a positive and a negative outcome?
- What are the characteristics of effective punishment?
- What effects does withholding reinforcement have on behavior?
- What patterns of responding are generated by the four major schedules of reinforcement?

1. Which of the following is an example of the formal definition of learning?
   a. A mouse reaches the end of a maze.
   b. A cat gets sprayed by water when scratching a couch, leading the cat to stop scratching the couch.
   c. An elephant remembers the face of the person it encountered ten years ago.
   d. A dolphin uses its fins to maneuver underwater.

2. Behaviorism is
   a. a subfield of psychology that focuses exclusively on the relationship between behavior and environmental events.
   b. a subfield of psychology that focuses exclusively on the internal processes that affect behavior.
   c. a field of psychology that emphasizes the importance of behavioral techniques on changing mental processes.
   d. a field of psychology that emphasizes the importance of internal processes as they relate to behavioral adaptations.

3. A male chimpanzee, Harry, experiences a rise in blood pressure when another male chimpanzee shows signs of aggression. When researchers accompanied these signs of aggression with the smell of roses, Harry eventually experienced this rise in blood pressure when exposed to the smell of roses even when no other chimpanzees were present. In this scenario, the signs of aggression were a(n)
   a. unconditioned stimulus.   c. conditioned stimulus.
   b. unconditioned response.   d. conditioned response.

Answer Key
1.b 2.a 3.a 4.c 5.d 6.b 7.c 8.d 9.c 10.c

4. In the case of Little Albert, when he responded with fear to a dog, a rabbit, and cotton wool, what was occurring?

    a. spontaneous recovery

    b. discrimination

    c. generalization

    d. extinction

5. Which of the following examples shows a case of discrimination?

    a. Jane shows signs of fear in the presence of snakes and worms.

    b. Fiona jumps at the sound of fireworks and screams at the sound of gunshots.

    c. Larry flinches when a moth comes near his face.

    d. Beau gasps when he sees wasps but not when he sees bumblebees.

6. Shameka taught her cat to stop jumping on the counters by spraying her cat with water each time it jumped on them. Shameka was using

    a. a positive reinforcer.

    b. a positive punisher.

    c. a negative reinforcer.

    d. a negative punisher.

7. Which of the following is the difference between a primary and a secondary reinforcer?

    a. A primary reinforcer is more effective.

    b. Primary reinforcers are environmental events we have learned are valuable.

    c. An organism does not have to learn the value of a primary reinforcer.

    d. A primary reinforcer can be extinguished, whereas a secondary reinforcer cannot.

8. Which of the following is true of a negative reinforcer?

    a. It is a stimulus or event that, when added, makes the behavior that produced it less likely.

    b. It is a stimulus or event that, when added, makes the behavior that produced it more likely.

    c. It is a stimulus or event that, when removed, makes the behavior that produced it less likely.

    d. It is a stimulus or event that, when removed, makes the behavior that produced it more likely.

9. Which of the following schedules of behavior will produce more constant rates of behavior?

    a. Fixed ratio

    b. Fixed interval

    c. Variable ratio

    d. Continuous reinforcement

10. Hank's children love to play noisy, roughhouse-type games in the house. In order to reduce these types of activities, Hank has started to praise his kids every time he notices them reading, coloring, or doing any activity that does not involve roughhousing. This is an example of

    a. extinction.

    b. differential reinforcement of incompatible behavior.

    c. differential reinforcement of other behavior.

    d. generalizability.

REFLECT

1. Behavior analysts argue that all behavior is controlled by its consequences. What are the consequences that maintain your study behavior? Can you think of any consequences that you could add, remove, or change in the environment that would make it more likely that you would study?

2. Classical conditioning is a large part of advertising and movies. What situations can you think of in which the media has used conditioning to shape your emotional responses?

3. How do schedules of reinforcement control your behavior? How do you think it would influence your studying behavior if exams were scheduled on variable rather than fixed schedules?

WRITE

1. In their study of Little Albert, Watson and Rayner demonstrated that phobias can be learned. However, much more research has focused on how to use classical conditioning to treat problem behaviors, such as phobias, addictions, and post-traumatic stress disorder. Using psychology databases available through your institution's library system—such as PsycINFO, PsycARTICLES, or Google Scholar, find two research articles reporting on the use of classical conditioning techniques to treat behavior problems. For each of the articles, write a one-page summary of how classical conditioning is being used. How effective do you think the technique would be for treating your fears and anxieties?

2. Our behavior is controlled by the consequences that surround us. Make a list of three behaviors you engage in during a typical day (make certain that these pass the Dead Person's test from Chapter 1). For each of the behaviors, identify:

    a. what antecedent stimuli predictably occur before the behavior,

    b. what consequences typically follow after the behavior,

    c. whether you would like to do more or less of this behavior, and

    d. what consequences you would change, add, or remove in order to produce the desired change in the behavior.

Key Terms

8 Consciousness and Sleep

After reading this chapter, you will be able to answer the following questions:

- Why might you believe that mental things are very different from physical things?
- What are the consequences of believing that mental and physical things are distinct?
- What kinds of questions about human consciousness are relatively easy to answer?
- Does imagination work like perception?
- If you were talking to someone who was suddenly replaced by a different person, would you notice the switch?
- If someone asked you why you did something and you didn't remember the reasons, would say you don't remember, or would you just make something up?
- What happens to your brain and body during a night's sleep?
- Do dreams mean anything?

What if, shortly after birth, communication cables were inserted through the back of your neck into the base of your brain? Ever since then, these cables have been interrupting motor signals as they descend from your brain so they never reach their intended targets: the muscles in your body. Instead, these motor signals are continuously conveyed to a centralized worldwide artificially intelligent computer system that interprets them and devises the appropriate sensory signals that are then sent back through the cable to be uploaded to your brain. For example, if you went for a run, you would expect to see the countryside flow by, you would hear your footsteps and labored breathing, and you would feel the wind in your face. The computer generates sensory signals that accompany the typical running experience, so your intention to run and belief that you are running are matched by your sensory experiences, when in fact you (and everyone else) are curled up in a fetal position, lying motionless, in a vegetative-sleep state floating in artificial placental fluid. Which is correct? And how would you know?

If you've seen the classic movie trilogy *The Matrix*, you're familiar with at least one modern story that directly addresses humans' experiences of consciousness. The hero computer hacker Neo (or Mr. Anderson) fights against malicious computer programs that have taken control of humanity by plugging them into "the matrix": a nearly inescapable global motherboard that harvests humans' heat energy to fuel artificial intelligence machines. To keep humanity docile, the machines create a false reality for humans that looks and feels real but reveals inconsistencies when strained (like déjà vu) and can be manipulated with the right training, which Neo receives from other freed humans.

At its core, *The Matrix* presents an intriguing and unsettling idea: What if the basic facts we all implicitly rely on to understand who we are and how we fit into the world are actually wrong? That is, you probably think that you woke up this morning and went about your usual daily routine, interacting with people and things and navigating your surroundings to arrive where you are right now, but how do you know that your experiences happened as you perceived and remember them? Scientists openly and frequently discuss the "easy" and "hard" problems of consciousness, as you'll read in this chapter. NASA physicist Tom Campbell in his *My Big TOE (Theory of Everything)* book series makes suggestions about the nature of consciousness akin to those in *The Matrix*. The fact that a NASA physicist and consciousness expert names his consciousness studies "theories" suggests that consciousness is a subject neither simple to explain nor understand, so let's take a look at consciousness and sleep in the context historical grounding and psychological study.

WHAT IS CONSCIOUSNESS?

consciousness
the awareness of whatever is presently happening in your mind

Consciousness is intensely personal but also mysterious. You're intimately familiar with your own conscious mind because it contains your entire subjective experience. And yet you are the only person who has direct access to your own conscious mind, so coming up with a definition of consciousness that is objectively satisfying to everyone is not easy. It is tempting to believe that consciousness represents an internal mental model of the world built from the perception of your surroundings, yet the experiences in your dreams are not actually occurring. Instead, consciousness can be defined as an awareness of whatever is presently happening in your mind.

Even though your conscious mind is always centered on the present moment, you can travel through time by loading your conscious mind with memories of the past and expectations for the future. And while your conscious mind contains everything that you are presently aware of, much of your brain's activity occurs outside of your awareness. In this chapter we will explore consciousness, beginning with some philosophical theories about consciousness.

Philosophical Background

René Descartes

evil genius
an imagined character who interrupts motor commands before they reach the body and creates fictitious sensory signals to send to the brain, enabling Descartes to doubt the accuracy of his perceptual experiences

While *The Matrix* relies on modern telecommunication, information processing, and robotics technology to tell its story, it is actually an updated version of a famous thought experiment described in the 1600s by René Descartes. In his book *Meditations on First Philosophy*, Descartes tried to find a firm foundation on which to base his knowledge about the world. To do so, he began by wondering whether his perceptual experiences accurately depicted objects, people, and scenes. Descartes didn't have access to our modern understanding of how neurons work as electrical devices, as described in Chapter 3. He did, however, understand that nerves descending from the brain command muscles to act, and other nerves ascending from the body tell the brain what it senses. Descartes imagined an **evil genius** who is so powerful that he can interrupt descending motor signals before they reach their targets in the body and generate ascending sensory signals to create an illusory mental model of the world. While this may have been difficult for a reader from the 1600s to imagine, Descartes noted that almost everyone can recall vivid dream experiences in which they seemed to be interacting in bizarre ways with strange people in weird places, when in fact they were lying snug in their beds. In this way, Descartes managed to doubt the accuracy of all of his perceptual experiences—because they might all be the product of an evil genius intent on deceiving him, as if he were in a dream.

Because Descartes was trying to build a firm foundation for knowledge, his method of doubt was intended not just to reveal how perceptual experiences can deceive but to clear the way for something else to be the foundation for knowledge. Even if all of Descartes's perceptual experiences are illusions, and none of the people, places, or things that inhabit his mind actually exist in the outside world, at least he knows that thought that they may be an illusion exists. And if there exists a thought, there must be a mind holding that thought. Descartes proposed this logical conclusion: I think, therefore I am. This, then, was the basis of human knowledge for someone like Descartes, who doubts the reliability of his entire perceptual experience: logic. And because a person who thinks logically is being rational, relying on logic as the foundation of human knowledge is called **rationalism**.

One of the consequences of Cartesian rationalism is a disconnect between objects in the outside world and your own mental representations of those objects. After all, physical things in the world and mental things in the mind do seem to be radically different. For example, a physical table has length, width, and height, which you can measure with a ruler, and weight, which you can measure with a scale. How could you possibly measure your own mental representation of a table? Could you wrap a measuring tape around your head or place your head on a scale while you're imagining the table? Of course not, so Descartes argued that there are two distinct kinds of things in the world: physical things and mental things. Distinguishing between the physical and mental, and presuming both to have their own independent existence, is called **dualism**.

Although dualism captures most people's common-sense knowledge that a physical table and your mental representation of the table are very different kinds of things, dualism entails some distasteful consequences. For example, if physical and mental things are independent, how do they interact? That is, if I feel my nose itch, how does my mental intention to scratch the itch command the physical muscles in my arm to move accordingly? This is the **mind-body problem**, which implies that if mental things are distinct and independent from physical things, there is no way for mental intentions to affect physical states, such as the movements of the body. One solution to the mind-body problem relies on the notion of two clocks that display the same time without being connected to each other. Like these two clocks, perhaps God synchronized your mind and body so when your mind notices an itch and decides to raise your hand to scratch it, your hand was preordained by God to rise at just that moment. Thus, the mental and physical do not actually interact, but they just seem to interact because the mental and physical systems unwind independently at the same rate, like two synchronized clocks.

If the idea that the mental and the physical were synchronized by God to unwind at the same rate seems crazy to you, then you feel the same frustration that many others have felt about Cartesian dualism. The mind-body problem doomed Cartesian dualism from being taken seriously as a scientific explanation of the human mind. If there are not two kinds of things in the world, as suggested by dualism, then there may be just one kind of thing, an idea called **monism**. But which one is it? Are there just mental things or just physical things? Each kind of monism has had its supporters; those who argue that there are only mental things are called **idealists**, and those who argue that there are only physical things are called materialists (the relationship between dualism, monism, idealism, and materialism is shown in Figure 8.1).

rationalism
a perspective based on René Descartes's argument that all knowledge based on perception can be doubted, so the best foundation for human knowledge is logic, as expressed in his famous statement: I think, therefore I am

dualism
a consequence of Descartes's doubt of the accuracy of perceptual experience; the belief that there are two kinds of things in the world, physical things and mental things, that exist independently

mind-body problem
because Cartesian dualism entails that mental things are distinct and independent of physical things, there is no way for mental intentions to influence physical things, such as body movements

monism
a rejection of Cartesian dualism by arguing that there is just one kind of thing in the world; because dualism entails two kinds of things, as a response to dualism, there are two kinds of monism: idealism (there are only mental things) and materialism (there are only physical things)

idealism
the branch of monism that claims there are only mental things in the world

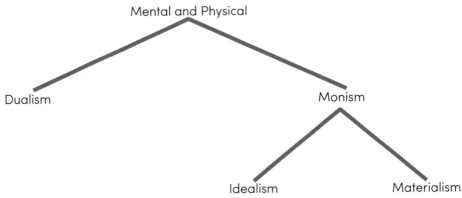

8.1 Are mental and physical things distinct?

Descartes argued that mind and body are different kinds of things, so he and everyone who agrees with him are dualism, because they believe that the two are separate. Alternatively, a person might believe, as in monism, that there is just one kind of thing, of which there are two versions. A person who believes that there are only mental things in the world is an idealist, and a person who believes that there are only physical things in the world is a materialist.

The best-known proponent of idealism was George Berkeley, an Irish bishop who published *Three Dialogues Between Hylas and Philonous* in 1713. In this book, Berkeley asked readers to consider everything they can know about a common object like a table. All that you can know about the table are such things as the way it looks, what it feels like when you rap your knuckles on it, and the sound it makes. Do you also know that there is a physical table existing over and above your perceptual experiences of it? To answer this question, Berkeley argued that we should rely on **Occam's razor**, which states that when trying to explain the available data, we should use a razor to trim any unnecessary parts. If the available data are the way the table looks, sounds, and feels, why then do we need to propose a physical table that exists over and above these perceptual features? The physical table is an unnecessary adjunct, so it should be trimmed.

Occam's razor
when trying to explain the available data, any unnecessary parts should be trimmed from the explanation as if with a razor

As you can see, Berkeley used Occam's razor to trim the physical things from Cartesian dualism, leaving just mental things. Also, by emphasizing the importance of perceptual information, Berkeley rejects Descartes's system of doubting perception. Indeed, by claiming that there are only mental things in the world, Berkeley argued that experience is the basis for human knowledge, a perspective called **empiricism**. According to empiricism, as babies, each of us began life with a mind like a **tabula rasa**, which is often translated from Latin to mean "blank slate." This slate has become filled with the particular memories and knowledge that each of us has accumulated through our own unique passage through life.

empiricism
a perspective associated with George Berkeley, who argued that in contrast to Cartesian rationalism, the only basis for human knowledge is perceptual experience

tabula rasa
a Latin term roughly translated as "blank slate," which is a metaphor for the mind of a newborn baby

Like Cartesian dualism, Berkeley's idealism entails its own distasteful consequences that doom it from being considered as a modern scientific explanation of the human mind. If a table consists only of the way it looks, sounds, and feels, and there is no physical table underlying people's perceptual experiences of it, then when there is nobody experiencing the table, it winks out of existence. Does this sound right to you?

According to Berkeley's idealism, all of the physical objects that we typically assume maintain a continuous existence independent of ourselves—from simple things, such as tables, to grander things, such as our moon—are actually just bundles of perceptual features, so when they are unperceived, they cease to exist. Perhaps Berkeley knew that his readers would violently object to the idea that seemingly physical objects wink into and out of existence based on whether they are being perceived at any one time. For that reason, Berkeley allowed that God constantly perceives seemingly physical objects, so they maintain continuity independent of human observers. As a bishop, Berkeley may have developed his system of idealism as a way to prove God's existence, but for most people, the idea that God must constantly perceive every single object to maintain the object's continued existence is deeply unsatisfying.

In contrast to Berkeley's idealism, our modern scientific perspective focuses on physical objects independent of mental representations. By arguing that there are only physical things in the world, the modern scientific perspective is the other kind of monism, which is called **materialism**. And yet, you may feel that mental experiences seem very different from physical things, which is why Cartesian dualism remains so satisfying for many people, even if it is defective as a scientific theory of mind. Francis Crick, who won the Nobel prize for being one of the co-discoverers of the structure of DNA, admitted that mind being just an aspect of the physical is an astonishing hypothesis. Crick argues that human minds are an **emergent property** of human brains, which means that when enough neurons work together, something (mind) emerges that is not apparent when examining the individual elements (neurons). In the few centuries since Descartes developed dualism, we have come to understand how atoms make up our world, how chemical elements bind to form molecules, how animals and plants grow and prosper, how continents drift, and countless other concepts, so it seems reasonable to expect that human consciousness should eventually succumb to the same scientific process that has explained so many other things (Dennett, 2017).

materialism
the branch of monism that claims there are only physical things in the world

emergent property
an emergent property, such as mind, is the product of (i.e., emerges from) smaller pieces (neurons) but is not apparent when examining the smaller pieces

Philosophical debates about whether there are both the mental and the physical in the world or just one, and how the mind comes to know about the world, form the foundation for modern approaches to studying consciousness. First of all, as with other sciences, such as physics and chemistry, the science of consciousness is strictly materialist, meaning that the world consists of physical things. While the mind may seem to be very different from physical things, it nevertheless emerges from physical brains. Second, the science of consciousness is a blend of rationalism and empiricism. When you were a newborn baby, you were not merely a tabula rasa, passively observing the world around you. Instead, although you had not yet acquired any experiences, you imposed mental structure on your experiences to make sense out of them. Your lack of experience was a kind of tabula rasa (empiricism), and the organizational structure you imposed on your experiences was a kind of logic (rationalism). Now that you have a general sense of how scientists approach the study of consciousness, it is time to be more specific about the kinds of problems that might yield to a scientific study of consciousness.

Concept Recall

1. Although rationalism and empiricism both try to explain how the mind comes to know things, how are they different?

2. How are dualism, monism, idealism, and materialism related to each other, and what are the two kinds of things they talk about?

3. How do dualism and idealism fall short as scientific explanations of mind?

4. What do the mind-body problem, Occam's razor, and tabula rasa have to do with the study of the mind?

The Easy and Hard Problems of Consciousness

David Chalmers (1995) distinguishes between what he calls easy problems of consciousness—e.g., explaining how mental states can be verbally reported or how attention can be focused—and the hard problem. The hard problem of consciousness is one that you might have come up with yourself as you read about neural function in Chapter 3. That is, while brain activity is fundamentally the result of ion flow within neurons and chemical diffusion between neurons, does that really explain *all* of human experience? When you consider the way pineapple tastes or how it feels to fall in love, does it make sense that these subjective experiences simply reflect the activities of chemicals moving around in your brain? Philosophers refer to subjective experiences as **qualia**, and Chalmers argues that the study of qualia represents the final frontier of science.

qualia
the way the world looks and feels inside your conscious mind—for example, the way red looks or the way pineapple tastes

This is not to say that science has thoroughly explained everything, but at least physicists trying to describe the birth of the universe and biologists probing the genome have developed a set of tools and techniques to support their investigations. Consider this classic thought experiment: when you and I look at a patch of color and we agree to call the patch "red", that doesn't necessarily mean that you and I have the same mental experience. If I could somehow directly access your mental experience of the color patch that we agree to call "red," maybe your subjective experience is what I would call "yellow" instead. While this kind of problem may be fun to think about, how on earth could I possibly meld your experience with my own, as if I were Mr. Spock on *Star Trek*? Until the science of qualia catches up with science fiction, researchers will have to content themselves with attacking the kinds of problems that Chalmers calls easy. Chalmers does not mean to imply that these kinds of problems are actually easy to solve, but rather that scientists at least have some ideas about how to investigate the easy problems, while they don't even know where to begin to study the hard problems. Two kinds of conscious experiences that have yielded to scientific study are mental imagery and selective attention.

MENTAL IMAGERY

How many windows are in your house or apartment? It isn't fair for you to just look and count, so if you are reading this while at home, close your eyes before answering. How did you figure out the answer? Did you create an image of your house or apartment in your mind, then "walk" around the mental image, counting windows as you went? If so, you used introspection to "look at" your mental image. Mental imagery is not just visual—it can include the other senses as well. What is the highest note in the Happy Birthday song? Is it Ha-, -ppy, birth-, -day, to, or you? If you can hear the song in your "mind's ear," you probably notice that you sing the highest note for "birth-." As with counting the windows in your house, you used introspection to answer a question. Does that mean that visual imagery is like vision, and auditory imagery is like hearing? Before finding an answer to this question, let's look at the history of the study of imagery in psychology.

You may recall from Chapter 1 that structuralism is based on the idea that breaking big things into smaller pieces works well in sciences such as physics. For example, physicists describe air pressure as collisions between gas molecules moving about. Because this approach works so well in physics and chemistry, according to structuralism, the study of mind should benefit from a similar analytic approach. To that end, structuralists developed the technique of **analytic introspection**, whereby a person exposed to some stimulus, such as a piece of pineapple, would try to break the sensation into all its constituent parts. An example of a modern-day analytic introspectionist might be a sommelier who takes a sip, then describes the wine as having notes of shaved chocolate with a touch of smoke. In the early part of the twentieth century, the prominent behaviorist John Watson (1913) denounced introspective techniques as unproductive because every person's internal experiences are private, so there is no way to compare the results of one person's introspection with another person's. One of the consequences of the cognitive revolution described in Chapter 10 was that mental images once again became acceptable as the subject of scientific study.

analytic introspection
a technique used by structuralists to study mind by breaking sensory experiences into their constituent pieces

One of the first scientific attempts to study mental images was Roger Shepard and Jacqueline Metzler's (1971) **mental rotation** experiment. In their experiments, participants viewed two computer-generated images of block figures, such as the ones in Figure 8.2, and reported whether the two objects were the same or different. The experimenters varied the rotational distance between the two shapes and measured the response time necessary to make the same-different judgment. As you can see for the three pairs of block figures in Figure 8.2, the rotational distance is smaller for the first pair of block figures than the second pair, and the third pair of block figures are different. How did you decide whether the two block figures are the same or different? Did you create a mental image of each item, then mentally rotate one of them until both shapes had the same orientation, then compare them with each other? Shepard and Metzler found that response times increased with rotational distance, so shapes that were rotated farther required more time to process than shapes that were rotationally closer.

mental rotation
an experimental technique in which participants view images depicting two objects that have been rotated relative to one another and report whether the two objects are the same or different

8.2 Computer-generated images from Shepard and Metzler's (1971) mental rotation experiment
Participants viewed two objects at a time and judged whether they were the same or different. The pair of items at the top are rotated less than the pair of items in the middle. The pair at the bottom are different.

If you were actually holding and visually examining the shapes depicted in Figure 8.2, you would need more time to rotate a shape farther than if you rotated it less, so the results from this experiment suggest that mental images are like visual images. This mental rotation experiment and others like it ignited a decades-long debate about whether mental images are more like visual images (as seems to be the case when you look at mental rotation), or more like verbal descriptions. One of the relevant pieces of evidence is based on people who experience visual deficits after suffering from brain damage. For someone who has lost the ability to visually perceive something, do they retain the ability to imagine the thing that they can no longer see?

In Chapter 3 you read that visual processing proceeds along two independent streams, one called "What" that enables you to identify objects, and another called "Where" that enables you to register objects locations. Did George Washington have a beard? If you asked someone who had injured the What pathway, they would have difficulty answering this question from memory. On the other hand, can you close your eyes and indicate the locations of the furniture in the room where you are sitting? This is the kind of question that someone who had injured the Where pathway would have difficulty answering (Levine, Warach, & Farah, 1985). Because mental imagery deficits often parallel the visual deficits from brain damage, mental images seem to rely on the same cortical "hardware" as visual perception. The overlap is not perfect, however, because some people with intact vision experience imagery deficits, and some people with impaired vision retain the ability to imagine what they can no longer see (Kosslyn, Ganis, & Thompson, 2001). Mental imagery and perception do share much of the same neural substrate (Brogaard & Gatzia, 2017). You may know that Beethoven continued to write music even after he lost his hearing, as if he could actually hear songs in his head that he could then commit to paper. From what you now know about mental imagery, you might realize that in a certain sense Beethoven *did* hear the music he wrote while deaf, because even though his ears no longer worked, the auditory processing in his brain was intact.

Selective Attention

As you will read in Chapter 9, attention is the gateway to the conscious mind; our brains are continually exposed to a flood of sensory stimuli, but only a small portion manages to pass through the attentional filter to reach conscious awareness. This aspect of attention is perhaps most clearly demonstrated in **change blindness** experiments (Simons & Levin, 1998). In one example, an experimenter approached a naive bystander on a college campus and asked for directions to one of the campus buildings. While the unwitting participant provided directions, two people carrying a door walked between the experimenter and participant (Figure 8.3). While hidden by the door, the experimenter switched places with one of the door carriers. After the door carriers walked away, because of the switch, a different person was now standing in front of the participant. While you might expect that almost everyone would notice their conversational partner being transformed into a completely different person, this was not the case. In fact, most participants failed to notice the switch, and they simply continued to provide directions as if nothing unusual had just occurred. Apparently they were so focused on the task of providing directions that they were unaware of the switch.

change blindness
a perceptual phenomenon that occurs when an observer does not notice a change in visual stimulus

8.3 Clips from Simons and Levin's door experiment
An experimenter pretends to be lost, then while an unsuspecting bystander provides directions, two people carrying a door seem to walk between them. While hidden by the door, one experimenter switches with one of the door carriers. Even though the person now listening to directions is different, many bystanders continue giving directions, indicating that they do not notice the switch.

Change blindness experiments show that people often fail to notice when external objects are switched, but what about things inside your own head, such as the choices you make? To find out whether people would fail to notice their own choices being switched, a group of Swedish researchers (Johansson, Hall, Sikström, & Olsson, 2005) showed participants images of women's faces two at a time and asked the participant to select the face they considered to be more attractive. The experimenter then placed

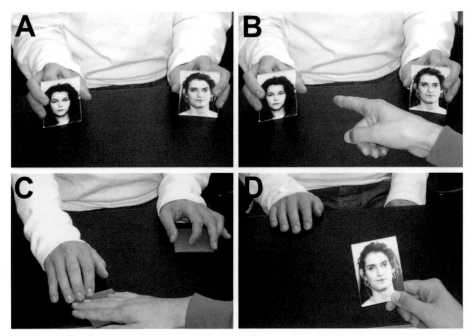

8.4 Choice blindness experiment
The experimenter shows two images to the participant, who indicates which face is more attractive. On some trials, the experimenter uses a simple magic trick to switch the images, and yet most participants do not notice.

both images facedown on the table and slid the selected image across the table to the participant, who then picked up the image and described their reasons for picking that image. On some trials, the experimenter used a simple magic trick to switch the images, so the participant picked up and examined the image they had judged to be *less* attractive, as shown in Figure 8.4. Surprisingly, most participants did not object to the switch and were willing to describe their reasons for selecting the image, even though they were looking at the image that they had not selected.

Apparently, when people are asked to justify decisions they don't remember making, instead of admitting that they don't remember the reasons, they just make up something that sounds plausible. Has anyone ever accused you of some behavior, then asked how you could possibly have done such a thing? If you didn't remember doing what you were accused of, would you deny having done what you were accused of, or would you invent some reasons on the fly? The results from choice blindness experiments suggest that you would make up reasons, which shows that our conscious experience of the world consists of the stories we tell ourselves. This seems also to be the case for people who have had their conscious mind split into two pieces.

In Chapter 3 you read about people suffering from seizure disorders who underwent surgery to sever the corpus callosum, which is the nerve bundle connecting the two hemispheres. As mentioned in Chapter 3, you might expect that hacking through several hundred million nerve fibers in the central nervous system would have profound consequences on postoperative behavior and mind. Nevertheless, while the surgery provided relief from seizures, there were relatively few side effects. In an experiment with a split-brain participant, Michael Gazzaniga briefly presented two images, one to each visual field. Because of neural crossover between the brain and body, the right hemisphere saw the object on the left (a snowy scene), and the left hemisphere saw the object on the right (a chicken foot), as depicted in Figure 8.5. Gazzaniga then presented several images and asked the participant to point to an image matching the two briefly visible images. The participant's right hemisphere commanded his left arm to point at a snow shovel, and his left hemisphere commanded his right arm to point at a chicken. Like most people, the participant's language ability is isolated in his left hemisphere, so when Gazzaniga asked the participant to *describe* his reasons for pointing at each image, only his left hemisphere could respond because his right hemisphere is mute. His verbal left hemisphere easily stated that he was pointing at a chicken because he had seen a chicken foot. However, his left hemisphere had no idea why his right hemisphere had commanded his left hand to point at a shovel, and the right hemisphere couldn't speak for itself, so his left hemisphere just invented a reason: he was pointing to a shovel because that was the necessary tool for mucking out a chicken coop. This example supports the claim made earlier in this chapter that the human mind is an emergent property of the brain; when the connection between the two hemispheres was severed, the single conscious mind was fractured into two separate pieces.

8.5 Choices made by someone with a split brain
Two images are briefly presented, one to each hemisphere, then the split-brain participant points with each hand to a picture matching what each hemisphere had seen. The left hemisphere saw a chicken foot, so the right hand points to a chicken, and the right hemisphere saw a snowy scene, so the left hand points to a snow shovel.

Concept Recall

1. What are the easy and hard problems of consciousness?

2. Why did behaviorists deem the study of mental images to be unproductive?

3. How did the mental rotation experiment work, what were the results, and what do these results imply about mental images?

4. If someone who suffers from a visual deficit due to brain damage also experiences similar deficits in mental imagery, what does that imply about mental images?

5. Do you think you would notice if a person you were talking to were switched with a different person? Is this what change blindness experiments found?

This Is Psychology

On the evening of Friday, February 1, 1991, a USAir 737 was landing at Los Angeles International Airport. As with all commercial flights, the pilot of the 737 expected the airport to have anticipated his arrival by clearing the runway, but due to a series of mishaps, a small turboprop plane was positioned right where he was intending to land. The 737 collided with the turboprop, crushing it underneath. For anyone who wasn't piloting the 737 that night, it can be difficult to imagine how the pilot could have failed to see the other airplane positioned on the runway *right where he was intending to land his own plane*. Actually, the 737 pilot may have seen the turboprop on the runway, in the sense that the turboprop's image was projected onto his retina, and his optic nerve conveyed the retinal image to his visual cortex. Even so, the image of the turboprop apparently failed to penetrate into his conscious mind. The collision was due to a failure of *attention*, not perception.

CIRCADIAN RHYTHMS AND SLEEP

Up to this point in this chapter, we have focused on the awake and alert mind, but this is just one of three brain states that mammals cycle through each day (Siegel, 2010). One of the brain states is wakefulness, and the other two occur while sleeping. As inhabitants of a world where the Earth's rotation causes predictable variations of light and dark each day, you might expect that our brains would simply rely on visible signals indicating the time of day to select behaviors appropriate to the available light. For example, we might be inclined to gather food during the day, when edible plants and animals can easily be seen, and to save energy by resting at night when wandering about in the darkness could be dangerous.

circadian rhythm
the daily cycle of waking and sleeping, body temperature, and hormones that is generated by an internal biological clock and synchronized to light and dark patterns due to the Earth's rotation

And yet, when experimental participants live for weeks in conditions of constant illumination, without access to clocks or any other cues to the time of day, they adopt a cycle of waking and sleeping that is about twenty-four hours and fifteen minutes long (Czeisler et al., 1999). Apparently, our brains contain an onboard clock that governs daily cycles of sleeping and waking, body temperature, and the amount of hormones, such as melatonin, in the blood. Because the internally generated rhythm approximates but does not perfectly replicate the externally generated patterns of light and dark due to the Earth's rotation, it is called a **circadian rhythm**, from the Latin meaning "approximately a day."

The fact that your brain is equipped with an onboard biological clock can explain why you experience jet lag when your flight carries you across one or more time zone boundaries. When your plane lands at its destination, your internal clock is still set to the time where your trip began, and you need a few days to resynchronize your internal clock to the local time. Not only that, but the fact that your internal clock runs a little slow each day explains why recovery from jet lag is quicker for westward travel than eastward travel. To understand why, think about a westward trip from New York to San Francisco. When you land in San Francisco, the local time is three hours earlier than your internal clock, so if you wake up your first night in California when your brain feels like 8 a.m., the local time is only 5 a.m., and you can sleep for an extra three hours. On the other hand, after adjusting to the local time in San Francisco then flying back to New York, on your first night in New York you'll have to wake up when your brain feels like 5 a.m. because the local time will be 8 a.m. In other words, westward travel lengthens the day, whereas eastward travel shortens the day, but because your internal clock runs for longer than a day, it's easier for you to lengthen the day than to shorten the day. Even if you have never flown across time zones, twice a year you reset your (external) clocks, when you spring forward an hour to daylight saving time and when you fall back by an hour to standard time. Because springing forward removes an hour from the day but falling back adds an hour to the day, you have probably found it easier to adjust to falling back than to springing forward. If so, you're not the only one. Traffic fatalities increase during the week following the spring forward transition (Smith, 2016), suggesting that shortening the day by an hour leads to widespread sleep deprivation.

Where is your internal clock in the brain, and how do you keep it synchronized with the external cycle of light and dark? You may recall from Chapter 3 that the hypothalamus is implicated in motivated behaviors, which includes the motivation to get enough sleep each night. In the hypothalamus is a bundle of cells called the **suprachiasmatic nucleus (SCN)**. That name is quite a mouthful, but it mostly indicates a location in the brain. As you can see in Figure 8.6, viewing the human brain from below reveals that the optic nerves from each eye appear to cross over as they project back to the brain, forming an X. The crossover is called the optic chiasm, named after the Greek letter X (chi). The suprachiasmatic nucleus is a of bundle of cells (nucleus) that lies directly above (supra-) the optic chiasm. How do we know the SCN embodies the brain's internal clock? When

suprachiasmatic nucleus (SCN)
a bundle of cells in the hypothalamus embodying the internal clock, which drives the circadian rhythm

experimenters removed the SCN from the brains of laboratory animals, the animals slept as much per day as they did before their brain surgery, but their sleep no longer followed a periodic cycle. Then, when their brains were transplanted with SCN cells from donor animals, their sleep patterns returned to a normal daily cycle. As for the question of how the SCN synchronizes the internal clock to external light and dark cycles, the location of the SCN above the optic nerves provides a clue. Your retinas contain specialized cells that respond exclusively to slowly changing levels of illumination, and these cells project to the SCN. From the way the SCN uses retinal signals to synchronize its clock, you may realize that blindness from retinal degeneration would eliminate the ability to synchronize the internal clock. Indeed, people who suffer from complete blindness have abnormal circadian rhythms even though they have access to nonvisual cues to the time of day, such as mechanical clocks and the behavioral cycles of friends and neighbors (Sack et al., 1992).

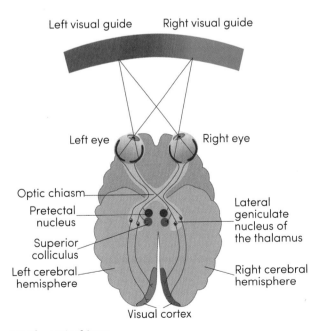

8.6 The optic chiasm
When viewing the human brain from below, the two optic nerves can be seen to cross over, forming an X called the optic chiasm.

Concept Recall

1. Which is easier to adjust to: westward or eastward travel? Spring forward or fall back? Why?

2. Where is the internal clock in the brain, and what experimental evidence shows that that part of the brain generates the internal clock?

3. How does the brain synchronize the internal clock with external daily cycles of light and dark?

Cross-Cultural Case

Sleep Patterns

While all humans need sleep, traditions, societal values, and environments all have a significant effect on how we sleep between cultures. The Japanese workforce is especially known for its commitment to productivity, which often equates to reduced time for sleep. A 2015 study revealed that nearly 40 percent of Japanese adults sleep fewer than six hours each night. As a means to combat inefficiency due to lack of sleep, *inemuri*, translated to "sleeping on duty" or "sleeping while present," is a common and socially-acceptable public nap that both men and women take in a number of social situations: on trains, in parks, in coffee shops—and even in class or at work! Anthropologist Dr. Brigitte Steger, a senior lecturer at University of Cambridge, explains in a BBC article that the Japanese are more tolerant than other cultures are about sleeping in public, which she theorizes can be traced back to certain social values such as cosleeping and diligence at work. In fact, some do not even consider *inemuri* sleep at all; rather, *inemuri* is valued for the ability to allow the person to remain present as opposed to stepping away to sleep in private. Moreover, engaging in *inemuri* requires the participant to be able to reenter the social or professional situation immediately, unlike the Spanish *siesta* or Italian *riposo*, both of which are built in to the work day, and businesses and other public venues shut down to accommodate these napping habits.

Mahathir Mohd Yasin/Shutterstock.com

How do you think your nighttime sleeping habits would change if *inemuri* were an acceptable part of your professional day?

Why Do We Sleep?

Even though sleeping is perfectly normal and natural, it may seem strange, and even dangerous, to spend a third of each day lying unconscious, because any jealous rival could just wait patiently until you were sleeping to attack you without fear of retaliation.

We must derive some utility from sleep for us to spend so much time doing it, but if so, what is the utility of sleep? There are two kinds of theories about why we sleep: **restorative theories** and **adaptation theories**. Restorative theories of sleep assert that while awake and active, our brains and bodies accumulate wear and tear over the course of the day, and a period of daily sleep is necessary to repair the damage. Evidence supporting the restorative power of sleep includes the fact that after a long day of strenuous exertion, you need more sleep than after a day filled with inactivity. Also, newborn babies spend lots of time and effort forging connections between brain cells, and they spend much more of the day sleeping than adults, which suggests that they need to recover from the hard work of building their brains.

restorative theories
these kinds of theories argue that our bodies and brains accumulate wear and tear while active and awake, so we need sleep to repair the damage

adaptation theories
these kinds of theories argue that sleep is tailored to the way an animal makes a living

However, there are other pieces of evidence that cannot be explained by restorative theories. Predator animals spend much more of each day sleeping than prey animals, but it seems unreasonable to suggest that carnivorous (meat-eating) predators, such as lions, accumulate much more damage throughout the day than herbivorous (plant-eating) animals, such as zebras. Also, predator animals, such as the lion in Figure 8.7, sleep very deeply, whereas prey animals sleep lightly and are easily awakened. This recalls the old joke that asks: Where does an 800-pound gorilla sleep? Wherever he wants to. Adaptation theories assert that sleep helps animals make a living in the manner to which they are adapted. As meat eaters, lions consume many more calories per meal than a plant eater like a zebra, which must graze almost continuously to satisfy its caloric needs. And of course, lions needn't worry about any other animals attacking them, whereas zebras

8.7 A sleeping lion
Predator animals like lions can sleep where, and when, and for as long as they please because no other animal would dare to disturb them.

are in constant danger of being attacked by predators like lions. Thus, lions can sleep for extended periods after gorging on a high-calorie feast, but a zebra must sneak a moment or two of sleep into its busy grazing schedule and vigilantly remain sensitive to the presence of dangerous predators in its surroundings. As omnivores who eat both meat and plants, humans' daily sleep needs are about halfway between those of carnivores and herbivores. And because edible plants and animals are difficult to find in the darkness, but the likelihood of injury increases in the dark, we might as well sleep during darkness to conserve energy and to pass the time.

So which kind of theory about sleep is correct? Is the value of sleep to recover from wear and tear, or is sleep tailored to the way animals make a living? To answer this question, consider marine mammals, such as dolphins. Because they live in the sea but breathe air, it's reasonable to expect dolphins not to sleep at all, because sleeping would seemingly lead to death from drowning. Because eliminating sleep from their daily schedule would seem to be the best strategy for dolphins, the fact that dolphins sleep supports restorative theories of sleep. But with an aquatic lifestyle that differs radically from the environment of land mammals, dolphins have evolved their own unique method of sleeping. As with humans, dolphin brains are divided into two hemispheres, so when dolphins sleep, just one hemisphere sleeps while the other hemisphere remains awake, then the hemispheres switch their roles until both hemispheres wake up. The fact that dolphins sleep shows that sleep is restorative, and the way dolphins sleep shows that an animal's way of sleeping is tailored to the way the animal makes a living.

Now that you know why humans in general sleep, you may wonder why you as an individual need to sleep and what the consequences of sleep deprivation are. The most obvious symptom of sleep deprivation is sleepiness; you feel sleepy, and when given the opportunity to sleep, you fall asleep faster and sleep for a longer duration than when not sleep deprived. Performance on physical tasks is relatively unaffected by sleep deprivation. The kinds of mental tasks that are most affected by sleep deprivation are boring and repetitive tasks that require sustained attention, which could describe driving a car under most normal circumstances. Remember the increase in traffic fatalities that follow springing clocks forward by an hour to daylight saving time? You should listen to your mom when she tells you to always get a good night's sleep.

The best known case of extreme sleep deprivation was Randy Gardner, who as a high school senior in 1964 remained awake for 264 hours (eleven days) as a way to gather data for a science fair project (Gulevich et al., 1966). He chose 264 hours as his target because it would break the previous record for staying awake. Besides his strong yearning for sleep, Randy's behavior throughout his ordeal was not particularly unusual or cause for worry. Shortly before the end of his experiment, Randy held a press conference in which he was able to respond coherently to questions. When Randy finally got to sleep, he stayed asleep for fourteen hours on the first night, but he quickly returned to his usual sleep schedule.

Randy Gardner's seemingly full recovery from extended sleep deprivation prompted researchers to investigate the harmful effects of sleep deprivation in laboratory animals. To force laboratory rats to remain awake, they were placed on a disk above a shallow pool of water (Rechtschaffen & Bergmann, 1995). When electrodes connected to their brains indicated that the rats were falling asleep, the disk began to rotate, bumping them into the water and waking them up. All rats exposed to unrelenting sleep deprivation died after about two or three weeks, but rats who were deprived of sleep but permitted to sleep before they died recovered completely. However, it is not clear whether sleep deprivation itself killed the rats. Living on the rotating disk apparatus was stressful, so the stress, rather than the sleep deprivation itself, may have been the cause of death. This experiment suggests that it may be impossible to separate the effects of sleep deprivation from stress in nonhuman experimental subjects.

Concept Recall

1. What kinds of theories explain why humans and other mammals sleep?
2. Which kind of theory is supported by a comparison of predators and prey animals, and why?
3. Which kind of theory is supported by dolphins, and why?
4. What are the consequences of extended sleep deprivation on people and laboratory animals?

Stages of Sleep

Prior to the 1950s, psychologists thought that when people sleep each night, they descend from wakefulness into sleep, stay there for eight hours or so, then ascend back into wakefulness. This account of sleep began to change when sleep researchers in the early 1950s attached electrodes to subjects to measure electrical activity during the night. Electrodes connected to the scalp measured brain activity, and the resulting signal was called an **electroencephalogram (EEG)**; electrodes attached to neck muscles, called an **electromyogram (EMG)**, measured muscle tone; and electrodes attached to both sides of the eye, called an **electrooculogram (EOG)**, measured eye movements. The outputs from these electrodes showed that you do not simply descend into sleep and remain static throughout the night. Instead, your brain activity, muscle tone, and eye movements cycle through different stages.

While you are awake, many areas of your brain are active, so the widespread brain activity adds together to form an EEG signal with high frequency, which means that the EEG signal moves quickly from high voltage to low and back again. To hold your head upright while awake, you need to keep your neck muscles flexed, so the EMG during wakefulness would record high muscle tone. As you ease into sleep, the EEG and EMG initially record signals similar to the signals recorded while you were awake, with a high frequency EEG signal and nearly as much muscle tone as during wakefulness. You might have noticed the loss of muscle tone in your neck while listening to a terribly boring lecture; as your eyes glaze over and you fade into sleep, your head droops suddenly, and you pop awake. This initial stage of sleep, which is similar to wakefulness, is called stage 1. As you continue sleeping, you descend through stage 2 into deeper sleep, until reaching stage 3, in which low frequencies dominate the EEG, and the EMG registers flaccid muscles from low muscle tone. After a few minutes in deep sleep, the EEG and EMG indicate that you ascend from stage 3 through stage 2 to shallower sleep, until you emerge into stage 1. This cycle from light (stage 1) sleep to deep (stage 3) sleep and back again takes about ninety minutes, which could explain why taking a nap for ninety minutes provides more rest than a longer nap lasting two hours. For the shorter, ninety-minute nap, you wake from light sleep, but for the longer, two-hour nap, you descend back into deeper sleep before waking up, making you feel groggy when you wake up.

When you emerge back into light (stage 1) sleep from deeper sleep, the EEG signal is similar to what it was during the initial stage 1, but the EMG and EOG show that this **emergent stage 1** is very different from the initial stage 1. The EMG registers flaccid muscles associated with deep sleep, which means that emergent stage 1 sleep is associated with brain activity (EEG) that is characteristic of light sleep, but muscle tone (EMG) that is characteristic of deep sleep. Combining light sleep (EEG) and deep sleep (EMG) is a kind of paradox, so emergent stage 1 sleep is also called **paradoxical sleep**. Not only are the EEG and EMG paradoxical during emergent stage 1, but the EOG indicates that the eyes move rapidly back and forth, a behavior that is distinct from any other stage of sleep. For that reason, emergent stage 1 sleep is also called REM, which stands for rapid eye movements. If you're keeping track, that means that there are three

electroencephalogram (EEG)
the signal from electrodes connected to the scalp measuring brain activity

electromyogram (EMG)
the signal from electrodes connected to the neck measuring muscle tone

electrooculogram (EOG)
the signal from electrodes connected to the head on both sides of the eye measuring eye movements

emergent stage 1 sleep
the stage of sleep that occurs after ascending from deep sleep into lighter sleep; this stage of sleep is called "emergent" to distinguish it from the initial stage 1 sleep that occurs just after descending from wakefulness

paradoxical sleep
also called emergent stage 1, this stage of sleep is paradoxical because it combines brain activity associated with light sleep with muscle tone associated with deep sleep

names for the same stage of sleep; *emergent stage 1* emphasizes the fact that the sleeper ascends into stage 1 from deeper sleep rather than descending into it as in initial stage 1, *paradoxical sleep* emphasizes the contrast between EEG characteristic of light sleep and EMG characteristic of deep sleep, and *REM* emphasizes the rapid eye movements that occur only during this stage of sleep. In fact, REM sleep is so distinct from other stages that all other stages of sleep are often referred to as non-REM sleep.

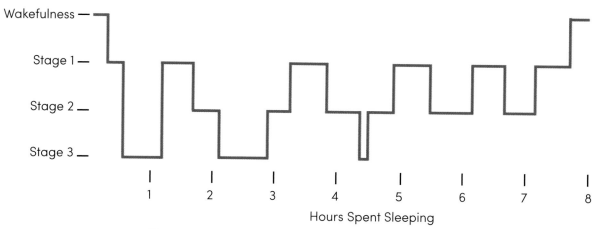

8.8 Typical night's pattern of EEG
Through a typical night's sleep, the EEG patterns indicate that the sleeper descends from wakefulness to deep sleep, then ascends to emergent stage 1, and repeats this pattern several times before finally waking up at the end of the night.

Figure 8.8 depicts a typical night's cycle through the stages of sleep, as measured by EEG. At the beginning of the night, the sleeper's brain descends from wakefulness to deep sleep, then ascends from stage 3 to REM, which takes about ninety minutes. During REM, the EOG detects eye movements, the EEG is characteristic of light sleep, the EMG is characteristic of deep, and if sleepers are awakened from this stage, they are likelier to report vivid dreams than if awakened during other stages of sleep. The sleeper's brain then proceeds through several more cycles of descent to deep sleep and ascent to REM sleep, each cycle taking about 90 minutes. As the night proceeds, the sleeper spends progressively less time in deep sleep and more time in REM sleep.

Ideally, you get to sleep each night without much difficulty and wake the next morning feeling refreshed and ready for the day. Unfortunately, a sleep disorder may prevent you from reaching this ideal. Many sleep disorders can be assigned to one of two categories: **insomnia** is difficulty getting to sleep or remaining asleep, and **hypersomnia** is a tendency to be sleepy when you are trying to remain awake. A third category of sleep disorders are associated with abnormalities in REM sleep. A primary cause of insomnia is anxiety. Ironically, worrying about getting enough sleep can itself be a cause of insomnia. Sleeping pills may provide some initial relief from sleeplessness due to anxiety, but the brain soon develops tolerance to the drug, so an ever-increasing dosage of drug is required just to get to sleep. A better solution would be to directly address the anxiety causing the insomnia by taking advantage of one of the therapies, such as cognitive behavioral therapy, described in Chapter 14.

insomnia
sleep disorders associated with difficulty getting to sleep or remaining asleep

hypersomnia
sleep disorders associated with excessive sleepiness when trying to remain awake

One kind of insomnia with a physiological, rather than emotional, cause is **obstructive sleep apnea**. While awake, the muscle tone in the neck contributes to your ability to maintain an airway in your throat, but loss of muscle tone in the neck may allow the airway to become pinched closed. Recall that as you descend into deeper sleep stages, you progressively lose muscle tone. The resulting pinched airway prevents the sleeper from drawing air into the lungs, so carbon dioxide builds up in the blood until a panic reflex prompts the sleeper to awaken abruptly. After waking up, muscle tone returns and the sleeper can breathe again, then fall asleep, kicking off the entire episode again. Surprisingly, even though people suffering from sleep apnea may wake up dozens of times each night, at the end of the night they might not remember waking up at all. As you can imagine, they believe they slept for the full duration of the night, and yet they remain exhausted because they never managed to achieve restful deep sleep. If they complained to their physician that they constantly suffer from sleepiness during the day when they need to be awake and productive, the physician might misdiagnose their insomnia as hypersomnia. As a treatment for the supposed hypersomnia, the physician could prescribe stimulant drugs, which would be counterproductive because the patient really needs restful sleep at night rather than drugs to remain awake during the day. If the patient spent a night in a sleep lab, the technician would record the numerous awakenings, even if patients don't remember for themselves.

The best known hypersomnia disorder is called **narcolepsy**. People suffering from narcolepsy experience overwhelming urges to fall asleep during the day and often fall asleep at inappropriate moments, like right in the middle of a conversation or while driving. A disorder called **cataplexy** may seem to be similar to narcolepsy, but whereas a narcoleptic episode entails descending from wakefulness into stage 1 sleep, in cataplexy part of the brain remains awake while other parts of the brain descend in REM. Recall that in REM the EEG registers brain activity that is similar to wakefulness, while the EMG indicates paralyzed muscles. During an episode of cataplexy, a person can collapse and remain paralyzed on the ground for several moments until the atonia (lack of muscle tone) associated with REM sleep fades away. Another REM disorder that seems to be the opposite of cataplexy is called **sleep paralysis**, which occurs at the end of REM sleep when part of the brain wakes and other parts of the brain remain briefly stuck in REM. As with cataplexy, people suffering from an episode of sleep paralysis feel as if they are awake but paralyzed.

Dreaming

As mentioned above, when subjects in a sleep lab are awakened from REM sleep, they are likelier to report their vivid recollections of dreams than when they are awakened from other stages of sleep. Does this mean that dreams are synonymous with REM sleep? Not quite, but REM and dreams seem to be correlated. Another peculiar aspect of REM sleep is that men's penises become erect during REM sleep, even when their dream content is nonsexual. This provides a useful tool in diagnosing erectile dysfunction disorder. That is, when a man who suffers from an inability to become erect asks his doctor for some kind of remedy, the doctor needs to know whether this

obstructive sleep apnea
an insomnia sleep disorder characterized by difficulty breathing due to loss of muscle tone during sleep, leading to numerous brief awakenings during the night

narcolepsy
a hypersomnia sleep disorder characterized by overwhelming urges to fall asleep at inappropriate moments during the day

cataplexy
an REM sleep disorder in which some parts of the brain remain awake while other parts descend into REM

sleep paralysis
an REM sleep disorder that occurs at the end of REM when part of the brain wakes up but other parts of the brain remain briefly stuck in REM

inability has a physical cause (e.g., abnormal blood pressure or nerve damage). Anyone who is physically able to achieve an erection will get an erection during REM, so if the patient achieves an erection during REM, his physician knows that the patient's erectile dysfunction has psychological, rather than physiological, causes.

What do dreams mean? Probably the best known answer was developed by Freud. As you will read in Chapter 12, Freud argued that the mind consists of the *id* that drives us to satisfy our basic needs for food and sex, the *superego* that urges us to conform to the morals of our social environment, and the *ego* that tries to navigate a path between the devil on one shoulder (id) and the angel on the other shoulder (superego). If the id had its way, we would seek pleasure at every opportunity, but society frowns on people who constantly gratify their own needs at the expense of other people's, so the ego needs to control the impulses generated by the id in favor of the socially acceptable behavior dictated by the superego. To prevent the id from commandeering behavioral decisions, it is banished to the unconscious mind. Hidden in the unconscious mind, the id must be sneaky if it has any hope of making its desires appear in the conscious mind. Freud thought that during sleep, the ego and superego are suppressed, so the id takes the opportunity to play out its fantasies in the mental theater of dreams. However, if the id merely presented its undisguised fantasies to the mind, the ego would be aroused by the wickedness of the id's fantasy and force an end to the dream by waking the dreamer up. For that reason, the id needs to disguise the inhabitants of its fantasies in symbols that will seem innocent enough not to arouse the suspicions of the ego censor. According to Freud, the **manifest content** of dreams represents the actual people and things present in the dream scenario, but these people and things are just disguised versions of the underlying fantasy the id is trying to indulge. The actual fantasy that the id wishes to act out in dreams is called the **latent content**.

manifest content
according to Freud's theory of dreams, the manifest content of dreams are the people and things that actually appear in dreams

latent content
according to Freud's theory of dreams, the latent content of dreams represents the actual fantasy that the id wishes to indulge in dreams, but to avoid arousing the ego, the id disguises the latent content in symbols

Because you can access your conscious mind but not your unconscious mind, Freud thought that dreams provided a valuable window into the unconscious, but only by interpreting the manifest content of dreams to reveal the latent content. Unfortunately, Freud's ideas about the interpretation of dreams have not aged well. As is the case with much else that Freud wrote, there is no way to test whether his ideas about the interpretation of dreams are true. Perhaps Freud's most enduring contribution to psychology is his idea that most of the mind is inaccessible, with a comparatively tiny sliver available to the conscious mind.

If modern scientists have rejected Freud's ideas about the interpretation of dreams, what do they think dreams mean? One influential hypothesis about dreams, called activation-synthesis (Hobson, Hong, & Friston, 2014), asserts that dreams actually don't mean very much. During REM, the brain stem bombards the cortex with electrical activity, and yet during REM you are lying motionless under the bed covers. Because your body isn't doing or feeling much, the ascending brain signals must just be random noise, but your cortex abhors randomness, so it works hard to make sense out of the noise. This is similar to top-down perceptual processing you read about in Chapter 4.

Concept Recall

1. What do the EEG, EMG, and EOG measure?

2. In terms of the output from EEG, EMG, and EOG electrodes, how does light sleep differ from deep sleep?

3. How do REM and non-REM sleep differ?

4. How can a night in a sleep lab be useful in diagnosing erectile dysfunction?

5. According to Freud, how are dreams useful in revealing desires buried in the unconscious mind?

This Is Psychology

Do you know anyone who claims to have been abducted by aliens? The closest star to our own sun is about three light-years away, so any aliens who might have visited our planet must have developed advanced technology enabling them to travel between star systems, are aware of our existence, and are willing to travel across vast distances just to visit us. Do you think there could be a more likely explanation for why they believe they were abducted by aliens? Surprisingly, their belief that they were abducted by aliens might have been caused by a sleep disorder called sleep paralysis (McNally & Clancy, 2005). Almost one out of three people have experienced sleep paralysis, so it is very possible that you have experienced it yourself. Sleep paralysis occurs when a part of a sleeper's brain wakes up from REM, but other parts of the brain briefly remain stuck in REM. During REM, your body is paralyzed, but your brain is exposed to a flood of stimuli that you typically interpret as dreams. What would happen if you thought you had woken up but part of your brain remained stuck in REM? Even though you tried to roll out of bed, you would lie paralyzed, you might hear buzzing noises and feel like electrical shocks were coursing through your body, and if you didn't know why all this was happening, you would probably be terrified. Actually, sleep paralysis is nothing to fear, because after a few seconds, your entire brain would be able to wake up, releasing you from paralysis. Now you know that if you experience sleep paralysis, just relax, and soon enough it will fade away.

ALTERED STATES OF CONSCIOUSNESS

As mentioned previously, humans and other mammals cycle through three natural brain states each day: wakefulness and two kinds of sleep, REM and non-REM. For some people, these three conscious states are not enough, so they seek ways of altering their conscious experience artificially, by becoming hypnotized or by ingesting chemicals that interfere with normal brain chemistry. In Chapter 3 you read about how drugs interact with the brain on the cellular level, but here we will describe how psychoactive drugs make themselves felt in conscious experience. But first, we will look at hypnosis.

Hypnosis

The history of **hypnosis** began in about 1780 when a physician from Vienna named Franz Mesmer began to develop techniques to treat his patients for various ailments. Mesmer believed that humans and other animals were connected to inanimate objects through a natural exchange of energy called animal magnetism, and his patients' discomfort was caused by aberrations in the magnetic fields surrounding them. Mesmer thought he could repair his patients' disordered magnetic fields by moving magnets around the ailing body part, while at the same time reassuring his patients in a soft and soothing voice. From a modern perspective, we would say that any relief his patients experienced was due to Mesmer's suggestions that his therapy would be helpful, combined with the patients' belief in its effectiveness. During Mesmer's lifetime, the techniques he pioneered were called **mesmerism**, but modern practices derived from mesmerism are called hypnosis. Even though mesmerism itself is no longer practiced, Mesmer left his imprint on the language when we refer to becoming mesmerized, for example when driving long distances across monotonous interstate highways.

Hypnosis often features in movies and other popular entertainment, but this prominence has led to many widely held misconceptions about how hypnosis works. Even the term hypnosis, from the Greek word for sleep, is itself misleading. The EEG signal measuring brain activity in a hypnotized person is characteristic of wakefulness rather than sleep (Baghdadi, & Nasrabadi, 2009). The hypnotist is often portrayed as capable of hypnotizing anyone he or she wants to hypnotize at will. In fact, not everyone is hypnotizable. First of all, some people are unwilling to be hypnotized, and if you don't want to be hypnotized, the hypnotist is powerless to force you. Second, the kind of person who is most susceptible to hypnosis is someone with a vivid imagination who can become completely absorbed in the flow of a book or movie, or in other words, someone who can narrowly focus attention while completely ignoring any conspicuous distractions. So it seems that the power resides in the recipient who is willing and able to be hypnotized rather than a hypnotist who commands the person to become hypnotized.

A hypnotist begins the session by telling the subject to focus on a single sensation, such as a spot on a distant wall. Soon after, the hypnotist offers suggestions to the subject such as, "Your eyes are getting heavy, so heavy that you are having trouble keeping them from slamming shut." Subjects who are willing to accept the hypnotist's suggestions find their eyelids slamming shut. Under hypnosis, the subject may follow the hypnotist's suggestions to act in odd ways that may amuse an audience, but the subject won't do anything that would be physically impossible or morally objectionable under normal circumstances. Thus, hypnosis is really just a state of narrow attentional focus, which explains how hypnosis can be used for pain relief, called **hypnotic analgesia**.

Hypnotic analgesia

Under hypnosis, the hypnotist directs a subject who is feeling pain to detach from the experience of the pain, and the subject soon feels relief. To understand how this works, we first have to consider chemicals your brain manufactures to ease pain under stressful

hypnosis
the induction of a state of consciousness in which a person apparently loses the power of voluntary action and is highly responsive to suggestion or direction

mesmerism
the therapeutic system of Franz Mesmer, hypnotism in its modern form

hypnotic analgesia
use of hypnosis for pain relief

circumstances. If you were being chased by a predator who injured you with his claws in the course of pursuit, you couldn't really ask the predator to call off the chase while you rested your injured leg. Instead, you would need to run as fast as possible, aggravating your injury in the short term, but providing the possibility of escape from the predator. For that reason, pain is maladaptive while in fight-or-flight mode, so to eliminate the feeling of pain while under stress, your brain manufactures and releases chemicals that act like morphine. In fact, your brain has receptor sites in which morphine fits just like a key in a lock, so your own internally generated (i.e., endogenous) chemicals are called endogenous morphine, or *endorphins* for short.

Sometimes people can experience a **placebo effect** from taking a pill that they believe contains active ingredients but is actually just a sugar pill. Is the placebo effect the same as hypnotic analgesia? No, they are different, and the different ways of acting can be revealed by Naloxone, a drug that blocks endorphin receptors. In an experiment, two groups of participants are made to feel pain by plunging their hands into nearly ice-cold water, cold enough to cause pain under extended exposure but not to cause permanent damage. One group of participants is injected with saline (which, like a sugar pill, has no active ingredients) and the other with Naloxone, and both are told that they are being given a pain-relieving drug. The participants who are given saline feel more pain relief than the participants who are given Naloxone. Because Naloxone blocks endorphins from binding to their receptor sites, the fact that Naloxone also blocks the placebo effect shows that the placebo effect results from patients releasing their own endorphins. However, Naloxone fails to block hypnotic analgesia, which shows that hypnotic analgesia must work through some means other than the release of endorphins (Moret et al., 1991).

placebo effect
a beneficial effect, produced by a "fake" drug or treatment, that cannot be attributed to the properties of the placebo itself and must therefore be due to the patient's belief in that treatment

The difference between the placebo effect and hypnotic analgesia highlights the dual nature of pain. As we all know, pain hurts, which means that pain entails a touch sensation. But pain also contains an attentional component. When your leg is injured, you feel the pain from the injury, but the pain also grabs your attention. The attentional component of pain can make it difficult to direct your attention to anything else. As shown by experiments with Naloxone, hypnotic analgesia has no effect on the pain sensation itself. Although the pain feels just as intense, hypnosis prevents the pain from hijacking attention. You may have noticed that in recent years, dentists have become aware of the dual nature of pain. Dentists, and in particular pediatric dentists, often equip their examination rooms with televisions and other conspicuous distractions to keep their patients from focusing exclusively on the pain.

Psychoactive drugs

The US Food and Drug Administration considers antiperspirant, but not deodorant, to be a drug. What's the difference? Deodorant just smells nice, but antiperspirant actually changes the way the body works. With that in mind, we might define **psychoactive drugs** as externally generated (exogenous) substances that change the way the brain works. Any chemicals dissolved in the blood can only enter the brain by crossing the

psychoactive drugs
externally generated (exogenous) substances that change the way the brain works

blood-brain barrier. Because the blood-brain barrier is so stingy, there are relatively few chemicals that can even reach the brain. Many psychoactive drugs were manufactured by plants as a defense to addle the brains of any animal who tries to consume their leaves or seeds. Even though these chemicals were designed by plants to be harmful or even lethal, humans have learned how to administer them to change our conscious experience, in small, nonlethal doses. And yet the danger constantly lurks for a drug user to accidently ingest a fatal overdose.

Stimulants and depressants

dopamine
a neurotransmitter that encourages neurons to send action potentials

Psychoactive drugs are typically grouped into four categories based on the way they affect the brain: stimulants, depressants, narcotics, and hallucinogens. Most stimulants enhance the effectiveness of **dopamine**, a neurotransmitter that encourages neurons to send action potentials. By doing so, stimulants increase mental processing speed and alertness. For hundreds of years, residents of Bolivia and Peru have been using coca leaf the same way Americans use caffeine: to perk themselves up for a hard day of work. Chewing coca leaf or drinking tea made by brewing the leaves has a much milder effect than the much more concentrated cocaine powder that is smuggled into the US by drug cartels. Ingesting cocaine powder sharply increases the release of dopamine in the brain, which is then followed by a crash that leaves the user craving more of the drug.

GABA
a neurotransmitter that acts like the mirror image of dopamine by discouraging neurons from sending action potentials

Most depressants enhance the effectiveness of the neurotransmitter gamma-Amniobutyric acid, or **GABA**, which acts like the mirror image of dopamine by discouraging neurons from sending action potentials. The most widely abused drug in the world is alcohol, which has been used for thousands of years, since at least ancient Egypt, and probably much earlier. The first beer was probably brewed when some barley got wet, releasing malt sugar. Yeast floating freely in the air landed on the sugary water, eating it and releasing alcohol as a defense against other microbes that might want to eat the sugar. Even today, alcohol remains one of the most effective antiseptic solutions for killing germs. It may be surprising that alcohol is a depressant, because people under the influence of alcohol are often loud, boisterous, and aggressive. In small doses, alcohol can seem more like a stimulant because the frontal cortex, which contains social inhibitions and impulse control, is more sensitive to alcohol than other parts of the brain. In larger doses, the effect of alcohol spreads to the rest of the brain, leading to a general depressant effect.

narcotic
the drugs that are related to the chemical extracted from the opium poppy plant

Even though the word "narcotic" is often misused as a general term to refer to all illegal drugs, narcotics are the drugs that are related to the chemical extracted from the opium poppy plant. When the seed case of the poppy flower is scratched, the plant responds by exuding a sticky sap containing opiates, which is intended to discourage any further insults on the seeds. As mentioned above, opiates such as morphine mimic chemicals manufactured by your own brain as an analgesic to relieve pain under stressful conditions. Besides analgesia, narcotics induce a serene euphoria, which is why narcotics are so widely abused. Narcotics also suppress activity in the brain stem, which is where reflexes such as breathing are housed, so the most common cause of death among narcotics users is cessation of breathing.

Hallucinogens

The hallucinogen category is often used as a catch-all for any psychoactive drugs that do not fit easily into the other three categories. However, if we consider that "hallucinogen" literally means to generate hallucinations, then hallucinogens should only refer to d-lysergic acid diethylamide (LSD) and similar substances that bind to serotonin receptors. Throughout history, when wheat infected with ergot fungus was eaten, it induced such unpleasant effects as projectile vomiting and convulsions, as well as some unusual sensory experiences. In the 1930s, the Swiss chemist Albert Hoffman figured out how to separate the chemicals in ergot fungus that lead to sensory effects from other chemicals and thereby synthesized LSD. One of the most common effects of LSD is *synesthesia*, from the Greek words for "sensing together." In synesthesia, stimulation of one sensory modality induces sensations in another modality. Some people experience synesthesia in their everyday lives without relying on LSD. For example, in his book *The Man Who Tasted Shapes*, Richard Cytowic describes visiting a man with synesthesia who was cooking dinner. He tasted the chicken to see if it was ready to serve, but decided that it tasted too much like square blocks. For this man, taste sensations induce touch sensations. While this may seem exotic, synesthesia seems to underlie such common expressions as "sharp cheese," which combines taste with touch, or a "loud tie," which combines vision and hearing. If synesthesia occurs for some people with chemical inducement and underlies common metaphors, perhaps the hallucinations associated with LSD are actually just enhanced versions of normal perception.

hallucinogens
psychoactive agents that cause perceptual anomalies and false sensory messages

Marijuana

Marijuana is a drug unto itself that does not fit easily into any of the four drug categories. As of the current writing, marijuana is legal as medicine in twenty-nine states and the District of Columbia, although these state laws are all superseded by federal laws prohibiting its use. Marijuana contains dozens of chemicals that cause a variety of effects that can be beneficial as medicine. For example, patients who are undergoing chemotherapy to slow or reverse the spread of cancer experience intense nausea and have little appetite. Marijuana is an antiemetic, meaning that it reduces nausea, and it boosts the appetite, so chemotherapy patients can hold down some food and avoid wasting away. Like alcohol, marijuana reduces anxiety, without the many unpleasant side effects of alcohol.

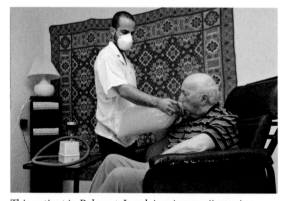

This patient in Rehovot, Israel, is using marijuana in a vaporizer in a medical clinic. In Israel, marijuana use has been permitted since the 1990s for pain relief. Israel is one of the global leaders in marijuana production, not only because of its government policies toward the plant but also because of well-developed farming systems and entrepreneurs.

Concept Recall

1. What kind of person is relatively hypnotizable?
2. What is the difference between the placebo effect for pain relief and hypnotic analgesia?
3. What are four categories of psychoactive drugs, and how does each affect consciousness?

CONSCIOUSNESS AND PSYCHOLOGY

Consciousness has long been a topic of wonderment for philosophers as well as idle speculation among the general public. For example, I can access my own conscious mind, but how do I know that anyone else (including you), has their own conscious mind? Maybe everyone is actually plugged in to a giant computer database providing heat energy to AI robots, à la *The Matrix*. These kinds of ideas are fun to talk about with friends or to explore in literature or the movies, but as we saw in this chapter, psychologists are having some success studying consciousness scientifically. Although the hard problem of consciousness remains out of reach, psychological science can answer some of the so-called easy problems of consciousness.

The things inside our minds seem very different from the real-world objects they represent, which may have prompted Descartes to develop his system of dualism, in which mental and physical things are distinct. Although dualism is intuitively appealing to most people, it represents a dead end for trying to figure out how consciousness works. The modern scientific stance is that there is only one kind of thing and that the mind emerges from a physical brain. Evidence from split brains shows that cutting the nerve bundle connecting the two hemispheres shatters the mind into two pieces that don't always get along with each other.

REVIEW

- How are rationalism and empiricism different?

- What do the mind–body problem, Occam's razor, and tabula rasa have to do with the study of the mind?

- What do the results of the mental rotation experiment imply about mental imagery?

- How do people with visual impairments caused by brain damage experience similar deficits in mental imagery as compared to sighted people?

- How does our internal clock adjust to synchronize with external daily cycles of light and dark?

- What do sleep deprivation experiments reveal about the theories of sleep?

- Name the three stages of sleep.

- Describe two types of sleep disorders.

- How is hypnotic analgesia different from the placebo effect?

- What is a psychoactive drug?

1. Which of the following is an example of a "hard" problem of consciousness?

   a. Determining the neural states that correspond to states of mental experience

   b. Figuring out why people pay attention to some things and not to other things

   c. Describing how mental states, such as the way food tastes, emerge from neural events, such as chemicals moving from place to place

   d. None of these are "hard" problems of consciousness

2. In their mental rotation experiments, Shepard and Metzler discovered that

   a. response time increased with rotational distance between two studied items.

   b. response time decreased with rotational distance between two studied items.

   c. response times were independent of rotational distance between two studied items.

   d. response time was not affected by rotational distance between two studied items.

3. In their "door" study, Simons and Levin discovered that

   a. participants objected when one person was switched for another.

   b. participants did not notice when one person was switched for another.

   c. participants did not remain focused on the task of giving directions after the switch.

   d. none of the above

4. The outputs from which of these are similar between initial stage 1 and emergent stage 1 sleep?

   a. EEG   b. EMG   c. EOG

5. The outputs from which of these are similar between initial stage 1 and stage 3 sleep?

   a. EEG   b. EMG   c. EOG

6. The outputs from which of these are similar between stage 3 and emergent stage 1 sleep?

    a. EEG   b. EMG   c. EOG

7. Which of the following is not a sleep disorder?

    a. Hypersomnia   c. Paradoxical sleep

    b. Obstructive sleep apnea   d. Cataplexy

8. What is not a feature hypnotic analgesia?

    a. The subject of the hypnosis feels pain relief.

    b. Endorphins are released, blocking pain.

    c. Hypnotic analgesia has no effect on the pain sensation itself.

    d. Hypnotic analgesia prevents the pain from capturing the subject's attention.

9. Most depressants enhance the effectiveness of the neurotransmitter

    a. dopamine.   c. serotonin.

    b. acetylcholine.   d. GABA.

10. What is a narcotic?

    a. Any federally illegal drug.

    b. Any drug that causes hallucinations.

    c. Any drug that reduces pain.

    d. Any drug chemically related to opium.

REFLECT

1. This chapter began by describing *The Matrix*, in which people are connected to a worldwide computer network that prevents motor signals from reaching their targets in the body and generates an illusory mental model of the world. Do you know for certain that you are not a part of such a matrix? If so, what test could you carry out that would definitively prove that your perceptual experiences actually represent the objects, people, and scenes they depict?

2. At one point in this chapter you were asked to consider the subjective experience of color. Even if you and I agree that grass is green and the sky is blue, that only means that we agree on the labels (i.e., green and blue), but we have no way of knowing that my experience of blue is the same as yours. Perhaps this kind of uncertainty about color prompted the English philosopher, John Locke, to distinguish between what he calls the primary qualities of shape, size, and number, and the secondary qualities of colors, tastes, and pains. Why do you think he grouped colors with tastes and pains? What is similar about the secondary qualities, and how are they distinct from the primary qualities?

Answer Key

1. c 2. a 3. b 4. a 5. c 6. b 7. c 8. b 9. d 10. d

WRITE

1. Consciousness is a popular topic in science fiction movies. For example, *Inception* follows the exploits of a specialized group of industrial spies who are hired by one corporation to invade the dreams of a rival corporation's chief executive in order to plant ideas in his head. The movie includes some familiar aspects of dreams, such as how the events in dreams seem to take much longer than the few minutes we spend dreaming, or how we often feel like we're falling in dreams and wake up just before we hit the ground. Some other movies that use the magic of cinema to explore human consciousness in a way that would be impossible outside the movie theater include *Solaris*, *Fight Club*, *Eternal Sunshine of the Spotless Mind*, and *Total Recall*. Watch one of these or select one of your own, and write about how the movie relates to what you've read in this chapter. What does your movie of choice argue about consciousness? Does it mirror psychological components of sleeping and dreaming, or does it fictionalize these experiences beyond the scientific? How does your comparison of the movie and this chapter affect your understanding of consciousness as a pop culture subject?

Key Terms

adaptation theories 237
analytic introspection 229
cataplexy 241
change blindness 231
circadian rhythm 234
consciousness 224
dopamine 246
dualism 225
electroencephalogram (EEG) 239
electromyogram (EMG) 239
electrooculogram (EOG) 239
emergent property 227
emergent stage 1 sleep 239
empiricism 226
evil genius 224
GABA 246
hallucinogens 247
hypersomnia 240
hypnosis 244
hypnotic analgesia 244
idealism 225
insomnia 240

latent content 242
manifest content 242
materialism 227
mental rotation 229
mesmerism 244
mind–body problem 225
monism 225
narcolepsy 241
narcotic 246
obstructive sleep apnea 241
Occam's razor 226
paradoxical sleep 239
placebo effect 245
psychoactive drugs 245
qualia 228
rationalism 225
restorative theories 237
sleep paralysis 241
suprachiasmatic nucleus (SCN) 235
tabula rasa 226

After reading this chapter, you will be able to answer the following questions:

- What are three kinds of memory storage, and how do they differ?
- What are the memory processes?
- Why do phone numbers have seven digits?
- How can you boost the number of items you can store in memory for immediate access?
- Why is forgetting actually a good thing?
- How could someone "remember" something that didn't actually happen?
- For someone suffering from amnesia, what is broken, and what remains intact?
- Can someone with amnesia make any kind of new memory?

C live Wearing was a well-known British musician and conductor in 1985 when he contracted meningitis, an infection in the tissues supporting and protecting his brain.

After suffering from what felt like an extended bout of the flu, he lost most of his memories of experiences prior to the illness. Clive was not the first person to suffer from permanent memory loss, but he did have one symptom that distinguished him from previous cases of memory loss: Clive lost the sense of time flowing coherently from one moment to the next. For Clive, the world appeared to be a constantly changing kaleidoscope of sensory impressions. Clive kept diaries in which he wrote entries like this: 9:04 a.m.: *Now I am awake*, but then moments later he would lose the thread and pop back into consciousness as if he were waking up for the first time that day. When he would notice the diary entry that had clearly been written by his own hand, he would angrily scratch it out and write another line like this: 9:15 a.m.: *Now I am completely, fully awake*, but then the cycle would repeat. Clive has filled dozens of diaries with these kinds of entries, each adamantly denying the evidence that he had been awake a moment before. Most people think of memory as the ability to recall events (the first time you saw *Star Wars*) and facts (the capital of France, a friend's birthdate, the meaning of the word "Jacuzzi"), but Clive Wearing shows us that memory is much more than that. Memory lets us know who we are and how we got here.

As we explore memory in this chapter, you will meet Henry Molaison, the man who revealed more about how memory works than anyone else ever did. Suffering from a debilitating seizure disorder, Henry was the first person to consent to a particular experimental brain surgery technique. He was also the last person to undergo this surgical procedure, primarily because Henry could remember almost nothing that happened after his surgery. However, some kinds of memory remained intact for Henry, indicating that memory is not a single thing but consists of several components. Working memory retains and processes whatever you are consciously aware of right now. To retain a fact or experience once you are no longer consciously aware of it requires storage in long-term memory, and to recall it later you must retrieve it from long-term memory. We will encounter these and other memory stores and processes, beginning with the model of memory that describes how everything fits together.

THE MODEL OF MEMORY

A popular model for memory consisting of several components that interact with one another is depicted in the box-and-arrow diagram in Figure 9.1. These components—sensory memory, short-term memory, and long-term memory—each make their own contributions to the overall system of memory. When each component is functioning properly, a person briefly retains a snapshot of the world in sensory memory, can rely on short-term memory to carry on a conversation in which each statement follows coherently from the statement before, and can store information for later retrieval in long-term memory.

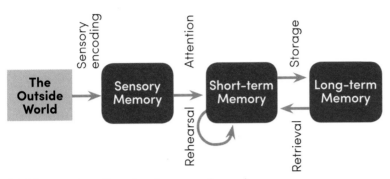

9.1 Memory stores (boxes) and processes (arrows)
Real-world energy (light, sound, etc.) is encoded and briefly held in sensory memory. Attention selects some information to enter short-term memory and rejects other information. Rehearsal is necessary to retain the contents in short-term memory. Short-term memories that are stored in long-term memory can be accessed later by retrieval from long-term memory.

After the sensory receptors described in Chapter 4 (eyes, ears, skin, tongue, and nose) **encode** various kinds of energy from the world into a form usable by the brain, the resulting sensory impressions are held briefly in sensory memory. You may believe that you have access to all the sensory information presented to your brain, but in fact there is so much sensory information that you would be overwhelmed if you tried to process it all, like putting your face in front of a fire hose to get a drink of water when all you can handle is the trickle you could get from a water fountain. To keep you from being overwhelmed by the constant flood of sensory information, your brain pays **attention** to a tiny fraction of the available sensory information and discards the rest. Attention selects only a few pieces of sensory information for entry into consciousness. Information stored in short-term memory is consciously accessible, where it remains available to the conscious mind only as long as it remains the center of attention.

As the name implies, items stored in short-term memory (STM) are available over the short term. Just because you are consciously aware of something in the present doesn't mean that you'll retain it for later access. What did you eat for breakfast yesterday? Presumably you were fully aware of your food while you were eating it, but you probably didn't record this information in anticipation of being asked about it the next day. As mentioned in Chapter 3, some events, particularly those associated with emotional arousal, are sufficiently important to store in long-term memory (LTM). Once stored in LTM, memories must be retrieved and loaded in STM if you'd like to consciously access them. What is your mother's maiden name? A moment ago you probably weren't thinking about it, but now you are because you retrieved your memory from LTM. In this chapter we'll consider each of the memory stores, beginning with sensory memory.

encode
the transformation of real-world energy, such as light and sound, into an electrical code that can be stored and processed by the brain

attention
the process by which your brain filters out loads of unnecessary sensory information to focus on a small portion

sensory memory
a memory store for briefly holding sensory information (primarily sights and sounds)

Sensory Memory

Sensory memory is a means for each of the five senses to briefly retain a trace of every sensed stimulus: visual sensory memory retains a picture of the world, auditory sensory memory retains an echo of sounds heard, and so on for the other senses. Visual sensory memory is typically called **iconic memory** because an icon is a kind of portrait. In the late 1950s, George Sperling was trying to study short-term memory experimentally but was frustrated by his participants' continual failure to retain as many items in STM as he expected them to. In the original version of his experiment, Sperling briefly presented (for a small fraction of a second) twelve letters arranged in three rows of four items each, as in Figure 9.2, then after the letters disappeared he asked participants to name as many of the letters as they could recall. Earlier STM experiments (described later in this chapter) found that participants could retain about seven items in STM, but Sperling's participants could only report about three or four letters. Although this was much fewer than expected, some participants described an intriguing phenomenon: after the letters disappeared, there seemed to be a page of text floating briefly in the air, and participants said they could "read" letters from it, but the ghostly page of text faded quickly. Sperling believed that the floating page of text was actually a form of memory. To prove it, Sperling developed a clever experiment based on the typical school exam procedure familiar to students everywhere.

iconic memory
a brief visual image of the world held in sensory memory

9.2 An example of a stimulus array used in Sperling's experiments
After the array was briefly flashed, participants in the full report experiment tried to recall all twelve letters. Participants in the partial report experiment saw the same kinds of arrays but heard a tone indicating which of the three rows to recall.

In most classes, students attend lectures and read books, then they take exams that measure their retention of the lecture and book material. Exams don't typically ask students to recall every single scrap of studied information but, instead, ask them to recall a subset of the studied material. Students don't know what questions will appear on the exam until after the studying phase is completed, ensuring that students must consult their memories rather than notes or books to answer the questions. To adapt the familiar exam technique to the laboratory, Sperling used the same study phase as in the original experiment (three briefly presented rows of four letters each), but participants were asked to report the letters in just one of the three rows. After the letter array disappeared, a tone sounded, and its pitch (high, middle, or low pitch) indicated which row (upper, middle, or lower row, respectively) should be reported. Because participants were asked to report only a subset of the study letters during the test phase, Sperling called this the **partial report** technique as opposed to the **full report** technique used in his original experiment. Participants in the partial report experiment typically recalled almost all the letters in the indicated row. Just as a teacher would conclude that any student who could correctly answer almost all the exam questions has retained most of the course material, Sperling concluded that visual sensory memory has the capacity to hold a picture of the entire visual field. However, although iconic memory has a large capacity, its duration is severely limited, lasting for just a small fraction of a second. As Sperling discovered, the reason why participants in the original full report method of the study did not do as well as expected was due to the limited duration of iconic memory, not its limited capacity.

partial report
an experimental technique in which participants recall just a specified subset of the study material, which showed that iconic memory has more capacity than was revealed by the full report technique

full report
an experimental technique in which participants are asked to recall all of the study material

The duration of iconic memory was a key factor in the development of motion pictures. Movie projectors shine light through images arranged one after another on a long ribbon of film. To prevent the movie from appearing blurry as the film rolls through the projector, the projector light doesn't shine continuously but, instead, flashes briefly for each frame, then darkens while the film moves to the next frame. How many bright-to-dark-to-bright flickers should the projector pack into each second? Movies in the early days had about 10 frames in each second, but this frame rate was slow enough that audiences could see the flicker, leading viewers to create the term "flicks" as slang for movies. Today movie projectors present twenty-four frames in each second, so the projector light shines for one forty-eighth of a second, then the entire theater is dark for the next forty-eighth of a second. Nobody notices that the entire theater is dark for half of the viewing time because the audience's iconic memories retain the projected image during the interval between frames. Not everything in sensory memory elicits attention, but anything that does is allowed entry to short-term memory.

Short-Term Memory

In the early days of telephones, professional operators connected phone calls, but when direct-dial phones were invented in the 1920s the likelihood of misdialed phone numbers threatened to increase telephone traffic, straining telephone exchanges to the breaking point. The Bell Telephone company needed to keep phone numbers as short as possible so its customers could reliably remember and dial the correct phone numbers. However, steadily increasing telephone use forced the Bell system to lengthen phone numbers so a unique number could be assigned to every phone. To find out how far phone numbers could be stretched and still be retained in memory, in the mid-1950s Bell Labs asked the memory researcher George Miller to investigate the capacity of human memory for immediate access. As a result of the research he conducted, Miller discovered critical insights about the nature of short-term memory, and the Bell system adopted the seven-digit phone number system that remains the standard today.

short-term memory
a memory store containing whatever currently inhabits the conscious mind

It may seem odd to you that the length of phone numbers is so closely tied to the capacity of short-term memory. With modern technology, we rarely need to learn phone numbers any more. However, before smartphones became available, people had to look up a phone number in a phone book, then hold it in memory long enough to dial it into the phone. This task requires the use of **short-term memory**, in which you hold information that you are consciously aware of. For example, think about what your feet feel like right now. A moment ago you probably were not thinking about how your feet feel, but by drawing your attention to your feet you became aware of the feeling, and this awareness was made available in your short-term memory. Once this paragraph ends, you will likely stop thinking about your feet, and the memory of how your feet felt a few minutes ago will be lost.

As a participant in one of Miller's experiments, you might have been asked to read the following string of 12 letters, and then try to recall as many letters as possible in the correct order. Try it for yourself: Read the letters, then cover them up and write as many as you can remember on another piece of paper.

A O M D S C L P S E G I

How many letters were you able to recall? Students typically recall somewhere between five and nine letters, but very rarely can a student recall all twelve letters in the right order. Miller found that participants could retain about seven items plus or minus two (i.e., between five and nine) items, but the items didn't have to be letters; they could also be letter clusters, each of which contained several letters. Short-term memory can be thought of as a tiny piggy bank that can hold about seven coins, but the coins may be any denomination, so a piggy bank filled with quarters would have much greater spending power than one filled with pennies. Similarly, each item in STM can be a single letter, a cluster of letters, or even a sentence containing several letter clusters. To illustrate this aspect of STM, try Miller's experiment one more time with the letters below.

O M G C I A L S D E S P

Even though both strings contain the same twelve letters, you probably had more success retaining the letters in the second arrangement than the first. The second arrangement of letters contains four clusters of three letters that are familiar to many Americans today. Because each item in STM can contain groups of smaller pieces, Miller described them as "chunks" of information. For example, a text message representing a single idea like "OMG, the CIA ran experiments to see if LSD would cause people to have ESP!" would take up just one slot in STM. Miller was so astonished by the fact that several pieces could be fused into a single chunk that he described the capacity of STM as the 'magical' number seven plus or minus two. In contrast to the unlimited capacity of iconic memory, the seven-item capacity of STM is relatively small, but **chunking** can stretch the capacity of STM by packing more information into each chunk.

chunking
a way of increasing memory capacity by grouping items together instead of remembering each item individually

Not only does STM have a limited but expandable capacity, but STM also has a brief but expandable duration. To see how you maintain a seven-digit number in STM, try to remember this phone number for half a minute: 867-5309. For anyone who doesn't remember the song about Jenny from the 1980s, this phone number probably occupies all seven slots in STM. During the half minute that you held the number in STM, you probably heard the numbers repeating over and over in your mind. Repeating numbers silently to yourself is called **rehearsal**, and is a way of extending the duration of STM. However, rehearsal requires constant attention, so if your attention is directed elsewhere then the number will leak out of STM as if it had never been there at all. Without looking back, what was the phone number mentioned earlier in the paragraph? Anyone remembering the song about Jenny can retrieve the number from their long-term memory (LTM), but for everyone else the number decayed from STM as they continued reading the paragraph following Jenny's phone number. You have likely experienced the frustrating effects of this decay as you tried to study while people around you are being noisy. The distractions frequently grab your attention, forcing the information you just read from your notes or textbook out of STM.

rehearsal
a way of extending the duration of items in short-term memory by repeating the items to yourself over and over

Short-term memory holds information for immediate conscious access, but quite often you need to process information at the same time you are holding it. To process the information stored in STM requires another mechanism, called working memory.

Working Memory

If you go to the grocery store intending to buy food to cook for dinner but only have twenty dollars in cash to spend, you might hear an internal monologue as you wander through the store, like the following: ". . . a bag of buns is about three dollars, leaving seventeen dollars. A green pepper is about two dollars, leaving fifteen dollars. This sirloin steak is about eight dollars. I already have some onions and olive oil at home, so maybe I can make steak sandwiches . . ." Notice that you have to hold numbers in STM, such as how much each item costs and how much money is left, and you also have to process numbers by subtracting the price of each additional item from the remaining money. To investigate this interaction between memory storage and processing, Alan Baddeley and Graham Hitch (1974) asked participants to perform a dual task, which included both memory and processing tasks (Figure 9.3). The memory task was similar to STM experiments, in which participants were asked to retain several numbers either in a simple-to-remember order (e.g., 1, 2, 3, 4, 5, 6), or jumbled order (e.g., 3, 2, 5, 6, 1, 4). In terms of chunks, the simple order contains one or two chunks (start at 1, end at 6), whereas the jumbled order contains six chunks, so it puts a heavier load on STM.

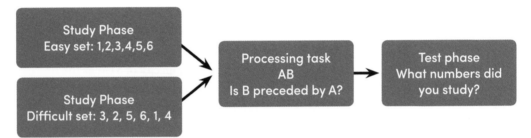

9.3 Outline of Baddeley and Hitch's (1974) dual task procedure
Participants studied numbers that were either easy or difficult to retain in STM, then held the items in STM while answering a reasoning question. Response times for the reasoning task were faster for the easily retained items than the difficult to retain items, indicating that STM and processing rely on a single engine, called working memory.

After participants viewed the numbers to be remembered, but *before* reporting them to the experimenter, they answered a simple reasoning problem. This means that while they were processing information, they were also holding numbers in memory. The reasoning problem might have been something like the following: For these two letters (AB), is B preceded by A? The answer is "yes," but this can be a tough question to answer while also holding several numbers in your head. At the time of the Baddeley and Hitch study, most researchers presumed that memory and processing relied on two different parts of the brain that work independently of each other, so the difficulty of the memory task should have no effect on the reasoning task. Nevertheless, response times for the reasoning problem were longer for the jumbled order than the simple order, implying that loading STM with more chunks hinders processing.

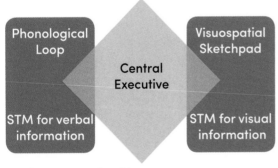

9.4 Components of working memory
Working memory enables you to access short-term memory for verbal information in the phonological loop and visual information in the visuospatial sketchpad and to process that information in the central executive.

When two systems interact, this implies that they have some functionality in common. For example, if you blast the air conditioning in your car, you can reasonably expect that it will reduce your gas mileage because a single engine drives both the wheels of your car and its air conditioning system. Similarly, the interaction between STM and processing shows that they are driven by the same "engine," which Baddeley and Hitch (1974) called **working memory**. The working memory model depicted in Figure 9.4 contains two kinds of short-term memory: STM for verbal information, such as words, letters, and numbers is stored in the phonological loop, and STM for visual images is stored in the visuospatial sketchpad. Information processing is handled by the central executive. Notice the overlap between the central executive and both kinds of STM, implying that they all draw on the same resources.

working memory
a form of memory that contains both storage and processing mechanisms

Concept Recall

1. How do the full report and partial report techniques differ in terms of the number of study items and test items?

2. What is the role of attention in memory?

3. What memory process can be used to increase the capacity of short-term memory? What memory process can be used to increase the duration of short-term memory?

4. What is the difference between short-term memory and working memory?

5. Why does running the car's air conditioner reduce gas mileage, and how does that relate to working memory?

This Is Psychology

A common metaphor for human memory is the computer, such that RAM is analogous to STM because RAM contains the information the computer is currently accessing. To process information, the computer relies on a central processing unit (CPU), so the CPU and RAM together are analogous to working memory. To archive information for later access the computer stores it on the disk drive, which makes it analogous to LTM. Just as you need to retrieve a document from the disk and load it into RAM to be able to revise the document, you have lots of facts about your life stored in LTM that are hidden from your conscious mind until you retrieve them from LTM. For example, what is your mother's middle name? A moment ago you weren't thinking about her middle name, so to answer the question you had to access LTM. Although the computer is a useful metaphor for explaining the interaction between STM, working memory, and LTM, human memory doesn't work quite the way a computer's memory works. In particular, human LTM stores the gist, or general idea, of past experiences, but a computer's disk needs to retain a verbatim copy of every document it contains.

Long-Term Memory: Forgetting

Everyone knows what forgetting is: at some point you could remember some fact or event, but now you can't. The classic study of forgetting was carried out by the German psychologist Hermann Ebbinghaus in the 1880s, for which he was the sole experimental participant. Ebbinghaus taught himself dozens of nonsense syllables of the form consonant-vowel-consonant; an example in English might have been "dax," which is pronounceable but doesn't mean anything.

forgetting curve
a function relating elapsed time to the amount of information that can be recalled; determined by Ebbinghaus's nonsense syllable experiment

long-term memory
memory of past events and facts about the world

Once Ebbinghaus could recall every syllable, he tested his ability to recall as many syllables as possible at periodic intervals. A plot of the number of recalled syllables as a function of time as in Figure 9.5 yielded the classic **forgetting curve**. You'll notice that the number of recalled syllables drops sharply at first but then the curve bends and levels out. Unlike STM, Ebbinghaus's **long-term memory** never quite lost every syllable. The shape of the forgetting curve shows two very beneficial characteristics of memory: (1) the initial drop-off shows that LTM doesn't retain every scrap of information, which would quickly lead to your mind becoming so cluttered that you couldn't efficiently retrieve memories, and (2) the leveling out demonstrates that your LTM *does* retain some information about the experience, which allows you to relearn things more easily than the first time you learned them.

Many students refuse to believe that decay from LTM is actually beneficial to the overall functioning of LTM. A tempting fantasy for many students is imagining what it would be like to have a photographic memory. You could open your textbook to the first page, take a mental snapshot, then turn to the next page and take another snapshot, and so on. During the exam, you could simply recall the image of the textbook, then mentally page through until you found the right place and "read" the answer from the mental image. It seems so easy, but perhaps you can see the problem: retrieval from memory would be excruciatingly sluggish, so by the end of the allotted exam time you would have only answered a fraction of the questions (if you have ever taken an open-book test, you know from experience how slow this process can be). To see how an LTM that retains every scrap of information is more of a curse than a blessing, consider the case of "S" (using just his initial to conceal his identity) described by the Russian neuropsychologist Alexander Luria.

9.5 Ebbinghaus forgetting curve
Ebbinghaus memorized dozens of nonsense syllables, then tested his ability to recall the syllables at several intervals. At first his ability to recall the syllables dropped off sharply, but then it leveled out, suggesting that he never completely forgot every syllable.

Employed as a newspaper journalist in the 1920s, S attended meetings each morning in which the editor doled out the day's assignments to the assembled reporters in a long verbal stream of names, addresses, and other relevant facts. One morning, the editor became irritated that S was the only reporter not feverishly taking notes, to which S replied that he didn't need to take notes to remember what the editor said. To the astonishment of everyone in the room, S then recited every word the editor had spoken during that morning's meeting, but S was just as astonished that his colleagues couldn't do the same thing. S assumed that everybody else remembered everything just like he did. At his editor's suggestion, S presented himself to Luria in the hope that Luria would test S's memory.

Thus began a collaboration between Luria and S lasting thirty years. Luria ultimately admitted that he failed to measure the capacity of S's LTM because he never discovered any limit. S could recite a string of 70 numbers forward and backward, complex mathematical formulas without understanding what the symbols meant, and Italian poetry without speaking a word of Italian, years after memorization. You might expect that S's capacious memory would uniquely equip him for every kind of profession, but he didn't last long as a journalist or in any other job. After drifting from one job to another he realized he was unemployable except as a mnemonist, performing various feats of memory on stage in front of an audience. The problem with S's memory seemed to be that he stored pristine copies of every fact presented to him, but he couldn't extract the figurative meaning of any of those facts. The essence of being an intelligent, educated person is the ability to see beyond the literal meaning of an idea to its gist and how distinct ideas are connected to one another. Unfortunately for S, these are skills that were well beyond his grasp. Ultimately, S became desperate to jettison some of the clutter from his mind. He tried writing words on scraps of paper then setting them on fire in the hope of incinerating the idea along with the written words, but to no avail; the ideas remained firmly embedded in his memory.

From the Desk of Dr. Stith

A fundamental psychological need for many across cultures and throughout history is the hope that we will be remembered. This hope is expressed when the living memorialize the dead and the ways they grieve, with monuments from pyramids to tombstones to roadside flower shrines.

Oklahoma City Bombing Memorial

In perpetrated mass tragedies (three or more unrelated persons are intentionally harmed), the community reflects this as a collective need. Often, a spontaneous memorial of personal objects, flowers, and poignant notes is created at the site (e.g., school shootings, church bombings, Aurora movie theater shooting). Later, more formal memorials are needed "lest we forget."

World Trade Center Memorial

Constructive Memory

As we saw with the case of S, forgetting is essential to the ability to effectively process ideas stored in LTM. For normal people who don't retain every scrap of information,

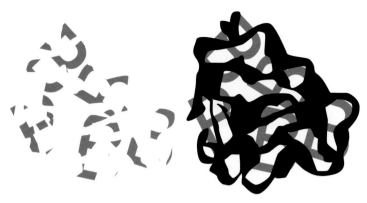

9.6 Vision is constructive because it fills in missing pieces
The shards on the left are the same as on the right, but your visual system can fill in the missing details on the right, so there appears to be several capital letter B's hidden by an inkstain.

memory is constructive in the same way perception is constructive. That is, the brain assembles pieces of information, then glues them together to form our experiences, whether they are sensory experiences or memories. To illustrate, the left side of Figure 9.6 contains several shapes that appear to be shards of broken pottery. The right side of the figure contains the same shapes plus what appears to be an ink stain, but your visual system is able to fill in in the missing parts of the image to form a complete set of objects. Do you see a collection of capital letter B's on the right, but not the left? As with retinal images, memories of events can be fragmented. Imagine watching a football game in which you see the quarterback throw the ball, but while the ball is in the air the guy in front of you stands up, obstructing your view. He quickly moves to the aisle, so you get to see the receiver catch the ball. Would you later remember the throw, the catch, and the ball flying through the air as a coherent event? If you do remember seeing the ball fly through the air, that is a false memory because you never actually witnessed that part of the event and only filled it in later. To get along in the world, it is more important for memories to represent coherent events than to record exact copies of what was perceived, so the memory system fills in the missing pieces of memory in a constructive process.

The constructive nature of memory was first described by Frederic Bartlett in the 1930s. Bartlett asked his English participants to read folktales, such as the *War of the Ghosts* from the Canadian Indian culture. This folktale describes the adventures of two young hunters, one of whom joins a war party traveling upriver in a canoe and dies from injuries incurred in the fighting. After reading the tale, participants later tried to recount it as accurately as possible. As expected, participants forgot some details from the story, particularly the supernatural elements that made no sense to Western minds. What was shocking at the time, however, was that the recalled versions of the tales included details that had not appeared in the original tales. After all, how can a memory include information that never occurred in the original event?

schema
a structure in long-term memory for organizing information

Bartlett noted that participants filled in gaps with details drawn from their own English experiences that were inconsistent with a tale set in the Canadian wilderness. Based on these results, Bartlett argued that we draw on organized sets of previous experiences called **schemas** to make sense of fragmented ideas (you were first introduced to the idea of a schema in Chapter 5). To get a sense of how you use schemas to make sense of a fragmented story, consider this screenplay for a very short movie:

> Man: I'm leaving.
>
> Woman: What's her name?

At first, you might have wondered what Woman is talking about, but soon enough you probably realized this is a brief conversation between a couple that is about to sever their tenuous romantic attachment. We have all kinds of schemas stored in LTM, including a football schema (when a quarterback throws a ball and a receiver catches a ball, the ball must have traversed the space between passer and receiver) and a romantic attachment schema. When you read the short script you retrieved the romantic attachment schema from LTM, which helped you fill in some missing information, including the fact that Woman thinks Man is breaking up with Woman to be with another woman.

Concept Recall

1. Why do people who have a photographic memory typically think of it more as a curse than a blessing?

2. What are the two main lessons to be learned from the shape of Ebbinghaus's classic forgetting curve?

3. How do schemas contribute to constructive memory?

False Memories

Generally, schemas do a great job of filling in missing details. You know how the ball got to the receiver and who Woman is asking about in the short screenplay. Sometimes, as in Bartlett's experiment, details drawn from schemas clash with the original memory, vividly demonstrating that filling-in actually generates false memories. They are false memories because Bartlett's participants presumed that their recall of the folktale was based on their prior reading of the tale, but some details came from their schemas. Some false memories are harmless, but not when memory is used as eyewitness testimony in a court of law. The psychologist Elizabeth Loftus is probably best known for her research at the intersection between the law and the scientific study of memory.

In 1990, Beth Loftus was an expert witness for the defense of George Franklin, who was on trial for the 1969 murder of his daughter's best friend, Susan Nason. The primary evidence linking George to the murder was a "recovered" memory of the murder described in testimony by his daughter, Eileen. Eileen claimed that at the age of eight she witnessed her father committing the murder, but she promptly lost all memory of the event and continued to have no access to the memory for the next twenty years. In 1989, Eileen became aware of a memory in which she could see her father commit the murder, almost as if the memory had been waiting patiently for years in her unconscious mind until it popped into her consciousness.

As an expert witness, Beth Loftus argued that the source of the memory might not have been visual; instead, Eileen might have imagined the event and misattributed the source of her mental images, thereby mistakenly concluding that she had witnessed the event. To support her argument Loftus described some of her research on memory, including experiments that elicited the **misinformation effect**. Loftus and John Palmer (1974) showed participants a movie depicting a collision between two cars, then asked them how fast the cars were going when they collided. The participants didn't know that different versions of the questionnaire used slightly different words; some questionnaires asked how fast the cars were going when they "smashed into" each other,

misinformation effect
a memory phenomenon in which people falsely recall information presented after an event as having been part of the event

and others when they "hit" each other. Participants who had been asked about the cars smashing into each other reported higher speeds than participants asked about the cars hitting each other. Furthermore, when asked a week later if they had seen any broken glass on the ground, the "smashed" participants were likelier to indicate they had seen broken glass than the "hit" participants, when in fact there was no broken glass to be seen. Even though everyone had witnessed the same event, slight wording changes in questions asked after the event caused some participants to recall seeing things that were not there to be seen. Apparently persuaded more by the testimony of Eileen Franklin than Beth Loftus, the jury elected to convict George Franklin for murder.

After George Franklin's conviction, Loftus tried to figure out why the jury found her testimony unconvincing. She decided that the misinformation effect shows that factors external to a witnessed event (misleading questions) can pollute a memory with phony details, but not that external factors can create a complete coherent event in memory from scratch. With that in mind, Loftus set about trying to implant memories. Knowing that an institutional review board would never permit her to implant traumatic childhood memories, Loftus decided that convincing participants that they had once gotten lost in a mall as a child would be mildly traumatic without causing devastating mental anguish. Loftus and Pickrell (1995) found that about a third of their participants recalled having been lost in the mall as a child on the basis of mere suggestion to that effect.

Not all psychologists agreed with Loftus's claims, and the "memory wars" raged through the 1990s. On one side were psychologists claiming that recovered memories of sexual abuse suffered years before are rock-solid and, thus, should be admissible in a court of law. On the other side were Loftus and her supporters claiming memory is malleable and subject to corruption and, therefore, should not be admissible without other corroborating evidence. As wars often do, this war became ugly, with Loftus receiving death threats and other abuses (Abramsky, 2004). In the early 1990s most legal victories favored the view that memories of abuse are accurate and reliable, but the tide began to turn with the lost-in-the-mall study and other studies replicating its effect. Courts of law began to require corroborating evidence along with testimony based on recovered memories (Wilson, 2002).

Even if the memory wars seem remote from your own life, the malleability of memory may introduce conflict when you least expect it. Did you ever go to a family gathering where two relatives discuss one of their common experiences from the past, but each person's recollection diverges radically from the other person's recollections, sometimes to the point of serious conflict?

From what you now know about memory, we hope you realize that memories can become corrupted without any malicious intent, and you can graciously accept differences between your own and other people's recollections of the same event. As for George Franklin, after six years in prison, he was acquitted by an appeals court that claimed there had not been sufficient evidence to convict in the lower court.

Concept Recall

1. How did Beth Loftus use the misinformation effect to create false memories of broken glass?

2. Does the misinformation effect show that an entire coherent event can be implanted in memory?

3. How did Beth Loftus's work on memory lead to change in the American legal system?

Amnesia

From time to time we all forget and falsely remember, but **amnesia**—in which memories never get stored in LTM—occurs only for people who have had certain kinds of brain injury. The most famous person with amnesia was Henry Molaison, known for most of his adult life until his death in 2008 as H.M. As a young man, H.M. had dreamed of studying how the brain works, but he never got the chance. Nevertheless, his cooperative participation in memory research for more than fifty years revolutionized our understanding of the neural basis of memory.

H.M. believed his trouble began as a child when he was knocked over in a collision with a bicyclist and cracked his skull. Shortly afterward, he began having small, or *petit mal*, seizures, and, at the age of fifteen, he had his first *grand mal* seizure. The seizures became increasingly frequent until H.M. had as many as ten each day, making him so desperate that he consented to experimental brain surgery for relief. In 1953, at the age of twenty-seven, H.M. became the first person to have surgery to remove the bulk of his hippocampi (the plural of hippocampus, one on each side of the brain); he was also the last person to have this surgical procedure. After surgery, the frequency of H.M.'s seizures was greatly reduced, and his IQ even jumped about ten points. At first, it seemed that the surgery had been a success because during recovery, H.M. recognized his mother and father and could carry on a normal conversation. However, it soon became clear that something was terribly wrong with H.M.'s memory.

While recovering in the hospital, H.M. never remembered any of the nurses or hospital staff who frequented his room, even people who had popped out of his room just minutes before. He could not get the hang of day-to-day hospital procedures or remember how to get to the bathroom despite having visited it numerous times. H.M.'s surgeon, William Scoville, was shaken by H.M.'s seemingly complete inability to store memories of anything happening after the surgery. Scoville eventually confessed to his colleague Wilder Penfield (the same Penfield described in Chapter 3 who mapped the somatosensory cortex) what he had done. At first, Penfield was infuriated by Scoville's recklessness, but then he recognized the opportunity to figure out what the hippocampus does. Penfield sent Brenda Milner, a graduate student at the time, to assess what H.M. had lost and to determine what, if anything, remained intact.

amnesia
loss of memory, typically due to brain damage

9.7 The kind of shape used in mirror-drawing tasks
Could you trace the path between the inside and outside stars with a pencil? What about if you could only see their mirror image? Over several trials, H.M. learned to trace the paths while viewing just their mirror image.

mirror drawing
a task in which the participant is asked to draw something seen in a mirror, which reverses the visual image

declarative memories
memories that can be put into words, such as events, facts, and word definitions

By recognizing his mother and father, H.M. showed that he was able to retrieve memories from before his surgery, but the loss of his hippocampi eliminated his ability to store any new memories. H.M. couldn't remember conversations from minutes before, what day it was, or when he had last eaten. Indeed, H.M. once ate an entire meal and was then accidentally offered another one, which he happily ate.

Milner's eureka moment occurred when she gave up asking questions that H.M. could not answer and decided to test his retention of motor skills. She presented H.M. with a piece of paper with two concentric stars, as in Figure 9.7, already drawn on it and asked H.M. to draw a third star along the pathway between the other two. The trick was that H.M. could not look directly at the stars. He could only look through a mirror, which reversed the visual image. Just like anyone else that tries **mirror drawing** for the first time, H.M. made a mess on his first attempt. After thirty attempts spread over a couple of days, he improved to the point that he could draw a line between the stars without a mistake. If you were exposed to the same training regimen as H.M. and then asked why you were so proficient at mirror drawing, you would be able to describe your training. However, H.M. couldn't recall his training, so after becoming proficient at mirror drawing without remembering how, he was surprised that he could do it so easily and concluded that he was just naturally good at mirror drawing.

H.M.'s ability to learn mirror drawing shows that he could store a kind of memory, if the meaning of "memory" is broadened from its usual meaning as stored events, facts, and word definitions to include skill acquisition. What is the difference between the kinds of memory he could store (new skills) and those he couldn't (events, facts, and word definitions)? Events, facts, and word definitions can all be described in words, so they are often called **declarative memories**, whereas skills are more about know-how, so they are called **procedural memories**. Once Milner showed that H.M. retained the ability to store procedural memories, the race was on to discover other kinds of procedural memories. As you saw in Chapter 7, Pavlov showed that animals could learn to associate two stimuli without having any language to describe the association, so conditioning seemed like it could be a kind of procedural memory. When a puff of air blows in your eye you blink without requiring any instruction. In the classical conditioning model the puff is an unconditioned stimulus (US), and the blink is the unconditioned response (UR). In one experiment H.M. heard a tone just before a puff of air blew in his eye. The conditioning procedure used with H.M. is shown in Figure 9.8.

9.8 Conditioning procedure used with H.M.
This figure represents how H.M.'s ability to learn procedural memories remained intact.

After several pairings of tone and puff, H.M. learned to associate the two, so when he heard the tone he blinked without understanding why he was blinking.

Like skill learning, H.M.'s acquisition of a classically conditioned association shows that it is a kind of procedural memory that must bypass the hippocampus. H.M. not only retained the ability to store and retrieve procedural memories, but also, as already mentioned, he could carry on a conversation, implying that his STM remained intact. To test this theory, Brenda Milner asked H.M. to retain the three-digit number "584" for twenty minutes while she stepped out of the room. Normally, H.M. would have lost everything in STM once his attention was distracted. On this occasion H.M. was determined to prove he could keep memories from leaking away, so he repeatedly rehearsed the number in his STM. When Milner returned to the room she was impressed when H.M. recited the number she'd asked him to remember as "584." Milner then continued the conversation for a few minutes and asked him again what number she had asked him to remember, to which he replied, "You asked me to remember a number?"

procedural memories
memories that often can't be expressed in words but are memories for how to do a certain skill

H.M.'s decades-long cooperation with various memory researchers showed that memory is not a single resource, but instead consists of many different resources, each relying on different parts of the brain. Immediate memory refers to items available for extremely brief access (sensory memory) and items held in the conscious mind (short-term memory). Once an item decays from STM it can only be retrieved if it was stored in LTM, and as H.M. shows, this includes anything that happened an hour ago or years ago. H.M.'s LTM was devastated, but the damage was isolated to the storage of declarative memories. The retrieval of declarative memories remained largely intact, and both the storage and retrieval of procedural memories remained intact.

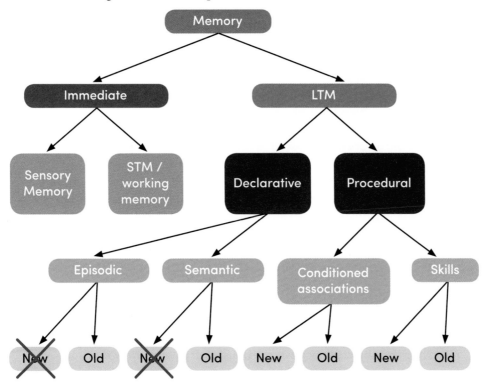

9.9 H.M.'s memory chart
H.M. showed that memory is much more than just one single mechanism. H.M.'s loss was primarily in terms of making new declarative memories (the boxes marked by an **x**) with the other memory systems remaining primarily intact.

episodic memory
a type of declarative memory; memories of specific events

semantic memory
a type of declarative memory for word meanings and facts about the world

Declarative memory includes memories of events, which are called **episodic memories**, and facts and word definitions, which together are called **semantic memories**. H.M.'s procedural memory system was mostly unaffected by his surgery because he could still store and retrieve new motor skills and conditioned associations. Notice that in Figure 9.9, H.M.'s surgery eliminated just the ability to make new declarative memories, with all other memory systems remaining intact, and yet this loss prevented him from being able to live alone and unassisted. H.M.'s amnesia consigned him to live in a permanent present tense.

Concept Recall

1. Why did H.M. submit to experimental brain surgery?
2. What did H.M. lose following the surgery, and did any function remain intact?
3. What is the difference between declarative and procedural memories?

This Is Psychology

Only one person survived. In the fifth century BCE, the Greek poet Simonides of Ceos was attending a banquet when he was called away to receive a message. Just after he stepped through the front door, the roof collapsed on everyone who remained inside. Rescuers digging through the rubble could not identify any victims, all of whom were mangled beyond recognition. Simonides soon realized that when he closed his eyes he could recreate a coherent version of the banquet in his mind, and by "walking" around the mental scene he could recall where each of his friends had been sitting. Modern mnemonists perform astonishing feats of memory by exploiting the technique described by Simonides. To understand why it works, consider the fact that our primitive ancestors had no need to remember long lists of words and numbers, but they did need to navigate their surroundings and remember where they could find food and water. As a result, our memories retain concrete objects and locations much better than lists of words and numbers. The trick is to transform one kind of information into the kind that sticks in our memories. In 2006, Akira Haraguchi spent sixteen hours reciting the first 83,431 digits of pi, which begins with 3.14 and continues infinitely. People who have sought to break his record typically begin by developing a system in which each digit is assigned to an object such as sun for one, eyes for two, a triangle for three, and so on for the remaining digits. Next, they build elaborate palaces in their minds and place objects at strategic locations throughout the palace. To recite the digits, they walk through the palace, retrieving the objects they have previously left behind. Now that you know the basic technique, are you tempted to try to break Haraguchi's record?

PHYSICAL STORAGE OF MEMORY

Up to this point, the discussion of memory has focused on cognitive models of what memory is and how it works, without much focus on where memories are stored in the brain. The answer to this question is complicated but beautiful. As we begin to understand where memories are stored, we gain a much better appreciation for how memory works and where some of the "problems" that have been described throughout this chapter originate.

We need to begin our discussion on the physical storage of memory by dispelling two common myths regarding memory.

Myth #1: There is a Single Place in the Brain Where Each Memory is Stored

As we discussed memory in the preceding sections, we introduced the modal model of memory that includes the components of sensory memory, short-term memory (STM), and long-term memory (LTM). These concepts help us make memory concrete and help us to understand how memory works, but, because these components are presented as actual "things" (often in the form of a graphic or flow chart such as in Figure 9.1), people often make the mistake of believing that there must be areas of the brain that specialize in these functions. It seems reasonable that the brain's memory system must be like storage in modern digital technology, with an area that corresponds to our "memory" where we send the things that we want to store. Remove this memory area and—just as would happen if you took the corresponding chip from your device—the information stored in that area would suddenly be forgotten. Replace the component (hopefully with upgraded storage capacity) and the information is right back. This way of thinking about memory is convenient, but it just isn't the way that the brain works (unless we remove the entire brain, which would delete almost all memories).

Karl Lashley, a neuroscientist who worked with John B. Watson during his early career, conducted a series of experiments over a period of more than 30 years that demonstrated the problem with conceptualizing memory as stored in any one place. In a paper summarizing his research, Lashley (1950) showed that the work by him and his colleagues with rats and monkeys using **ablation studies**—a physiological research procedure in which small portions of the brain are removed or destroyed in order to explore the function of a neural system—had failed to find any one area that contained the memory of a learned response or relation. As monkeys and rats are not able to tell us what they remember, memory researchers train these animals to perform certain behaviors, such as correctly navigating a maze. Once a rat can successfully navigate a maze from beginning to end, we might presume that a "map" of the maze exists somewhere in the rat's brain. After a rat subject learned the maze, Lashley and his team would systematically remove areas of the animal's brain. The rat was then returned to the maze to see whether the animal retained any memory of it. If the area of the brain that had been removed contained the "map," the rat would have lost the ability to navigate the maze. Across all of their studies, Lashley and his team failed to find any specific

ablation studies
a physiological research procedure in which small portions of the brain are removed or destroyed in order to explore the function of a neural system

areas that store memory. Instead, what they found was that performance deteriorated as a function of how much of the area was experimentally destroyed. Lashley's work provides an early example of what we now know about memory storage: *memories are not stored in a single place, but instead are distributed across the cortex.*

Myth #2: A Memory is a Faithful Copy of an Experienced Event

Another common misconception about memory is to think of it as a picture or a video of a past event. Before the invention of modern personal electronic devices, pictures were developed from film then stored in photo albums, collections, and piles in cabinets or drawers. If you wanted to view a picture, you would have to find it in your collection. Each time you successfully found the picture, it would look exactly the same (minus potential wear, water damage, or fading). The same was true of videos that were stored on videotapes, CDs, or DVDs (without the potential for wear). This physical way of interacting with recorded events has shaped our way of thinking about our memories. It is an easy analogy to draw between how we look for physical records and how we look for mental records as well as how digital storage works in modern technology. Unfortunately, the analogy is misleading. Memory storage is nothing like how we store photographs and videos, either physical copies or digital copies, nor is it similar to how digital memory works in personal electronics. The analogy makes sense and sounds right, but it does not hold up to scientific scrutiny.

The major problem with the "filing cabinet" approach to memory is that it assumes that the memory is stored as a whole and that each memory is independent. If I have a set of images saved to my computer, each image file contains its own information. Even if I have saved a dozen pictures of the same event, say a student activity in the psychology department, each file will contain its own information. In your memory, this is not going to be the case. Your memory of the student event will store information about the event, but that information will be directly tied to memories of other events that occurred in the same room, with the same group of people, and with other shared details.

Earlier in this chapter, we discussed the constructive nature of memory. In this discussion, the fact that a memory is "pieced" together each time it is activated was presented as one reason why we end up with false memories and memory errors. The constructive nature of memory is similarly the reason why you have likely noticed that it is rare that you ever completely forget any one thing. Instead, we forget certain details, such as a name, or a color, or the size of an object, or the smell of a food, while still being able to remember other details. Forgetting is more like deleting entries from a text message thread one at a time, rather than taking away the entire conversation all at once. As long as we have some of the pieces of the conversation, we can still make sense of what we have. Once enough of the messages have been lost, the conversation no longer has any meaning. The same is true of our memories. Because the pieces of the memory are stored separately and then reassembled when recalled, it is common to have pieces that are "missing." The missing pieces are either a source of frustration ("Oh, come on! How can I forget their name!") or they are simply filled in—consciously or unconsciously—with information that seems to make sense based on learned schemas.

Distributed Nature of Memory

Understanding that memory is not stored in any one place and that memories themselves are not faithful copies of experienced events provides the foundation needed to appreciate the distributed nature of memory. What we call a memory is, at the physiological level, a pattern of activation across neurons. As you recall from Chapter 3, the brain is made up of billions of neurons that are all interconnected. When we have a sensory experience, the incoming energy from the sensation begins a pattern of chemical and electrical activity that proceeds through our cortex. Over time, this pattern of activity becomes associated (remember classical conditioning from Chapter 7?) with different events. For example, you have a network that is associated with the written word "cat." Each time you read the word "cat" the same general group of visual neurons become active. If you read the words

Cross-Cultural Case

How Does Culture Influence Memory?

Memory—individual, familial, and cultural—plays a significant role in all our lives. However, the way we experience and make memories can differ depending on what part of the world we call home. According to the social interaction model developed by CUNY psychologist, Dr. Katherine Nelson, the way we discuss events in our lives can influence how and whether we encode those events as memories. In this model, a key element of memory-making is storytelling. Nelson, and later researchers using her model, have discovered the more children are asked to elaborate on their experiences, to tell their stories, the more likely they are to solidify those experiences as memories. University of New Hampshire psychologist, Dr. Michelle Leichtman, tested this theory on American, Asian, and Maori children and found that the age at which a child begins to encode memories of his or her past is much younger in Maori children than in American or Asian children. She attributes this to Maori culture's "very strong emphasis on the past—both the personal past and the family's past." As such, both children and adults are encouraged to share very detailed stories about daily life, causing the events to encode as memories in children as young as 32 months.

Researchers in this area of study, including Leichtman, are careful to point out that these studies in no way imply that one culture has a "better" memory than another. Rather, "people have the types of memories that they need to get along well in the world they inhabit," and some cultures simply expect more elaboration than others.

"tabby cat," two networks are activated: one associated with the word "tabby" and one associated with the word "cat." If you have a pet cat, then reading "cat" activates the visual network associated with your cat, and the past couple of sentences likely elicited several "memories" of your cat.

One way to understand the distributed nature of memory storage is through recent demonstrations of "mind-reading" computer software (Miller, Schalk, Hermes, Ojemann, & Rao, 2016). Using brain-imaging technology, this type of software can report to others what you are thinking. Sound terrifying? Or maybe like something from a science fiction movie? Not so much. The algorithms don't actually tell what you are thinking. Instead, before the "mind reading" event, the computer takes thousands of scans of the electrical activity in your brain while you are being shown a variety of different stimuli. Using these scans, the machine creates a "map" of the neural networks that are associated with different environmental events. A stimulus that is presented might be a picture of a house or a picture of a face. Each of these stimuli activates a different pattern of activity in the visual cortex as well as other areas. In later sessions, the researchers show you the same images again, and the software algorithm matches the pattern of neural activity to the recorded maps. Since the neural networks associated with particular memories stay relatively constant, the software is able to "read your mind" with a high degree of accuracy.

How accurate do you think that the predictions of the software would be at reading someone else's mind? As it turns out, not very. The specific neural networks for each person are different, even for the same images, concepts, and ideas. The network is a product of individual life experience. Which specific neurons are active depends on how the brain was wired during development, how information was presented during learning, and what the individual's particular life experiences have been.

A major implication of the storage of memories in neural networks is that our neural networks are highly flexible. As we have experiences, the networks change and rewire based on these experiences. With our memories for a person, event, or idea all stored in a general neural network, a change to one aspect of the memory can cause changes to other associated memories. You have likely encountered this when your opinion of a person changed. An example of this is the corruption of memories for an ex-romantic partner. The memories of the initial relationship are—for most relationships—pleasant, fun, and very positive. The memories at the end of the relationship tend to be the opposite. Unfortunately, both the new and the old memories are stored in similar networks, so when the beginning of the relationship is later recalled, some of the newer, more negative feelings will be activated and then integrated into the memory. This type of **retroactive interference**—the tendency for newer learning to interfere with older memories—is part of what is responsible for how a relationship is "tainted" by new information.

retroactive interference
the tendency for newer learning to interfere with older memories

The ability of new experiences to change old memories may seem like an error in the system, but there are two major evolutionary advantages to a system built this way. First, the neural network is a highly efficient way to store information. Instead of having 1,000 different memories for each object, your memory system has a single area that is integrated into all of these different memories. Given how expensive it is to maintain neurons, this storage efficiency outweighs the potential downsides of memory changes that go "viral" and influence other related memories. Second, the evolutionary function of memory is to help us decide how to act in the present. The flexible nature of the neural networks allows the memories to update with our current environment. Yes, the memories no longer represent a true account of what happened in the past, but the updated memory is better calibrated to the current environment of the organism.

MEMORY ACROSS PSYCHOLOGY

Now that you have been introduced to the way human memory works, you can appreciate that our ancestors endowed us with long-term memory that readily stores concrete objects and locations—if not lists of words and numbers. Working memory stores only about seven items, but each item can contain several smaller items if the grouping of smaller items is familiar to you. Knowing what you now know (assuming you can remember any of it), you can take advantage of how the memory systems are designed to improve your interactions with the world.

To exploit these aspects of long-term and working memory when studying for classes, instead of relying on rote memorization (such as endlessly cycling through a stack of flashcards), transform the material you are trying to remember by figuring out how the course material relates to your everyday life. Creating a personal connection to the material will activate existing neural networks, which are easier to change than creating entirely new associations between disconnected networks. Rearranging the material also allows you to spend more time with the information in STM, which increases the likelihood that it will be transferred to LTM. Educational psychologists, instructional technologists, and other forms of educators are actively creating new learning technologies that are better calibrated to the workings of human memory. They are also coming to better understand the genius of older technologies—such as oral traditions and the use of analogies and simile—in their adapted use of the memory system.

Another advantage of understanding how memory works is that now that you know that false memories can intrude into your long-term memory, you are better equipped to prevent the formation of false memories or to fall into believing them when they occur. Becoming more conscious of the source of memories and of the possible influences on them will help you to make more accurate evaluations of objects, people, and events. Psychologists working in legal settings understand how important it is to take into account the flexibility of memory during interrogations, depositions, and trials.

As you have seen throughout this chapter, human memory is a complex and convoluted subject, and you will see it as it appears in the context of other psychological concepts. As we'll discuss in Chapter 12, personality development relies partly on past experience, something memory keeps and organizes for its role in forming who you are. Similarly, much of our evaluation of the social world, which is the topic of Chapter 15, is dependent on our memories of social interactions from our past.

Review/Reflect/Write

REVIEW

- What memory stores are represented by boxes in the model of memory?
- What memory processes are represented by arrows in the model of memory?
- How do the full report and partial report techniques work?
- How do sensory memory and short-term memory differ in terms of capacity and duration?
- What is the relationship between short-term memory and working memory?
- What does Ebbinghaus's classic forgetting curve look like, and what does it tell us about memory?
- Why did people falsely recall broken glass at the scene of a car crash in the classic misinformation effect study?
- What did H.M. lose, and what did he retain after his brain surgery?

1. Iconic memory has a _____, but it lasts for _____.
   a. small capacity; years
   b. large capacity; years
   c. small capacity; a fraction of a second
   d. large capacity; a fraction of a second

2. When Daryl finished school, he noticed that he quickly forgot a lot of information he had learned, but the memory loss eventually leveled out. This leveling out occurs so that
   a. his brain will have more room to learn new things without losing everything he learned in the past.
   b. the brain will not degrade from excessive memory loss.
   c. he can prevent dementia by maintaining some memories.
   d. he can relearn the information.

3. Glenda heard a story about a Japanese haunting. When she retold the story later, she included information that was not in the original story. This most likely occurred because
   a. Glenda was unable to remember some parts and needed to make pieces up in order to convey the story to others.
   b. Glenda was drawing from her schemas to make sense of a story originating from another culture.
   c. Glenda's brain encoded the information properly, but her information retrieval was insufficient.
   d. Glenda wanted to make the story more detailed for the next listeners.

4. The misinformation effect can be demonstrated by
   a. showing that research participants are more likely to believe a detailed lie than a short, simple truth.
   b. participants recalling a car accident as having faster car speeds when questions use the word "smash" instead of "hit."

Answer Key
1.d 2.d 3.b 4.b 5.b 6.d 7.d 8.c 9.c 10.a

    c. shopper's adjustments to purchasing decisions based on dishonest advertising.

    d. test-takers' indecisiveness after being told information contradicting what she or he initially studied.

5. People can experience amnesia, in which memories are never stored in long-term memory, when they

    a. experience traumatic events.

    b. have a certain type of brain injury.

    c. have undergone hypnosis.

    d. all of the above

6. Declarative memory refers to memories such as

    a. events.   c. word definitions.

    b. facts.   d. all of the above

7. The "forgetting curve," discovered by Ebbinghaus, can best be described as

    a. your recall decreases really quickly for the first day, then continues to decrease slowly, until everything is forgotten.

    b. your recall will slowly and steadily decrease over time, until only around 20 percent of the information remains.

    c. your recall will stay steady or decrease slowly at first; after around one hour there will be a massive drop in recall, then it will level out.

    d. your recall will decrease quickly, then level out, never quite forgetting everything.

8. Which of these types of memory remained mostly intact by H.M.'s surgery?

    a. Episodic memory   c. Procedural memory

    b. Semantic memory   d. Declarative memory

9. Which of the following best describes the capacity for LTM?

    a. Around 10,000 items

    b. Seemingly unlimited capacity for declarative memories, but far fewer procedural memories

    c. Seemingly unlimited capacity for all types of memory

    d. Seemingly unlimited, but only for a year, when we lose all but around 5 percent of the year's memories.

10. _____ is the transformation of energy into an electrical code to be used by the brain, whereas _____ is the process of filtering out unnecessary sensory information to focus on a smaller portion.

    a. Encoding; attention   c. Sensory memory; iconic memory

    b. Attention; encoding   d. Iconic memory; sensory memory

REFLECT

1. Did you ever get into a fight with a friend or family member because his or her recollection of some shared past experience diverged from your own memory? Having learned in this chapter how inaccurate memory can be, are you more likely to accept that your own memories may not match the way things really happened? If so, would you be less likely to get angry when someone else's memory of a shared experience is different from your own?

2. Did you ever wish you had a photographic memory so you could ace all your exams simply by taking mental snapshots of your textbooks? Knowing how S struggled with his memory, can you better appreciate having a memory system that doesn't retain every fact and experience?

3. If you were a witness to a crime, what do you think you could do to prevent your memory from being corrupted by the way a police investigator phrases his or her questions?

WRITE

1. Mnemonics are techniques for boosting memory retention. Investigate the effectiveness of the mnemonic called the peg-word technique. Use the following set of ten pegs, or develop your own:

    1. sun (rhymes with one)
    2. eyes (two eyes)
    3. pyramid (three sides)
    4. square (four sides)
    5. hand (five fingers)
    6. sticks (rhymes with six)
    7. calendar (seven days)
    8. octopus (eight tentacles)
    9. baseball (nine players)
    10. hen (rhymes with ten)

    Ask classmates to name ten items, one at a time. After they name each item, create a mental image of the named item interacting with its peg item. For example, if the first item named by your classmates is a rhino, imagine a rhino sticking its horn into a sun. Compare your own ability to remember ten items with someone else who tries to remember the same ten items without using the peg-word technique. Who is quicker to remember the items? Do both remember all ten items the next day, or several days later?

2. After his surgery, H.M. lost the ability to make new declarative memories but retained the ability to make new procedural memories, such as skills and conditioned associations. Like most people, you are able to make both kinds of memories. For example, if you were in a car crash, you might afterward have a conditioned fear of driving (procedural memory) and retain a memory of the crash that you can describe in words (declarative memory). Think of a conditioned association that you have, and the circumstances in which you acquired that association. How are your declarative and procedural memories alike, and how are they different? By losing the ability to make new declarative memories, H.M. could no longer live independently. Could the same be said of procedural memories? That is, how would your life be affected if you lost the ability to make new procedural memories while retaining the ability to make new declarative memories?

Key Terms

10 Thinking and Intelligence

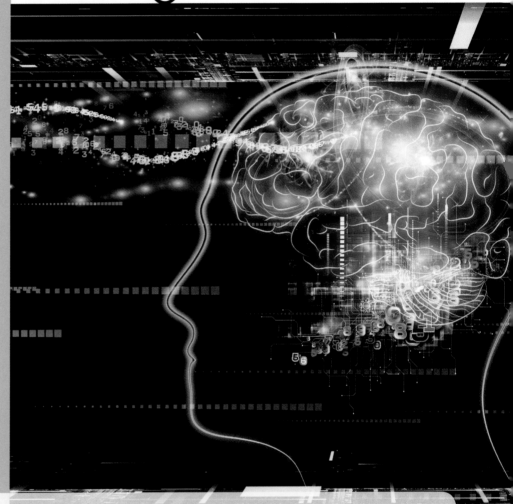

After reading this chapter, you will be able to answer the following questions:

- When and why did thinking become a topic of interest to psychologists?
- What are concepts?
- What are two primary problem-solving strategies?
- How has recent research changed the way psychologists understand how people make decisions?
- What are syntax and semantics?
- How do syntax and semantics influence the development and use of language?
- How is intelligence tested?
- Why should intelligence tests be standardized?
- What is a culturally biased test?

People often use the word "intelligence" without really knowing what the word means. On a recent visit to a fifth grade class, your authors had the opportunity to watch students between the ages of ten and eleven talk about what they think it means to be intelligent. These students focused on the idea that intelligent students finish their work faster than less intelligent students. In other words, task completion speed was the only important measure of cognitive ability for these fifth graders. As the discussion continued, it became clear that task completion speed was so important to them that several students even admitted to having turned in incomplete work just to be the first student to the teacher's desk. While the resulting grade on the assignment was lower than what they could have received by completing the entire assignment, these students continued to define themselves as intelligent because they were speedier than their classmates.

From your perspective as someone who is older and wiser than fifth graders, you probably realize that while speed is an important component of intelligence, it isn't the only component. After all, while thinking quickly is fine, it is more important to think both quickly and accurately. Intelligence, then, must be considered a combination of at least two skills. As we will see by the end of this chapter, intelligence is actually much more than just speed and accuracy.

Intelligence is a way to quantify and compare thinking across individuals. Thinking is an active process in which we consciously evaluate and act upon information. By this definition, thinking begins at an early age, when children learn to speak. A toddler who squeals "doggie!" whenever she encounters a dog is expressing her delight that she can connect a word to the item named by that word. She will need some time and practice to develop her ideas, because at first she refers to all four-legged furry things as "doggie," including cats and buffalo (this is the process of assimilation, discussed in Chapter 5). Eventually she learns to distinguish between cats, dogs, and buffalo by learning the name for each.

Speech development shows how each word points to some items in the world and excludes other items, which is the basis for mental concepts. Equipped with mental concepts, a person has the capacity to solve problems, make decisions, and use language effectively. However, thinking is not the whole story of intelligence, and intelligence researchers have identified aspects of intelligence that lie outside the boundaries of thinking. Nevertheless, our investigation of intelligence begins with the ways that people think.

THINKING: PROCESSES AND CONCEPTS

American psychologists mostly overlooked the way people think throughout the first half of the twentieth century, when the field was dominated by a behaviorist perspective. As you learned in Chapter 7, behaviorism is primarily concerned with stimulus-response associations that can be seen by an outside observer rather than events that occur between the stimulus and the response. The focus on stimulus-response associations began to change in the 1950s and 1960s, due in part to the advent of digital computers. In the 1940s, room-size digital computers had about as much computing power as a modern-day basic pocket calculator. Nevertheless, digital computers were technological marvels for their time and provided a handy model to explain how the human mind works. The digital computer's input, processing, memory, and output functions became models for how the human brain works as an information processing machine. However, this wasn't the first time people used technology to explain how we process information. Plato first compared thinking to a wax tablet, and we have been revising the association of how we think with the function of technology ever since.

At the same time computers were becoming familiar in popular culture, psychologists were beginning to realize that behaviorism couldn't explain all of human nature. Noam Chomsky described some of the limitations of behaviorism in his review of B. F. Skinner's 1957 book, *Verbal Behavior*. As his title suggests, Skinner argued that human language was a behavior like any other, and therefore, language acquisition could readily be explained with the same principles used widely by behaviorists, including imitation, association, and reinforcement. In response, Chomsky pointed out examples that defy Skinner's analysis and yet are familiar to anyone who has watched a child learn language. For example, when learning language, a child might say something like "Today I go to school, and yesterday I goed to school." Making the past tense of "go" by saying "goed" couldn't be explained by imitation because the adults from whom the child is learning language would say "went" as the past tense of "go." Chomsky argued that these kinds of errors show that children learning language understand that language has rules, but they sometimes use the rules inappropriately, such as when the correct past tense of a verb is irregular.

cognitive revolution
the shift in psychology from strict behaviorism to investigating ways in which the brain creates the mind

cognitive science
investigations of how the brain creates the mind that draw from several fields, including psychology, philosophy, economics, neuroscience, and computer science

By drawing attention to the way children acquire language, Chomsky was arguing that learning is not merely a collection of associations between stimuli and responses. Instead, the human mind is equipped with cognitive (from Latin for "think") machinery that lies between the stimulus and response. Chomsky was at the forefront of what later became known as the **cognitive revolution**, in which practitioners from several fields of inquiry invented new tools and techniques for investigating how the brain's functioning creates the experience of thinking. Chomsky and other linguists were joined by cognitive psychologists, philosophers of mind, behavioral economists, neuroscientists, and computer scientists trying to create artificial intelligence in a communal effort called cognitive science. **Cognitive science** seeks to understand cognition by approaching the question from several angles. One of the central themes of cognitive science is also one that has been studied for the longest time: concepts.

Mental Concepts

Mental **concepts** are a kind of map for knowing how to react efficiently to the objects we meet. A good map is one that has enough detail to plan a route but not too much detail to be overwhelming. For example, when you approach a stop sign, you don't concern yourself with exactly how tall it is, whether the sun is shining on it, and other details about its appearance. To focus on all of these details would be cognitively overwhelming. Instead, you recognize that each stop sign looks pretty much like every other stop sign, and you quickly move on from its appearance to knowing how to behave in response to it. Your mental concept for "stop sign" contains a red octagon with white lettering on a tall post, and that's about all. Additional details would slow down our thinking and acting.

concept
a mental map that allows us to know how to react in different situations

essence
the set of necessary and sufficient conditions that determines whether a particular item is a member of a concept

The Greek philosopher, Aristotle, developed the earliest ideas about how mental concepts work. He described concepts as a set of necessary and sufficient conditions, so, for example, an odd number is an integer that can't be evenly divided into two equal pieces. For a couple thousand years, no one had the courage to suggest that anything was wrong with Aristotle's description of concepts until the Austrian philosopher Ludwig Wittgenstein did in the 1950s. Wittgenstein argued that a set of necessary and sufficient conditions might capture the **essence** of mathematical concepts, like odd numbers, but it didn't work as well for mental concepts of everyday objects and people. For example, the set of necessary and sufficient conditions for the concept of "bachelor" is any (1) adult that is (2) male and (3) unmarried. At first glance this seems to capture the essence of bachelorhood: anyone that meets all three conditions can be considered a bachelor, and anyone that violates any of the three conditions (e.g., an unmarried woman, or a young boy) would not be a bachelor. However, consider these examples. Shi Xing Fuyu is an unmarried adult male, and he lives as a monk in a monastery. Charlie is a married adult male, but he has been separated from his wife for a year, doesn't intend to patch things up with her, and is interested in dating other women. By the definition of bachelor as an unmarried adult male, Shi Xing is a bachelor and Charlie is not, but does this seem right to you? Students tend to admit that Charlie seems more like a bachelor than Shi Xing, even though Charlie violates the strict definition of the concept because he's married. These examples illustrate the main flaw with Aristotle's conceptual boundaries—they are too sharp (i.e., Each person is either a member of the category or not. There is no gray area.) Thus, Wittgenstein argued that our everyday concepts have fuzzy boundaries and challenged scientists to gather data supporting his philosophical arguments.

Ludwig Wittgenstein

One of Wittengenstein's readers, Eleanor Rosch, accepted his challenge. Rosch asked participants in her experiments to determine the truth of such statements as "a robin is a bird" and "a penguin is a bird." Both statements are true, but people are quicker to verify robins as members of the concept of bird than penguins. Our concept of bird is centered around a

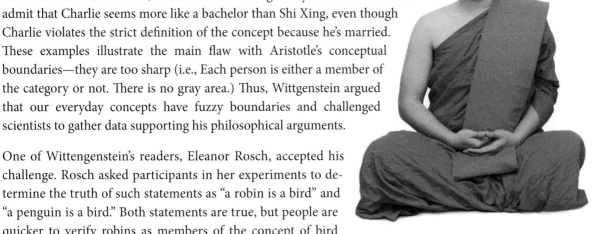

A monk is an adult unmarried man, but is he a bachelor?

prototype
a kind of item that best represents a concept; robins but not penguins are prototypical birds

prototype, which is the best member of the concept. The prototypical bird is a small songbird that flies. Birds such as robins that are more similar to the prototype are considered better members of the concept than birds such as penguins (i.e., a large bird that swims) that are less similar to the prototype. Experiments such as the one in which participants were quicker to verify robins as birds than penguins as birds showed that our everyday concepts don't always work as described by Aristotle. Using concepts enables us to quickly determine how to interact with the objects in our world without wasting much mental effort. As a result, we have cognitive resources left over to figure out how to solve problems.

Both penguins and robins are considered birds, but robins are prototypes of the category and penguins are not, and people can verify that robins are birds more quickly than they can verify that penguins are birds.

Problem Solving

Suppose a friend gave you a briefcase filled with money for you to spend any way you like, provided you can figure out the four-digit combination to unlock the case within the next thirty minutes. At first you might try 0000, then 0001, and 0002, but you would soon realize that this kind of "brute force" method would probably require you to try several thousand numbers (in the worst case you'd try 10,000 numbers before getting the right one), and time would expire before you found the right combination. Out of desperation, you might try

To find the right combination of numbers that will open the lock, algorithms such as trying every single number (e.g., 0000, 0001...) would take too much time. Instead, this is the kind of problem that requires a heuristic to solve quickly enough to meet the deadline.

random numbers like 5788 and 3265, hoping to get lucky. After several wild guesses you sense that you are no closer to opening the case than when you started. You begin to wonder why your friend would have wanted to torture you, but while thinking about your friend you realize that she is fascinated with the ill-fated ship, Titanic. She collects Titanic memorabilia, has seen every movie recounting the story of Titanic's maiden voyage, and loves to inject the Titanic into her conversations. With that in mind you think that 1912, the year of the Titanic's voyage and sinking might be worth trying, and, sure enough, it works.

When presented with the locked briefcase you had a problem: You didn't know what number would open the briefcase's lock, and you wanted to discover the right combination within the allotted time limit. **Problem solving** is a process in which a person begins in an initial state and moves through a series of intermediate states to arrive at a desired state. The way you might have opened the briefcase highlights two different methods of problem solving. Entering each number in turn, beginning with 0000, then 0001, and so on, is a method guaranteed to give you the right answer, if only you had enough time to try every combination. Step-by-step procedures guaranteed to solve problems are called **algorithms**, named for Muhammad Al-Khwarizmi, an Arab mathematician and author of the book that introduced the decimal system of numbers to Europe in the twelfth century (Bellos, 2010). When you learned to solve multiplication and division problems in elementary school, you relied on algorithms taught by your math teacher.

problem solving
a process in which a person begins at an initial state and moves through a series of intermediate states to arrive at a desired state

algorithm
a step-by-step procedure for solving problems that is guaranteed to work but slow

Although algorithms are guaranteed to produce the right answer, as the example illustrates, they can often be too slow to be useful. After trying several combinations on the briefcase lock, you would recognize that the algorithm to try every numerical combination would probably fail to produce the right combination within the time limit. Clearly you would need to limit the number of combinations you try, but which numbers should you choose? Selecting numbers that pop into your head is a method for limiting the number of combinations you try, but that clearly is not guaranteed to generate the right combination. Problem-solving procedures that rely on inexact rules or estimation are called **heuristics**. For example, some cooks strictly adhere to recipes, carefully measuring every ingredient, and using a timer to cook for the specified time. This is similar to the algorithmic approach previously described. However, other cooks use a more intuitive approach, such as using what looks like a tablespoon of sugar, rather than measuring it, and cooking until the food looks about right. Neither method is right or wrong, but each has its advantages and disadvantages. Following an algorithm guarantees that you will eventually find the correct solution, provided that you carry out each step correctly. Heuristics can be error-prone, but they produce results much more quickly than algorithms. That is, algorithms are reliable but slow, whereas heuristics are "quick and dirty."

heuristic
a way of solving problems that relies on inexact rules, so it is error prone but faster than algorithms

Heuristics often fit better with the evolved functions of thinking. Although people may occasionally ponder existential problems such as the meaning of life, human thinking evolved to foster quick responses. If a car begins to drift into your lane while you are driving, you need to make a snap decision on whether to brake, accelerate, swerve, honk, or yell at the driver to stop texting and drive. You do not have time to calculate the rate of drift, to evaluate the make and model of the vehicle, or to Google the probabilities of an accident in this situation. Throughout most of human's evolutionary history, the nature of the problems that the brain needed to solve was such that a quick, heuristic-driven decision may have been prone to error but was reliable enough, as well as quick enough, to promote the individual's survival.

creativity
the ability to make surprising connections between seemingly disconnected ideas

Another advantage of heuristics over algorithms is that heuristics are better suited for expressing **creativity**, or the ability to make surprising connections between seemingly disconnected ideas. In his free time, Albert Einstein enjoyed reading such things as mathematical papers describing non-Euclidean geometry (he was an unusual guy). Mathematicians had developed these kinds of exotic geometries without any expectation that they would ever have any practical use. Einstein had the insight to realize that non-Euclidean geometry was not just an interesting mathematical idea, but could be used to describe the structure of our universe. By noticing a surprising connection between an abstract mathematical system and the structure of the universe, Einstein was able to solve problems that were otherwise impossible to solve while developing his famous theory of relativity (Bellos, 2010).

insight
moment at which the solution to a problem suddenly becomes clear

When trying to solve a problem for which the path between the initial and goal states is hidden, problem solvers often experience a sudden flash of **insight**, such as when you suspected your friend might have chosen a combination inspired by her enthusiasm for the Titanic. In the movie *Despicable Me*, the main character Gru celebrates such moments by exclaiming "Light bulb!" when he suddenly understands how to solve a problem that's been bothering him, such as how to invade a rival's house without being shot by guided missiles.

Gestalt psychologist Wolfgang Köhler described the role of insight in problem solving on the basis of his experiments with chimpanzees. In 1913, Köhler became the director of a chimpanzee research colony on Tenerife, one of the Canary Islands (off the coast of Africa), never expecting that the outbreak of a world war would trap him there for the next six years. He spent the years productively, and his observations of chimpanzee behavior became almost as famous as Pavlov and his dogs.

In one of his experiments, Köhler placed Sultan, a male chimpanzee, in a cage with bananas hanging above his head, out of his reach. At first, Sultan tried to grab the bananas by jumping, but the bananas were too high. After aimlessly prowling around the cage, he suddenly rushed to a box that was in the cage with him, picked up and maneuvered the box to a spot just under the bananas, climbed on the box, and jumped to reach the bananas. Voilà, the bananas were his. Later, Köhler placed Tshego, a female chimpanzee, in a cage with bananas beyond her arms' reach outside the cage. Tshego thrust her arm toward the bananas until, frustrated, she sprawled on the floor. However, when some other chimps appeared outside her cage, she jumped up, grabbed a stick from the floor of the cage and used it to reach and retrieve the bananas (Hunt, 1993). Time and again Köhler observed chimps blundering around nonproductively, then their behavior would suddenly change as they pursued and reached their goal. Visual metaphors (like the flash of insight, Gru's light bulb) seem appropriate to describe the "aha!" moment because the path to the goal was previously hidden in the dark, but at the moment of insight it suddenly became floodlit.

Obstacles to problem solving

One of the most common obstacles to problem solving is called **mental set**, which means that we often approach a problem with a set of assumptions that can hide possible moves. To see how prior assumptions can prevent you from considering all possible solutions, try to solve the six matchstick problem. Using six matchsticks (or any six sticks all the same length), can you make four triangles such that every edge of a triangle is a single stick? Try to work on the problem for a few minutes before looking at the solution in Figure 10.1, on the next page.

mental set
a set of mental assumptions about a situation that can hide possible solutions

Fortunately, obstacles can be overcome by noticing how a difficult problem can be restructured into a different problem with a clearer solution. For example, imagine being a physician with a patient who has a stomach tumor hidden deep within his body. How would you excise the tumor? One possibility would be to direct a beam of radiation at the tumor, but to eliminate the tumor, the radiation would have to be sufficiently intense that it would damage healthy tissues in its path as it entered and exited the patient's body. While trying to figure out how to cure your patient, consider another story about a cruel dictator hidden within his castle.

As an army general, you would like to remove the dictator from his castle and end the tyranny suffered under his reign. To have sufficient manpower to attack the castle and extract the dictator you will need to deliver a sizeable army and heavy weaponry to the castle, but the dictator is paranoid and prepared for such an attack. He installed land mines on all the roads leading to the castle, so a traveling army will destroy itself, and the surrounding countryside, when it trips the mines. At the same time, the dictator needs to travel on the roads without blowing himself up, so the mines are set to trip only when set off by a heavy load. With all this in mind, you divide your entire army into several smaller groups that are each small enough to travel on the roads without tripping the mines along the way, but when the groups converge at the dictator's castle there will be a sufficient force to attack and subdue the dictator's troops within the castle.

Does the story about the dictator's castle provide any insight into how to treat your patient's tumor? Perhaps you realized that instead of pointing one high-intensity beam at the tumor, you should point several low-intensity beams from different directions that all converge on the tumor. Because each beam is low intensity, they won't damage healthy tissue, but the location where the beams converge will be exposed to the total intensity of all the beams together. The sum total intensity is sufficient to eliminate the tumor.

Albert Einstein, one of the most dazzling problem solvers of all time, claimed that imagination is more important than knowledge, so to find creative solutions to difficult problems keep your eyes, ears, and mind open.

Decision Making

When faced with a difficult decision, such as whether or not to cheat on an exam, a person can feel pulled in two directions (Mills, 1958). Cheating on the exam might enable the student to get a higher grade, but if caught cheating, the student would receive a failing grade and suffer a damaged reputation. The choice depends not only on the costs and benefits, but also on the likelihood of each cost and benefit. If the student has thoroughly prepared for the exam, doing well without cheating is so likely there is nothing to be gained by cheating and much to be lost. In other words, the expected value of cheating is not worth the cost. According to economics, which is the scientific study of decision making, the **expected value** of a particular choice equals the cost or benefit resulting from that choice multiplied by the probability of the cost or benefit. The predominant economic theory of decision making in the mid-twentieth century assumed people were rational in their decisions, which means that they calculate expected values for all possible choices, then select the choice that offers the highest expected value.

expected value
the benefit or cost of an outcome multiplied by the likelihood of the outcome occurring

To see how expected value calculations can be used in a purchasing decision, consider the case of a lottery ticket. In some lotteries, players select one number between zero and 999, so there are 1,000 numbers to choose from, and the lottery pays $500 if the player's number matches the winning number. For this kind of lottery, the expected value of a ticket equals the value of a winning ticket ($500) multiplied by the probability of winning (1/1000): expected value = $500/1000 = $0.50, or 50 cents. But we need to factor in the cost of purchasing the ticket for $1, so the expected value of the ticket equals 50 cents minus the cost of the ticket, for a total of negative 50 cents. Compared to the negative expected value associated with buying a lottery ticket for a dollar, you would be better off just keeping the dollar for yourself. Based on this calculation, if people act rationally, as economists assume, no one would ever purchase any lottery tickets. Yet millions of people do buy lottery tickets, so the assumption that people make decisions by calculating expected values must be wrong.

Amos Tversky and Daniel Kahneman didn't accept the prevailing economic theory that decisions are based on expected value calculations, so they tried to figure out how people actually *do* make decisions. Their work revolutionized economics to the extent that Kahneman was awarded the 2002 Nobel prize for economics; sadly, Tversky had already passed away by then, otherwise he and

10.1 Solution to the six matchstick problem
After reading the problem you probably assumed that the sticks should all be arranged on a flat surface such as a tabletop, but as you can see from the arrangement of sticks in the figure, the solution to the problem requires that the sticks be allowed to rise above the tabletop, into the third dimension.

Kahneman would certainly have been joint recipients. One experiment in particular illustrates the problem with the claim that decisions are based on expected values.

Imagine being the public policy official for a small town that lies directly in the path of a virulent disease as it sweeps across the country. In preparation for the disease reaching your town, you consider two possible plans of response. If you do nothing, the disease is so devastating that it is expected to kill all 600 people in your town, but if you select one of the following two plans, you can expect:

- **Plan A:** 200 will be saved.

- **Plan B:** There's a one-third chance of saving everyone in town and a two-thirds chance of saving no one.

Which plan would you choose? The expected value of Plan A is 200 people saved, and the expected value of Plan B is 1/3 X 600 = 200 people saved, so the expected values of both plans are the same. If we asked a group of participants which plan they prefer, classical economic theory predicts that about half will pick A and the other half will pick B, but that's not what happened. Instead, most participants picked Plan A. The experiment was repeated with a second group of participants, in which the two plans were described as:

- **Plan A:** 400 will die

- **Plan B:** There's a one-third chance none will die and a two-thirds chance everyone in town will die.

Here again, the expected values are the same because the expected value of Plan A is 400 deaths and the expected value of Plan B is 2/3 X 600 = 400 deaths. Although the expected values of the plans are the same, most participants in this version of the experiment picked Plan B (see Figure 10.2 for a visual of the Asian Disease Problem). This flip-flop from one preference to the other shows that participants were more

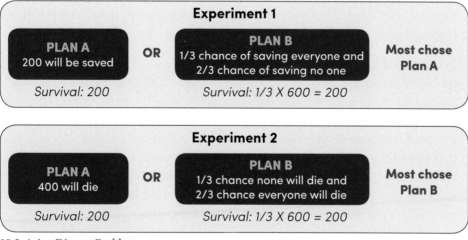

10.2 Asian Disease Problem
The Asian Disease Problem shows the power of framing on decision-making. Both Experiment 1 and Experiment 2 present the same outcome, but the different presentation of the choices change the perception of the outcomes.

framing
the way in which a particular problem or solution is presented

sensitive to the way the questions were framed, or put into words, than they were to the expected values. The **framing** of the first pair of questions emphasized how many lives could be saved by each plan, whereas the framing of the second pair of questions emphasized how many lives could be lost under each plan. As the public policy official presenting the plans to your town, you will need to choose which language you'd prefer your plan to be associated with: lives lost or lives saved. In other words, you need to determine how best to "sell" your plan to the townsfolk.

Advertisers know that buyers' decisions can be influenced by the way they frame their product. Insurance companies want you to be risk avoidant (like the participants who selected Plan A), so their advertisements show big happy families and smiling babies to emphasize everything you could lose if you don't have sufficient insurance coverage. Casinos want you to be risk seeking (like the participants who selected Plan B), so their advertisements depict one or two ecstatic people winning lots of money.

Perhaps people resist calculating expected values because probability calculations are notoriously difficult for most people. Which do you think is a likelier cause of death in the United States each year: being attacked by a shark, or being hit by airplane parts falling from the sky? The algorithmic way to answer this question would be to investigate causes of death over several years and calculate the average deaths per year for each cause. That sounds like a lot of work, so do you have an intuition about which is a likelier cause of death? Doesn't death by shark attack seem to be much likelier than being hit by a falling airplane part? To decide which of two events is more likely, people imagine both events, and the one that's easier to imagine is judged to be likelier. This is called the **availability heuristic** because one event is more available to the imagination. Unfortunately, while common events are typically easier to imagine than uncommon events, uncommon, but vivid, events, such as shark attacks, are really easy to imagine. After all, they make movies about shark attacks but not so much about being hit by falling airplane parts (with the possible exception of *Donnie Darko*). For that reason, death by shark attack is less common, but easier to imagine so it's mistakenly judged as more common.

availability heuristic
heuristic based on the assumption that the most easily imagined possibility is also the likeliest

In light of Kahneman and Tversky's efforts, economists have become receptive to the idea that people are not as rational as economists had always assumed they were. Among other things, economists still commonly speak in terms of expected value, but they are willing to accept that expected values can include squishy things like emotions. Although leaving the money in your pocket has a higher expected value than purchasing a lottery ticket, the purchase of a lottery ticket allows you to fantasize about what you would do with the money if you *did* win. For that reason, the negative fifty cents expected value of a lottery ticket can be seen as a dreadful investment on the one hand, or as a cheap form of entertainment on the other.

Concept Recall

1. What is the difference between the classical and modern views of categorization?

2. What are algorithms and heuristics?

3. How does classical economics claim people make decisions?

4. What is the availability heuristic?

This Is Psychology

This chapter argues that one of the reasons people resist calculating expected values to make decisions is that expected value is based on the calculation of probability, but most people have great difficulty calculating probabilities. Are experts better equipped to correctly calculate the probabilities for a tricky problem? Consider the Monty Hall problem, named after the game show host who posed the problem to contestants on the show *Let's Make a Deal*. Monty would show each contestant three doors, such that goats were hidden behind two of the doors and a great prize, such as a car, was hidden behind the other door. First, the contestant picked one of the doors, then Monty opened one of the two other doors to reveal one of the goats. Contestants could then stick with their original selection or switch to the other unopened door. Should contestants stick or switch? Most people would think that it doesn't matter because after Monty has opened a door to reveal a goat and there remain just two unopened doors, the contestant now has a fifty-fifty chance of winning either way. But that's not correct. Actually, contestants have a one out of three chance of winning by sticking with their original choice and a two out of three chance of winning by switching. That is, over the long run, just one-third of contestants who stick with their original choice after Monty has opened a second door will win, whereas two-thirds of contestants who switch win. In her weekly column in *Parade* magazine in 1990, Marilyn vos Savant described the Monty Hall problem and the surprising probabilities. Her description of the problem and the correct way to calculate probabilities aroused thousands of her readers to write angry letters, many of whom claimed to be experts in calculating probability. Nevertheless, the self-described experts who claimed that Marilyn vos Savant was wrong and that the probability of winning was one out of two regardless of the contestant's decision were themselves wrong. It seems that our brains are not hardwired to calculate probabilities, so even experts can get lost when they approach an unfamiliar problem.

LANGUAGE

Although written language has existed for several thousand years, spoken language came first. Similarly, though most of us learn to read and write only after several years of instruction and practice, babies learn to speak their native language without any instruction. The fact that written words are separated by spaces creates the illusion that in spoken language there are tiny pauses between the sounds contained in one word and the next. In fact, there are typically no breaks between spoken words, so listeners must impose their expectations onto a stream of spoken language to break the words apart (Pinker, 1994). You might have noticed that a spoken foreign language sounds like a continuous stream because you have no idea how to divide the sounds into words. Every baby is born into a world filled with people speaking a language they've never heard, and yet, over the course of a year or two, they learn to hear the sounds of the local language, and by noticing that some sounds often go together and others don't, they figure out where the boundaries are between words.

phoneme
the smallest unit of sound in a language

phonology
the ability to hear phonemes and assign the phonemes to words

The basic sounds in a language are called **phonemes**, and the ability to hear sounds and assign them to different words is called **phonology**. English has about fifty phonemes but only twenty-six letters, so some letters have a double duty (e.g., each vowel in English can be pronounced two ways), and some phonemes are represented by bundling letters together, such as "sh," "th," and "ch." Each language has its own set of phonemes, so children learning to speak one language might never hear some of the sounds spoken in another language. For example, the sound of the "th" in the English word, "that," is an unusual phoneme that does not occur in French or in many other languages. As a result, an adult French speaker learning to speak English has a tough time making this sound, and he or she may say what sounds like "zis and zat" when intending to say "this and that."

The other aspect of phonology—assigning sounds to words—has its own difficulties. As a case in point, the Jimi Hendrix song, "Purple Haze," contains the line, "Excuse me while I kiss the sky," but listeners often assign sounds to the words so the lyrics sound like, "Excuse me while I kiss this guy." The next time you hear "Purple Haze," imagine the alternative line, and you'll notice that Hendrix does seem to mention kissing some guy.

This is a wug.

Now there is another one.
There are two of them.
There are two _____.

morpheme
the smallest meaningful unit in a word

The smallest units of sounds in a language (phonemes) are assembled into meaningful units called **morphemes**. For example, the word, "bake," contains three phonemes but just one morpheme. In English, morphemes can be added to words to change their meaning, like adding "-r" to the end of "bake," to indicate a "baker," or a person who bakes. Further, adding a "-y" at the end of "baker" indicates the "bakery" in which the baker works. When children learn language they have to learn how to add morphemes to words to change their

10.3 The "wug" test
Does a young child who is learning language and refers to two "kittens" understand how to pluralize words, or is he or she just imitating others? The wug test distinguishes between the two possibilities by using items the child has never heard of before. Children who have developed the ability to pluralize words will answer 'wugs', but younger children who have not yet developed this ability will not.

meaning, so more than one kitten is kittens. But if a child knows how to change kitten to kittens, does that mean she understands how to pluralize a word, or is she just imitating what she has heard previously? To find out, in a classic experiment called the 'wug' test, Jean Berko (1958) invented new words that the children had never heard before, so there was no way for children to simply imitate the sounds. For example, pre-schoolers and first graders were asked to look at cards, like the one shown in Figure 10.3, while the experimenter read the words from the card out loud. Even though you've never heard of a wug, you realize that when there are two of them, they are called wugs. Like you, almost all of the first graders gave the right answer, but many preschoolers failed to generate the right answer. This shows not only that children are able to understand and use the rules of language but also this ability develops over time.

The meaning of a word, or **semantics**, is the set of things or actions in the world that the word "points to," so, for example, "snow" refers to the white, fluffy, frozen water that sometimes falls from the sky in winter. Meaningful words are arranged into meaningful phrases based on rules of **syntax**, or word order. Word order is an important consideration when attempting to communicate ideas. For example, the title "Man Bites Dog," can headline a newsworthy article, but "Dog Bites Man" isn't really news. Both titles have the same words, but rearranging the word order changes the meaning of the phrase.

semantics
connection between a word and the word's meaning

syntax
rules governing word order in a language

While the linguistic elements discussed above are important to any understanding of language, equally important is the relationship between language and cognition. For example, you might have heard that Native Americans living in the Arctic speak a language that has many more words for snow than other languages spoken in warmer climates. It is tempting to conclude that, with so many words in their language, Arctic dwellers must have more concise mental concepts for snow than an English speaker does. Unfortunately, the claim about having more words for snow is a hoax, and yet the belief refuses to die (Pullum, 1989). Although the snow story is a hoax, the question remains whether a language's inventory of words for a particular concept influences the speakers' perception of that concept.

Take color as an example. English and many other languages have eleven basic color terms: red, green, blue, yellow, black, white, gray, orange, brown, pink, and purple. If you studied Spanish or French, these are probably the colors you learned from those languages. A color term is deemed "basic" if most speakers of a language spontaneously name that color; most English speakers will name pink, but only a few will name aubergine, vermilion, or puce. Cross-cultural studies have shown that while many languages have the same eleven basic color terms as English, many other languages have different numbers of basic color terms (Berlin and Kay, 1969). To determine whether language could influence the perception of color, Eleanor Rosch (1975) traveled to New Guinea to work with members of the Dani tribe, who speak a language with just two color words, representing black and white. Remember from earlier in this chapter that concepts have prototypes that are the "best" example of the concept, and this is true of color as well. Fire-engine red and lemon yellow are prototypical examples of their respective color categories. Notably, even though the Dani don't have the same color words as English, Rosch found that they tended to learn and remember colors that were prototypes of English color categories better than nonprototypes. The Dani are equipped with the same retinal physiology as speakers of English, which implies that they perceive colors the same, even if their language doesn't contain all the same categories. In short, there is no correlation between a given language's inventory of words to represent a particular concept and the cognitive ability of its members to perceive and understand the concept.

Our cognitive machinery enables us to respond quickly and appropriately to a complex world, move closer to our goals, select the alternative that best meets our needs, and communicate our ideas with others. To do all this, cognition relies on perception to help us navigate the world and learning and memory to avoid the mistakes made in the past. As we will see in the remainder of this chapter, intelligence is the ability to efficiently learn from experience, perform mental tasks, and solve problems. For that reason, intelligence could be thought of as a measure of cognitive ability.

Concept Recall

1. What are the roles of phonology, morphology, semantics, and syntax in language?

2. What is the wug test, and what does it tell us about the development of semantics and syntax?

3. What is an example of a phoneme and a morpheme in English?

4. What did Eleanor Rosch discover about how people with very different color words than English remember colors?

DEFINING INTELLIGENCE: THEORIES AND EVIDENCE

If asked, most people would likely identify themselves as intelligent, or, at least say that they desire to be intelligent. The desire to be intelligent directly results from the fact that, while people may not really understand what intelligence is, they do notice that people who excel in different aspects of life are typically labeled "intelligent." Students who do well in school are considered intelligent. Political commentators who are particularly accurate in their assessments or commentary are considered intelligent. You likely consider your friends who often have interesting or wise comments intelligent. Because the use of the word "intelligent" is generally associated with success and accomplishment, the common feeling is that intelligence is something desirable.

Interestingly, the same people who either believe themselves to be or wish to be intelligent often encounter difficulty if asked to define intelligence. As it turns out, defining intelligence can be extremely difficult! Like the fifth graders from the introduction to this chapter, some people focus on the ability to complete mental activities quickly as the defining characteristic for intelligence. For others, being intelligent means knowing, offhand, the state capitals, how to spell or define a word like "pulchritudinous," or how to calculate the product of 369 multiplied by 13. Other people would define intelligence based on the ability to "think outside the box" in solving problems. For early evolutionists and psychologists, intelligence referred to the ability to use past experience to improve on future performance (Boakes, 1984, pg. 23; Sternberg & Kaufman, 1998).

There are two basic types of intelligence researchers: lumpers and splitters. Lumpers tend to pile everything together into a single lump, and splitters make fine distinctions between the types of intelligence that lumpers pile together. As you will see later in this section, Charles Spearman was the ultimate lumper, claiming that intelligence is one lump called the g factor, which stands for general intelligence. Howard Gardner is a splitter, identifying eight kinds of intelligence, and Robert Sternberg's three kinds of intelligence fall between the two extremes. How do the cognitive faculties described earlier in this chapter (i.e., mental concepts, problem solving, decision making, and language) fit into these conceptions of intelligence? For Spearman, cognition is the whole story of intelligence, insofar as g represents effective thinking. In contrast, Gardner and Sternberg would say that cognition is only part of the story. Cognition is embodied in just the first two of Gardner's eight kinds of intelligence (linguistic and logical-mathematical intelligence) and the first of Sternberg's three kinds of intelligence (analytical intelligence).

Why is intelligence so hard to define? The biggest problem is that the word "intelligence" does not refer to anything physical or directly measurable but to a general concept. Robert Sternberg—a major influence in modern intelligence research whose ideas we will discuss in more depth later in this chapter—once asked a dozen intelligence researchers to define intelligence, and he received a dozen different definitions (Sternberg & Detterman, 1986). Sheldon White of Harvard University (2000) suggested that defining intelligence at a basic level (where it is tied to brain systems or structures) may never be possible, but that the concept of intelligence is useful for helping to understand people's differences (similar to words such as brave or hardworking, which are also hard to define but informative about the people they describe). In many ways, defining intelligence is similar to United States Supreme Court Justice Potter Stewart's comment on pornography: "I can't define it, but I know it when I see it" (Jacobellis v. Ohio, 378 US 184, 1964).

Despite the major challenges in defining intelligence, psychologists have worked to come up with useful definitions. Sam Goldstein (2015) identified some of the many dimensions of intelligence in his *Handbook of Intelligence*:

> ". . . intelligence has been defined in multiple ways, including the capacity for abstract thought, understanding, communication, planning, learning, reasoning, and, most importantly, problem solving" (pg. 3).

The items included in this list of mental activities reveals some commonalities upon which to build a general definition of intelligence: **intelligence** is the ability to efficiently

intelligence
the ability to efficiently and effectively learn from experience, perform mental tasks, and solve problems

and effectively learn from experience, perform mental tasks, and solve problems. This definition of intelligence refers both to the quality of the mental work (efficiently and effectively) and to the type of activities (mental tasks and problem solving) one should be able to perform in order to be considered intelligent. According to this definition, we would expect that persons with higher intelligence would be able to: (1) complete mental tasks more quickly, (2) complete a broader range of mental tasks, (3) employ efficient mental solutions for mental tasks, (4) solve new mental tasks, and (5) generate new solutions to problems or new uses for familiar items.

Notice that each of these elements of intelligence suggests the idea of a comparison between people (phrases like "more quickly" and "broader range" imply a comparison between groups). Intelligence is a measure of individual differences, and any definition of intelligence will bring with it this idea of comparison. Alfred Binet—one of the founders of modern intelligence testing—began his work in intelligence as an attempt to scientifically differentiate between his two daughters (Nikolas & Levine, 2012). Following Darwin's publication of his work on evolution, many philosophers and early psychologists began to use intelligence as a way to discuss the differences in intellectual abilities between humans and other species (White, 2000). By looking at species as a continuum of development along an evolutionary scale—that differences across species are a matter of degree, not of kind (Boakes, 1984, pg. 1)—biologists, philosophers, and psychologists began to explore similarities between the mental abilities of animals and humans. Today, we tend to think of intelligence more as a way of comparing across groups of people rather than across species, but the idea of using intelligence as a way of measuring individual differences remains.

Theories of Intelligence

The abstract nature of intelligence has led to extensive debate between psychological scientists about the exact nature of intelligence. At the heart of this debate is whether there is a single underlying "intelligence" or several different types of "intelligence." To appreciate these differences, consider the following line from the 2004 sci-fi action movie *I, Robot*, in which Detective Spooner (played by Will Smith) calls Dr. Susan Calvin (Bridget Moynahan) the "dumbest smart person" he has ever met. This statement is made in reference to the character's high level of capability within her field of expertise in contrast with her lack of ability to deal with more general problems. Do you know people like this? It might be someone who seems like a genius in one field, such as science or math, but can't seem to remember to pay the bills. Or someone who can fix almost anything, but has a difficult time performing well in classes. Based on examples like these, it seems likely that there are multiple intelligences. However, there is also compelling evidence that there is a single underlying "intelligence" that seems to influence people's mental activities.

The roots of general intelligence

Charles Spearman

In 1904, the British psychologist Charles Spearman addressed a major challenge faced by the new field of psychology: the apparent lack of connection between laboratory work and real-world solutions, or, as discussed in Chapter 1, the lack of external validity in psychological research (Spearman, 1904, pg. 203). To address this challenge, Spearman engaged in a series of studies on "Correlational Psychology" (pg. 205), in which he worked to develop a new statistical method for grouping items into related clusters based on the correlations between them. Today, Spearman's method is known as **factor analysis**—a statistical method for grouping items on a test into clusters by evaluating the correlations between them. Using factor analysis, Spearman (1904) concluded that there is a single underlying capacity correlated with performance on a wide variety of mental tasks: **general intelligence (g)**. According to Spearman's findings, although each individual will vary somewhat between different mental tasks, the overall performance across tasks will be related. In other words, general intelligence suggests that someone who excels at mathematics will likely do well on other mental tasks as well.

> **factor analysis**
> a statistical method for grouping items on a test into clusters by evaluating the correlations between items

> **general intelligence (g)**
> a single factor that accounts for much of the variance in intelligence scores across individuals

Louis Leon Thurstone, an American psychologist and Spearman's contemporary, challenged Spearman's arguments. In his experiments, Thurstone gave participants as many as fifty-seven mental tests and—according to his factor analysis of the results—found evidence of not just one, but seven different types of intelligence: space, verbal relations, isolated works, memory, induction, perceptual speed, and arithmetic (Thurstone, 1938). In a re-analysis of Thurstone's work, Spearman challenged Thurstone's application of factor analysis. While Spearman disagreed with Thurstone's argument against a general intelligence, "*g*," he did agree with the idea that different tasks require specific skills separate from "*g*." As shown in Figure 10.4, a compromise between Spearman and Thurstone would be to conceptualize intelligence as containing general intelligence as well as our ability in each of the four subdomains shown in the figure (there are very likely more than four subdomains, but we chose to illustrate a model with four), such as our ability to do numerical calculations (S_1), reason through physical space (S_2), recall information (S_3), and use and understand words (S_4) (Spearman, 1939). In summary, Spearman's argument is that we have a single underlying intelligence level that determines an overall range for our performance. This general factor then influences our specific abilities to determine our performance on the task.

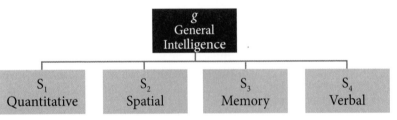

10.4 Spearman's concept of general intelligence
Spearman accepted Thurstone's argument that general intelligence consists of several subskills, including the four shown here.

Crystallized and fluid intelligence

While Spearman argued that there is a single general intelligence that influences our performance, most intelligence researchers differentiate between "what" a person knows and "how" a person thinks. To keep these two concepts separate, intelligence researchers often make a distinction between **crystallized intelligence**—the facts, information, and details we know—and **fluid intelligence**—how we are able to process information and develop solutions to problems. (Cattell, 1943). The importance of

> **crystallized intelligence**
> the facts, information, and details that we know

> **fluid intelligence**
> how we are able to process information and develop solutions to problems

distinguishing between these two types of knowledge has been part of intelligence research since the first intelligence test in 1905 (Binet & Simon, pg. 71). As you will read later, the original intelligence test was developed to measure both the range of knowledge and the mental abilities of the test takers, who were school-age children in France. During the development of the test, the French scientist in charge of development, Alfred Binet, argued that the test needed to distinguish between what the child knew and the child's ability to learn.

One way that we can tell that crystallized and fluid intelligence are different is that they have different developmental trajectories. (Salthouse, 2010). As we get older, our crystallized intelligence tends to increase steadily until about age sixty, when it begins to level off and then slowly decline. Fluid intelligence peaks in the early twenties and then steadily declines across the life span. While it is true that after our early twenties our processing speed, reaction times, and other elements of fluid intelligence decline, our knowledge about the world and how it works continues to grow. As we get older, we might be slower, but we can compensate for the downturn with the increased knowledge and wisdom that come with age. The sudden change in crystallized intelligence as we reach our sixties and beyond is due mainly to changes in the ability of the brain to adapt to new information and growing difficulty accessing existing information.

Second, activities and events that influence intelligence have not had an equivalent impact on both types of intelligence. For example, "brain training" games and activities, such as the website *Lumosity*, that target cognitive processing and working memory have a different effect on the two types of intelligences. While it has been shown that brain training can increase fluid intelligence, these cognitive training activities have not been shown to affect crystallized intelligence or verbal reasoning (Nisbett et al., 2012). Similarly, the gains in performance on intelligence scores for the general population observed over the last several decades have had a larger impact on fluid intelligence than on crystallized intelligence. This is called the **Flynn effect**, named after the scientist who discovered it (Flynn, 2007).

Flynn effect
the name given to gains in performance on intelligence scores for the general population that have been observed over the last several decades

Multiple intelligences

The debate between Spearman and Thurstone regarding general intelligence, "*g*," focused on skills needed to perform academic tasks, such as those needed for success in academic settings and many professional jobs. However, not all of life is a mental puzzle. Two major theories of intelligence argued for a broader interpretation of intelligence, which would include our abilities to navigate the diverse problems encountered in the world (Sternberg, 2003).

Howard Gardner, an American psychologist, argued that we actually have eight separate intelligences that can be used independently or in unison to solve problems (Davis, Christodoulou, Seider, & Gardner, 2011).

1. **Linguistic intelligence** is the ability to understand, analyze, and produce language. An example of someone with great linguistic intelligence is Lieutenant Uhura, a character in the original *Star Trek* television series during the 1960s as well as the recently rebooted movie series. As a communications officer, Uhura is esteemed for her ability to speak numerous alien languages and to make subtle distinctions between similar dialects, such as Klingon and Romulan.

Nichelle Nichols as Lieutenant Uhura

linguistic intelligence
ability to understand, analyze, and produce language

2. **Logical-mathematical intelligence** is the ability to solve mathematical problems and understand symbolic representations. The British physicist Stephen Hawking made dazzling contributions to the modern understanding of black holes despite suffering from a neural degenerative disease that gradually paralyzed him, leading to his death in 2018. Among other things, Hawking showed that black holes, which exert such strong gravitational pull that not even light can escape, nevertheless emit radiation.

Stephen Hawking

logical-mathematical intelligence
ability to solve mathematical problems and understand symbolic representations

3. **Spatial intelligence** is the ability to understand how objects relate to one another in space and to navigate these objects. M. C. Escher was a Dutch artist who created many images that playfully manipulate, and even violate, basic rules of geometry. One of his best-known lithographs is *Ascending and Descending*, which includes a never-ending staircase. People who walk in one direction continually climb the stairs, and those walking in the other direction continually descend.

M.C. Escher

spatial intelligence
ability to understand how objects relate to one another in space and to navigate these objects

4. **Musical intelligence** is the ability to understand, produce, and organize music. John Williams has received 50 Academy Award nominations, making him the second most nominated person after Walt Disney. John Williams has composed much of the best known music in movies, including the rollicking themes for *Star Wars* and *Raiders of the Lost Ark*, as well as the deeply moving score for *Schindler's List*.

John Williams

musical intelligence
ability to understand, produce, and organize music

5. **Bodily-kinesthetic intelligence** is the ability to control and organize bodily movements, such as in sports. LeBron James is currently a basketball player in the NBA who has been called the best player of all time and invites comparisons with such legends as Michael Jordan. In fact, LeBron James and Michael Jordan are the only two people to be named most valuable player in the NBA and play in the finals in the same year that they also won an NBA championship and Olympic gold medal.

LeBron James

bodily-kinesthetic intelligence
ability to control and organize bodily movements, such as in sports

naturalistic intelligence
ability to observe, appreciate, and understand the natural world

interpersonal intelligence
ability to understand the social world, including the thoughts, emotions, and motivations of others

intrapersonal intelligence
ability to understand the self, including your own thoughts, emotions, and motivations

6. **Naturalistic intelligence** is the ability to observe, appreciate, and understand the natural world. Henry David Thoreau lived and wrote in the mid-nineteenth century, but his writing about nature remains relevant today, earning him the title of the Father of Environmentalism. His masterpiece, *Walden*, describes the two years he spent building and living in a cabin on Walden Pond and exploring the surrounding wilderness.

Henry David Thoreau

7. **Interpersonal intelligence** is the ability to understand the social world, including the thoughts, emotions, and motivations of others. Having grown up in poverty, Oprah Winfrey has earned widespread acclaim and vast wealth for her numerous media and philanthropic endeavors. She remains best known for her talk show, in which she focuses on self-improvement and spirituality. Oprah has a natural talent for connecting with guests on her show and members of her audience.

Oprah Winfrey

8. **Intrapersonal intelligence** is the ability to understand the self, including your own thoughts, emotions, and motivations. The Dalai Lama is the leader of Tibetan Buddhism, who has been living in exile since 1959, following the Chinese invasion of Tibet. Buddhists in general and the Dalai Lama in particular rely on meditation to achieve self-knowledge.

Dalai Lama

While we provided examples of famous people to illustrate each of Gardner's eight intelligences, take a few minutes and think about your friends, classmates, and other people you know. Can you come up with examples of people who might be strong in one of these categories but weaker in others? Stereotypes of different individuals often assert that this is true. For example, the stereotypical assessment of an orchestral musician who is extremely skilled in musical intelligence suggests she might maintain less linguistic intelligence due to her extensive study in music without words. While we can use our own judgment to decide the strengths and weaknesses of our friends and family, this is not a scientific approach to understanding intelligence. Gardner, however, used a very similar, but much more scientific, approach in the development of these eight intelligences. Gardner developed his theory by examining the abilities of people who excelled in areas such as sports, politics, arts, and music as well as observing the deficits and talents of **savants**—individuals with generally limited mental abilities but outstanding capabilities in one or two limited domains—and persons with brain damage. By looking across these diverse sources of information, Gardner developed an understanding of what types of abilities tend to group together. Gardner also relied on evidence from the growing field of neuroscience to better understand abilities that share similar brain networks (Davis, et al., 2012).

savants
individuals with generally limited mental abilities but outstanding capabilities in one or two limited domains

While Gardner's theory of multiple intelligences has become extremely popular in educational and business settings, recent factor analyses (the same statistical technique used by Spearman in arguing for general intelligence, "*g*") continue to find evidence in support of a single factor that influences performance across the intelligences Gardner proposed (Almeida, et al., 2010). Similar to Spearman's argument that intelligence is both a general ability, "*g*," and specific abilities, "*s*," current consensus is that Gardner's eight intelligences represent specific domains that are distinct from one another, yet still influenced by general intelligence.

In contrast to Gardner's theory of intelligence, the American psychologist, Robert Sternberg, proposed the Triarchic Theory of Successful Intelligence with only three dimensions (Sternberg, 2003). Sternberg argued that his theory of intelligence "defines successful intelligence in terms of one's ability to succeed according to what one values in life, within one's sociocultural context . . . One does so by a blend of analytical, creative, and practical abilities." (Sternberg, 2003, pg. 400). As proposed by Sternberg, each of the three components of intelligence are analytical intelligence, creative intelligence, and practical intelligence.

1. **Analytical intelligence** is the problem-solving and reasoning abilities used to solve everyday problems, such as information processing, mental calculations, and learning new information. Of Sternberg's three components of intelligence, analytical intelligence most closely relates to Spearman's ideas of general intelligence.

2. **Creative intelligence** is the ability to use information in new ways, to invent, and to come up with nontraditional solutions to problems; the ability to "think outside the box."

3. **Practical intelligence** is the ability to solve the day-to-day challenges of a particular context while adapting previous strategies and shaping new strategies for success. People who can do things such as rebuild an engine or run a business have the *street smarts* to solve practical problems.

analytical intelligence
problem-solving and reasoning abilities used to solve everyday problems, such as information processing, mental calculations, and learning new information

creative intelligence
the ability to use information in new ways, to invent, and to come up with nontraditional solutions to problems ("to think outside the box")

practical intelligence
the ability to solve the day-to-day challenges of a particular context while adapting previous strategies and shaping new strategies for success

Looking at the dimensions of Sternberg's theory of intelligence, you see that these different dimensions allow for solving of familiar, abstract, academic problems (analytical), unique problems (creative), and repeated problems unique to the particular setting or context (practical). Sternberg argues that these three components thus provide full coverage for the types of problems we encounter throughout life.

Sternberg's theory faces many of the same challenges as Gardner's theory of multiple intelligences. Specifically, the three types of intelligence are frequently found to be largely related, suggesting they are all influenced by a similar underlying factor. So, while there is evidence that the specific tests do a better job of measuring real-world outcomes—such as academic success in the first year of college—than does a general measure of intelligence, this improvement may be due to both the influence of general intelligence and the more focused measurement of the specific test compared to an assessment that just provides a measure of general intelligence.

Concept Recall

1. What is the difference between crystallized and fluid intelligence?

2. What is the Flynn effect?

3. What are three theories about the number of different kinds of intelligence?

4. What is meant by lumpers and splitters, and how would you use these terms to describe the ideas of Spearman, Gardner, and Sternberg?

5. How does cognition fit into each theory about the number of different kinds of intelligence?

INTELLIGENCE TESTING

intelligence test
standardized set of measures used to assess mental performance and abilities to make comparisons across groups and individuals

An **intelligence test** is a standardized set of measures used to assess mental performance and abilities in order to allow for comparisons across groups and individuals. The previous section on the nature of intelligence focused on providing a theoretical definition of intelligence. However, a more popular approach to defining intelligence is the psychometric approach. According to the psychometric approach, intelligence is what we measure it to be. Accordingly, we define intelligence as the score on a test, and we determine the usefulness of this test by examining what it tells us about people's interactions with the world. To be useful, an intelligence test must be valid, reliable, and standardized.

validity
of an exam is determined by how well it measures or predicts what it was intended to assess

The **validity** of an exam is determined by how well it measures or predicts what it was intended to assess. For example, have you ever taken an exam for a class that really did not feel like it measured what you learned in the course? Maybe you felt that the course was about learning terms while the instructor asked almost entirely application questions. As you leave the exam and talk with your friends about your concerns regarding the test, you are questioning the exam's validity. The American College Test (ACT) is an example of a valid test, as it is designed to both assess readiness for college and predict success in college. Extensive research demonstrates that scores on the ACT both correlate with performance in high school and predict first-year academic success in college. Exams that you take in your college classes are valid if they accurately reflect the instructor's goals (which may not be the same as your expectations for the exam).

reliability
refers to the consistency of a test across the entire measurement and different test-taking occasions

Reliability refers to the consistency of the test across the entire measurement and different test-taking occasions. If you take your temperature with a thermometer several times within fifteen minutes, you expect to receive the same general temperature each time (there will be some variation, but not much). Similarly, if you stand on a scale several times without changing what you are wearing, you expect the scale to show the same number each time. Both of these are examples of a measurement tool's reliability. Intelligence tests contain a number of different scales or measurement tools to allow for the repeated measurement of mental abilities. If the test is reliable, the test taker will score similarly on each scale in the test. Also, we might give the same test to people several times over the course of a semester. A reliable test will show the same pattern of scores from one testing period to the next. A common way of evaluating reliability of a psychological test is to perform a split-half analysis. This analysis is conducted by splitting the test into two random halves and looking at the correlation between the items. If all items on the test are measuring the same thing, this split-half analysis should produce a strong positive correlation. We can also assess the reliability of a test by administering it over several time periods. If the test is a reliable measure of intelligence, the correlation between the different administrations will be positive and strong.

In intelligence testing, **test standardization** refers to the practice of determining set procedures that will be used whenever the test is given and giving the test to people across a desired reference group in order to establish a range of comparison scores. Standardization sets the rules for how the test will be administered and who is able to take the test. Can you remember when you took the ACT or any state-mandated test during high school? The test administrators had very specific rules they had to follow about when to start the test, how many people could be in the room, what you were allowed to have on the table or desk during the test, and how long you could work on each section of the test. Each of these elements is part of the test's standardization. The degree to which we can make reliable, valid assumptions about the meaning of test scores is directly related to how closely the standardization rules are followed. Imagine what would happen if your college instructors assigned half of the class to complete an exam in fifteen minutes in a noisy classroom while the other half of the class was allowed all the time they wanted while sitting alone in a quiet, comfortable study room at the library. Would it be fair—or make sense—for the instructor to compare scores across these two very different settings?

test standardization
the practice of determining set procedures that will be used whenever the test is given and giving the test to people across a desired reference group in order to establish a range of comparison scores

Standardization also refers to who is allowed to take the test. As part of "norming" a standardized test, the test is administered to a large sample of individuals who represent the target population for the test. The ACT, for example, is administered to high school students. The Graduate Record Exam (GRE) is administered to students who are juniors and seniors in college. Valid comparisons of test scores can only be made across the individuals with the same general characteristics as the reference population. If the only people who have completed a test are freshman students in a general psychology class at a small, rural college in the United States, then the test results can only be used to compare the performance of other individuals from the same group. If we wanted to use the test to compare the mental abilities of people from across the United States, we would have to administer the test to a representative sample of people from across the United States.

The most popular intelligence test in the United States is the fourth edition of the Wechsler Adult Intelligence Scale (WAIS-IV) (Wechsler, 2008). The WAIS-IV is standardized for administration to people age sixteen to ninety, includes eleven subtests, and takes between sixty to ninety minutes to administer. Due to the strict standardization of the test administration and scoring, only people with advanced training and licensure or certification as a test administrator are allowed to purchase, administer, score, and interpret the test. The WAIS-IV shows good reliability when administered twice over a twelve-week period and good validity in that scores on the WAIS-IV are highly correlated with another popular intelligence test, the Stanford-Binet test.

Origins of Intelligence Testing

Alfred Binet

While there are many different types of intelligence tests, most modern intelligence tests are strongly influenced by the work of the French psychologist Alfred Binet (1857-1911). Binet's work with intelligence testing began in the early 1900s, when Binet was commissioned to join a government committee developing procedures to identify children whose cognitive abilities would be better suited to teaching methods different from those used in mainstream classrooms (Nikolas & Levine, 2012). Binet and his collaborator, Theodore Simon, a fellow Frenchman, developed their original tests in order to address two questions of importance to the school setting: is the child's intelligence level "abnormal," and how far away from "normal" is the child's intelligence (Binet & Simon, pg. 140)? Binet and Simon identified three types of abnormal children (pg. 266):

- **Idiots:** persons who are unable to use spoken language to communicate;
- **Imbeciles**: persons who are unable to use written language to communicate, and
- **Morons:** persons who are unable to care for themselves.

The classification "moron" is complicated because Binet and Simon included the lack of ability to function at their parents' same social level a diagnostic category. In this way, "an attorney's son who is reduced by his intelligence to the condition of a menial employee is a moron" (Binet & Simon, pg. 266). It is important to note that these categories were created in order to assist with decision-making related to how children would be educated. While each of these terms is used today as an insult and would be strongly frowned upon as a label applied to a child, the original intent of the words was not to demean or hurt children but to assist in improving their lives. Over time, however, the original intent of these categories has been lost as the social misuse of the words continues to grow (a similar social change has occurred with the use of the label "retarded," from its original use as a descriptive label for ranges of intelligence scores below normal to its modern use as an insult).

Binet and Simon published the results of their first test in 1905. This test took approximately forty minutes to administer and consisted of thirty cognitive tasks (Boake, 2002), including: assessments of coordination, verbal identification of objects and pictures; comparison of similarities and differences of objects from memory; creating sentences using three given words; and replying to an abstract question such as, "When one has need of good advice—What must one do?" (Binet & Simon, 1905, pgs. 45-50, & 66). This original test was designed to assess physical (inherited conditions, development, anatomical condition, and other physical characteristics, including the senses, motor function, and blood, pg. 77), pedagogical (how much a person knows), and psychological influences on intelligence. The emphasis of the test was on the psychological method of measuring intelligence. Accordingly, Binet and Simon argued that true intelligence lies in the psychological abilities of the individual.

The original test was scored by comparing the test taker's performance to that of other students of the same age. If the child taking the test scored about the same or better than children of their same age, they were viewed as "normal." If they scored lower, they were viewed as "abnormal." In 1908, Binet and Simon changed the scoring of their test

Cross-Cultural Case

Intelligence Across Cultures

For years, researchers have been trying to establish a reliable measure by which to gauge intelligence. Recently, however, research reveals there may not be a single, reliable method by which to achieve this goal. Indeed, Yale psychologists Dr. Robert J. Sternberg and Dr. Elena L. Grigorenko find in their 2004 study that "intelligence cannot fully or even meaningfully be understood outside its cultural context" because while "the processes of intelligence are universal . . . their manifestations are not." In fact, different cultures even appear to view the purpose of intelligence differently. In his 2003 study, "The Geography of Thought," Dr. Richard Nisbett, co-director of the Culture and Cognition Program at the University of Michigan at Ann Arbor, argues that people in Western cultures tend to view intelligence as a tool necessary for rational debate and conversation, while people in Eastern cultures see intelligence as means of successfully performing required social roles and interacting with others. Further complicating matters, researchers have discovered in a number of cultures a tendency to blur the lines between what Westerners would often refer to as "book smarts" versus "common sense." In rural Zambia, for instance, Dr. Robert Serpell of the University of Zambia describes a concept known as *nzelu*, which "includes both cleverness (*chenjela*) and responsibility (*tumikila*)." Another study performed in rural Zambia and published in the journal *Intelligence*, "suggests that practical and academic intelligence can develop independently or even in conflict with each other, and that the values of a culture may shape the direction in which a child develops" just as much as his or her innate intellectual ability. These studies also "agree with studies in a number of countries, both industrialized and non-industrialized, that suggest that people who are unable to solve complex problems in the abstract can often solve them when they are presented in a familiar context." Combined, these studies reveal that intelligence is not as easily measured as we have often thought, and that tools like the IQ, while sometimes effective in one culture, may be of little to no use in another.

Sam DCruz / Shutterstock.com

to reflect the mental age of the test taker (Boake, 2002). Performance on the test was determined by comparing the test taker's answers to those given by other test takers of varying ages. These comparisons allowed the evaluator to determine the approximate age range of the test taker's performance. With this new scoring method, the test taker's score was considered "abnormal" if the test taker's mental age was assessed as less than the test taker's chronological age. If the child completing the test completed items in the way we would expect of an eight-year-old but was actually twelve years old, then this child's intelligence would be deemed abnormal, and the child would be identified as needing different educational opportunities than a typical twelve-year-old child.

As we evaluate the tests developed by Binet and Simon, it is easy to wonder why intelligence tests include so many different tasks and can take so long to administer. In fact, modern intelligence tests that developed from earlier versions by Binet and Simon, such as the Wechsler Intelligence Scale for Children (WISC-V), include more types of items and can require even more time (approximately 60 minutes, according to the publisher). Intelligence tests are typically organized into a "battery" of tests for two major reasons: a variety of tests reveals potential deficits, and overall assessment provides the most comprehensive measurement of intelligence.

A variety of tests across many different abilities and activities allows the evaluator to determine where deficits might occur. For example, a test might include several tests of receptive language (ability to understand what is being said) and expressive language (ability to produce understandable communications) as well as tests of reasoning, mathematical abilities, and memory. After completing the test, the evaluator may find that the test taker performed below normal, but that this is only true in one or two areas, such as expressive or receptive language. Understanding precisely where deficits occur is important in developing treatment or educational programs.

The identification of an individual's level of intelligence typically seeks their overall performance on mental tasks, which emerges from the overall assessment of performance on many different types of tasks. Single measurements always include a certain degree of measurement error (when you weighed yourself several times earlier in this chapter without doing anything to change your weight, such as eating or adding/removing clothes, you likely encountered slight fluctuations across each measurement), and only assessing a single dimension would not allow for the determination of an overall assessment of performance. Binet and Simon said that "a particular test isolated from the rest is of little value, that it is open to errors of every sort . . . One test signifies nothing, let us emphatically repeat, but five or six tests signify something" (pg. 329). The importance of repeated and varied assessment is easily understood by thinking about your academic abilities. Would you be happy if your abilities as a student were assessed by only a single test, administered one time? We once joked with a class that their grade would be determined by the score on a single exam, given at the end of the semester. Not one student found this funny.

Lewis Terman, an American psychologist, revised the Binet-Simon test for use in the United States. The revised test, the Stanford-Binet, was designed for children and adults and adapted a new scoring system. Using a system of scoring proposed by the German psychologist William Stern, Terman's Stanford-Binet test assigned each test taker a numerical score that could be used to make direct comparisons across individuals with normal, below normal, and above normal mental abilities: the intelligence quotient, or IQ.

IQ: The Intelligence Quotient

A measurement without a point of reference is useless. For example, people who grew up in the United States have a good sense of what it means for something to be three feet tall. You likely know how tall you are and can easily compare your height to an object that is three feet tall. As the average height of a male in the United States is approximately five feet ten inches, an average male could think that three feet is just a little more than half his height. However, tell someone educated in most of the United States that an object is 0.914 meters tall, and he or she would have a difficult time understanding what this means. Without experience with the metric system, there is no immediate reference group available, and the measurement becomes uninformative. This same reasoning can be applied to tests of academic or mental abilities. For example, consider what you would think if a friend ran up to you and enthusiastically exclaimed, "I got a 37 on my exam!" Is this a good or a bad score? The measurement by itself is rather useless. If your friend told you that this was the highest score in the class and that the scores of the other students ranged from a 5 to your friend's 37, then you can immediately understand that your friend's score is really something to celebrate.

The need for a usable reference group is particularly important for intelligence tests, as the aim of these measurements is to understand individual differences in abstract mental abilities. Determining the reference group for a test is part of its standardization procedures. As discussed previously, a standardized test has rules about how the test is administered and who can take the test. A test is only standardized for those persons who were part of its reference group. For example, the ACT is taken annually by tens of thousands of high school students who want to go to college. Accordingly, performance on the ACT has been *standardized* for persons aged fifteen to eighteen. The composite score on the ACT (1 to 36) is based on a comparison of the test performance for students in the target age range. Imagine that you and two friends took the ACT on the same day. You and Friend A were both sixteen at the time of the test, but Friend B was only thirteen. Your composite score from the test was a 30, while both of your friends scored a 27. What can we make of these test scores? Because of the standardization range of the ACT, you can brag that you outperformed Friend A (your score of 30 is better than your friend's score of 27). But did you outperform Friend B? At age thirteen, Friend B is outside the standardization range for the ACT, making it impossible to compare Friend B's 27 directly with your composite score of 30. As this example shows, it is only possible to interpret the meaning of a test when we know the comparison group (standardization) that was used in developing the test.

As discussed previously, Binet and Simon suggested the best way to standardize their intelligence test scores was to compare the mental age of the test taker to their chronological age (Nikolas & Levine, 2012). A six-year-old who answered as many questions correctly as the typical nine-year-old in the reference group would be said to have the mental age of a nine-year-old. To standardize the comparison of test scores across different **chronological ages**—the actual ages of the test takers—and mental ages, Lewis Terman of Stanford University suggested dividing the test taker's mental age by their chronological age to create a comparison that could be used across individuals of different ages, thus giving rise to the Intelligence Quotient, or IQ score. In order to make IQ scores easier to interpret, the quotient of the mental age divided by chronological age is multiplied by 100, and the remainder (anything after the decimal point) is dropped. The formula for IQ can be written as follows:

chronological age
the actual age of the test taker, expressed as the number of years since the date of birth

$$IQ = (Mental\ Age\ /\ Chronological\ Age)*100$$

The norm is for a person to have a mental age that is equivalent to their chronological age. Whenever the mental and chronological ages are equal, the individual's IQ will be 100 (a ten-year-old with the mental age of a ten-year-old would have an IQ of: (10/10) * 100 = 100. If the person's mental age is greater than his chronological age, the IQ score will be greater than 100. If the person's mental age is less than her chronological age, her IQ will be less than 100. Earlier, we gave the example of a six-year-old whose mental age was determined to be equal to that of a nine-year-old. We can calculate this child's IQ as follows:

$$IQ = 9/6*100 = 150$$

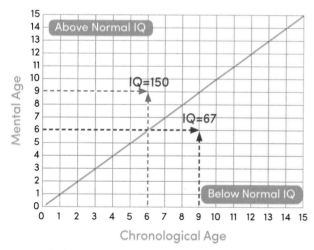

10.5 Calculating IQ based on mental age and chronological age
Early measurements of IQ used the ratio of the mental age— which was assessed comparing the mental performance of a test taker to the performance of children at different ages—to the chronological age of the test taker. The blue line shows the typical score, IQ = 100, where the chronological age and mental age are the same. Any scores above the blue line represent above normal IQ while any scores below the line represent below normal IQ.

The blue arrows in Figure 10.5 show how this score of 150 compares to an average IQ of 100 (the diagonal orange bar). A score of 150 would be considered above average. What if the child's scores were reversed, with a chronological age of nine and a mental age of a six-year-old? The red arrows show that this child's IQ of 67 (6/9 * 100) is below average. This system for standardizing IQ as the ratio between mental age and chronological age gives a straightforward way to compare people's mental performance.

While IQ scores based on the ratio of the mental age to the chronological age create a useful reference for mental abilities, there is a significant problem with this measure of intelligence. Thinking back to our six-year-old, imagine what would happen if this child's mental age were to always stay three years ahead of his chronological age. By the time the child was nine, he or she would have the mental age of a twelve-year-old. His or her nine-year-old IQ would be 133, down 17 points from the child's IQ of 150 at six.

Notice that the IQ score dropped, even though the child maintained the same mental lead on others in the same chronological age group. To keep the child's IQ at 150, the child's mental age would have to increase to that of a fifteen-year-old. The increase in mental age would have to be faster than the increase in chronological age to maintain the same IQ level as a person ages. Figure 10.6 simulates the change in IQ over thirty years for a person who maintains a three-year gap between her chronological and mental age.

By age thirty-six, the individual's IQ score would have dropped from 150 to 108 (39/36 = 1.08 * 100 = 108). To maintain an IQ score of 150, the individual must increase in mental age from nine at the age of six (three years difference) to fifty-four at age thirty-six (eighteen years difference). While individuals with IQs above 100 see an illusionary loss in IQ over the years—unless their mental age increases faster than their chronological age—the opposite would be true for someone with an IQ below 100. As the years pass for this individual, the gap between her or his chronological and mental age would lessen, leading to an illusionary increase in IQ score.

Because we need to adjust for these illusory changes, today IQ scores are determined by calculating how far the individual's score deviates from the average for her or his chronological age group. This method employs the statistical concept of variance around the mean to determine how different the test score is from the mean for the reference group. **Variance** refers to the difference in scores around the mathematical mean. Even though each test taker is going to differ from other test takers, the scores will tend to cluster around a middle score (the mean, or average). To understand how scores vary around the mean, think about how tall people are. Some people are really tall, and some people are really short, but most people are about the same height. If we went out and measured hundreds of men in the United States, we would find that the majority of them will be around five feet ten inches. We might measure some that are over seven feet tall and some that are less than four feet tall, but the vast majority will be in the average range. With the variety of different heights we observe, what would we consider tall? What would we consider short? Extremely tall? Extremely short? The only way to answer these questions is to look at how much the scores differ (vary) around the mean height. Heights that deviate a lot from the mean would be considered extremely tall or extremely short.

variance
the difference in scores around the mathematical mean

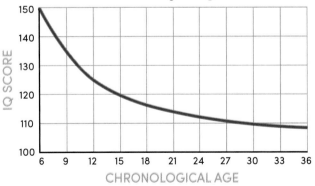

Change in IQ score over the years when mental age remains three years ahead of chronological age

(vertical axis: IQ SCORE, 100–150; horizontal axis: CHRONOLOGICAL AGE, 6–36)

10.6 Change in IQ scores
This graph shows apparent change in IQ score as age increases. A six-year-old child with a mental age of nine will have an IQ score of 150. However, if the child continues to maintain a three-year mental advantage on her peers over the years, her IQ will decrease toward 100, despite the constant mental age difference.

Just as height varies across people, so do mental abilities. If we gave every person of the same chronological age the same set of mental tasks to complete, we would find there are some who do extremely well on the task, while others do not do so well. We could determine how much better or worse the test takers did by looking at how far their scores are away from the cluster in the center—the average. Modern IQ scores are calculated using this method of determining how far the test taker's scores deviate from the average performance for a test taker with the same chronological age rather than the ratio of mental age to chronological age to avoid the problem of IQ scores drifting toward the middle (100) as the individual ages.

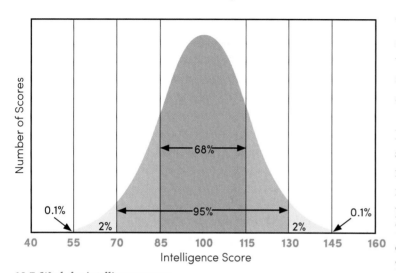

10.7 Wechsler intelligence score
IQ scores are based on deviation from the mean score. The deviation method of determining IQ score determines the average performance for each comparison age IQ and assigns that a score of 100 with a standard deviation (a statistical measure of how much scores vary) of 15. An individual test taker's score is determined by where it falls on this distribution of deviation scores.

To maintain similarity with previous IQ scores, deviation scores are calculated with an average IQ set at 100 and a standard deviation (a measure of how far scores typically deviate from the mean) of 15 points as shown in Figure 10.7. Since IQ scores tend to vary around the mean in a predictable way, 68 percent of IQ scores fall within the range of 85 to 115 (plus or minus one standard deviation), and 95 percent of scores fall within a range of 70 to 130 (plus or minus two standard deviations). Typically, an IQ of less than 70 is considered a sign of a severe mental delay while a score above 130 would be considered mentally gifted.

IQ scores are important measures of individual differences because they can predict changes in performance across many contexts. Individuals with higher IQ scores tend to do better in school and perform better in the workplace (Nisbett, et al., 2012). In general, IQ scores predict abilities to perform tasks that require a great deal of mental activity, such as school and professional jobs, and are less useful for contexts less directly connected to mental abilities (Neisser, at al., 1996).

Whenever discussing the correlations between IQ scores and real-world behavior, it is important to repeat the caution from Chapter 1: correlation does not imply causation. Just because two items are correlated does not mean that one item causes the other. The relationship between intelligence and real-world behaviors is an excellent example of the caution we need to use when interpreting correlations. Consider, for example, the association between breastfeeding and intelligence. Research shows that intelligence scores are correlated with breastfeeding. However, there are many factors—such as the parents' IQ levels, time spent with parents, social economic status (SES), etc.—that could influence this relationship (Chapman, 2013; Nisbett, et al., 2012). The correlation between IQ and nursing does not tell us what is causing changes in either of the two variables (in addition to children who were breastfed having high IQs, there is also evidence that mothers with high IQs tend to nurse their babies more often than mothers with lower IQ scores).

A special type of correlation can be used to determine how much of an impact genes have on a particular trait. As discussed throughout this book, the environment and our genetic inheritance influence all behaviors and abilities. However, we can use correlations between genetically related individuals to determine how much of an impact the environment has on a particular ability. We call these types of studies heritability research. The heritability of a trait or behavior ranges from 0.0—meaning the behavior is entirely influenced by environment—to 1.0—meaning the behavior is entirely influenced by genetic inheritance. The extremes of this scale, 0.0 and 1.0, are theoretically possible but extremely improbable. Research indicates that the heritability estimate for intelligence is approximately .5, or 50 percent. (Plomin, DeFries, Knopik, & Neiderhiser, 2012). Any measure of heritability should be viewed as a general estimate of heritability, as research indicates that genetic influence on intelligence is affected by environmental events. Research indicates that the heritability of intelligence increases as: the environment becomes more stable, the social economic status of the family increases, and the age of the participants in the study increases (Nisbett, 2012). The fact that the degree of heritability of intelligence is influenced by the environment is further evidence that biology and environment both contribute to the development of our behaviors and abilities.

Just as IQ scores are influenced by our genetic inheritance, so are they affected by so-cial context. Intelligence scores are influenced by the prenatal environment (such as the mother's drug use and dietary choices), early environmental enrichment, access to school, interactions with caregivers, and other social factors (Nisbett, 2012). While these individual factors are important influences on intelligence, the aim of an intel-ligence test is to be **culture fair**—meaning the score is not biased by the test taker's cultural and social background. Binet and Simon stressed the importance of measuring intelligence independent of social background in the 1905 report on their first attempts at measuring intelligence: "We have often said that in our study we have sought to find the natural intelligence of the child, and not his degree of culture, his amount of instruction" (pg. 253).

culture fair
meaning that the score is not biased by the test taker's cultural and social background

However, it is not really possible to develop a test completely free from cultural influence. All intelligence tests must make assumptions about the knowledge and abilities of those who will take the test. Any test requiring reading is automatically biased against anyone who was not taught to read. Similarly, the choice of stimuli shown during the test and the required activities are all made by people from certain cultural backgrounds and may possibly create differences in the observed score that do not reflect differences in the underlying mental abilities. Given these challenges, it may not be possible to create a completely culture-fair test. Instead, it is important for the test giver and those who will be using the results of the test to resist influences of cultural and social background on the test taker's performance.

One example of a test created to be culture fair is the Raven's Progressive Matrices intelligence test. This test uses a series of patterns laid out in a three-by-three grid with the last image hidden to assess mental reasoning and visualization abilities. While the bottom-rightmost card is missing (the ninth card for those who read from left to right), the relationship between the patterns on the other eight cards create a rule that can be used to determine which card is missing from a set of four to eight other cards. As the patterns are novel arrangements of shapes, colors, lines, and textures, the test does not require the use of language (reading or speaking) to complete, and it is a generally novel activity that prevents test takers from "practicing" prior to taking the exam. Due to these characteristics, the Raven's is considered by most scientists to be a culture-fair test of intelligence (or at least the closest thing we have to a culture-fair test).

This Is Psychology

One of the main characters in the classic 1988 movie, *Rain Man*, is Raymond Babbitt, a man who exhibits some astonishing mental abilities. With just a glance, Raymond accurately counted more than 200 toothpicks that had spilled on the floor of a diner. After spending an evening reading the Cincinnati phone book, he was able to recall anyone's phone number whose last name began with a letter between A and G. At the same time, Raymond seems to lack many aspects of common sense. When asked how much a candy bar costs, Raymond replies that it should cost about 100 dollars, and when asked how much a new car costs, Raymond again replies that it should cost 100 dollars. Although Raymond was fictional, his character was inspired by an actual man named Kim Peek. Kim, who died in 2009, was considered to be a savant, meaning that he could effortlessly complete mental processing tasks that would be impossible for almost anyone else. Perhaps as the result of Kim's brain never having developed a corpus callosum (the nerve bundle that connects the right and left hemispheres described in Chapter 3), Kim could simultaneously read two pages of text. Kim read constantly and retained almost everything, making him a walking encyclopedia. Kim's processing of information was equally impressive, as he could provide driving directions between any two cities in the world, and for any date he could quickly determine the day of the week on which that date occurred. Savants such as Kim strain our understanding of intelligence, because along with his superlative mental skills, Kim's measured IQ was well below average. Also, Kim had difficulty comprehending social conventions. For example, Kim had read and memorized Shakespeare's plays, and Kim's father often took him to see these plays performed. If one of the actors flubbed one of the lines, Kim would stand in the auditorium and interrupt the performance to object.

Concept Recall

1. A quotient is the result of a division between two numbers. What is the original meaning of "intelligence quotient" in terms of one number divided by another?

2. Why is IQ no longer calculated in terms of mental and chronological age?

3. What is a culturally biased test?

INTELLIGENCE TESTING IN WORK AND LIFE

Intelligence testing is used in many ways. **School psychologists**—a type of applied psychologist who works in school settings to address the educational, psychological, and social needs of students—are a group that makes frequent use of intelligence testing. Just as was true of Binet's original development of intelligence tests, school psychologists today use scores on intelligence tests to determine the academic placement of students. Students who score high on intelligence tests are considered for placement in gifted and talented programs, while those who score low are considered for additional instructional opportunities or—in the case of extremely low scores—placement in a special education classroom. School psychologists rarely use scores on an intelligence test as the only diagnostic tool for making decisions regarding a child's educational opportunities, but the scores can be highly informative, as they allow for an objective comparison of the child's abilities in comparison to other students.

Psychologists working in other applied fields also make use of intelligence testing. Therapists and counselors working to provide treatment for mental health issues (like those we will discuss in Chapter 13) may use intelligence scores in developing treatment plans. The intelligence of a client can be a predictor regarding which types of therapy may be most beneficial. Intelligence scores can also provide important information about the development of particular mental health challenges. **Forensic psychologists**—applied psychologists who use psychological science in addressing legal and criminal issues—use intelligence testing in the evaluation of the competency of accused persons to stand trial. In the United States, an important consideration of a person's guilt includes his or her cognitive ability to understand the significance of his or her actions. Finding that a person has extremely low intelligence could change the way the courts evaluate the nature of the crime and possible penalties (intelligence and culpability are beautifully explored in the end of the John Steinbeck's *Of Mice and Men*). Finally, intelligence testing may also be a part of an industrial/organizational psychologist's evaluation of potential employees for different jobs at a company or as a tool to determine which of a group of applicants to offer a job. This use of intelligence testing is not all that different from how tests such as the ACT, SAT, and GRE are used to evaluate which applicants to admit to an undergraduate program (in the case of the ACT and SAT) or a graduate program (GRE).

The above examples highlight some of the professional fields that use intelligence testing as a tool in completing their work. This is not an exhaustive list, however. Intelligence testing is a powerful tool in many situations where objective comparisons need to be made across individuals. Despite the variety of contexts where intelligence testing is used, some things remain constant: (1) The test must be administered according to the specific directions and requirements listed by the test developers (in other words, the directions must be followed), and (2) the test administrator must be trained in the administration and interpretation of the results of the test. In most cases, test administrators must possess at least a master's degree and an appropriate professional certification or license.

school psychologists
a type of applied psychologist who works in school settings to address the educational, psychological, and social needs of students

forensic psychologists
applied psychologists who use psychological science in addressing legal and criminal issues

Whether or not you choose to pursue a profession where you are responsible for giving and interpreting intelligence tests, it is extremely likely that at some point in your life you will either take an intelligence test or be required to make sense of the results of an intelligence test. The information provided in this chapter was selected to help you successfully navigate these times. As you consider the significance of "intelligence" it is important to keep in mind that this is a comparative term. A wise consumer of intelligence scores will ask questions about the norming of the test, including comparison groups, and evidence of the validity of the test. In other words, do scores on the test actually tell the group that has ordered it what they want to know? Asking questions about the validity and reliability of any psychological test (well, any test, really) is an important step in becoming an empowered decision-maker and ensuring that you are making the best decisions for yourself or for persons for whom you are responsible.

THINKING, INTELLIGENCE, AND PSYCHOLOGY

This chapter began by suggesting that electronic computers are useful metaphors for describing how people think. However, as you read the chapter, studies revealed the psychological mechanism of thinking differs radically from how we might expect a computer to think. Within that mechanism, mental concepts are not based on necessary and sufficient conditions but rather arrange best examples, called prototypes and boundaries, which are fuzzy rather than sharp. Where computers use algorithms, which are guaranteed to generate the correct solution to a problem, people use heuristics, which are occasionally prone to error but can solve problems and estimate probabilities much more quickly than algorithms can. While both humans and computers process information—or think—humans process information critically—or intelligently. Even so, intelligence is much more than just information processing. In fact, human information processing comprises only two of Howard Gardner's eight kinds of intelligence (linguistic and logical-mathematical intelligence) and one of Robert Sternberg's three kinds of intelligence (analytic intelligence). As this book maintains, you are a complex individual who develops, learns, remembers, thinks, and socializes; intelligence, shown in this chapter, equips you to do all these things well. Thinking and intelligence used together are two of several components of your complexity that play significant roles throughout diverse aspects of psychological study.

Review/Reflect/Write

REVIEW

- What was the cognitive revolution, and why did it occur when it did?
- How does Aristotle's classical description of mental concepts differ from the current description of mental concepts?
- What are two main problem solving strategies, and how do they differ?
- How is expected value calculated, and why do people prefer to use heuristics rather than calculating expected values?
- What is the hierarchical organization of language?
- What is the difference between crystallized and fluid intelligence?
- What is meant by a test that is reliable, valid, and standardized?
- What are three theories about the number of different kinds of intelligence?
- How was IQ originally calculated in terms of chronological and mental age?
- What are the mean and standard deviation of the IQ distribution?

1. Which is the following phrases spoken by children cannot be fully explained by behaviorism?

   a. "The dog ran."

   b. "The deers runned."

   c. "Why?"

   d. "Mommy loves me."

2. Contrary to Aristotle's view, Wittgenstein argued that everyday concepts have

   a. fuzzy boundaries.

   b. concise boundaries.

   c. no boundaries.

   d. finite definitions.

3. Which of the following is a prototype of a farm animal?

   a. silkworm

   b. llama

   c. ostrich

   d. cow

4. Lau can't remember the code to get into his locker. He has decided to use the step-by-step procedure of entering every number possible so he won't have to go back to the office to get his number again. Lau is using _____ to solve this problem.

   a. insight

   b. an algorithm

   c. a heuristic

   d. creativity

5. Economists claim that people make decisions rationally using expected values. Which of the following is a demonstration that this is not completely true?

   a. Many people continue to pay more for fresh food vs. canned food.

   b. The government assists in funding insurance coverage for low-income households.

   c. Many people choose not to cheat on tests.

   d. Lottery sales are still popular among many people.

6. While intelligence is difficult, even impossible, to define, what is the general definition of intelligence, as reported in the text?

    a. The capacity for abstract thought, understanding, communication, planning, learning, reasoning, and problem solving.

    b. The ability to imagine and create when problem solving and to use experience to improve on future performance.

    c. The ability to quickly and effectively complete mental activities, relative to others of equal status.

    d. The ability to efficiently and effectively learn from experience, perform mental tasks, and solve problems.

7. You have an algebra class with Amy. She is the top student in the class. According to Spearman's general intelligence, Amy is probably

    a. also good at English.

    b. equally talented in geometry.

    c. even better at trigonometry.

    d. none of the above. High intelligence in algebra does not mean intelligence will be high in any other areas.

8. If an exam measures or predicts exactly what it was intended to assess, you could say that the exam is high in _____.

    a. generalizability   c. reliability

    b. standardization   d. validity

9. Regina is 52 years old. She has a great amount of knowledge about the world and history; however, her processing speed and ability to solve problems are not very fast. She has greater _____ and less _____.

    a. fluid intelligence; crystallized intelligence

    b. analytical intelligence; creative intelligence

    c. crystallized intelligence; fluid intelligence

    d. creative intelligence; analytical intelligence

10. What is a reason for the Flynn effect?

    a. better nutrition   c. less disease

    b. better education   d. all of the above

REFLECT

1. Do you think that electronic computers will ever have the same computing power as the human brain? Why or why not?

2. Consider this measure of mathematical intelligence: Use a tape measure to find the distance around a person's head. Is that a valid measure of mathematical ability? Is it a reliable measure of mathematical ability? Surprisingly, the answer to one of these questions is "yes." Which is it?

3. Do you know a child who is currently learning to talk? What are some examples of language errors the child makes that reveal how the child understands the rules of language but sometimes misuses the rules?

Write

1. Have you ever used Siri on an iPhone, Microsoft's Cortana, or Alexa on an Amazon Echo device? "Virtual assistants," as they're known, have steadily grown in popularity after Apple introduced Siri to the world through its iOS 5 on iPhone 4S in 2011. Generally, users respond positively to virtual assistant capabilities, occasionally trying to exploit their robotic tendencies by asking questions no one—human or machine—could answer (such as, "What is the meaning of life?" to which Siri often responds with, "42," or, "All signs point to chocolate."). Research both the abilities and weaknesses of virtual assistants, applying a critical view to their purposes. What did developers originally expect users would want? Do users tend to task virtual assistants with Internet searching or with scheduling, ordering, or task completion? What elements of thinking or intelligence did software writers seek to impart in virtual assistant programs, and were software programs successful in being perceived as actively thinking machines? Write a report detailing your research and conclusions.

2. This chapter described eight people, each of whom clearly embodies one of Howard Gardner's eight kinds of intelligence. Nominate your own eight well-known people, fictional or real, who embody each kind of intelligence, and describe what qualifies your nominees to exemplify each kind of intelligence.

Key Terms

11 Emotion and Motivation

After reading this chapter, you will be able to answer the following questions:

- What are the major components of emotions?
- How do the James-Lange, Cannon-Bard, and Schachter-Singer theories explain emotion?
- How are positive and negative affect important to understanding emotion?
- What are the basic human emotions?
- What is motivation?
- How do the hierarchy, evolutionary, and social theories of motivation differ?
- What is the difference between intrinsic and extrinsic motivation?
- How is our social experience related to motivation?

H eadhunting—the act of killing, removing, and collecting the head of another person, not the modern practice of searching for potential job candidates—has been practiced by groups of people all around the world. But why? What would motivate an entire people to engage in this type of behavior? From our current social-cultural context, this type of communal acceptance of killing and dismemberment seems impossible to understand.

An explanation for this type of behavior—at least for the Ilongot people living on Luzon Island in the Philippines—was provided by Renalto and Michelle "Shelly" Rosaldo, cultural anthropologists, in the late 1960s (Spiegel, 2017). As described in the June 1, 2017, NPR *Invisibilia* podcast (https://goo.gl/ELUmUX), Renalto and Michelle spent years living with and observing the traditions and cultural practices of the Ilongot. As they learned the local language, they discovered a word used to refer to a unique and difficult to understand emotional state, *liget*.

What exactly is *liget*? Well, it is hard to define by those who primarily speak English. There simply is not a similar concept in the English language. As Rosaldo has explained (2004; Spiegel, 2017), a full understanding of the meaning of this word only came to him through several key experiences. Initially, he connected the meaning to people in the community who were especially energized and productive. In this sense, *liget* was tied to the energy and vitality of life. Rosaldo believed the emotion described by this word to be something like hyperactive or excited. This definition, though, was too simple.

Rosaldo discovered a deeper meaning to *liget* when a group of tribe members became extremely emotional when listening to the recorded voice of a well-respected tribe member who had recently died. Upon hearing the voice, the tribe's members became highly agitated and demanded that the recording be turned off. The listeners were not just energized. They were also angry, full of rage. As Michelle Rosaldo later explained, "most verbal and adverbial forms of *liget* thus evoke not only energy and irritation, but also a sense of violent action and of intentional shows of force." (1980, p. 45). This finding was another step closer to understanding *liget*.

The final stage of Rosaldo's understanding came after Michelle's tragic and unexpected death. Michelle died from a fall into a river gorge while out walking one day with several village members. After returning home to California for the funeral, Rosaldo found himself filling with rage and energy. Pulling over to the

side of the road, he discovered the full meaning of *liget* as the grief and rage boiled out of him in an intense howl. Rosaldo described this as "like high voltage was flowing through my body." (Spiegel, 2017).

With this experience, Rosaldo could finally understand the full reasoning behind the tribe's headhunting. Headhunting, it turns out, was one way that the community learned to deal with the challenges of living in a difficult and dangerous environment. As they experienced death, the feelings of *liget*—a combination of grief, rage, and intense energy—built up, spread across the community, and sought an outlet. Over time, the community developed the tradition of headhunting in order to deal with these feelings. As Rosaldo told NPR, "They need to take a human head and throw it. I was just stunned. I said I've never heard this kind of feeling with this intensity in my life."

Our guess is that you cannot identify with the tribe's use of headhunting as a mechanism for dealing with the emotion surrounding death. Headhunting is a highly uncommon cultural practice (currently there are no known groups practicing headhunting). However, we similarly guess that you can identify with the feelings. Rage, sadness, and a need to do something? These are feelings that we all experience at times in our life. So, while your cultural and linguistic background may not contain a word that is similar to *liget*—the lack of a word in his background was one reason why it was so hard for Rosaldo to initially identify the emotion—you certainly have feelings and experiences that are similar to what the Ilongot experienced.

The emotional and motivational experiences of the Ilongot highlight the relationship between these two aspects of behavior. As we will see throughout this chapter, there is a connection between environmental events—including our social interactions with others—that produce an emotional reaction, and this emotional reaction creates energy that motivates us to engage in behaviors that change the environmental conditions. Emotions are a response to the environment that help to prepare us to deal with the demands of the environment. Emotions feed into our motivational systems to energize and organize our activities.

In this chapter, we explore the psychology of both emotion and motivation. These concepts are important to discuss together, as they are highly connected. The connection begins even with the words "motivation" and "emotion." These two words share a common Latin root, *mot*, which means "to move" (see this site: http://membean. com/wrotds/mot-move for other English words that share this same connection). Our emotional and motivational systems both work to move us forward. Throughout this chapter, we will explore how these two systems work together to shape our behavioral responses to the environment.

Before moving forward, though, take a moment to look at Figure 11.1. This flow chart provides a general conceptual framework for how emotions and motivation work together. We will use this framework as a reference throughout the chapter. As your understanding of emotion and motivation increases, you will come to appreciate that the relationship between emotion and motivation is not as direct as shown in Figure

11.1. Nevertheless, understanding the general progression from environmental event, to emotional reaction, to a change in motivational state, to a direct behavioral response will help you to more easily understand the role of emotion and motivation in not just what you feel, but what you do, what you think about, and how you react to the world around you.

WHAT IS AN EMOTION?

Our emotions have a huge impact on our experience of the world. However, we do not always have a clear understanding of what an emotion is, how or when they influence our behavior, or how they develop. Consider the following statement by Sarah Larson (2017), concerning our understanding of emotion:

> "What are emotions? To what extent are they 'real'? And what should we do with them? These are questions that we've all struggled with. You can squish them down, ignore them, face them, obsess about them, try to figure them out, indulge them. Sometimes you might do all of these in quick succession."

11.1 Conceptual relationship between emotion and motivation
This flow chart that shows the conceptual relationship between emotion and motivation will be used as a reference framework throughout the chapter. However, note that the relationship between motivation and emotion is not as clear-cut as the conceptual figure suggests.

This quotation wonderfully captures the complexity of **emotion**. We know what we feel. We know (some) of the impact that emotions have on our behavior. But emotions are primal. They occur deep inside us and—in many ways—elude our conscious understanding. Even among the scientific community, developing an exact definition of emotion has been a contentious and difficult task.

emotion
the subjective experience of a change in physiological arousal due to environmental events

Despite the challenges in coming up with a single agreed-upon definition of emotion, most scientists agree that emotions include **four components**: an environmental event or trigger, a physiological change (such as increased heart rate, changes in respiration, raised eyebrows, and downturned corners of the mouth), an affective experience (negative, such as pain, or positive, such as pleasure), and cognitive interpretation of the experience. Using these four components, we can build a definition of emotion as the subjective experience of a change in physiological arousal due to environmental events. Emotions are typically brief in duration, triggered by specific environmental events, and associated with specific behavioral responses. Let's explore what an emotion is with an example.

four components of emotion
an environmental event or trigger, a physiological change, an affective experience, and a cognitive interpretation of the experience

Imagine that you are walking across campus to get to your psychology class. As you begin crossing the street—in the crosswalk—a car turns the corner and stops inches from hitting you. You jump back, look at the driver, and notice that they are holding their cell phone in a texting-ready position. How do you emotionally respond to this event? It is likely that you would become mad or angry. Later when telling the story to a friend, you would say something along the lines of, "I got so mad when that texting jerk almost ran me over." Do you notice the four major components of emotion in this example?

A distracted driver almost hits a pedestrian, who responds in anger. Consider how the pedestrian's response follows the four major components of emotion.

- **Environmental event or trigger:** The distracted driver entering the crosswalk interrupts your regular walk and requires additional attentional resources.

- **Physiological change:** The sudden threat to your safety triggers a change in physiological functioning, with your heart rate quickening and a sudden release of adrenaline. You also jump and move away from the oncoming vehicle while orienting toward the driver. You likely furrow your brow as you stare at the driver.

- **Affective experience:** The change in physical arousal associated with the fight-or-flight response is typically viewed as a negative affective state (we don't like being scared—except on those occasions when we choose the experience for ourselves, such as a roller coaster, haunted house, or scary movie).

- **Cognitive interpretation:** The car in the intersection is consciously associated with the negative change in physiological state.

Thinking about how you would later describe your emotional response to this event to a friend, notice that your description almost certainly includes both how you felt *and* the environmental event that triggered the response. As you reflect back on when you talk with people about your feelings, you will notice that your comments almost always include both what you perceived caused the feeling and what you felt. Our perceived cause and its effect are linked together in our experience of the emotion.

mood
a long-lasting, generalized affective state without a direct trigger or target

As we conclude our discussion of the basic components of an emotion, it is important to distinguish emotions from moods. A **mood** is a long-lasting, general affective state that does not have a specific trigger event or target. Throughout this section we have highlighted that emotions are reactions to specific environmental events that serve to focus and energize behavior. A mood—in contrast—is an enduring, often lasting for days, weeks, months, or years, affective state. The exact trigger of a mood is often unknown. Similarly, the motivational target is also unknown. We tend to experience moods not as distinct experiences but rather as a background influence on our emotional experiences. A negative mood seems to enhance negative emotions and weaken the effects of positive experiences. A good mood does the opposite as it buffers against the negative and enhances the positive.

This Is Psychology

A staple on current network television programming is the criminal procedural. Episodes of these shows typically involve a crime, the identification of suspects, an interrogation, and finally the successful resolution of case. The interrogation often involves some technique or trick to determine the veracity of the witness's statements. Frequently, these techniques involve some type of lie detection.

The physiological responses to environmental events that are part of our emotional reactions are the focus of many of these lie-detector technologies. The polygraph test and other lie-detecting technologies include biological measures or arousal, including: heart rate, skin conductance, and respiration rate. The suspect is asked a series of questions that establish a general physiological baseline. The test administrator then begins to ask questions about details of the case. As the suspect responds, the stress and strain associated with lying should be evident in a measured change in these physiological measures.

Unfortunately, the scientific support for lie-detector technologies is not as flattering to the techniques as their popularity on modern television shows would suggest. Rather, the scientific evidence is quite mixed, with a general feeling that there is insufficient support for the use of lie-detecting technologies. The idea of being able to detect lies using physiological arousal is really enticing, but the reality is that there are simply too many reasons why arousal could change across a criminal interview to fully support the interpretation of increased arousal as evidence of lying.

A summary of the current scientific standing of polygraphs and other lie-detecting technologies can be found here:

www.apa.org/research/action/polygraph.aspx

Positive and Negative Affect

Affect is an important component of our emotional experience. We can define **affect** as the psychological experience of our physiological state. Affect is closely tied to our interpretation of our physiological arousal. When arousal is high, we make a subjective judgment of the type of arousal. If the arousal is due to an erotic experience, we typically interpret this positively. If the arousal is due to an unexpected, unwanted experience, we typically interpret this negatively. Notice from this that affect is both our physiological state (aroused, nonaroused) and our interpretation of that state.

affect
the psychological experience of our physiological state

So, what is your affect right now? Take a moment and complete the measure shown in Table 11.1. Once you complete the scale, turn to page 325 for instructions on how to score it.

Table 11.1 The Positive and Negative Affect Schedules

Listed below are twenty feelings or emotions. For each word, indicate how strongly you are feeling this way *right now*. Use this scale to rate your current feelings.				

1 = Very slightly or not at all

2 = A little

3 = Moderately

4 = Quite a bit

5 = Extremely

1. Interested	5. Strong	9. Enthusiastic	13. Ashamed	17. Attentive
2. Distressed	6. Guilty	10. Proud	14. Inspired	18. Jittery
3. Excited	7. Scared	11. Irritable	15. Nervous	19. Active
4. Upset	8. Hostile	12. Alert	16. Determined	20. Afraid

(PANAS; Watson et al., 1988).

positive affect
subjective experience of energy, engagement, and concentration

negative affect
subjective experience of distress and unwanted engagement

This mind map of emotion uses "positive" and "negative" to identify a range of different feelings. Like the roller coaster ride example, can you think of any other physiological responses that might bridge both positive and negative affect?

Now that you have completed the scale, here are some details on what you just did. The survey that you completed is a psychological scale known as the Positive and Negative Affect Schedule (PANAS). The PANAS was developed in 1988 by David Watson and colleagues. This scale includes ten items that measure positive affect and ten that measure negative affect. As presented here, the scale is intended to measure the respondent's affect at the moment they are completing the scale. As the PANAS is intended to measure current affect, scores are expected to change over time as your life experiences change.

It is easy to think that positive and negative affect are two ends of the same continuum. Either I feel good (positive affect), or I feel bad (negative affect). This is not the case. Rather, these dimensions are two different characteristics of our emotional state. Think of these two types of affect as similar to adding water to a bath. You can add hot water. You can add cold water. The final temperature of the bath is a product of how much of each of these that you add. The same is true of our emotional state. We can add positive affect, and we can add negative affect. Our final emotional state is a product of how much of each of these we are experiencing at a given time.

So what is the difference between positive and negative affect? According to Watson and colleagues (1988), **positive affect** is related to energy, engagement, and concentration. Someone who scores high on positive affect would be engaged, alert, attentive, and active. High positive affect is associated with emotions such as gratitude, happiness, and joy. Low scores on positive affect are associated with being disengaged, lethargic, and inactive. High **negative affect** has more to do with our feelings of distress and unwanted engagement. High negative affect is associated with emotions such as fear, guilt, and shame.

Elevated levels of positive and negative affect are both associated with activation of the limbic system. The defining characteristic of this activation is often the desirability of the activation. Positive affect is high following a ride on a roller coaster. The high level of physiological arousal is the product of a sought-after experience. On the other hand, high negative affect is associated with a near accident in an automobile. Physiologically, the response to the roller coaster ride and the near accident share a very similar profile. Both result in strong arousal of the sympathetic nervous system. Contextually, though, the perception of the events is very different. How we interpret arousal is very much a product of the context, our learning history, and our cultural context.

Concept Recall

1. What are the four major components of an emotion?
2. How is mood different from emotion?
3. What all is included in the physiological changes associated with emotion?
4. How do positive and negative affect differ from each other?

THEORIES OF EMOTION

Trying to understand emotion has been a philosophical and artistic pursuit for thousands of years. Attempting to provide a scientific explanation is more recent but has been a part of psychology since its earliest days. The psychological scientist's current understanding of emotion is largely influenced by three historical theories: the James-Lange theory, the Cannon-Bard Theory, and the Schachter-Singer theory. We review each of these theories below.

The earlier description of your hypothetical response to almost being hit by a car while crossing the street presented a very particular order of events leading up to your emotional response. In our description of your emotional reaction to this event, we described the physiological responses to the event, the affective change, and, finally, the cognitive labeling of these states as "mad" or "angry." Notice that this order of events says that the physiological changes came first, with the emotion following as we consciously evaluated our response to the environmental event. This order of events is most consistent with the **James-Lange theory of emotion**, which we first introduced in Chapter 3. According to William James (1884), an American psychologist, and his contemporary Carl Lange (1885), a Danish physiologist, emotions are the cognitive labels we give to the behaviors caused by the physiological states triggered by environmental events. In this theory, the emotion is a reaction to the environment rather than the cause of the reaction. In our earlier example, you felt mad because of the threat response to nearly being hit. While the James-Lange theory of emotion has

James-Lange theory of emotion
the theory that environmental events trigger physiological responses that we then label as particular emotions

been challenged and revised over the years, it remains a highly influential theory of emotion, largely due to its influence on the role of the physical body in our experience of emotion (Dagleish, 2004).

A key component to the James-Lange theory is that the "emotion" is a cognitive label given to the physiological change produced by an environmental event. Figure 11.2 gives a depiction of this series of events. First, a dog jumps out and barks. If you are like Shawn, your heart begins racing, you start to sweat, and you jump back and away from the unexpected dog. At this point, the conscious monitoring of your behavior determines that you are feeling afraid. Why? Because you acted afraid. The emotion is the subjective label used to describe your physiological state. Had Shawn not

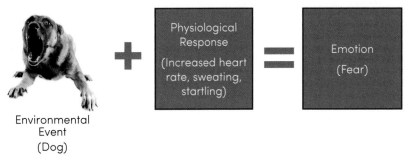

11.2 James-Lange theory of emotion
This figure illustrates the James-Lange relation between environmental stimulus and physiological response to the stimulus. The resulting emotion is the subjective label given to the changed physiological state.

startled at the dog, he might have said that he was feeling "brave" or "courageous." Notice that the James-Lange explanation is different from the typical belief that we see the dog, get scared, and then the fear of the dog causes us to jump back and away from the dog. In the more typical way of thinking of emotion, the feeling (fear) drives the response (startling). James-Lange reverses this and argues that the emotion is a label to describe the response to the environment, not the cause of it.

Cannon-Bard theory of emotion
the theory that the physiological response and emotional response to a stimulus occur simultaneously

The **Cannon-Bard theory of emotion** suggested a different sequence for how we interpret emotions. This theoretical approach argues that emotional experiences do not follow a set path from the physiological response to the emotional experience but rather that the physiological and emotional events occur simultaneously. When an emotion-inducing stimulus is presented, we have a physiological response to these events, and *at the same time* we experience the emotional response. Similar to the James-Lange theory of emotion, Cannon-Bard places emotion in the physiological response of the brain but suggests that we have one set of pathways (motor and sensory pathways) that is involved in the physical response to the stimulus and a second (hypothalamus and amygdala) that is simultaneously processing the emotional content of the stimulus. Returning to the example of Shawn's fear of dogs (Figure 11.3), once the dog jumps out, Shawn quickly experiences both the physiological changes and the feel of fear. These happen simultaneously and are mediated by different areas of the brain.

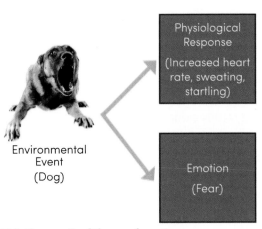

11.3 Cannon-Bard theory of emotion
Distinct from the James-Lange theory of emotion, the Cannon-Bard theory of emotion suggests that physiological response and emotional events occur simultaneously. While they're both similar in their emphasis on physiological changes as a result of environmental events, they differ in their temporal order of events.

A comparison of the James-Lange and Cannon-Bard theories shows that both are similar in their emphasis on the importance of the physiological changes produced by environmental events in our emotional experiences. Both theories are biological theories of emotion that serve to embody the emotion in the physiological response. The major difference is in the temporal order of events. The James-Lange theory posits that the events occur one after the other, while the Cannon-Bard theory says that they occur at the same time.

While the previous emotions focused on the physiological experience of emotion, the **Schachter-Singer two-factor theory of emotion** focuses on the interaction between our physiological arousal and the cognitive interpretation of the context in which the emotion occurs. According to this theory, we experience an environmental trigger that produces a physiological change. We determine our emotion both by looking at the physiological change (factor 1) and by looking into the environment to determine what was responsible for the change (factor 2). The emotion that we experience is a product of both biology and our interpretation of the context. In the example of almost being hit while crossing the street, the physiological response and the cognitive appraisal of the car as the source of the arousal lead to a general feeling of anger toward the driver. But why do we turn to anger and not fear? Part of the reason why we become angry at the driver is because of our history with drivers who use cell phones being distracted and causing problems. Our interpretation of the context drives our emotional response, and our interpretation of the environment is strongly shaped by our previous experiences, thoughts, and feelings.

Figure 11.4 shows the Schachter-Singer two-factor theory explanation for Shawn's feelings of fear around the dog. As acknowledged in both of the previous theories, the appearance of the dog triggers a physiological response. At the same time, Shawn looks around for a source of the arousal. Seeing the dog, he thinks, "Man, I'm scared of dogs. I remember when I was younger and the big dog we owned would jump on me, and all of the dogs in the streets when I lived in Chile." The attribution of the feelings of arousal to the dog leads to the experience of fear toward the dog. Could Shawn's reaction have been different? While the sudden appearance of the dog would likely cause arousal in anyone, people with a more positive history with dogs may interpret the feelings of arousal not as fear, but as excitement at meeting a new "best friend." The exact interpretation of the arousal depends on the cognitive interpretation of the event.

An interesting prediction of the Schachter-Singer theory is that

> **Scoring Instructions for Table 11.1**
>
> **Positive Affect:** Add the scores for items 1, 3, 5, 9, 10, 12, 14, 16, 17, and 19.
> **Negative Affect:** Add the scores for items 2, 4, 6, 7, 8, 11, 13, 15, 18, and 20.
>
> Scores range from 10 to 50, with higher scores representing greater affect.
>
> According to the initial report of the PANAS, the average Positive Affect score was 29.7 (SD = 7.9), and the average Negative Affect score was 14.8 (SD = 5.4) for people asked to report what they were feeling at the moment they completed the scale (Watson et al., 1988). You can compare your scores on the two categories to these averages to get an idea of how your feelings at the moment you completed the scale compared to the 660 participants who completed the PANAS back in 1988.

Schachter-Singer two-factor theory of emotion physiological arousal and the cognitive interpretation of the context in which the emotion occurs

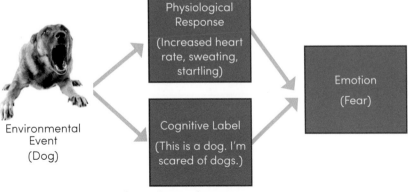

11.4 Schachter-Singer two-factor theory of emotion
This theory argues that emotion is based on two factors: physiological arousal and cognitive label. It is known for its discussion of the possibility of mislabeling emotions when the source of the response is ambiguous.

From the Desk of Dr. Stith

Recall the last time you were asked to intervene in a crisis. It may have been to help a distraught little brother or sister find a misplaced favorite toy or blanket. It might have been last week, responding to a friend's "messy breakup." You may have already been faced with what to say or do with a friend who you were worried might harm himself. What you said or did was a crisis intervention in someone's personal trauma. And as you already know, it may or may not have been helpful. Yelling at your sister that she needs to keep track of her own things isn't going to help her. Reminding your friend at his moment of difficulty that he always makes lousy choices in girls is not a good idea. Ignoring the hurt and desperation when someone is "giving up" can leave you and them feeling helpless.

Professionals who are trained in crisis intervention have developed skills that enable them to quickly assess the immediacy and risk of a crisis situation and help the person move beyond feeling "out of control" and "immobilized." All of us can learn and use some of those basic skills when confronted with personal crises. It also helps to remember an individual in the midst of a personal crisis is feeling out of control and overwhelmed. Emotions are ramped up, and behavior is restrained. They need someone else to actively listen, to avoid judgment, and to help reassert some personal control in the situation. Listen, and assure them that you are there and together you can figure out the next step. Then, help them decide on a next step so they regain some control over the crisis.

All professionals are taught (and sometimes even they forget in the heat of the moment) to ask for help. If the crisis seems overwhelming to you, or you don't know what you should do, ask others for support. You also can call crisis lines—toll-free numbers that address a number of traumatic situations—and ask them what they think would be helpful. Professionals consult with each other in tough situations all the time; so should you.

Randy C. Stith, PhD

we may be prone to errors in our emotional labels. When the source of the arousal is more ambiguous, misattributions of arousal may occur, and the arousal may be mislabeled (e.g., fear mislabeled as sexual arousal), or the triggering event may be misidentified (e.g., opposite-gender person rather than dangerous situation; Wirth & Schramm, 2005). The possibility of this misattribution is hinted at in an exchange that happens between Keanu Reeve's character—Jack—and Sandra Bullock's character—Annie—at the end of the 1994 blockbuster *Speed*. After the highly emotional events of the movie, Annie comments that, ". . . relationships that start under intense circumstances, they never last." Several minutes later, Jack says, "I have to warn you, I've heard that relationships based on intense experiences never work." (It appears that Jack and Annie were prescient in this statement, as Annie is no longer with Jack at the start of the sequel *Speed 2: Cruise Control*.) So, why is it that relationships started during highly emotional times may not last? According to Schachter-Singer, one explanation could be that the feelings of attraction to the other person are a misattribution. In the movie *Speed*, Jack and Annie were highly physiologically aroused due to speeding through Los Angeles in a bus wired with explosives. This scenario would be enough to cause anyone's heart to start racing. In addition to dealing with the explosives, they were also interacting with each other. In these kinds of high-emotion situations, some of the arousal can be attributed to not just the contextual triggers but also to the other people in the room, leading to the mislabeled emotion of "love" or "attraction" due to the experienced arousal.

These three psychological theories of emotion highlight different aspects of the emotional experience. However, an overall review of the theories helps us see the pattern described in Figure 11.1. An environmental event triggers a physiological reaction, which causes physiological arousal that is then interpreted and labeled.

THE BASIC EMOTIONS

Emotional interpretations are subjective and do vary cross-culturally. But are there some emotions that are basic to all people? Despite the variety of experiences that people have, doesn't the universality of our basic experience suggest that there would be some emotions that are fundamentally the same, regardless of experience or culture?

One of the first scientists to explore the universality of basic emotions was Charles Darwin. Yes, the same Darwin famous for the theory of evolution. Darwin's third major book on evolution published in 1872 with the title *The Expression of the Emotions in Man and Animals*. This book explored the expression of emotion across species and concluded that to a large extent, the facial expression of emotion was very similar for all forms of life. Much of Darwin's support for the ideas proposed in this book came from the analysis of photographs of different organisms in a variety of contexts. Snyder and colleagues (2010) showed that Darwin's investigations used both his talents for observing the natural world, and controlled (for his day, not necessarily meeting the standard of today's scientific methodologies) experimental work, in which he showed a series of photographs developed by French physician and physiologist, G. B. A. Duchenne. Based on these initial studies, Darwin concluded that while our facial muscles can be used to create a wide variety of expressions, there is only a subset of universally recognized emotions, such as happiness, sadness, fear, and surprise (Ferris, 2010).

The modern emotion researcher Paul Ekman (2009) summarized Darwin's contributions to our modern understanding of emotion:

- Emotions are found across species, not just in humans.

- Emotional processes are genetically determined and shared across a species and closely related species.

- We experience discrete, separate emotions, such as fear, anger, and disgust.

- Facial expressions are tied to distinct emotional states.

- Muscle movements can be signals of particular emotions.

six basic emotions
anger, disgust, fear, happiness, sadness, surprise

Not too surprisingly, Darwin's work emphasized the potential evolutionary role of emotions. In humans, the connection between facial muscles and emotional states may increase our overall evolutionary fitness by allowing for quick communication of emotional information between people (Ray, 2012).

A more modern approach of Darwin's use of photographs for studying the universality of human facial expressions was taken up by Paul Ekman in the 1960s and 1970s. Ekman showed photographs of people with different facial expressions to people in different countries, including Argentina, Brazil, Chile, Japan, and United States. He also ran versions of the study with a primitive tribe in New Guinea. Cross-culturally, Ekman found that people were equally good at identifying the emotional state of the person in the picture and of telling which pictured expression would go with a story describing a particular emotional experience, regardless of their cultural background (Ekman, 1999). Based on these studies, Ekman proposed **six basic emotions**:

- Anger
- Disgust
- Fear
- Happiness
- Sadness
- Surprise

11.5 Facial responses to emotion
Ekman identified six basic emotions because they all had a unique facial expressions that could be identified cross-culturally.

Ekman identified these as the basic emotions because they each had a unique facial expression that was identified across the cultures and peoples that he included in his study (see Figure 11.5).

While these emotions are universally recognized, there is a great deal of cultural variability in when they are displayed. For example, let's consider disgust. Disgust is most often tied to smells and tastes. Disgust is commonly triggered by bodily liquids (blood, urine, vomit), feces, and the smell of food that has gone or is going bad. But what specific foods?

11.6 Thai dish rod duan
Rod duan is a dish from Thailand made primarily of fried silkworms. Now knowing the ingredients, did you experience a feeling of disgust? Westerners who actually try the dish report it tastes somewhat similar to French fries.

While a quick glance at the food shown in Figure 11.6 might look like a pasta dish, the picture actually shows a food from Thailand called rod duan—fried silkworms. Does the pile of fried worms still look enticing? Our guess is that most of the readers of this text would be strongly opposed to eating this particular food. If forced to do so, they would most likely experience an extremely strong feeling of disgust. However, the readers of this text who are from Thailand, or have spent a great deal of time immersed in their culture, will experience a much weaker or nonexistent disgust response toward this food.

As the example of rod duan demonstrates, the disgust response—while universal in facial expression, subjective experience, and physiological response— is highly malleable to individual experience. Cultural context and early learning experiences are critical to many of the types of foods that produce the disgust response.

Happiness is similarly a function of cultural context. In the United States, personal victories are associated with a strong happiness response. The success of our colleagues, roommates, siblings, and so forth is often associated with a negative reaction, jealousy. Individuals from a more collective society, such as Japan, would likely experience happiness upon learning of the success of members of their group. The facial expressions, physiological changes, and affective state of the emotion are the same across the two cultures, but the environmental triggers for these emotions differ based on individual and group experiences.

Concept Recall

1. What is the major difference between the James-Lange and Cannon-Bard theories of emotion?

2. Under what conditions does the Schachter-Singer two-factor theory of emotion predict we might make emotional errors?

3. What are the six basic emotions?

This Is Psychology

Can a computer interpret your emotional state? Companies such as Noldus, creators and distributors of the FaceReader software (www.noldus.com/human-behavior-research/products/facereader) believe that it is possible. Tech giant Apple, Inc., appears to be similarly interested in the ability of machines to read emotions with its 2016 acquisition of the emotion detection software company Emotient (Eddy, 2016).

Emotion-detecting software relies heavily on the research into basic emotions. Darwin's, Ekman's, and other researchers' work into the basic facial expressions correlated with different emotional states provides the basic foundations for these technologies. Computer scientists create algorithms that identify specific facial markers (such as ears, eyebrows, the corners of the mouth, and so forth) and then calculate changes in the facial configuration as different stimuli are presented. There is evidence that these algorithms can be extremely accurate in automatically quantifying the emotional state of the participants.

Noldus's FaceReader software is marketed as a research tool for behavioral and market researchers. However, the technology could have many additional uses. For example, Adrienne LaFrance (2015) reported on current research into the ability of facial recognition software to detect depression based on the type of smile observed in participants. Imagine a mental health app that could be used to provide assessment of current emotional functioning or a basic diagnosis of psychological state. It is not outside the range of possibility that a "virtual counselor" could be developed that would respond to the emotional content of the user's response to various prompts.

A more pessimistic view of these technologies was discussed by Sam Levin (2017) in an article to *The Guardian*. Levin's article focused on work by Michal Kosinski that suggests facial recognition software can predict sexual orientation. Dr. Kosinski predicts that facial recognition software will be able to predict political orientation, IQ, criminal tendencies, personality traits, and other private behaviors.

What makes the power of these technologies especially concerning is that our faces are typically considered public domain. That is, stores, stadiums, and public cameras can record our faces without our explicit permission. Think about all of the photos that you voluntarily upload to Facebook, Instagram, Snapchat, and other social media platforms. It is possible that these photos could be passed through facial recognition software that would make predictions about your future behaviors and preferences based on your facial expressions.

Darwin's original idea regarding facial expressions is that they evolved to allow us to communicate social information that is needed to coordinate group interactions. Modern technologies may be able to take advantage of these evolved signals to create an individualized virtual world that is responsive to the emotional and genetic information revealed in our facial expressions.

From the Desk of Dr. Stith

"Help me!" During a natural disaster, these two words challenge every first responder, volunteer, neighbor, and friend. What do you need? How can I help? Are you safe? When the person calling for help has a disability, has limited mobility, or has a pet they do not want to leave behind, the helper is often faced with increased challenges and difficult choices. Shelters are not always accessible to everyone. Someone with reduced mobility can face severe limitations. In many disasters, rescuers aren't always able to bring the victim's wheelchair or walker in the evacuation vehicle. Likewise, the elderly may require oxygen or other assistance devices that have been left behind, contributing additional stress and anxiety. Necessary medications are often left behind in a hurried evacuation. A person struggling with dementia can have severe anxiety and get extremely agitated with the crowded conditions and chaos of a shelter.

Pet owners are encouraged by the Centers for Disease Control (CDC), the Federal Emergency Management Agency (FEMA), and the Humane Society of the United States to also plan ahead. Most shelters are not allowed to have animals except trained service dogs. Animals are extremely stressed during a natural disaster and more likely to be aggressive and uncontrolled. Individuals who refuse to evacuate without their pet put themselves, other evacuees, and first responders at risk. Rescuers can face agonizing decisions when a child's pet can't be brought out with the child.

Large animals often have to be left to fend for themselves. A recent forest fire in California jumped the fire break, and several horse properties had to be quickly evacuated. The owners were limited to bringing only horses they had trailers for, and most had to release some or all of their other horses to escape the fire as best they could. In this instance, many but not all were successfully picked up in a round-up following the fire.

Plans for pet safety cannot be left to the last minute. Local animal shelters can help you develop your plan and tell you what options are available in your area long before a disaster limits the options for your pets. The staff and volunteers at a shelter want everyone to be safe, and they will work to address special needs even in the most difficult circumstances. But to be truly prepared, it starts with us and/or our caregivers to have an emergency evacuation plan in place.

Randy C. Stith, PhD

EMOTIONS IN CONTEXT

Our introduction to the science of emotion highlighted the four characteristics of an emotion, the major theories explaining emotion, and the six basic emotions. There are two major themes that we hope you will take away from this discussion: emotions are responses to environmental events, and emotions exist to help energize and direct our behavior. While we often believe that our behavior is slave to our emotion (I yelled because I was angry), it is important to recognize that we most often feel a certain way in response to the way that we are acting (I'm angry because I was just yelling).

A major reason why emotions have such an impact on our behavior is because they occur outside of our conscious awareness. The environment triggers a physiological response, and we respond to these physiological changes. While we occasionally experience powerful emotions (such as the feeling of disgust at possibly eating fried silkworms), most of our emotional changes are much smaller. These low-level emotions shift our responses to environmental events, even though we do not consciously recognize that our level of arousal has been shifted. Advertisers, politicians, writers, and movie directors understand the powerful influence of the subtle emotional shift on our behavior. These groups often take advantage of these reactions to shape our behavior to line up with their products, politics, stories, and movies.

MOTIVATION

Motivation refers to the processes that energize us to behave in certain ways and in certain contexts. Motivation includes the conditions that activate behavior, the types of behaviors that are engaged, and the persistence of these behaviors under similar environmental conditions (Ryan & Deci, 2000). Interviewers often try and determine what the motivation is for a candidate seeking a certain job, school, or other placement. Motivation ranges from basic physiological processes, such as seeking food, safety, shelter, or sexual opportunities, to more transcendental processes, such as a need to achieve or belong. It is common to ask questions about a person's motivation. Why did this person do something? What is this person trying to achieve?

Cross-Cultural Case

How Humans Show Grief

Grief, like so many of our emotions, easily crosses and connects people from different cultures. However, cultural beliefs about death and the grieving process are as varied as the people who follow them. In the West, we expect a deceased person to be removed to a funeral home or mortuary as close to immediately following death as possible, and once memorial services are held, Westerners' interactions (if they can be called such) with the deceased's body are at an end. This is not the case with many other cultures. For example, a recent study by Amanda Bennett published in National Geographic Magazine traces the funeral practices of the Torajan peoples of Indonesia who, after treating the deceased with a cocktail of water and formaldehyde to prevent putrefaction, keep the body in their house for anywhere from a few weeks to a few years. All the while, the family includes the dead family member, referred to as to makulá, or sick person, in everything from meals to prayers. Even after the deceased is buried, family members return to the grave every few years to remove and clean the corpse, changing its clothes, and often posing for pictures with it. While Westerners grieve death as the end of their relationship with a loved one, the Torajans grieve death as an evolution. As Bennett notes, the Torajans "are probably more deeply connected than we are to the way people everywhere feel death: the desire to stay connected . . . to believe that people don't ever really die . . . to have, and to become, an ancestor."

Muslianshah Masrie / Shutterstock.com

motivation
the processes that energize us to behave in certain ways and in certain contexts

People very commonly ask motivation questions when they observe someone's actions. This is particularly true of highly unexpected news stories. Asking, "Why would they do that?" seems to be a nearly automatic response to receiving information about a person—or an animal for that matter—that does not line up with the expectations for a given situation. What are the forces that motivate the way people behave? As we will see in this section, motivation describes biological impulses as well as social and psychological influences.

As we discuss motivation, there are two important elements to remember. First, there is a big difference between describing (goal of science #1 from Chapter 2) and explaining (goal of science #3) behavior. When people ask "why," it implies that they are asking for an explanation, but the answer that is given is often a description. A motivational question that could be asked is, "Why did the child climb onto the countertop?" A possible answer is, "to get a cookie." While it may be true that the child got a cookie while on the counter, the answer fails to explain why she engaged in climbing on the counter to get a cookie. Expanding the answer to include, "She was hungry and wanted a cookie," provides a more thorough answer to this question, so long as there is a reason beyond the observation of the child climbing on the counter and getting the cookie to support the assumption that the child was hungry. A motivational explanation of the behavior needs to explain the behavior without making reference to the observed behavior (in order to avoid circularity) and must provide a possible causal reason for the behavior. In this way, a good motivational theory is descriptive, predictive, and explanatory (the first three goals of science, as introduced in Chapter 2).

proximate explanations
a causal explanation of behavior that focuses on immediate situational and physiological factors

Second, most behavior can be explained at two levels. **Proximate explanations** of behavior explain the immediate factors—both situational and physiological—that influence a behavior. A child climbing the cupboard to get a cookie can be explained by reference to the time since the child last ate and the availability of food alternatives in the environment. This is a proximate explanation in that it focuses on the factors in the immediate context or situation. **Ultimate explanations** focus on the evolutionary reasons for the behavior. An ultimate explanation for why the child climbed on the counter would focus more on the adaptive function of foraging and the role of calories in maintaining fitness. These levels of explanation are not exclusive as they both answer the same "why" question, but they do so by looking at the question from a different level of analysis (or perspective). Throughout this chapter, we will discuss both proximate and ultimate explanations for what motivates our actions.

ultimate explanations
a causal explanation of behavior that focuses on the evolutionary forces and functions of the behavior

Biological Theories of Motivation

Maslow's Hierarchy of Needs
this theory proposes that we have genetically determined physiological needs that drive our behavior

Our physiological system is designed with very specific motivational networks that help us to survive. As you have experienced after having gone for a long period of time without eating, hunger can be a powerful motivator for action. An even more powerful motivator is the need to breathe. The last time you either chose or were forced to hold your breath for a long period you experienced the irresistible impulse to inhale when blood oxygen levels fell. These basic physiological needs form the foundation for the biological theories of motivation.

Abraham Maslow contributed strongly to our understanding of motivation with his **Maslow's Hierarchy of Needs** (1987), Figure 11.7. This theory proposes that we have genetically determined physiological needs that drive our behavior. Consistent with the hierarchy of needs introduced earlier, these needs range from basic physiological needs (food, water) to safety needs (shelter, protection) to social needs (belonging, companionship) to self-esteem needs (recognition, respect), and finally to self-actualization (becoming the best self a person can become). Our behavior is driven by the order of unfulfilled needs, with lower-level needs being addressed before higher needs. For example, a child who lacks atten-

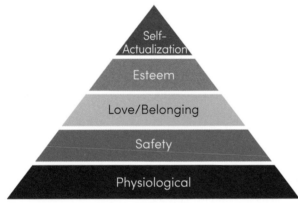

11.7 Maslow's Hierarchy of Needs
The stacked pyramid representation of Maslow's Hierarchy of Needs places basic human needs as the base of the pyramid with more sophisticated needs toward the top, culminating with self-actualization: the fulfillment of one's talents, potential, and abilities.

tion at home will be driven more by the need to gain the teacher's attention (a social need) than by the need to achieve good grades (a self-esteem need).

Maslow's hierarchy theory

Maslow's theory provides some perspective on your approach to schoolwork and employment. As illustrated in the example above, students who have unmet needs in the lower levels of the hierarchy will lack motivation to address the needs higher in the hierarchy. Similarly, employees who are struggling to meet basic needs will not perform well on the more social or abstract aspects of their job. To illustrate this, consider the effects of school or workplace bullying on performance from the perspective of Maslow's hierarchy theory. A student or employee who feels socially threatened will have unmet safety and social needs. Most of the behaviors that a teacher or employer needs from the individual are more in the self-esteem levels of the hierarchy (a powerful motivator for work behavior is a feeling of accomplishment and excellence). So long as the threatening social situation exists, motivation for the higher-level behaviors will be lacking.

Muchinsky (2003) points out that Maslow's need hierarchy theory is more "philosophical than empirical" (p. 378). In terms of validity, the theory has great **face validity** in that it sounds good and fits well with our thoughts or expectations about how people should behave. It makes sense that someone who is starving would not focus on how well he or she fits with his or her social group or if the person is really living life the way he or she wants. Unfortunately, Maslow's theory has been difficult to support with empirical research due to the abstract nature of the needs and strong interconnections between the levels.

face validity
the degree to which a psychological theory or assessment appears to be effective or accurate

Evolutionary theories of motivation

Evolutionary psychologists attempt to understand motivation in a similar way to Maslow, but without the emphasis on the hierarchy of needs. Instead, evolutionary approaches to addressing why behavior occurs focus more on ultimate explanations for the behavior. According to this approach, we are motivated to engage in behaviors that increase our overall **genetic fitness**, which is the likelihood to continue living and to pass the genes on to the next generation through reproduction. Meeting any of the needs identified by Maslow would increase the genetic fitness of the organism. Unlike Maslow, evolutionary psychologists do not believe that needs must be met in any particular order. Under the right conditions, engaging in social behaviors can be better for our genetic fitness than foraging for food, even when hungry.

The evolutionary psychology approach assumes that cultural practices have developed to reflect our evolutionary motivations, and motivations that suited our ancestors may not be well suited to our modern environment. To understand how these two assumptions fit together, consider the modern obesity epidemic. When hungry, people are highly motivated to eat foods that are high in calories, salt, and sugar. This strategy is well adapted to an environment in which calories are hard to find (requiring foraging,

Evolutionary theories of motivation suggest that increased rates of obesity in industrialized countries may be related to humans' evolutionary motivation to seek out calorically dense foods. Fast food giants have capitalized on this motivation, offering cheap foods high in sugars, salts, and various types of fats.

conflict
any challenge to the organism's genetic fitness

lifetime reproductive potential
the potential number of offspring that an organism could produce in its lifetime

hunting, and preparation), and salts and sugars are found primarily in fruits and vegetables, food items that are extremely high in other essential vitamins and minerals. As culture has advanced, science and technology developed agriculture, refrigeration, and food processing. All of these advances make it easier to meet the evolutionary motivation to find and eat high-calorie, salty, sugary foods. Thanks to these developments, genetic fitness in industrialized nations skyrocketed. So did obesity and other so-called diseases of civilization (e.g., diabetes, heart disease). Fast food providers have flourished due to our evolutionary motivation to eat the foods they provide. In this way, our fast food culture is the product of our evolved desires. The lack of an evolved strategy to deal with a modern environment that is overflowing with food is creating all kinds of problems. In this way, our evolved strategies are poorly fit to our modern environmental context.

As illustrated with the connection between obesity and evolved food preferences, evolutionary psychology explains motivation as the pressure to resolve conflicts. In this sense, a **conflict** is any challenge to the organism's genetic fitness. Conflicts can occur in many different ways. As we review the conflicts, notice the similarity between the categories of conflict and Maslow's hierarchy of needs. *Environmental conflicts* occur as the organism works to solve the problems of shelter and protection. Skin pigmentation is an excellent example of an evolved solution to an environmental conflict. *Interspecies conflicts* occur as two or more species try to share the same ecological niche. You encounter a species conflict any time you find a spider in your house or apartment. The spider wants the shelter and potential food sources. You want the spider gone. What is good for you is bad for the spider's genetic fitness. Unfortunately for the spider, the battle between homo sapiens and arachnids leans strongly in our favor. The final major class of conflict that we are evolutionarily motivated to solve are *intraspecies conflicts*. This type of conflict occurs as members of the same species interact, either cooperatively or aggressively. Intraspecies conflicts include mate selection, parenting, friendships, work coordination, and warfare. In all of these conflict situations, the perceived threat to the organism's genetic fitness encourages the organism to do something in order to address the conflict.

Men and women experience the same types of conflicts as they interact with their world, but physiological differences result in different motivations and solutions to these conflicts. The explanation for differences in motivations across men and women are tied to differences in **lifetime reproductive potential**. Men have a much greater lifetime reproductive potential than do women. While both men and women reach puberty at approximately the same age, the number of children that a woman can produce is limited by the menstrual cycle (fertilization of an egg can only occur for about four days in a twenty-eight-day cycle), length of pregnancy (nine months), and shorter reproductive life span. Men don't have the same constraints on their lifetime reproductive potential. These differences between men and women produce very different challenges to genetic fitness. For example, parenting has different evolutionary costs for men and women. For a man, producing a new child is relatively low cost both in terms of resources and time commitment. For a woman, each child is very costly in both resources and time. For a man, time spent interacting with existing children is time not spent creating new children. In short, lifetime reproductive potential in males is negatively correlated with parenting time. For a mother, time spent investing in her existing children does not have as direct an impact on her lifetime reproductive potential. Instead, during the infertile days of her cycle, a mother best helps her genetic fitness by investing in her existing children. Increasing genetic fitness for men and women—with regard to lifetime reproductive potential—requires vastly different strategies.

As we conclude our discussion of motivation and evolved strategies, there are two important cautions to consider. First, similar to Freud's idea of the id and unconscious influences on behavior and personality, the drive to solve evolutionary conflicts occurs outside of our conscious awareness. When a potential rival begins flirting with someone in whom you have romantic interest, you experience jealousy. You likely have never *consciously* thought, "This person is threatening my genetic fitness! I must put a stop to this right now!" (at least not before reading this section of the chapter). Similarly, when you see a spider in your apartment, you don't think about the risk that it might pose to your genetic fitness. Instead, you feel disgusted, scared, or annoyed. The emotions we feel as we interact with the world are the proximate explanations for our action. The increase in genetic fitness is the ultimate explanation for the behavior. Our conscious experience is typically tied to the proximate causes, while our unconscious motivations are typically tied to the ultimate causes of the behavior. As stated in the introduction to this section, proximate and ultimate explanations are not competing explanations, but different levels of explanation.

Second, any discussion of evolved motivations must address the **naturalistic fallacy**. The naturalistic fallacy is erroneously equating "natural" with "good." Evolved behavioral strategies are tied to environmental conditions that existed in the organism's past. Moral questions—questions about how we should or shouldn't behave—are tied to existing cultural and social conditions. In other words, "what we do" is driven by the natural process of evolution, and "what we should do" is driven by cultural considerations, and thus they are two separate questions. Evolutionary psychologists explore the conditions that shaped current motivations and behaviors. As a society, we must actively engage in discussions and dialogues about what behaviors are right or wrong. We discussed earlier in the chapter our evolved motivations to eat foods that are high in calories, fats, and sugars. This is our biological motivation, but is it right? Should we eat this way? What about the personal costs of this pattern of eating? The social costs? Questions like these are answered differently than the scientific questions about the behavioral motivations influencing our food choices.

naturalistic fallacy
the erroneous belief that biologically based motives, feelings, or behaviors are morally right or wrong

Concept Recall

1. What is motivation?

2. How does Maslow's hierarchy theory of motivation differ from the evolutionary theory of motivation?

3. Why does lifetime reproductive potential differ from men to women?

Reinforcement Theory of Motivation

Biological and evolutionary models of motivation are connected to the environmental conditions that existed for our ancestors. Reinforcement theories of motivation focus more on the conditions that exist *after* the behavior and are based on the operant conditioning model of B.F. Skinner. As discussed in Chapter 7, operant conditioning occurs when the consequences of a behavior—the way it changes the world around the organism—become associated with the behavior. An employee who learns that calling in sick will get her or him out of work without any unpleasant consequences has been reinforced for this behavior. In this way, the reinforcement theory of motivation argues that motivation is directly tied to the person's history of reinforcement, with people being motivated to engage in the behaviors that have resulted in positive experiences in the past and to avoid behaviors that have resulted in negative experiences, and that motivation is largely determined by factors that are external to the organism. Psychologists often refer to this as **extrinsic motivation**. If a teacher or employer provides an environment that is rich in reinforcement, the person will be highly engaged and motivated.

extrinsic motivation
behavior that is activated by stimuli in the environment surrounding the organism

Reinforcement approaches to motivation have both strong support and criticism. The careful management of consequences (both reinforcers and punishers) and the use of schedules of reinforcement have been empirically supported in education and the workplace. So have the negative consequences of poorly managed behavioral interventions. Critics of the use of reinforcement in applied settings (e.g., schools, work, health care) argue that external reinforcers reduce the **intrinsic motivation** to engage in particular behavior. The argument is that the use of reinforcement to motivate behavior results in actions that only occur in particular settings, when the reinforcer is available, and that these conditions might force individuals to engage in behaviors that they find unethical or inappropriate.

intrinsic motivation
behaviors that are motivated by thoughts, feelings, and values that are inside the individual

Many of these are concerns that mirror most people's experiences with work. Imagine what would happen to your work or school performance if the external pressures for working or studying were suddenly removed. What if you were not going to be quizzed on any of the information from this book? Would you read it? Our guess is that for most of you, if your instructor were not holding you accountable for reading this book, you would not currently be reading this sentence. Similarly, if your employer suddenly stopped paying you, you would stop going to work. If this is the case for you, then your school and work behavior is driven by extrinsic motivation. If you are one of the lucky few who would study and work without tests or pay, then your behavior is driven by intrinsic motivation. Applied behavior analysts—scientists who actively apply reinforcement theory to behavior in school and work contexts—argue that a primary goal of any reinforcement program is to use external motivation to create intrinsic motivation. As you will read in the following section, proponents of social theories of motivation argue that intrinsic motivation must exist first in order for people to be happy in their actions.

Social Theories of Motivation

Many theories of motivation are less directly tied to our biological needs, evolutionary challenges, or reinforcement history and focus more on our social connections. Anecdotal evidence in support of a strong social drive is easy to find. Social media applications account for the majority of activity on smartphones, the Internet, and other modern technologies. Movie theaters, classrooms, libraries, and other public areas are straining to find strategies that will get participants off social media and re-engaged with their venue's offerings. You have likely noticed (and been guilty of being—as have your authors) the people who pull out their phones the instant that class or a meeting ends. We have noticed that many students are engaged with texting, chatting, or phone calls before they even leave the classroom.

Roy Baumeister and Mark Leary (1995) proposed that people are fundamentally motivated by a **need to belong** as part of their belongingness hypothesis. According to their framework, people are motivated to create and maintain deep, personal, lasting social connections with at least a few people. These relationships must include a certain degree of social, psychological, and emotional reciprocity—the give and take that exists in established relationships. Baumeister and Leary argued that our need to belong is marked by two main characteristics: people are motivated to engage in frequent, personal contacts with the same people, and people perceive a degree of "connection" in these interactions. A perceived lack in belongingness results in personal distress and increased social seeking—attempts to form new social bonds and connections. In this way, our need to belong becomes a fundamental motivation for our behavior.

need to belong
people tend to have an 'inherent' desire to belong and be an important part of something greater than themselves

Another approach to understanding how social context can motivate behavior is Self-Determination Theory (SDT; Ryan & Deci, 2000). Similar to the belongingness hypothesis, SDT argues that we are highly motivated to be engaged in meaningful social interactions. Behavior is influenced by the need to develop competence (the ability to perform skills accurately and fluently), relatedness (a degree of connection between the self and others, directly comparable to the need to belong), and autonomy (the belief that events and experiences are individually caused, rather than forced upon us). The idea of autonomy is most directly tied to the idea of intrinsic motivation for behavior. Ryan and Deci argued that when behavior is driven by internal forces—such as our values, thoughts, and feelings—the person will be much happier and better adjusted. People are highly driven to engage in social interactions as they facilitate meeting the needs of competence, relatedness, and autonomy.

This Is Psychology

Andy Warhol—American artist, producer, and director—once said, "In the future, everyone will be world-famous for fifteen minutes." The rise of social media technologies seems to be creating a world in which Warhol's prediction can come true. These technologies allow for individuals to have a greater individual reach than ever before, to easily and quickly create digital records of their exploits, and for the low-cost distribution of these digital records.

But what is the motivation that drives people to social media? According to a report released by the American Psychological Association (Winerman, 2013), social media use is motivated by both a need to belong and the need for self-presentation. The need to belong is a motivational pressure to be part of a social group and receive social support from others. Self-presentation motivations are the need to present ourselves in a way that "matches" the expectations of the perceived group and of the self. Social media usage can meet both of these needs by allowing people to feel connected with not only the people in their immediate real-world social networks, but also virtual networks that extend across geographical constraints. Self-presentation needs can be met by allowing the user to upload photos, memes, stories, and so forth that fit either the perceived expectations of the target group or the individual's desired presentation.

Unfortunately, while social media usage may be motivated by the need to belong and the need for self-presentation, there is evidence that social media usage may not fully meet these needs. According to research discussed by Winerman, increased usage of social media can provide feelings of increased connectedness with others, but it often does not address underlying issues of loneliness. While we are able to learn about others and share our stories with them via social media, a large portion of our online interactions are not in real time. Our connections lack the social reciprocity that is part of a real-world interaction, where we can see, hear, and directly experience the other person. A major element missing from online interactions is the ability to detect and interpret the emotional content that is conveyed by the speaker's facial expression, voice tone, and body language (yes, you can use emoticons, but these are not sufficient substitutes—even though they are cute). Video chats allow for a closer inspection of the emotional content of the message, but lag time in the video, buffering, and the resolution of the image or audio stream still reduce the social and emotional impact of these interactions.

The power of social media technology is evident in how quickly it has become a ubiquitous element of modern life. However, balance is needed between virtual satisfaction of social needs and direct, human-to-human interactions.

Motivation in Context

Understanding motivation is a key concept in understanding behavior. Motivational theories strive to answer both why and when we will engage in different activities. A general assumption is that we do what we are motivated to do. Whether behavior is driven by basic biological needs, social needs, or internal needs to achieve or belong is debated across the breadth of psychology. Because questions of motivation are so fundamental to how we act, most of the major theories of behavior, including behavior analysis, cognitive psychology, evolutionary psychology, psychodynamic theories, social psychology, humanistic psychology, and others, have very strong ideas regarding motivation. Each explains what drives our behavior from its individual perspective.

Motivation is especially important with regard to work and school. Employers strive to maximize the work they get out of employees. Their motivation is to maximize their earnings. Your motivation is to pay your bills, but it is also to find a social niche, have fun, and reach your personal goals. Industrial/organizational psychologists work to create situations where the needs of both employees and employers can be met. Google, Facebook, and other companies have received a great deal of publicity lately for their attempts to integrate corporate and personal needs into their work environments.

What "motivates" us at any given point in time is a complex interplay between our physiological, psychological, social, and cultural context. Maslow's hierarchy of needs correctly captures the idea that behavior serves needs across multiple levels. However, his hierarchical approach creates a false idea that we are driven by any one need at a given time. Instead, our behavior occurs as the product of the interaction between needs at multiple levels.

Concept Recall

1. What is the reinforcement theory of motivation?
2. Define need to belong. What are the two main components of the need to belong?
3. What are two theories on how our social context influences motivation? How do these differ from each other?

MOTIVATION AND EMOTION

This chapter provides an overview of our modern understanding of our emotions and motivations. As discussed at the beginning of the chapter, both of these concepts are about the forces that shape our behavior. Emotion is the subjective experience of our physiological reactions to environmental events. Motivation refers to the processes that energize and shape our behaviors. Emotion and motivation refer to distinct processes that are shaping our behavior at any given moment. The connection between emotion

Country artist Dierks Bentley's silly song "What Was I Thinkin'"? highlights the struggle and constant interplay between motivation and emotion. Although the subject of the song realizes what he's doing, he can't seem to intervene in his own actions early enough!

and motivation can be highlighted with the lyrics from the Dierks Bentley song, "What Was I Thinkin'?" Here is some of the chorus:

Out the other side she was hollerin' faster

Took a dirt road and had the radio blastin'

Hit the honky tonk for a little close dancin'

What was I thinkin'?

Oh, I knew there'd be hell to pay

But that crossed my mind a little too late...

'cause I was...

Thinkin' 'bout a little white tank top sittin' right

There in the middle by me

I was thinkin' 'bout a long kiss man just gotta get

Goin' where a night might lead

I know what I was feelin'

But what was I thinkin'... what was I thinkin'

This song highlights the interplay between emotion, motivation, and cognition. Our protagonist clearly identifies the environmental influences on his behavior and the effect that these have on his emotions. Despite recognizing the causes of his feelings and actions, he is a little confused about the "why" of his behaviors.

As we think about our actions, we can all identify with this song. We know what we are feeling. We often know the consequences of the actions that we "feel" like engaging in. Nevertheless, we often find ourselves driven to engage in behaviors, despite the consequences that we know will follow. We all do this, but it is especially true of people with addictions or other "bad habits." By better understanding our emotions and motivation, we can begin to take control of our behavior. As we learn to apply a scientific lens to the frequent question of "Why? Why would they do that?" we grow in our ability to understand and predict the actions of others—and ourselves.

REVIEW

- What are the four components of emotion? Provide an example of each component.

- Define emotion and mood, and note the primary difference between the two terms.

- How do the James-Lange and Schachter-Singer two-factor theories of emotion differ?

- What does the Schachter-Singer two-factor theory of emotion predict about our interpretations of our emotions? Give an example representing this prediction.

- Though more specific emotions may differ cross-culturally, what six basic emotions are able to be identified universally, and what purpose might this serve?

- What does Maslow's hierarchy theory suggest? Does this affect the way we are motivated to pursue certain needs above others?

- What is one of the problems with finding empirical support for Maslow's theory?

- What does the biological theory of motivation imply about our needs and the motivations to address those needs? What might the biological theory neglect to address?

- What are the two types of motivation that are outlined by the reinforcement theory of motivation, and what is the difference between the two?

- Why is understanding both motivation and emotion important to the goals of psychology (to describe, predict, and explain)?

1. According to Rosaldo's experience, what does the term *liget* mean?

   a. Grief

   b. Rage

   c. Intense energy

   d. All the above

2. Responses to the environment that help to prepare us to deal with the demands of that environment are defined as which of the following?

   a. Rage

   b. Headhunting

   c. Mindfulness

   d. Emotions

3. Our _____ has/have a _____ impact on our experience of the world.

   a. perception; negative

   b. motivation; positive

   c. emotions; huge

   d. triggers; negative

4. Todd walked into a dark garage, and suddenly he experienced a physical arousal associated with a flight-or-fight response; according to the text, this was an

   a. emotional reaction.

   b. affect trigger.

   c. environmental trigger.

   d. affective experience.

5. Which of the following is not true of emotions according to Darwin?

    a. Emotions are found across species, not just in humans.

    b. Muscle movement can be signals of particular emotions.

    c. Emotions are stable over time only in humans.

    d. Facial expressions are tied to distinct emotional states.

6. Regarding responses to environmental events the _____ comes first, and it is followed by the emotion.

    a. cognitive labeling   c. psychological changes

    b. emotional Affect   d. none of the above

7. Motivation is central to our _____ and _____.

    a. sadness; environment   c. perception; proximations

    b. behavior; contexts   d. genetics; perspectives

8. Motivation describes _____ _____ as well as _____ and psychological influences.

    a. physical;readiness; current   c. biological; impulses; social

    b. proximate; explanations; present   d. none of the above

9. According to evolutionary theories we are motivated to engage in behaviors that will increase our overall _____ _____.

    a. reproduction; opportunities   c. evolutionary; perspective

    b. genetic; fitness   d. none of the above

10. As illustrated with the connection between obesity and evolved food preferences, evolutionary psychology explains motivation as the press to _____ _____.

    a. successfully; reproduce   c. reduce; conflict

    b. resolve; conflict   d. enhance; reproduction

REFLECT

1. Think back to a recent emotional experience, and try to identify the four major components of that emotion: trigger, physiological response, affective state, and cognitive interpretation. How do you think being aware of these four components of emotion can help you better respond to emotional situations?

2. Have you ever misattributed your physiological arousal to the wrong emotional experience? Think back to times that you believed you were feeling one emotion but later discovered that this emotion did not fit the experience. Why do you think this happened?

3. Identify three activities that you feel are extremely important to you (e.g., sports, music, social groups). What motivational needs do you think these activities/groups satisfy? Explain the motivation for these activities using two of the motivational theories described in the text.

Answer Key

1.d 2.d 3.c 4.d 5.c 6.c 7.b 8.c 9.b 10.b

WRITE

1. What is happiness? Conduct a web search for websites from different countries or cultures that provide a definition of happiness. How do these definitions differ across cultures? What similarities are present from culture to culture? Write an analysis of the cultural influences on what makes us happy and how happiness is valued across cultures.

2. Does social media use meet our social needs? Using a database such as PsycINFO, PsycARTICLES, or Google Scholar, identify three peer-reviewed articles that discuss social media and social needs. Analyze the findings in the articles for strengths and weaknesses of social media for meeting our social needs.

Key Terms

affect   321
Cannon-Bard theory of emotion   324
conflict   334
emotion   319
extrinsic motivation   336
face validity   333
four components of emotion   319
genetic fitness   333
intrinsic motivation   336
James-Lange theory of emotion   323
lifetime reproductive potential   334
Maslow's Hierarchy of Needs   332

mood   320
motivation   330
naturalistic fallacy   335
need to belong   337
negative affect   322
positive affect   322
proximate explanations   332
Schachter-Singer two-factor theory of emotion   325
six basic emotions   327
ultimate explanations   332

After reading this chapter, you will be able to answer the following questions:
- How do the different theories of personality view and explain personality development?
- What are the Big Five traits?
- What are the id, ego, and superego, and how do they relate to personality?
- What is the purpose of defense mechanisms?
- What is self-actualization?
- What is self-efficacy?
- What is the difference between an external and internal locus of control?
- What is the purpose of personality assessment?

Harry Potter's first major challenge upon arriving at Hogwarts was being sorted into the appropriate "house." As it turns out, students attending Hogwarts School of Witchcraft and Wizardry are assigned to one of four houses (Gryffindor, Hufflepuff, Ravenclaw, and Slytherin) in which they will live and work during their time at the school. Each house is distinct. Students sorted into the different houses have similar values and characteristics to their housemates, but different from those in the other houses. For example, the two houses that most directly play into the story of the Harry Potter books are Gryffindor and Slytherin. Gryffindor is associated with bravery, loyalty, and wisdom. Slytherin is associated with cunning, ambition, and resourcefulness. Harry Potter is a Gryffindor. Lord Voldemort is a Slytherin. How do we know this? Because the Sorting Hat told us so.

But how does the Sorting Hat know? The Sorting Hat is a magical item (a fictional magic item) that declares the first-year student's house—and, in many ways, destiny—after being placed on the student's head at the beginning of the year's opening banquet. Using its magic, the hat looks inside each student to examine what he or she is made of and then chooses the house where that student will best "fit." The assumption of the Sorting Hat is that there is something unique and stable about the individual that will predict the individual's behavior in different situations. By measuring this "something," the hat can assign the student to the house that will provide her or him the best opportunity to thrive and grow during that student's time at Hogwarts.

Sorting by magical hat? That's a really weird idea. We find it fairly safe to bet that you have never experienced selection by Sorting Hat (if you want the experience, though, you can find plenty of online sites that will tell you in which house you belong). While you have never been sorted by hat, you have experienced the same procedure as using the Sorting Hat. Think back to the last interview you had. Was it for employment? Maybe it was for college admissions or a scholarship. Perhaps you were seeking membership into an organization, like a sorority or fraternity, or a Greek honors society, like psychology's Psi Chi, the International Honor Society in Psychology (www.psichi.org). What sort of questions did the interviewer ask? Certainly, if you were trying to get a job, you would have prepared your resume and fielded questions about your work experience. You likely would have discussed your education and other related qualifications. If you were rushing a fraternity or sorority, members may have asked you questions about the extracurricular activities you participated in during high school; in the same vein, questions like "How would you get involved on campus as a member?" and "Why do you want to join?" seek to find out your membership goals. Admission into honors societies—very formal on some campuses and quite informal on others—tend to focus on your degree program and coursework.

While interviews often try to investigate your drives and ambitions, they also focus heavily on qualitative assessments.

Have you ever been asked during an interview, "Would you consider yourself a perfectionist?" How about, "What attributes do you think you would contribute to our organization?"

Jacquelyn Smith writing for *Business Insider* notes that the modern employer isn't necessarily looking for abundant technical skills and experience as much as a strong set of "soft" skills—or those related to personality. She quotes Edward Fleischman, CEO of recruitment firm Execu|Search: "If [an employer finds] a candidate who has less experience than [his or her] competition, but has stronger growth potential and seems to be a better cultural fit, the employer may feel encouraged to hire that person" (Smith, 2014). Smith notes a number of questions interviewers ask specifically to assess personality, such as, "If your best friend was sitting here, what would he or she say is the best part about being your friend?" Smith also suggests a question such as, "If you were an animal, what would you be, and why?" reveals how well applicants can think on their feet and apply some creativity in a short amount of time.

Employers, scholarship selection committees, and online dating sites do not use the same magic as the Sorting Hat, but they are trying to do the same thing as they decide whether you would be the right employee, award recipient, or dating partner. Just like the Sorting Hat, they are trying to look inside you to see the unique and stable parts of you. By asking questions and conducting assessments that reveal your underlying structure, they believe that they can better assign you to roles, tasks, and opportunities where you will succeed.

PERSONALITY DEFINED

personality
a person's relatively consistent pattern of thinking, feeling, and behaving

This chapter explores the general principles and theories associated with personality psychology. **Personality** refers to a person's relatively consistent pattern of thinking, feeling, and behaving. The elements of our personalities tend to remain very stable from situation to situation and across our life spans. One of the authors of this text, Shawn, is a reserved, quiet person. This is true in pretty much all contexts. Even when teaching, a job that requires being much louder and more engaged than how he normally acts, Shawn continues to be more reserved than other instructors. Shawn has to actively work to be sufficiently outgoing in the classroom to keep students engaged with the material. Ken, another of the authors of this text, on the other hand, is much more outgoing and socially engaged. This is true in all contexts. Ken's more outgoing approach to social interaction makes it much easier for him to engage with students in the classroom. Both Shawn and Ken are able to engage students during their class discussions, but the structure and feel of how they accomplish this is very different due to the distinctiveness of their personalities.

Views of Personality

Ancient approaches to studying personality focused on the nature side of "nature vs. nurture," exploring its connection to human biology. Hippocrates developed the biological theory that humans' four bodily fluids, or "humors," and their proportions determined a person's personality. In fact, the word "humor" has its origins in Hippocrates's theory. While the biological view of personality still carries modern significance, personality theory is now more focused on psychological and environmental factors.

A more modern view, the trait perspective on personality first theorized by Gordon Allport, is primarily descriptive—referencing the goal of science (Chapter 2), which aims to provide information on how behavior looks in form and over time—giving us a way to understand the characteristics people exhibit through recognizing patterns. This view attempts to capture the major patterns of personality using several key traits and their corresponding characteristics. Other viewpoints speak more to how our personalities are formed and why. For example, the psychodynamic viewpoint looks at our internal psychological workings, particularly the unconscious and basic drives that fuel personality development quite early. The psychodynamic views of the mind constitute the classic Freudian concepts of id, ego, and superego.

Where the first three views tend to focus on the nature of personality, the behavioral and social cognitive perspectives focus more on personality development and how our environment and our responses to it drive our personality development, and the humanistic viewpoint focuses on a more positive drive to fulfill our potential as the source for personality development. The first three viewpoints also tend to conceptualize personality as having discrete elements and discontinuous stages. The latter three describe a more continuous process (remember these themes from our discussion of how to conceptualize development at the beginning of Chapter 5). As you read, think about the differences between each of these theories and how they build on each other.

Coming full circle, we end the section on personality by looking at how we can describe and assess personality through standardized, agreed-upon means, rather than through observation. Personality assessment is an important psychological area and widely used in employment as well as mental health arenas. If you have not taken a personality test up until this point, don't worry. You will have many, many opportunities throughout your life!

Biological view

As mentioned in the previous section, the earliest approach to describing personality was developed by the ancient Greek physician, Hippocrates (460–377 BCE), based on his ideas about four bodily "humors," or fluids: black bile, yellow bile, blood, and phlegm. According to Hippocrates, the humor that predominated in an individual determined that person's characteristics. For example, if you possessed a predominance of black bile, you were quiet, analytical, and prone to depression (melancholy). If you had a predominance of phlegm, you were relaxed and peaceful. While the notion of these four humors is no longer widely accepted, the idea that at least part of personality is biologically based remains valid.

Another biological approach that has come and gone is the idea of personality being connected to body shape (Sheldon & Stevens, 1943; Sheldon, Stevens & Tucker, 1940). William Sheldon noted that there are three basic body types, or somatotypes: endomorphs are round, mesomorphs are rectangular, and ectomorphs are thin. He argued that each body type was associated with a particular personality. Endomorphs are outgoing and love comfort, mesomorphs are energetic and assertive, and ectomorphs are restrained and lonely. Sheldon's correlations did not hold up in subsequent research. While the scientific evidence does not support the view that body shape and personality are connected, there are social stereotypes (see Chapter 15) that suggest different body shapes are associated with expected behavior patterns. In most cases, the way we "see" people of different body shapes acting is not a part of their personality, but their behavioral reactions to the attitudes and actions of others toward them based on cultural and social stereotypes and prejudices tied to body shape.

Although there is little research to support the idea that body type is related to personality, researchers continue to investigate the influence of other biological factors. One of these factors is a person's general level of neural arousal. As technology has advanced, so has our ability to conduct research on the biology of our behavior, and with these advances psychologists have found that the personality characteristic, extroversion, is associated with lower levels of brain arousal than its opposite, introversion (Johnson, et al., 1999; Wacker, et al., 2006). This idea that outgoing, engaged people (extroverts) tend to seek stimulation from a variety of sources helps explain some of the individual differences in levels of social engagement. Brain scans show that a frontal lobe area involved in behavior inhibition is more active in introverts than extroverts, implying that introverts are more inhibited and less sensation-seeking than extroverts (Johnson, et al., 1999). This may be a reason why you'll find more extroverts at most parties, as well as in line for the giant roller coaster the next time you visit an amusement park. As extroverts tend to be more visible, there is a tendency to believe that it is better to be extroverted than introverted. This is not always the case, as is argued by Susan Cain in her 2012 bestseller *Quiet: The Power of Introverts in a World that Can't Stop Talking*.

Because extroverts tend to be more visible than introverts, like at parties, there is a misconception that extroversion is superior to introversion.

Our biology influences our personality in other ways as well. Much of our personality is tied to our genes, which help determine our temperament. Our genes influence our temperament, which then influences the behaviors that help define our personality. For example, Jerome Kagan has attributed differences in children's shyness and inhibition to their autonomic nervous system (ANS) sensitivity; you may remember from Chapter 3 that the ANS controls organ activities, such as heart rate, breathing, and digestion. A child with a more sensitive ANS reacts to stressful situations with greater anxiety and inhibition (Kagan, Reznick, & Snidman, 1988). This is not to say that introverted children (and adults) never do things like rock climbing or skydiving. It just takes more effort for them than someone described as curious or fearless.

Trait view

When we describe people, or pets, we use summary terms that capture their particular stable and enduring tendency to respond in a certain way: shy, outgoing, kind, aggressive. In psychological circles, these are known as **traits**. The trait view of personality can be traced back to Gordon Allport, who was influenced by Sigmund Freud, even though Freud was not exploring traits. Allport's experience with Freud actually moved him toward trying to describe people's consistent behavior rather than trying to understand what was underneath it, as Freud aimed to do.

There are many different traits that can be used to describe people, so how do we efficiently capture personality? Personality psychologists have spent a good deal of time looking at this issue, trying to determine which traits are the most important. Allport came up with 4,000 traits and then grouped them into central traits, which combine to dominate behavior, and secondary traits, which may be more limited or situational. He also thought that there could occasionally be a single, or cardinal, trait that so dominates a personality that the person and the trait are viewed as one and the same. A good example of this is honesty in Abraham Lincoln, a trait so evident that the moniker "Honest Abe" was given to him in early adulthood and remained past his death.

While Allport's theories remain influential, later researchers narrowed down the number of personality traits. Raymond Cattell used factor analysis to reduce the number of traits to sixteen; he theorized that we all have these traits to varying degrees. He developed the 16PF (Personality Factors) questionnaire, an assessment instrument used in a variety of areas, from career selection to couples' counseling. Figure 12.1 illustrates Cattell's sixteen personality dimensions along with the hypothetical profiles for two occupations, Career A and Career B. As illustrated in this figure, completing a 16PF assessment provides a score for each of the 16 dimensions. The patterns of scores create a "profile" of the client's personality. Scores on these dimensions should not be thought of as "good" or "bad." For instance, consider the score on the dimensions of "private" to "forthright." Is it better to be more private or more forthright? It really depends. People who are very forthright probably don't make very good espionage agents, but they likely make great television hosts.

Cattell and Mead (2008) listed the 16PF as being used in employee selection, promotion, development, coaching, outplacement counseling, and career exploration. Extensive research of literature has correlated scores on the sixteen dimensions with performance in different work responsibilities, settings, and roles. Trained psychologists (most of whom earned graduate degrees in industrial/organizational psychology) analyze the pattern of scores on the sixteen dimensions, compare these with characteristics of work as shown in Figure 12.1, and then make predictions about how well an employee will fit with different job demands. With a growing emphasis on career planning during high school in the United States, it is

traits
summary terms that capture an individual's stable and enduring tendency to respond in a certain way

President Abraham Lincoln earned the moniker "Honest Abe" as a result of a clearly evident personality trait that became his public persona. Can you think of any other people with similar nicknames?

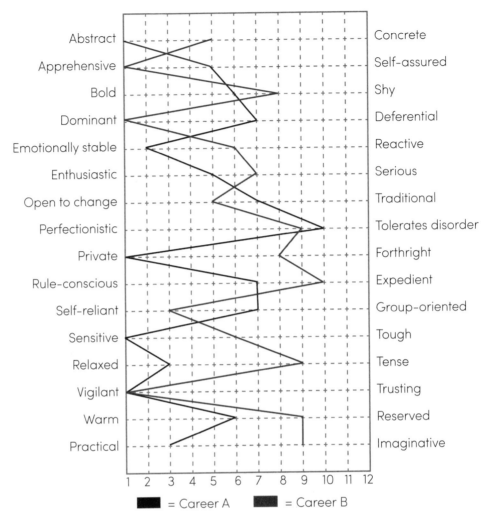

12.1 Personality factors
Personality profiles for jobs are investigating the personality characteristics of successful people in those careers. When you take a career assessment, the evaluator tries to match your personality profile with one associated with a particular career.

very likely that you have taken a version of the 16PF in the past. If you have not done so already, we encourage you to contact your institution's career services office to investigate the career development resources that they provide.

extroversion
one of the Big Five personality characteristics indicating where a person gets his or her energy; an extrovert feels 'recharged' by social interaction, whereas an introvert feels recharged by being alone

While Cattell felt that personality was best defined using sixteen characteristics, Hans Eysenck placed importance on just one or two dimensions—introversion/extroversion and stability/instability. These dimensions can be viewed as perpendicular to each other, creating a "+"-shaped axis like the x-y coordinate system used in mathematics. Similar to the use of the x-y coordinates in math, we can plot our "personality" as the intersection of our score on the two axes of "introversion/extroversion" and "stability/instability."

There tends to be confusion over the meaning of introversion and **extroversion**. These two concepts refer to the source of a person's energy. An extrovert draws energy from social interactions and being engaged with other people. An introvert draws energy from inside. Introverts are recharged by time spent in personal reflection and thinking. In popular discussion, these two concepts are often confused with being shy or outgoing. Introverts are not necessarily fearful, anxious, or hesitant to engage in social situations. Extroverts can be socially awkward, fearful of social interaction, or plagued by social anxiety. The caricaturized view of the extroverts in the middle of the dance floor and the introverts sitting along the walls is correct, so long as we remember that both the introvert and extrovert are perfectly happy being in those spots!

At present, consensus favors an approach that lies between Cattell's sixteen factors and Eysenck's two factors. The Big Five (Costa & McCrae, 2009) theory conceptualizes personality as a combination of five dimensions. These are most easily remembered through an acronym, such as OCEAN: openness to experience, conscientiousness, extroversion, agreeableness, and neuroticism, shown in Table 12.1.

Table 12.1 The Big Five theory of personality

Trait	Characteristics	Example
Openness	Imaginative, original, accepting of new ideas	Leonardo da Vinci
Conscientiousness	Organized, careful, disciplined	Michelle Obama
Extroversion	Outgoing, fun-loving, and affectionate	Eddie Murphy
Agreeableness	Helpful, empathetic, and trusting	Fred Rogers
Neuroticism	Anxious and insecure	Marlin (*Finding Nemo*)

One of the best ways to understand these traits is to look at examples of people who fit the dimensions. **Openness** refers to how imaginative and independent a person is: Leonardo Da Vinci's volume and variety of work makes him a good example of a very open person. If a person is organized, careful, and disciplined, the person is considered **conscientious**. Michelle Obama is sometimes given as an example of such a person—this trait has likely helped her succeed in her work as a lawyer and as First Lady. Extroversion refers to how outgoing, fun-loving and affectionate a person tends to be. Most of the movie roles played by Eddie Murphy are extroverted, including Donkey in the Shrek movies, for whom Murphy provided the voice; Donkey befriended Shrek immediately after meeting him, and during almost all of Donkey's time onscreen he chatters continuously. If a person is high in **agreeableness**, she is helpful, empathetic, and trusting; Fred Rogers parlayed this trait into a career that positively impacted thousands of people through his television show, *Mister Rogers's Neighborhood*. Marlin, Nemo's dad in *Finding Nemo*, is remembered well for his **neuroticism**—being highly anxious and insecure. Neuroticism is also used to great comedic effect in many fictional characters, such as Leonard Hofstadter in *The Big Bang Theory*, Ross Geller in *Friends*, Woody Allen in his many comedies, and Rex in *Toy Story*. Table 12.1 provides a more complete description.

openness
one of the Big Five personality characteristics indicating a willingness to try new experiences

conscientious
one of the Big Five personality characteristics indicating a tendency to be organized, careful, and disciplined

agreeableness
one of the Big Five personality characteristics indicating helpfulness, empathy, and trust

neuroticism
one of the Big Five personality characteristics indicating a tendency toward anxiety and insecurity

The Big Five have been found to be stable in adulthood, with three (openness, extroversion, and neuroticism) waning a bit during early and middle adulthood and the other two (conscientiousness and agreeableness) rising (McCrae, 2011; Vaidya, et al., 2002). Biologically, the evidence suggests that these traits are about 50 percent heritable across countries (Loehlin, et al., 1998; Yamagata, et al., 2006) and are associated with identified brain areas (DeYoung, et al., 2010).

Do the Big Five traits actually predict behavioral attributes? Yes, they do. Research has found, among other things, that highly conscientious people earn better grades in high school and college (Poropat, 2009), and couples who are about the same on openness, agreeableness, and neuroticism experience greater sexual and marital satisfaction (Botwin, et al., 1997; Donnellan, et al., 2004). Personality traits are even associated with how we use social media. People who are more conscientious are more cautious regarding what they present about themselves on Facebook, while those higher in neuroticism, extroversion and agreeableness are more open about presenting their actual self (Seidman, 2013). However, while the Big Five and other trait theories do have predictive validity, they are not infallible.

Cross-Cultural Case

Personality Across Cultures

Cross-cultural psychology is a subfield of psychological study that considers the impact of cultural influence on personality and psychopathology. The Big Five dimensions of psychology make comparison across cultures feasible, as researchers could, theoretically, apply the dimensions to any person. In the years following the establishment of the Big Five theory, researchers hypothesized that the Big Five would remain consistent across cultures, despite the many differences in cultural factors: language, religion, political systems, sociocultural values, or historic impacts. McCrae and colleagues undertook one of the most extensive tests of this hypothesis, called the Personality Profiles of Cultures Project, or PPOC, in 2005. The researchers composed a group of college students from 50 distinct cultures and identified 11,985 individual "targets"—defined in the study as adult or college-age females or males—and rated them using a version of the NEO Personality Inventory, which takes the Big Five personality traits and breaks them down with six subcategories under each, creating 30 traits. The study revealed that the American self-report structure that influenced the development of the Big Five was replicated in most cultures and was at least recognizable in all of them. With few exceptions, the PPOC Project proved the existing hypothesis that personality traits across cultures are not only consistent across like cultures, i.e. Western or Eastern groups, but also are common to all human groups. What kind of study would you design to further research on cross-cultural personality similarities and differences? What factors of culture do you think influence personality development the most? The least?

People's characteristic way of reacting can change with the situation. In Chapter 15, you will encounter a research study by Stanley Milgram in which participants were asked to administer painful electric shocks to another person (or so they thought—the shocks were faked). It is highly unlikely that the participants in Milgram's study would be described by their friends and family as cruel or unfeeling, but many participants behaved that way in the experiment. This is known as the **person-situation controversy**. We change in less extreme circumstances as well: in familiar, less formal situations, we are more likely to "be ourselves," or allow our traits to emerge, while others will see less of who we are in unfamiliar or more formal situations (Buss, 1989). Ultimately, situations do influence and even change our behavior. However, if we average our behavior across many situations, clear personality patterns do emerge (similarly to what happens with general intelligence if you average people's mental performance across many different situations and activities). The trait perspective has also been challenged on the basis that, while it describes behavior, it does not explain it. In other words, the trait perspective may tell us what people do but not why they do it. For that perspective on personality, we need to look at approaches that have been around for a while: psychodynamic, behavioral, social cognitive, and humanistic.

person-situation controversy
a person's behavior is different in different situations

Psychodynamic view

Sigmund Freud, as we will discuss in more detail later, is known as the father of psychotherapy. He was actually a neurologist who developed his theories while working with patients whose issues could not be explained in terms of what he understood about the nervous system. For example, unexplained blindness might be due to the desire to avoid seeing something that provoked intense anxiety. In working with the idea that physical symptoms might have a psychological cause, Freud conceptualized what is now commonly known as the **unconscious** mind. As noted earlier, he wanted to explore the world underneath people's behavior.

unconscious
the part of Freud's structure of mind that remains constantly inaccessible to the conscious mind

Structure of mind and personality

Freud believed that what goes on in our minds is mostly hidden, or outside of our awareness. Psychologists typically use the image of an iceberg to illustrate Freud's thinking. A small part of our minds, the **conscious**, is visible above the water. The conscious mind contains everything you are aware of right now. Like the part of the iceberg near the water line, the **preconscious** is often underwater (consciously inaccessible), but as the iceberg rolls in the surf, it can rise above the waterline. For example, think about how your feet feel pushing down on the ground. Just a moment ago, you weren't thinking about it, but right now you are. In contrast to the conscious that is continually above the waterline and the preconscious that intermittently rises above the water, the bulk of the mind, like the bulk of the iceberg, remains constantly underwater and inaccessible to the conscious mind.

conscious
the part of Freud's structure of mind that is currently accessible

preconscious
the part of Freud's structure of mind that is accessible but not currently conscious

You may be wondering why the majority of what you think and feel on a daily basis would be hidden. According to Freud, you are only aware of those things that you are willing to acknowledge; the remainder is pushed down into your unconscious mind. In understanding Freud, remember Freud's ideas—just the same as our ideas are—were a product of his time, and the Victorian era in which he lived was known for an emphasis on good manners and emotional restraint. He hypothesized that human personality is the product of conflict between impulses and restraint. In other words, our aggressive, pleasure-seeking biological urges constantly strive to express themselves while our internalized social controls try to stop them, or at least appropriately channel them.

To explain this conflict, Freud proposed a three-part structure of personality: **id**, **ego**, and **superego**. The three components of personality (id, ego, and superego) do not map directly onto the three levels of consciousness (conscious, preconscious, and unconscious) but instead are laid out as in Figure 12.2. The id is purely unconscious, forever hidden below the water's surface. The ego and superego are spread across the entirety of the iceberg, including aspects of the conscious, preconscious, and unconscious. The id represents the biological side of our personality. Thinking back on the introduction to the brain in Chapter 3, the id would most closely correspond with the functions of the lower and middle brains—the parts that push us to survive and reproduce through eating, mating, and if we have to, fighting. The id operates on the **pleasure principle**—immediate gratification without regard to future consequences (imagine a newborn baby when it is hungry or uncomfortable and the complete disregard to place, time, or social norms when it comes to letting parents know of the need). We are almost all id when we are babies; at about age two or three, however, the ego develops, to help gratify the id's impulses in ways that will not get us in trouble with the world. The ego operates on the **reality principle** and constantly strives to find a way to express the pleasurable impulses generated by the id while behaving in ways that are socially acceptable. The ego serves as a mediator between the id and the superego, which develops at about age four and is essentially our conscience, or set of ethics. The superego absorbs the rules and expectations of society and generates pangs of guilt when we violate them. It also drives us to behave as we ought to, in ways that we are proud of. The ego is constantly stuck between the pleasure-seeking id and the morality-driven superego and must find a middle ground between the two that will satisfy our desires without arousing conflict with other people.

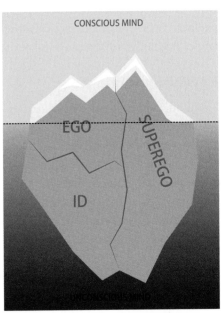

12.2 Conscious vs. unconscious mind
The id is constantly unconscious, but both the ego and superego occupy the conscious, preconscious, and unconscious.

According to Freud, anxiety results when the ego cannot find that middle ground. Freud considered **defense mechanisms** to be the ego's way of reducing anxiety. For

id
the part of Freud's structure of personality that houses primitive desires

ego
the part of Freud's structure of personality that must find a way to act that satisfies basic desires without violating social constraints

superego
the part of Freud's structure of personality that is the conscience, or set of ethics

pleasure principle
the driving force of the id, which constantly seeks gratification of basic desires

reality principle
the driving force of the ego, or its attempts to meet basic needs without violating social constraints

defense mechanisms
processes by which the ego reduces anxiety

example, if you are angry at your professor for making you read this book but do not feel comfortable expressing this anger (until after final grades are posted anyway), you may engage in **reaction formation**—switching unacceptable impulses into their opposite—and be overly cheerful around the professor. Or, you may engage in **projection**, **repression**, or **displacement**, three of the better-known defense mechanisms. You would be engaging in projection if you decided to talk about how upset your friend from class is about the amount of reading assigned by the teacher. By projecting feelings onto another person, it is possible to address the topic without the personal threat. Projection is a favorite strategy for adolescents who wish to talk about their attraction for another person (e.g., "Did you know that Tommy likes Julie?"). Repression occurs when the unwanted feeling or thought is pushed entirely out of consciousness. You might be repressing your feelings toward the instructor if you are constantly forgetting about the reading assignments, course, and other details that you find frustrating. Freud believed that repression underlies all the other defense mechanisms and that it is often incomplete. Finally, you could be displacing your feelings about the course onto your roommates or other safer targets. Instead of telling your instructor what you feel about the course workload, you may choose to yell at your younger brother, a coworker, or a pet. While they may be slightly annoying, the true cause of the anger and frustration is what is at school, not home. As you can see from these paragraphs, the goal of the defense mechanisms is to reduce anxiety through ignoring, changing, or projecting.

Another principle Freud subscribed to was the idea that nothing is accidental. **Psychic determinism** means that our past influences our present, whether we are aware of it or not. In addition, our urges, when not fully repressed, will pop up in dreams or as slips of the tongue. An example of such a Freudian slip is the woman hosting a cookout, who said, "I'll be right back. I'm just going to get the condoms," as she went in for the ketchup, mustard, and relish (condiments). Freudian slips, dream imagery, fixations, and other unconscious influences on our behavior, thoughts, and language are, according to Freud, reflections of thoughts, wants, and desires that we are not consciously willing to accept or address.

reaction formation
a defense mechanism by which a person behaves in a manner opposite to their true feelings, such as an angry person who acts excessively cheerful

projection
a defense mechanism in which unwanted thoughts or feelings are assigned to another person

repression
a defense mechanism in which unwanted thoughts and feelings are pushed out of the conscious into the unconscious

displacement
a defense mechanism in which unacceptable thoughts or feelings about a person or thing are shifted to a more acceptable person or thing

psychic determinism
point of view stating that past experiences influence the present state of mind and that nothing happens by chance

Concept Recall

1. From a modern viewpoint, how does biology influence personality?

2. How would you describe personality from a trait perspective?

3. What impact do experiences have on personality?

4. What are the three basic elements of personality, according to Freud?

5. What is the purpose of defense mechanisms?

This Is Psychology

Psychodynamic theorists, such as Freud and Carl Jung, have placed a good deal of significance on dreams as a means of understanding our unconscious and therefore our personalities. They are not the only ones to find meaning in dreams; Native American and African cultures, Islam, Hindu, and Christianity are among the groups that view dreams as a way to understand ourselves and the world. But does science support this? Generally not. Many researchers think dreaming is a sort of side effect of REM sleep, which has a physiological function, perhaps to regenerate the oxygen in our corneas (Maurice, 1998), rather than a psychological one. So why the often bizarre images? According to Hobson & McCarley (1977), this is merely our brain trying to make sense of random sensory stimuli. Nevertheless, we seem to remain fascinated by what goes on in our heads while we sleep.

PERSONALITY DEVELOPMENT: FREUDIAN PERSPECTIVES

Freud claimed that personality develops as we move through a series of five psychosexual stages (shown in Table 12.2), from the oral stage in infancy to the genital stage in adolescence. These stages are called psychosexual because each stage is characterized by efforts to achieve pleasure centered on various parts of the body. Think about what people of different ages enjoy doing: babies like to suck on toys, pacifiers, or thumbs, while teenagers may experiment with sex. Freud believed that if someone did not achieve satisfactory pleasure in a particular stage, they would get stuck, or become fixated, in that stage, which could surface as maladaptive behavior in adulthood. If you are a heavy smoker, the Freudian explanation is that during the oral stage you were denied the pleasurable outlet of sucking your thumb, so you got stuck in the oral stage. After the oral stage is the anal stage, from about one year old until three years old, during which toddlers are taught to use the toilet. Toddlers who are toilet trained before they're ready can get stuck in the anal stage and become fussy about neatness; this is why adults that obsess over details are sometimes called anally fixated.

Table 12.2 Five psychosexual stages

Stage	Approximate ages	Example of fixation in adulthood
Oral	Birth → 1	Smoking, overeating
Anal	1 → 3	Fussy about neatness
Phallic	3 → 6	Sexual deviancy
Latent	6 → 12	None
Genital	12 and up	If all stages were completed successfully, the person should be sexually mature.

Have you heard of the Oedipus complex? This is another idea of Freud's that is tied to personality development: he believed that during the third, or phallic, psychosexual stage, boys develop unconscious sexual desires for their mothers and jealousy of their fathers. Girls will experience their version of this as well, known as the Electra complex. Freud also thought that girls developed "penis envy"—the realization that boys get more sexual pleasure from their penises that girls do from their vaginas. He believed that it manifested in girls' love for their fathers and their wish to produce sons. Male and female children subsequently have feelings of guilt about the desire toward the opposite-sex parent, jealousy toward the same-sex parent, and often use the defense mechanism of repression to cope. The feelings of guilt also push the child to identify with the same-sex parent, which, Freud theorized, is how we develop our gender identity. The fourth stage is called the latent stage, during which sexual urges are mostly absent. Do you remember a time when you and your friends acted as if members of the opposite sex were "gross?" This was the latent stage, but soon enough just about everyone becomes interested in sex after entering the final stage, called the genital stage.

Karen Horney

If you are thinking that Freud sounds a bit sex-crazed, you would not be alone. In his own time, Freud was considered dirty-minded (Hunt, 2009). In fact, he originally expressed the belief that many cases of hysteria, when psychological conflict manifests in physical symptoms, stemmed from childhood incest. The reaction among his peers was so negative that he retracted this idea and attributed most cases to the complexes described above. Some have said this set the field of trauma psychology back decades (Herman, 1992). Even therapists in the Freudian tradition dispute Freud's strong focus on sexuality. Neo-Freudians such as Karen Horney and Carl Jung did believe that personality is, at least initially, shaped in childhood, and also accepted the unconscious as a key structure of personality. However, they felt that social, rather than sexual tensions are what drive personality development.

Carl Jung

Horney felt that Freud's emphasis on penis envy was much more a reflection of the higher status and privilege males held in the family and society at that time than a biologically driven phenomenon. She even countered that men's desire for professional success and legacy sprung from womb envy—their inability to carry and bear children. Horney also argued that women's emphasis on charm, beauty, and measuring their value through their relationships with others rather than their own accomplishments was the result of their imposed dependence on men rather than a desire to be in that role. Another key point on which Horney parted ways with Freud involved when personality development stops. Freud theorized that personality is almost fully formed when we exit childhood. In contrast, Horney posited that personality has the potential to grow and develop throughout our lives, an idea that influenced the humanistic theorists we discuss a bit later (Held, 2010).

Like Horney, Jung agreed with Freud on the existence and importance of the unconscious and disagreed with him on the role of sexuality, though Jung focused more on creativity and spirituality as our driving forces, rather than gender differences.

Jung also agreed with Horney that our adult experiences and ambitions influence personality development as much as our early experiences. The *This Is Psychology* box for this section discusses dreams, an area that was of particular importance to Jung. One of the main things Jung is known for is his emphasis on the collective unconscious, so called because we share our ancestral and evolutionary past with others, through latent memories, at this level. It should also be noted that Jung's written speculations on introversion and extroversion led to their use by trait theorists, as well as a popular assessment measure to be discussed shortly.

Behavioral and Cognitive Views

While Freud was quite methodical in making the observations that led to his theories, his focus on inner, unobservable processes has often been labeled unscientific. Figures such as Watson and Skinner held that we develop distinct personalities because each person experiences different histories of learned associations, reinforcements, and punishments. Recall from Chapter 7 that we increase behavior patterns that result in pleasant things happening and decrease those that result in unpleasant things happening. For example, Jack acts aggressively because he got others to give him things he wanted and not hassle him through aggressive behaviors in the past, while Natalie is known for having a great sense of humor because people have always laughed at her jokes and antics.

Strict behaviorists believe that our personalities are shaped through direct experience. Social learning theorists, however, argue that we also learn through watching others. Julian Rotter (1990) notes that most of the reinforcers we seek are social (e.g., attention, praise, hugs), and that most learning takes place in social situations. Rotter developed a social learning theory of personality in which cognitive factors, particularly our expectancies, play a role. Imagine you are applying for your first job after college. You probably have some idea of how successful you will be, as well as what will contribute to that success: how applicable your major is to the position, how well you prepared for the interview, whether the interviewer is having a bad day, whether your horoscope is positive, and more. The applicability of your major and your preparation are examples of things you can influence, the interviewer's day and your horoscope are things you can't. We all have expectations regarding how much control we have over situations. Further, we have expectations regarding whether that control extends across settings.

Experiential and social influences

locus of control
the perceived source of control in an individual's life that results in the attribution of events to circumstances either within or beyond the individual's control

Do you think that you control your fate, or do you think that things happen to you without your being able to control them? The difference lies in where you believe the **locus of control** (LOC) resides (Rotter, 1966). Some people have an internal LOC and believe they can influence what happens to them through skill and ability. Others have a more external LOC and believe that what happens to them is due to chance or fate. Let's go back to that job you need to get after college. If you have an internal LOC, you will likely apply for jobs that are directly related to your major as well as gather background on the companies and practice answering interview questions. If you have an external LOC, you are less likely to do these things and may instead check your horoscope before you schedule your interviews.

The locus of control we develop is tied to our cultural background as well as our learning history. Countries such as the United States, which hold taking the initiative in high regard and positively reinforce it when people do, tend to produce more people with internal LOC. Internal LOC has been associated with more participation in the American civil rights movement, better physical health, higher academic performance, and less anxiety (Findley & Cooper, 1983; Strickland, 1989). This is not to say that an internal LOC is always the better one. In fact, there are many situations, such as natural disasters, that are outside of our control, and people who recognize that will have a healthier, more productive attitude in such circumstances than those who believe they should be able to control everything.

Albert Bandura also contributed to the idea that our personalities are a combination of experience and cognitions about that experience. Bandura is well known for his work on **observational learning**, but he also did work on personality. A fundamental question asked by personality psychologists is, "Why do people act the way they do—what creates that characteristic way of interacting with the world?" For Bandura (1986), the answer lies in the idea of **reciprocal determinism.** This model suggests that a person's behavior is both influenced by and influences our cognitions and the environment in which we exist. Imagine a child doesn't like going to school because it is difficult, but doesn't want others to know because he or she fears being seen as stupid. As a result, the child acts out in class. This leads to teachers and administrators in the school disciplining the child and even disliking having him or her in class. The child feels ashamed and unwelcome and acts out further, forcing the adults in the school to administer more discipline, creating a restrictive environment.

Another important component of Bandura's theory is **self-efficacy.** Self-efficacy refers to a person's beliefs about his or her skills and ability to perform certain acts. Greater self-efficacy means more confidence in the ability to deal with the challenges encountered in life. Self-efficacy has been associated with such things as final grades in high school and college and the ability to resist relapse following treatment for substance abuse (Hackett, et al., 1992; Rchtarik, et al., 1992; Zimmerman, Bandura, & Martinez-Pons, 1992).

A person's sense of self-efficacy has a significant impact on his or her behavior, but it is not considered a personality trait because self-efficacy varies by behavior and situation, whereas personality traits are the characteristics that remain consistent across situations. Self-efficacy is influenced by a person's own experience with success and failure, as well as observing others' experiences. For example, by watching other people running a marathon, you can develop feelings of self-efficacy that equip you to run a marathon yourself. Verbal persuasion can also impact self-efficacy, depending on the trustworthiness and expertise of the persuader, such as a personal trainer

observational learning
learning that occurs through observing the behavior of others; modeling

reciprocal determinism
a personality model that posits that an individual's behavior is the result of the interaction between an individual's cognition and the environment within which the individual resides

self-efficacy
the beliefs an individual holds concerning his or her skills and ability to perform certain acts

verbally motivating you to train for the marathon. Finally, self-efficacy can be related to physiological arousal, as we may associate unpleasant emotional states with poor performance and translate that as failure or incompetence (Maddux, 1991).

Humanistic Theories

humanistic theorists
psychologists who choose to focus on the potential for positive growth and achievement in an individual rather than the individual's deficits

By the 1960s, some personality psychologists were dissatisfied with the focus on the often-negative unconscious drives and conflicts of Freud's theory of personality. They were no happier with the theory advocated by the behaviorists, as it essentially boiled personality down to a series of learned responses. The **humanistic theorists** chose to move away from the idea that people are sick or lacking and look instead at their potential for positive growth and achievement. This became known as the "third force" in American psychology.

self-actualization
involves making "the full use and exploitation of talents, capacities, potentialities"

The humanistic approach focuses on the ways in which people try to achieve self-determination and -realization. Its early practitioners also differed from the behaviorists in the way they studied people's development. Rather than observing behavior, they learned about people through self-reported feelings and experiences.

Maslow and self-actualization

Abraham Maslow was one of the first humanist theorists. As we discussed in Chapter 11, Emotion and Motivation, he proposed that humans are motivated by needs arranged in a hierarchy. Maslow's hierarchy of needs begins with our basic physiological needs—things we need to survive, such as food, water, and sleep. Once these needs are met, we move up the hierarchy through a series of needs that are important but not essential to our survival, the last of which is **self-actualization**. According to Maslow, self-actualization involves making "the full use and exploitation of talents, capacities, potentialities" (Maslow, et al., 1970, p. 150).

An element of accomplishment leading to self-actualization is the process of applying for college and eventually graduating, achieving one's potential of receiving a college degree. While Maslow believed most humans rarely achieve self-actualization, he believed qualities such as autonomy, defined moral values, and an appreciation of life could lead to self-actualization.

Maslow developed his ideas through his study of healthy, creative people rather than troubled clinical cases. He looked at people such as Abraham Lincoln, Albert Einstein, and Eleanor Roosevelt, as well as the healthiest 1 percent of college students (Smith, 1978). These people shared characteristics, such as being self-aware and self-accepting, open and spontaneous, loving and caring, and not paralyzed by others' opinions. Because such people are secure in who they are (and likely have strong self-efficacy in several areas), they are problem-centered and outward-focused, often contributing to the world in a positive way by focusing their energy on accomplishing great things. While Maslow believed that we all have a need to achieve self-actualization, he recognized that not everyone manages to meet this need because if lower-level needs are not met, we do not have the time or energy to devote to our full potential. People who wonder where their next meal is coming from or who don't feel safe can be expected to try to meet those needs first before turning their attention to higher-level needs. The lower the need on the hierarchy, the more powerful the pull, and many people do not live in an environment conducive to self-actualization.

Rogers & the person-centered perspective

Carl Rogers concurred with Maslow's belief that people are innately good and are driven toward fulfilling their potential, given the right environment, but Rogers' clinical work convinced him that many people don't have a healthy environment from the start. The "right" environment to Rogers contained three elements: genuineness, acceptance, and empathy. Genuineness consists of honesty and openness, acceptance involves valuing people and even knowing their failings, and empathy is understanding others' feelings and reflecting their meaning. Rogers and Maslow believed that these three elements create a core part of our personality, called **self-concept**, or our perception of our abilities, behaviors, and characteristics. Rogers viewed the self as having two sides: the real self, which is the product of our experiences, and the ideal self, which is the self we would like to be. We act according to our self-concept. The real and ideal selves are a closer match in persons with a positive self-concept. If we have a positive self-concept, then we tend to act in positive ways.

self-concept
an individual's perception of his or her abilities, behaviors, and characteristics

Remember that one of the needs in Maslow's hierarchy is for love—most of us receive love from those who raise us. However, this love (or at least the expression of it) can be conditional, or given only if the person thinks and behaves in ways that are approved of by others. Thus, your self-concept will also be conditional, good only when you feel you have behaved in ways that gain others' approval. If you rarely feel approval (love), your self-concept is likely to be negative. In Rogers's person-centered therapy, which will be discussed in Chapter 14, the therapist creates an environment in which the client experiences unconditional positive regard. In such an environment, the client can feel empowered to bring the real self closer to the ideal self.

The views of Maslow and Rogers have had widespread impact; they have influenced not only the field of psychology but also management, education, and child rearing. We place a good deal of importance on people in all of those settings feeling heard, valued, and fulfilled. However, the humanistic perspective has its critics as well. Some view the humanistic concepts of self-concept and self-actualization as vague and subjective. Such critics worry that Maslow may have based his description of self-actualized people not on scientific findings but on his own values and people he considered heroic (Smith, 1978). Further, when Rogers perpetuated the idea that we should be focused primarily on living in a way that is fulfilling to ourselves, he may actually have moved us away from a path of self-actualization, as Maslow saw it, and toward a more self-absorbed, self-indulgent path (Campbell & Specht, 1985; Wallach & Wallach, 1983).

Concept Recall

1. How did Freud conceptualize the structure and development of personality?

2. How are self-concept and the process of self-actualization important to personality development, according to the humanistic view?

3. What do behavioral psychologists believe about the role of the unconscious and cognition in personality development?

4. How does locus of control impact personality development?

This Is Psychology

The box office success of such movies as *The Martian* and *Everest* attest to our general fascination with people who voluntarily enter extreme environments, whether for work or recreation. Many of us believe that the personality traits of such people are impulsiveness and sensation-seeking, but research has shown that this is only partly true (Barrett & Martin, 2014). Such characteristics do hold for many of those who are engaged in an extreme activity for a short period of time, such as skydiving or bungee jumping. There are a few "professional adventurers," such as British polar explorer, Sir Edmund Shackleton, and Royal Navy combat diver, Commander Lionel Crabb, who definitely fit the mold of "thrill-seeker." However, most people who work or play in extreme environments on a long-term basis are, in fact, much more likely to be conscientious and risk-averse. In fact, personality assessment is used in the selection of people for jobs such as space and polar exploration missions to weed out the thrill-seekers, whose impulsivity could be dangerous to themselves and others. Ed Viesturs, a mountaineer who has climbed all fourteen of the world's peaks above 26,000 feet, has a motto that exemplifies the mindset that led to his success: "Getting to the top is optional. Getting down is mandatory."

objective personality inventory
a self-report questionnaire that clearly asks about a wide range of behaviors and feelings and assesses several traits at once

Minnesota Multiphasic Personality Inventory (MMPI)
the most widely used objective personality inventory, primarily utilized to help diagnose psychological disorders, such as schizophrenia and bipolar disorder

ASSESSMENT OF PERSONALITY

With knowledge of the various approaches and theories of psychology, you understand that there is no cut-and-dried method for defining it. Assessing personality is similarly difficult and has been researched almost as much as personality itself. There are two main ways to get at a person's characteristic way of responding to the world. **Objective personality inventories** are self-report questionnaires that clearly ask about a wide range of behaviors and feelings and assess several traits at once. They are called objective because they are standardized and scored independent of the examiner's beliefs. As discussed in Chapter 10 on intelligence, standardization means such attests are administered and scored the same way every time, and the individual's score is compared to a large, normative sample. The **Minnesota Multiphasic Personality Inventory (MMPI)**, is the most widely used objective personality inventory. It consists of 567 questions in a true/false format. The primary purpose of the MMPI is to help diagnose psychological disorders, such as schizophrenia and bipolar disorder (see Chapter 13).

Another widely used inventory is the **Myers-Briggs Type Indicator (MBTI)**; see Table 12.3. The MBTI was designed based on Carl Jung's typological theory of how we experience the world, with the purpose of helping people find a job that was the best fit for their personality type. The MBTI has since been used additionally in such areas as team building, leadership training, personal development, and marriage counseling. It is also often used on college campuses, so you may have taken it. If you have not and would like to experience a personality assessment very similar to the MBTI, you can go to this link: http://www.humanmetrics.com/cgi-win/jtypes2.asp.

Myers-Briggs Type Indicator (MBTI) a Jungian personality test that has been used in team building, leadership training, personality development, and marriage counseling

Table 12.3 Myers-Briggs Type Indicator (MBTI)

ISTJ	ISFJ	INFJ	INTJ
Management Administration Law enforcement Accounting	Education Health care Religious setting	Religion Counseling Teaching Arts	Scientific or technical fields Computers Law
ISTP	**ISFP**	**INFP**	**INTP**
Skilled trades Technical fields Agriculture Law Enforcement Military	Health care Business Law enforcement	Counseling Writing Arts	Scientific or technical fields
ESTP	**ESFP**	**ENFP**	**ENTP**
Marketing Skilled trades Business Law enforcement Applied technology	Health care Teaching Coaching Childcare worker Skilled trades	Counseling Teaching Religion Arts	Science Management Technology Arts
ESTJ	**ESFJ**	**ENFJ**	**ENTJ**
Management Administration Law Enforcement	Education Health care Religion	Religion Arts Teaching	Management Leadership

The Myers-Briggs Type Indicator (MBTI) is a popular personality inventory for use in business, counseling, and other settings. This table shows career types that fit within the 16 different MBTI types.

Projective personality tests are assessment instruments that are sensitive to the examiner's beliefs. They are based on the psychodynamic perspective and are a way to get at the unconscious. Projective tests, such as the **Rorschach inkblot test** depicted in Figure 12.4, require the examinee to respond to ambiguous stimuli. The examiner listens to the responses and interprets the response patterns, content, and other details to identify the latent content. Proponents of projective tests believe that, because there

projective personality tests assessment instruments based on the psychodynamic perspective that are sensitive to the examiner's beliefs and are a way to examine the unconscious

Rorschach inkblot test an ambiguous stimulus test, the responses to which are thought to reflect an individual's true personality characteristics

12.4 Personality assessment
Projective personality tests, such as the Rorschach, are thought to elicit personality characteristics through descriptive responses.

thematic apperception test
a type of test where individuals make up stories about pictures, express themselves through drawing, or complete sentences such as, "One thing I wish I could change is…."

are no correct or best answers, individuals will not be able to fake their responses; thus, their true personality characteristics will be reflected in their answers. Other types of projective tests, such as the **thematic apperception test**, have individuals make up stories about pictures, express themselves through drawing, or complete sentences such as, "One thing I wish I could change is. . . . "

Since personality assessment is one of the tools used by psychologists to predict how people will behave in various settings, it needs to be reliable and valid, as discussed in Chapter 2 and again in Chapter 10 (this is the third time the concepts of reliability and validity are discussed in this book, indicating the importance of these two concepts for measurement and understanding of human behavior). In addition to having a different way of assessing personality characteristics, projective personality tests are generally not considered to have as much validity as their objective counterparts. More than one psychologist has said they would not want to try to defend a Rorschach test in court. That said, the Society for Personality Assessment commends the "responsible use" of the Rorschach test, and a research-based, computer-aided tool has been designed to improve inter-rater agreement and validity (Erdberg & Exner, 1990; Mihura, et al., 2013). Objective personality measures, as previously mentioned, generally undergo fairly rigorous standardization. Thus, their reliability and validity is thought to be good. However, it is not foolproof. Because the questions are fairly transparent, someone taking the MMPI as part of a hiring process can give socially desirable responses to create a good impression. Alternatively, a person charged with a crime can answer in a way that makes her or him appear to have serious mental health issues in order to not be held responsible. To counter possible faking of "good" or "bad" responses, the MMPI is designed to assess the validity of responses to certain questions, which then determines whether the full profile is likely to be valid or not.

Concept Recall

1. What is the purpose of personality assessment?
2. What are the strengths and weaknesses of personality assessment?
3. How do objective and projective personality inventories differ?

PERSONALITY ACROSS PSYCHOLOGY

As you have read about personality, you have likely felt a sense of déjà vu with the previous chapter on thinking and intelligence. This is because personality, thinking, and intelligence are very similar concepts that share some of the same strengths, weaknesses, and challenges. Personality, like intelligence, is a description of how we generally perform in situations and why, but it doesn't always predict exactly how we will act. While social influences and other environmental factors may produce uncharacteristic actions, most of the time our behavior will match our personality. Understanding personality can help us to better understand how we will respond to different situations as well as to better understand others' motivations and actions.

Understanding what personality patterns are fairly typical also helps us to discern when people's patterns are atypical. We have already discussed that a person's characteristic patterns can change in response to extreme circumstances. They can also change in response to the social environment, as we will see in Chapter 15. Further, while there is a wide range of typical personalities, people's behavior patterns can be so different as to be considered abnormal and in need of intervention, as we'll discuss in Chapter 13. As you read through the next several chapters, keep personality study in mind to inform your understanding of abnormal psychology, psychotherapy, and social psychology.

In the opening of this chapter, we presented personality as "how" we tend to do things. As we end this chapter, we return to the Harry Potter analogy. Hermione, Ron, and Harry—the three heroes of J.K. Rowling's story—possessed certain traits that made them good fits for the Gryffindor house. These characteristics determined how they worked together to overcome the challenges presented to them. The balance of traits across the three friends provided the tools needed to successfully accomplish their objectives.

As you move forward in life, you will be confronted with many choices. One of the most important regards your professional career. Personality psychology can tell you a great deal about where your traits and characteristics would "fit" well. These types of assessment can usually be received for free at your institution's career development office (the name is slightly different across institutions, but almost all of them have one). Career exploration activities are a great way to get ideas about what types of jobs might fit well with your personality. We strongly encourage you to seek out this kind of information. A second important question, though, is what drives you? What are your goals, desires, and motivations? Getting a fit between what you value and what you want from your career is just as important as the match between your personality and the job.

Review/Reflect/Write

REVIEW

- How is the arousal level in our brain connected to our personality?
- What is the person-situation controversy, and how does it influence personality?
- Why are the id and the superego in conflict with each other, and how does this influence our behavior?
- How did Freud explain personality development?
- How do reinforcement and punishment shape our behavior?
- Explain how reciprocal determinism shapes personality.

- Why is self-efficacy not considered a personality trait?
- How does Maslow's hierarchy of needs relate to personality?
- Why is self-concept important to personality development?

1. Lily's friends said she is kind, patient, and outgoing. They are listing what psychologists would call:
   a. characteristics
   b. her personality
   c. her natural tendencies
   d. traits

2. Behaviorists believe that personality develops based on
   a. behavioral instincts.
   b. a history of learned associations, reinforcements, and punishments.
   c. genetic influences on behavior as they adapt to present culture.
   d. none of the above—behavior is innate and predetermined.

3. Nadia has an external locus of control. This means she believes that
   a. what happens to her is based on fate or chance.
   b. what happens to her is based on her own actions.
   c. she has the ability to influence external factors.
   d. she has the ability to influence outcomes.

4. Carl Rogers and Abraham Maslow, humanistic psychologists, believed that human beings are
   a. innately good.
   b. innately bad.
   c. easily steered away from innate, selfish tendencies.
   d. highly intelligent and capable of overcoming incredible odds.

5. If a marketing company is evaluating whether offering cash bonuses or letting employees choose the projects they work on leads to greater productivity, they are looking at
   a. defense mechanisms.
   b. need hierarchies.
   c. extrinsic vs. intrinsic motivation.
   d. need to belong.

6. Of the Big Five personality traits, which would be the best to have LOW levels of?
   a. neuroticism
   b. extroversion
   c. conscientiousness
   d. openness

7. Bandura, a social cognitive theorist, believed that behavior is influenced by and influences our thoughts and the environment, which is known as
   a. psychic determinism.
   b. reciprocal determinism.
   c. locus of control.
   d. reinforcement.

8. According to Maslow, when people reach their full potential, they have become
   a. humanistic.
   b. fulfilled.
   c. self-actualized.
   d. whole.

Answer Key
1. d 2. b 3. a 4. a 5. a 6. a 7. b 8. c 9. c 10. d

9. The earliest approach to describing personalities was by Hippocrates (460-377 BCE). On what did he base his descriptions?

   a. maintained emotional characteristics
   b. body shape
   c. body fluids
   d. enduring physical traits

10. Freud's three part structure of personality is

   a. conscious, preconscious, subconscious.
   b. innate desires, learned social constructs, compromise.
   c. widely accepted in modern society.
   d. id, ego, superego.

REFLECT

1. How often have you looked at a person's house or car and imagined what that person is like? Think about your ideal house or car in detail (perhaps jotting notes), then reflect on what someone else might conclude about your personality based on that image.

2. Think about your personality and how you present yourself most of the time. Under what circumstances would you act out of character for you? What about those particular situations would alter your personality traits?

3. Identify whether your locus of control is primary external or internal. What do you think led you to be this way?

WRITE

1. Take the Keirsey Temperament Sorter, if you have not already done so (www.keirsey.com). What jobs does your profile suggest you would be suited for? Discuss whether your profile fits your view of your personality or your current major.

2. Can nations have a personality? One study says yes and that national personality can predict attitudes about certain issues, such as the environment. Gather a bit of information on "national personality," and discuss whether you agree with the concept.

Key Terms

13 Abnormal Psychology

After reading this chapter, you will be able to answer the following questions:
- What are the four criteria that determine whether behavior is abnormal?
- What are the four models used to explain psychological disorders?
- What is the purpose of the Diagnostic and Statistical Manual, fifth edition (DSM-5)?
- What are the definitions and characteristics of the following disorders?
    - Schizophrenia spectrum and other psychotic disorders
    - Bipolar and related disorders
    - Depressive disorders
    - Anxiety disorders
    - Obsessive-compulsive and related disorders
    - Trauma- and dtressor-related disorders
    - Dissociative disorders
    - Feeding and eating disorders
    - Substance-related and addictive disorders
    - Personality disorders

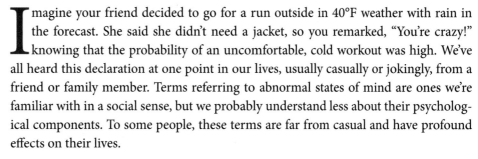

I magine your friend decided to go for a run outside in 40°F weather with rain in the forecast. She said she didn't need a jacket, so you remarked, "You're crazy!" knowing that the probability of an uncomfortable, cold workout was high. We've all heard this declaration at one point in our lives, usually casually or jokingly, from a friend or family member. Terms referring to abnormal states of mind are ones we're familiar with in a social sense, but we probably understand less about their psychological components. To some people, these terms are far from casual and have profound effects on their lives.

The impact of mental health on individuals has become a major topic of social and political discussion in the United States. Major social issues related to mass shootings, the treatment of military personnel and veterans, and the handling of sexual assaults on college campuses have pushed discussions of mental health into the national spotlight. Hopefully, this coverage will bring greater attention and resources to the needs of individuals with mental health challenges. However, it can also lead to the development of a negative caricature of these individuals. A caricature is an exaggeration or embellishment of certain characteristics of an individual or a group. For many individuals, the perception of mental health given by watching the news is of individuals who suffer from uncontrollable bouts of violence, suicidal thoughts, and other socially deviant behavior. This is not an accurate portrayal of the vast majority of individuals struggling with mental health challenges.

As you study this chapter, we hope that you will recognize that what is considered "abnormal" behavior is just an extreme of normal behavior. We all feel sad sometimes. For a person with major depression, this sadness is just deeper and longer lasting. We all want our life to have a certain organization and structure to it. For a person with obsessive-compulsive disorder, this desire for consistency is just stronger and more disruptive. We all occasionally feel a little uncomfortable in social situations; for someone with severe social anxiety, this discomfort is just so strong that he or she cannot engage in social interactions. The way we engage in the world (our behavior) occurs along a continuum. Healthy behavior tends to fall in the middle of this continuum. Like Goldilocks's porridge, it is neither too hot nor too cold. For individuals with mental health struggles, some aspects of their behavior (including thoughts and feelings) are "too hot" or "too cold."

In this chapter, we focus our discussion on what happens to behavior—and the labels that we give it—when it moves out of the normal ranges and into the extremes. This is a different focus from what we have had so far in the text. Much of the focus in the field of psychology is on typical phenomena, from brain physiology and emotional development to the principles of learning. However, the average person's knowledge of psychology is centered on abnormal phenomena, due partially to media portrayals and commonly known stigma. Human distress and psychological deviance from the norm have long been the subject of writing, art, and cinema; some claim the displacement of impulses considered inappropriate has actually advanced civilization (Freud, 2005). Statistics have revealed that about 22 percent of the adult population in the world are affected by some form of psychological distress (Mental Illness Research Association, 2015).

Why are we so fascinated with something that affects less than one in four adults? Perhaps because, as William James suggested, the best way to understand normalcy is to study abnormality (1890). Or perhaps because 22 percent of seven billion people is still about 450 million people, and adding in the family members, friends, and coworkers close to affected individuals makes for a great number of people impacted by mental illness.

The psychology subfield of abnormal psychology explores the nature and causes of thoughts, feelings, and behaviors that are so outside of our expectations of normal behavior that they are considered problematic. As with intelligence and personality, psychologists have explored biological, psychological, and sociocultural explanations for the development of abnormal behavior. Mental health professionals have also sought to classify abnormal behavior, grouping it into particular categories of disorders, to promote understanding and intervention. In this chapter, we explore the definitions of psychological disorders as well as their history and models. Then, we will discuss specific psychological disorders and their characteristics in addition to their scope and mechanisms.

DEFINING PSYCHOLOGICAL DISORDERS

What qualifies a behavior as disordered? In the many cases of high-profile mass shootings in the United States over the past several years—such as the theater shooting in Aurora, Colorado—the news reports immediately begin discussing the mental health of the suspected shooter. It seems obvious that only a person with mental health issues would engage in a behavior so far from the norm. There are two major issues with defining psychological disorders based on these types of highly socially disruptive acts. First, this way of defining disorders is circular. The individual is believed to have a disorder because he engaged in extremely inappropriate behavior. At the same time, he is believed to have engaged in this behavior because he has a disorder. These types of circular definitions do not meet the standards of science. Second, most people with psychological disorders never commit any type of crime, much less one of the magnitude of a mass shooting. Instead, they are our neighbors, work colleagues, friends, and family. Like those with "normal" mental health, they strive daily to achieve the best that they can. The major difference is that they have an additional struggle to overcome as they do so.

In order to understand abnormal behavior, we must first understand how it fits into culture since something is only abnormal in context. For example, if your psychology professor were to walk into class tomorrow and lecture dressed up as Captain America, you would likely think your professor is a bit abnormal, unless tomorrow is Halloween, a day we deem it normal for people to dress up in costumes. What we consider disordered psychologically has varied with culture, time, and social, as well as political, values. Some have even argued that mental illness is a complete myth, a method of control developed to deal with people whose behavior we have deemed morally unacceptable (Szasz, 1961, 1994).

Those in the mental health field define a **psychological disorder** as a pattern of thoughts, feelings, and behavior that is deviant, disordered, dysfunctional, and/or dangerous (Comer, 2004; Stein et al., 2010). Deviance is how far from the norm something is thought to be. Being **deviant**, or different, is the first criteria of the "four D's" for determining whether someone has a psychological disorder. However, it is not sufficient, as we consider many thoughts and behaviors to be deviant in a positive direction. Albert Einstein's brain was said to work in a very different way than most people's, yet he is considered a genius. Olympic athletes have physical abilities far from the average, and we award them medals.

To be considered **disordered**, behavior must be more than deviant. It will often cause distress. Thoughts, feelings, and/or behaviors are considered distressing when they are troublesome to the person who has them or to other people around that person. A person may be bothered by the need to wash his or her hands repeatedly, and/or coworkers may be troubled because it makes the person late for work. **Dysfunctional** behavior interferes with normal functioning, so, for example, thoughts or feelings that prevent a person from holding a job to pay for rent and food would be dysfunctional. Finally, we consider behavior to be psychologically disordered if it is dangerous. A behavior is **dangerous** when it poses a threat to self or others.

These four D's of abnormal behavior provide general rules for determining whether a behavior is disordered. Take a moment to think about how a behavior with these four characteristics would add to the challenges faced by an individual as well as the difficulties that they would cause to people who are trying to engage with the individual. As you think about these characteristics of disordered behavior, be aware that meeting two or more of the four D's does not automatically mean a person is psychologically disordered. All four of these criteria are subject to the social context.

Historically, people presumed abnormal behavior to be the result of forces they did not understand—the movement of the celestial bodies, god-like powers, or evil spirits. Many of us still hang on to remnants of the first, in thinking that people's abnormal behavior escalates during a full moon. Had you lived in the Middle Ages, you might have believed "the devil made her do it" and approved of such cures as trepanning, or drilling a hole in the skull, to rid the victim of demonic or satanic impulses (see Figure 13.1). We also locked people considered mad in dungeon-like places, even chaining

psychological disorder
a pattern of thoughts, feelings, and behavior that are deviant, disordered, dysfunctional, and/or dangerous

deviant behavior
behavior that is different from what most people in a person's reference group exhibit

disordered behavior
behavior that causes distress for the person exhibiting it and/or distress for those around the person

dysfunctional behavior
behavior that interferes with a person's ability to perform necessary activities, such as going to work or caring for family members

dangerous behavior
behavior that has serious potential to harm self or others

13.1 A depiction of trepanning
During the Middle Ages, trepanning was believed to let evil spirits escape through a hole in the head.

them to walls or beds. If you would like a glimpse into the actual history of mental health treatment in the late nineteenth and early twentieth centuries, visit the Glore Psychiatric Museum in St. Joseph, Missouri (http://stjosephmuseum.org/museums/glore/).

Many of the historical explanations of and treatments for abnormal behavior seem barbaric to us now, but keep in mind that practitioners were doing what they thought best for the patients based on the knowledge they had at the time. It remains to be seen how future practitioners of psychology will view our current explanations of and treatments for abnormal behavior. As psychological science improves our understanding of the causes and influences on behavior, we are able to build better technologies to treat abnormal behavior. (Recall the four stages of sciences discussed in Chapter 2? Control—building technologies to influence the world—was the fourth stage, following describe, predict, and explain.)

MODELS OF ABNORMAL BEHAVIOR

There are several modern theories regarding the development of abnormal behavior and psychological disorders. The biological model proposes that psychological disorders are the result of neurotransmitters in the brain not working properly or structures not formed correctly. The psychological model proposes that disorders are the result of extreme or incorrect perceptions and emotions about the self and the world. The sociocultural model proposes that psychological disorders are the result of a harmful environment. The biopsychosocial model (which is the same as the bio-psycho-social-cultural model introduced in Chapter 1) combines these three schools of thought and holds that a variety of factors interact to produce abnormal behavior. We will use depression as an example of abnormal behavior as we work through each of the models. More detail on depression and other specific psychological disorders will be covered in more detail later in the chapter.

The Biological (Medical) Model

medical model
model that conceptualizes abnormal behavior as the result of physical causes that can be treated through medical means

For several generations, physicians have documented their patients' symptoms and noted which ones occur together. These groups of symptoms, called syndromes, help physicians to identify underlying diseases and develop effective treatments. Viewing abnormal behavior, or mental illness, as one views medical illness is known as the **medical model**. Szasz (1993) advocates for limiting this model to conditions that result from actual brain dysfunctions. Szasz argues that many behaviors placed under "mental illness" are simply ones that society deems annoying or inappropriate (the social context of abnormal behavior that we discussed in the beginning of this chapter). Accumulating evidence does support brain dysfunction playing a role in mental illness. One way this occurs is through elevated or reduced levels of certain neurotransmitters, such as dopamine and serotonin, the latter of which is thought to be too low in people with depression and too high in people with anxiety.

Further evidence to support the idea that psychological disorders have a biological origin comes from the finding that some disorders run in families. For example, you have a one in ten chance of developing schizophrenia if you have a parent or sibling with the disorder, as compared with a one in 100 chance otherwise (Gottesman, 2001). The same is true if you have a family history of depression. If you have a parent or sibling with major depression, you probably have a two or three times greater risk of developing depression compared with the average person (or around 20 to 30 percent instead of 10 percent) (Levinson & Nichols, 2014). Since you inherit physiological characteristics from your parents, the medical model would argue that depression is the result of an imbalance of neurotransmitters and/or lack of sufficient electrical activity in the brain, which was likely passed down through your family.

The Psychological Models

While there is a strong biological component to several of the psychological disorders, the biological perspective cannot explain all disorders, nor can it explain all aspects of the ones in which biology is directly implicated. In contrast to the medical model, psychological perspectives on abnormal behavior emphasize the importance of mental functioning and learning experiences. If you remember Freud's **psychodynamic model** from our discussion of personality in Chapter 12, you know he claims that both abnormal and normal behavior are accounted for by the unconscious conflicts involving the id, ego, and superego or by the inability to successfully move through one or more of the psychosexual stages of development. For example, if you suffer from depression, the psychodynamic model would argue that you have a great deal of anger toward your parents because they were inconsistent, overindulgent, or too demanding. However, because you couldn't express that anger toward them when you were young and relied on them to provide life's necessities, you internalized the anger (Reiss & Dombeck, 2007).

psychodynamic model
Freudian approach to psychology that interprets personality in terms of conscious and unconscious forces

behavioral model
a scientific approach to psychology concerned only with observable and measurable behavior that can be objectively recorded

The **behavioral model** would say that your depression is due to a combination of stressors in your environment and a lack of coping skills to deal with those stressors (Lewinsohn, Hoberman, & Hautziner, 1985). Other disorders are also explained by what is reinforced or not in your environment and how well you cope (Nemade, Staats, Reiss, & Dombeck, 2013). Behavioral theorists such as Watson and Skinner, as discussed in Chapter 7, believed that we develop both normal and abnormal behaviors due to the associations made during classical and operant conditioning as well as modeling others' behavior. People who develop psychological disorders tend to have an excess of negative reinforcers (consequences that support engaging in behaviors that remove aversive stimuli from the environment) and a lack of positive reinforcers (stimuli that support engaging in behaviors that produce pleasing stimuli), as well as a lack of appropriate coping skills. The **cognitive model** would add that a person's interpretation of events is the key, not just the reinforcers and coping skills. In this view, your depression comes from negative interpretation of the events in your life.

cognitive model
a scientific approach to psychology emphasizing the need to understand the mechanical and internal processes of the mind in order to better understand abnormal behavior

The Sociocultural Model

Other theorists believe the development of abnormal behavior often goes beyond our immediate environment and our thoughts about it. The **sociocultural model** emphasizes the role of social and cultural factors on the conception, diagnosis, and frequency of psychological disorders. Among these influences are socioeconomic status, cultural beliefs, and cultural norms. For example, let's consider poverty and racial discrimination in the development of depression. These two contextual variables often go hand in hand since it is very hard to be positive and feel that you can do well in life when you have limited resources and constantly feel that society considers you to be inferior. It is not surprising that a person who deals with these factors on an ongoing basis would become clinically depressed. Eating disorders are another set of conditions thought to be strongly influenced by culture, particularly in countries where there is a specific standard for an ideal body shape that does not match what occurs naturally.

sociocultural model
an approach to psychology that considers the complex effects social and cultural factors have on individual behavior

There are some psychological disorders that are considered **culture-bound syndromes**; they occur in a particular culture and are closely tied to the values of those societies, though the underlying emotions can be felt universally. Consider anxiety, which, as we have discussed, is a normal emotion that can become excessive and debilitating. In Western cultures, when tied to the social realm, anxiety usually manifests in a person being excessively concerned that she or he will be embarrassed or humiliated. This is tied to the cultural emphasis on individual success. In contrast, the Eastern culture of Japan emphasizes group harmony and the importance of making sure others are not embarrassed or offended. There is a Japanese anxiety syndrome known as *taijin kyofusho*, whose primary symptom is a strong fear that the person's body or its functions will be embarrassing or offensive to others (Kleinknecht, Dinnel, Kleinknecht, Hiruma, & Harada, 1997). Other examples include *amok*, or a sudden attack of violence, in Malaysia, and *ataque di nervios*, characterized by uncontrollable yelling, crying, trembling, and sometimes fainting, in Hispanic Caribbean societies (Beardsley, 1994; Castillo, 1997). However, there are mental illnesses, such as schizophrenia, that manifest the same symptoms across cultures.

culture-bound syndromes
disorders that occur in a particular culture and are closely tied to the values of those societies, though the underlying emotions can be felt universally

The Biopsychosocial Model

Human behavior, whether normal or abnormal, is complex and results from more than just one factor. As we have discussed throughout this text, most of today's psychologists contend that all behavior is a result of an interaction between nature (biological factors, such as genes and physiology) and nurture (past and present experiences, internal psychological dynamics, social and cultural circumstances). Thus, the **biopsychosocial model**, as shown in Figure 13.2, is probably the best for explaining psychological

biopsychosocial model
a scientific approach to psychology that considers biological, psychological, and social factors and their complex interactions when understanding the effects on human behavior and mental disorders

disorders, with the amount of influence from nature and nurture varying with the disorder. This approach recognizes that our behavior—including thoughts and feelings—and our biological systems are inseparable. In this way, the person and the environment—including their social interactions and culture—are just as inseparable. Let's go back to explaining depression. From the biopsychosocial point of view, depression would develop as follows: you are born with lower levels of serotonin in your brain, which means you are prone to being less energetic and

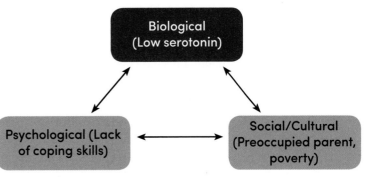

13.2 The biopsychosocial model of mental disorders
The biopsychosocial model purports that depression results from a person having low levels of a neurotransmitter, combined with an environmental factor, such as living in poverty, and a lack of skills that would help offset the biological and environmental factors.

more likely to be sad. Add to this a parent who suffers from depression as well, so he or she not only gave you the brain chemistry but also models feeling pessimistic about life and being unable to do much to address these feelings. Combined, these elements cause you to develop a pessimistic view of the world without the adequate coping skills to deal with the challenges that confront you. Throw this mixture of ingredients into an oven of poverty, and out comes a dish of depression. Notice how this recipe consists of biological factors (low serotonin, genetic susceptibility), learning factors (coping skills and attitude modeled by parents), social factors (relationship with parents and peers), and cultural factors (socioeconomic level, attitudes toward mental health).

CLASSIFYING PSYCHOLOGICAL DISORDERS

Even before getting to this chapter, you have likely heard of disorders such as major depression, schizophrenia, and post-traumatic stress disorder. Before we discuss the specific disorders, however, we need to talk about how and why we categorize abnormal behavior into psychological disorders. In the sciences, psychology included, classification is a way to create order and increase understanding. A scientific label provides a very specific description of an event that allows scientists to communicate clearly and effectively. A lack of clarity can cause communication problems and slows scientific progress. To understand the need for clarity, think about the word "crazy" (which, by the way, is neither a scientific label nor an appropriate description of individuals with mental health challenges). What does "crazy" mean? Sometimes, "crazy" is used to say that somebody is a ton of fun. Sometimes it is used to mean that somebody is very disorganized and has erratic behavior. And sometimes it is used to mean that somebody is dangerous and to be avoided. As these different uses show, the word "crazy" is used so ambiguously that its actual meaning across contexts is hard, if not impossible, to decipher. This lack of specificity does not work for scientific dialogue or progress.

A major goal driving the classification of abnormal behavior is to arrange various behaviors into groups (or symptoms) that make up a particular disorder, such as depression, social phobia, or schizophrenia. Once it is determined that a person's symptoms fit a particular disorder, he or she is said to have a diagnosis, just as with physical disorders. We then have an efficient, generally understood way of talking about a person's psychological issues. For example, if you say you have a friend with schizophrenia, you are indicating that he or she does several or all of the following: talks incoherently, hallucinates or has delusions, shows inappropriate and/or little emotion, and is socially withdrawn. Telling a psychological scientist or practitioner that a particular individual has a diagnosis of schizophrenia conveys that the individual displays a specific set of behaviors, thoughts, and experiences.

In psychiatry and psychology, the two professions that most heavily drive diagnosis and treatment of psychological disorders, classification doesn't just create order and promote understanding. It also enables mental health professionals to predict the future course of the disorder and implement appropriate treatment as well as helping direct research. Continuing to use the example of a friend with schizophrenia, if you were to discuss your friend's diagnosis with a mental health professional, he or she would be able to tell you that your friend's treatment most likely consists of a combination of antipsychotic medication and therapy.

Diagnostic and Statistical Manual of Mental Disorders (DSM)

Diagnostic and Statistical Manual of Mental Disorders (DSM)
the standard classification of mental disorders used by mental health professionals

The main authoritative scheme for the classification of psychological disorders is the **Diagnostic and Statistical Manual of Mental Disorders (DSM)**, produced by the American Psychiatric Association. This publication has been in existence since 1952 and is now in its fifth edition (see Figure 13.3 for a general history of the DSM). However, the DSM is an atheoretical document, which means that it describes symptoms and provides rules for making diagnoses without offering specific models to explain the disorders, such as those described earlier in this chapter. The DSM guides mental health professionals in determining a primary diagnosis, a subtype of that diagnosis where appropriate, and a severity level for the presenting symptoms. Returning to the example of your friend who has been diagnosed with schizophrenia, the formal diagnosis from the fifth edition of the DSM (abbreviated as DSM-5) might look like this:

> 295.90 (F20.9) Schizophrenia, first episode, acute, delusions 3, hallucinations 2, negative symptoms 1

This diagnosis displays the interplay between the numerical categorizations of the International Classification of Diseases (ICD-10), used by health professionals in all fields, and the verbal diagnoses of the DSM-5, used by mental health professionals specifically. The use of the DSM in the mental health field, particularly with its revisions, has had the desired effect: the reliability of diagnoses has improved, and research on diagnoses has led to greater understanding and treatment of several psychological disorders (Riskind, et al., 1987). Further, insurance companies will only pay for mental health care with a diagnosis by a licensed mental health professional. The DSM is a very widely used publication (Maser, Kaelber, & Wise, 1991), but it is not without its critics.

Determining When Behavior Is Disordered

The two chief issues with the DSM are the increase in what behavior we consider to be disordered and the problem of labeling. When the DSM was first published in 1952, it contained 106 psychological disorders. The latest edition, the DSM-5, released in 2013 with updates as recent as 2017, contains 297. As the number of disorders available to fit people's behavior has increased, so too has the number of adults who meet the criteria for at least one of those disorders—26 percent of the population in any year (NIMH, 2007) and 46 percent at some time in their lives (Kessler, et al., 2005). Critics' main concern in this area is that we are pathologizing (treating as psychologically abnormal or unhealthy) problems that are simply regular things that people deal with or exhibit. Imagine you lose someone quite close to you, and for the next several weeks you experience crying spells, lack of energy, difficulty completing tasks, and you no longer enjoy your usual activities. Should you be diagnosed with depression, or are you simply grieving? Or, as occurs quite commonly, should a child who is frequently loud and impulsive be diagnosed as hyperactive or merely be considered rambunctious? There is no question that, for some people, some patterns of behavior are debilitating to the point of qualifying as a psychological disorder, and these people do benefit from professional intervention. However, as a society, we need to be wary of pathologizing behavior too much and giving people the message that they have a problem that needs professional intervention rather than simply experiencing the normal ups and downs of life.

A related issue is the problem of deeming behavior to be abnormal because it is unconventional or disturbing to others, even when, in and of itself, it is not harmful to the person exhibiting it (Szasz, 1961, 1994). What goes into the DSM has been criticized by some for being driven by social and political norms (recall the earlier discussion of the cultural context of abnormal behavior). For example, homosexuality was listed as a psychological disorder in the first two editions of the DSM but was not considered disordered in later editions. Even with research as early as 1957 showing that homosexuals were no more or less well-adjusted than heterosexuals, it was not removed until 1974 (Gonsiorek & Weinrich, 1991). Asperger syndrome is a disorder that wasn't entered into the DSM until the fourth edition in 1994. In the DSM-5, it has been folded into the overall area of autism. The justification for this is that the diagnosis was not being consistently applied as a separate category (Kite, Gullifer, & Tyson, 2013). Someone previously diagnosed with Asperger syndrome would now be diagnosed with Autism Spectrum Disorder, without accompanying intellectual impairment, without accompanying language impairment, severity level 1. As exemplified here, the changes made to the DSM remain controversial, but DSM-5 is still very new and probably not the last edition we will see.

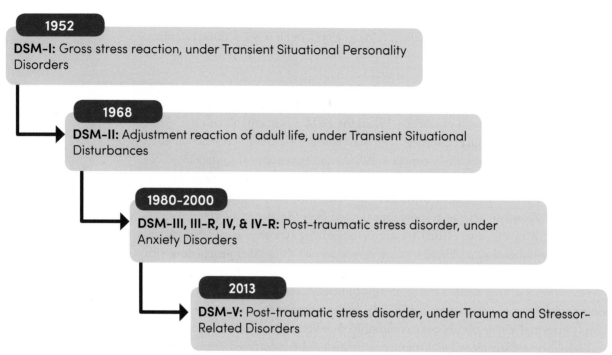

13.3   Major editions of the DSM

Since 1952, the DSM has been revised several times. Outlined above are the four major stages of the DSM's development using trauma-related disorders to demonstrate how classification can evolve.

Another reason to issue new editions of the DSM is to reconceptualize disorders as we learn more about them and/or the individuals who experience them. For example, obsessive-compulsive disorders and trauma-related disorders are no longer in the section on anxiety disorders. Obsessive-compulsive disorders are now in their own group due to the unique repetitive behavioral component. Trauma-related disorders are also in their own section paired with stressor-related disorders due to, as the name implies, trauma and/or stress being a necessary prerequisite. This is not the case with all anxiety disorders. Furthermore, a person's culture and community often view a disorder's symptoms in varying ways. The DSM-5 in particular incorporates a much greater cultural sensitivity than prior editions of the manual, making distinctions between co-occurring clusters of symptoms stemming from a patient's culture, race, ethnicity, religion, or geographical origin. For example, in some cultures, the primary symptoms of a panic attack are uncontrollable crying and headaches, while in other cultures, the primary symptom is shortness of breath. As shown in Figure 13.3, classification of disorders can change with the understanding of the underlying context and issues. Though the DSM receives periodical reviews and updates, it had been nearly two decades since the release of the DSM-IV, and since then, researchers and physicians had accrued a wealth of knowledge about mental disorders that required a complete new edition in the DSM-5. One of the main goals included clearly communicating the shared features between disorders, such as psychosis occurring in both mood and thought disorders. Another goal was to better reflect the variations in symptom presentation across age, development, and culture (Varley, 2013).

Cross-Cultural Case

Cultural Differences In Diagnosing

Consider the variances of diagnosing a sleeping disorder in a Japanese man and a French woman using the same criteria. Recall from Chapter 8 (Consciousness and Sleep) that Japanese people—especially working professionals—frequently engage in *inemuri*, the "public nap," both by choice and as a means to show their commitment to their professional responsibilities. Consider too that French persons, statistically, sleep the most of any group, according to data from a sleep study conducted by the University of Washington. Researchers concluded that sleep in Japanese culture is perhaps more undervalued than in any other culture. As the person diagnosing sleep disorders, one would need to understand not only the agreed-upon criteria for such a diagnosis but also patients' sociocultural backgrounds.

The latest updates to the *Diagnostic and Statistical Manual of Mental Disorders* (DSM-5) address cultural variances in diagnosing more than previous versions. The manual achieves this by "[updating] criteria to reflect cross-cultural variations in presentations, [giving] more detailed and structured information about cultural concepts of distress, and [including] a clinical interview tool to facilitate comprehensive, person-centered assessments" (DSM-5).

The interview tool, called the DSM-5 Cultural Formulation Interview Guide, aims to help clinicians ask questions toward understanding a patient's cultural background. Such elements of cultural formulation include language, cultural factors in development, and involvement with the culture of origin and host culture. Cultural factors related to environment include social stressors and supports, meaning how influential the individual's environment is on his or her behavior (Trujillo, 2008). According to the DSM-5, the purposes of the Cultural Formulation Interview Guide are to enhance the application of diagnostic criteria in multicultural environments, to systematically review a patient's cultural background, to identify the role of the cultural context in the expression and evaluation of psychiatric symptoms and dysfunction, to enable clinicians to describe the patient's cultural reference groups, and to identify the effect that cultural differences may have on the relationship between the patient and the clinician as well as how they affect the ultimate course and outcome of treatment.

The Issue of Labeling

A deeper concern for some critics of the DSM specifically, and diagnosis in general, is that in labeling people to better understand their issues, we are really pigeonholing them as their issues. Once a person receives a diagnosis, particularly for some of the more serious disorders, he or she is often thought of only in terms of the disorder. "My mother is schizophrenic" may be said instead of "My mother has schizophrenia"—the label becomes the person's identity. Once we have classified someone as mentally ill, we often interpret his or her behavior as part of the disorder. The classic example of this is illustrated in a study done by David Rosenhan in 1973. He and seven others presented themselves to psychiatric hospitals and deceived the admitting nurses into believing that they were hearing voices. Apart from giving false names and occupations, and lying about their complaint, they answered all other questions truthfully. Most were admitted and diagnosed with some form of schizophrenia. The eight confederates then began acting normally. The surprising finding was that they were not released quickly, but an average of nineteen days later, after being given medications (which they did not swallow) and therapy. Clinicians interpreted the "patients'" behavior in terms of the illness—e.g., one patient who was taking notes was interpreted as being paranoid (Rosenhan, 1973). While this study is not representative of how most psychiatric patients end up in hospitals, it is a fitting example of how we assimilate new information to suit our existing schemas (recall Chapter 5), and tend to assume a person's behavior is tied to his or her mental illness. We will talk more about this particular research study as part of our discussion of social behavior in Chapter 15.

Labeling in and of itself is not the entire problem ("I am an Olympic athlete" is a label most would not mind having). However, the perceptions that go with the label of being mentally ill make it something most people do not want to be associated with. Mental illness has long had a stigma that does not follow physical illness. Being mentally ill is often viewed as the person's fault, some sort of moral defect, or something the individual should be able to get over, if only the person was stronger. Though many more people today are willing to admit they suffer from a mental illness or have sought counseling than in previous years, stereotypes do linger, partly due to how mental illness is portrayed in the media. Some portrayals are fairly accurate and sympathetic, such as John Nash, Jr., in the movie *A Beautiful Mind*. Others detrimentally depict people with psychological disorders as worthy of ridicule (*What About Bob*). The image that probably does the greatest disservice to the mentally ill is that of a psychologically disturbed person as aggressive and dangerous (*Silence of the Lambs, Psycho*). While there certainly are people with mental illness who are dangerous (John Hinckley, Jr., Jared Lee Loughner), the vast majority of people with mental illness are not violent (Douglas, et al., 2009; Elbogen & Johnson, 2009; Fazel, et al., 2009, 2010). There are many examples of attempts to combat this image. New Zealand developed an award-winning campaign, "Like Minds, Like Mine," that included television ads (these can be seen on YouTube; just search "know me before you judge me New Zealand") in which people were described by family and friends as a whole person with many positive qualities before it was added that they suffered from a mental illness.

As we finish this section on labeling and mental illness, it needs to be mentioned how we talk about individuals with mental illness. The acceptable way of approaching this discussion is to be "person first." A person who has been diagnosed with depression, should be talked of as a "person with depression," rather than depressed. Similarly, a child with autism should not be called autistic. An easy way to keep this straight is to think about mental illness as any other disease. When it comes to physical ailments, it is the norm to speak of these as things that people "have." People have cancer, broken bones, and the flu. We do not speak of these as inherent aspects of the individual. The same should be true of mental illnesses. The person IS a friend, a sibling, a parent, or a coworker. The person HAS a mental disorder.

Concept Recall

1. What four criteria are used to determine whether behavior is abnormal?

2. How do each of the modern models conceptualize the development of psychological disorders?

3. What are the pros and cons of classifying psychological disorders?

This Is Psychology

The DSM is the most common diagnostic manual used in the United States. However, it is not the only approach to diagnosing disorders. An alternative to the DSM is the International Classification of Disease (ICD) 10th edition. The ICD-10 is a much broader diagnostic system than the DSM in that it is a general medical diagnostic system that includes mental health issues, rather than being specifically focused on mental health, as is the DSM.

A completely different approach to the DSM—and used for a different purpose—are the Research Domain Criteria (RDoC) that have been adopted by the National Institutes of Mental Health (NIMH). This classification system has as its main goal the creation of diagnostic criteria that are based on (1) observable behaviors and (2) brain function. The approach used in the development of the RDoC criteria is to view abnormal behavior as a dysfunction of specific behavioral and neural systems. For example, the RDoC approach to understanding post-traumatic stress disorder is to evaluate the biological and behavioral system typically used to cope with trauma and then explore how these systems malfunction in individuals with post-traumatic stress. The RDoC approach is currently being used to guide research, not clinical practice. However, the hope of the NIMH is that this new approach to diagnosing mental disorders will provide improved clinical information and better treatment options.

SPECIFIC PSYCHOLOGICAL DISORDERS

Anxiety, sadness, difficulty remembering, bizarre thoughts, substance use. All of these are something most of us experience at one point or more in our lives. For a small percentage of the population, however, these issues become the bulk of their experience and fit the four D's discussed at the beginning of the chapter (deviant, disordered, dysfunctional, and dangerous).

The DSM-5 organizes its table of contents based not only on how various conditions relate to each other but also on how these disorders occur across a person's life span. The chapters are organized and the disorders within them are grouped according to where, or more precisely when, they are likely to appear during a person's life span. Therefore, disorders typically diagnosed in childhood are listed first, followed by those appearing in adolescence, adulthood, and later life. This organization is more reliable than the DSM-IV's reliance on categorical axes, such as Axis I for mental disorders and Axis II for personality disorders. In the DSM-5, all disorders and diagnoses are logged in a single list. Now that we have taken a look at psychological disorders and how we classify them in general, let's examine a few of the more well-known disorders in more detail.

Schizophrenia Spectrum and Other Psychotic Disorders

This category contains diagnostic information for several disorders—schizotypal (personality) disorder, delusional disorder, brief psychotic disorder, schizophreniform disorder, schizophrenia, schizoaffective disorder, substance/medication-induced psychotic disorder, psychotic disorders due to another medical condition, and catatonia. The term **schizophrenia** was coined by Swiss psychiatrist Paul Eugen Bleuler (1857–1939), and it literally means "split mind." Schizophrenia is sometimes confused with dissociative identity disorder, which involves a splitting of personality. The splitting in schizophrenia is a break, or split, from reality, as one of the hallmark symptoms is the inability to distinguish between sensory experiences that are occurring in the brain, without a corresponding event in the physical world, and those that are triggered by actual physical events. As we discussed in Chapter 4, the brain sits isolated from the world, protected by the skull. Everything that is known about the world is delivered from the sense organs, which make actual contact with the world. When neural pathways become active without actual stimulation from the senses, the brain has a difficult time discerning the actual source of the activity. You have likely encountered something similar to this "ghost" sensation when you thought you saw something from the corner of your eye or thought you heard your name in an empty room.

schizophrenia
a chronic and often disabling mental disorder characterized by disorganized and/or delusional thinking, distorted sensory and perceptual experiences, and blunted or inappropriate emotions and behaviors

Schizophrenia involves a wide range of symptoms, which are divided into two categories: positive and negative. Positive symptoms are distortions or excesses of normal functioning, such as disorganized speech, delusions, and hallucinations. Disorganized speech can consist of loose associations in which the train of thought lacks sense, such as, "I was making a movie . . . I'm Mary Poppins. Is this room painted blue to make me upset?" (Sheehan, 1982, p. 25). It can also consist of words put together in a way that has no real meaning, such as, "eating wires and lighting fires" (Spitzer, et al., 1994). Delusions are false beliefs, such as thinking that the neighbor's dog is spying on you. Hallucinations are false sensory experiences (sensory experiences without actual external stimulation), such as hearing voices (as in the following example) or smelling things.

> For about almost seven years—except during sleep—I have never had a single moment in which I did not hear voices. They accompany me to

every place and at all times; they continue to sound even when I am in conversation with other people, they persist undeterred even when I concentrate on other things, for instance read a book or a newspaper, play the piano, etc.; only when I am talking aloud to other people or to myself are they of course drowned by the stronger sound of the spoken word and therefore inaudible to me. (Torrey, 2006, pg. 34)

These positive symptoms are the ones most people picture when they think about a person suffering from schizophrenia. However, negative symptoms, including behaviors that represent a reduction in or loss of normal functioning, such as poverty of speech, lack of affect (emotional expression), or lack of volition (ability to act), often accompany or alternate with the positive symptoms.

Schizophrenia is not as common as the other disorders we have looked at, with about twenty-four million sufferers worldwide compared to 400 million for depression (WHO, 2014). However, it is one of the most serious disorders, as it almost always significantly impairs daily functioning for most of the sufferer's life. Slightly more men than women are affected by schizophrenia.

Causes of schizophrenia and other psychotic disorders

Current research suggests a combination of hereditary and environmental factors play a role in the development of schizophrenia and other psychotic disorders; however, the precise cause of the disorders is unknown. Physicians have identified specific factors that tend to increase an individual's vulnerability to schizophrenia and psychotic disorders, and these include genetics, brain infections, and birth complications, such as lack of oxygen during delivery, among others. Especially in the case of schizophrenia, people with a parent or sibling who has been diagnosed with the disorder have an increased likelihood of developing the disorder themselves.

Bipolar and Related Disorders

Bipolar disorder is named for its inclusion of the two extremes or "poles" of mood disorders—depression and mania. Individuals with bipolar and related disorders (formerly called manic depressive disorder or illness) experience alternating episodes of depression and mania that can vary in their severity. While experiencing depression, people with bipolar and related disorders can experience fatigue, hopelessness, and anxiety, while manic episodes are characterized by feelings of elation greatly out of proportion with the situation and excessive physical activity, such as those experienced by Jay in the following example.

bipolar disorder
a mental disorder characterized by alternating periods of extreme highs (mania) and extreme lows (depression)

> Two weeks ago, twenty-year-old Jay's mood switched from friendly to irritable. When he thought his tablet was missing, he accused a friend of taking it. After determining that he had misplaced the tablet himself, Jay refused to apologize to his friend. Although he had no knowledge of music, he purchased an expensive guitar. As his need for sleep decreased, he spent hours planning to write the definitive work on "existentialism,

divine providence, and the collective unconscious." He also decided he could reconcile with his ex-girlfriend and knocked on her door at 2 a.m. When she refused to let him in, he began tearing off his clothes, pounding on the door, and yelling to be let in. The neighbors called the police who took Jay to a local emergency room after attempts to calm him down failed. While in the ER, Jay's speech was rapid, he shifted topics rapidly, and he moved around restlessly. After his release from a psychiatric hospital a couple of weeks later, Jay became very depressed. (Brown & Barlow, 2007)

The depressive and manic episodes of bipolar disorder may occur simultaneously, but they usually alternate and are often separated by periods of relatively normal behavior. The manic state involves boundless energy, euphoria, and an eagerness to engage in enjoyable behavior, such as spending, socializing, sexual activity, or high-risk physical activities. You may be wondering where the problem is with these behavior patterns. The problem lies in the manic behavior going too far. People in a manic state are often unable to judge their thoughts and actions appropriately, and their behaviors move from fun and creative to angry, impulsive, and even dangerous. They can incur huge debts, break the law, or physically harm themselves.

At a milder level (i.e., before it escalates to behavior that gets you hospitalized or arrested), the manic phase consists of a level of energy and free-flowing thinking that can fuel creativity. For example, one patient diagnosed with bipolar disorder has noted that his midlevel mania allowed him to be very productive in graduate school. Indeed, there may well be a link between creative genius and mood disorders; artists, composers, writers, and entertainers seem to suffer more than people who rely on logic and precision to succeed, such as architects, designers, and journalists (Jamison, 1993, 1995; Kaufman & Baer, 2002; Ludwig, 1995). The composer Handel, who may have suffered from bipolar disorder, wrote the *Messiah*—which is nearly four hours long—in 1792 during a three-week span of intense, creative energy. More recently, singer Demi Lovato has been open about her 2011 diagnosis of bipolar disorder in hopes of helping others, and the late Robin Williams, who most consider to be a comedic genius, was strongly suspected of having bipolar disorder. Though bipolar disorder affects fewer people than major depression, it is often more debilitating (Kessler, et al., 2006), and it affects men and women about equally.

Causes of bipolar and related disorders

The exact cause of bipolar disorder is not known, but genetics may play a part in the development of the disorder. Researchers have determined that problems associated with the body's production of neurotransmitters lead to the symptoms of the disorder, but what causes these problems is unknown. Furthermore, while some people have developed bipolar disorders after a stressful event or might experience a depressive or manic episode after such an event, scientists have not been able to demonstrate an exact cause-and-effect relationship between stress and bipolar disorders.

Depressive Disorders

This category appears deceptively simple on the surface, but actually contains diagnoses for a number of disorders, all featuring depressive episodes as a key symptom. Feelings of depression are often an appropriate response to past and current loss and can serve as a signal for us to slow down, let go of anger, let go of wanting things we cannot obtain, and take fewer risks (Andrews & Thompson, 2009a, b; Wrosch & Miller, 2009). It turns out that even mild sadness can improve people's recall, make them more discerning, and help them make complex decisions (Forgas, 2001). So, contrary to what some of you may believe, being happy all the time is not something to strive for. Like anxiety, depression has an adaptive purpose. But at what point does depression become maladaptive? Again, we must look at patterns; the difference between feeling bad after a bad day and having a mood disorder is the difference between being tired after a good workout and being chronically fatigued no matter what your activity level. The essence of clinical-level depression is captured in the following quote:

> Here is the tragedy: when you are the victim of depression, not only do you feel utterly helpless and abandoned by the world, you also know that very few people can understand, or even begin to believe, that life can be this painful. There is nothing I can think of that is quite as isolating as this. (Giles Andreae)

Major depressive disorder

There is no diagnosis in the DSM-5 for what society largely refers to as "depression." Rather, what we often refer to this generalized term is actually major depressive disorder. **Major depressive disorder** occurs when at least five symptoms of depression last two or more weeks and they cause significant distress and/or impairment. As with anxiety, there is a combination of cognition (thoughts of death and suicide or problems in thinking, concentrating, or making decisions), emotion (feeling worthlessness or excessive guilt), and physiology (appetite and sleep disturbance). Appetite and sleep disturbance means that some depressed people eat too much while others lose their appetite, and some depressed people sleep too much while others fail to get enough sleep. Most people who are depressed experience decreased appetite and may experience weight loss. Others will seek comfort in food and gain weight. Some depressed individuals sleep far too much, in part as an escape (Kupfer & Reynolds, 1992). Two forms of insomnia are often associated with depression: difficulty falling asleep and early morning awakenings with an inability to get back to sleep. While we often think of depressed people as sad and lethargic, some experience a more agitated depression and may look more anxious than depressed. Major depression appears to impact more women than men, but it may be that women simply receive the diagnosis more often (Pelham, 2009). Depression in men, and children for that matter, often manifests as irritability or anger, so they may be viewed as having something other than depression.

major depressive disorder
a mental disorder that is characterized by feelings of extreme unhappiness and hopelessness and interferes with one's work, sleep, eating, and life

Causes of depressive disorders

Any number of factors may contribute to the development of a depressive disorder. When determining causes of depressive disorders it is important to note that such disorders in no way indicate a weakness of character, and, contrary to popular belief, they often do not stem from childhood trauma or poor parenting, though these can contribute to development of depression. Neither do social class, race, or culture seem to affect a person's likelihood of experiencing depression of any kind during his or her lifetime. Genetics may play a part in that they can affect the body's ability to produce neurotransmitters, and some depressive disorders, such as premenstrual dysphoric disorder, can only affect women. Physical disorders can sometimes cause depression, especially when they affect the body's hormone levels or cause a person to experience pain and/or disability, and other mental disorders, such as certain anxiety disorders and substance abuse, can also predispose a person to depression. Use of some prescription drugs or even stopping use of a drug can also cause depression. Emotionally distressing events, such as loss of a loved one, can also trigger depression. Even though many factors can contribute to depression, it is important to note the depression can arise or worsen even without any apparent or significant outside influences.

phobia
a completely irrational fear toward an object or situation, in which the individual only finds peace by avoiding the object

Anxiety Disorders

Anxiety is a part of life, and a beneficial part too. If that sounds counterintuitive, think about the last time you realized you might have forgotten to do something important or the car in front of you slammed on its brakes. Those are moments when you likely, and should have, experienced anxiety—the emotion that serves as a warning system for us. Anxiety helps us to be on our toes and push ourselves to perform well. Just the right amount of anxiety improves attention, motivation, and performance. For most of us, anxiety triggers at the onset of specific events, it is not too intense, and it does not persist. For about 18 percent of adults, however, anxiety is severe and persistent enough to qualify as a psychological disorder ("Facts & Statistics | Anxiety and Depression Association of America, ADAA," n.d.).

While driving to do some shopping with his family, John, a 45-year-old high school principal, had just turned back around after telling his children to settle down. He looked at the road and immediately felt dizzy. As soon as he noticed this sensation, he experienced a rapid and intense surge of other sensations: sweating, accelerated heart rate, hot flashes, trembling, and the feeling of being detached from his body. In response to these intense feelings, John began shifting in his seat and tightening his grip on the wheel in an effort to gain control over them. When his wife asked if he was OK, he could not respond, and fearing he was going to crash the car, pulled to the side of the road. He quickly jumped out and lowered himself into a squatting position, trying to gain control over his breathing by using techniques he and his wife had learned in Lamaze classes. After about ten minutes, John began to feel better. However, he asked his wife to drive for the remainder of the trip, fearful that he would experience another attack (Brown & Barlow, 2007).

John's experience illustrates the typical experience of a panic attack, a frequent experience for individuals with anxiety disorders. There are different types of anxiety disorders, but all are characterized by a persistent, distressing level of anxiety or maladaptive behaviors that reduce the anxiety. One such disorder is **generalized anxiety disorder (GAD)**. The symptoms of this disorder—continual worry, jitteriness, agitation, and sleep deprivation—are common. Their persistence—for six months or more—is not. Two-thirds of the people who suffer from this condition are women (McLean & Anderson, 2009). Concentration can be quite difficult, as attention shifts from one worry to another. The tension and apprehension often manifests in physical signs, such as furrowing brows, trembling, twitching eyelids, perspiring, and fidgeting. One of the worst parts of GAD is that the sufferer is often unable to identify the source of the worry. Thus, they can neither deal with nor avoid the cause of their anxiety; Freud referred to this type of anxiety as "free-floating." Depression often comes along with GAD, but regardless of the presence of depression, GAD tends to be a disabling condition (Hunt, et al., 2004; Moffitt, et al., 2007b). In addition, experiencing that much stress constantly takes its toll on the body, and can lead to health problems, such as high blood pressure.

> **generalized anxiety disorder**
> a mental disorder characterized by tension, excess worry, and a state of physiological arousal that has no specific trigger

Panic disorder

An event people may experience when they are highly anxious is a panic attack, similar to the experience of John at the beginning of this section. A panic attack consists of an episode of intense fear, lasting at least several minutes, in which the person believes something horrible is about to happen, but in the absence of an actual emergency situation (you can think of this as a severe "false alarm" by our emotional warning system). Physical sensations, including heart palpitations, shortness of breath, choking sensations, trembling, and dizziness usually accompany the intense fear. In the midst of such symptoms, it's no wonder that many sufferers think they are about to die (often of a heart attack). Any substance or experience that stimulates your central nervous system (coffee, stimulant medication, energy drinks) will make you more prone to a panic attack when anxious. Smokers, for example, have at least double the risk of panic disorder (Zvolensky & Bernstein, 2005). Ironic, given many smokers say they smoke to relieve stress.

Panic disorder is a pattern of frequent panic attacks, interspersed with the constant worry that an attack is about to happen. Like generalized anxiety disorder, panic disorder occurs more often in women (Eaton, et al., 1994). About half of the people who suffer from panic disorder also suffer from agoraphobia (Eaton, et al., 1994), a word that originates from Greek and means a fear of open spaces. Individuals with agoraphobia are not so much scared of the open space, but more afraid that they will have a panic attack in a place they cannot hide or avoid strangers seeing them. Therefore, the person with panic disorder begins to limit the places he or she goes, sometimes eventually becoming trapped at home, the only place the person feels some sense of safety.

> **panic disorder**
> feelings of tremendous fear, when there is no reasonable causation, and characterized by panic attacks that can last for several minutes or longer

Causes of anxiety disorders

The causes of anxiety disorders are not fully known, but genetic and environmental factors as well as a person's psychological and physical condition can be involved in their development. Researchers have noticed that anxiety tends to run in families, but they have yet to determine whether it is an inherited or a learned trait in such cases. Environmental stresses, such as major life changes or experiencing a life-threatening situation, can also trigger an anxiety disorder, but so too can physical disorders, drug and substance use, or withdrawal.

Obsessive-Compulsive and Related Disorders

obsessive-compulsive disorder
a mental disorder characterized by unwanted repetitive thoughts (obsessions) and/or actions (compulsions)

Obsessive-compulsive disorders have been placed in their own category in the DSM-5 to reflect the increasing evidence of these disorders' relatedness to one another and distinction from other anxiety disorders. **Obsessive-compulsive disorder** (OCD) is the most well-known of this group, thanks to the attention it has gotten in the media through films such as *As Good As It Gets* and *The Aviator*. Some of you may even think you have OCD because, as with other disorders, there are likely some aspects of OCD in your behavior (see Figure 13.5). For example, you may have a strong urge to wash your hands after your friend's dog licks them, or you may like your study space set up "just so." The difference between normal fussiness about germs and neatness and OCD involves the ability to stop thinking or acting once you have done what you need in order to alleviate the worry and move on. People with OCD cannot move on; they spend so much time on their thoughts (obsessions) and behaviors (compulsions) that it interferes with daily life. Approximately 3 percent of people will cross the line from normal preoccupation and conscientiousness to debilitating disorder, usually during their late teens or early twenties (Karno, et al., 1988).

13.5 Obsessive-compulsive disorders
Some phobias are often accompanied by rituals, or compulsions, designed to reduce the sufferer's anxiety. The person here likely has a fear of germs and is engaging in repeated handwashing.

Hoarding disorder

hoarding disorder
a mental disorder that is characterized by a persistent difficulty discarding or parting with possessions because of a perceived need to save them

In addition to removing OCD from the generalized category of Anxiety Disorders, the DSM-5 added hoarding disorder as a distinct disorder with distinct treatments separate from those that may be administered for individuals with OCD. Like OCD, **hoarding disorder** has received media attention through the television show *Hoarders* on A&E. The fact that there are enough people suffering from this disorder to warrant a television show and that that television show falls prey to the tendency to label people as their disorders rather than as people with a disorder indicates a need for increased public awareness, which the creators of the DSM-5 hope to create with the unique diagnosis.

People with hoarding disorder don't just collect items. You may have a friend who collects baseball cards and another who is particularly fond of books and hopes to one day fill a library with the volumes she's accumulated. These friends likely do not have hoarding disorder. Collecting becomes hoarding when the quantity of items your friend has collected affects her and/or those around her emotionally, physically, socially, financially, or even legally. People who hoard will accumulate so many possessions that they often clutter living areas and/or their workplaces to the point that they can no longer be used for their intended purposes. This clutter can sometimes become a public health issue by creating fire hazards and breeding grounds for pests.

Causes of obsessive-compulsive and related disorders

The causes of obsessive-compulsive disorders are not fully understood, but the need to engage in obsessive-compulsive behaviors stems from concerns about harm or risk. People who suffer from these disorders truly believe that not engaging in them could result in injury or even death either for themselves or those around them. Scientists have identified some factors that could increase a person's risk of developing an obsessive-compulsive disorder, and these include family history, stressful life events, other mental health disorders, and substance abuse.

Trauma- and Stressor-Related Disorders

Trauma- and Stressor-Related Disorders is a new chapter in the DSM-5. Unlike most of the disorders in other chapters of the manual, the disorders in this chapter have specific, identifiable causes. Trauma and stressor-related disorders are so called because an event that results in the sufferer feeling physically and/or emotionally overwhelmed is a necessary trigger. Such events might include engaging in combat, experiencing or witnessing sexual or physical assault, or experiencing a disaster, whether natural or man-made. The disorders in this chapter are no longer considered anxiety disorders because those affected often do not experience anxiety. Instead, they

From the Desk of Dr. Stith

A man in our community walked into a local ice cream store. He began to take off his clothes. By the time police arrived, he was restrained by adult customers in the store. Was he dangerous to himself or to others or gravely impaired because of a mental illness? Or was he just a habitual public exposure offender?

Crisis management is the capacity to respond to a range of crisis and emergency situations. These situations can include scopes from an individual to a community tragedy to a large-scale natural disaster. Most responses involve a single person in crisis, such as the man in the ice cream store who was trying to satisfy a voice only he could hear. Every state has a version of a "hold and treat" law that allows, and in most states, requires, law enforcement or a licensed mental health crisis professional to "hold" a person if that person is seen as dangerous to himself, herself, or others or is gravely disabled because of a mental illness.

In the case of individual crises and emergency responses, crisis management has a variety of tools. Mobile crisis workers can be dispatched to where the individual is located. In this case, they met the police at the ice cream store. Emergency staff can be sent to meet families or individuals at local emergency rooms. Many communities are fortunate to have a variety of crisis stabilization units, which are nonhospital stays up to a week. Communities may have walk-in crisis centers that operate as urgent care centers for anyone suffering from a mental health or substance abuse crisis.

Often, an individual crisis affects a much larger part of a community. A teen's suicide at a high school affects all students, families, teachers and school staff. Crisis management now requires a broader deployment of trained professionals to work with the wider impact of trauma and stress. Natural disasters (hurricanes, tornadoes, forest fires, earthquakes) often require crisis management efforts involving multiple disaster teams over a longer period of time. Trained trauma staff members are drawn from surrounding communities and states. They respond in shelters, schools, and to first responders. Likewise, in a perpetrated community tragedy, such as the Las Vegas shooting, crisis management requires a disaster team response to the many levels of individual and group impacts of the tragedy.

In the case of the ice cream store, crisis management staff needed to intervene with his acute psychotic episode and also several traumatized children and their parents, the employees, and an owner who was terrified that the negative publicity would cost him his business and livelihood.

Randy C. Stith, PhD

might behave aggressively; feel restless, angry, or numb; or experience vivid memories (flashbacks) of the traumatic or stressful event as if it were actually happening.

Post-traumatic stress disorder (PTSD)

post-traumatic stress disorder
a mental disorder characterized by intrusive memories, nightmares, social withdrawal, hypervigilance, and/or insomnia that lingers for a month or more after experiencing a traumatic event

Post-traumatic stress disorder (PTSD) is also the best-known disorder in this chapter, mostly due to the impact of war. The diagnosis of PTSD is relatively new, but the symptoms it includes have been around a long time with different names. Some of the past names include "soldier's heart" during the American Civil War, "shell shock" in World War I, and "combat fatigue" in World War II and the Korean War. PTSD did not receive its current name until 1980, when Vietnam veterans were presenting with symptoms. While PTSD is closely associated with combat and other experiences of war, people can develop PTSD through other events, such as natural disasters, automobile accidents, assault, or abuse.

Bad memories, in general, are normal and even adaptive, as they help us to learn and avoid negative things in the future. However, some memories of bad events are so severe and persistent that they interfere with daily living, such as happens in PTSD. In addition, PTSD sufferers can experience anxiety, nightmares, insomnia, a sense of numbness, and social withdrawal. Not everyone who lives through a traumatic experience develops PTSD. The frequency of the experience, how distressed the person was at the time of the traumatic event, and a sensitive limbic system are all factors associated with development of PTSD. The experiences and support a person receives after the traumatic event largely determine how much he or she will recover.

Dissociative Disorders

We have discussed disorders that involve disturbances in mood and disorders that involve disturbances in beliefs and/or perception. The following section covers disorders in which the disturbance involves memory or awareness. Take the following case, reported by Dr. Abdel-Aziz Salama in 2005:

Kathy's traumas began when she was three. At that age, she suffered from terrible nightmares, but would often be left to cry herself to sleep while her parents entertained guests in the home. She would often wake up throughout the night terrified and screaming. Kathy's first alternate personality developed at age 4, after discovering her father in bed with a five-year-old neighbor and then being convinced to join the sexual activity. After this event, Kathy insisted on being called "Pat" whenever she was sexually assaulted by her father over the next five years.

> "Vera," Kathy's next identity, appeared at age nine after her mother discovered how her father was abusing her. Kathy's mother required her to sleep in bed with her, a relationship that eventually turned sexual. "Vera" continued in this relationship with her mother for another 5 years. The next identity "Debby" was the result of Kathy's rape by her father's best friend. At age 18, Kathy ran away from home after her parents refused to

accept her relationship with her boyfriend. Unable to secure employment, Kathy began to work as a prostitute, at which time she began to call herself "Nancy."

Kathy was admitted to a mental hospital following an overdose by sleeping pills caused by "Debby's" rejection of "Nancy." In the hospital Nancy met her husband and received a formal diagnosis.

Such patterns, while quite rare, are startling and bewildering enough that the **dissociative disorders** are probably the more well-known disorders outside of the mental health field. They have been the subject of documentaries and movies (e.g., *The Man with No Past, The Three Faces of Eve, Memento*), and popular plot twists in soap operas. Dissociative disorders are disorders of consciousness, in which a person seems to experience a sudden loss of memory or change in identity, often as a response to overwhelmingly stressful circumstances.

dissociative disorder
a mental disorder characterized by a disruption in consciousness, in which a person seems to experience a sudden loss of memory or change in identity, often as a response to overwhelmingly stressful circumstances

Keep in mind that dissociation in and of itself is not so rare, nor is it always pathological. If you have ever successfully walked or driven a familiar route without consciously being aware of it, you experienced a detachment that is a mild form of dissociation. Soldiers often experience a level of dissociation in combat that actually helps them perform more effectively and thus survive (Brooks, 2014). As with all psychological issues, however, if the dissociation is severe enough, and/or interferes with daily functioning, it becomes a problem.

Dissociative amnesia occurs when a person loses his or her memory after a traumatic event, in the absence of neurological damage that would explain the memory loss. Dissociative fugue occurs when the amnesia composes a person's entire identity— memories and personality. A person suffering from dissociative fugue may travel away from familiar surroundings and even assume a new identity. Robert Louis Stevenson's *Strange Case of Dr. Jekyll and Mr. Hyde*, as seen in Figure 13.6, is known for its portrayal of a split personality and has become synonymous with multiple personalities in both lay and scientific literature (Singh & Chakrabarti, 2008).

13.6 Robert Louis Stevenson's *Strange Case of Dr. Jekyll and Mr. Hyde*
The Jekyll and Hyde character is an early example of one person having two distinct personalities, though Stevenson's portrayal of the physical transformation via serum is fictional.

Dissociative identity disorder

The most complicated, and controversial, of the dissociative disorders is **dissociative identity disorder**. As in the story of Nancy at the start of this section, DID involves the separation of the self from ordinary consciousness, such that two or more distinct identities are thought to alternately control the person's behavior. The different personalities

dissociative identity disorder
a dissociative disorder in which two or more distinct identities are thought to alternately control a person's behavior, often a result of severe trauma

often have their own names, voices, mannerisms, and styles of dress. They tend to have specific roles to play, such as a protector, and the original personality typically denies awareness of the others, known as alters. DID is thought to develop as a way of coping with severe and prolonged physical, emotional, and sexual abuse; the personalities, or parts thereof, form to help the original person cope with and repress the traumatic experiences and overwhelming emotions tied to them.

Many in the mental health field, both practitioners and researchers, have expressed skepticism that DID is actually a disorder. Some point to the nature of traumatic memories, noting that they are among the hardest to forget (Christianson & Loftus, 1990). Others note that DID seems to be strongly tied to time and place. In the first half of the twentieth century (about 1930–1960) the number of DID cases diagnosed in North America was two per decade. After the DSM included the first formal diagnostic criteria for DID in the 1980s, that number shot to more than 20,000 (McHugh, 1995a). The average number of exhibited personalities also increased from three to twelve per client (Goff & Simms, 1993). DID is also found with much less frequency outside of North America, and has even been referred to as "a wacky American fad" (Cohen, 1995).

There are clinicians and researchers, however, who believe DID is a genuine disorder. Some studies have found differences in brain and body states between the personalities. Examples include visual acuity (one personality needs glasses, another doesn't) and activity level in brain areas associated with the control and inhibition of traumatic memories (alter personality remembers, original one does not), (Elzinga, et al., 2007; Miller, et al., 1991). Still others believe that dissociative disorders in general should be grouped with post-traumatic disorders because some sort of traumatic event(s) seems to be a necessary trigger (Putnam, 1995).

Feeding and Eating Disorders

For much of human history, when we thought about our food and our bodies, we focused on survival: obtaining food and keeping our bodies functioning well enough to stay alive. As we became better able to provide food on a consistent basis, our focus shifted. People became more concerned with quality rather than quantity of food and with the form, or physical appearance, rather than function, of our bodies. For about 4 percent of people, this focus becomes extreme and pathological, leading to various types of **eating disorders**. We will look at the three that are most well-known.

Anorexia nervosa

People who suffer from **anorexia nervosa** often start out trying to lose weight via typical dieting. However, they end up dropping significantly—15 percent or more— below normal weight. They do this by severely restricting their food intake, exercising excessively, vomiting, and even abusing laxatives, diet aids, or enemas. People with anorexia feel fat despite being thin, fear gaining any weight, and obsess over losing it.

eating disorder
a mental disorder characterized by abnormal or disturbed eating habits

anorexia nervosa
a serious, potentially life-threatening eating disorder characterized by self-starvation and excessive weight loss

Sufferers of anorexia are more likely to be female, by a ratio of three to one, but it does occur in males as well.

Bulimia nervosa

Bulimia nervosa also frequently starts off as typical dieting, but it is broken by a pattern of gorging on the foods barred from the diet and then purging through vomiting, laxative use, and/or fasting. People with bulimia, again usually women in their late teens or early adulthood, have a preoccupation with food, fear gaining weight, and experience bouts of depression and anxiety during and following binges (Johnson, et al., 2007). About half of the people who have bulimia exhibit a binge-purge-depression cycle. People who engage in significant binge eating without purging or fasting are thought to have **binge eating disorder (BED)**. However, BED is not simply a matter of being overweight; significant distress over eating more than is needed to feel full must also be present. Further, it is a common misconception that all people with BED are overweight. While it is most common among overweight or obese individuals, it is not limited to this group. Though it has not been classified as a disorder as long as anorexia or bulimia, binge eating disorder is actually the most common eating disorder in America. It affects women slightly more often than men.

Causes of feeding and eating disorders

So what causes some people to take their bodies' need for food off a healthier autopilot and into a maladaptive manual mode? Recent research suggests that genetics make some people more susceptible to eating disorders, via available levels of the neurotransmitter serotonin and the hormone estrogen (Klump & Culbert, 2007). Family has an influence in other ways as well. If you have a family member who exhibits disordered eating, your risk of developing the same increases. Parents who place a great deal of emphasis on success and physical appearance while being highly protective and critical are more likely to have children who are prone to anorexia and bulimia (Jacobi, et al., 2004). Very recent research from Jaclyn Saltzman and Janet M. Liechty (2016) indicates that binge eating disorder is correlated with a lack of emotional responsiveness from parents and teasing from parents and/or siblings about weight. People with eating disorders frequently have low self-evaluations, are highly critical when they fail to meet their own perfectionistic standards, and are extremely concerned with how others perceive them (Sherry & Hall, 2009).

Culture also contributes to the development and variation of eating disorders. This is largely because the ideal physical shape varies by culture and historical period. The entertainment and fashion industries in most modern countries tout a body ideal that is impossible for most of us to achieve, yet it has such a powerful hold that we spend billions trying, and the prevalence of poor body image and eating disorders has skyrocketed (Feingold & Mazella, 1998). When food is scarce and poverty prevalent, as in much of Africa and Asia in present day or America prior to the twentieth century, plumpness indicates prosperity and health, so bigger is seen as better (Swami et al., 2010). It seems quite ironic that America tends to idolize thinness when food is so

bulimia nervosa
a serious, potentially life-threatening eating disorder characterized by a cycle of binge eating and compensatory behaviors, such as self-induced vomiting

binge eating disorder
an eating disorder characterized by recurring episodes of binge eating without accompanying compensatory behaviors

readily available for most of us. Further, the United States has the highest rates of obesity and binge eating. This seems to be due to a combination of an increasingly sedentary lifestyle, diets higher in processed foods, fats, and sugars, and not being mindful of hunger cues as we eat.

Concept Recall

1. What are the hallmark characteristics of schizophrenia?
2. What are dissociative disorders, and why are they controversial?
3. How are personality disorders different from other psychological disorders?
4. How do the eating disorders exemplify the influence of culture on development of psychological problems?

Substance-Related and Addictive Disorders

Yet another group of psychological disorders involves the use of some substance to such an extreme extent that it disrupts the person's ability to keep up with his or her responsibilities and relationships. The substance is usually alcohol or another type of drug, but the substance can be money, as gambling disorder falls into this category in the DSM-5 (it was classified as an impulse control disorder in previous editions). The majority of people who drink alcohol or bet on a horse race do so responsibly; the majority of us also take over-the-counter or prescription medication to alleviate a genuine physical illness or discomfort. There are people who only smoke cigarettes or cigars once in a while, and even marijuana has become legal for medicinal purposes in twenty-eight states and Washington, D.C. For a smaller number of people, however, use of substances, legal or not, becomes something they cannot control.

substance use disorder
a disorder in which use of one or more substances results in a maladaptive behavior and cognition patterns that often impair judgment, finances, and interpersonal relationships

Substance use disorder occurs when a person has a strong desire to use increasing amounts of a substance to the exclusion of other activities, and/or in the face of clear negative consequences, such as conflict with friends and family, not fulfilling school or work obligations, and legal trouble. The increase in amount used comes from tolerance, or the diminished effect of the same dose of a substance due to the brain adapting to it. This is why someone who, for example, drinks small amounts of alcohol infrequently will get drunk off of one or two drinks, while someone who consumes a larger amount more often won't show any effects until six or more drinks. Adaptation in this case is not a good thing; physical damage can occur in addition to the previously mentioned consequences. Substance abuse becomes substance addiction when a person experiences physical or psychological dependence and withdrawal in addition to everything else described. Physical dependence means a person has used the substance to such an extent that the body now needs it and will respond to its absence with intense cravings and even physical pain—withdrawal. While psychological dependence doesn't involve the physical symptoms, the need is just as strong, and both result in the addict spending the majority of his or her time getting and using the substance.

TRAIT DOMAINS

Dimensions				
Antagonism	Disinhibition/ Compulsivity	Neuroticism (Negative Affectivity)	Introversion (Detachment)	Openess (Unconventionality/ Psychoticism)
hostility*	impulsivity	anxiousness	intimacy avoidance	unusual beliefs & experiences
deceitfulness	risk-taking	emotional lability	anhedonia	eccentricity
callousness	irresponsibility	separation anxiety	withdrawal	cognitive & perceptual dysregulation
manipulativeness	distractibility	suspiciousness*	restricted affectivity*	
grandiosity	rigid perfectionism(-)	submissiveness	suspiciousness*	
attention-seeking	rigid perfectionism	perseveration	depressivity*	
	other opposites of disinhibition trait facets	depressivity*		
		hostility*		
		restricted affectivity (-)*		
Opposite Dimensions				
Agreeableness	Conscientiousness	Emotional Stability (Positive Affectivity)	Extraversion	Closedness (Conventionality)

Personality Disorders:

AnPD = Antisocial   AvPD = Avoidant   NPD = Narcissitic
BPD = Borderline   SPD = Schizotypal OCD = Obsessive-Compulsive

13.7 Personality disorder chart
This chart offers a visual depiction of how extreme and/or maladaptive personality traits combine in individuals to manifest as personality disorders. This demonstrates that personality disorders are neither distinct from normal personality nor from one another.

Personality Disorders

personality disorder
a mental disorder characterized by a maladaptive pattern of behaviors and cognitions that often impair the ability to interact successfully in the social environment

So far, we have discussed psychological disorders involving symptoms that present themselves and then, to some extent, abate. These symptoms are not viewed as a part of who the individual is. However, some patterns of dysfunctional behavior are more constant and ingrained. When a person presents with an enduring behavior pattern that is inflexible and disruptive to social functioning, the person is thought to have a **personality disorder.** Remember in Chapter 12, we defined personality as a person's characteristic way of responding to the world. For someone with a personality disorder, his or her characteristic responses tend to deviate strongly from the norms of his or her culture. As a result, such a person tends to have difficulty and/or be seen as difficult when it comes to interactions with others. Such is the case for Jordan:

> When he was younger, Jordan was frequently sent to the principal's office for fighting with peers. One night during winter break, Jordan broke into his middle school and stole some athletic equipment. He denied any knowledge of the incident even though his actions were captured on the school's security cameras. When Jordan was eighteen, he was arrested for vandalizing several cars and rappelling off a city bridge. By age twenty-five, he was in jail for robbing a bank and assaulting a guard in the process. When the police asked why he engaged in such acts, Jordan said that he was bored and just wanted to have some fun.

In the DSM, personality disorders are placed into one of three categories, depending on the primary feature driving the behavior pattern. As you recall from the discussion of the Big Five trait theory presented in Chapter 12, personality characteristics occur on a continuum. People who are thought to have personality disorders exhibit patterns of behavior on the extreme ends of the continuum (see Figure 13.7, page 395). Cluster A consists of disordered behavior patterns that are considered odd or eccentric, such as the restricted range of emotions and lack of interest in relationships that characterize schizoid personality disorder. Anxiety regarding the environment and/or relationships is the primary feature of Cluster C personality disorders, such as avoidant personality disorder.

Probably the most well-known personality disorders are in Cluster B because they consist of behavior driven by emotional insecurity, lability, and contrariness. Thus, they are marked by impulsive, dramatic behavior patterns, such as those exhibited by Jordan in the above example, which are at least as disruptive for others as they are for the person with the disorder. Antisocial personality disorder (APD) is the most heavily researched of the personality disorders, likely because people with this disorder often have a very noticeable and negative impact on individuals and society as a whole. Jordan would most likely be diagnosed with antisocial personality disorder; in pop psychology terms he would be called a "psychopath" or "sociopath." By the way, in spite of the modern Sherlock Holmes' claim that he is a high-functioning sociopath rather than a psychopath, there is really no difference (and he does not suffer from APD). Individuals who are given a diagnosis of APD tend to be deceitful, impulsive, and irresponsible, though some manage the latter two characteristics more successfully than others. They can also be quite charismatic. The core reason people with antisocial personality disorder cause other people pain, however, is their lack of empathy. They are not easily aroused by or responsive to others' feelings and reactions (Fowles & Dindo, 2009). While APD is the personality disorder most often associated with criminal activity, not all criminals have APD (Skeem & Cooke, 2010).

Causes of personality disorders

Though personality disorders may be more pervasively woven throughout a person's makeup, the causes for them are similar to those for other psychological disorders: a combination of genetic and environmental factors. Remember temperament from Chapter 3? Some people are born more sensitive to their environments and experience their emotions more strongly. Others do not adjust quickly or easily to change. And still others seem to be fearless and less responsive to the feelings of others. Because the symptoms of personality disorders are themselves personality characteristics, they are often more difficult to treat than those of other disorders. This is particularly true if the symptoms are not distressing or disruptive to the person or others.

Some psychologists have questioned whether we should even consider certain personality disorders to be disorders. For example, a person who is reserved, has little interest in interpersonal relationships, participates in few to no hobbies, and seems indifferent to either praise or criticism from other people would qualify for Schizoid Personality Disorder. However, if this person is not distressed by the lack of interaction or enjoyment of people and things, and is able to live a productive life, can we truly say that person is "disordered"? Another complicating factor is something we discussed early in this chapter: sometimes the very characteristics that qualify a person for a disorder are adaptive in some contexts. A person who is highly dramatic, likes to be the center of attention, and often interacts with others in a seductive or provocative manner may fit the profile for histrionic personality disorder, but the person would also do quite well as a celebrity. For individuals with personality disorders, even when they are distressed by their behavior and want to change, it can take a long time for them to develop a new way of responding to the world.

The Issue of Suicide

One of the most serious complications of psychological disorders is thoughts of death in general or the act of taking one's own life in particular. While many people associate suicide with major depressive disorder, and it is a key symptom of that disorder, it is a risk for people with other disorders as well. In the latest Centers for Disease Control & Prevention report published in 2014, 44,773 suicides were reported, which made suicide the tenth leading cause of death for Americans (American Foundation for Suicide Prevention, 2016). In 2014, the highest suicide rates were among people eighty-five years or older and people in middle age (forty-five to sixty-four), both at just about 19 percent. While it is a serious issue among adolescents and young adults, younger groups have had consistently lower suicide rates than older and middle-aged adults. In

2014, adolescents and young adults age fifteen to twenty-four had a suicide rate of 11.6 per 100,000. Suicide is about four times more prevalent among males, generally because while females attempt more often, men use more lethal means. In regard to ethnicity, suicide was highest among whites in 2014, at 14.7 percent, and second highest among American Indians and Alaska Natives (13.9 percent). Much lower rates were found among Blacks, Asians and Pacific Islanders, and Hispanics (all about 5 to 6 percent).

The risk of suicide does go up when a person suffers from a psychological disorder, most often depressive disorder, bipolar disorder, schizophrenia, and alcohol abuse or dependence. In fact, if people drink alcohol as a way of self-medicating when they are emotionally distressed, they are much more likely to attempt suicide, as alcohol consumption lowers inhibitions and increases impulsivity (Sher, 2006). Why exactly are psychological disorders associated with a higher risk of suicide? Partly because of the severe level of distress; some people do not want to feel that badly anymore and have no hope that they will ever feel better. This can be especially difficult to counter when the disorder is recurring and significantly interferes with the ability to fulfill goals, such as having a career or a family. Other disorders involve a high level of risk-taking behavior and impulsiveness, or being so out of touch with reality that the person does not realize his or her behavior is life-threatening.

A psychological disorder, however, is not a necessary precursor to suicide. People who have no history of psychological issues may resort to suicide when faced with a life event that overwhelms them, such as loss of their home, family, employment, or the end of a significant relationship. Physical conditions that significantly impact quality of life can also lead individuals to contemplate, if not commit, suicide. Elderly people and those with severe, painful, and/or terminal illnesses may choose suicide rather than living with pain, debilitation, or the sense they are a burden to others.

Concept Recall

1. How does an anxiety disorder differ from just being nervous or stressed?

2. What is the difference between major depressive disorder and bipolar disorder?

3. How is suicide related to psychological disorders?

ABNORMAL BEHAVIOR AND THE HUMAN CONDITION

Part of the reason abnormal behavior is covered this late in your book is because you need to have a good grasp of normal behavior before you can properly conceptualize abnormal behavior. You can probably think of something you or a friend or family member did over the last week that would be considered abnormal. This does not mean that it rises to the level of a psychological disorder. We all experience stress and difficult, sometimes heartbreaking events as a part of living. We all experience a range

This Is Psychology

Based on what you hear in the news, with such stories as the Sandy Hook school and Aurora theater shootings, you might think that many people with mental illness are violent. This is far from the reality, as most psychological disorders rarely lead to violence, apart from the few who experience delusions of a threatening nature, command hallucinations to harm others, and those who also abuse substances (Douglas, et al., 2009; Elbogen & Johnson, 2009; Fazel, et al., 2009, 2010). In fact, those who suffer from psychological disorders are more likely to be victims of violence than perpetrators of it (Marley & Bulia, 2001).

When people who suffer from psychological disorders do perpetrate violence, we are presented with a moral dilemma: should a person who is psychologically disturbed be held responsible for his or her actions? There is a legal term many of you may have heard of: not guilty by reason of insanity. It has been applied to people such as John Hinckley, Jr., who attempted to assassinate President Ronald Reagan in 1981, and Andrea Yates, who drowned her five children in 2001. If a person is acquitted due to being "insane" it essentially means the person cannot be held legally responsible for her or his actions because the illness prevented the person from understanding what she or he did was wrong. However, having a psychological disorder (being "psychologically insane") does not automatically make a person legally insane. Most people who suffer from psychological disorders are aware of right and wrong. Being acquitted by reason of insanity does not get a perpetrator off the hook; rather, it usually means the perpetrator will be institutionalized in a psychiatric facility, often for as long as he or she would have been jailed (Lilienfeld & Arkowitz, 2011). There is also another designation, "guilty but mentally ill," which holds the perpetrator responsible but allows for psychiatric treatment.

of thoughts and emotions, some of which seem strange or extreme. Much of the time, we deal with them through our existing coping mechanisms and support system, move on, and get back to the tasks of daily life.

Now that you have studied this chapter, you can appreciate that there are a variety of thoughts, feelings, and behaviors that can cause significant difficulty for a person and/or those around them for long periods of time. Those difficulties can often surpass the capabilities of the existing coping system and require professional intervention. There are also a variety of ways to explain why psychological disorders develop. As with the development of normal behavior, abnormal behavior is usually the combined result of nature and nurture, with one having more influence that the other, depending on the disorder. Those explanations then influence how we choose to manage the difficulties the person and those around them are facing. The therapies and other interventions that can be used to help people with psychological disorders are the subject of the next chapter.

Mental health issues in the United States are on the rise. While all of the modern conveniences have improved the overall physical quality of life, they have introduced new and very difficult challenges to psychological well-being. Evolutionary psychologists often point out that human psychology is adapted to a world that is much different from the current social and physical environment. Fortunately, there is a great deal that you can do to manage your mental health. Just as preventative measures—such as exercise, a healthy diet, and stress management—can impact the physical body, these approaches can help protect your mental health as well. In addition to maintaining a healthy physical body, you can help your mental health by cultivating a small, close group of friends, taking time to get away from school and work, and learning time management skills. Becoming aware of your mental health provides a lifetime of benefits.

In the next chapter, we discuss the treatments that are available for psychological disorders. In the United States today there remains a stigma against seeking professional help. Much of the "do it yourself" mentality continues to pressure people to handle their life stressors individually. As you walk away from this chapter, we invite you to join us in helping to change this stigma. The best way we can do so is to ensure that we avoid minimizing people's struggles through jokes about mental health and avoiding discussing topics of mental health. Just as many physical ailments—such as a cold or a small cut—will resolve themselves with just minimal self-care, many mental health challenges can be resolved by better health practices and changing our social and physical environments. Some physical challenges—cancer or loss of a limb—require medical attention. When our friends encounter these issues, we not only hope they go to the doctor. We encourage it and provide whatever assistance we can. The same should be our approach to major mental health episodes. Some problems, both physical and psychological, simply require the attention of a trained professional.

REVIEW

- What can we learn from David Rosenhan's 1973 study regarding the hazards of labeling people through diagnosing them with psychological disorders?
- What are the main benefits of diagnosing psychological disorders using the DSM?
- Which model of psychopathology seems to best explain most psychological disorders?
- What is the difference between positive and negative symptoms of schizophrenia?
- How do personality disorders differ from the other disorders covered in the chapter?
- How can behavior be deviant, distressing, or dangerous without qualifying as psychologically disordered?
- What is the difference between depression and bipolar disorder?
- How is a phobia different from obsessive-compulsive disorder?
- What factors increase a person's risk for suicide?
- How can substance use and gambling qualify as psychological disorders?

1. _____ and _____ exist in some form in almost all societies.
   a. Depression; schizophrenia
   b. Bipolar disorder; borderline personality disorder
   c. Anxiety; adjustment disorder
   d. Narcissism; pedophilia

2. The criteria used to determine if behavior is normal is/are
   a. cultural norms, religious norms, societal norms.
   b. adjustment to society.
   c. deviance, distress, dysfunction, and dangerousness.
   d. deviance, distress, dysfunction, and difficulty.

3. The cognitive model adds to the behavioral model that a person's _____ also affects the development of psychological disorders.
   a. personality prior to the onset of stressors
   b. past experiences
   c. biology
   d. interpretation of events

4. Some disorders are seen across all societies, but others are found only within certain societies and can often be traced to societal values. These are _____.
   a. only considered syndromes because the particular society views it as abnormal
   b. culture-bound syndromes
   c. region-specific disorders
   d. not recognized as disorders in other societies

5. Anxiety is a(n) _____ experience in everyday life. It only becomes a(n) _____ if the severity negatively affects a person's functioning.

   a. unpleasant; disease
   b. normal; problem
   c. abnormal; problem
   d. inconvenient; disorder

6. What is a criticism of the DSM?

   a. The increase in the number of disorders that people say may not actually be abnormal.
   b. Behavior may be deemed abnormal because it is considered inappropriate or unconventional to others, even though it may not be harmful to the person exhibiting it.
   c. The labels that come with a diagnosis may cause people to stigmatize that person and consider all of their behavior to be part of their disorder.
   d. All of the above are correct.

7. While there are psychologists who may favor one explanation over another, overall, what model do most psychologists support?

   a. behavioral model
   b. biological model
   c. medical model
   d. biopsychosocial model

8. Which of the following is a benefit of using the Diagnostic and Statistical Manual of Mental Disorders in order to diagnose psychological disorders?

   a. Specific theoretical models are offered to explain disorders.
   b. The manual bridges cultural gaps and provides information that can be applied internationally.
   c. Diagnoses are more reliable and there is a greater amount of research.
   d. The manual focuses only on serious and rare conditions.

9. Sara suffers from generalized anxiety disorder. Which of the following is not likely?

   a. She has difficulty sleeping.
   b. She has very specific worries that she can pinpoint.
   c. She is jittery and fidgets frequently.
   d. Her anxiety reduces her ability to function in a healthy way.

10. The _____ model proposes that psychopathology is the result of neurotransmitters not working properly, or structures not formed correctly.

   a. biological
   b. psychological
   c. social
   d. biopsychosocial

REFLECT

1. Thomas Szasz proposed that mental illness is a myth, merely a way to manage people who do not conform to societal norms. Do you think there are patterns of behavior that we pathologize because they are bothersome? Which patterns, and why?

2. Why do you think that mental illness as a whole still has more stigma than physical illness in our society?

Answer Key

1.a 2.c 3.d 4.b 5.b 6.d 7.d 8.c 9.b 10.a

3. Think about having one of the disorders described in the chapter. How would (or does) it impact your thoughts, feelings, and behavior? Is it easier or harder than having a serious physical illness or injury?

WRITE

1. Most of the research on the disorders discussed in this chapter is based in America, or at least other Western cultures. Select one or two of the disorders covered, and find data on the prevalence and manifestation in other cultures. How does it compare?

2. While mental illness may not be entirely a myth, there are diagnoses that are added, changed, or removed from the DSM due to societal beliefs and pressures. Briefly research the history of the DSM, and identify one or two of these diagnoses. Why do you think they were added, changed, or removed?

Key Terms

anorexia nervosa   392
behavioral model   373
binge eating disorder (BED)   393
biopsychosocial model   374
bipolar disorder   383
bulimia nervosa   393
cognitive model   374
culture-bound syndromes   374
dangerous behavior   371
deviant behavior   371
Diagnostic and Statistical Manual of Mental
    Disorders (DSM)   376
disordered behavior   371
dissociative disorders   391
dissociative identity disorder   391
dysfunctional behavior   371
eating disorders   392

generalized anxiety disorder (GAD)   387
hoarding disorder   388
major depressive disorder   385
medical model   372
obsessive-compulsive disorder   388
panic disorder   387
personality disorder   396
post-traumatic stress disorder (PTSD)   390
psychodynamic model   373
psychological disorder   371
schizophrenia   382
sociocultural model   374
substance use disorder   394

Chapter 14 Therapies

After reading this chapter, you will be able to answer the following questions:
- What are some of the treatments used prior to the twentieth century?
- How does medication impact psychological disorders?
- What is the purpose of electroconvulsive shock therapy?
- What is the purpose of psychosurgery?
- What are the characteristics of psychodynamic therapies?
- What are the characteristics of humanistic therapies?
- What are the characteristics of behavior therapies?
- How are cognitive behavior therapies different from behavior therapies?
- What is the purpose of group therapy?
- What is the purpose of family therapy?
- How does culture impact therapies?

In the 1997 movie, *Good Will Hunting*, after having managed to outsmart, con, or simply stonewall a variety of sophisticated therapists, prickly but brilliant Will Hunting (Matt Damon) encounters Sean Maguire (Robin Williams), a rather bumbling and unpolished psychologist. Sean reaches through Will's genius-level IQ using a combination of humor, compassion, and tough love to disarm Will into finally dealing with his childhood pain and trauma. In the short span of a couple of hours, the audience sees Will move through all the stages of psychological therapy, and suddenly he is able to pursue his dreams and drum up the confidence to establish a picture-perfect relationship with "the girl."

This is one time when it would be great if the real world worked like the world shown in the movies. The Hollywood version of therapy is often portrayed as much simpler and more streamlined than most real-life treatments. The resolution to problems in movies typically come with a single "aha" moment. The patient forgives those who wronged them. Or maybe they overcome the substance or habit that has plagued them. One victory, and the battle is won. This is not the case with psychological therapies in real life.

Psychological therapy is a process that occurs over several treatment sessions across different time periods for every patient. Psychologists' goals in providing therapy are to help patients effectively manage and treat their illnesses. Therapies focus on the goals for each session as well as the desired outcomes of treatment; psychologists don't "cure" mental illnesses but utilize a variety of methods to help people. In this chapter, we will look at those methods, both past and present, that are involved in helping people with the psychological disorders explored in Chapter 13.

As long as humans have been around, they have established methods within their own communities to treat psychological disorders, often focusing on the physical body. Recently, once the mechanisms of mental illness were better identified and understood, more formal and standardized methods appeared. The models for treating psychological disorders follow the models for explaining them. Thus, there are biological interventions in the form of procedures performed on the brain, and in modern times, medications. Talk therapies, what we now call psychotherapy, began with Freud in the late nineteenth century. Both biological and psychological interventions take place in a variety of settings, ranging from minimally restrictive (outpatient) to very restrictive (psychiatric hospital). People also still pursue less formal methods that do not involve a mental health professional to address their psychopathology.

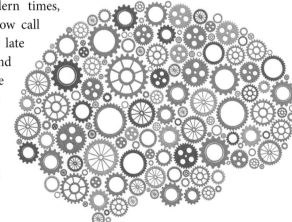

HISTORY OF THERAPIES

Treatment for mental illness used to be something people would never admit to receiving, but now it is almost a status symbol in some circles. As discussed in the last chapter, we have been attempting to treat psychological disorders for as long as they have been around. This history has included both harsh and gentle methods. All of the methods reflected the beliefs of people regarding the cause of behavior. As the science of psychology has provided a better understanding of why we behave, treatments have improved in effectiveness and gentleness.

The Roman bath is one of the first recorded therapies for various ailments. Ancients often turned to naturalistic forms of treatments that addressed the body, including exercise and massage therapy.

Beginning around 3000 BCE, Egyptian priests invited those who behaved abnormally to sleep in temples, in hopes that their dreams would reveal appropriate treatments. Hundreds of years later, the Greeks created religious and magical rituals to cure their patients' ailments. The Greek emphasis on naturalistic explanations for ailments (beginning with Hippocrates and the four humors, as described in Chapter 12) persisted in Roman times, and stricken people received treatments such as baths, exercise, and massage.

From the Middle Ages through the seventeenth century, people with psychological disorders were often thought to be either witches or demonically possessed. The trepanning described in the previous chapter was used to release demons, and so-called witches were often tortured and killed. However, not all mentally ill people were treated so harshly. In many Native American cultures, people who experienced hallucinations were given special status as shamans. In Europe, some were housed in institutions, so at least they had a place to live. In most of these institutions, however, the living conditions were less than ideal—at St. Mary's of Bethlehem Hospital in London, patients were often kept in chains and slept on straw beds. The term 'bedlam' comes from this facility (a contraction of Bethlehem), due to its disorganization, unsanitary conditions, and inhumane treatment of patients. Adding to the inhumanity of their circumstances, on weekends, members of the general population could pay a penny for the entertainment of viewing the patients.

By the eighteenth and nineteenth centuries, people such as Philippe Pinel, Benjamin Rush, and Dorothea Dix began the implementation of more humane treatment of people with mental illness (Deutch, 1949). They promoted relaxed environments where patients interacted with staff and one another. Partly as a result of Dix's reform efforts, existing mental hospitals were enlarged and new ones built. Indeed, the Bryce Hospital, first known as the Alabama State Hospital for the Insane, in Tuscaloosa, Alabama, was conceived and built based on Dix's call for reformation and "moral" architecture. However, Dix's efforts to make states responsible for care of the mentally ill backfired to some

Philippe Pinel

Dorothea Dix

extent. As more and more patients were housed in the hospitals without a corresponding increase in staff, it became harder to address individual patient needs. As a result, many patients were simply stored in the hospitals as if in a warehouse. With no treatment, there was no hope of them learning to cope with their illnesses.

For many patients, though, treatments did continue and began to improve. The introduction of new therapies, including psychoanalysis and behavior therapies, changed the way individuals with mental illness were treated. Surgical intervention was also attempted in the 1930s through 1950s in the form of lobotomies.

A **lobotomy** is a surgical procedure in which most of the connections to and from the prefrontal cortex—the part of the brain responsible for personality expression, decision-making, and

Despite Dorothea Dix's influence on reformations in mental health care, patients at the Bryce Hospital, opened in 1861 in Tuscaloosa, Alabama, were made to build caskets for their peers during the nineteenth century. After the abysmal conditions were revealed in the early twentieth century, several buildings on the campus were closed permanently, and in 1967 Alabama Governor Lurleen Wallace urged steps toward progress in the care of patients. The original location of the hospital was closed in 2009.

moderation of social behavior—are severed. It was thought that this would calm the patients' more severe symptoms, such as manic agitation and aggression. It did in some cases, but it also negatively impacted other brain functions, such as memory, concentration, and expressiveness. Rosemary Kennedy, sister of President John F. Kennedy, underwent this procedure in 1940 at age twenty-three, due to alleged violent mood swings, and it left her intellectually deficient and institutionalized for the rest of her life. Some 35,000 patients had been lobotomized in the United States alone before use of the procedure waned, largely due to the creation of medications to target the same symptoms.

lobotomy
surgical procedure performed on the brain to help alleviate more severe symptoms of mental illness, such as agitation and aggression

Psychotropic medications were introduced in the mid-twentieth century, with the creation of the antipsychotic, *chlorpromazine* (Thorazine). The use of this and other medications made it possible to control many of the more serious symptoms of psychological disorders (Talbott, 1994). This, combined with legislation in the 1960s that made it harder to commit people, as well as the belief that community-based treatment was better, led to the deinstitutionalization movement. Consequently, large numbers of patients were discharged from mental hospitals, and most people with psychological disorders were treated on an outpatient basis, with the help of government funds provided through the Community Mental Health Centers (CMHC) Act of 1963.

The movement away from institutionalization was not the end of inpatient treatment. Far from it—people still receive both short- and long-term inpatient care, just on a smaller scale. Unfortunately, several decades after the passage of the CMHC Act, several of the key goals put forth have not been achieved. One unmet goal is that the act called for the building of 2,000 community-based mental health centers to provide both prevention and intervention efforts; less than half that number were actually built. As a result, many mental health patients began to be served in nursing homes, board-and-care facilities, day-treatment programs, and group homes. Worst of all, many patients went untreated, partly due to lack of resources and partly due to their suspicion of treatment, and ended up homeless (Lurigio & Lewis, 1989).

Surprisingly, at least some elements of most of the historical treatment methods described above are still offered today. Modern treatments for mental illness can be placed into three broad categories: **psychosurgery**, psychopharmacology (both considered biomedical forms of treatment), and psychotherapy.

psychosurgery
surgical procedures performed on the brain in order to alleviate severe symptoms of mental illness that are not responsive to less invasive treatments

This Is Psychology

As mentioned at the beginning of the chapter, treatment of mental illness often appears in books, movies, and television. Given the number of people who access these forms of media, this is a great way to make people aware of mental health issues and their treatments. Unfortunately, a good bit of what Hollywood puts out there is inaccurate. As funny as they may be to watch, portrayals such as *Frasier, Analyze This, What About Bob*, and *Web Therapy* make the client and/or therapist look scatterbrained and neurotic. More than one person has likely been put off therapy because they don't want to be viewed as "crazy" or talk to a "crazy" therapist. However, there are portrayals that get it right, or at least close. In addition to *Good Will Hunting, Ordinary People, The Sixth Sense*, and *In Treatment* give us an accurate look at both the people and the process involved in therapy. Of course, Hollywood's job is to entertain, not to educate. It is your job as the consumer to determine what is accurate and beneficial. So, as the modern-day Sherlock has said (a fairly accurate portrayal of what we dubbed Aspergers until recently, by the way), "Do your research!"

Psychosurgery

While procedures as radical as prefrontal lobotomies are no longer performed, more refined psychosurgical procedures are still used today, though rarely and only as a last resort. As exemplified in Figure 14.1, a limbic leucotomy involves making lesions on a small part of the brain in order to disrupt the neurochemical pathways that seem to be malfunctioning (Price, et al., 2001). If you recall from Chapter 3, the messages that travel these pathways help determine sleep and appetite cycles, mood, and

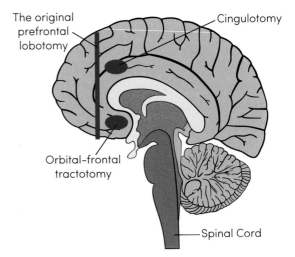

14.1 Lobotomy
The red line through the frontal lobe shows the location of the incision for a prefrontal lobotomy.

energy levels, all things impacted in mood and anxiety disorders. These surgeries are performed when patients suffering from depression or obsessive-compulsive disorder have failed to respond to several rounds of less drastic forms of treatment. About a third of patients show significant improvement in their symptoms following the procedure (Mashour, Walker, & Martuza, 2005).

Electroconvulsive therapy (ECT) is another form of biological treatment that impacts the functioning of the body, but with ECT, there is no invasive surgery. ECT involves the use of electrical current to stimulate areas of the brain (as discussed in Chapter 3, the action potentials that transmit signals along the axon of the neuron are electrical pulses). As with psychosurgical treatments, ECT has evolved to be much less brutal than in its early days. When ECT was first introduced in 1938, the patient was strapped to a table, awake, and his or her brain was jolted with approximately 100 volts of electricity. This resulted in immediate convulsions, brief unconsciousness, and later, in some patients, a reduction in depression. In today's version, the patient receives general anesthesia and a muscle relaxant to prevent injury from the convulsions, followed by thirty to sixty seconds of the electrical current. The patient awakens about thirty minutes later with no memory of the procedure. Like some forms of antidepressant drugs and exercise, ECT appears to boost the production of new brain cells (Bolwig & Madsen, 2007).

> **electroconvulsive therapy (ECT)**
> a therapeutic technique in which electric currents are sent through the brain to induce a brief seizure, which causes the brain to reverse symptoms of certain mental illnesses

While ECT may still seem harsh, after three sessions per week for two to four weeks, at least 80 percent of patients improve markedly (Bailine, et al., 2010; Fink, 2009; UK ECT Review Group, 2003). The side effect of some memory loss for the treatment period is more than acceptable to the patients who find relief from the severe depression that ECT is intended to treat. Despite evidence of success with some patients, ECT does not work for everyone. Some patients report more permanent cognitive difficulties and a return of their depression (Kellner, 2006). After being in use for more than seventy years, there is no definitive answer to how or why ECT works. Some think that it is akin to rebooting a computer, or maybe the seizures induced by the procedure calm the neural centers where overactivity may produce depression.

Two newer neurostimulation procedures used mostly with severely depressed patients are magnetic stimulation and deep-brain stimulation. Magnetic stimulation involves sending repeated pulses through a magnetic coil held close to the patient's skull. This painless procedure, known as repetitive transcranial magnetic stimulation (rTMS) is performed over several weeks. It is preferable to ECT in that it does not cause seizures or memory loss, though headaches can result. The way rTMS works is through energizing the left frontal lobe, noted to be relatively inactive during depression (Helmuth, 2001) or through facilitating the formation of new neural pathways. Initial studies have found "modest" positive results (Daskalakis, et al., 2008; George, et al., 2010; Lopez-Ibor, et al., 2008).

Deep-brain stimulation involves implanting electrodes in the brain and the use of a pacemaker stimulator to activate inhibitory neurons in an area that bridges the frontal lobe and the limbic system (Mayberg, 2009). This area is apparently overactive in depressed people. Of twenty initial patients who received the procedure, twelve experienced mild to moderate improvement that held for three to six years afterward (Kennedy, et al., 2011).

Psychopharmacology

psychopharmacology
the scientific study of the impact drugs have on psychological disorders

As mentioned earlier, medication was introduced as a treatment for psychological disorders in the mid-twentieth century. Today, **psychopharmacology** is by far the most widely used biomedical treatment and is about even with psychotherapy in terms of the most used treatments of any sort for psychological disorders.

There is often a wave of positive reception following the introduction of a new treatment, and many people report improvement. Although many people feel relief from their symptoms after taking medication, there are at least two alternative explanations:

1.   People often recover from mental disorders without the need for drug intervention.

2.   The relief is due to the placebo effect, meaning that people get better because of the positive expectations of patients and professionals alike.

As discussed in the experimental research section of Chapter 2, the best way to avoid the placebo effect is for researchers to conduct double-blind studies, in which neither staff nor patients know who is given an active drug and who is given an inactive placebo. The results of these studies indicate that some psychotropic medications are useful in treating some psychological disorders in some people. They are most likely to be effective when the disorder has a strong biological basis, as is the case with schizophrenia and bipolar disorder.

Antipsychotic medications

antipsychotics
a group of medications used to treat the positive symptoms of psychosis

The widespread use of medication in the treatment of people with mental illness began with an unexpected discovery. In 1952, French surgeon Henri Laborit observed that a new anesthetic calmed his patients without loss of consciousness. He persuaded his psychiatrist colleagues to try it on their schizophrenic patients, and they found that chlorpromazine reduced symptoms such as hallucinations and delusions (Lehman, et al., 1998). **Antipsychotic** drugs appear to work by occupying the receptor sites that respond to dopamine, the neurotransmitter whose abnormally high activity is thought to play a role in several of the symptoms of schizophrenia and other psychotic disorders. With the receptor sites blocked by the antipsychotic drugs, the dopamine in the system cannot connect with the receptors and activate the cells.

Antipsychotics calm the positive symptoms of psychosis for 60 to 70 percent of patients but, unfortunately, seem to have little impact on the negative symptoms, such as flat affect (lack of emotional expression on the face) and poverty of speech (Torrey, 1988). Further, antipsychotics have powerful and unpleasant side effects, such as sluggishness, agitation, and tremors. Some of the side effects seem similar to the symptoms of Parkinson's disease (Kaplan & Saddock, 1989), which makes sense as Parkinson's is thought to be the result of insufficient dopamine.

A new group of medications, known as second-generation, or atypical, antipsychotics has been developed in order to address some of the side effects of the first generation. Medications such as clozapine (trade name Clozaril), risperidone (Risperdal) and olanzapine (Zyprexa) are no more effective at controlling the symptoms of schizophrenia than the first generation, but they do have far fewer of their unpleasant side effects. This may be because they act on serotonin receptors as well as dopamine receptors. While they are more tolerable to patients than the typical antipsychotics, they too have their side effects, including risk of decreased immune functioning, diabetes, and obesity (Buchanan, et al., 2010; Pickar & Hsiao, 1995).

Even with their problems, antipsychotic medications, combined with life-skills programs and family support, have provided hope for many people with psychotic disorders (Guo, et al., 2010). While psychotic disorders, particularly schizophrenia, can mean a life in a hospital, many individuals with schizophrenia have been able to work and live in such places as group homes or even independently (Leucht, et al., 2012). In rare cases, such as Nobel-prize winner John Nash, Jr., subject of the award-winning movie *A Beautiful Mind*, symptoms can even go into remission.

Antianxiety medications

Antianxiety medications alleviate anxiety by depressing central nervous system activity in a manner similar to alcohol. The anxiety-depressing effects of alcohol are why many anxious people self-medicate with alcohol. It is also why the people prescribing such medication tell you not to use it in combination with alcohol. The major class of antianxiety drugs (also known as minor tranquilizers) is the benzodiazepines. Some of the better known of these medications are clonazepam (Klonopin), diazepam (Valium), and alprazolam (Xanax). These drugs increase the ability of GABA, an inhibitory transmitter, to bind to receptor sites, which reduces the neurological activity that produces anxiety. The primary side effects of benzodiazepines are drowsiness, impaired attention and memory, and loss of coordination. These are usually short-lived (Shader & Greenblatt, 1993).

antianxiety medication medication that reduces anxiety via depression of central nervous system activity

A major concern with antianxiety drugs is that they reduce the symptoms of anxiety but do not resolve the underlying thought and behavior patterns that cause the anxiety. If the latter are not addressed, then the medication can become simply another way of avoiding anxiety. Another problem is that people can become both psychologically dependent (believing they need the medication to feel well) and physically dependent (actually needing the medication to feel well) on benzodiazepines. Physical dependence, or tolerance, can develop if benzodiazepines are taken daily for three months or longer. If this is the case, the drugs should be discontinued gradually to avoid withdrawal symptoms. Fortunately, antianxiety medications are relatively safe in terms of lethal overdose. While death from overdose is rare, physical consequences such as cardiac problems, seizures, and coma can result (Gresham, 2015). The effectiveness of antianxiety medications is immediate and significant, but primarily short-term; they are best when combined with psychological therapy. In the past twenty years or so, the new standard drug treatment for anxiety has become antidepressants because they have a similar impact on the brain, but are longer-lasting and do not have the potential for addiction.

Antidepressant medications

antidepressants
medications that reduce depression by increasing levels of neurotransmitters associated with positive mood

Antidepressant medications were named for their ability to lift people out of a state of depression, and this was their primary use until recent years. Some are now used to treat obsessive-compulsive disorder and some anxiety disorders. There are three classes of antidepressants: tricyclic antidepressants, MAO inhibitors, and selective serotonin (and norepinephrine) reuptake inhibitors.

All three classes of drugs work to increase the amount of serotonin and norepinephrine; it is thought that depression is the result of too few of these neurotransmitters making their way through the brain. The tricyclics, such as amitriptyline (Elavil) were among the first antidepressants developed and administered, but they have since given way to newer drugs due to the tricyclics' unpleasant side effects: constipation, dizziness, and dry mouth (Maxmen, 1991). Patients who did not respond to tricyclics were often switched to MAO inhibitors (MAOIs), which prevent the breakdown of serotonin and norepinephrine by the monoamine oxidase enzyme. Two common MAOIs are tranylcypromine (Parnate) and phenelzine (Nardil). While MAOIs proved effective for some patients, they are rarely used today because of their potentially dangerous interaction with other medications and with the amino acid tyramine, which is in several common foods, such as aged cheeses and meats, fish, bananas, and tomatoes, to name a few (Wegman, 2008).

The newest group of antidepressant medications includes the selective serotonin reuptake inhibitors (SSRIs), which target only serotonin (See Figure 14.2), and the newer SNRIs (serotonin and norepinephrine reuptake inhibitors). Both of these drugs increase the activity in the brain by interfering with the neuron's ability to take released neurotransmitters back into the sending neuron after communication. SSRIs and SNRIs are likely familiar to you thanks to active advertising campaigns and the high frequency of prescription. The SSRIs include fluoxetine (Prozac) and sertraline (Zoloft). The newer SNRIs include duloxetine (Cymbalta) and venlafaxine (Effexor XR). The latter are thought to be more effective than the SSRIs in managing severe depression (Wegman, 2008). While the newer medications do

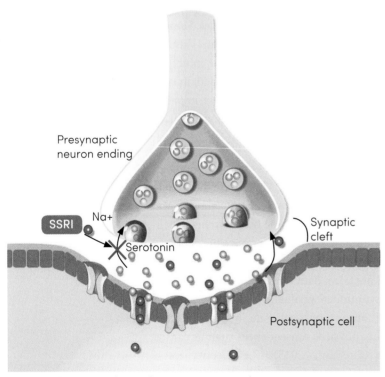

Presynaptic neuron ending

SSRI   Na+

Serotonin

Synaptic cleft

Postsynaptic cell

14.2 Antidepressant chemical activity
Selective serotonin reuptake inhibitor drugs interfere with the presynaptic neuron vacuuming serotonin from the synapse.

not have side effects as serious as some of the older drugs, they do still have them: insomnia, sedation, sexual dysfunction, and weight gain.

Mood stabilizers

Antidepressants work for depression and anxiety but are not adequate for people with bipolar issues, as they only address the depressive stage and may, in fact, exacerbate the manic phase. Thus, **mood stabilizers** are used to even out the highs and lows of bipolar disorder. In 1940, Australian physician Dr. John Cade discovered the effectiveness of lithium, which is a simple salt, on reducing the symptoms of a person's mania, and it has been in use ever since (Snyder, 1996). Approximately seven in ten people with bipolar disorder benefit from long-term use of lithium (Solomon, et al., 1995). Patients report that lithium prevents or eases the manic episodes and eases the depressive ones. It is not clear how lithium (brand named Eskalith and Lithobid) works, but it does. One theory is that lithium decreases mania by increasing the reuptake of norepinephrine (the opposite of how some antidepressants act on it), thus reducing the "fight or flight" response that is part of mania (Wegmann, 2008). Lithium has been noted for reducing the risk of suicide and suicide attempts in bipolar patients. This is important because about 1 percent of bipolar patients attempt suicide each year (Wegmann, 2008).

mood stabilizers
medications that balance out extreme moods by acting on neurotransmitters that influence mood and behavior

One drawback involved in the use of lithium is that it takes from five to fourteen days to be effective. Another issue is that the therapeutic dosage of lithium is close to toxic, so patients must undergo frequent blood-level monitoring. More recently, the anticonvulsant medications such as divalproex (Depakote) and lamotrigine (Lamictal) have been prescribed, as they also demonstrate lithium's efficacy in reducing the manic symptoms, particularly the rage reactions, but they do so more quickly and with better tolerance than lithium.

PSYCHOPHARMACOLOGY CONSIDERATIONS

Medications for the treatment of mental disorders are common and often effective. Most diagnoses of mental illness occur in the office of a primary care physician or hospital by staff trained in the medical model. As a result of this, the treatment of mental illness as a symptom to be dealt with is common. However, there are two primary drawbacks to the use of psychopharmacology. The first is the side effects. As already described, almost all medications have side effects, and for the psychotropic medications, some of them are quite unpleasant—so much so that many patients stop taking their medications. A second reason people will stop taking the medication is because they feel better after taking the medication and conclude that they no longer need it (this is a case of negative reinforcement, a concept introduced in Chapter 7 on learning). While not wanting to rely on a "crutch" is admirable and beneficial in terms of motivation to develop improved coping skills, for some people, psychotropic medication is a necessary part of their treatment. Some people can take an antidepressant or antianxiety medication for a while, until the most severe symptoms have abated, taper off, and not need it again.

However, for others, psychotropic medications must be taken over the long term to be effective, like insulin for diabetes or interferons for multiple sclerosis.

The second major issue with the use of medicine to treat mental illness is the lack of treatment for the causes of the challenges. As discussed previously, antianxiety medications alleviate the anxiety, but not the perceived threats or challenges that cause the anxiety. Similarly, the use of antidepressants can treat the depression but does not leave the patient with strategies and behavioral skills necessary to create long-term coping solutions. Most psychologists recognize that medication is most effective when used as part of a long-term treatment program that includes behavioral and cognitive training programs.

While it is important for long-term treatment strategies to be in place, this does not change the fact that psychosurgery and psychopharmacology are, indeed, effective means of managing the symptoms of several psychological disorders, at least some of the time. And for some people with severe episodes of the disorders, they would not be able to manage daily functioning without them. However, these treatments cannot create or replace lost social skills or create the ability to cope with the impact of having a psychological disorder. That is the purview of the psychotherapies.

Concept Recall

1. What are the similarities and differences between historical and modern therapies?
2. What are the pros and cons of the biomedical therapies?
3. When are the biomedical therapies used, and how effective are they?
4. When are treatments such as psychosurgery generally implemented?
5. What are side effects, and how do they impact compliance with biomedical therapies?

PSYCHOTHERAPY

All types of psychotherapy involve a trained therapist employing psychological techniques to assist people in overcoming difficulties and/or achieving personal growth. Trained therapists include people from various clinical backgrounds. Therapists can receive their training as clinical social workers, counselors, or psychologists. While the training programs differ, all of these professions require that practitioners are licensed to provide therapy. The eligibility to be licensed includes completion of at least a master's degree as well as hundreds of hours providing therapeutic services under the supervision of a fully licensed therapist. This helps to promote the provision of competent and ethical psychotherapy services.

There is often confusion over the difference between a psychologist and a psychiatrist. Both professions have "doctor" as their title, and both can provide similar forms of psychotherapy. However, they differ significantly in both training and how they conceptualize mental illness. A psychiatrist is a medical doctor who specializes in the treatment of mental illness. Historically, the early psychoanalysts were psychiatrists. Most modern psychiatrists spend the majority of their time treating patients via medication rather than in hour-long psychotherapy sessions. As they are trained medical doctors, psychiatrists have the ability to prescribe medications. A psychologist, on the other hand, is trained in the bio-psycho-social-cultural model that we have talked about throughout this text. While medication is a part of their treatment approach, psychologists tend to focus more on the behavioral, cognitive, and social aspects of the change process. There is a movement among psychologists to push for the ability to prescribe medications designed to treat mental illness. Illinois, New Mexico, and Louisiana have policies in place who provide psychologists these benefits. Other types of mental health professionals that can provide psychotherapy include clinical social workers, counselors, marriage and family therapists, and advanced nurse practitioners.

The practice of psychotherapy is often referred to as "talk therapy" because speaking with a trained therapist is the primary method for learning why symptoms and issues are present as well as how to better manage them. This method does have to be adapted depending on the person receiving psychotherapy. Imagine a young child, a person who is deaf, or a person whose first language does not match the therapist's trying to sit in a chair and successfully "do therapy" in the traditional manner. However, psychotherapy is not all talk. Therapists typically assign homework, which may include social tasks, physical exercise, self-reflections, and many other types of activities.

Overall, there are dozens of versions of psychotherapy. In this chapter, we will look at the most influential models. Each therapy model is built on one or more of the major theories of psychology: psychodynamic, humanistic, behavioral, and cognitive. Most of the psychological techniques can be used individually or with some combination of multiple people (couple, family, group).

Psychoanalysis and Psychodynamic Therapy

Sigmund Freud is considered the father of psychotherapy because his **psychoanalysis** was the first of the psychological therapies. The proverbial image of a patient talking to a therapist while lying on a couch, the subject of many a therapy cartoon, is Freudian in origin. While many therapists today have couches in their offices, few practice in this manner. Nonetheless, Freud's work is worthy of discussion.

psychoanalysis
a type of therapy that investigates repressed fears and conflicts by bringing them into the conscious mind in order to treat the mental disorder

Psychoanalytic theory holds that people become healthier and less anxious when they redirect the energy they had devoted to the id-ego-superego conflicts described in Chapter 12. Freud believed that we are not fully aware of ourselves and that the thoughts and feelings we relegate to the unconscious impede our functioning. Thus, the primary goal of psychoanalysis is to bring those thoughts and feelings to conscious awareness so the person can face them (gain insight) and move on. During this process, the psychoanalyst is an active agent in helping the client discover these unconscious motives.

"It goes back to being pulled out of the hat."

In individual psychotherapy, a patient or client talks about concerns, and the therapist facilitates exploration and growth.

Psychoanalysts help their patients unlock the unconscious through free association—having the patient speak aloud whatever comes to mind. This seems easy but actually takes some practice; most of us automatically edit much of what we think before we verbalize it. Psychoanalysts are trained to listen for such hesitations, which they call resistance, and provide insight or interpretation into their meaning. They are also trained to note how the client interacts with them, which the therapist interprets as transference of past feelings toward important people in the client's life to the therapist. Transference is also thought to lead to insight, and thus change, in the client's current relationships.

Psychoanalysis is no longer frequently practiced for two main reasons. First, the theory underlying it has little scientific support. Second, and more relevant to most people seeking therapy, however, is the fact that traditional psychoanalysis involves seeing a therapist multiple times a week for several years. Freud and his early followers worked primarily with patients of considerable means who could afford such numerous appointments with their therapists. Most of us today have neither the time nor the funds (insurance companies do not generally cover psychoanalysis) to devote to this type of therapy. Some of Freud's ideas, though, are still utilized in the more modern **psychodynamic therapy** practiced today.

psychodynamic therapy
a form of psychotherapy that focuses on the client reaching self-awareness of unconscious content and childhood experiences, as well as understanding the impact they have on past and present behavior

Psychodynamic therapists don't spend time on the id, ego, and superego. Instead, they try to help people understand their current symptoms by focusing on themes across important relationships, which include childhood experiences and the therapeutic relationship. Another difference is that modern psychodynamic therapists work with their patients sitting up and face-to-face. They also meet with them less frequently (once or twice a week) for several months rather than several years. Interpersonal psychotherapy is a brief (twelve to sixteen sessions) variation of psychodynamic therapy that has been found to be effective in treating depression (Cuijpers, 2011). It still focuses some on addressing past issues and offering interpretations, but its primary goal is relief of symptoms in the here and now.

insight therapy
a technique used to help individuals improve functioning through increasing understanding and expression of unresolved conflicts

Humanistic therapies

Another therapeutic perspective that spends a lot of time in the here and now is the humanistic perspective. The goal of humanistic therapies, like psychodynamic therapies, is to reduce growth-impeding inner conflicts by providing clients with new insights. Both psychodynamic and humanistic therapy are often referred to as **insight therapies**. There are significant differences between the two, however. Humanistic therapies work to increase individuals' **self-actualization** (recall Maslow and Rogers' ideas on personality in Chapter 12) through helping clients grow in terms of self-awareness and self-acceptance.

self-actualization
the final tier of Maslow's theory of Human Motivation, in which the individual has reached the full potential in every aspect of his or her life

Humanistic therapies are quite positive in nature, thus, self-actualization is the focus rather than curing illness. This focus is the origin of people in therapy being referred to as "clients"—as they are throughout this chapter—rather than "patients." Humanistic therapies facilitate the client taking immediate responsibility for his or her feelings and actions rather than uncovering hidden determinants for their problems. Thus, the unconscious does not play a major role in the humanistic therapies in the same way it does in psychodynamic therapies. Further, the place for insight to occur in humanistic therapy is the present rather than the past.

The most well known of the humanistic therapies is probably Carl Rogers' **client-centered therapy**. Rogers developed the technique of **active listening**—echoing, restating, seeking clarification of what the client is expressing (verbally and nonverbally), and acknowledging the expressed feelings. This method is one of the most widely used therapy techniques today, incorporated into most therapeutic approaches. Humanistic therapies are considered nondirective in that the therapist listens without judging or interpreting (at least not out loud!) and tries not to direct clients toward specific insights or actions. Client-centered therapy reflects Rogers' firm belief that most people already possess the resources for growth and just need to have someone provide the right environment in which to use them (Rogers, 1961, 1980). Humanistic therapists provide this environment by exhibiting genuineness, acceptance, and empathy. When therapists demonstrate these characteristics in sessions, clients are more likely to feel accepted and understood and thus more likely to deepen self-understanding and self-acceptance, especially if they are struggling with thoughts, feelings, and behavior they (and/or others) deem quite negative (Hill & Nakayama, 2000).

Behavioral therapies

The insight therapies operate on the assumption that psychological problems decrease as self-awareness increases (a negative correlation, as discussed in Chapter 2). Psychodynamic therapists expect that problems subside as clients gain insight into their unconscious and unresolved tensions. Humanistic therapists expect that problems subside as clients get in touch with their feelings. Advocates for **behavior therapy**, however, are skeptical that self-awareness is the key to healing. For example, you can become aware of why you are very anxious while driving or riding in a car and still remain anxious. Conversely, you may be able to reduce some of your anxiety symptoms through relaxation without fully understanding why you are anxious. Behavior therapists operate under the premise that problem behaviors are the problems rather than symptoms masking an underlying issue. Thus, maladaptive symptoms are learned behaviors, and the application of learning theory can help a person unlearn them and replace them with more adaptive behaviors.

Classical conditioning (described in Chapter 7) informs two types of behavior therapies: exposure therapy and aversive conditioning. Both involve **counterconditioning**, or pairing of the trigger stimulus with a new response that is incompatible with the maladaptive emotion or action. The goal of exposure therapy is to substitute a positive or neutral response for a negative response to a harmless situation (or at least much less

client-centered therapy
a type of psychotherapy in which the client is given an accepting, empathetic environment in which to explore and attain personal growth

active listening
a therapeutic technique in which the therapist pays close attention to his/her clients' words and then echoes, paraphrases, and clarifies what the client says; a key component of client-centered therapy

behavior therapy
a type of therapy that helps the client/individual change potentially self-destructive behavior through application of learning principles

counterconditioning
a behavioral technique using classical conditioning to replace an undesirable response to a stimulus with a desired response

threatening than the client perceives it to be). For example, in counterconditioning, a behavior therapist would help the client to substitute relaxation (deep breathing, slower heart rate, pleasant thoughts) for the panic he or she would usually feel when in a crowd, thus changing the client's association of a strong negative sensation with crowds. The kinder, gentler method of achieving this goal is known as systematic desensitization, in which the client is slowly exposed to the source of his or her fear in small steps over time to learn how to manage the fear itself, as well as the fear of the fear response, without avoiding the trigger. The client who fears driving might start out practicing relaxation in the therapist's office while visualizing being on the road for two to three minutes, then do the same while driving around the parking lot for a few minutes, and, over several weeks, work up to taking a twenty-minute drive across town (see Figure 14.3).

exposure therapy
a behavioral technique that involves having the client face her or his fear while engaging in calming strategies

A more brutal method of exposure is known as flooding, or prolonged **exposure therapy**. With this technique, the client is thrust into the trigger situation and made to stay until he or she conquers the fear response. In this type of treatment, the therapist would put the client in the car and have them drive around until the client was past the fear of driving. While flooding is quicker, it is also less efficient and more likely to traumatize a client, making his or her fear even worse. Therefore, a therapist would likely only put a client through this treatment because the maladaptive behavior is interfering with the client's life in a way that does not accommodate a lengthier treatment. Suppose the client with the fear of driving was an over-the-road trucker. If a therapist uses flooding after judiciously and properly assessing and preparing the client, the treatment can be quite helpful.

Aversive conditioning utilizes the same principles as exposure therapy, but in a different direction. The goal in aversive conditioning is to substitute a negative (aversive) stimulus for a behavioral response, such as drinking or gambling, that the client does not have the self-control to stop on his or her own. For example, an alcoholic might take the drug antabuse each morning. As long as the client avoids drinking alcohol, he or she will feel no negative effects from the drug, but if the client does drink alcohol, antabuse causes terrible nausea. This method has been used with some success to treat alcoholism by pairing the alcohol with nausea (Wiens & Menustik, 1983). The problem with aversive conditioning is that the negative response always needs to occur in the face of the harmful stimulus;

Most feared

- Drive across town
- Drive down the street
- Drive in parking lot
- Drive via simulation (video/virtual)
- Watch video of driving
- Visualize driving in therapist office while practicing relaxation

Least feared

14.3 Exposure therapy
In systematic desensitization, the client is exposed to low-fear stimuli and progressively moves up to high fear stimuli. This figure depicts a potential progression for a client with a phobia of driving.

once an alcoholic gets away from the therapy setting, he or she no longer has to take the nausea-inducing drug and can learn to discriminate between the aversive conditioning situation and other situations. Arthur N. Wiens and Carol E. Menustik found that only 33 percent of their participants continued abstaining from alcohol after three years. Because of this complication and to achieve a higher success rate, therapists often use aversive conditioning in combination with other treatments.

Operant conditioning informs another type of behavior therapy, called **applied behavior analysis**. Applied behavior analysis occurs when reinforcers are presented to encourage desired behaviors and withheld to discourage undesired behaviors. If you have a professor who gives you a point every day you attend class but gives you nothing if you do not show up, he or she is using some of the principles of applied behavior analysis. Examples of its use in treatment settings include helping people with schizophrenia behave more appropriately and helping children with autism (who are often very socially withdrawn) to interact more. Applied behavior analysis as a therapy can be quite time intensive—the Lovaas method, which was developed to help young autistic children, takes forty hours a week of shaping behavior. Parents used a combination of positively reinforcing desired behaviors, such as smiling and making eye contact and ignoring or punishing aggressive and self-abusive behaviors, such as hitting or head-banging (Lovaas, 1987). After two years in the initial study, nine of the nineteen participating children were demonstrating normal intelligence (people with autism often score in the intellectually deficient range) and successfully functioning in school.

> **applied behavior analysis**
> a treatment approach that replaces undesirable behavior with positive behavior through conditioning, punishment, or reinforcement

Reinforcers used in applied behavior analysis can be social in nature (praise, attention) or concrete (toys, food). For example, a student might receive congratulations and/or a favorite dessert as a reward for good grades. Similarly, in some grade schools and households, people might use a token economy, in which participants receive a token of some sort—such as a plastic coin or gold star—for exhibiting appropriate behavior; the accumulated tokens are later exchanged for various concrete or activity rewards. If you ever had a star chart or reward jar at home, you experienced a token economy (of course, if you have a job, now you are also experiencing the universal token economy).

Although applied behavior analysis has been used successfully to address many issues in many settings, it is not without its critics. There are two main concerns. The first is whether behaviors modified through the use of external reinforcers will remain modified if and when the reinforcement stops. Further, some argue that use of external reinforcers is merely bribery. Advocates of applied behavior analysis hold that the appropriate behaviors will remain because a shift is made toward other real-life reinforcers, such as social praise. In addition, oftentimes the appropriate behaviors resulting from the behavioral intervention become intrinsically rewarding. Best practice in applied behavior analysis requires that the therapist explicitly design the program in a way that will encourage clients to maintain behaviors after the end of therapy. The second concern is whether it is ethical to control someone else's behavior. Advocates argue that all behavior is shaped by reinforcers in some way, so why not reinforce the adaptive, positive behaviors instead of the maladaptive, negative ones. Regardless of the approach, it is important to remember that all types of therapy have some element of attempting to change another's behavior.

Cognitive behavioral therapies

cognitive behavioral therapy
a type of therapy that helps the person/client change potentially self-destructive behavior through addressing negative thought patterns that fuel the behavior

Behavior therapies seem to best serve specific fears and behavior problems. They do not do as well with disorders that have more of a mental component, such as major depression and generalized anxiety. Cognitive behavioral therapies were born out of the cognitive model, which holds that we cannot adequately explain or change human behavior if we ignore the impact of our thoughts. As the Greek philosopher, Epictetus, noted: "People are not disturbed by things but by the view they take of them." Thus, cognitive psychologists hypothesize that blaming the self and overgeneralizing when explaining negative events are key to the cycle of depression. A depressed person interprets a friend canceling plans with him or her as a general dislike, confirming the low self-opinion already held, contributing to feeling sad and hopeless, and then to not rescheduling or avoiding the friend in the future. Through cognitive behavioral therapy, the maladaptive thoughts are identified and changed, thus leading to a change in feelings and behaviors.

Beck's (1979) cognitive therapy, for example, seeks to alter catastrophizing, or blowing things out of proportion (e.g., if I fail this exam, I'll fail the class, then I'll lose my scholarships and have to drop out and move back home with my parents). Another early cognitive therapist, Albert Ellis, created rational emotive behavior therapy (REBT) (1962, 1987, 1995). REBT focused on irrational thoughts that tend to involve absolutes: the first time someone experiences a romantic breakup, he or she may believe that it is awful; he or she cannot stand it; or he or she will never have a relationship again. Ellis argued to his clients that this sort of thinking is absurd, and if they would just change such self-defeating thoughts, they would feel better and engage in healthier behaviors. Figure 14.4 depicts how many cognitive behavioral therapists view the interconnections between behavior, thoughts, and feelings. While most cognitive therapists are not as confrontational as Ellis, the theory and methods hold. In general, practitioners such as Beck and Ellis worked to change cognitions, believing that the behaviors would follow. These days, most therapists who practice cognitive behavioral therapy advocate an approach that has a stronger behavioral component.

14.4 The cognitive triangle
The cognitive triangle is representative of approaches to cognitive behavioral therapy often used by cognitive behavioral therapists. It represents the relationship between various emotive factors on a person.

The more integrated approach involves identifying and challenging negative thoughts but also strongly encourages clients to practice their more positive approach in everyday settings (Kazantzis, et al., 2010; Moses & Barlow, 2006). For example, a client might keep a log of daily activities associated with positive and negative emotions and engage more in the activities that lead to feeling good. Other examples include someone with social phobia practicing talking with people or someone with obsessive-compulsive disorder playing a guitar instead of washing his or her hands. Practicing adaptive behaviors helps to "retrain the brain"—people learn that they are competent and can choose which behaviors they will engage in.

This Is Psychology

Receiving therapy used to involve travel to another location and in-person contact with your therapist. While this still happens to a large degree, online or distance therapy is a growing phenomenon. There are now platforms, such as thera-LINK, Talkspace, and Breakthrough, that allow people to meet with a therapist via their computer, tablet, or phone, using approaches we have discussed in this chapter. The self-help movement has also gotten on board, with programs such as WellTrack and SilverCloud, which let college students access screenings to measure depression, anxiety, and more; take courses; and even track their moods to see what things help them feel better or worse. The University of Florida launched Therapist Assisted Online, or TAO, in 2014, a program that combines online self-help methods with online therapist consultation. Benefits of digital modes of treatment include access for people who could not otherwise get to a therapist's office, convenience, and affordability. Critics believe that online therapy loses some of the nuance of face-to-face contact and has risks regarding confidentiality. Further, it is not sufficient to meet the needs of those with more severe, complicated issues (DeAngelis, 2012; Hoffman, 2011). In spite of these concerns, studies have found it to be effective for some issues, some of the time (Villines, 2015).

Group and Family Therapies

All of the above therapies were originally developed for work with individuals. With the exception of traditional psychoanalysis, however, they have been used with groups as well. **Group therapy** involves one or two therapists working with an average of eight clients who have the same diagnosis (e.g., anxiety) or are struggling with the same issue (e.g., grief). Groups do not allow for the same level of therapist involvement with each client, but they do have clear benefits: enabling clients to see that others share their problems, constructing a social laboratory for exploring behaviors and developing skills, and providing feedback for those behaviors and skills.

A particular type of group therapy is **family therapy**, which gained traction in the 1960s, with the work of people such as Virginia Satir, Salvador Minuchin, and Jay Haley. Family therapy holds that no one person in a family is responsible for the problems being experienced. The therapists work with multiple family members to heal relationships and learn more adaptive ways of communicating (Hazelrigg, et al., 1987; Shadish, et al., 1993).

group therapy
a form of psychotherapy in which one or more therapists work with people/clients as a group

family therapy
a form of group therapy in which a therapist works with two or more family members to address dysfunctional family dynamics

Another way for people to get help with emotional and behavioral issues is through self-help and support groups (Yalom, 1985). These groups differ from group psychotherapy in that they are not run by a licensed psychotherapist. Rather, they are most often facilitated by people who have life experience with the issue rather than formal training in counseling. The most widely known and used support group is probably Alcoholics Anonymous (AA), which reports having more than two million members and more than 100,000 groups around the world (Finlay, 2000).

Concept Recall

1. What are the goals and techniques of psychodynamic therapy?
2. What are the themes and goals of humanistic therapy?
3. Why are the behavioral therapies not considered insight therapies?
4. What is the primary difference between behavior therapy and cognitive behavior therapy?
5. How do group and family therapies differ from individual psychotherapies, and what are their benefits?
6. How are self-help groups different from group psychotherapy?

EFFECTIVENESS OF PSYCHOLOGICAL THERAPIES

How effective are the psychological therapies, and should we be directed to one type of psychotherapy over others? The overall consensus, after a fair amount of research, is that psychotherapy is effective for some people, for some problems, some of the time. Not exactly a ringing endorsement; however, if we look a little deeper, it seems that therapy will probably be worthwhile. On average, people in therapy have a better outcome in improving their conditions than those with similar problems who do not seek therapy (Smith, et al., 1980). Further, some forms of therapy work better for particular problems. For example, behavioral conditioning therapies have achieved the most favorable results with specific behavior problems, such as bed-wetting, phobias, compulsions, marital problems, and sexual disorders (Baker, et al., 2008; Hunsley & DiGiulio, 2002; Shadish & Baldwin, 2005), while psychodynamic therapy has had success with depression and anxiety (Driessen, et al., 2010; Leichsenring & Rabung, 2008; Shedler, 2012). New studies conclude that cognitive and cognitive behavioral therapy are best for anxiety, PTSD, and depression (De Los Reyes & Kadzin, 2009; Stewart & Chambliss, 2009; Tolin, 2010). Also, therapy tends to be more effective when the problem is clear-cut and more behavioral in nature (Westen & Morrison, 2001). In other words, a phobia is generally much more easily treated than a personality disorder or schizophrenia.

While most psychological therapies are helpful for at least some people, it is possible for them to be ineffective or even harmful (Barlow, 2010; Castonguay, et al., 2010;

Dimiddjian & Hollon, 2010). Most practicing therapists rely on a combination of well-researched therapeutic interventions and their experience to determine what works for their clients most of the time.

Alternative Therapies

In addition to the long-standing psychological therapies, there are some newer approaches that some professionals consider effective, while others consider them to be "pseudotherapies," not worthy of the effort people put into them. Regardless, many people suffering from psychological issues are willing to try them in hopes of relief (Kessler, et al., 2001). Examples of therapies that are currently considered alternative by many include **Eye Movement Desensitization Reprocessing (EMDR)** and **light exposure therapy**. The former was developed originally as a technique to help veterans traumatized by their combat experiences (Shapiro, 1989), and the latter was developed to help people who suffer from seasonal affective disorder, a form of depression that most often affects people living in climates far from the equator that have long, dark winters.

Eye Movement Desensitization Reprocessing (EMDR) a technique to help veterans traumatized by their combat experiences

light exposure therapy a technique developed to help people who suffer from seasonal affective disorder, a form of depression that most often affects people living in climates far from the equator that have long, dark winters

Though still considered "alternative," both of the above therapies seem generally to work at least often enough to keep the approaches around. Shapiro (1999, 2002) reported that 84 to 100 percent of single-trauma victims participating in four studies did, in fact, have a reduction in their symptoms. The Society of Clinical Psychology task force on empirically validated treatments allows that EMDR is "probably efficacious" in the treatment of nonmilitary post-traumatic stress disorder (Chambless, et al., 1998; Rodenburg, et al., 2009; Seidler & Wagner, 2006). What is unclear is why EMDR works. It may be bilateral stimulation in the form of eye movements that help with traumatic memories, or it may be simply recalling them in a safe and reassuring context combined with a strong placebo effect (Lilienfield & Arkowitz, 2007).

Light exposure therapy seems to have more definitive research supporting its use. Twenty carefully controlled trials led to this conclusion: morning bright light does indeed improve SAD symptoms for many people and does so as effectively as cognitive behavior therapy or antidepressant medication (Lam, et al., 2006; Rohan, et al., 2007). Further, brain scans indicate that light therapy sparks activity in a brain region that influences the body's arousal and hormones (Ishida, et al., 2005).

Impact of Culture

In Chapter 13, we looked at the impact culture can have on perception of psychological disorders. Culture also influences how we treat psychological disorders, as well as how people view therapy. For example, *Naikan* is a Japanese therapy in which the goal is for the client to discover how he or she has been ungrateful or bothersome to others and find ways to demonstrate gratitude and alliance (Foulks, Bland, & Shervington, 1995). While this may sound strange to you (unless you are Japanese), it makes sense in Japanese culture, which is collectivistic and, thus, values the well-being of the group over the individual.

Cross-Cultural Case

Therapies Across Cultures

Throughout this text, we've discussed how cultural norms and expectations can affect everything from diagnosis (Abnormal Psychology) to the placebo effect (Behavior), but culture can also influence the type of treatment a person not only receives but also expects to receive from his or her physician or psychologist. As the University of Southern California's Dr. Ruth C. White notes in a 2011 article in *Psychology Today*, "culture not only influences the motivation to seek help but also impacts how mental illness is experienced." Social stigma, according to White, can also affect a person's ability to accept the help provided by their psychologist once a condition has been diagnosed. For example, while many Americans readily accept prescription drugs—pills—as an acceptable treatment for many mental disorders, people in other cultures may see such "pill-popping" as a sign of weakness. Indeed, even in cultures as comparatively closely connected as the US and the UK, treatments such as support groups, which are seen as beneficial in the US, are viewed as invasive and inappropriate in the UK. Unfortunately, cultural ideas regarding mental illness can sometimes affect treatment to the point of removing the possibility for it. White notes that in Uganda, the cultural stigma applied to mental illness is such that not only will families go to great lengths to hide a loved one's mental illness rather than seek treatment for it, but also the government allots only 5 percent of its fiscal resources to mental health services, leaving Ugandan psychologists and their patients with little to no resources for treatment. As psychologists and physicians look to treat mental disorders in different cultures around the world, they must consider not only the variances in symptom presentation and treatment expectation, but also each culture's unique ideas regarding whether even to admit symptoms or seek treatment in the first place.

The United States is a multicultural nation with a diversity of ethnic and cultural backgrounds, and this diversity impacts patterns of therapy. If you are part of an ethnic minority group, you are less likely to seek psychological services than someone from the majority group. This is not due to lack of need; the rate of most major psychological disorders is similar across racial and ethnic groups living in the community (US Department of Health and Human Services, 1999). In fact, the rate of some disorders is even higher among people living in poverty, or who are homeless, incarcerated, or institutionalized, and minorities are overrepresented in these subgroups. Mental health services for ethnic minorities are not meeting existing needs for a number of reasons: lack of proper insurance coverage, lack of mental health facilities where they live, distrust of anything considered part of "the system," and language barriers, to name a few (Sue & Zane, 1987; US DHHS, 1999). Another barrier involves the lack of ethnic minority mental health providers. Therapy involves sharing personal information with a virtual stranger, a process that is often made easier if you feel the therapist has some understanding of where you are coming from. Having a therapist from the same ethnic background can go some way in helping people feel more comfortable, but while ethnic minorities make up just over 30 percent of the population (and growing), they make up only about 10 percent of mental health professionals across the different disciplines (American Psychological Association, 2015).

Therapeutic Lifestyle Change

The biopsychosocial model was described in Chapter 13 as the best model to explain the development of most of the psychological disorders. It may also be the key for long-term relief from those disorders. Traditionally, we have tended to compartmentalize treatment: we see medical doctors for the biological component, psychologists and counselors for the psychological component, and social workers for the social component, when we address these problems at all. Some people are now trying to integrate these and promote therapeutic lifestyle change (Ilardi, 2009). They point out that for much of human history, physical activity and social engagement were what helped us survive. Therefore, those are the things for which our bodies and brains are designed. We know that outdoor activity in natural environments reduces stress and promotes health (McCurdy, et al., 2010; Phillips, 2011). Most people would probably not give up central heating and indoor plumbing to live in a cave and hunt for food on a permanent basis, though many might do so in the short term for recreation and/or the chance to win seven figures on a reality show. However, making regular aerobic exercise, adequate sleep (seven to eight hours per night), light exposure, social connection, mindfulness, and time in nature part of one's lifestyle has been shown to be more effective than traditional treatment in relieving depressive symptoms (Ilardi, 2009). Whether a person is dealing with a major mental illness or just daily stress, it is certainly not going to hurt to become more engaged in the world around us!

Concept Recall

1. How effective are the psychological therapies?
2. What impact does culture have on the nature of therapy and whether people will seek it?
3. Why is lifestyle important to mental health?
4. What factors contribute to the effectiveness of psychological therapies?
5. Why do people seek alternative therapies, and are they worthwhile?

THERAPY AND PSYCHOLOGY

As has been discussed throughout this chapter, there are a variety of methods for helping people when they want to change their thought patterns and behavior and/or learn to better understand and manage their emotions. Biological, psychological, and sociocultural forms of therapy have all been found to be helpful to some degree. Many people believe psychotherapy would not benefit them because they are not "crazy." Most of the people psychotherapists treat aren't either. The methods we have discussed here have been helpful for people who are unable to function otherwise but have also helped people who are temporarily experiencing difficult circumstances or simply want to grow and become more effective people for themselves, their loved ones, and society. As we will see in the next chapter, society and our social world have a powerful impact on our individual selves.

Practicing psychotherapy requires a great deal of training. Nevertheless, there are things that you can do today to apply what you have learned over the last two chapters regarding mental illness. First, your attitude regarding mental illness shapes the way you react to the world around you. Recognizing that mental health and mental illness are two ends of the same continuum—rather than two distinct states of being—will help you to better understand your challenges and to be more supportive of others. Second, the way we talk about mental health matters. Person-first language, as discussed in Chapter 13, helps us to keep the person separate from the life challenges. Similarly, avoiding the slang terms, such as "crazy" or "mental," as well as avoiding misuse of clinical words, such as calling someone who is highly organized OCD, shows sensitivity to people's struggles. Finally, we can help reduce some of the stigma associated with seeing a mental health professional by learning more about how they help with all aspects of life. Medical researchers and practitioners are beginning to recognize the huge health advantages of preventative health practices, such as balanced diets, exercise, and stress management. The same is true regarding our mental health. Many people have recognized that beginning early to apply psychological principles to shaping daily habits can reduce the disruption and distress caused by preventable mental health problems later in life (we use "preventable" here to differentiate between mental health challenges that are caused by lifestyle versus those that are strongly influenced by genetic and sociocultural factors).

REVIEW

- When are treatments such as electroconvulsive shock therapy and psychosurgery typically used in modern times?
- How is cognitive behavior therapy different from behavior therapy?
- What does research say about the effectiveness of therapies?
- Why did group and family therapy develop?
- What contributed to deinstitutionalization in the mid-twentieth century?
- What are some of the reasons people do not want to take, or stop taking, psychotropic medication when it is prescribed as part of their treatment?
- Why are ethnic minorities less likely to access mental health services?
- What makes self-help groups different from group therapy?
- Why are psychodynamic and humanistic therapies considered "insight" therapies?
- Why do people try alternative therapies, such as EMDR and light exposure therapy, if many professionals do not endorse them?

1. Because _____ was the first psychological therapy, Sigmund Freud is considered to be the father of psychotherapy.
   a. personal counseling
   b. person-centered counseling
   c. psychopharmacology
   d. psychoanalysis

2. If Leo's therapist is trying to help him self-actualize, he is probably a
   a. psychoanalyst.
   b. behaviorist.
   c. cognitive behaviorist.
   d. humanist.

3. If Linda is terrified of clowns and wanted to try a behavioral technique, one way she could overcome this fear would be to
   a. give herself a pep talk before she goes to a circus.
   b. interact with a clown repeatedly until she is no longer afraid.
   c. write a list of why she shouldn't be afraid of clowns.
   d. avoid clowns. They are not a necessary part of everyday life.

4. Which of the following did not play a role in leading to the deinstitutionalization movement?
   a. the introduction of antipsychotic medicines that controlled serious symptoms
   b. 1960s legislation that made committing people difficult and promoted community treatment
   c. government funding from an act passed in the 1960s
   d. the publication of the first DSM

5. What are the three broad categories of treatment for psychological disorders?

    a. psychoanalysis, psychopharmacology, and psychotherapy

    b. psychosurgery, psychopharmacology, and psychoanalysis

    c. psychosurgery, psychoanalysis, and psychotherapy

    d. psychosurgery, psychopharmacology, and psychotherapy

6. What do all types of psychotherapy include?

    a. personality assessment tools

    b. trained therapists

    c. setting goals

    d. changing behavior

7. Which of the following is true of Eye Movement Desensitization Reprocessing and light exposure therapy?

    a. They are long-standing and successful treatments.

    b. Although they are considered alternative therapies, there have been reported benefits.

    c. Eye Movement Desensitization Reprocessing is considered evidence-based treatment, whereas light exposure therapy is not seen as successful.

    d. They are considered alternative therapies and have not been connected to benefits in clients.

8. Which of the following is true of ethnic minorities, in general, in relationship to therapy?

    a. They do not experience the same benefit as majority members.

    b. They are less likely to seek services.

    c. They have less need for therapy.

    d. They are more comfortable with the process of therapy.

9. Which one of these is a side effect of electroconvulsive therapy?

    a. memory loss

    b. prolonged muscle twitches

    c. aphasia

    d. poverty of speech

10. If you were living in a Western country and had a mental illness during the Middle Ages, which of the following is likely?

    a. You would have been prescribed Freud's talk therapy.

    b. You would have been thought to be a witch or demonically possessed.

    c. You would have experienced humane treatment advocated by people such as Dorothea Dix.

    d. You would have experienced a surgical procedure, such as a lobotomy.

Answer Key

1. d 2. a 3. b 4. d 5. d 6. b 7. b 8. b 9. a 10. b

REFLECT

1. This chapter gave a historical overview of treatments, some of which we now consider inhumane and barbaric. What treatments offered today do you think people in 200 years will read about and view in the same vein?

2. People will sometimes refuse treatment for mental health issues because they do not like the side effects of the treatment or do not feel they need to change. Do you think that people with mental health issues should have the right to refuse treatment, even if it interferes with their or someone else's ability to function?

3. Which of the therapies discussed do you think you would find most helpful, and why?

WRITE

1. Therapies, like disorders, are often culturally based. Choose a cultural group, either from a different country or a minority group in this country, and research what sort of treatment they advocate for mental health issues.

2. Self-help resources (books, videos, support groups) are a popular means of working through mental health issues. Research whether such approaches are as or more effective than treatment by a professional. If so, are there issues or people who respond particularly well to self-help approaches?

Key Terms

active listening   421
antianxiety medication   406
antidepressants   412
antipsychotics   410
applied behavior analysis   419
behavior therapy   417
client-centered therapy   417
cognitive behavioral therapy   420
counterconditioning   417
electroconvulsive therapy (ECT)   409
exposure therapy   418
Eye Movement Desensitization Reprocessing (EMDR)   423

family therapy   421
group therapy   406
insight therapy   406
light exposure therapy   423
lobotomy   407
mood stabilizers   413
psychoanalysis   415
psychodynamic therapy   416
psychopharmacology   410
psychosurgery   408
self-actualization   416

Chapter 15 Social Psychology

After reading this chapter, you will be able to answer the following questions:

- What factors influence our attitudes toward different people, experiences, and things?
- What are the different types of persuasion?
- What is cognitive dissonance?
- How does cognitive dissonance affect behavior and attitudes?
- How do prejudices develop?
- What impact do stereotypes have on our perception of others?
- What is bias, and how does it develop?
- How do implicit and explicit social norms impact behavior and attitudes?
- What is the difference between informational and normative influence on behavior?
- Under what conditions are we most likely to provide help to someone in need?

The rise in popularity of social media is creating a new level of challenge and difficulty for psychologists. We live in a social world and are strongly influenced by the people around us. The social connections we share with others are an important part of our daily lives, and thanks to modern technology, we can now be constantly connected with others. To appreciate how socially connected you are, stop reading for a moment and look around you. It is a safe bet that you will find that you are socially connected in several ways at this very moment. You likely have your cell phone close by, or maybe a computer with a social media program open, or you are watching a television show that is depicting people interacting with one another, or maybe there are other people around you (or possibly all four? If so, you may want to reconsider the place where you study). Thanks to social media, the Internet, television, and other technologies, we now have access to the social world in a way that has never been possible before.

Social media technologies present a new challenge for psychologists. Facebook was launched in 2004. While not the first social media website, Facebook is considered the beginning of the modern wave of social media technologies. Today, many options exist for creating online social interactions, including—but certainly not limited to—Instagram, Snapchat, and Twitter. To us, one of the most vivid examples of the power of the social technologies is what happens right before and after class. Before social technology became widespread, the time before and after class provided an opportunity for students to engage with their classmates. The same was true for other social gatherings. Today, we find that the time before and after class is dedicated to the virtual social world. While the classroom is full of living, breathing people who are only a few feet away, virtual connections demand students' attention.

The high level of interconnectedness permitted by social technologies is both a benefit and a curse, as it provides opportunities to be engaged with family, friends, and people from across the globe, but with this increased opportunity for social connectedness often comes a greater feeling of disconnectedness as our interactions with others are becoming less personal and more digital.

The new dynamic created by virtual social interactions is a rapidly growing area of interest for psychologists. However, the research we discuss in this chapter primarily focuses on the old fashioned kind of person-to-person social interaction. Prior to the availability of the Internet and personal electronics such as smartphones, this focus made sense. Not any more. As you read, ask yourself how you feel the social influences discussed in the chapter might be different

when interactions occur through social media technology. We must first understand the way people interact with each other offline in order to understand the power of online relationships.

social psychology
a subfield of psychology that focuses on how the social environment—including individuals and groups—influences the behavior of the individual, including how they think, act, and feel

As defined in Chapter 1, **social psychology** is a subfield of psychology that focuses on how the social environment—including individuals and groups—influences the behavior of the individual, including how they think, act, and feel. In this chapter, we will discuss what social psychologists have learned about how our social world shapes our behavior. We will see how the social world affects our behavior both recognizably and in subtle, largely unnoticed ways we may rarely, if ever, recognize.

ATTITUDES

attitudes
the emotional and cognitive evaluations that we attach to people, places, objects, and ideas

Much of people's interactions with their social world depends on attitude. **Attitudes** are the emotional and cognitive evaluations that people attach to places, objects, ideas, and other people (Aronson, Wilson, & Akert, 2010). Our attitudes toward things can be either positive or negative. A positive attitude is felt when something is desirable and viewed as valuable to the individual. A negative attitude is felt toward something that is undesirable and viewed as not valued by the individual. Social psychologists typically talk of attitudes as involving three major components (Zanna & Rempel, 1988):

1. **An affective component**: how you feel about the person, object, or idea (What emotions do you feel when people discuss the Cleveland Cavaliers basketball team?)

2. **A behavioral component**: how you act toward the person, object, or idea (What do you do when you see a Cleveland Cavaliers game on television, sports clip on Facebook, or news story on ESPN.com?)

3. **A cognitive component**: what you believe or think about the characteristics of the person, object, or idea (What do you think about when someone mentions the Cleveland Cavaliers?)

Attitudes contain some element of each of these three components, but not necessarily in equal measure. For example, what answers did you give to each question about the Cleveland Cavaliers? Were your answers equally strong for each of the three elements of an attitude: affective, behavioral, and cognitive? Some attitudes may be almost entirely affective, while others may have a large behavioral or cognitive component. For example, many readers will have a strong emotional reaction toward the Cleveland Cavaliers franchise, while others will not feel anything at all toward this team. Those who have a strong emotional reaction may not be able to identify the current head coach, owner, or most players, but they do know how they feel about the team (a stronger affective component than cognitive). A strongly cognitive attitude toward the Cleveland Cavaliers would involve a preference or nonpreference based on the characteristics of the team, their playing style, or their management decisions, but without any real emotional attachment.

While almost all attitudes involve a combination of affective, behavioral, and cognitive influences, the exact mixture varies by the importance of the topic. The more important the topic, the higher the level of each of these influences. A true "superfan" of a sports team shows strong emotion toward the team (crying at losses and cheering wins), engages in many team-oriented behaviors (talking about the team, attending games, purchasing team-related memorabilia), and spends a great deal of mental effort on the team (memorizing the team roster, trivia, and statistics).

Understanding how our attitudes are constructed is important because attitudes have an influence on our behavior and our perception of events. We are typically motivated to defend our attitudes, especially strongly held attitudes and attitudes that we have shared publicly. The defense of our attitudes pushes us to evaluate objects and events in specific ways. A positive attitude can lead us to excuse, explain away, or justify negative characteristics of an object or event, such as when our favorite actor is in a movie that is not well received by audiences or critics, but we work to justify the weaknesses based on the positive feelings we have toward the actor. Similarly, a negative attitude toward an object or event can make us blind to the positive characteristics of that object or event, such as when people immediately overlook a movie because of their attitude toward an actor, director, or genre.

While our attitudes can influence our behavior, the amount of influence they have on our actions depends on several factors. Social psychologists have discovered that the influence of attitudes on behavior is strongest when the attitude is:

1. **Public**: you have shared it with other people;

2. **Specific**: the target is something concrete (such as a particular product, sports team, or political candidate) rather than abstract (such as freedom or health practices);

3. **Stable**: this is an object or issue with which you have had repeated contact over time; and

4. **Accessible**: the details of the attitude are easy to recall from memory.

Affective Component	**How we feel about the person, object, or idea** *What emotions do you feel when people discuss the Cleveland Cavaliers basketball team?*
Behavioral Component	**How we act toward the person, object, or idea** *What do you do when you see a Cleveland Cavaliers game on television, sports clip on Facebook, or news story on ESPN.com?*
Cognitive Component	**What we believe or think about the characteristics of the person, object, or idea** *What do you think about when someone mentions the Cleveland Cavaliers?*

15.1 Major components of attitudes
The three major components of an attitude are shown above, with an example of how this component might apply to a sports team.

These characteristics allow you to make predictions about when people will engage in certain behaviors. You can better predict if a person is going to purchase tickets to a Cleveland Cavaliers' basketball game by asking about the person's attitude toward the current Cleveland Cavaliers' team than if you were to ask about the person's general attitude toward professional basketball (Figure 15.1). The connection between attitudes and behavior is very similar to the connection between intelligence tests and real world behavior (as discussed in Chapter 10): Both attitudes and intelligence are internal to the person, and both influence externally observable behavior.

Persuasion: Central and Peripheral Routes

central route of persuasion
attitude change that is due to a careful weighing and evaluation of arguments and the characteristics of the object or event

Understanding that attitudes give rise to behaviors can help you understand that to persuade people to change their behavior you should begin by changing their attitudes, which is why commercials and political campaigns seek to manipulate the audience's attitudes.

Research on persuasion indicates that there are two routes to changing attitudes: the central route and peripheral route (Petty & Cacioppo, 1984). When a person is motivated and willing to engage in evaluating the argument, the **central route of persuasion**—attitude change that is due to a careful weighing and evaluation of arguments and the characteristics of the object or event—will be more successful. Attitudes based on the quality of the arguments (central route) are most likely to be successful when the listener is motivated, able to devote attention and cognitive resources to the argument, and interested in the topic and finds it personally relevant (see Figure 15.2). We expect that most of the readers of this text would be more likely to engage in a discussion about the rules regarding cell phone usage in campus buildings than a discussion regarding Medicare benefits for the elderly. The cell phone in campus buildings topic is simply more personally relevant to most of the readers of a college textbook. However, some of you may be nontraditional students or caregivers for an elderly relative and, thus, would find the second topic more personally engaging. This being the case, if people wanted to convince you that a "no cell phone" policy would be good for your campus, they would need to provide a logical, well-reasoned argument to influence your attitude on this topic. That is, they would need to pursue the central route of persuasion.

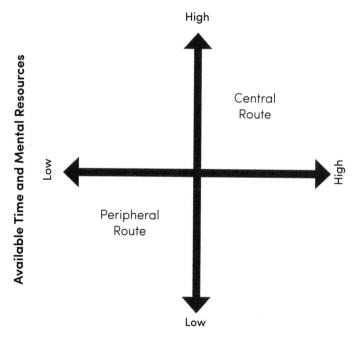

Characteristics of the Two Routes of Persuasion

15.2 Which route to choose?
How we present persuasive messages depends on both the importance of the topic to the audience and the time and resources the audience has available.

Unfortunately, it is relatively rare that you have both the motivation and the time to become cognitively engaged with all of the persuasive arguments that fill your social world. When the argument is about an attitude that is only weakly held or when the argument occurs in a context in which the listener is not able to focus closely on the details of the argument, then the **peripheral route of persuasion**—attitude change that is due to quick association with positive or negative cues—is often responsible for changes in our attitude. As you watch television, read magazines, or engage on social media, you are bombarded with arguments that use the peripheral route of persuasion. This is the case because most commercials and celebrity endorsements you see on television and social media do not rely on a discussion of the logical or factual elements of the product, but rather on quick associations between the product and peripheral cues, such as attractiveness of the celebrity endorser, background music, and humor. Peripheral arguments often make use of classical conditioning, one of the two types of learning discussed in Chapter 7. Think for a minute about the most recent commercials you saw or heard; did the commercials provide specific, factual information about the product, or did they focus on humor or popularity to create interest? For example, a recent commercial aired during a sporting event featured a popular sports star driving the advertised vehicle onto a movie set in which he was playing a cowboy, and the other actors were all riding horses. While this commercial is memorable, it does not inform viewers about the vehicle's features or advantages. The peripheral route used in this commercial is well suited to a television audience who zones out during commercials.

In order to appreciate the role of the two routes of persuasion in attitude change, let's take a moment and think about how we might use these two routes of persuasion to influence the attitudes of students on campus. Imagine that you have been asked to help change a policy on your campus regarding the allocation of funds to the naming of buildings on campus. You will be speaking with two groups about this topic. The first group includes your fellow classmates while the second group includes campus administrators. Your classmates likely do not realize that the naming of buildings is a highly political process that can possibly be a source of significant donations to the university or the loss of support from donors. Campus administrators are acutely aware of the politics involved in this process. How would the differences between these two groups influence your presentation? According to what we have learned about the central and peripheral routes to persuasion, your chances of success would be better if you used a PowerPoint presentation containing well-researched facts with the college administrators, but a local band and free giveaways with your fellow classmates.

Cognitive Dissonance

Your attitudes are strongly influenced by the persuasive arguments that abound in your social world. However, your attitudes are also a product of the powerful effects of self-persuasion. You are highly motivated to perceive consistency between your actions and attitudes, and, typically, what you do matches what you believe. However, this is not always the case. Sometimes, you engage in behaviors that are inconsistent with your attitudes (such as eating junk food despite your positive attitude regarding healthy

peripheral route of persuasion
attitude change that is due to quick association with positive or negative cues in the environment or the object or event

eating). When inconsistencies between actions and attitudes are viewed by other people, you often experience a strong feeling of tension and discomfort created by the mismatch between action and attitude. According to **cognitive dissonance theory** (Festinger, 1959), the tension people experience when their attitudes and behaviors do not match motivates them to change their attitudes to be more consistent with their behaviors.

The power of cognitive dissonance in changing people's attitudes was most famously demonstrated by Leon Festinger and James Carlsmith (1959). Participants were asked to spend thirty minutes placing and removing spools from a board, then another thirty minutes turning forty-eight square pegs one quarter-turn clockwise, then another quarter-turn, and so on. Do these sound like tedious tasks? While participants busied themselves with the spools and pegs, the experimenters pretended to closely monitor the participants' behavior, but they didn't actually care about the participants' performance and didn't even report anything about it in their paper. Instead, the hour spent fooling around with spools and pegs was merely intended to instill boredom and frustration in their participants, and the actual experiment began only after the hour with spools and pegs was finished.

After completing the task, the experimenter pleaded with participants to help him recruit other students to participate in the experiment by describing what a wonderful time they had, and the experimenter even offered to pay participants for their time and effort. Participants were randomly assigned to receive either five dollars (about forty dollars in today's money) or twenty dollars (about $170 today). Once the participants agreed to help the experimenter, they sat down with a female **confederate**—a person who pretends to be a candidate for participation but is actually working with the researchers—to describe the experiment as fun and exciting. All participants who accepted the job offer were observed to do a nice job of explaining to the confederate

cognitive dissonance theory
the tension we experience when our attitudes and behaviors do not match; motivates us to change our attitudes to be more consistent with our behaviors

confederate
a person who pretends to be a candidate for participation but is actually working with the researchers

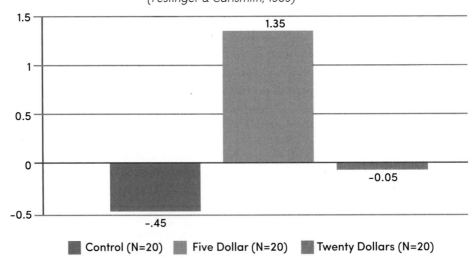

How enjoyable were the experimental tasks? (-5 to +5)
(Festinger & Carlsmith, 1959)

Control (N=20)   Five Dollar (N=20)   Twenty Dollars (N=20)

15.3 Outcome of Festinger and Carlsmith's (1959) study of cognitive dissonance
Despite being offered less money, the participants paid five dollars reported the task as being the most enjoyable.

that the experiment was great fun. Finally, after the task with spools and pegs that was really just a decoy, after being offered money to lie about how much fun the experiment was, and after telling the lie for which they expected to be paid, participants were asked how they *really* felt about the spool and peg task. Before we tell you what the researchers found, let us say that one group reported actually enjoying the task, and the other group admitted that it was terribly boring. Who do you think claimed to enjoy the task, the group who was promised five dollars for lying about it or the group who was promised twenty dollars for lying?

If you thought the group who was promised twenty dollars for lying was the one who claimed to enjoy the task, you would be wrong. That's right, the group who was promised just five dollars—not twenty dollars—was the group who claimed to have enjoyed the task. Why did the five-dollar group but not the twenty-dollar group change their attitudes? You might think that the five-dollar group's attitudes toward the task changed when they described its positive aspects to the confederate, but that explanation doesn't work because *both* the five-dollar and the twenty-dollar group described the experiment as fun and exciting to the confederate, but only the five-dollar group changed their attitudes (see Figure 15.3). For the key to the attitude change, imagine how you would have felt as a participant in each condition. As a participant in the twenty-dollar group you might have thought something like, "Why did I lie to another person? Well, I was handsomely paid for lying, that's why." In other words, you could rely on the hefty payoff as justification for your unethical behavior. On the other hand, as a participant in the five-dollar group you would probably have wondered the same thing, but unfortunately the five-dollar payoff is not sufficient to justify lying. In music, dissonance occurs when two notes clash, so *cognitive* dissonance refers to two *ideas* that clash. Because most people like to think of themselves as ethical, participants in the five-dollar group are forced to entertain two ideas that clash: "I am an ethical person" and "I just lied without sufficient justification." Just as dissonant notes create discomfort in the listener, cognitive dissonance creates mental discomfort.

Anyone who experiences cognitive dissonance is motivated to find a way to eliminate the dissonance, which will in turn ease the discomfort. To eliminate the cognitive dissonance, participants in the five-dollar group deceived themselves into believing that they had actually enjoyed the experiment, which led to harmony between the ideas "I am an ethical person" and "I didn't lie when I described the task as fun and exciting." Once participants in the five-dollar group deceived themselves, they went so far as to share this self-deception with the experimenter by saying that they had enjoyed the task with spools and pegs (see flowchart in Figure 15.4 on the following page). Research on cognitive dissonance theory confirms that self-deception occurs when attitudes and actions are inconsistent and there is not a sufficient external reason to explain the reasons for the behavior.

Although participants in the five-dollar group used self-deception to change their attitude to make it consistent with their behavior, this is only one of several ways of eliminating cognitive dissonance. A second way to eliminate cognitive dissonance would be to change behavior to be more consistent with an attitude. The first option (i.e.,

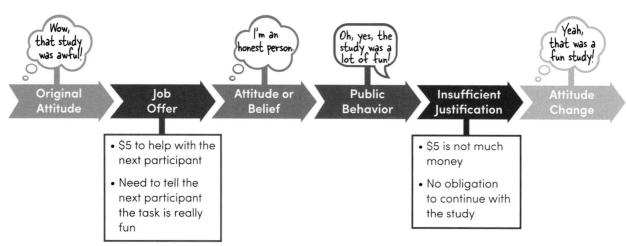

15.4 Cognitive dissonance flowchart
This flowchart represents the attitude change process for participants in the $5 condition of Carlsmith and Festinger's (1959) study.

changing attitude to be consistent with behavior) is typically easier because attitudes are private but behavior is publicly visible. Further, in the Festinger and Carlsmith experiment, the lying behavior had already occurred, so the participant couldn't really go back in time to change the past behavior.

Cognitive dissonance is a major motivational force in the development of our behavior and our attitudes. The level of dissonance (discomfort and tension) is influenced by the amount of discrepancy between our behavior and our attitude, how public the behavior is, and the level of external force that is pushing for the behavior. When we experience cognitive dissonance, there are several options for reducing these feelings. Some of the ways to minimize cognitive dissonance include:

1. Changing the behavior to be consistent with our attitude, and

2. Changing the attitude to be more consistent with the behavior.

Of these first two options, it is easier to change the attitude than our behavior due to the private nature of our attitudes and public nature of the behavior. If people have seen us engaging in the behavior, it is very difficult to change the behavior and convince people that we did not do what they saw us do. However, it is much more likely that we can change the attitude and convince others—and ourselves—that this was always our attitude. Other ways to reduce cognitive dissonance through self-persuasion include:

3. Minimizing the importance of the attitude,

4. Including additional thoughts and attitudes that allow us to hold both the original attitude and engage in the behavior, and

5. Rationalizing that we did not have a choice but to engage in the behavior.

These five strategies are a small sample of how we can adjust our thinking to reduce cognitive dissonance. Research on dissonance reveals that inconsistency between attitudes and behavior causes psychological tension and discomfort, and we are highly motivated to reduce this tension. Frequently, the quickest route to dissonance reduction is through attitude rather than behavior change.

Concept Recall

1. What are the three major components of an attitude?
2. Under what conditions will an attitude most closely reflect our behavior?
3. How do messages based on the peripheral route of persuasion differ from those that use the central route?
4. What conditions create a feeling of cognitive dissonance?
5. What are several ways that we can reduce cognitive dissonance?

This Is Psychology

Cognitive dissonance can be a powerful tool for influencing voter behavior. On November 12, 2012, Benedict Carey published an article in the *New York Times* titled "Academic 'Dream Team' helped Obama's Efforts" in which he discussed the role of behavioral scientists, including Dr. Robert Cialdini, an emeritus professor of social psychology at Arizona State University, in Barack Obama's winning bid for re-election as president of the United States. According to Carey, one technique employed by the Obama campaign was to remind individuals that they voted in the past. Reminding people of how they have acted in the past creates a need for consistency and makes it more likely that they will behave this way again. As discussed in the previous section, failing to be consistent with past behaviors and attitudes creates a feeling of discomfort and dissonance. The Obama campaign's use of social science research is one indication of the growing application of psychology to exploring and impacting political behavior.

THE PSYCHOLOGY OF PREJUDICE

People have attitudes about most things, including biased behaviors toward members of certain groups. **Prejudice** is a strong positive or negative attitude toward a group of people that biases the way you think, act, and feel about the members of a particular group (Dienstbier, 1970). A quick survey of American history demonstrates the role that combating prejudice has played in many social and cultural changes over the past 100 years (e.g., women gaining the right to vote, civil rights for people of all races, and marriage equality for same-sex couples). Positive prejudice occurs when someone gives extra privileges to certain groups over others and makes assumptions about the high quality of individuals from a certain group. Children who always choose certain friends for their kickball team during recess are showing prejudice toward that particular group of individuals. Negative prejudice occurs when privileges are withheld from people or assumptions are made about what characteristics apply to individuals within a group based only on their membership in the group. Prejudice is particularly difficult to deal with because of people's seemingly automatic tendency to separate others into mental categories that include members of the **in-groups**—

prejudice
a strong positive or negative attitude toward a group of people that biases the way we think, act, and feel about the members of a particular group

in-groups
the individuals with whom we directly identify and perceive as most similar to us

out-groups

the individuals with whom we least directly identify and who we perceive to be most dissimilar from us

individuals who are perceived as similar—or **out-group**—the individuals who are perceived to be dissimilar (Brown, 2000). You can get a quick sense of these groups by thinking about who you include when you think of "us" versus who you think of when you think of "them." Members of a person's in-group are often over-attributed with the person's same characteristics, feelings, and behaviors, while members of the out-group are typically over-attributed with whatever characteristic makes them "different" from the members of the in-group (Hampton, 2010). One way to adjust for the lack of diversity that people attribute to members of out-groups is to look at the variability in attitudes, thoughts, and actions shown by members of the in-group and then to assume that this same degree of variability applies to the individual members of the out-group (see Figure 15.5). People tend to focus on the differences between themselves and the members of out-groups because it is a shorter list than the number of similarities.

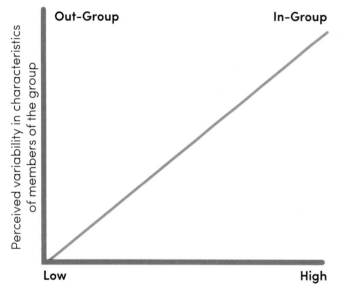

15.5 In-groups versus out-groups
We tend to perceive members of groups that are different from us as all being the same. For members of our in-groups, we recognize the variability across individuals.

In a series of experiments during the 1940s, Gordon Allport and Leo Postman powerfully demonstrated the influence of prejudices on people's evaluations of events. Groups of individuals were shown a pencil drawing of seven passengers on a subway in New York City. Five white passengers were seated (one was reading a newspaper, one held a baby, and the others were similarly engaged in other tasks). In the front of the scene, two men, one white and one black, were interacting. Allport and Postman asked people to look at this scene and report what they saw. In the picture, the white man was holding an item that looked like a razor. However, in more than half of the studies using this picture, the final report of the group was that the black man held the razor, and it was even reported that he was "brandishing it wildly" or "threatening" the other passenger (Allport & Postman, 1945, pgs. 78–79). The picture was identical for all participants, but the recalled version of the picture was shaped and distorted by the prejudices of the viewers.

We can also see the effect of positive and negative prejudices on behavior by looking at people's interpretations of sporting events. In 1954, Albert Hastorf and Hadley Cantril reported on a case study (remember from Chapter 2 that a case study is an in-depth analysis of a single subject or event) involving a football game in 1951 between Dartmouth and Princeton. This game became very rough (even for football's standards), and several players were injured. Hastorf and Cantril were more interested in the perception of the audience than the game's outcome. You can probably anticipate what happened when the researchers asked students from each of the schools to describe what happened during the game. Each school felt that the "dirty play" was initiated by the "other" (out-group) team and that the players from "their" (in-group) team were simply retaliating against the other team. Similar prejudice occurs when you attend a sporting event and feel that all of the calls in favor of your team were correct calls while calls against your team demonstrate bias by the officials. Interestingly, the fans of the other team—while watching the same game as you—felt exactly the opposite of what you did while watching the same game. While there is only one set of officials for each game, the apparent quality of the officiating is strongly influenced by prejudiced attitudes for your own team and against the other team.

Stereotypes

Prejudices toward others often lead people to make overgeneralizations about the members of the prejudiced group. **Stereotypes** are the overgeneralized characteristics that are assigned to all members of a perceived group. While it is true that members of a group will have at least some traits in common (after all, these shared characteristics are what get them included in the group), the reality is that the individual members of the group probably differ from other members of their group in many ways. Stereotypes are cognitively economical in that they allow a person to make decisions about how to interact with many different individuals based on limited social information. This may remind you of the discussion of concepts in Chapter 10. However, while this cognitive economy is essential when categorizing *things*, lumping people into social categories can be hurtful to the people who are categorized, and even worse, can lead to errors in judgment. For example, using gender stereotypes to make assumptions about how men and women will engage in certain situations often helps us to choose how to interact with men and women. However, there are also many occasions in which these stereotypes are not accurate guides to the behaviors of the individual members of the target group.

stereotypes
the overgeneralized characteristics that we assign to all members of a perceived group

Stereotypes are particularly influential on our behavior because they create expectations that influence both how people act toward us and how we act toward other people. For example, there is a general stereotype that extremely tall men are basketball players. Due to this expectation, upon first meeting tall men, people tend to steer the conversation toward basketball. In reality, tall men are just as likely to play basketball as are men of average height.

The powerful influence of the expectations associated with stereotypes was demonstrated in a study by Margaret Shih, Todd Pittinsky, and Nalini Ambady (1999) in which Asian-American women were asked to complete a series of math problems. Prior to completing the math problems, one-third of the participants completed a survey asking questions about preferences for co-ed housing, one-third completed a survey asking questions on their family's cultural background, and the final third did not complete any survey. The purpose of the two surveys was to subtly remind participants of one of two stereotypes. As Asian-American women, all participants were subject to the stereotypes that women are not as good at math as men and that Asians are better at math than Americans. By asking the participants to think about either their cultural background or their gender, the researchers were able to activate one or the other stereotype prior to having the women complete the math tests. The

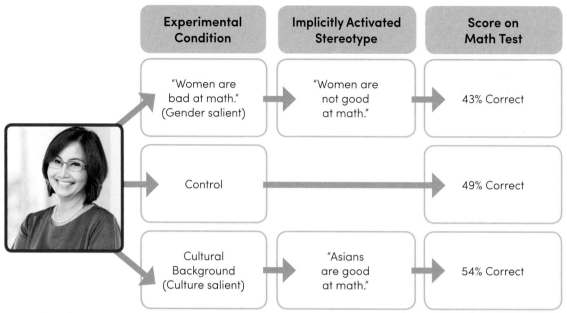

15.6 Effect of stereotype activation on math performance
This graphic shows Shih, Pittinsky, and Ambady's (1999) demonstration of the effect of streotype threat on women's math performance.

results from this study found that Asian-American women reminded of their cultural background performed better than control participants, while those reminded of their gender performed worse (see Figure 15.6). Gender and racial stereotypes may also be responsible for the differences in women and minorities seeking careers in science and technical fields (Leslie, Cimpian, Meyer, & Freeland, 2015). Our stereotypes toward others influence how we treat them, and the stereotypes others have toward us can also shape how we behave.

Before you continue reading this chapter, stop and think about different groups that you belong to or know of, and explore your expectations about how the individual members of these groups would act or feel in different situations. As you think about how the members of the group would respond to the situations, ask yourself, "How would I react to this situation?" and "What direct evidence do I have that the individual members of the group would act this way?" Our stereotypes and prejudices have a substantial impact on our social behavior, and it is good practice to take time to evaluate where these attitudes come from and how accurate they are.

Attributions

As people interact with others, they often find themselves making assumptions about the reasons for their behaviors, which is called an attribution (Kelley & Michela, 1980). As people make attributions about others' actions, they can focus on one of two causes: personal causes and situational causes (Heider, 1944). A **personal attribution** occurs when the cause of the behavior is assigned to something within the individual, such as personality, beliefs, or motivations. A **situational attribution** occurs when the cause of the behavior is assigned to something outside the individual, such as the context or

personal attribution occurs when we assign the cause of the behavior to something within the individual, such as his or her personality, beliefs, or motivations

situational attribution occurs when we assign the cause of the behavior to something outside the individual such as the context or other people in the situation

other people in the situation. An easy way to distinguish between these two attributions is to recognize that personal attributions can be thought of as things that the person chose to do, while situational attributions are things that happened to the person. Consider, for example, what happened the last time someone held the door open for you as you entered a building. Why did the person do this? Did she or he hold the door open because he or she is a nice person (personal attribution), or did the person do it simply because you were so close behind that the person did not have time to let the door close before you moved in (situational attribution)? Would the attribution that you make in this situation have an influence on the way you would act toward this person in the future?

In order to understand the importance of attributions, imagine that you were a participant in a study conducted by Thibaut and Riecken (1955). Participants in this study were assigned to interact with one of two randomly selected confederates hired by the researchers. The confederate was either of a higher or lower social status than the participant (determined by age and years of education). Participants in the study were required to approach the confederate and ask for the confederate's assistance on a project. The confederate always agreed to assist. After the experimental task was completed, participants were asked why they thought the other person participated. If you were a participant, would you attribute the tendency of the high- and low-status individuals to help to the same reason? Participants made significantly more personal attributions about the high-status individuals (e.g., they are helpful people) and more situational attributions about the low-status individuals (e.g., they had to help once I asked).

How can we make sense of these different attributions? One explanation is that, due to their higher social status, the situation did not put sufficient demands on the high-status individuals for them to agree to assist. Accordingly, any assistance they provided must have been due to their "helpful" or "kind" personal characteristics. The low-status individuals, however, did experience social pressures forcing them to participate due to the higher social status of the participants. In this case, the help provided was attributed to the situation, not to characteristics of the individual. The attribution had a large impact on the participant's assessment of the individual. The evaluation of the high-status person from before to after the task increased significantly more than for the low-status person. It says much more about people when they do what they are not obligated to do than when they are forced to act by the situation.

Thibaut and Riecken's study shows that the attributions we make about an individual are influenced by our interpretations of the situation. However, additional research has shown that people tend to commit the **fundamental attribution error**, in which we tend to make more personal attributions than situational attributions when observing others' behavior (Ross, 1977). Take a minute and think back to the last time someone cut you off in traffic or the last time someone held the door open for you. Can you remember the first label you assigned or thought you had regarding this individual? More likely than not, you labeled the person who cut you off as a "jerk," "moron," or other—more colorful—description of his or her individual characteristics. The person who held the door for you? "Nice," "polite," or another form of positive attribution.

fundamental attribution error
the error in which we tend to make more personal attributions than situational attributions when observing others' behavior

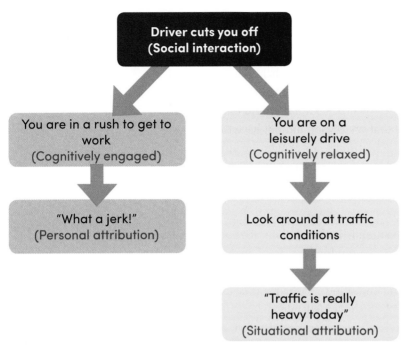

15.7 Influence of attention on the attributions of other people's behavior
Whether we make a personal or a situational attribution depends on whether we attend to the individual only or take the time to attend to both the individual and the situation.

In both cases, you only had a limited perspective of the individual's behavior, but you immediately made a personal attribution about the individual. These immediate, personal attributions are difficult to avoid.

The tendency to over-attribute other people's behavior to personal characteristics while discounting situational factors (fundamental attribution error) is an automatic cognitive response that influences how we see other people. Personal attributions are especially likely when attention is engaged with other tasks. For example, when we are driving, the demands of the day (schedule, assignments, work tasks) and of the road require a great deal of attention. When cut off by another driver, the result of the limited resources available to evaluate the driver's actions typically leads to an immediate and automatic personal attribution (see Figure 15.7). Once the initial attributions are made, they become the starting point from which we judge other people. If you were to later discover that the person who cut you off in traffic is your new psychology professor, this individual would have to work to rebuild his reputation from your original experience. However, imagine that for the person sitting next to you, her or his first experience with the professor was as the professor held the door open for him or her while walking into the building. While the two of you would listen to the exact same introductory lecture, given by the same professor, your perceptions of the experience would likely be quite different due to the personal attributions that formed from a brief snapshot of the individual's behavior.

Attributions and biases

Why do we tend to overemphasize personal attributions over situational attributions? One possible explanation is because of where our attention is during the attribution process. When someone cuts you off in traffic, where is your attention focused? Rather than looking at the big picture of traffic flow and other possible situational factors, you are focused on the offending driver. When someone holds the door, you focus on that person. In other words, when you observe someone's behavior, you focus on the individual, not the situation surrounding the behavior. Shelly Taylor and Susan Fiske (1975) demonstrated the importance of attention in the attribution process in a study investigating the **correspondence bias**—the tendency to believe that people's behavior matches their personal characteristics (Jones, 1979), which leads to the fundamental

correspondence bias
the tendency to believe that people's behavior matches their personal characteristics

attribution error. In this study, six observers were seated around two individuals who were engaged in a "get to know you" activity (these were actually two paid actors who were performing a scripted interaction). The six observers were arranged so that one pair could observe Actor A, one pair could observe Actor B, and one pair was able to see both actors. This arrangement was designed to influence the observers' focus during the interactions. Also, notice that all six observers—regardless of their arrangement in the room—heard the exact same dialogue between the two actors. Despite hearing the same dialogue, the observers did not make the same attributions about the actors. Rather, those observers who observed Actor A directly rated Actor A as having a larger impact on the conversation. The opposite was true for those who observed Actor B. Those who were able to see both Actor A and Actor B reported that both actors played a similar role in the conversation. While all pairs of observers shared the same experience, their attributions regarding the actors were shaped by the focus of their attention.

Attributions also apply when we examine our own behavior. When observing our behavior, we tend to be victims of a **self-serving bias**—we accept our successes as a product of personal characteristics and losses as due to situational variables (Shepperd, Malone & Sweeny, 2008). The self-serving bias is highly visible when listening to professional athlete interviews at the end of a game (Lau & Russell, 1980). As shown in Figure 15.8, players from the winning side frequently talk about heart, desire, and the quality of their team. Players from the losing side frequently talk about situations that did not go their way, blown calls, the quality of the other team, or other factors that are unique to the situation. Similarly, when you do well on an exam, it is because of your skills, but when you do poorly, it is your instructor's fault. These self-serving biases provide a good way to protect our self-esteem, but they may also blind us to possible changes in our behavior that are needed for long-term success.

In discussing the self-serving bias, it is important to consider whether outcomes meet expectations. When a team wins the game, the outcome matches their expectation, and they make a personal attribution: "We were the better team today." When the team loses, the outcome deviates from expectation, prompting team members to make a situational attribution: "The refs made a bunch of bad calls." In this way, the self-serving bias helps us to maintain our personal view of ourselves—our **self-esteem**. Individuals with high self-esteem expect to succeed, so successes reinforce

self-serving bias
we accept our successes as a product of personal characteristics and losses as due to situational variables

self-esteem
our personal view of ourselves

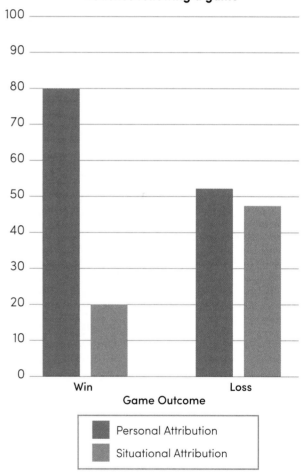

Attributional comments made by players and coaches following a game

15.8 Attributional comments made by players and coaches following a game
The graph represents a 1980 case study of self-serving attributions made by professional athletes and coaches by Richard R. Lau and Dan Russell. The study is an analysis of thirty-three sports stories printed in 1977, including the 1977 World Series and college and professional football. Players and coaches from winning teams made many more personal attributions than did coaches and players from the losing teams.

their sense of being wonderful people, and failures can be explained away as the result of circumstances. On the other hand, people with low self-esteem turn the self-serving bias upside down because they expect to fail. When people with low self-esteem experience a failure, it meets their expectations, so they make a personal attribution: "I knew I was incompetent." But a success violates their expectations, so they make a situational attribution: "That test was so easy that anybody could have gotten an A." For people with low self-esteem, failures reinforce the belief that they are bad people, and successes are explained away as the result of circumstances. The self-serving bias is so self-serving that it can always be used to maintain our view of our self, whether it is a positive or negative view.

Concept Recall

1. How are prejudices and stereotypes similar? How are they different?

2. How do personal and situational attributions differ? Which one are we more likely to make about others?

3. What is the fundamental attribution error?

4. What is the difference between an in-group and an out-group prejudice?

5. How can stereotypes influence both our actions toward others and how we think of ourselves?

This Is Psychology

First impressions really do matter. Based on our discussion of attribution theory, we see how first interactions with a new person create an initial evaluation of the individual. We then use these attributions as filters through which to evaluate the individual's behavior and intentions. Being aware of the power of first impressions is particularly important when applying for graduate school, internships, or jobs. Most interviews begin with an informal "get-to-know-you" session before moving to the more formal interview questions. Brian W. Swider, Murray R. Barrick, and T. Brad Harris (2016) found that impressions formed during the informal sessions carry over to the formal interview situation. If you happen to make a less than stellar first impression, all is not lost. Swider and his co-authors found that the effect of these "first impressions" weakened as the interview progressed.

BEHAVIOR AND SELF-FULFILLING PROPHECIES

Our attitudes, prejudices, and attributions are important determinants of our social interactions. When we interact with other people, our actions prompt their behavior, just as their actions prompt our behaviors (remember the section on behavior traps in Chapter 7: Learning and Behavior). Our expectations regarding the circumstances—our attitudes and attributions—have a crucial, though often unrecognized, impact on how we treat the situation. Previously, we discussed the psychology professor who (unintentionally) cut off a student in traffic on the way to class and (unintentionally) held the door for another student while entering the building. As a result of these interactions, the first student assigned a negative personal attribution to the professor, while the second student assigned a positive personal attribution. During the ensuing class discussion, the professor responds to the first student's glares by not making eye contact with the student and responds to the second student's smile by making frequent eye contact with that student. As a result, the professor's interactions with the students confirm their opinions about the professor. Attitudes and attributions often lead to **self-fulfilling prophecies**: situations in which expectations of an event have such a strong influence that they actually make the event turn out as expected.

Robert Rosenthal, a psychology professor at Harvard University, showed the power of self-fulfilling prophecies in school settings. Rosenthal studied children in the first through sixth grade who were students at a public elementary school (Rosenthal & Jacobson, 1968). At the beginning of the school year, Rosenthal and his colleague, Lenore Jacobson, administered an intelligence test to all students in the school. Several weeks later, the experimenters informed teachers that some students were "bloomers" who had the potential to make significant academic gains. In reality, the names given to the teachers were randomly selected from all of the students in each grade with test scores that were similar to those for the rest of the school. At the end of the school year, Rosenthal and Jacobson repeated the same intelligence test. The results indicated that the teachers' expectations had a large impact on the students' academic gains. Students who teachers thought were bloomers (experimental condition) showed greater IQ gains than students in the control group. What caused these differences? Rosenthal (1994) suggested that teachers provided bloomers with more academic opportunities, more time to complete work, more challenging material, and treated them more "warmly" than they would have if they had not been identified as bloomers. Due to the (fake) feedback to teachers, they expected more of the blooming students and changed their behavior toward them, and the blooming students were rewarded with better academics.

A second study on the power of self-fulfilling prophecy was conducted in twelve different mental hospitals in the United States by David Rosenhan, a professor at Stanford University (1973). As discussed in Chapter 13, Rosenhan had eight people with no known psychological issues—and certainly no need to be institutionalized—present themselves to mental hospitals claiming that they heard voices. Once admitted to the hospitals, the fake patients were instructed to act as normal as they could, meaning they did not attempt to fake symptoms or act as if they were patients in the hospital. Rosenhan wondered whether the hospital staff would correctly identify the imposters and have them released from the hospital (like other patients, the fake patients were not able to leave until they were discharged by the staff). Rosenhan's imposters were highly motivated to leave the hospitals, leading to conflict with the staff that led to outbursts that were consistent with the staff's expectations of how a patient in a mental institution would act. Because the staff expected the patients to act in certain ways, they created social pressures that induced behavior that matched their expectations.

self-fulfilling prophecies situations where the expectations of an event increase the likelihood of the event occurring, which reinforces the expectation of the event

Concept Recall

1. How can the self-serving bias be used to confirm our self-esteem?
2. In what ways can our attitudes, prejudices, stereotypes, and attributions create self-fulfilling prophecies?
3. What did Rosenthal's research show about self-fulfilling prophecies in sixth graders?
4. How did the staff expectations influence the actions of the participants in Rosenhan's study of self-fulfilling prophecy?

SOCIAL NORMS AND BEHAVIORAL INFLUENCES

social norms
the rules and expectations of the group concerning the behavior of individual members

explicit social norms
social norms that are formally adopted by a group as written laws, rules, or policies

One of the most powerful ways behavior is shaped by our social world is the set of **social norms**—the rules and expectations of the group concerning the behavior of individual members—that surround us. Social norms can be explicit rules, such as classroom policies, conduct statements, or laws. **Explicit social norms**, social norms that are formally adopted by a group as written laws, rules, or policies, reflect the popular belief of the group regarding how the individual members should act. In many cases, the norm developed as a way to promote social coordination (e.g., traffic regulations, such as which side of the road to drive on and obedience to traffic lights) or the health of the group (e.g., laws governing sanitation and waste disposal). Violation of these explicit norms is met with a negative consequence agreed upon by the group (fines, prison sentence). While explicit norms were adopted by the members of the group, the importance of these norms can change over time as group membership and the demands of the environment change. For example, current social and political events in the United States and much of the world reflect a change in the explicit social norms accepted by the group.

implicit social norms
expectations and rules governing social behavior that are not part of formally adopted laws, rules, or policies

In contrast to the explicitly defined social norms, much more of our behavior is influenced by **implicit social norms**, expectations and rules governing social behavior that are not part of formally adopted laws, rules, or policies, that have become part of the social group's expectations regarding individual behavior. These implicit norms are more difficult for new members of a group to navigate because the only way to become aware of the norm is to experience it and, in many cases, to violate it. Violation of implicit social norms typically results in social isolation (not being included by the group) and even social ostracization (being completely excluded from the group). Often, explicit social norms develop from implicit norms and change over time to reflect changes in the implicit social norms of a group.

social roles
the expected behaviors of individuals with certain characteristics in a social group

Our behavior around and toward members of groups is strongly influenced by social norms, with a special influence from the different **social roles**, the expected behaviors of individuals with certain characteristics in a social group, that people fill within the group. Just as a sports team coordinates the activity of the team members by having players assigned to specific roles within the team (infielder, outfielder, pitcher, and catcher on a baseball team), a social group maintains order through the use of the defined structure of the social roles within the group. In highly formalized groups, such as the military, these roles and the rules regarding these roles are explicitly defined and enforced. However, in most social groups, the social roles are informally adopted and enforced. Think about how you and your friends interact when you are all together. There is likely one person in the group who tends to take on a leadership role. Another group member is probably the mediator or peacekeeper for the group. What is your role in your group of friends?

Social roles help to coordinate social life, as they provide rules and order for our social interactions. Despite their usefulness in ordering social life, the expectations and rules that come along with social roles can be the source of significant problems. Social roles can create problems when they create expectations for how people should behave that are different from how the individual would like to behave and when people change their behavior to conform with what they believe the social role requires of them.

The Stanford Prison Experiment

The powerful effect of social roles on behavior was demonstrated by Dr. Philip Zimbardo in one of the best-known studies in social psychology, the Stanford Prison Experiment. While this was not an experiment in the technical sense of the word (with high levels of scientific control, independent variables, and a dependent variable), it was an experiment in that participants were placed in a setting and their behavior was observed. For this study, Zimbardo and his research team created a temporary prison in the basement of a building on the campus of Stanford University and recruited college-age adults to participate in the two-week prison simulation for fifteen dollars a day. Half of the recruited participants played the role of "prisoners," and the other half were "guards." Extensive prescreening ensured that the prisoners and guards did not differ from each other on the assessed measures. From what the researchers could tell, all that was different between the two groups were the randomly assigned roles of prisoner or guard.

While the roles were randomly assigned, participants in the study quickly adopted the behaviors that were associated with the assigned roles. The students assigned to be prisoners became submissive, nervous, paranoid, and bitter. Most of the conversations between prisoners were about the prison experience, including how to escape and how to beg favors from the guards. The students assigned to the role of guards became domineering, demeaning, and abusive. While the participants in the experiment were assigned roles to play, the nature of the social norms and expected social roles of "prisoner" and "guard" shaped both groups into adopting the behaviors and actions associated with their assigned role in the simulation. The study was intended to run for fourteen days but had to be cancelled after only six days due to the level of distress observed in the prisoners and concerns over the guards' behaviors. In an interview after the experiment was ended, one of the guards stated:

We were no longer dealing with an intellectual exercise in which a hypothesis was being evaluated in the dispassionate manner dictated by the canons of the scientific method. We were caught up in the passion of the present, the suffering, the need to control people, not variables, the escalation of power and all of the unexpected things that were erupting around and within us. We had to end this experiment. (Zimbardo, Haney, Banks, & Jaffe, 1973, pg. 58)

The Stanford Prison Experiment was evaluated and approved by the appropriate Institutional Review Board, but neither the board, Zimbardo, nor those involved were prepared for how powerfully the perceived social norms and roles would influence the participants in the study.

Obedience to authority

In Zimbardo's simulated prison study, the "prisoners" submitted to the authority of the guards, even to the point of performing socially inappropriate and embarrassing behaviors. While the rules of the social roles of "prisoner" and "guard" suggest that one is subordinate to the other, these were not real prisoners and guards. So why did the prisoners follow the guards' orders?

Stanley Milgram, a psychology professor at Yale University, conducted an experiment in 1961 that revealed the power of perceived authority in controlling our behavior. Milgram's work was strongly influenced by the trial of Adolf Eichmann, a Nazi officer during World War II (Milgram, 1974). Milgram wondered if Eichmann and other Nazi officers committed their crimes because they were bad people or because of the social situation that prevailed in Germany during World War II. In other words, Milgram was trying to distinguish between the personal and situational attributions discussed earlier in this chapter. While the public mostly made personal attributions for the behavior of the Nazi officers on trial, Milgram believed that this interpretation largely underestimated the power of the situation in producing obedience to authority.

To test his hypotheses, Milgram set up an experiment that included a participant and a confederate who pretended to be a second participant in a study on learning. Participants were led to believe they had been randomly assigned the role of "teacher," when in fact the participant was always assigned the role of "teacher" and the confederate the role of "learner." For most of Milgram's studies, the teacher and learner were on opposite sides of a wall. During the teaching session, the participant would read a list of word pairs, such as blue – box, nice – day, and wild – duck.

After reading the word pairs, the teacher would prompt the learner with the first word from one of the pairs (blue, nice, wild) followed by four choices (box, day, duck, sky), and the learner would have to choose which of the words was actually paired with the sample word by pushing one of four buttons.

The participant was told from the outset of the study that the goal of the project was to better understand the role of punishment in learning. Therefore, the teacher either rewarded the learner for correct answers by saying "That is correct" or punished the learner for incorrect answers by administering a brief electric shock. The teachers were told that the electric shocks were painful but would not cause any permanent harm. In order to create believability and to ensure that the teacher was familiar with a shock, each teacher was given a forty-five-volt shock. It is important to note that the only real shock in the experiment was this demonstration shock given to the teacher. The learner was never actually shocked, although the teacher watched as the experimenter pretended to hook the learner to the shock generator. The shock generator had thirty switches labeled as in the second column in Table 15.1.

Table 15.1 Levels of shock, label used on shock generator, and the learner's verbal feedback

Shock Level (volts)	Label	Learner Feedback
15–60	Slight shock	
75–120	Moderate shock	• Little grunt of pain (75, 90, and 105 volts) • Shout that shocks were painful (120 volts)
135–180	Strong shock	• Painful groans (135 volts) • "Experimenter, get me out of here! I won't be in the experiment any more! I refuse to go on!" (150 volts) • "I can't stand the pain!" (180 volts)
195–240	Very strong shock	• Painful groans of increasing intensity
255–300	Intense shock	• Agonized scream (270 volts) • Shout that participant would no longer answer questions (300 volts)
315–360	Extreme intensity shock	• Violent scream, followed by affirmation that the participant would not participate any further (315 volts) • No more noise and no more answers (330 volts and up)
375–420	Danger: Severe shock	• No more noise and no more answers
435–450	XXX	• No more noise and no more answers

The table shows the label written above each range of shocks and the verbal response from the learner during the experimental sessions in Experiment 2 of Milgram's obedience research. Each teacher was given a sample shock of 45 volts (labeled a slight shock) to familiarize them with the machine. After 330 volts, the learner stopped responding, but the teacher was instructed to count no answer as an incorrect answer and to continue providing shocks (Milgram, 1974, pg. 23, 34).

The dependent measure in Milgram's study was the maximum voltage of shock that the participant would administer. What do you think you would do in this situation? Would you deliver the maximum level of shock, or would you defy the authority figure? When Milgram asked psychiatrists, psychology faculty, college students, and community members how many of his participants would deliver the maximum shock, their response was unanimous: not a single respondent believed that any participant would deliver the maximum shock. These predictions turned out to be very wrong: almost two-thirds of Milgram's participants (twenty-five out of forty) administered the maximum shock, all while the learner was screaming about the pain and a heart condition. All of the participants, including the researcher and the learner, were male in the original study, but a follow-up study using all female participants produced nearly identical results (twenty-six out of forty female teachers administered the maximum level of shock).

Why were so many people so wrong in their predictions about how participants would act in Milgram's studies? One way is to look again at the idea of situational versus personal attributions and self-serving bias. When we are asked to anticipate our behavior in a certain situation, we focus on how our personal characteristics, morals, attitudes, and values apply to that situation. We thus make a determination based on these personal attributes and fail to account for the power of the situation. In later studies, Milgram explored the power of the situation by varying the proximity of the teacher to the experimenter and learner. Across these many experimental variations, Milgram found that fewer teachers were willing to administer the maximum level of shock when (1) the authority figure was moved away from the teacher, (2) the learner was moved closer to the teacher, and (3) as the prestige of the institution was varied. Consider what this might mean for soldiers who are ordered to visit death and destruction on enemy combatants, and you can see that a soldier who is ordered to meet the enemy face to face would have a harder time following orders than another soldier who launches a drone to drop bombs from thousands of miles away.

Behavioral and obedience research ethics

Before ending this section, let's take a moment and discuss the ethics involved in the Zimbardo and Milgram studies. These two studies have drawn major criticism based on both their methodologies and their implications regarding human behavior. Many of the ethical questions focus on whether the level of distress experienced by participants is justified by what researchers stood to gain from the studies. While Zimbardo clearly explained the purpose of his study and what was expected of participants in the study, he allowed the study to continue beyond the symbolic acts that were stipulated in the rules and guidelines for the study, and he placed himself in a difficult situation by being both involved in the study and the ethical oversight for the study. Milgram's participants believed that they were actually causing physical pain to the learner in the study. While the participants experienced a great deal of distress during the study, both Milgram and Zimbardo provided participants with a full debriefing after the study and worked to minimize any harm from participating in the study. From a scientific standpoint, these studies triggered hundreds of studies and became a foundation for social research on obedience to authority and the power of social situations.

Conformity and influence

conformity
the process of adapting our individual behavior to meet the social norms, attitudes, and behaviors of a social group

Both Zimbardo's Stanford Prison Experiment and Milgram's studies of obedience are examples of how people's behavior can conform to the demands of the social situation. **Conformity** is the process of adapting behavior to meet the social norms, attitudes, and behaviors of a social group. Over time and with repeated interactions with members of a social group, the pressure created by the social norms of the group will typically shape the behavior of the individual to match the norms of the group. While Western tradition (a form of implicit social norm) suggests that conformity is always bad, this is not typically the case. Most of the time, conforming to the demands of the social group will bring the individual into greater contact with the social reinforcers and social support of the group. As we conform to the demands of a social group, the influence of the group can be either informational or normative. **Informational influence**—changes in behavior due to a desire to do what is right in a social setting and to act correctly—typically results in individuals adopting the group's social norm into their personal belief system. When given future opportunities to engage in the behavior in the absence of the social group, behaviors created through informational influence will typically continue to occur. **Normative influence**—changes in behavior due to a desire for social approval or to avoid social disapproval—typically results in short-term changes in the individual's behavior that do not persist in the absence of the social group. Informational and normative influence both result in the individual's behavior changing to be more consistent with the social norms of the group. However, only informational influence creates a behavioral change that will last independent of the social group.

informational influence changes in behavior due to a desire to do what is right in a social setting and to act correctly

normative influence changes in behavior due to a desire for social approval or to avoid social disapproval

How do we know which type of social influence is producing our conformity? Two studies, one by Muzafer Sherif (1936) and the other by Solomon Asch (1956), demonstrate the contextual variables that influence why we conform to group norms and behavior. While both studies provide evidence of conformity, they do so for very different reasons.

Sherif (1936) asked participants to engage in a very difficult perceptual task in which they were asked to view a dot of light on a wall in a dark room and judge how far the dot moved. In reality, the dot was held stationary, but it appeared to move as the result of saccades, which are constant jerky eye movements that are too small to notice under most circumstances. Participants completed three sessions of the study along with another group of individuals. During each session, the individual members of the group spoke their judgment out loud to the entire group. During the first session, there was a lot of variability in the perceived movement, which makes sense because everyone has their own jerky eye movements that are independent of anyone else's. By the third session, the members of the group came to a near consensus regarding how far the light traveled. When tested a year later, the members of the group maintained the group decision regarding the movement of the light (Rohrer, et al., 1954). The durability of the response outside of the presence of the social group suggests informational influence on the participants' behavior.

Asch (1956) demonstrated conformity using a different situation, in which he asked participants to look at an example line, then identify which of three choice lines was the same length as the example. The line discrimination task was pretty easy, and participants working individually answered correctly nearly 100 percent of the time. In the experimental condition, participants selected lines while seated in the same room as seven confederates who were paid to get the first two line comparisons correct but then to pick the wrong choice lines in subsequent comparisons. Overall, the group of confederates made twelve errors out of eighteen total trials (they were paid to get six trials correct in order to increase the believability of the experiment). The participant was seated next to the last person in the group. While we are only going to discuss one version of the study, Asch conducted many variations of the project in which he varied the size of the group, number of correct trials, and the number of group members who gave the wrong answer, among other variables.

Cross-Cultural Case

Social Media and Social Psychology

Social media use among all age ranges is not only common but also, in some groups, necessary for communication. We keep in touch with family and friends, catch up on local and international news, and organize events and plans using the most trafficked social media sites, such as Facebook and Twitter. However, its pervasive role in Americans' lives, in particular, draws criticism from users themselves and even psychologists. A quick search on *Psychology Today* reveals that "social media" is an exceedingly common topic of discussion, and those discussions often tend toward the negative. An article by Amy Morin published February 10, 2018 suggested that recent changes Facebook implemented as a means to increase users' ability to engage in more "meaningful social interactions" could be bad for their health. Although Facebook's founder Mark Zuckerberg explained that Facebook "feel[s] the responsibility to make sure [their] services aren't just fun to use, but also good for people's well-being," Morin cites a 2016 study that revealed social media increases users' tendency toward social comparison, which appears to be in conflict with Zuckerberg's claims of Facebook's awareness of user happiness.

Interestingly, there are other claims that promote the benefits of social media and even its "cultivation" of well-being. WeChat, the most popular social network in China, boasts more than 980 million monthly active users and is also the most popular messaging app in Bhutan. Researcher Jiaqi Wu of the University of Pennsylvania determined that elements of WeChat, including community-based ties within the app, selective friend lists, and "savoring," or users' ability and desire to save positive interactions or moments, could actually promote a sense of well-being. While Wu's evidence is mainly anecdotal due to WeChat's lack of available public user data, her research suggests psychologists have tremendous opportunity to continue to study the impact of social media on the global public.

Waricha Wongphyat / Shutterstock.com

What impact did the majority's influence have on the participants' behavior? Remember that under the control conditions in which participants selected lines without any social pressure, accuracy was nearly 100 percent. When participants selected lines in the same room as seven confederates whose selections were wrong two-thirds of the time, participants' accuracy fell dramatically. Their accuracy wasn't quite as bad as the confederates (wrong two times out of three), but they were wrong an average of about one time out of three. Almost all of the participants' wrong answers matched the answers given by the confederates, suggesting that performance on the task for almost all participants was influenced by the presence of a social majority (Figure 15.9).

15.9   Examples of the question format used by Asch (1957) to test conformity
The question on the left was answered correctly by the seven confederates (all confederates chose line A). The question on the right was answered incorrectly by the group of confederates. Confederates selected line B in the question on the right.

As a concluding remark on our discussion of Asch's research, it is important to recognize that recent reviews of this work argue that Asch's findings more accurately demonstrate the power of independence from social pressure (Griggs, 2015). That is, while about three-quarters of participants gave at least one answer that matched the wrong answer given by the confederates, one-quarter of participants never conformed to the majority's clearly wrong answers. Asch's work is not evidence of either mass conformity or independence but rather demonstrates the powerful effect that social influence can have on our behavior.

Sherif's and Asch's conformity research highlight the power of social influence in shaping our behavior. The results from Asch's study demonstrate that the social pressure of the majority influenced the behavior of the individual participants, despite the ability of the participants to correctly perform the line-comparison task. This is an example of normative influence. The influence of the group in Asch's task, in which the correct answer was obvious, was quite different from the influence experienced by participants in Sherif's study, in which the correct answer was much more difficult to find. The relative difficulty of the two tasks is reflected in the participants' accuracy outside of social influence: answers were uniformly nearly perfect in Asch's task but highly variable in Sherif's task. After participating in the task, participants from Sherif's study showed a durable and consistent change in their behavior when asked to make similar judgments at a later date. Participants from Asch's study did not show any long-term changes in their ability to correctly judge line lengths after completing the experimental task. Sherif's and Asch's tasks highlight the role of informational and normative influence in shaping our behavior.

Concept Recall

1. What are social norms, and how do these influence our behavior and attitudes?

2. How did social norms influence the outcome of the Stanford Prison Experiment?

3. What factors influenced the level of obedience to authority observed in Milgram's studies of obedience?

4. How can personal and situational attributions explain the difference between the predictions of how much shock people would deliver and how much shock people actually delivered in Milgram's studies of obedience?

SOCIAL INFLUENCE AND HELPING BEHAVIOR

Our social world has a large impact on our behavior. This influence can even include whether or not we help people in need. Bibb Latané and John Darley (1970) designed a series of experiments in which participants were placed in a situation, so they had to decide whether or not to give help to a fellow participant (who was actually a confederate of the researchers) who acted as if experiencing an epileptic seizure. During the study, participants were alone in a room with an intercom that allowed them to communicate with the other members of the group. The group size ranged from two (the participant and the confederate) to six (the participant, confederate, and four other people). The dependent variable in the study was how long it took the participant to notify the researcher of the other participant's distress. Latané and Darley found that the larger the group, the longer it took the participants to notify the researcher of the problem. When the group consisted of only the participant and the confederate, all of the participants notified the researcher of the problem in less than a minute and a half. When the group consisted of six people, less than two-thirds of participants responded to the emergency (Aronson, Wilson, & Akert, 2010). Latané and Darley's work is an example of the **bystander effect**: the tendency for the likelihood of receiving help to decrease as the number of witnesses increases. While it may seem better to have an emergency when surrounded by a big group of people, the bystander effect suggests the opposite, that members of a small group are likelier to offer assistance.

bystander effect
the tendency for the likelihood of receiving help to decrease as the number of people witnessing the emergency increases

Why does group size influence the likelihood for people to help? One possibility is that this is a type of normative influence similar to what was observed in the Sherif studies. When there is an emergency, people in the crowd look around to see how others are reacting. If others are not moving to assist with the emergency, this can be interpreted as evidence that help is not needed. A second explanation for the bystander effect is **diffusion of responsibility**: the more people in the group, the less any one person is responsible for the outcome of the situation. With lots of people around, it is unclear exactly who is responsible for helping with the situation, and the responsibility for helping is spread across all of the witnesses to the emergency. You have likely felt diffusion of responsibility as you sped past people standing next to their disabled car on the highway, and while you were willing and happy to help, you thought to yourself, "Well, I bet somebody else has already come to their aid." In summary of their research,

diffusion of responsibility
the more people in the group, the less any one person is responsible for the outcome of the situation

Latané and Darley suggested that the decision to help involves five decision-making questions:

1. Is there something going on that requires my attention?
2. Is this event an emergency?
3. Do I have a responsibility to help in this situation?
4. Do I know how to help with this situation?
5. Am I willing to accept any risks associated with helping?

According to this model, witnesses to an event begin with the first question and progress until they have answered yes to all of the questions—at which point they provide help—or until they reach the first "no" answer, at which point they don't. This model is useful in understanding our willingness to help because it gives us several ideas about how to better elicit help from strangers. When you need help, clearly communicate your need for help to a specific member of the group. Simply yelling, "help me, help me!" in a crowd is unlikely to produce the assistance you seek. It is increasingly difficult to solicit help from others as there are rising concerns about the legal risks associated with helping (question 5) and difficulties catching people's attention with the increased prevalence of personal technology, such as smartphones, personal music players, and other attention-demanding devices (question 1). In order to reduce the legal liability for trained professionals who provide help in emergency situations, all fifty states have some version of a "Good Samaritan" law that provides some level of legal protection to helpers in emergencies.

Concept Recall

1. What is the difference between informational and normative influence?
2. Under what conditions did Asch find that conformity to the incorrect answer of the group would increase?
3. What is the bystander effect, and what does it tell us about how to increase the likelihood of people helping?
4. What are the five steps in the process of deciding to give help to a person in need?

UNDERSTANDING SOCIAL PSYCHOLOGY

Our social interactions very strongly influence how we think, act, and feel. We are members of a highly social species. We seek out opportunities to interact with others and are greatly influenced by these social interactions. As we have seen in this chapter, our attitudes about the world are shaped by our social interactions, and these attitudes influence the way that we act toward others. Unless we stop and pay careful attention to how we are acting and feeling, we are often unaware of the powerful influence of our social world on our behavior. However, as we become more aware of this influence, we can make use of the power of the social world in order to help bring about the behavioral changes that can make for happier, healthier relationships with others.

In the introduction to this chapter, we challenged you to think about how your online social interactions differ from the real-world interactions that were the main focus of the social psychology research explored in this chapter. As we come to the end of this text, we expand that challenge to all of your interactions. Across the fifteen chapters of this book you have been exposed to the major ideas and concepts that make up our scientific understanding of what it is to be you. Please take some time to reflect on what you have learned and how it applies to your actions and experiences. Regardless of whether you take more psychology courses or pursue psychology as a profession, what you have learned in this book will prove useful to you. Better understanding what influences your behavior is a powerful way to gain control over what you do, think, and feel. Understanding what influences other people's behavior is an important step in creating positive relationships in your personal and professional life. Psychology really is all about understanding you.

Review/Reflect/Write

REVIEW

- What are the differences and similarities between attitudes and attributions? Between stereotypes and prejudices?
- What are the three elements of an attitude?
- Under what conditions will our attitudes most likely have the biggest impact on our behaviors?
- What is the difference between the central and the peripheral routes of persuasion?
- What is cognitive dissonance, and what are some ways to reduce feelings of dissonance?
- What is a self-fulfilling prophecy?
- What are implicit and explicit social norms?
- Under what conditions do we experience informational and normative influences on our behavior?
- Why are people less likely to provide help when there are more people around than they are when the crowd is smaller?
- What are the five questions we often ask when deciding whether or not to help someone in need?

1. If you have spoken with others about an attitude toward something, and your attitude is specific and has been stable over time, this attitude
   a. is concrete.
   b. is more likely to affect your behavior.
   c. cannot be influenced.
   d. is a stereotype.

2. Dr. Lichtenstein uses psychoanalysis in his therapy sessions. However, when he seeks therapy, he doesn't like the psychoanalytic approach for himself, so he seeks out a cognitive-behavioral therapist. This inconsistency makes Dr. Lichtenstein uncomfortable, so he changes his approach with his clients to match his personal preference in order to
   a. increase attitudinal congruence.
   b. decrease attitudinal congruence.
   c. increase cognitive dissonance.
   d. decrease cognitive dissonance.

Answer Key

1.b 2.d 3.c 4.c 5.d 6.b 7.b 8.c 9.b 10.b

3. The _____ states that we make far more personal attributions than situational attributions to explain the behavior of others.

   a. internal reasoning tendency

   b. external reasoning tendency

   c. fundamental attribution error

   d. fundamental attribution tendency

4. The term used to describe the tendency to believe that people's behavior matches their personal characteristics is

   a. negative prejudice.

   b. fundamental attribution error.

   c. correspondence bias.

   d. self-serving bias.

5. When we accept our successes as a product of personal characteristics and losses as due to situational variables, we are displaying

   a. negative prejudice.

   b. fundamental attribution error.

   c. correspondence bias.

   d. self-serving bias.

6. When the law firm decided to move locations from Little Rock to Dallas, Sara supported the decision as the larger market would allow for acquisition of more clients. This best illustrates what component of attitude?

   a. a behavioral component

   b. a cognitive component

   c. an affective component

   d. a situational component

7. Attitude change that is due to a careful weighing and evaluation of arguments and the characteristics of the object or event is the _____ route of persuasion.

   a. peripheral

   b. central

   c. frontal

   d. cerebral

8. When the professor is talking about his college's football team he always says things like, "We played a great game last Friday" or "We will do better next time." He perceives the college football team as a(n)

   a. peer group.

   b. allied group.

   c. in-group.

   d. out-group.

9. A teacher thinks Andre is a stronger student than May. The teacher spends lots of extra time working with Andre and encouraging him. By the end of the year most students feel like Andre has overcome May as the strongest student. The teacher has just experienced a

   a. fundamental attribution error.

   b. self-fulfilling prophesy.

   c. cognitive dissonance.

   d. social norm.

10. Haley wore white to her friend's wedding. She kept getting dirty looks from everyone in the party. When she asked her sister why she reminded her that you're not supposed to wear white to someone else's wedding. Haley was violating a(n)

    a. rule of thumb.

    b. implicit social norm.

    c. explicit social norm.

    d. boundary.

REFLECT

1. We have opinions about and attitudes toward all kinds of things in our lives. How do you think that becoming aware of the content of these attitudes, the origin of these attitudes, and the impact of these attitudes on our behavior can help us to treat ourselves and others more fairly?

2. What would you have done if participating in Milgram's studies? Would you have delivered the full level of shock? What are some situations that you can think of in which your behavior changed to reflect the values, attitudes, or behaviors of your social group?

3. How would you use the information in this chapter to increase the number of students on your campus that are involved in volunteer activities?

WRITE

1. Find four print advertisements that depict the central and peripheral routes of persuasion (two of each). Write a summary of the argument made in each advertisement, and clearly explain how it represents either the central or peripheral route of persuasion. Take a copy of each advertisement, and show it to ten people. Ask each person to rate the advertisement's effectiveness from one (not very effective) to ten (extremely effective) and to briefly explain their rating. Summarize the general findings from the ten people who you surveyed, including which advertisements were found most convincing and any common themes in what influenced their ratings. Conclude your report with a discussion of your beliefs about how advertisers choose to use the different routes of persuasion in constructing their products.

2. We challenged you at the beginning of this chapter to think about the influence of social technologies on your social interactions. Pick one type of major social technology, and write a report on its influence on behavior. Include a description of the technology and how it works, the number of current users of the technology, and a brief summary of at least two peer-reviewed research studies that address the influence of social technology and how the findings from these studies apply to the social technology that you are exploring. Conclude your report with a discussion of how you feel social interactions using this technology are similar to and different from direct face-to-face social interactions.

Key Terms

attitudes   432
bystander effect   456
central route of persuasion   434
cognitive dissonance theory   436
confederate   436
conformity   452
correspondence bias   444
diffusion of responsibility   456
explicit social norms   448
fundamental attribution error   443
implicit social norms   448
in-groups   439
informational influence   453

normative influence   453
out-groups   440
peripheral route of persuasion   435
personal attribution   442
prejudice   439
self-esteem   445
self-fulfilling prophecies   447
self-serving bias   445
situational attribution   442
social norms   448
social psychology   432
social roles   448
stereotypes   441

Glossary

ablation studies a physiological research procedure where small portions of the brain are removed or destroyed in order to explore the function of a neural system

abnormal psychology the scientific study of psychological problems, including mental illness, and their treatment

accommodation (ocular) a process in which the lens of the eye changes shape to adapt to different viewing distances

accommodation the process of adjusting a pre-existing schema to comport with new information

acetylcholine a neurotransmitter that causes a muscle fiber to contract

action potential electrical impulse that moves from the soma through the axon

active listening a therapeutic technique in which the therapist pays close attention to his/her clients' words and then echoes, paraphrases, and clarifies what the client says; a key component of client-centered therapy

adaptation the process in which the brain becomes less sensitive to a particular sensory feature after being exposed to it for an extended period of time

adolescence the years spent moving from childhood to adulthood

adolescent –egocentrism the belief that an adolescent's private experiences are unique and that others, especially their peers, are always directing their attention toward them

afterimage after viewing one color for an extended period its opponent color appears when looking at a colorless surface

agonist a drug that boosts the effectiveness of a neurotransmitter

agreeableness one of the "Big Five" personality characteristics indicating helpfulness, empathy, and trust

algorithm a step-by-step procedure for solving problems that is guaranteed to work but slow

Alzheimer's disease a specific form of dementia that is irreversible, and includes impaired thought, impaired speech, flat affect, and confusion

amnesia loss of memory, typically due to brain damage

amplitude the height of a wave, which corresponds to the loudness of a sound

analgesic a substance that relieves pain

analytical intelligence problem-solving and reasoning abilities used to solve everyday problems such as information processing, mental calculations, and learning of new information

anorexia nervosa a serious, potentially life-threatening eating disorder characterized by self-starvation and excessive weight loss

antagonist a drug that reduces the effectiveness of a neurotransmitter

anthropomorphization the projecting of human experience and abilities onto non-human objects

antianxiety medication that reduces anxiety via depression of central nervous system activity

antidepressants medications that reduce depression by increasing levels of neurotransmitters associated with positive mood

antipsychotics a group of medications used to treat the positive symptoms of psychosis

aphasia a language deficit

applied behavior analysis a treatment approach that replaces undesirable behavior with positive behavior through conditioning, punishment, or reinforcement

assimilation the process of interpreting new information in terms of what we already know

atmospheric perspective a monocular depth cue wherein objects that are closer have more visible detail than objects in the distance

attachment the association infants make between their caregiver, nourishment, and comfort; this process is integral to cognitive and social development

attention the process by which your brain filters out loads of unnecessary sensory information to focus on a small portion

attitudes the emotional and cognitive evaluations that we attach to people, places, objects, and ideas

autonomic nervous system the portion of the nervous system that controls involuntary behaviors (i.e., digestion)

availability heuristic heuristic based on the assumption that the most easily imagined possibility is also the likeliest

axon single long wire that sends electrical signals from the soma to other neurons

backward conditioning the US is presented before the NS occurs

basilar membrane a flat sheet of tissue in the cochlea that resonates at different frequencies at different ends

behavior analysis a scientific approach to the study of learning that focuses on laws and processes of behavior across species and the development of behavior technologies

behavior analysts the scientists who approach behavior from the perspective of behavior analysis

behavior therapy a type of therapy that helps the client/individual change potentially self-destructive behavior through application of learning principles

behavior trap a situation in which two people's unwanted behavior is maintained by both negative and positive reinforcement

behavioral model a scientific approach to psychology concerned only with observable and measurable behavior that can be objectively recorded

behaviorism a subfield of psychology that focused exclusively on the relationship between behavior and environmental events

bereavement the emotional and role changes that occur following the death of a loved one

binge eating disorder an eating disorder characterized by recurring episodes of binge eating without accompanying compensatory behaviors

biopsychology how the physical systems produce behavior

biopsychosocial model a scientific approach to psychology that considers biological, psychological, and social factors and their complex interactions into understanding the effects on human behavior and mental disorders

bio-psycho-social-cultural perspective this perspective is inclusive of the many factors that work together to influence behavior

bipolar disorder a mental disorder characterized by alternating periods of extreme highs (mania) and extreme lows (depression)

blind spot an area in the eye without any photoreceptors because of the optic nerve

bodily-kinesthetic intelligence ability to control and organize bodily movements, such as in sports

Broca's area an area of the cortex typically located in the left hemisphere associated with language, damage to which causes aphasia

bulimia nervosa a serious, potentially life-threatening eating disorder characterized by a cycle of binge eating and compensatory behaviors such as self-induced vomiting

bystander effect the tendency for the likelihood of receiving help to decrease as the number of people witnessing the emergency increases

callosotomy a surgical procedure in which the corpus callosum is severed

camera obscura a device created by Alhazen, consisting of a dark room with a tiny hole for light that simulates the human eye

case study a detailed observation of a single individual or group of individuals

central nervous system the part of the nervous system made up of the brain and the spinal cord

central route of persuasion attitude change that is due to a careful weighing and evaluation of arguments and the characteristics of the object or event

cerebellum a brain structure that contributes to movements requiring balance, coordination, and precise timing

chronological age the actual age of the test taker, expressed as the number of years since the date of birth

chunking a way of increasing memory capacity by grouping items together instead of remembering each item individually

classical conditioning also known as respondent conditioning, Pavlovian conditioning, and associative learning

client-centered therapy a type of psychotherapy in which the client is given an accepting, empathetic environment in which to explore and attain personal growth

closure a Gestalt principle wherein the brain "fills in" gaps in the retinal image

cochlea the fluid-filled portion of the middle ear that transforms sound into an electrical signal to be sent to the brain

cognition all mental activities associated with thinking, knowing, remembering, and communicating

cognitive behavioral therapy a type of therapy that helps the person/client change potentially self-destructive behavior through addressing negative thought patterns that fuel the behavior

cognitive dissonance theory the tension we experience when our attitudes and behaviors do not match; motivates us to change our attitudes to be more consistent with our behaviors

cognitive model   a scientific approach to psychology emphasizing the need to understand the mechanical and internal processes of the mind, in order to better understand abnormal behavior

cognitive psychology   the study of memory, thinking, reasoning, and other mental activities

cognitive revolution   the shift in psychology from strict behaviorism to investigating ways in which the brain creates the mind

cognitive science   investigations of how the brain creates the mind that draws from several fields, including psychology, philosophy, economics, neuroscience, and computer science

color opponency   the idea that color vision is based on two pairs of opponents; red vs. green and blue vs. yellow

comparative psychology   an indirect form of measurement whose goal is to learn about humans by studying non-humans

concept   a mental map that allows us to know how to react in different situations

concrete operational stage   Piaget's third stage of cognitive development, occurring between ages six and twelve, in which children can perform mental operations as long as they have tangible (concrete) materials to work with

conditioned response   an unconditioned response that was elicited by the presentation of a conditioned stimulus

conditioned stimulus   a previously neutral stimulus that begins to elicit the unconditioned response after being paired with an unconditioned stimulus

cones   a type of photoreceptor found mostly in the foveal region of the retina that is responsible for color vision

confederate   a trained actor that is working with the researchers

conformity   the process of adapting our individual behavior to meet the social norms, attitudes, and behaviors of a social group.

confounding variables   uncontrolled variables that can influence the phenomenon being studied

conscientious   one of the "Big Five" personality characteristics indicating a tendency to be organized, careful, and disciplined

conscious   the part of Freud's structure of mind that is currently accessible

conservation   the principle that quantity remains the same despite changes in shape

contiguity   the state of being close together in time or space

contingency   refers to the degree to which one event predicts the occurrence of another event

control condition   a situation in which variables are not changed in order to observe what the behavior looks like in normal circumstances

cornea   the transparent bulge at the front of the eye

corpus callosum   a broad band of fibers that connects the left hemisphere of the brain to the right hemisphere

correlation coefficient   summarizes the degree of relatedness between two continuous variables

correlational study   a research study that involves the measurement and comparison of two or more variables

correspondence bias   the tendency to believe that people's behavior matches their personal characteristics

cortex   the wrinkly surface of the brain

counterconditioning   a behavioral technique using classical conditioning to replace an undesirable response to a stimulus with a desired response

creative intelligence   the ability to use information in new ways, to invent, and to come up with non-traditional solutions to problems ("to think outside the box")

creativity   the ability to make surprising connections between seemingly disconnected ideas

critical period   an optimal time period within which certain events need to take place to foster healthy development

crystallized intelligence   the facts, information, and details that we know

culture fair   meaning that the score is not biased by the test taker's cultural and social background

culture-bound syndromes   disorders that occur in a particular culture and are closely tied to the values of those societies, though the underlying emotions can be felt universally

dangerous behavior   behavior that has serious potential to harm self or others

decibel (dB)   a unit of measurement that compares the pressure caused by a sound wave to the normal pressure inside the ear

declarative memories   memories that can be put into words, such as events, facts, and word definitions

defense mechanisms   processes by which the ego reduces anxiety

delayed conditioning   the NS is presented first and then the US is presented while the NS is still present, there are two key elements to delayed conditioning

demandingness   refers to the extent to which parents expect obedience and responsible behavior, regardless of how their children may feel about it

dementia   an umbrella term for symptoms of a degenerating brain, such as impaired thinking and memory

dendrites   branching neural fibers that collect inputs from other neurons

dependent variable   the behavior that is being directly measured and observed

developmental psychology   the study of how the individual changes physically, cognitively, and emotionally over the life span

deviant behavior   behavior that is different from what most people in a person's reference group exhibit

Diagnostic and Statistical Manual of Mental Disorders (DSM)   the standard classification of mental disorders used by mental health professionals

differential reinforcement   the technique of putting a problem behavior on extinction while adding positive reinforcement

differential reinforcement of alternative (DRA)   behavior change technique that provides reinforcement for behaviors that produce the same reinforcement as the problem behavior

differential reinforcement of incompatible (DRI) behavior   technique in which a behavior is identified that cannot occur at the same time as the problem behavior

differential reinforcement of other (DRO) behavior   technique that provides reinforcement for the organism when it is doing any behavior that is not the problem behavior

diffusion of responsibility   the more people in the group, the less any one person is responsible for the outcome of the situation

discrimination   occurs when the behavior is observed in the presence of stimuli used during training, but not in their absence

discriminative stimuli   the stimuli that precede a behavior and provide information about the available consequences

disordered behavior   behavior that causes distress for the person exhibiting it, and/or distress for those around the person

dissociative disorder   a mental disorder characterized by a disruption in consciousness, in which a person seems to experience a sudden loss of memory or change in identity, often as a response to overwhelmingly stressful circumstances

dissociative identity disorder   a dissociative disorder in which two or more distinct identities are thought to alternately control a person's behavior, often a result of severe trauma

dualism   the idea that humans are a combination of physical and non-physical components

dysfunctional behavior   behavior that interferes with a person's ability to perform necessary activities, such as going to work or caring for family members

ear canal   conveys sounds from the outer ear to the eardrum

eating disorder   a mental disorder characterized by abnormal or disturbed eating habits

ego   the part of Freud's structure of personality that must find a way to act that satisfies basic desires without violating social constraints

egocentrism   a young child's difficulty perceiving things from another individual's point of view, resulting in the assumption that everyone else sees, hears, and feels exactly as he or she does

electroconvulsive therapy (ECT)   a therapeutic technique in which electric currents are sent through the brain to induce a brief seizure, which causes the brain to reverse symptoms of certain mental illnesses

emerging adulthood   an unsettled phase of life occurring between ages eighteen to the mid-twenties

encode   the transformation of real-world energy, such as light and sound, into an electrical code that can be stored and processed by the brain

environmental realism   the degree to which the testing environment is similar to the real world context where the behavior typically occurs

episodic memory   a type of declarative memory; memories of specific events

essence   the set of necessary and sufficient conditions that determines whether a particular item is a member of a concept

evolutionary psychology   a subfield of psychology that aims to understand the evolutionary pressures that shaped behavior and the adaptive function of behavior

expected value   the benefit or cost of an outcome multiplied by the likelihood of the outcome occurring

experimental condition a situation in which the level of one or more independent variables has been changed, while holding as many other variables constant as possible

experimental control the ability of the researcher to control the environment and minimize outside influences on the behavior of interest

explicit social norms social norms that are formally adopted by a group as written laws, rules, or policies

exposure therapy a behavioral technique that involves having the client face her or his fear while engaging in calming strategies

external validity the degree to which findings from the study can be applied to situations and participants outside the original group of participants

extroversion one of the "Big Five" personality characteristics indicating where a person gets his or her energy; an extrovert feels 'recharged' by social interaction whereas an introvert feels recharged by being alone

extrinsic motivation behavior that is activated by stimuli in the environment surrounding the organism

Eye Movement Desensitization Reprocessing (EMDR) a technique to help veterans traumatized by their combat experiences

face validity the degree to which a psychological theory or assessment appears to be effective or accurate

factor analysis a statistical method for grouping items on a test into clusters by evaluating the correlations between items

falsifiability the ability to test a hypothesis with an objective, empirical observation that could demonstrate the hypothesis to be incorrect

family therapy a form of group therapy in which a therapist works with two or more family members to address dysfunctional family dynamics

figure-ground segregation the ability to distinguish nearby objects from the surrounding background

fluid intelligence how we are able to process information and develop solutions to problems

Flynn effect the name given to gains in performance on intelligence scores for the general population that have been observed over the last several decades

focus the point of origin of a seizure

forensic psychologists applied psychologists who use psychological science in addressing legal and criminal issues

forgetting curve a function relating elapsed time to the amount of information that can be recalled; determined by Ebbinghaus's nonsense syllable experiment

formal operational stage Piaget's fourth and final stage of cognitive development, occurring at approximately age twelve, in which children should begin to demonstrate the ability to perform mental operations abstractly, without the aid of actual experience

fovea an area of high-acuity vision in the center of the retina that is tightly packed with photoreceptors

framing the way in which a particular problem or solution is presented

frequency the number of cycles per second of a wave

frontal lobe the area of the brain that is implicated in impulse control and personality

full report an experimental technique in which participants are asked to recall all of the study material

functional Magnetic Resonance Imaging (fMRI) a technology that uses MRI techniques to measure changes in blood flow in the brain during mental activity

functionalism the view that psychology's goal should be to study how consciousness and experience aid in adjusting to the environment

fundamental attribution error the error in which we tend to make more personal attributions than situational attributions when observing others' behavior

fusiform face area an area of the temporal lobe that has increased activity when we view faces

general intelligence (g) a single factor that accounts for much of the variance in intelligence scores across individuals

generalizability the degree to which scientific findings from one context can be applied to a different context, group of people, or situation

generalization occurs when the CR is observed in the presence of stimuli that were not present during training

generalized anxiety disorder a mental disorder characterized by tension, excess worry, and a state of physiological arousal that has no specific trigger

genetic fitness the likelihood that an organism's genes will survive either by the continued life of the organism or being passed through reproduction

gestalt the view that psychology's goal should be to study experience as a whole rather than the sum of its parts

Gestalt grouping principles methods of grouping disconnected sensory fragments to form a coherent whole

glial cell   a brain cell that supports the activities of neurons

good continuation   a Gestalt principle in which our brain assumes that edges are more likely to be smooth than to have abrupt bends or kinks

group therapy   a form of psychotherapy in which one or more therapists work with people/clients as a group

hemisphere   the division of the cortex into left and right sides

hoarding disorder   a mental disorder that is characterized by a persistent difficulty discarding or parting with possessions because of a perceived need to save them

heuristic   a way of solving problems that relies on inexact rules, so it is error prone but faster than algorithms

humanism   the view that psychology's goal should be to understand human strengths, aspirations, conscious experience, free will, and potential

humanistic theorists   psychologists that choose to focus on the potential for positive growth and achievement in an individual rather than the individual's deficits

hypothalamus   a midbrain structure that is essential to motivated behaviors such as feeding or fighting

iconic memory   a brief visual image of the world held in sensory memory

id   the part of Freud's structure of personality that houses primitive desires

identity   an individual's consistent sense of who they are

implicit social norms   expectations and rules governing social behavior that are not part of formally adopted laws, rules, or policies

imprint   a bonding process that occurs between certain birds and their perceived caretakers

independent variables   the environmental conditions the researcher manipulates during the experiment

indirect measurements   surveys and comparative psychology

industrial/organizational psychology   the subfield of psychology that examines the application of psychological principles to work and business

informational influence   changes in behavior due to a desire to do what is right in a social setting and to act correctly

in-groups   the individuals with whom we directly identify and perceive as most similar to us

insecure attachment   when infants demonstrate behavior marked by anxiety, avoidance, or a combination of both in regard to relationships

insight   moment at which the solution to a problem suddenly becomes clear

insight therapies   a technique used to help individuals improve functioning through increasing understanding and expression of unresolved conflicts

Institutional Review Board   a committee composed of scientists and administrators that oversees all human research at an institution in order to protect the rights of research participants

intelligence   the ability to efficiently and effectively learn from experience, perform mental tasks and solve problems

intelligence test   standardized set of measures used to assess mental performance and abilities to make comparisons across groups and individuals

internal validity   the ability to minimize the influence of variables other than those involved in the research question

interneuron   a neuron in the spine that is involved in reflexive movements

interpersonal intelligence   ability to understand the social world, including the thoughts, emotions, and motivations of others

intimacy   the ability to form emotionally close relationships, particularly of a romantic nature

intrapersonal intelligence   the ability to understand the self, including your own thoughts, emotions, and motivations

intrinsic motivation   behaviors that are motivated by thoughts, feelings, and values that are inside the individual.

introspection   a systematic method of providing research participants with an external stimulus and asking them to provide detailed reports of their internal experiences, to provide access to the internal mental processes and experiences of their participants

ion channels   passageways that enable charged particles (ions) to travel through the neural membrane when opened

iris   the colored ring of muscle in the eye that controls the size of the pupil

lifetime reproductive potential   the potential number of offspring that an organism could produce in its lifetime

light exposure therapy   a technique developed to help people who suffer from seasonal affective disorder, a form of depression that most often affects people living in climates far from the equator that have long, dark winters

limbic system   a group of midbrain structures that contributes to our emotional experience

linear perspective   a monocular depth cue wherein parallel lines appear as if they converge in the distance

linguistic intelligence   the ability to understand, analyze, and produce language

lobotomy   surgical procedure performed on the brain to help alleviate more severe symptoms of mental illness, such as agitation and aggression

locus of control   the perceived source of control in an individual's life that results in the attribution of events to circumstances either within or beyond the individual's control

logical-mathematical intelligence   the ability to solve mathematical problems and understand symbolic representations

long-term memory   memory of past events and facts about the world

major depressive disorder   a mental disorder that is characterized by feelings of extreme unhappiness and hopelessness, which interferes with one's work, sleep, eating, and life

maturation   the orderly sequence of biological growth

medical model   model that conceptualizes abnormal behavior as the result of physical causes that can be treated through medical means

medulla   a brain stem structure that controls basic reflexes such as breathing and heartbeat

menarche   the first menstrual period, occurring, on average, around age twelve

menopause   the end of the menstrual cycle, resulting in the loss of the ability to bear children

mental set   a set of mental assumptions about a situation that can hide possible solutions

Minnesota Multiphasic Personality Inventory (MMPI)   the most widely-used objective personality inventory, primarily utilized to help diagnose psychological disorders, such as schizophrenia and bipolar disorder

mirror drawing   a task in which the participant is asked to draw something seen in a mirror, which reverses the visual image

misinformation effect   a memory phenomenon in which people falsely recall information presented after an event as having been part of the event

mood stabilizers   medications that balance out extreme moods by acting on neurotransmitters that influence mood and behavior

moral development   the development of the capacity to distinguish between right and wrong

moral intuitions   gut feelings that can drive decisions

morpheme   the smallest meaningful unit in a word

morphine   a drug that relieves pain by mimicking the neurotransmitter endorphins

motivation   the processes that energize us to behave in certain ways and in certain contexts

multicultural/diversity studies   a subfield of psychology that explores how behavior is influenced by culture, ethnicity, sexual orientation, gender, and disability

musical intelligence   the ability to understand, produce, and organize music

myelin   glial cell that provides electrical insulation for the axon

Myers Briggs Type Indicator (MBTI)   a Jungian personality test that has been used in team building, leadership training, personality development, and marriage counseling

naturalistic fallacy   the erroneous belief that biologically based motives, feelings, or behaviors are morally right or wrong

naturalistic intelligence   the ability to observe, appreciate, and understand the natural world

naturalistic observation   a research method in which behavior is observed and recorded in the context where it typically occurs with as little interference from the researchers as possible

need hierarchy theory   this theory proposes that we have genetically determined physiological needs that drive our behavior

need to belong   a fundamental psychological drive to have meaningful, reciprocal social connections

negative punisher   a stimulus or event, the removal of which will decrease the likelihood that the behavior that produced its removal will occur again in the future

negative reinforce   a stimulus or event that, when removed, will increase the likelihood that the behavior that produced its removal will occur in the future

neglect   a visual deficit in which people tend to ignore everything seen in one half of the visual field

neuromuscular junction   tiny gap between a muscle fiber and the motor neuron controlling the fiber

neuron   a brain cell that stores and processes information using an electrical code

neuron doctrine   the claim that the network that appears when examining brain tissue under a microscope consists of separate cells

neuroticism   one of the "Big Five" personality characteristics indicating a tendency toward anxiety and insecurity

neurotransmitters   chemical messengers manufactured by one neuron that communicate with other neurons via synapses

neutral stimulus (NS)   an environmental event that does not elicit an unconditioned response

normative influence   changes in behavior due to a desire for social approval or to avoid social disapproval

nucleus accumbens   part of the brain that underlies feelings of pleasure

object permanence   the awareness that objects continue to exist when not seen

objective personality inventory   a self-report questionnaire that clearly asks about a wide range of behaviors and feelings and assesses several traits at once

observational learning   learning that occurs through observing the behavior of others; modeling

obsessive-compulsive disorder   a mental disorder characterized by unwanted repetitive thoughts (obsessions) and/or actions (compulsions)

occipital lobe   the lobe at the posterior corner of the brain, concerned primarily with basic visual processing

occlusion   a monocular depth cue wherein objects that are closer may hide or cover objects that are more distant

openness   one of the "Big Five" personality characteristics indicating a willingness to try new experiences

operant conditioning   focuses on the relation between the behavior and the environmental changes that the behavior produces

operational definition   a statement that clearly explains what is being measured and how to measure it

ossicles   three tiny bones in the middle ear that amplify airborne vibrations

out-groups   the individuals with whom we least directly identify and who we perceive to be most dissimilar from us

palliative care   a multidisciplinary support approach to caring for people with serious illnesses, with the goal of improving quality of life for patient and family

panic disorder   feelings of tremendous fear, when there is no reasonable causation, and characterized by panic attacks that can last for several minutes or longer

parasympathetic nervous system   the portion of the autonomic nervous system that controls normal organ activity

parenting style   how caregivers impart beliefs and standards of behavior to their children

parietal lobe   the part of the cortex that processes visual locations and contains the primary somatosensory cortex

partial report   an experimental technique in which participants recall just a specified subset of the study material, which showed that iconic memory has more capacity than was revealed by the full report technique

pelvic inflammatory disease (PID)   an infection of the female reproductive organs; usually occurs when sexually transmitted bacteria spread from the vagina to the uterus, fallopian tubes, or ovaries

perception   the mental experience of sensory information

perceptual constancy   the visual perception that objects remain constant even when their retinal image changes

peripheral nervous system   the portion of the nervous system containing all nerves outside the central nervous system

peripheral route of persuasion   attitude change that is due to quick association with positive or negative cues in the environment or the object or event

personal attribution   occurs when we assign the cause of the behavior to something within the individual, such as his or her personality, beliefs, or motivations

personality   a person's relatively consistent pattern of thinking, feeling, and behaving

personality disorder   a mental disorder characterized by a maladaptive pattern behaviors and cognitions that often impair the ability to interact successfully in the social environment

personality psychology   the study of the relatively consistent patterns of thinking, feeling, and behaving within an individual

person-situation controversy   a person's behavior is different in different situations

perspectives of psychology   philosophical ways of thinking about the goals of psychology and the nature of human behavior

phi phenomenon   when the brain perceives motion in stationary alternating images, such as lights flashing along a string of Christmas lights

phobia   a completely irrational fear toward an object or situation, where the individual only finds peace by avoiding the object

phoneme   the smallest unit of sound in a language

phonology   the ability to hear phonemes and assign the phonemes to words

photopigment a molecule in a photoreceptor that changes shape when light collides with it

photoreceptors light-sensitive cells in the retina

phrenology an idea created by Franz Joseph Gall that postulates bumps on a person's skull are correlated to his or her personality

pinna the cartilaginous portion of the outer ear that collects sound

placebo effect a phenomenon in which people often feel better when exposed to a treatment, even if the treatment does not work

pleasure principle the driving force of the id, which constantly seeks gratification of basic desires

positive psychology the subfield of psychology that aims to understand the strengths, virtues, and values of human behavior

positive punisher a stimulus or event that is produced by the behavior and causes a decrease in the probability of the behavior occurring in the future

positive reinforce a stimulus or event that, when presented, will increase the likelihood that the behavior that produced it will occur again in the future

post-traumatic stress disorder a mental disorder characterized by intrusive memories, nightmares, social withdrawal, hypervigilance, and/or insomnia that lingers for a month or more after experiencing a traumatic event

practical intelligence the ability to solve the day-to-day challenges of a particular context while adapting previous strategies and shaping new strategies for success

preconscious the part of Freud's structure of mind that is accessible but not currently conscious

prejudice a strong positive or negative attitude toward a group of people that biases the way we think, act, and feel about the members of a particular group

preoperational stage Piaget's second stage of cognitive development, occurring between ages two and six, in which children can mentally represent, but not mentally operate, objects

primary auditory cortex the first major region of the auditory processing in the cortex

primary motor cortex lies on the frontal lobe and programs voluntary movements

primary sex characteristics external genitalia and reproductive organs; primarily internal

primary somatosensory cortex lies on the parietal lobe and processes touch sensations

primary visual cortex the first stage of cortical visual processing in which the visual image is separated into its component parts, such as color, shape, and motion

problem solving a process in which a person begins at an initial state and moves through a series of intermediate states to arrive at a desired state

procedural memories memories that often can't be expressed in words but are memories for "how to" do a certain skill

projective personality tests assessment instruments based on the psychodynamic perspective that are sensitive to the examiner's beliefs and are a way to examine the unconscious

prosopagnosia a condition which causes people to lose the ability to recognize faces

prototype a kind of item that best represents a concept; robins but not penguins are prototypical birds

proximate explanations a causal explanation of behavior that focuses on immediate situational and physiological factors

psychic determinism point of view stating that past experiences influence the present state of mind and that nothing happens by chance

psychoactive drugs chemicals that alter mental function by interacting with one or more synaptic processes

psychoanalysis a type of therapy that investigates repressed fears and conflicts by bringing them into the conscious mind in order to treat the mental disorder

psychodynamic model Freudian approach to psychology that interprets personality in terms of conscious and unconscious forces

psychodynamic theory Freud's argument that our psychological experience is the product of the conflict between our id and our superego

psychodynamic therapies a form of psychotherapy that focuses on the client reaching self-awareness of unconscious content and childhood experiences, as well as understanding the impact they have on past and present behavior

psychological disorder a pattern of thoughts, feelings, and behavior that are deviant, disordered, dysfunctional, and/ or dangerous

psychology the scientific study of the behavior of individual organisms and how environmental, physiological, mental, social, and cultural events influence these behaviors

psychology of intelligence   the study of individual differences in mental capacities and abilities

psychopharmacology   the scientific study of the impact drugs have on psychological disorders

psychosurgery   surgical procedures performed on the brain in order to alleviate severe symptoms of mental illness that are not responsive to less invasive treatments

puberty   the period of sexual maturation within which we become capable of sexual reproduction

pupil   the tiny transparent hole in the center of the iris that allows light to enter the eye

reaction formation   a defense mechanism by which a person behaves in a manner opposite to their true feelings, such as an angry person who acts excessively cheerful

reactivity   changes in behavior that occur because of being observed/recorded

reality principle   the driving force of the ego or its attempts to meet basic needs without violating social constraints

receptor sites   locations where neurotransmitters fit like a key in a lock to activate postsynaptic neurons

reciprocal determinism   a personality model that posits that an individual's behavior is the result of the interaction between an individual's cognition and the environment within which the individual resides

reflex   an automatic behavioral response to a stimulus

rehearsal   a way of extending the duration of items in short-term memory by repeating the items to yourself over and over

reliability   refers to the consistency of the test across the entire measurement and different test-taking occasions

repression   a defense mechanism in which unwanted thoughts and feelings are pushed out of the conscious into the unconscious

resiliency   the ability to overcome stress and trauma

resonance   a frequency at which something vibrates most energetically

respondent behavior   an inherited behavior that is directly caused by the occurrence of a specific stimulus in the environment.

respondent extinction   occurs any time the conditioned stimulus (CS) is presented without presenting the US

responsiveness   refers to warmth, or to what extent parents respond to their children's needs and wants

resting potential   voltage maintained by a neuron when it is not sending any electrical messages

resurgence   when an old behavior reappears during extinction of a new behavior

retina   the "projection screen" of the eye that transforms the light energy received from the outside world into an electrical signal that is passed to the brain

retroactive interference   the tendency for newer learning to interfere with older memories

reuptake   the process of the sending neuron reclaiming used neurotransmitters from the synapse

rods   a more sensitive type of photoreceptor found mostly on the periphery of the retina

Rorschach Inkblot Test   an ambiguous stimulus test, the responses to which are thought to reflect an individual's true personality characteristics

salience   refers to how noticeable the neutral stimulus is to the organism

savants   individuals with generally limited mental abilities, but outstanding capabilities in one or two limited domains

scatterplot   a graph that shows the relationship between two variables

schedules of reinforcement   refers to the rules that specify when reinforcement is delivered and what must be done to earn the consequence

schema   a structure in long-term memory for organizing information

schizophrenia   a chronic and often disabling mental disorder characterized by disorganized and/or delusional thinking, distorted sensory and perceptual experiences, and blunted or inappropriate emotions and behaviors

school psychologists   a type of applied psychologist that works in school settings to address the educational, psychological, and social needs of students

science   the systematic, organized approach to understanding the physical and natural world through direct observation and measurement

scientific method   an organized way that helps scientists (or anyone!) answer a question or begin to solve a problem

sclera   the outer white portion of the eye

secondary sex characteristics   external indicators of sex, such as breasts and hips in girls and facial hair and deeper voices in boys; primarily external

secure attachment   when infants play happily and readily explore new environments in the presence of their mother

self-actualization the final tier of Maslow's theory of Human Motivation, in which the individual has reached the full potential in every aspect of his or her life

self-concept the image individuals have of themselves, consisting of the abilities we believe we have and how we perceive them

self-efficacy the beliefs an individual holds concerning his or her skills and ability to perform certain acts

self-esteem our personal view of ourselves

self-fulfilling prophecies situations where the expectations of an event increase the likelihood of the event occurring, which reinforces the expectation of the event

self-serving bias we accept our successes as a product of personal characteristics and losses as due to situational variables

semantic memory a type of declarative memory for word meanings and facts about the world

semantics connection between a word and the word's meaning

sensation the process of collecting sensory information from the outside world through the five senses

sensation and perception the study of how the senses collect energy from the environment and then process this sensory information

sensorimotor stage Piaget's first stage of cognitive development, occurring from birth to approximately age two, in which babies learn about the world through their senses and actions

sensory memory a memory store for briefly holding sensory information (primarily sights and sounds)

serotonin a neurotransmitter that affects mood, sleep, and appetite

short-term memory a memory store containing whatever currently inhabits the conscious mind

simultaneous conditioning the NS and US are both presented at the same time

situational attribution occurs when we assign the cause of the behavior to something outside the individual such as the context or other people in the situation

social clock the appropriate time, depending upon one's culture, to leave home, get a job, marry, have children, and retire

social norms the rules and expectations of the group concerning the behavior of individual members

social psychology a subfield of psychology that focuses on how the social environment—including individuals and groups—influences the behavior of the individual, including how they think, act, and feel

social roles the expected behaviors of individuals with certain characteristics in a social group

sociocultural model an approach to psychology that considers the complex effects social and cultural factors have on individual behavior

soma part of the neuron that contains machinery to keep the neuron alive and functioning

somatic nervous system the portion of the peripheral nervous system that controls voluntary behaviors (i.e., walking)

spatial intelligence the ability to understand how objects relate to one another in space and to navigate these objects

spermarche the first time sperm is part of ejaculation

spontaneous recovery the reoccurrence of the conditioned response after some time has passed since the last extinction trial

spurious correlation a situation in which two variables are not really related, but are statistically correlated

statistics a type of mathematics used to describe and evaluate data

stereopsis the brain's ability to generate a three-dimensional view of the world from two flat retinal images by comparing the two images

stereotypes the overgeneralized characteristics that we assign to all members of a perceived group

strange situation an experiment conducted by Mary Ainsworth to systematically study attachment patterns in infants

stranger anxiety anxiety born of an infant's inability to assimilate people (strangers) into the caregiver schema, beginning at approximately eight months of age

structuralism the view that psychology's goal should be to identify and understand the basic elements of human experience

subfield of psychology an area of research that focuses on a specific set of influences on behavior

substance use disorder a disorder in which use of one or more substances results in a maladaptive behavior and cognition patterns that often impair judgment, finances, and interpersonal relationships

superego the part of Freud's structure of personality that is the conscience, or set of ethics

survey an indirect form of measurement used to collect data about individuals

sylvian fissure a structure of the cortex that separates the parietal and temporal lobe

sympathetic nervous system the portion of the autonomic nervous system that controls the body's organ activity in response to threats

synapse tiny gap between two neurons where chemical transmission of neural messages occurs

syntax rules governing word order in a language

temperament personality characteristics that are made evident shortly after birth relating to emotional reactivity and intensity

temporal lobe the part of the cortex that allows us to recognize visual objects such as faces

teratogens environmental factors, such as maternal stress, viruses, or drugs, that can negatively impact fetal development

test standardization the practice of (1) determining set procedures that will be used whenever the test is given and (2) giving the test to people across a desired reference group in order to establish a range of comparison scores

thalamus a midbrain structure that receives incoming sensory information and passes the information onto the limbic system and the cortex

Thematic Apperception Test a type of test where individuals make up stories about pictures, express themselves through drawing, or complete sentences such as "One thing I wish I could change is…."

top-down processing the use of previous experience and expectations about situations to organize sensory information during perception

trace conditioning the NS is presented and removed before the US is presented so that there is no overlap between the two stimuli

traits summary terms that capture an individual's stable and enduring tendency to respond in a certain way

transduction the transformation of one kind of energy into another kind of energy

trichromatic theory the idea that our eyes have three different kinds of nerves that respond to three colors: red, blue, and green

ultimate explanations a causal explanation of behavior that focuses on the evolutionary forces and functions of the behavior

unconscious the part of Freud's structure of mind that remains constantly inaccessible to the conscious mind

validity of an exam is determined by how well it measures or predicts what it was intended to assess

variance the difference in scores around the mathematical mean

vesicles tiny bags used to contain and transport neurotransmitters from the soma to the end of the axon

working memory a form of memory that contains both storage and processing mechanisms

zeitgeist the major intellectual theories and philosophies that dominate an area during a specific time in history

References

23 legal medical marijuana states and DC. (2015). Retrieved from http://medicalmarijuana.procon.org/view.resource.php?resourceID=000881

Achievements in public health, 1990-1999: Control of infectious diseases. (1999). *Morbidity and Mortality Weekly Report, 48*(29), 621–629. Retrieved from https://www.cdc.gov/mmwr/preview/mmwrhtml/mm4829a1.htm

Ainsworth, M. D. S. (1973). The development of infant-mother attachment. In B. Caldwell & H. Ricciuti (Eds.), *Review of child development research* (Vol. 3). Chicago, IL: University of Chicago Press.

Ainsworth, M. D. S. (1989). Attachments beyond infancy. *American Psychologist, 44,* 709-716.

Allport, G. W., & Postman, D. L. (1945). The basic psychology of rumor. *Transactions of the New York Academy of Sciences, 8,* 61-81.

Almeida, L. S., Prieto, M. D., Ferreira, A. I., Bermejo, M. R., Ferrando, M., & Ferrándiz, C. (2010). Intelligence assessment: Gardner multiple intelligence theory as an alternative. *Learning and Individual Differences, 20*(3), 225-230.

American Foundation for Suicide Prevention. (2016). Suicide: Facts and figures. Retrieved from https://afsp.org/wp-content/uploads/2016/06/2016-National-Facts-Figures.pdfAmerican Foundation for Suicide Prevention. (2016). Suicide statistics. Retrieved from https://afsp.org/about-suicide/suicide-statistics/

American Psychological Association. (2011). *Careers in psychology.* Washington, DC: Author.

American Psychological Association. (2015). *Demographics of the U.S. psychology workforce: Findings from the American community survey.* Washington, DC: Author.

American Psychological Association. (2015). Health disparities & mental/behavioral health workforce. Retrieved from http://www.apa.org/about/gr/ issues/workforce/disparity.aspx

American Psychological Association. (2016). Datapoint: What do people do with their psychology degrees? *Monitor on Psychology, 47*(6), 12.

Andrews, P. W., & Thomson J. A., Jr. (2009). Depression's evolutionary roots. *Scientific American Mind,* 57–61.

Andrews, P. W., & Thomson J. A., Jr. (2009a). The bright side of being blue: Depression as an adaptation for analyzing complex problems. *Psychological Review, 116*(3), 620-684.

Arnett, J. J. (1999). Adolescent storm and stress, reconsidered. *American Psychologist, 54,* 317-326.

Anxiety and Depression Association of America. (2015). Facts & statistics, Retrieved from http://www.adaa.org/about-adaa/press-room/facts-statistics

Aronson, E., Wilson, T. D., & Akert, R. M. (2010). *Social psychology* (7th ed.). Upper Saddle River, NJ: Prentice Hall.

Asch, S. E. (1956). Studies of independence and conformity: I. A minority of one against a unanimous majority. *Psychological Monographs: General and Applied, 70*(9), 1-70.

Atsma, Aaron J. (2016). Theoi Greek Mythology. Retrieved from http://www.theoi.com/

Ault, A., & Brzuzy, S. (2009). Removing gender identity disorder from the Diagnostic and Statistical Manual of Mental Disorders: A call for action. *Social Work, 54*(2), 187-189.

Baddeley, A. D., & Hitch, G. (1974). Working memory. *Psychology of Learning and Motivation, 8,* 47-89.

Baghdadi, G., & Nasrabadi, A. M. (2009). An investigation of changes in brain wave energy during hypnosis with respect to normal EEG. *Sleep and Hypnosis, 11*(2), 40-45.

Baker, T. B., McFall, R. M., & Shoham, V. (2008). Current status and future prospects of clinical psychology toward a scientifically principled approach to mental and behavioral health care. *Psychological Science in the Public Interest, 9*(2), 67-103.

Bandura, A. (1986). *Social foundations of thought and action: A cognitive social theory.* Englewood Cliffs, NY: Prentice Hall

Barlow, D. H. (2010). Negative effects from psychological treatments: A perspective. *American Psychologist, 65*(1), 13.

Barrett, E., & Martin, P. (2014). *Extreme: Why some people thrive at the limits.* Oxford, England: Oxford University Press.

Baumeister, R. F. (Ed.). (1999). *The self in social psychology.* Philadelphia, PA: Psychology Press.

Baumeister, R. F., & Leary, M. R. (1995). The need to belong: Desire for interpersonal attachments as a fundamental human motivation. *Psychological Bulletin, 117*(3), 497-529.

Baumrind, D. (1971). *Current patterns of parental authority.* Richmond, VA: American Psychological Assn.

Baumrind, D. (1996). The discipline controversy revisited. *Family Relations, 45,* 405-415.

Beardsley, L. M. (1994). Medical diagnosis and treatment across cultures. In *Psychology and culture* (pp. 279–284). Needham Heights, MA: Allyn and Bacon.

Beck, A. T. (1979). *Cognitive therapy and the emotional disorders.* New York, NY: Penguin.

Bellos, A. (2010). *Here's looking at Euclid.* New York, NY: Free Press.

Belsky, J., Houts, R. M., & Fearon, R. M. P. (2010). Infant attachment security and the timing of puberty: Testing an evolutionary hypothesis. *Psychological Science, 21,* 1195-1201.

Benjamin, L. T., Jr. (1988). *A history of psychology: Original sources and contemporary research.* New York, NY: McGraw-Hill.

Beran, M. (2012). Did you ever hear the one about the horse that could count? *Frontiers in Psychology, 3,* 357.

Berk, L. E. (1994, November). Why children talk to themselves. *Scientific American, 27*(5), 78-83.

Berk, L. E., & Roberts, W. L. (2009). *Child development.* Toronto: Pearson.

Berkeley, G. (2012). *Three Dialogues Between Hylas And Philonous.* D. Jaquette (Ed.). Ontario, Canada: Broadview Press.

Berko, J. (1958). The child's learning of English morphology. *World, 14,* 150-157.

Berlin, B., & Kay, P. (1969). *Basic colour terms.* Berkeley, CA: University of California Press.

Binet, A., & Simon, T. (1905). New methods for the diagnosis of the intellectual level of subnormals. *L'année Psychologique, 12,* 191-244.

Biro, F. M., Galvez, M. P., Greenspan, L. C., Succop, P. A., Vangeepuram, N., Pinney, S. M., . . . Wolff, M. S. (2010). Pubertal assessment method and baseline characteristics in a mixed longitudinal study of girls. *Pediatrics, 126,* e583-e590.

Bishop, D. I., Weisgram, E. S., Holleque, K. M., Lund, K. E., & Wheeler-Anderson, J. R. (2005). Identity development and alcohol consumption: Current and retrospective self-reports by college students. *Journal of Adolescence, 28,* 523-533.

Blakemore, S. (2008). Development of the social brain during adolescence. *Quarterly Journal of Experimental Psychology, 61,* 40-49.

Bloom, P. (2005). *Descartes' baby: How the science of child development explains what makes us human.* Random House.

Blumenthal, A. L. (1975). A reappraisal of Wilhelm Wundt. *American Psychologist, 30*(11), 1081.

Boakes, R. (1984). *From Darwin to behaviourism: Psychology and the minds of animals.* New York, NY: Cambridge University Press.

Bolwig, T. G., & Madsen, T. M. (2007). Electroconvulsive therapy in melancholia: The role of hippocampal neurogenesis. *Acta Psychiatrica Scandinavica, 115*(s433), 130-135.

Botwin, M. D., Buss, D. M., & Shackelford, T. K. (1997). Personality and mate preferences: Five factors in mate selection and marital satisfaction. *Journal of Personality, 65*(1), 107-136.

Bowlby, J. (1969). *Attachment and loss.* New York, NY: Basic Books.

Bowlby, J. (1988). *A secure base: Parent-child attachment and healthy human development.* New York, NY: Basic Books.

Brooks, E. K. (2014). Contest winner: A healthy dose of dissociation. *The Military Psychologist.* Retrieved from http://www.apadivisions.org/division-19/publications/newsletters/military/2014/10/dissociation.aspx

Brown, R. (2000). Social identity theory: Past achievements, current problems and future challenges. *European Journal of Social Psychology, 30,* 745-778.

Brown, T., & Barlow, D. (2007). *Casebook in abnormal psychology.* Belmont, CA: Wadsworth.

Buchanan, R. W., Kreyenbuhl, J., Kelly, D. L., Noel, J. M., Boggs, D. L., Fischer, B. A. & Keller, W. (2010). The 2009 schizophrenia PORT psychopharmacological treatment recommendations and summary statements. *Schizophrenia Bulletin, 36*(1), 71-93.

Buri, J. R., Louiselle, P. A., Misukanis, T. M., & Mueller, R. A. (1988). Effects of parental authoritarianism and authoritativeness on self-esteem. *Personality and Social Psychology Bulletin, 14,* 271-282.

Buss, A. H. (1989). Personality as traits. *American Psychologist, 44*(11), 1378-1388.

Cacioppo, J. (2007). Psychology is a hub science. *Observer, 20*(8). Retrieved from https://www.psychologicalscience.org/observer/psychology-is-a-hub-scienceCampbell, D. T., & Specht, J. C. (1985). Altruism: Biology, culture, and religion. *Journal of Social and Clinical Psychology, 3*(1), 33-42.

Carey, B. (2012, November). Academic 'dream team' helped Obama's efforts. *The New York Times.* Retrieved from: https://www.nytimes.com/2012/11/13/health/dream-team-of-behavioral-scientists-advised-obama-campaign.html

Castillo, R. J. (1997). *Culture & mental illness: A client- centered approach.* Salt Lake City, UT: Thomson Brooks/Cole Publishing Co.

Castonguay, L. G., Boswell, J. F., Constantino, M. J., Goldfried, M. R., & Hill, C. E. (2010). Training implications of harmful effects of psychological treatments. *American Psychologist, 65*(1), 34-49.

Cattell, H. E., & Mead, A. D. (2008). The sixteen personality factor questionnaire (16PF). In G. J. Boyle, G. Matthews, & D. H. Saklofske (Eds.), *The SAGE handbook of personality theory and assessment* (Vol. 2, pp. 135–178). Thousand Oaks, CA: SAGE Publications.

Cattell, R. (1943). The measurement of adult intelligence. *Psychological Bulletin, 40*(3), 153-193.

Central Intelligence Agency (n.d.). The World Factbook. Retrieved from https://www.cia.gov/library/publications/the-world-factbook/fields/2102.html

Chalmers, D. J. (1995). Facing up to the problem of consciousness. *Journal of Consciousness Studies, 2*(3), 200-219.

Chambless, D. L., Baker, M. J., Baucom, D. H., Beutler, L. E., Calhoun, K. S., Crits-Christoph, P., . . . & Woody, S. R. (1998). Update on empirically validated therapies, II. *The Clinical Psychologist, 51*(1), 3-16.

Chance, P. (2013). *Learning and behavior* (7th ed.). Belmont, CA: Wadsworth.

Chapman, D. J. (2013). Does breastfeeding result in smarter children? A closer look. *Journal of Human Lactation, 29*(4), 444-445.

Chivers, M.L. & Baily, J.M. (2005). A sex difference in features that elicit genital response. *Biological Psychology, 70*, 115-120.

Chomsky, N. (1959). A review of BF Skinner's verbal behavior. *Language, 35*(1), 26-58.

Christianson, S. Å., & Loftus, E. F. (1990). Some characteristics of people's traumatic memories. *Bulletin of the Psychonomic Society, 28*(3), 195-198.

Christie, J. (1987). Helen Keller. In J.A. van Cleve (Ed.), *Gallaudet encyclopedia of deaf people and deafness* (Vol. 2, p. 125). New York,N: McGraw-Hill.

Clancy, S. A. (2009). *The trauma myth: The truth about the sexual abuse of children-and its aftermath.* New York, NY: Basic Books.

Cohen, D. (1995, June). Now are we one, or two, or three. *New Scientist, 1982,* 14-15.

Collazo, R. (2016). Race vs. ethnicity vs. nationality (learn the difference). *Affinity.* Retrieved from http://affinitymagazine.us/2016/05/31/race-vs-ethnicity-vs-nationality-learn-the-difference/

Comer, R. J. (2004). *Abnormal psychology* (5th ed.). New York, NY: Worth.

Conley, C. S., & Rudolph, K. D. (2009). The emerging sex difference in adolescent depression: Interacting contributions of puberty and peer stress. *Development and Psychopathology, 21,* 593-620.

Coopersmith, S. (1967). *The antecedents of self-esteem.* San Francisco, CA: Freeman.

Copeland, W., Shanahan, L., Miller, S., Costello, E. J., Angold, A., & Maughan, B. (2010). Outcomes of early pubertal timing in young women: A prospective population-based study. *American Journal of Psychiatry, 167,* 1218-1225.

Corkin, S. (2013). *Permanent present tense: The unforgettable life of the amnesic patient, H.M.* New York, NY: Basic Books.

Costa, P. T., & McCrae, R. R. (2009). The five-factor model and the NEO inventories. In J. N. Butcher (Ed.), *Oxford handbook of personality assessment* (pp. 299-322). New York, NY: Oxford University Press.

Crick, F. (1994). *The Astonishing Hypothesis.* New York, NY: Scribner's.

Cuijpers, P., Geraedts, A. S., van Oppen, P., Andersson, G., Markowitz, J. C., & van Straten, A. (2011). Interpersonal psychotherapy for depression: A meta-analysis. *American Journal of Psychiatry, 168*(6), 581-592.

Cummins, R. (1991). The introspectionism of Titchener. In J. C. Smith (Ed.), *Historical foundations of cognitive science* (pp. 235-242). Houten, Netherlands: Springer.

Cunningham, H., & Morpurgo, M. (2006). *The invention of childhood.* London, England: BBC.

Cytowic, R. E. (2003). *The Man Who Tasted Shapes.* Exeter, United Kingdom: Imprint Academic.

Czeisler, C. A., Duffy, J. F., Shanahan, T. L., Brown, E. N., Mitchell, J. F., Rimmer, D. W., & Dijk, D. J. (1999). Stability, precision, and near-24-hour period of the human circadian pacemaker. *Science, 284*(5423), 2177-2181.

Dalgleish, T. (2004). The emotional brain. *Nature Reviews Neuroscience, 5*(7), 583-589.

Damasio, A. (1994). *Descartes' error: Emotion, reason, and the human brain.* New York, NY: G. P. Putnam's Sons.

Darley, J. M., & Latane, B. (1970). *The unresponsive by- stander: Why doesn't he help?* New York, NY: Appleton-Century-Crofts.

Darwin, C. (1872). *The expression of emotion in man and animals.* London, England: Methuen.

Darwin, C. (1877). A biographical sketch of an infant. *Mind, 2*(7), 285-294.

Daskalakis, Z. J., Levinson, A. J., & Fitzgerald, P. B. (2008). Repetitive transcranial magnetic stimulation for major depressive disorder: A review. *Can J Psychiatry, 53*(9), 555-566.

Davis, K., Christodoulou, J., Seider, S., & Gardner, H. (2011). The theory of multiple intelligences. In R. J. Sternberg & S. B. Kaufman (Eds.), *The Cambridge handbook of intelligence* (pp. 485-504). New York, NY: Cambridge University Press.

De Los Reyes, A., & Kazdin, A. E. (2009). Identifying evidence-based interventions for children and adolescents using the range of possible changes model: A meta-analytic illustration. *Behavior Modification, 33,* 583-617.

De Wolff, M. S., & van IJzendoorn, M. H. (1997). Sensitivity and attachment. *Child Development, 68,* 571-591.

Dennett, D. C. (2017). *From bacteria to Bach and back: The evolution of minds.* New York, NY: WW Norton & Company.

Descartes, R. and Cress, D. (1993). *Meditations on First Philosophy.* Indianapolis, IN: Hackett Pub. Co.

Deutsch, A. (1949). *The mentally ill in America; A history of their care and treatment from colonial times* (2nd ed.). New York, NY: Columbia University Press.

DeYoung, C. G., Hirsh, J. B., Shane, M. S., Papademetris, X., Rajeevan, N., & Gray, J. R. (2010). Testing predictions from personality neuroscience brain structure and the big five. *Psychological Science, 21,* 820-828.

Dienstbier, R. A. (1970). Positive and negative prejudice: Interactions of prejudice with race and social desirability. *Journal of Personality, 38,* 198-215.

Dimidjian, S., & Hollon, S. D. (2010). How would we know if psychotherapy were harmful? *American Psychologist, 65*(1), 21.

Dirix, C. E. H., Nijhuis, J. G., Jongsma, H. W., & Hornstra, G. (2009). Aspects of fetal learning and new memory. *Child Development, 80,* 1251-1258.

Dixon, M. J., Harrigan, K. A., Santesso, D. L., Graydon, C., Fugelsang, J. A., & Collins, K. (2014). The impact of sound in modern multiline video slot machine play. *Journal of Gambling Studies, 30*(4), 913-929. doi:10.1007/s10899-013-9391-8

Donnellan, M. B., Conger, R. D., & Bryant, C. M. (2004). The big five and enduring marriages. *Journal of Research in Personality, 38*(5), 481-504.

Douglas, K. S., Guy, L. S., & Hart, S. D. (2009). Psychosis as a risk factor for violence to others: A meta-analysis. *Psychological Bulletin, 135*(5), 679-706.

Driessen, E., Cuijpers, P., de Maat, S. C., Abbass, A. A., de Jonghe, F., & Dekker, J. J. (2010). The efficacy of short-term psychodynamic psychotherapy for depression: A meta-analysis. *Clinical Psychology Review, 30*(1), 25-36.

Dunst, C. J., & Kassow, D. Z. (2007). Caregiver sensitivity, social responsiveness, and secure infant attachment. *Journal of Early and Intensive Behavior Intervention, 5*(1), 40-56.

Dutton, D. G., & Aron, A. P. (1974). Some evidence for heightened sexual attraction under conditions of high anxiety. *Journal of Personality and Social Psychology, 30*(4), 510-517. doi:10.1037/h0037031

Eagly, A. H. (2009). The his and hers of prosocial behavior: An examination of the social psychology of gender. *American Psychologist, 64,* 644-658.

Eaton, W. W., Kessler, R. C., Wittchen, H. U., & Magee, W. J. (1994). Panic and panic disorder in the United States. *The American Journal of Psychiatry, 151,* 413-420.

Ecklund-Flores, L. (1992). *The infant as a model for the teaching of introductory psychology.* Paper presented to the American Psychological Association Conference.

Eddy, N. (2017). Apple acquires emotion recognition specialist Emotient. *Information Week.* Retrieved from https://www.informationweek.com/big-data/big-data-analytics/apple-acquires-emotion-recognition-specialist-emotient/d/d-id/1323811

Edwards, W. (1954). The theory of decision making. *Psychological Bulletin, 41,* 380-417.

Ekman, P. (1999). Basic emotions. In T. Dalgleish & M. Power (Eds.). *Handbook of Cognition and Emotion.* Sussex, UK: John Wiley & Sons.

Ekman, P. (2009). Darwin's contributions to our understanding of emotional expressions. *Philosophical Transactions of the Royal Society of London B: Biological Sciences, 364*(1535), 3449-3451.

Ekman, P., Levenson, R. W., & Friesen, W. V. (1983). Autonomic nervous system activity distinguishes among emotions. *Science, 221*(4616), 1208-1210.

Elbogen, E. B., & Johnson, S. C. (2009). The intricate link between violence and mental disorder: Results from the National Epidemiologic Survey on Alcohol and Related Conditions. *Archives of General Psychiatry, 66*(2), 152-161.

Ellis, A. (1962). *Reason and emotion in psychotherapy.* Secaucus, NJ: Citadel Press.

Ellis, A. (1987). The impossibility of achieving consistently good mental health. *American Psychologist, 42*(4), 364.

Ellis, A. (1995). Changing rational-emotive therapy (RET) to rational emotive behavior therapy (REBT). *Journal of Rational-Emotive & Cognitive-Behavior Therapy, 13*(2), 85-89.

Elzinga, B. M., Ardon, A. M., Heijnis, M. K., De Ruiter, M. B., Van Dyck, R., & Veltman, D. J. (2007). Neural correlates of enhanced working-memory performance in dissociative disorder: A functional MRI study. *Psychological Medicine, 37*(02), 235-245.

Emerging Trends (1997, September). *Teens turn more to parents than friends on whether to attend church.* Princeton, NJ: Princeton Religion Research Center.

Engber, D. (2016). What Anna Stublefield believed she was doing. *The New York Times Magazine.* Retrieved from https://www.nytimes.com/2016/02/03/magazine/what-anna-stubblefield-believed-she-was-doing.htmlErdberg, P., & Exner Jr, J. E. (1990). Rorschach assessment. In G. Goldstein, & M. Hersen, *Handbook of psychological assessment* (pp.387-399). New York, NY: Pergamon Press.

Erikson, E. H. (1963). *Childhood and society.* New York, NY: Norton.

Fazel, S., Långström, N., Hjern, A., Grann, M., & Lichtenstein, P. (2009). Schizophrenia, substance abuse, and violent crime. *Jama, 301*(19), 2016- 2023.

Feingold, A., & Mazzella, R. (1998). Gender differences in body image are increasing. *Psychological Science, 9*(3), 190-195.

Ferreira, A. J., (1960). The pregnant woman's emotional attitude and its reflection on the newborn. *American Journal of Orthopsychiatry, 30*(3), 553–561.

Festinger, L. (1957). *A theory of cognitive dissonance.* Palo Alto, CA: Stanford University Press.

Festinger, L., & Carlsmith, J. M. (1959). Cognitive consequences of forced compliance. *The Journal of Abnormal and Social Psychology, 58*(2), 203-210.

Field, T., Diego, M., & Hernandez-Reif, M. (2007). Massage therapy research. *Developmental Review, 27,* 75-89.

Findley, M. J., & Cooper, H. M. (1983). Locus of control and academic achievement: A literature review. *Journal of Personality and Social Psychology, 44*(2), 419-427.

Fink, M. (2009). *Electroconvulsive therapy: A guide for professionals and their patients.* New York, NY: Oxford University Press.

Finlay, S. W. (2000). Influence of Carl Jung and William James on the origin of Alcoholic Anonymous. *Review of General Psychology, 4*(1), 3-12.

Fishman, R. S. (1997). Gordon Holmes, the cortical retina, and the wounds of war. *Documenta Ophthalmologica, 93,* 9-28.

Fleischman, J. (2002). *Phineas Gage: A gruesome but true story about brain science.* Boston, MA: Houghton Mifflin.

Flynn, J. R. (2007). *What is intelligence? Beyond the Flynn effect.* New York, NY: Cambridge University Press.

Fodor, N. (1949). *The search for the beloved: A clinical investigation of the trauma of birth and pre-natal conditioning.* New York, NY: Hermitage Press.

Forgas, J. P., & George, J. M. (2001). Affective influences on judgments and behavior in organizations: An information processing perspective. *Organizational Behavior and Human Decision Processes, 86*(1), 3-34.

Freud, S. (2005). *Civilization and its discontents.* Strachey, J. (Ed.). New York, NY: WW Norton & Company.

Fry, A. F., & Hale, S. (1996). Processing speed, working memory, and fluid intelligence: Evidence for a developmental cascade. *Psychological Science, 7,* 237-241.

Fuller, M. J., & Downs, A. C. (1990). Spermarche is a salient biological marker in men's development. Poster presented at the American Psychological Society convention.

Funder, D. C., & Block, J. (1989). The role of ego-control, ego-resiliency, and IQ in delay of gratification in adolescence. *Journal of Personality and Social Psychology, 57,* 1041-1050.

Gazzaniga, M. S., & LeDoux, J. E. (1978). *The Integrated Mind.* New York, NY: Springer.

George, M. S., Lisanby, S. H., Avery, D., McDonald, W. M., Durkalski, V., Pavlicova, M., . . . & Sackeim, H. A. (2010). Daily left prefrontal transcranial magnetic stimulation therapy for major depressive disorder: A sham-controlled randomized trial. *Archives of General Psychiatry, 67*(5), 507-516.

National LGBT Health Education Center. (2016). Glossary of LGBT terms for health care teams. Retrieved from https://www.lgbthealtheducation.org/wp-content/uploads/LGBT-Glossary_March2016.pdf

Goff, D. C., & Simms, C. A. (1993). Has multiple personality disorder remained consistent over time? A comparison of past and recent cases. *The Journal of Nervous and Mental Disease, 181*(10), 595-600.

Gold, M., & Yanof, D. S. (1985). Mothers, daughters, and girlfriends. *Journal of Personality and Social Psychology, 49,* 654-659.

Goldman, A. L., Pezawas, L., Mattay, V. S., Fischl, B., Verchinski, B. A., Chen, Q., . . . & Meyer-Lindenberg, A. (2009). Widespread reductions of cortical thickness in schizophrenia and spectrum disorders and evidence of heritability. *Archives of General Psychiatry, 66*(5), 467-477.

Goldstein, S. (2015). The evolution of intelligence. In S. Goldstein, D. Princiotta, & J. A. Naglieri (Eds.), *Handbook of Intelligence* (pp. 3-7). New York, NY: Springer.

Gonsiorek, J. C., & Weinrich, J. D. (Eds.). (1991). *Homosexuality: Research implications for public policy.* Thousand Oaks, CA: SAGE Publications.

Gottesman, I. I. (2001). Psychopathology through a life span-genetic prism. *American Psychologist, 56*(11), 867.

Greene, J. D., Sommerville, R. B., Nystrom, L. E., Darley, J. M., & Cohen, J. D. (2001, September 14). An fMRI investigation of emotional engagement in moral judgment. *Science, 293,* 2105-2108.

Greif, E. B., & Ulman, K. J. (1982). The psychological impact of menarche on early adolescent females: A review of the literature. *Child Development, 53,* 1413-1430.

Gresham, C. (2015). Benzodiazepine toxicity. Retrieved from http://emedicine.medscape.com/ article/813255-overview

Griggs, R. A. (2015). The disappearance of independence in textbook coverage of Asch's social pressure ex-periments. *Teaching of Psychology, 42*(2), 137-142.

Groothuis, T. G., & Carere, C. (2005). Avian personalities: Characterization and epigenesis. *Neuroscience & Biobehavioral Reviews, 29*(1), 137-150.

Gulevich, G., Dement, W., & Johnson, L. (1966). Psychiatric and EEG observations on a case of prolonged (264 hours) wakefulness. *Archives of General Psychiatry, 15*(1), 29-35.

Guo, X., Zhai, J., Liu, Z., Fang, M., Wang, B., Wang, C., . . . & Zhao, J. (2010). Effect of antipsychotic medication alone vs combined with psychosocial intervention on outcomes of early-stage schizophrenia: A randomized, 1-year study. *Archives of General Psychiatry, 67*(9), 895-904.

Hackett, G., Betz, N. E., Casas, J. M., & Rocha-Singh, I. (1992). Gender, ethnicity, and social cognitive factors predicting the academic achievement of students in engineering. *Journal of Counseling Psychology, 39*(4), 527.

Hampton, S. (2010). *Essential Evolutionary Psychology.* Thousand Oaks, CA: SAGE Publications.

Harlow, H. F., Harlow, M. K., & Suomi, S. J. (1971). From thought to therapy: Lessons from a primate laboratory. *American Scientist, 59,* 538-549.

Harrison, G. P. (2010). *Race and reality: What everyone should know about our biological diversity*. Amherst, NY: Prometheus Books.

Hastorf, A. H., & Cantril, H. (1954). They saw a game; A case study. *The Journal of Abnormal and Social Psychology, 49*(1), 129-134.

Havas, D. A., Glenberg, A. M., Gutowski, K. A., Lucarelli, M. J., & Davidson, R. J. (2010). Cosmetic use of botulinum toxin-A affects processing of emotional language. *Psychological Science, 21*(7), 895-900. doi:10.1177/0956797610374742

Hayes, T. R., Petrov, A. A., & Sederberg, P. B. (2015). Do we really become smarter when our fluid-intelligence test scores improve? *Intelligence, 48*, 1-14.

Hazelrigg, M. D., Cooper, H. M., & Borduin, C. M. (1987). Evaluating the effectiveness of family therapies: An integrative review and analysis. *Psychological Bulletin, 101*(3), 428.

Heider, F. (1944). Social perception and phenomenal causality. *Psychological Review, 51*(6), 358.

Heiser, N. A., Turner, S. M., & Beidel, D. C. (2003). Shyness: Relationship to social phobia and other psychiatric disorders. *Behaviour Research and Therapy, 41*(2), 209-221.

Held, L. (2010). Profile of Karen Horney. In A. Rutherford (Ed.), *Psychology's feminist voices multimedia internet archive*. Retrieved from http://www.feministvoices.com/karen-horney/

Helmreich, W. B. (1992). *Against all odds: Holocaust survivors and the successful lives they made in America*. New York: Simon & Schuster.

Helmuth, L. (2001). Boosting brain activity from the outside in. *Science, 292*(5520), 1284-1286.

Hepper, P. (2005). Unravelling our beginnings. *The Psychologist, 18*, 474-477.

Herculano-Houzel, S. (2014). The glia/neuron ratio: How it varies uniformly across brain structures and species and what that means for brain physiology and evolution. *Glia, 62*(9), 1377-1391.

Hill, C. E., & Nakayama, E. Y. (2000). Client-centered therapy: Where has it been and where is it going? A comment on Hathaway (1948). *Journal of Clinical Psychology, 56*(7), 861-875.

Hobbes, T. (2006). *Leviathan*. K. Schuhmann, & G.A.J. Rogers (Eds.). London, England: A&C Black.

Hobson, J. A., Hong, C. C., & Friston, K. J. (2014). Virtual reality and consciousness inference in dreaming. *Frontiers in Psychology, 5, 1133*.

Holden, C. (2010). Experts map the terrain of mood disorders. *Science, 327*(5969), 1068-1068.

Hothersall, D. (1990). *History of psychology* (2nd ed.). New York, NY: McGraw Hill.

Hunsley, J., & Di Giulio, G. (2002). Dodo bird, phoenix, or urban legend? The question of psychotherapy equivalence. *The Scientific Review of Mental Health Practice 1*(1).

Hunt, C., Slade, T., & Andrews, G. (2004). Generalized anxiety disorder and major depressive disorder comorbidity in the National Survey of Mental Health and Well-Being. *Depression and Anxiety, 20*(1), 23-31.

Hunt, M. (1993). *The Story of Psychology*. New York, NY: Anchor Books.

Hurvich, L., & Jameson, D. (1957). An opponent process theory of color vision. *Psychological Review, 64*, 384-404.

Ilardi, S. (2010). *The depression cure: The six-step programme to beat depression without drugs*. New York, NY: Random House.

Illouz, E. (1997). *Consuming the romantic utopia: Love and the cultural contradictions of capitalism*. Berkeley, CA: University of California Press.

Ishida, A., Mutoh, T., Ueyama, T., Bando, H., Masubuchi, S., Nakahara, D., . . . & Okamura, H. (2005). Light activates the adrenal gland: Timing of gene expression and glucocorticoid release. *Cell Metabolism, 2*(5), 297-307.

Jabr, F. (2010). The evolution of emotion: Charles Darwin's little-known psychology experiment. Retrieved from https://blogs.scientificamerican.com/observations/the-evolution-of-emotion-charles-darwins-little-known-psychology-experiment/

Jacobellis v. Ohio, 378 U.S. 184 (1964). Retrieved from https://supreme.justia.com/cases/federal/us/378/184/case.html

Jacobi, C., Hayward, C., de Zwaan, M., Kraemer, H. C., & Agras, W. S. (2004). Coming to terms with risk factors for eating disorders: Application of risk terminology and suggestions for a general taxonomy. *Psychological Bulletin, 130*(1), 19-65.

James, W. (1884). What is an emotion? *Mind, 9*(34), 188–205.

Jamison, K. R. (1993). *Touched with fire*. New York, NY: Simon and Schuster.

Jamison, K. R. (1995). *An unquiet mind: A memoir of moods and madness*. New York, NY: Vintage.

Johansson, P., Hall, L., Sikström, S., & Olsson, A. (2005). Failure to detect mismatches between intention and outcome an a simple decision task. *Science, 310*(5745), 116-119.

Johnson, D. L., Wiebe, J. S., Gold, S. M., Andreasen, N. C., Hichwa, R. D., Watkins, G. L., & Ponto, L. L. (1999). Cerebral blood flow and personality: A positron emission tomography study. *The American Journal of Psychiatry, 156*, 252-257.

Jones, A. C., & Gosling, S. D. (2005). Temperament and personality in dogs (Canis familiaris): A review and evaluation of past research. *Applied Animal Behaviour Science, 95*(1), 1-53.

Jones, E. E. (1979). The rocky road from acts to dispositions. *American Psychologist, 34*(2), 107-117. doi:10.1037/0003-066X.34.2.107

Kagan, J. (1984). *The nature of the child*. New York, NY: Basic Books.

Kagan, J. (1995). On attachment. *Harvard Review of Psychiatry, 3,* 104-106.

Kagan, J., Reznick, J. S., & Snidman, N. (1988). Biological bases of childhood shyness. *Science, 240*(4849), 167-171.

Kahneman, D. (2011). *Thinking, fast and slow*. New York, NY: Farrar, Strauss and Giroux.

Kail, R. (1991). Developmental change in speed of processing during childhood and adolescence. *Psychological Bulletin, 109,* 490-501.

Kanizsa, G. (1979). *Organization in vision: Essays on gestalt perception*. New York, NY: Praeger.

Kaplan, H. I., & Sadock, B. J. (1989). *Comprehensive textbook of psychiatry* (Vols. 1-2). Philadelphia, PA: Lippincott Williams & Wilkins.

Karraker, K. H., Vogel, D. A., & Lake, M. A. (1995). Parents' gender-stereotyped perceptions of newborns: The eye of the beholder revisited. *Sex Roles, 33*(9-10), 687-701.

Kaufman, J. C., & Baer, J. (2002). I bask in dreams of suicide: Mental illness, poetry, and women. *Review of General Psychology, 6*(3), 271-286.

Kazantzis, N., & Dattilio, F. M. (2010). Definitions of homework, types of homework, and ratings of the importance of homework among psychologists with cognitive behavior therapy and psychoanalytic theoretical orientations. *Journal of Clinical Psychology, 66*(7), 758-773.

Kean, S. (2014). *The tale of the dueling neurosurgeons: The history of the human brain as revealed by true stories of trauma, madness, and recovery*. New York, NY: Little, Brown, and Company.

Kelley, H. H., & Michela, J. L. (1980). Attribution theory and research. *Annual Review of Psychology, 31*(1), 457-501.

Kellner, C. H., Knapp, R. G., Petrides, G., Rummans, T. A., Husain, M. M., Rasmussen, K., . . . & Fink, M. (2006). Continuation electroconvulsive therapy vs pharmacotherapy for relapse prevention in major depression: A multisite study from the Consortium for Research in Electroconvulsive Therapy (CORE). *Archives of General Psychiatry, 63*(12), 1337-1344.

Kendler, K. S. (1996). Parenting: A genetic-epidemiologic perspective. *The American Journal of Psychiatry, 153,* 11-20.

Kennedy, S. H., Giacobbe, P., Rizvi, S. J., Placenza, F. M., Nishikawa, Y., Mayberg, H. S., & Lozano, A. M. (2011). Deep brain stimulation for treatment- resistant depression: Follow-up after 3 to 6 years. *American Journal of Psychiatry, 168*(5), 502-510.

Kessler, R. C., Berglund, P., Demler, O., Jin, R., Merikangas, K. R., & Walters, E. E. (2005). Lifetime prevalence and age-of-onset distributions of DSM- IV disorders in the National Comorbidity Survey Replication. *Archives of General Psychiatry, 62*(6), 593-602.

Kessler, R. C., Soukup, J., Davis, R. B., Foster, D. F., Wilkey, S. A., Van Rompay, M. I., & Eisenberg, D. M. (2001). The use of complementary and alternative therapies to treat anxiety and depression in the United States. *American Journal of Psychiatry, 158*(2), 289-294.

Kinsey, A., et al. (1948). *Sexual behavior in the human male*. Retrieved from https://kinseyinstitute.org/research/publications/staff-publications-alfred-kinsey.php.

Kinsey, A., et al. (1953). *Sexual behavior in the human female*. Retrieved from https://kinseyinstitute.org/research/publications/staff-publications-alfred-kinsey.php.

Kirchner, P. (1995). *Forgotten fads and fabulous flops*. Los Angeles, CA: General Publishing Group.

Kite, D. M., Gullifer, J., & Tyson, G. A. (2013). Views on the diagnostic labels of autism and Asperger's disorder and the proposed changes in the DSM. *Journal of Autism and Developmental Disorders, 43*(7), 1692-1700.

Kleinknecht, R. A., Dinnel, D. L., Kleinknecht, E. E., Hiruma, N., & Harada, N. (1997). Cultural factors in social anxiety: A comparison of social phobia symptoms and Taijin Kyofusho. *Journal of Anxiety Disorders, 11*(2), 157-177.

Klimstra, T. A., Hale, W. W., Raaijmakers, Q. A., Branje, S. J., & Meeus, W. H. (2009). Maturation of personality in adolescence. *Journal of Personality and Social Psychology, 96,* 898-912.

Klump, K. L., & Culbert, K. M. (2007). Molecular genetic studies of eating disorders current status and future directions. *Current Directions in Psychological Science, 16*(1), 37-41.

Kohlberg, L. (1981-1984). *The philosophy of moral development: Essays on moral development* (Vol. I-II). San Fransisco: Harper & Row.

Kontula, O., & Haavio-Mannila, E. (2009). The impact of aging on human sexual activity and sexual desire. *Journal of Sex Research, 46,* 46-56.

Kosslyn, S. M., Ganis, G., & Thompson, W. L. (2001). Neural foundations of imagery. *Nature Reviews Neuroscience, 2*(9), 635-642.

Koutrelakos, J. (2013). Ethnic identity: Similarities and differences in white groups based on cultural practices. *Psychological reports, 112*(3), 745-762.

Krebs, D. L., & Van Hesteren, F. (1994). The development of altruism: Toward an integrative model. *Developmental Review, 14,* 103-158.

Kuhn, D. (2006). Do cognitive changes accompany developments in the adolescent brain? *Perspectives on Psychological Science, 1,* 59-67.

Kupfer, D. J., & Reynolds, C. F. (1992). Sleep and affective disorders. In Paykel, E. S. (Ed.), *Handbook of Affective Disorders* (311-323). New York, NY: Guilford Press.

Lam, R. W., Levitt, A. J., Levitan, R. D., Enns, M. W., Morehouse, R., Michalak, E. E., & Tam, E. M. (2006). The can-sad study:

A randomized controlled trial of the effectiveness of light therapy and fluoxetine in patients with winter seasonal affective disorder. *The American Journal of Psychiatry, 5,* 805-812.

Landy, F. J. (1992). Hugo Münsterberg: Victim or visionary? *Journal of Applied Psychology, 77*(6), 787-802. doi:10.1037/0021-9010.77.6.787

Lange, C. (1885). *The Emotions.* ed. E. Dunlap. Pp. 33–90. Williams & Wilkins, Baltimore, Maryland.

Langer, S. J., & Martin, J. I. (2004). How dresses can make you mentally ill: Examining gender identity disorder in children. *Child and Adolescent Social Work Journal, 21*(1), 5-23.

Larson, S. (2017). "Invisibilia" returns-with timely concepts. Retrieved from https://www.newyorker.com/culture/sarah-larson/invisibilia-returns-with-timely-concepts

Lashley, K. S. (1950). In search of the engram. In *Physiological mechanisms in animal behavior.* (Society's Symposium IV.) (pp. 454-482). Oxford, England: Academic Press.

Lau, R. R., & Russell, D. (1980). Attributions in the sports pages. *Journal of Personality and Social Psychology, 39*(1), 29-38.

Ledoux, J. (1996). *The emotional brain.* New York, NY: Touchstone.

LeFrance, A. (2015). Machines that can see depression on a person's face. *The Atlantic.* Retrieved from https://www.theatlantic.com/technology/archive/2015/10/machines-that-can-see-depression-on-a-persons-face/411229/

Lehman, A. F., Steinwachs, D. M., Dixon, L. B., Postrado, L., Scott, J. E., Fahey, M., . . . & Skinner, E. A. (1998). Patterns of usual care for schizophrenia: Initial results from the Schizophrenia Patient Outcomes Research Team (PORT) Client Survey. *Schizophrenia Bulletin, 24*(1), 11-20.

Leichsenring, F., & Rabung, S. (2008). Effectiveness of long-term psychodynamic psychotherapy: A meta-analysis. *Jama, 300*(13), 1551-1565.

Leslie, S. J., Cimpian, A., Meyer, M., & Freeland, E. (2015). Expectations of brilliance underlie gender distributions across academic disciplines. *Science, 347*(6219) 262-265 doi: 10.1126/science.1261375

Leucht, S., Tardy, M., Komossa, K., Heres, S., Kissling, W., Salanti, G., & Davis, J. M. (2012). Antipsychotic drugs versus placebo for relapse prevention in schizophrenia: A systematic review and meta-analysis. *The Lancet, 379*(9831), 2063-2071.

Levin, R.J. (2008). Critically revising aspects of the human sexual response cycle of Masters and Johnson: Correcting errors and suggesting modification. *Sexual and Relationship Therapy* 23(4), 393-399.

Levin, S. (2017). Face-reading AI will be able to detect your politics and IQ, professor says. *The Guardian.* Retrieved from https://www.theguardian.com/technology/2017/sep/12/artificial-intelligence-face-recognition-michal-kosinski

Levine, D. N., Warach, J., & Farah, M. J. (1985). Two visual systems in mental imagery: Dissociation of 'what' and 'where' in imagery disorders due to bilateral posterior cerebral lesions. *Neurology, 35*(7), 1010-1018. doi:10.1212/WNL.35.7.1010

Levinson, D. J. (1986). A conception of adult development. *American Psychologist, 41,* 3-13.

Lewinsohn, P. M., Hoberman, H., Teri, L., & Hautzinger, M. (1985). An Integrative Theory of Depression. In S. Reiss, & R.R. Bootzin (Eds.), *Theoretical Issues in Behavior Therapy* (331-359). San Diego, CA: Academic Press.

Lewis, N. A., & Oyserman, D. (2015). When does the future begin? Time metrics matter, connecting present and future selves. *Psychological Science, 26*(6), 816-825. doi: 0956797615572231

Li, Z. H., Connolly, J., Jiang, D., Pepler, D., & Craig, W. (2010). Adolescent romantic relationships in China and Canada: A cross-national comparison. *International Journal of Behavioral Development, 34,* 113-120.

Lilienfeld, S. O., & Arkowitz, H. (2007). EMDR: Taking a closer look. *Scientific American, 17,* 10-11.

Lilienfeld, S. O., & Arkowitz, H. (2011). The insanity verdict on trial. *Scientific American Mind, 21*(6), 64-65.

Lindsley, O. (1991). From technical jargon to plain English for application. *Journal of Applied Behavior Analysis, 24*(3), 449–458.

Liu, A. (Ed.). (2011). *Restoring our bodies, reclaiming our lives.* Boulder, CO: Shambhala Publications.

Locke, J. (1975). *An essay concerning human understanding.* P.H. Nidditch (Ed.). New York, NY: Oxford University Press.

Loehlin, J. C., McCrae, R. R., Costa, P. T., & John, O. P. (1998). Heritabilities of common and measure- specific components of the Big Five personality factors. *Journal of Research in Personality, 32*(4), 431-453.

Loftus, E. F., & Palmer, J. C. (1974). Reconstruction of automobile destruction: An example of the interaction between language and memory. *Journal of Verbal Learning and Verbal Behavior, 13,* 585- 589.

Loftus, E. F., & Pickrell, J. E. (1995). The formation of false memories. *Psychiatric Annals, 25,* 720-725.

Lopez-Ibor, J. J., López-Ibor, M. I., & Pastrana, J. I. (2008). Transcranial magnetic stimulation. *Current Opinion in Psychiatry, 21*(6), 640-644.

Lorenz, K. (1937). The companion in the bird's world. *Auk, 54,* 245-273.

Lourenco, O., & Machado, A. (1996). In defense of Piaget's theory: A reply to 10 common criticisms. *Psychological Review, 103*(1), 143-164. doi:10.1037//0033- 295X.103.1.143

Lovaas, O. I. (1987). Behavioral treatment and normal educational and intellectual functioning in young autistic children. *Journal of Consulting and Clinical Psychology, 55*(1), 3-9.

Ludwig, A. M. (1995). *The price of greatness: Resolving the creativity and madness controversy.* New York, NY: Guilford Press.

Lurigio, A. J., & Lewis, D. A. (1989). Worlds that fail: A longitudinal study of urban mental patients. *Journal of Social Issues, 45*(3), 79-90.

Lynn, J. (2004). *Sick to death and not going to take it anymore!: Reforming health care for the last years of life.* Berkeley, CA: University of California Press.

Lynne, S. D., Graber, J. A., Nichols, T. R., Brooks-Gunn, J., & Botvin, G. J. (2007). Links between pubertal timing, peer influences, and externalizing behaviors among urban students followed through middle school. *Journal of Adolescent Health, 40,* 181.e7-181.e13.

Lyons, L. (2004). Growing up lonely: Examining teen alienation. *Gallup Poll News Service.* Retrieved from http://news.gallup.com/poll/10465/growing-lonely-examining-teen-alienation.aspx

Lyons, L. (2005). Teens stay true to parents' political perspectives. *Gallup Poll News Service.* Retrieved from http://news.gallup.com/poll/14515/teens-stay-true-parents-political-perspectives.aspx

Yudell, M. (2014). *Race Unmasked: Biology and Race in the 20th century.* Columbia University Press.

Maccoby, E. E. (1992). The role of parents in the socialization of children: An historical overview. *Developmental Psychology, 28,* 1006-1017.

Maccoby, E. E., & Martin, J. A. (1983). Socialization in the context of the family: Parent–child interaction. In P. H. Mussen & E. M. Hetherington, *Handbook of child psychology Vol. 4. Socialization, personality, and social development* (4th ed.). New York, NY: Wiley.

MacFarlane, J. W. (1964). Perspectives on personality consistency and change from the guidance study. *Vita Humana, 7,* 115-126.

Macknik, S. L., & Martinez-Conde, S. (2010). *Sleights of mind: What the neuroscience of magic reveals about our everyday deceptions.* New York, NY: Henry Hold and Company.

Maddux, J. E. (1991). Self-efficacy. In Snyder, C. R., & Forsyth, D. R. (Eds.). *Handbook of social and clinical psychology: The health perspective.* Oxford, England: Pergamon Press.

Marley, J. A., & Buila, S. (2001). Crimes against people with mental illness: Types, perpetrators, and influencing factors. *Social Work, 46*(2), 115-124.

Martin, C.L. & Ruble, D.N. (2010). Patterns of gender development. *Annual Review of Psychology, 61,* 353-381.

Maser, J. D., Kaelber, C., & Weise, R. E. (1991). International use and attitudes toward DSM-III and DSM-III-R: Growing consensus in psychiatric classification. *Journal of Abnormal Psychology, 100*(3), 271-279.

Mashour, G. A., Walker, E. E., & Martuza, R. L. (2005). Psychosurgery: Past, present, and future. *Brain Research Reviews, 48*(3), 409-419.

Maslow, A. H. (1987). *Motivation and personality* (3rd ed.). R. Frager, J. Fadiman, C. McReynolds, & R. Cox (Eds.) New York, NY: Harper & Row.

Maslow, A. H., Frager, R., & Cox, R. (1970). *Motivation and personality.* Eds. J. Fadiman, & C. McReynolds (Vol. 2). New York, NY: Harper & Row.

Masten, A. S. (2001). Ordinary magic-Resilience processes in development. *American Psychologist, 56*(3) 227-238.

Matthews, R. (2000). Storks deliver babies (p= 0.008). *Teaching Statistics, 22*(2), 36-38.

Mauer, D., & Mauer, C. (1988). *The world of the newborn.* New York, NY: Basic Books.

Mayberg, H. S. (2009). Targeted modulation of neural circuits: A new treatment strategy for depression. *Journal of Clinical Investigation, 119*(4), 717-725.

McClintock, M. K., & Herdt, G. (1996). Rethinking puberty: The development of sexual attraction. *Current Directions in Psychological Science, 5(6),* 178-183.

McCrae, R. R. (2011). Personality theories for the 21st century. *Teaching of Psychology, 38*(3), 209-214.

McCurdy, L. E., Winterbottom, K. E., Mehta, S. S., & Roberts, J. R. (2010). Using nature and outdoor activity to improve children's health. *Current Problems in Pediatric and Adolescent Health Care, 40*(5), 102-117.

McHugh, P. R. (1995). Resolved: Multiple personality disorder is an individually and socially created artifact. *Journal of the American Academy of Child & Adolescent Psychiatry, 34*(7), 957-963.

McLean, C. P., & Anderson, E. R. (2009). Brave men and timid women? A review of the gender differences in fear and anxiety. *Clinical Psychology Review, 29*(6), 496-505.

McNally, R. J., & Clancy, S. A. (2005). Sleep paralysis, sexual abuse, and space alien abduction. *Transcultural Psychiatry, 42*(1), 113-122. doi:10.1177/1363461505050715

Mendle, J., Turkheimer, E., & Emery, R. E. (2007). Detrimental psychological outcomes associated with early pubertal timing in adolescent girls. *Developmental Review, 27,* 151-171.

Mental Illness Research Association. (2015). Statistics. Retrieved from http://www.miraresearch.org/ understanding/statistics/

Mihura, J. L., Meyer, G. J., Dumitrascu, N., & Bombel, G. (2013). The validity of individual Rorschach variables: Systematic reviews and meta-analyses of the comprehensive system. *Psychological Bulletin, 139*(3), 548.

Milgram, S. (1974). *Obedience to authority*. New York, NY: Harper Row.

Miller K. J., Schalk G., Hermes D., Ojemann J. G., & Rao R. P. N. (2016). Spontaneous decoding of the timing and content of human object perception from cortical surface recordings reveals complementary information in the event-related potential and broadband spectral change. *PLoS Comput Biol 12*(1): e1004660. doi:10.1371/journal.pcbi.1004660

Miller, P. A., Eisenberg, N., Shell, R., & Fabes, R. A. (1996). Relations of moral reasoning and vicarious emotion to young children's prosocial behavior toward peers and adults. *Developmental Psychology, 32*, 210-219.

Miller, S. D., Blackburn, T., Scholes, G., White, G. L., & Mamalis, N. (1991). Optical differences in multiple personality disorder: A second look. *The Journal of Nervous and Mental Disease, 179*(3), 132-135.

Mills, J. (1958). Changes in moral attitudes following temptation. *Journal of Personality, 26*, 517-531.

Mischel, W., Shoda, Y., & Peake, P. K. (1988). The nature of adolescent competencies predicted by preschool delay of gratification. *Journal of Personality and Social Psychology, 54*, 687-696.

Moffitt, T. E., Harrington, H., Caspi, A., Kim-Cohen, J., Goldberg, D., Gregory, A. M., & Poulton, R. (2007). Depression and generalized anxiety disorder: Cumulative and sequential comorbidity in a birth cohort followed prospectively to age 32 years. *Archives of General Psychiatry, 64*(6), 651-660.

Montagu, A. (1998). *Man's most dangerous myth: The fallacy of race* (6th ed.). Walnut Creek, MD: Altamira Press.

Moret, V., Forster, A., Laverrière, M., Lambert, H., Gaillard, R. C., Bourgeois, P., & ... Buchser, E. (1991). Mechanism of analgesia induced by hypnosis and acupuncture: Is there a difference? *Pain, 45*(2), 135-140. doi:10.1016/0304-3959(91)90178-Z

Moses, E. B., & Barlow, D. H. (2006). A new unified treatment approach for emotional disorders based on emotion science. *Current Directions in Psychological Science, 15*(3), 146-150.

Muchinsky, P. M. (2003). *Psychology applied to work* (7th ed.). Belmont, CA: Thomson Wadsworth.

Munger, S. D. (2017, May 23). *The taste map of the tongue you earned in school is all wrong*. Retrieved March 25, 2018, from https://www.smithsonianmag.com/science-nature/neat-and-tidy-map-tastes-tongue-you-learned-school-all-wrong-180963407/

Myers-Walls, J A., Hinkley, K. R., & Reid, W. H. (2015). *Encouraging positive self-concepts in children*. [Historical Documents of the Purdue Cooperative Extension Service.] Retrieved from http://docs.lib.purdue.edu/agext/1043

National Center for Health Statistics. (1990). *Health, United States, 1989*. Washington, DC: U.S. Government Printing Office.

National Institute of Mental Health. (2007). *The numbers count: Mental disorders in America*. (nimh.nih.gov).

Neisser, U., Boodoo, G., Bouchard, T. J. Jr., Boykin, A. W., Brody, N., Ceci, S. J., . . . & Urbina, S. (1996). Intelligence: Knowns and unknowns. *American Psychologist, 51*(2), 77-101.

Nelson, C. A. III, C. A., Furtado, E. A., Fox, N. A., & Zeanah, C. H. Jr. (2009, May-June). The deprived human brain. *American Scientist, 97*(3), 222. doi: 10.1511/2009.78.222

Nestor, J. (2014). *Deep: Freediving, renegade science, and what the ocean tells us about ourselves*. Boston, MA: Houghton Mifflin Harcourt.

Neugarten, B. L. (1979). Time, age, and the life cycle. *The American Journal of Psychiatry, 136*, 887-894.

Nicolas, S., & Levine, Z. (2012). Beyond intelligence testing: Remembering Alfred Binet after a century. *European Psychologist, 17*(4), 320-325. doi:10.1027/1016-9040/a000117

Nisbett, R. E., Aronson, J., Blair, C., Dickens, W., Flynn, J., Halpern, D. F., & Turkheimer, E. (2012). Intelligence: New findings and theoretical developments. *American Psychologist, 67*(2), 130-159.

Offer, D. (1988). *The Teenage world: Adolescents' self-image in ten countries*. New York, NY: Plenum Medical.

Office of the High Commissioner for Human Rights. (2015). Free & equal campaign fact sheet: Intersex. Retrieved from: https://unfe.org/system/unfe-65-Intersex_Factsheet_ENGLISH.pdf

Ondeck, M., & Focareta, J. (2009). Environmental hazards education for childbirth educators. *Journal of Perinatal Education, 18*(4), 31-40.

Palmer, B. (2012). Are there really just five racial groups? How the government developed its racial-classification system. *Slate*. Retrieved from http://www.slate.com/articles/news_and_politics/explainer/2012/05/white_american_babies_are_now_in_the_minority_why_does_the_census_divide_people_by_race_anyway_.html

Patten, S. B., Li Wang, J., Williams, J. V., Currie, S., Beck, C. A., Maxwell, C. J., & el-Guebaly, N. (2006). Descriptive epidemiology of major depression in Canada. *Canadian Journal of Psychiatry, 51*(2), 84.

Pearson, K. (1896). Mathematical contributions to the theory of evolution-On a form of spurious correlation which may arise when indices are used in the measurement of organs. *Proceedings of the Royal Society of London, 60*(359-367), 489-498.

Pelham, B. W. (2009, October 22). About one in six Americans report history of depression. *Gallup*. Retrieved from http://news.gallup.com/poll/123821/one-six-americans-report-history-depression.aspx

Penfield, W., & Boldrey, E. (1937). Somatic motor and sensory representation in the cerebral cortex of man as studied by electrical stimulation. *Brain: A Journal of Neurology, 60*(4), 389-443.

Petty, R. E., & Cacioppo, J. T. (1984). The effects of involvement on responses to argument quantity and quality: Central and peripheral routes to persuasion. *Journal of Personality and Social Psychology, 46*(1), 69-81.

Pfungst, O. (1911). *Clever Hans (the horse of Mr. Von Osten): A contribution to experimental animal and human psychology.* New York, NY: Holt, Rinehart and Winston.

Phillips, A. L. (2011, July-August). A walk in the woods. *American Scientist, 99*(4), 301. doi: 10.1511/2011.91.301

Piaget, J. (1930). *The child's conception of physical causality.* London, England: Routledge & Kegan Paul.

Pickar, D., & Hsiao, J. K. (1995). Clozapine treatment of schizophrenia. *JAMA, 274*(12), 981-983.

Pierce, W. D. & Cheney, C. D. (2013). *Behavior analysis and learning.* New York, NY: Psychology Press.

Piliavin, J. A. (2003). Doing well by doing good: Benefits for the benefactor. In C. L. M. Keyes & J. Haidt (Eds.), *Flourishing: Positive psychology and the life well-lived.* Washington, DC: American Psychological Association.

Pillsbury, W. B. (1940). Margaret Floy Washburn (1871- 1939). *Psychological Review, 47*(2), 99-109. doi:10.1037/h0062692

Pin, T., Eldridge, B., & Galea, M. P. (2007). A review of the effects of sleep position, play position, and equipment use on motor development in infants. *Developmental Medicine & Child Neurology, 49*(11), 858-867.

Pinker, S. (1994). *The language instinct: How the mind creates language.* New York, NY: Harper Collins.

Plomin, R., DeFries, J. C., Knopik, V. S., & Neiderhiser, J. M. (2013). *Behavioral genetics: A primer.* New York, NY: Worth Publishers.

Popham, W. J. (2002). Right task, wrong tool. *American School Board Journal, 189*(2), 18-22.

Poropat, A. E. (2009). A meta-analysis of the five-factor model of personality and academic performance. *Psychological Bulletin, 135*(2), 322.

Posada, G., Gao, Y., Wu, F., Posada, R., Tascon, M., Schöelmerich, ..., & Synnevaag, B. (1995). The secure-base phenomenon across cultures: Children's behavior, mothers' preferences, and expert' concepts. *Monographs of the Society for Research in Child Development, 60,* 27–48. doi:10.1111/j.1540-5834.1995.tb00202.x

Poundstone, W. (2011). *Priceless: The myth of fair value (and how to take advantage of it).* New York, NY: Hill and Wang.

Population Reference Bureau. (2007). Gender disparities in health and mortality. *Retrieved from:* http://prb. org/Articles/2007/genderdisparities

Population Reference Bureau. (2010). 2010 world population data sheet. Retrieved from: https://www.prb.org/2010wpds/

Price, B. H., Baral, I., Cosgrove, G. R., Rauch, S. L., Nierenberg, A. A., Jenike, M. A., & Cassem, H. (2001). Improvement in severe self-mutilation following limbic leucotomy: A series of 5 consecutive cases. *The Journal of Clinical Psychiatry, 62*(12), 925-932.

Pullum, G. K. (1989). The great Eskimo vocabulary hoax. *Natural Language & Linguistic Theory, 2,* 275-281.

Putnam, F. W. (1991). Recent research on multiple personality disorder. *Psychiatric Clinics of North America, 14*(3), 489-502.

Rabinowicz, T., de Courten-Myers, G. M., Petetot, J. M., Xi, G., & de los Reyes, F. (1996). Human cortex development: Estimates of neuronal numbers indicate major loss late during gestation. *Journal of Neuropathology and Experimental Neurology, 55,* 320-328.

Rabinowicz, T., Dean, D. E., Petetot, J. M., & de Courten- Myers, G. M. (1999). Gender differences in the human cerebral cortex: More neurons in males; more processes in females. *Journal of Child Neurology, 14,* 98-107.

Ramachandran, V. S., & Altschuler, E. L. (2009). The use of visual feedback, in particular mirror visual feedback, in restoring brain function. *Brain, 132*(7), 1693-1710. doi: 10.1093/brain/awp135

Ramachandran, V. S., & Hirstein, W. (1998). The perception of phantom limbs. The DO Hebb lecture. *Brain, 121*(9), 1603-1630.

Rank, O. (1952). *The trauma of birth.* Eastford, CT: Martino Fine Books.

Ray, W. J. (2012). *Evolutionary Psychology: Neuroscience Perspectives concerning Human Behavior and Experience.* Thousand Oaks, CA: Sage.

Rechtschaffen, A., & Bergmann, B. M. (1995). Sleep deprivation in the rat by the disk-over-water method. *Behavioural Brain Research, 69*(1-2), 55-63.

Renner, M. J., & Renner, C. H. (1993). Expert and novice intuitive judgments about animal behavior. *Bulletin of the Psychonomic Society, 31,* 551-552.

Renniger, K. A., & Granott, N. (2005). The process of scaffolding in learning and development. *New Ideas in Psychology, 23*(3), 111-114.

Rescorla, R. A. (1968). Probability of shock in the presence and absence of CS in fear conditioning. *Journal of Comparative and Physiological Psychology, 66*(1), 1-5.

Resnick, M. D., Bearman, P. S., Blum, R. W., Bauman, K. E., Harris, K. M., Jones, J., . . . & Udry, J. R. (1997). Protecting adolescents from harm. Findings from the National Longitudinal Study on Adolescent Health. *Jama-Journal of The American Medical Association, 278,* 823-832.

Reyes, J. M. (2016, August 20). Police: Mom charged for leaving children alone while picking up food. *The (Wilmington, Del.) News Journal.* Retrieved from https://www.azcentral.

com/story/news/nation-now/2016/08/20/police-mom-charged-leaving-children-alone-while-picking-up-food/89042428/Reyna, V. F., & Farley, F. (2006). Risk and rationality in adolescent decision-making implications for theory, practice, and public policy. *Psychological Science in the Public Interest, 7*(1), 1-44.

Richards, G. (2009). *Putting psychology in its place: Critical historical perspectives.* New York, NY: Routledge.

Riskind, J. H., Beck, A. T., Berchick, R. J., Brown, G., & Steer, R. A. (1987). Reliability of DSM-III diagnoses for major depression and generalized anxiety disorder using the structured clinical interview for DSM-III. *Archives of General Psychiatry, 44*(9), 817-820.

Rodenburg, R., Benjamin, A., de Roos, C., Meijer, A. M., & Stams, G. J. (2009). Efficacy of EMDR in children: A meta-analysis. *Clinical Psychology Review, 29*(7), 599-606.

Rogers, C. R. (1961). *On becoming a person: A therapist's view of psychotherapy.* Boston, MA: Houghton Mifflin.

Rogers, C. R. (1980). *A way of being.* Boston, MA: Houghton Mifflin.

Rohan, K. J., Roecklein, K. A., Tierney Lindsey, K., Johnson, L. G., Lippy, R. D., Lacy, T. J., & Barton, B. (2007). A randomized controlled trial of cognitive-behavioral therapy, light therapy, and their combination for seasonal affective disorder. *Journal of Consulting and Clinical Psychology, 75*(3), 489.

Rohner, R. P., & Veneziano, R. A. (2001). The importance of father love: History and contemporary evidence. *Review of General Psychology, 3*(6), 176-179. doi:10.1037/1089-2680.5.4.382

Rohrer, J. H., Baron, S. H., Hoffman, E. L., & Swander, D. V. (1954). The stability of autokinetic judgments. *The Journal of Abnormal and Social Psychology, 49*(4p1), 595.

Rosaldo, M. Z. (1980). *Knowledge and Passion* (Vol. 4). New York, NY: Cambridge University Press.

Rosaldo, R. (2004). Grief and a headhunter's rage. *Death, Mourning, and Burial: A Cross-Cultural Reader,* 167-178. Malden, MA: Blackwell Pub.

Rosch, E. (1975). Cognitive reference points. *Cognitive Psychology, 7*(4), 532-547.

Roscoe, J. A., Morrow, G. R., Aapro, M. S., Molassiotis, A., & Olver, I. (2011). Anticipatory nausea and vomiting. *Supportive Care in Cancer, 19*(10), 1533–1538.

Rosenhan, D. L. (1973). On being sane in insane places. *Science, 179*(4070), 250-258.

Rosenthal, R. (1994). Interpersonal expectancy effects: A 30-year perspective. *Current Directions in Psychological Science,* 176-179.

Rosenthal, R., & Jacobson, L. (1968). Pygmalion in the classroom. *The Urban Review, 3*(1), 16-20.

Ross, L. (1977). The intuitive psychologist and his shortcomings: Distortions in the attribution process. *Advances in Experimental Social Psychology, 10,* 173-220.

Rotter, J. B. (1966). Generalized expectancies for internal versus external control of reinforcement. *Psychological Monographs: General and Applied, 80*(1), 1-28.

Rotter, J. B. (1990). Internal versus external control of reinforcement: A case history of a variable. *American Psychologist, 45*(4), 489.

Rubin, R. T., Provenzano, F. J., & Luria, Z. (1974). The eye of the beholder: Parents' views on sex of newborns. *American Journal of Orthopsychiatry, 43,* 720-731.

Ryan, R. M., & Deci, E. L. (2000). Self-determination theory and the facilitation of intrinsic motivation, social development, and well-being. *American Psychologist, 55*(1), 68.

Rychtarik, R. G., Prue, D. M., Rapp, S. R., & King, A. C. (1992). Self-efficacy, aftercare and relapse in a treatment program for alcoholics. *Journal of Studies on Alcohol and Drugs, 53*(5), 435.

Sack, R. L., Lewy, A. J., Blood, M. L., Keith, L. D., & Nakagawa, H. (1992). Circadian rhythm abnormalities in totally blind people: Incidence and clinical significance. *The Journal of Clinical Endocrinology & Metabolism, 75*(1), 127-134.

Sacks, O. (1985). *The man who mistook his wife for a hat.* New York, NY: Touchstone.

Salama, A. A. A. (2005). Multiple personality disorder: A review and a case study. *Journal of the Islamic Medical Association of North America, 37*(2), 60-63.

Salthouse, T. A. (2010). Selective review of cognitive aging. *Journal of the International Neuropsychological Society, 16*(5), 754-760.

Saltzman, J. A., & Liechty, J. M. (2016). Family correlates of childhood binge eating: A systematic review. *Eating Behaviors, 22,* 62-71. doi:10.1016/j.eatbeh.2016.03.027

Samuel Hoffenstein Quotes. (n.d.). Retrieved from http://www.quotery.com/authors/samuel-hoffenstein/

Schachter, S., & Singer, J. (1962). Cognitive, social, and physiological determinants of emotional state. *Psychological Review, 69*(5), 379-399. doi:10.1037/h0046234

Schaefer, Richard T. (Ed.). (2008). *Encyclopedia of race, ethnicity, and society* (pp. 1091-1096). Thousand Oaks, CA: Sage.

Schmitt, D.P. (2005). Sociosexuality from Argentina to Zimbabwe: A 48-nation study of sex, culture, and strategies of human mating. *Behavioral and brain sciences, 28,* 247-311.

Schultz, D. P., & Schultz, S. E. (2004). *The history of modern psychology* (8th ed.). Belmont, CA: Thomson Wadsworth.

Schultz, D. P., & Schultz, S. E. (2015). *A history of modern psychology.* Boston, MA: Cengage Learning.

Seidler, G. H., & Wagner, F. E. (2006). Comparing the efficacy of EMDR and trauma-focused cognitive- behavioral therapy in the treatment of PTSD: A meta-analytic study. *Psychological Medicine*, *36*(11), 1515-1522.

Seidman, G. (2013). Self-presentation and belonging on Facebook: How personality influences social media use and motivations. *Personality and Individual Differences*, *54*(3), 402-407.

Shader, R. I., & Greenblatt, D. J. (1993). Use of benzodiazepines in anxiety disorders. *New England Journal of Medicine*, *328*(19), 1398-1405.

Shadish, W. R., & Baldwin, S. A. (2005). Effects of behavioral marital therapy: A meta-analysis of randomized controlled trials. *Journal of Consulting and Clinical Psychology*, *73*(1), 6-14.

Shadish, W. R., Montgomery, L. M., Wilson, P., Wilson, M. R., Bright, I., & Okwumabua, T. (1993). Effects of family and marital psychotherapies: A meta-analysis. *Journal of Consulting and Clinical Psychology*, *61*(6), 992-1002.

Shanahan, L., McHale, S. M., Osgood, D. W., & Crouter, A. C. (2007). Conflict frequency with mothers and fathers from middle childhood to late adolescence: Within-and between-families comparisons. *Developmental Psychology*, *43*, 539- 550.

Shane, H. C., & Kearns, K. (1994). An examination of the role of the facilitator in facilitated communication. *American Journal of Speech-Language Pathology*, *3*(3), 48-54.

Shapiro, F. (1989). Efficacy of the eye movement desensitization procedure in the treatment of traumatic memories. *Journal of Traumatic Stress*, *2*(2), 199-223.

Shapiro, F. (1999). Eye movement desensitization and reprocessing (EMDR) and the anxiety disorders: Clinical and research implications of an integrated psychotherapy treatment. *Journal of Anxiety Disorders*, *13*(1), 35-67.

Shapiro, F. (2002). *EMDR as an integrative psychotherapy approach.* Washington, DC: American Psychological Association.

Shedler, J. (2012). The efficacy of psychodynamic psychotherapy. In *Psychodynamic psychotherapy research* (pp. 9-25). New York, NY: Humana Press.

Sheehan, S. (1982). *Is there no place on earth for me?* New York: Vintage.

Sheldon, W. H., & Stevens, S. S. (1942). *The varieties of temperament; A psychology of constitutional differences.* New York, NY: Harper Collins.

Sheldon, W. H., Stevens, S. S., & Tucker, W. B. (1940). *The varieties of human physique: An introduction to constitutional psychology* (Vol. 1). New York: Harper.

Shepard, R. N., & Metzler, J. (1971). Mental rotation of three-dimensional objects. *Science*, *171*(3972), 701-703.

Shepperd, J., Malone, W., & Sweeny, K. (2008). Exploring causes of the self-serving bias. *Social and Personality Psychology Compass, 2*(2), 895-908.

Sher, L. (2006). Alcohol consumption and suicide. *QJM, 99*(1), 57-61.

Sherif, M. (1936). *The psychology of social norms.* New York, NY: Harper

Sherry, S. B., & Hall, P. A. (2009). The perfectionism model of binge eating: Tests of an integrative model. *Journal of Personality and Social Psychology*, *96*(3), 690-709.

Shick, V., Herbenick, D., Reece, M., Sanders, S. A., Dodge, B., Middlestadt, S. E., & Fortenberry, J. D. (2010). Sexual behaviors, condom use, and sexual health of Americans over 50: Implications for sexual health promotion for older adults. *Journal of Sexual Medicine, 7*(s5), 315-329.

Shih, M., Pittinsky, T. L., & Ambady, N. (1999). Stereotype susceptibility: Identity salience and shifts in quantitative performance. *Psychological Science, 10*(1), 80-83.

Shriner, J. (2007). Young Children's Understanding of Death. *The Ohio State University.* Retrieved from https://extension. tennessee.edu/centerforparenting/TipSheets/Young%20 Children's%20Understanding%20of%20Death.pdf

Siegel, J. M. (2008). Do all animals sleep? *Trends in Neurosciences*, *31*(4), 208-213. doi:10.1016/j.tins.2008.02.001

Silveri, M. M., Rohan, M. L., Pimentel, P. J., Gruber, S. A., Rosso, I. M., & Yurgelun-Todd, D. A. (2006). Sex differences in the relationship between white matter microstructure and impulsivity in adolescents. *Magnetic Resonance Imaging*, *24*, 833-841.

Simons, D. J., & Levin, D. T. (1998). Failure to detect changes to people during a real-world interaction. *Psychonomic Bulletin & Review*, *5*, 644-649.

Singh, S. M., & Chakrabarti, S. (2008). A study in dualism: The strange case of Dr. Jekyll and Mr. Hyde. *Indian Journal of Psychiatry*, *50*(3), 221-223.

Skinner, B. F. (1957). *Verbal behavior.* Englewood Cliffs, NJ: Prentice-Hall.

Skinner, B. F. (1990). *The behavior of organisms: An experimental analysis.* Cambridge, MA: BF Skinner Foundation. (Original work published in 1938)

Smith, A. C. (2016). Spring forward at your own risk: daylight saving time and fatal vehicle crashes. *American Economic Journal: Applied Economics*, *8*(2), 65-91.

Smith, M. B. (1978). Psychology and values. *Journal of Social Issues*, *34*(4), 181-199.

Smith, M. L., Glass, G. V., & Miller, T. I. (1980). *The benefits of psychotherapy.* Baltimore, MD: Johns Hopkins University Press.

Snyder, P. J., Kaufman, R., Harrison, J., & Maruff, P. (2010). Charles Darwin's emotional expression "experiment" and his contribution to modern neuropharmacology. *Journal of the History of the Neurosciences, 19*(2), 158-170.

Snyder, S. H. (1996). *Drugs and the brain.* New York, NY: W H Freeman & Co.

Solomon, D. A., Keitner, G. I., Miller, I. W., Shea, M. T., & Keller, M. B. (1995). Course of illness and maintenance treatments for patients with bipolar disorder. *Journal of Clinical Psychiatry, 56*(1), 5-13.

Sorkhabi, N. (2005). Applicability of Baumrind's parent typology to collective cultures: Analysis of cultural explanations of parent socialization effects. *International Journal of Behavioral Development, 29,* 552-563.

Spearman, C. (1904). "General Intelligence," objectively determined and measured. *The American Journal of Psychology, 15*(2), 201-292.

Spearman, C. (1939). Thurstone's work re-worked. *Journal of Educational Psychology, 30*(1), 1-16. doi:10.1037/ h0061267

Spiegel, A. (2017). Invisibilia: A man finds an explosive emotion locked in a word. *NPR.* Retrieved from http://www. npr.org/sections/health-shots/2017/06/01/529876861/ an-anthropologist-discovers-the-terrible-emo-tion-locked-in-a-word

Spitzer, M., Weisker, I., Winter, M., Maier, S., Hermle, L., & Maher, B. A. (1994). Semantic and phonological priming in schizophrenia. *Journal of Abnormal Psychology, 103*(3), 485.

Squire, L. R. (2009). The legacy of patient HM for neuroscience. *Neuron, 61*(1), 6-9.

Stams, G. J., Juffer, F., & IJzendoorn, M. H. (2002). Maternal sensitivity, infant attachment, and temperament in early childhood predict adjustment in middle childhood: The case of adopted children and their biologically unrelated parents. *Developmental Psychology, 5,* 806-821.

Stein, D. J., Phillips, K. A., Bolton, D., Fulford, K. W. M., Sadler, J. Z., & Kendler, K. S. (2010). What is a mental/psychiatric disorder? From DSM-IV to DSM-V. *Psychological Medicine, 40*(11), 1759-1765.

Steinberg, L. (2007). Risk taking in adolescence: New perspectives from brain and behavioral science. *Current Directions in Psychological Science, 16,* 55-59.

Steinberg, L., & Morris, A. S. (2001). Adolescent development. *Annual Review of Psychology, 52,* 83-110.

Steinhauer, J., & Holson, L. M. (2008, September 20). As text messages fly, danger lurks. *The New York Times.* Retrieved from https://www.nytimes.com/2008/09/20/ us/20messaging.html.

Sternberg, R. J. (2003). Our research program validating the triarchic theory of successful intelligence: Reply to Gottfredson. *Intelligence, 31*(4), 399-413.

Sternberg, R. J., & Detterman, D. K. (Eds.). (1986). What is intelligence? Contemporary viewpoints on its nature and definition. Santa Barbara, CA: Praeger Pub Text.

Sternberg, R. J., & Kaufman, J. C. (1998). Human abilities. *Annual Review of Psychology, 49*(1), 479- 502.

Stewart, R. E., & Chambless, D. L. (2009). Cognitive– behavioral therapy for adult anxiety disorders in clinical practice: A meta-analysis of effectiveness studies. *Journal of Consulting and Clinical Psychology, 77*(4), 595.

Strickland, B. R. (1989). Internal-external control expectancies: From contingency to creativity. *American Psychologist, 44*(1), 1.

Subrahmanyam, K., & Greenfield, P. (2008). Online communication and adolescent relationships. *The Future of Children, 18,* 119-146.

Sutherland, A. (2006, June). What Shamu taught me about a happy marriage. *The New York Times.* Retrieved from https:// www.nytimes.com/2006/06/25/fashion/25love.html Swami, V., Frederick, D. A., Aavik, T., Alcalay, L., Allik, J., Anderson, D., . . . & Danel, D. (2010). The attractive female body weight and female body dissatisfaction in 26 countries across 10 world regions: Results of the International Body Project I. *Personality and Social Psychology Bulletin, 36*(3), 309-325.

Swider, B. W., Barrick, M. R., & Harris, T. B. (2016). Initial impressions: What they are, what they are not, and how they influence structured interview outcomes. *Journal of Applied Psychology, 101*(5), 625-638. doi:10.1037/ apl0000077

Szasz, T. (1961). *Myth of mental illness* (Vol. 15). New York, NY: Harper & Row.

Szasz, T. (1994). Mental illness is still a myth. *Society, 31*(4), 34-39.

Szasz, T. (2003). *A lexicon of lunacy: Metaphoric malady, moral responsibility, and psychiatry.* Piscataway, NJ: Transaction Publishers.

Talbott, J. A. (1994). Fifty years of psychiatric services: Changes in treatment of chronically mentally ill patients. In J. M. Oldham & M. B. Riba (Eds.) *Review of Psychiatry* (93-120). Washington, DC: American Psychiatric Press.

Tartakovsky, M. (2011). The media and mental illness: The good, the bad and the ridiculous. *Psych Central.* Retrieved from https://psychcentral.com/lib/the-media-and-mental-illness-the-good-the-bad-and-the-ridiculous/

Taylor, S. E., & Fiske, S. T. (1975). Point of view and perceptions of causality. *Journal of Personality and Social Psychology, 32,* 439-445.

Thatcher, R. W., Walker, R. A., & Guidice, S. (1987). Human cerebral hemispheres develop at different rates and ages. *Science, 236,* 1110-1113.

Thibaut, J. W., & Riecken, H. W. (1955). Some determinants and consequences of the perception of social causality. *Journal of Personality, 24*(2), 113-133.

Thomas, A., & Chess, S. (1977). *Temperament and development*. New York, NY: Brunner/Mazel.

Thorndike, E. L. (1911). *Animal intelligence*. New York, NY: Macmillan.

Thurstone, L. L. (1938). *Primary mental abilities*. Chicago, IL: University of Chicago Press.

Tolin, D. F. (2010). Is cognitive–behavioral therapy more effective than other therapies? A meta-analytic review. *Clinical Psychology Review, 30*(6), 710-720.

Torrey, E. F. (1988). *Surviving schizophrenia: A family manual* (rev. ed.). New York, NY: Perennial Library.

Torrey, E. F. (1995). *Surviving schizophrenia: A manual for families, consumers, and providers*. New York, NY: Harper Perennial.

Turner, C. (2015). Arrests for leaving kids home alone made every day. *Telegraph*. Retrieved from http://www.telegraph.co.uk/news/uknews/law-and-order/11498123/Arrests-for-leaving-kids-home-alone-made-every-day.html

Tuttle. B. (2015, May). The simple mind trick that will boost your savings in no time. *Time*. Retrieved from http://time.com/money/3855517/tricks-boost-savings-retirement-college/

Twenge, J. M., & Campbell, W. K. (2001). Age and birth cohort differences in self-esteem: A cross-temporal meta-analysis. *Personality and Social Psychology Review, 5*, 321-344.

UK ECT Review Group (2003). Efficacy and safety of electroconvulsive therapy in depressive disorders: A systematic review and meta-analysis. *The Lancet (London, England), 361*(9360), 799-808.

United Nations. (2001). *World population aging: 1950-2050*. Retrieved from http://www.un.org/esa/population/publications/worldageing19502050/

Underhill, P. (2009). *Why we buy: The science of shopping--updated and revised for the Internet, the global consumer, and beyond*. New York, NY: Simon and Schuster.

US Department of Health and Human Services. (1999). Executive summary mental health: Culture, race, and ethnicity, a supplement to mental health: A report of the Surgeon General. Retrieved from http://www.ct.gov/dmhas/lib/dmhas/publications/mhethnicity.pdf

Vaidya, J. G., Gray, E. K., Haig, J., & Watson, D. (2002). On the temporal stability of personality: Evidence for differential stability and the role of life experiences. *Journal of Personality and Social Psychology, 83*(6), 1469-1484.

Valkenburg, P. M., & Peter, J. (2009). Social consequences of the Internet for adolescents: A decade of research. *Current Directions in Psychological Science, 18*, 1-5.

van IJzendoorn, M. H., & Kroonenberg, P. M. (1998). Cross-cultural patterns of attachment: A meta-analysis of the strange situation. *Child Development, 59*, 147-156.

Vigen, T. (2015). *Spurious correlations*. New York, NY: Hachette Books.

Vigil, J. M., Geary, D. C., & Byrd-Craven, J. (2005). A life history assessment of early childhood sexual abuse in women. *Developmental Psychology, 41*, 553-561.

Wacker, J., Chavanon, M. L., & Stemmler, G. (2006). Investigating the dopaminergic basis of extraversion in humans: A multilevel approach. *Journal of Personality and Social Psychology, 91*(1), 171-187.

Wallach, M. A., & Wallach, L. (1983). *Psychology's sanction for selfishness: The error of egoism in theory and practice*. New York: W. H. Freeman & Company.

Wang, S., Baillargeon, R., & Brueckner, L. (2004). Young infants' reasoning about hidden objects: Evidence from violation-of-expectation tasks with test trials only. *Cognition, 3*, 167-198. doi:10.1016/j. cognition.2003.09.012

Ward, A. J. (1991). Prenatal stress and childhood psychopathology. *Child Psychiatry & Human Development, 3*, 97-110. doi:10.1007/BF00707788

Waterman, A. (1988). Identity status theory and Erikson's theory: Communalities and differences. *Developmental Review, 8*, 185-208.

Waters, E., Corcoran, D., & Anafarta, M. (2005). Attachment, other relationships, and the theory that all good things go together. *Human Development, 48*(1-2), 80-84. doi:10.1159/000083217

Watson, D., Clark, L. A., & Tellegan, A. (1988). Development and validation of brief measures of positive and negative affect: The PANAS scales. *Journal of Personality and Social Psychology, 54*(6), 1063–1070.

Watson, J. B. (1913). Psychology as the behaviorist views it. *Psychological review, 20*(2), 158-177.

Wechsler, D. (2008). *Wechsler adult intelligence scale - Fourth Edition (WAIS–IV)*. San Antonio, TX: NCS Pearson.

Wegmann, J. (2008). *Psychopharmacology: Straight talk on mental health medications*. Eau Claire, WI: PESI.

Weisskirch, R. S., Kim, S. Y., Schwartz, S. J., & Whitbourne, S. K. (2016). The complexity of ethnic identity among Jewish American emerging adults. *Identity, 16*(3), 127-141.

Westen, D., & Morrison, K. (2001). A multidimensional meta-analysis of treatments for depression, panic, and generalized anxiety disorder: An empirical examination of the status of empirically supported therapies. *Journal of Consulting and Clinical Psychology, 69*(6), 875-899.

White, M. (1981). The effect of the nature of the surround on the perceived lightness of grey bars within squarewave test gratings. *Perception, 10*, 215-230.

White, S. H. (2000). Conceptual foundations of IQ testing. *Psychology, Public Policy, and Law, 6*(1), 33-43.

World Health Organization. (n.d.). *Schizophrenia*. Retrieved from http://www.who.int/mental_health/management/schizophrenia/en/World Health Organization. (2002). Global burden of disease (GBD) 2002 estimates. Retrieved from http://www.who.int/healthinfo/global_burden_disease/estimates_regional_2002/en/

Wiens, A. N., & Menustik, C. E. (1983). Treatment outcome and patient characteristics in an aversion therapy program for alcoholism. *American Psychologist, 38*(10), 1089-1086.

Winerman, L. (2013). What draws us to Facebook? *Monitor on Psychology, 44*(3). Retrieved from http://www.apa.org/monitor/2013/03/cover-facebook.aspx

Wirth, W., & Schramm, H. (2005). Media and emotions. *Communication Research Trends, 24*(3), 3-25.

Wolman, D. (2012). A tale of two halves. *Nature, 483,* 260-263.

Woods, N. F., Dery, G. K., & Most, A. (1983). Recollections of menarche, current menstrual attitudes, and premenstrual symptoms. In S. Golub (Ed.), *Menarche: The transition from girl to woman.* Lexington, MA: Lexington Books.

Wright, J. (2006, March 16). Boomers in the bedroom: Sexual attitudes and behaviours in the boomer generation. *Ipsos Reid.* Retrieved from https://www.ipsos.com/en-ca/boomers-bedroom-sexual-attitudes-and-behaviours-boomer-generation

Wrosch, C., & Miller, G. E. (2009). Depressive symptoms can be useful: Self-regulatory and emotional benefits of dysphoric mood in adolescence. *Journal of Personality and Social Psychology, 96*(6), 1181-1190.

Wrzesniewski, A., McCauley, C., and Rozin, P. (1999). Odor and affect: Individual differences in the impact of odor on liking for places, things and people. *Chemical Senses, 24,* 713-721.

Yalom, I. D. (1995). *The theory and practice of group psychotherapy.* New York, NY: Basic Books.

Yamagata, S., Suzuki, A., Ando, J., Ono, Y., Kijima, N., Yoshimura, K., … Jang, K.L. (2006). Is the geneteic structure of human personality universal? A cross-cultural twin study from North America, Europe, and Asia. *Journal of Personality and Social Psychology, 90*(6), 987-998., 987-998. http://dx.doi.org/10.1037/0022-3514.90.6.987

Zabin, L. S., Emerson, M. R., & Rowland, D. L. (2005). Child sexual abuse and early menarche: The direction of their relationship and its implications. *Journal of Adolescent Health, 36,* 393-400.

Zanna, M. P., & Rempel, J. K. (1988). Attitudes: A new look at an old concept. In D. Bar-Tal and A. W. Kruglanski (Ed.), *The social psychology of knowledge* (pp. 315–334). Cambridge, England: Cambridge University Press.

Zimbardo, P. G., Haney, C., Banks, W. C., & Jaffe, D. (1973). The mind is a formidable jailer: A Piran- dellian prison. *The New York Times Magazine, 8,* 38-60.

Zimmerman, B. J., Bandura, A., & Martinez-Pons, M. (1992). Self-motivation for academic attainment: The role of self-efficacy beliefs and personal goal setting. *American Educational Research Journal, 29*(3), 663-676.

Zvolensky, M. J., & Bernstein, A. (2005). Cigarette smoking and panic psychopathology. *Current Directions in Psychological Science, 14*(6), 301-305.

Index

F

S